PSYCHOLOGICAL
FOUNDATIONS
OF EDUCATION

Learning and Teaching

PSYCHOLOGICAL FOUNDATIONS OF EDUCATION

LEARNING AND TEACHING

B. CLAUDE MATHIS
Northwestern University

JOHN W. COTTON
University of California, Santa Barbara

LEE SECHREST
Northwestern University

ACADEMIC PRESS   New York and London

ACADEMIC PRESS, INC.
111 Fifth Avenue, New York, New York 10003

United Kingdom Edition published by
ACADEMIC PRESS, INC. (LONDON) LTD.
Berkeley Square House, London W1X 6BA

LIBRARY OF CONGRESS CATALOG CARD NUMBER: 78-107561

PRINTED IN THE UNITED STATES OF AMERICA

CONTENTS

5. Forgetting and Extinction: The Elimination of Behavior   149

6. Thinking and Concept Formation   192

11. Motivation and Learning Theory   374

12. Motivation and Schooling   428

PREFACE

Nearly a decade has elapsed since the funding by the Carnegie Corporation of a proposal advanced by Northwestern University which had as its major objective the development of closer working relationships between a department of psychology known for its experimental commitments and a school of education which has some reputation for plotting an independent course in teacher education. Among the contributions of Northwestern faculty members to that project were papers by Benton J. Underwood on verbal learning and education, Donald T. Campbell (with Julian Stanley) on experimental and quasiexperimental designs in education, Carl P. Duncan on problem solving, Robert I. Watson on the history of educational psychology, Winfred F. Hill on learning theory and identification, and Lee Sechrest (with R. Wray Strowig) on teaching machines and programmed instruction. In addition, a symposium on learning, "Can the Laws of Learning Be Applied in the Classroom?," produced papers by Kenneth Spence and Arthur Melton.

The Carnegie Project at Northwestern stimulated much interaction between psychologists and educators on the problems and challenges of education. One result of this interaction is *Psychological Foundations of Education,* which includes content from both general and educational psychology using the classroom as the organizer of the material. We feel this approach has at least two implications. First, it requires some deemphasis of topics such as sensory and animal psychology, which are often dominant in the general psychology curriculum. Second, given the present conceptual status of basic problems in psychology such as learning, motivation, and development, it suggests that the apparent dichotomies of knowledge represented by the classifications of general and educational psychology are no longer realistic, if indeed they ever were.

An examination of textbooks available today for general and educational psychology courses reveals an overlap of basic topics with the latter course often appearing to be a furbishing of general psychology material with classroom examples and references to educational research. A prime criterion for including any topic in an educational psychology book is relevance to teaching, which is a worthy standard. If the topic, however, represents one previously learned in a general psychology course, then a second criterion, the conscious effort to produce overlearning and transfer of repeated material, must also exist. Or perhaps this duplication of material may be less than conscious, deriving simply from intraprofessional differences among psychologists. *Psychological Foundations of Education* suggests an alternate answer to the problem of the bifurcation of general and educational psychology in the curriculum of teacher preparation. Our solution is provisional and has obvious imperfections. We offer it, however, in the hope that we may stimulate discussion of the problem and other solutions and/or explicit justifications for past practice.

This text should have a variety of uses in classes where students are preparing for teaching. It was written specifically for those situations in which the prospective teacher is introduced to psychology through a one- or two-semester integrated sequence. The instructor in such a situation may wish to use the chapters in the order in which they appear. Administrative convenience may prevent such an arrangement; therefore, we offer some alternate organizations of chapters for other teaching situations. Instructors in a general psychology course intended for future teachers may wish to cover Chapters 1, 3, 5, **6**, 7, 9, **10**, 11, 13, **14**, and 16. Instructors in an educational psychology course with a general psychology prerequisite may wish to present Chapters 1, 2, 3, 4, **6**, 8, **10**, 12, **14**, 15, and 17. The boldface numbered chapters in each case represent possible sources of overlap between the two courses, to be omitted or not as local conditions and the instructor's judgment dictate.

We do not consider our coverage of the material exhaustive, but we have attempted to organize all the chapters so that their relevance for teaching is either implicit or explicit. We hope the future educator who reads this book will leave it with a clearer understanding of psychology as a science and the contributions the science can make to teaching and the process of education. One of the major values held by educators today is the concept of relevance. Our attempts at relevance will be particularly noted in the chapters recommended above for the educational psychology course. There the explicit focus is upon students and teachers in their respective educational roles.

Reading this book in no way substitutes for perceptive, meaningful experiences with students in a classroom. Learning to teach is more than understanding a textbook. However, if the contents of this book help future teachers prepare for methods courses, practice teaching, and the professional teaching career itself, we shall be content.

No book would be complete without an acknowledgment of the efforts of the many persons other than the authors whose contributions have helped to produce that volume. We would especially like to recognize Cleo Dietz and Dorothy Damewood for their help in typing the manuscript, Cynthia George for the many permission letters which she wrote, Dennis Ridley for assistance with the Index, Michael Byer for his editing skills, and Carolyn Cotton for her skills in proofreading.

Writing a textbook is inevitably a family affair. Our wives and children are to be commended for the patience and support which they gave to a project which all too frequently required the subordination of their interests to the priorities of the manuscript.

Last, we should like to recognize the invaluable assistance given by those with whom we worked at Academic Press.

1

PSYCHOLOGY AND EDUCATION

Although psychological lore is so familiar, few of us attain a well-rounded understanding of psychology from everyday experience.

This book reports some unusual facts of psychology and includes many topics you may not be familiar with. Since this book is intended primarily for persons interested in teaching, our emphasis is on the aspects of psychology relevant to education. However, the chapters presented here should give readers a clearer understanding of the science of psychology generally, and of the commitments and points of view of psychologists who translate the science into professional activity.

What Is Psychology?

Psychology is two things: an academic discipline and a technology. As an academic discipline, psychology is the scientific study of the behavior of human beings and of animals. As a technology, psychology is the means of changing behavior by applying the findings of academic psychology, combined with intelligent guesses where knowledge is lacking. Let us pursue what is meant by these two statements. Behavior—what living things do—is the *raison d'etre* of psychology. At some time or another psychologists have studied almost all aspects of life. Some of the activities studied seem to fit better in fields other than psychology. However, regardless of its relevance to biology, political science, religion, or other disciplines, all behavior can be explained in part by psychological principles and all deserve psychological investigation.

To say that psychology is a scientific study is to say that psychologists choose to do research governed by scientific standards. Science, when approached abstractly, may appear to have one set of absolute standards for what is or is not scientific. As long as the product of science results from the activity of men, there will be variations in the interpretation of the standards representing science. Nevertheless, scientists generally agree on some of the basic attributes of scientific activity necessary to any discipline that deserves the label "scientific." Several of these basic standards will be illustrated in this book. In general, scientists typically favor:

1. Fact over "expert" opinion
2. Logic over intuition
3. Purity of research methods over speed of gaining knowledge

To learn whether one unidentified cola drink actually tastes sufficiently different from another to be correctly identified consistently one must look for factual evidence (3). When seeking facts, one does not ask one's neighbor for an opinion nor judge by statements in a television commercial. To find out whether a "burning desire" to win is enough to make an athlete the world's champion high jumper, we need to ask two logical questions. First, how can we express a "burning desire to win" in a way that can be measured, and second, how does it relate to the jumping performance of the athlete? Similarly, to find out about the improvement of elementary school children's reading skills, one does not ask their parents. The scientific answer to the question could involve the assessment of evidence from many different sources (7).

Now look at psychology as a technology. This aspect of psychology can best be understood by observing the psychologists who apply the facts of psychology in their professional relationships. An applied psychologist is much like other psychologists in that he tries to influence people's actions. The many kinds of applied psychologists try to influence people in different ways. An industrial psychologist works to improve employee morale, increase production, and decrease labor turnover. A clinical psychologist works to alleviate or even prevent people's emotional disorders. An educational psychologist helps school planners develop the best in learning methods and techniques for students.

Comparisons suggest that applied psychologists and nonpsychologists often try to achieve the same goals. What distinguishes the actions of the psychologist from the nonpsychologist? The difference is twofold. First, each uses different tools for his tasks: For example, a psychologist gives individual intelligence tests, but a teacher does not. Second, even when doing the same tasks, each emphasizes different aspects. In counseling a child with reading problems, a psychologist uses a different body of

TABLE 1-1
Distribution of Psychologists among the Various Subfields of Psychology (4)

	Percentage		
	1960	1962	1964
	$N = 15,257$	$N = 16,791$	$N = 16,804$
Subfield	%	%	%
Clinical	39	37	37
Counseling and guidance	12	12	11
Developmental psychology	2	3	3
Educational psychology	8	9	8
Engineering psychology[a]			2
Experimental, comparative, and physiological psychology	11	13	11
General psychology	1	1	1
Industrial and personnel psychology	10	10	8
Personality	3	3	3
Psychometrics	3	3	3
School psychology	5	4	6
Social	5	4	6
Other	1	1	1

[a] Did not appear on the Specialties List of the 1960 and 1962 surveys.

research findings and professional practices than does a social worker or a teacher.

Some of the many areas of specialization within the field of psychology are listed in Table 1-1, showing the percentage of psychologists engaged in each. These data, summarized for the years 1960, 1962, and 1964, were obtained from a recent study of manpower in psychology reported by the American Psychological Association (4). Table 1-2, also from this study, shows how these psychologists are distributed vocationally—that is, where they work. The tables indicate that many psychologists are employed in an educational setting, either in a college or university or in a public school system. But in all the subfields of psychology the common denominator is people studying human behavior scientifically. In this book the area of specialization emphasized is educational psychology. However, it will be apparent that the scientific approach is shared by all psychologists.

The Purposes of Psychological Study

If psychology is an academic discipline employing scientific methods for the study of behavior, what is the purpose of this study? For some it may be a curiosity to discover what people are like, prompting the

TABLE 1-2
Employers of Psychologists (4)

Subfield	N	College and university %	Secondary and school systems %	Federal government %	Other government %	Military %	Nonprofit organizations %	Industry %	Self-employed %	Other %	Not employed or not reported %
Clinical	6,151	22	7	10	22	1	14	2	14	2	5
Counseling and guidance	1,831	51	10	10	8	<1	10	2	4	1	3
Developmental	510	65	3	3	6	1	9	<1	2	2	9
Educational	1,427	56	20	2	6	<1	4	3	1	3	4
Engineering	377	7	0	14	1	7	9	60	<1	1	1
Experimental, comparative, and physiological	1,912	68	1	9	3	2	6	7	1	1	4
General	141	76	1	2	3	1	4	0	1	0	12
Industrial and personnel	1,367	19	1	9	3	2	5	51	6	2	3
Personality	479	67	2	7	7	1	7	1	3	1	4
Psychometrics	467	50	1	16	5	1	10	11	1	1	3
School	939	10	68	1	10	0	1	1	<1	3	6
Social	1,004	70	1	6	3	2	7	5	2	1	3
Other	199	35	2	6	9	1	11	6	6	1	23
All subfields	16,804	39	10	8	11	1	9	8	7	2	5

observer to watch what they do and record his findings. Other psychologists may study behavior because they want to understand behavior. Still others would like to be able to predict what will happen in certain situations. A fourth type of psychologist may seek to influence or control other people.

Research directed primarily by curiosity can answer whatever questions the curious person may raise: At what age can the average child first say a three-word sentence? How soundly do most people sleep? Do left-handed people learn differently from right-handed people? Can babies select a balanced diet if free to choose? Do children learn to read better by one method than by another? Is pica or elite type easier to read? Is prolonged hunger more severe than prolonged thirst? The hundreds of facts garnered from the answers to such a group of questions could comprise the material for a handbook on behavior.

But if a psychologist's curiosity is completely unchanneled, the questions he answers may be as unrelated as those just raised. He functions to produce a *descriptive* psychology, which tells much about many things but does not connect any one thing to anything else. If, however, the answer to one question leads him to ask one related to it, he is helping to build an organized body of knowledge. After finding at what age a child first says a three-word sentence, he asks: What words are most often found in the child's vocabulary at this period? How large must his vocabulary be before he utters such a sentence? How many words like "wa-wa" will an infant create for use with his own family before he replaces them with the actual words his parents employ? The result of this proliferation of research on related questions is a developing psychology which is systematic as well as descriptive. We are still describing behavior, but we are trying to describe it in a systematic way. Only thus can the hypothetical handbook mentioned above contain chapters on infant speech, sleep, animal memory, food preferences, running speeds of rats, legibility of different types, comparisons of different needs, and so on.

Yet the psychologist who wants to *understand* behavior will still be dissatisfied (1). If he finds that babies can select a balanced diet for themselves (5), he wants to know why. He may have discovered many facts about this food-selection procedure, but he is dissatisfied until he knows *why* it occurs. Do the organs of taste become more sensitive to the foods the child needs but has not been getting? Does a needed food taste better than an unneeded one? If two foods of different food value taste very much the same, like sugar and sucaryl, will the child choose the one he needs? These questions are in fact hunches or *hypotheses* about the reasons for the findings. As the psychologist learns which hypotheses are right and which are wrong, he understands better why people act as they do.

Everyone realizes, however, that a complete explanation of a phenomenon is impossible. We may learn that taste rather than need enhances a food's palatability, and that neural discrimination of foods is not related to changing needs (13). These facts tell us that food choices are based on certain cues that are present before eating, and that more than a simple sensory mechanism operates in selecting needed foods. No matter how long research on the problem continues, however, new questions will arise. Would the organism eat the food if he could see but not taste that it was a needed food? Does such selectivity preclude eating poisonous objects having a characteristic taste? Partial explanations multiply as new answers lead to new questions, and vice versa, but a single cause is not to be found. Even when one seems to exist, the so-called cause requires limitless investigation.

The psychologist with a pragmatic (i.e., practical) orientation considers that understanding or explaining behavior is too contemplative, even metaphysical. Since full explanations are never available, why not content oneself with *predicting* what will happen, what a person will do in a certain situation, and not ask why? Other psychologists may spend their lives trying to prove or disprove the proposition that learning never occurs without motivation, but the pragmatist is satisfied to know how much learning to predict from a certain classroom, a certain teacher, and certain motivating instructions.

Emphasizing prediction as the essential function of science is far more defensible than searching for shallow explanations or understandings; it is also much less intellectually pure than the quest for the most thorough possible understanding. A solely emotional attempt to understand Johnny in the classroom provides neither the basis for predicting what he will do in the future nor the basis for a thorough description of what he was doing under specified conditions in the past. This defect becomes clear when one asks for evidence that such understanding has practical value. On the other hand, the pragmatist's attempts to predict behavior by any means and at any cost—though sometimes successful—make no significant scientific contribution to understanding why a specific behavior is as it is. If asked to choose between the "blind" prediction that an individual will become neurotic within a year if his preference for one of a pair of designs like this

conforms to a certain listing of "neurosis-proneness responses" and the prediction that he will become neurotic within a year if his mother is feigning heart attacks as a means of preventing his imminent marriage, the choice would certainly be the latter. The designs are used because they are diagnostic aids—not because the relation between them and neurosis has been scientifically investigated. On the other hand, there is a great deal of information concerning parent-child relationships and neurotic personality which confirms the prediction that neurosis may stem from the behavior of the mother. This is an important link in a body of knowledge. However, it is not now possible to perfectly predict neurosis; nor is it likely to become possible in the next hundred years. This book cites many examples of moderately successful predictions of behavior. Whether or not complete success is a practical hope can be told only after lengthy research.

Once prediction is feasible, *control* of behavior becomes a real possibility. Many psychologists agree with B. F. Skinner, the influential Harvard professor, that psychological principles could be used not only in teaching children, raising families, training employees, and stimulating desires for creature comforts, but also in planning the institutions and practices of a town or country. A psychologist's version of a scientific *Brave New World* (9) would utilize the psychologist's knowledge of reasons for people's actions to induce them to comply with his wishes. Such a psychologist, like Mr. Frazier, the hero of Skinner's utopian novel, *Walden Two* (17), would make benevolent plans for his charges, leaving neither education, personality development, marriage choice, vocational selection, nor community organization to spontaneous (and hence unscientific) modification by other individuals or groups. Skinner has Mr. Frazier describe one of the techniques of control used in *Walden Two* as follows:

> We have had to *uncover* the worthwhile and truly productive motives— the motives which inspire creative work in science and art outside the academies. No one asks how to motivate a baby. A baby naturally explores everything it can get at, unless restraining forces have already been at work. And this tendency doesn't die out, it's *wiped* out.
>
> We made a survey of the motives of the unhampered child and found more than we could use. Our engineering job was to preserve them by fortifying the child against discouragement. We introduce discouragement as carefully as we introduce any other emotional situation, beginning at about six months. Some of the toys in our air conditioned cubicles are designed to build perseverance. A bit of a tune from a music box, or a pattern of flashing lights, is arranged to follow an appropriate response—say pulling on a ring. Later the ring must be pulled twice, later still three or five or ten times. It's possible to build up fantastically perseverative behavior without encountering frustration or rage.

Though *Walden Two* is fiction, it deserves serious thought because its author has done research on the problem of controlling behavior. We agree with Skinner that controlling behavior of people, either singly or in groups, is practicable.

Moreover, controlling others' behavior has been moderately successful throughout the history of man. Kings have controlled their populaces, popes have controlled kings, generals have controlled armies, and bankers have controlled manufacturers, all without the benefit of psychological principles now available. One cannot read Machiavelli's *The Prince* or Montesquieu's *The Spirit of Laws* without realizing that intelligent men have long been trying to understand the methods of psychological control, even when factual solutions were absent. Today modern devices such as public opinion polls, surveys of buying habits, and assessments of abilities make it possible to predict and control behavior more precisely than was previously possible.

This fact may make you think of science in general—and psychology in particular—as a creator of bondage. Why should you learn more ways of restricting other people's freedom? Aren't there enough individuals trying to manipulate others' lives without adding psychologists? Even if science can give us wealth, physical health, or mental health, isn't the loss of freedom too great a price to pay? One answer is that science is no more culpable than any other discipline or profession which aims to establish control over behavior. The psychologist has neither the ability nor the desire to exercise the degree of control envisaged in *Walden Two*. In his limited capacity, he no more deserves blame for an intention to restrict individual freedom than does the average parent for trying to guide his children. Any special stigma attached to the psychologist probably stems from his greater efficiency (because of more careful factual analysis of the situation) rather than from his attempt to exercise control.

The scientist not only shares the goal of controlling behavior with other groups of people, he is also controlled by them. In his professional capacity he is likely to be an instrument of control operated by government, industry, or labor. In such a case the psychologist does not decide who should be influenced to do what but only how this influence can be gained most practicably. Should the influence desired be an immoral one (for example, if the psychologist were to develop the means of teaching children unquestioning acceptance of all adult authority), the responsibility is shared by the employer (in this case, the local school board or national ministry of education) and the psychologist. The onus is not on the psychologist alone, as would be the case in a community like *Walden Two*.

You may ask, is not any control of this kind automatically unacceptable to free people? Our reply must be that it is neither desirable nor possible to prevent one man from trying to influence another nor one group from trying to affect another. Many such attempts are either benevolent or harmless. Control that is undesirable, or malevolent, cannot be eliminated by renouncing the use of control techniques but by placing better means of control in the hands of responsible citizens. Without doubt psychological techniques will sometimes be used improperly. Nonetheless, subject to the restrictions of common decency, good taste, and existing laws there is no more reason to refuse to use psychological methods of control than to refuse to use geological knowledge in seeking oil fields.

We belabor this point because psychology, a relatively new discipline, does touch hitherto forbidden areas of man's life. We all realize that the intelligence test, the personality test, the time-and-motion study, and the teaching machine diminish our privacy and reduce the use of initiative. Nor is this all: We not only do object to being so well controlled by others, we fear being understood scientifically, either as individuals or as a species. Distinguished scholars have many times objected to research on sexual behavior as improper; ministers and philosophers have complained about materialistic emphases in learning theory; the typical student clings to the conviction (or is it a hope?) that behavior is unpredictable. Yet the psychologist perseveres, convinced that whatever people do deserves scientific study, that if psychology has overemphasized materialistic concepts new research will detect the error, and that we cannot know if behavior is predictable without trying to predict it.

How Psychological Knowledge Grows

Perhaps an example of psychological research on a single question will tell you something about the way knowledge about psychology develops. This problem involves research emphasizing the description and understanding of a particular behavior rather than the prediction or the control of behavior. Although prediction and control are more highly regarded by the psychologist than description and understanding, the latter are more typical of psychological research. First, a simple fact: The moon (or the sun viewed through dark glasses) looks bigger if it is near the horizon than if it is overhead. This phenomenon is called the moon illusion. Over the centuries many men have discovered this mysterious fact and have tried to explain it. Early studies of the illusion provided insight into its properties, but only recently through the experimental work of the late Harvard psychologist E. G. Boring and his associates, do we understand the phenomenon reasonably well.

As has often been the case with scientific puzzles, explanations of the moon illusion had been made for many centuries before a complete description of it was recorded in about A.D. 140. Ptolemy (15) said of it, "Of the celestial bodies which subtend the same angles between the visual radii, those appear smaller which are close to the point right over our head. Those close to the horizon, on the other hand, appear bigger (in a different size) and more in accordance with the familiar." Fifteen hundred years later, when so much more was known about physics, astronomy, physiology, optics, and psychology, many theories had been proposed but no one had significantly added to Ptolemy's statement about its properties. But in 1651 Riccioli (15) made measurements indicating at least the size of the illusion: The moon seemed to be about 40 minutes (two-thirds of a degree) larger at the horizon than at the zenith. This now appears to have been a considerable underestimate of the illusion. In 1909, Pozdena (14) found that the moon appeared 2.5 times as large at the horizon as at the zenith. More recent evidence (see Fig. 1-1) indicates that a ratio of 2.0 to 1 is more accurate.

The discrepancy between Riccioli and Pozdena's findings is due to different methods employed by them. Riccioli's seventeenth-century procedures for measuring were crude compared with those used by Pozdena in the twentieth century. A common method was to compare the apparent size of an artificial moon of constant size with the actual moon, moving the artificial moon away from the observer until it looked exactly the size of the actual moon at one position. Then the experimenter waited

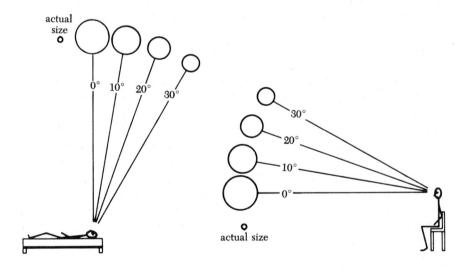

Fig. 1-1.

for the real moon to change position and permitted the observer to judge again where—to match the real moon in apparent size—the artificial moon had to be placed. But this caused an underestimation of the illusion, explainable as follows: People are known to see objects, no matter how far away they are, as the same size—a principle known as *size constancy.* Actually, size constancy makes distant objects appear too large. Thus the comparison moon, when used with the horizontal moon, has to be moved extra far away to appear small enough; whereas, when used with the moon at its zenith, it will be close because the zenith moon seems smaller, and it will require little correction (moving away) for size constancy. The outcome of the size constancy phenomenon was that it made a bigger difference between the settings of the artificial moons for the moon in its extreme positions, and thus made the illusion seem greater than it was.

In Pozdena's experiment the size constancy effect does not appear because the artificial moon was kept at a constant distance from the observer, which allowed the observer to adjust its size until it matched the apparent size of the actual moon.

A Modern View of the Moon Illusion

Because of the perceptual phenomenon of size constancy, the moon looks larger to people at every elevation than a camera would record. When the eyes are tilted up or down, however, it looks smaller than when they are pointed straight ahead. Apparently, then, some cues associated with eye movements are required to produce the illusion.

Holway and Boring varied head positions for a fixed position of the eyes, showing that head movements alone do not produce the illusion. Taylor and Boring also found no illusion in monocular persons (people with only one functioning eye) or normal persons viewing the moon with only one eye. Thus Boring and his associates (2, 8, 18) have verified earlier hypotheses about the perceptual source of the moon illusion, and yet, by showing that the illusion does not occur monocularly, have left almost as big a puzzle as the one with which they began.

Psychologists continue to show determined interest in the problem of the moon illusion. One recent report by Kaufman and Rock (10, 16) voices skepticism about the conclusions of Boring and his collaborators and presents an excellent summary of the various conclusions which psychologists have reached concerning explanations for the phenomenon. Another recent study demonstrates that the magnitude of the illusion is greater for children than for adults (11). The conclusion offered is that the moon illusion is the result of a normal developmental process and is dependent on the perceptual experience of the subject.

Although psychologists still disagree about the explanation for and cause of the moon illusion, they continue to devise experimental tests of possible interpretations. The problem of the moon illusion is an excellent illustration of scientific persistence practiced on a behavioral problem long before the profession of psychology emerged.

This treatment of the history of the moon illusion problem in psychology is important for reasons other than the conclusions and interpretations which experimental psychologists have offered, for it is a good example of how the research psychologist works. The study of the moon illusion introduces a problem in behavior that was identified long before the profession of psychology emerged. By the time the psychologists got to the problem, there was a great store of opinions on which to base hypotheses for empirical testing. Answers were not obtained and verified in one experiment. Psychologists have continued to study the phenomenon, and by a series of successive approximations have moved closer to obtaining reliable explanations for the moon illusion. The process of seeking to understand behavior by chipping away at a problem through a series of researches is analogous to taking a number of small steps to reach a goal rather than attempting to get there in one large leap. The moon illusion is one of those topics in psychology that have not been satisfactorily concluded and set aside. As such, it exemplifies almost all the research topics psychologists pursue in their study of behavior.

The moon illusion is also a good example of a basic fact in psychology which makes the study of behavior a most interesting and complex undertaking. The illusion of difference between actual—or physical—size and perceived—or psychological—size in observing the moon under certain conditions clearly indicates that the way we experience the world is not necessarily related to the way the world is physically constructed. This difference between the physical world and the psychological world has been the starting point for a great deal of research in psychology in an attempt to discover why we perceive external reality as we do.

Much of what you read about education and psychology in this book is based on research that has followed a pattern of development similar to that for the moon illusion problem. If you attempt to generalize from the facts of psychology to the specfics of an individual student in the classroom you will encounter as a basic difficulty the differences between individuals perceiving and reacting to a given physical situation. Behavior expresses the way we interpret the world and ourselves, not what the world really is or what we really are. This is one reason that psychological principles cannot be applied arbitrarily in all seemingly appropriate instances. To say that a phonics approach is generally better than other methods of teaching reading to first-graders is not to say that all the children with whom you use a phonics approach will learn to read better than will all the children who have been taught with methods not based on phonics. The hypotheses of any science are successive approximations of certainty. The quest of any science is the challenge to eliminate error from its content.

Much has been written about the scientific method as a way of solving problems. The scientist does use a method, but it is not always so rigid as is usually defined. The scientific method emphasizes: (a) stating a definition of the problem to be studied, (b) forming questions or hypotheses to be tested, (c) constructing an experiment, a series of controlled observations, or a series of experiments to test the hypotheses, (d) interpreting the data obtained, and (e) stating the conclusions, which usually contain avenues for further investigation.

The scientific method thus stated might lead to a stereotyped image of science to someone who does not realize that the method is not an abstraction. Actually, it becomes meaningful as a strategy for discovering knowledge only through the activities of the scientist engaged in research on some problem. The steps in this method can usually be identified in the scientist's behavior as he goes about his task of doing research.

The scientist, whether a psychologist or a chemist, is committed to a common strategy for discovering knowledge that involves finding some way other than through philosophical speculation to answer questions. In science, truth is discovered by empirical methods, that is, by methods that rely on experimentation and observation rather than reason alone. The scientist's approach to the problems he investigates may be either inductive or deductive, but he must seek his answers in an orderly way that can be duplicated by other scientists to ascertain the validity and reliability of his results. Scientific methods of discovering knowledge, then, are based on the experimentation and experience of many rather than on the private thoughts of one. The history of any science shows that initial efforts to seek facts reflect an inductive process which contributes many unrelated questions about discrete events. The answers to these questions lead to generalizations which in turn stimulate deductive approaches emphasizing theories (12).

The methods of science, and its meaning as a strategy for the discovery of knowledge, will become increasingly apparent as you read more about scientific investigations in psychology. You will find that to be useful, psychological research has to be critically evaluated by the consumer. Research is not valid and reliable simply because it is research. In psychology this is especially true, since much that is studied about human behavior involves inferences and assumptions which are probably true but which lack the certainty one might find in research in, say, the field of chemistry. Errors in interpreting data or in the conclusions of research in psychology can be made quite easily. A common error is to over-generalize the results of an investigation by applying the results inappro-priately. For instance, the findings of a study of I.Q.s of native-born United States citizens cannot be applied indiscriminately to all other groups. To do so is to commit an error which completely misinterprets the original data. Another problem is caused by accepting experimental results based on observations or experimental procedures which are lax and not sufficiently controlled to minimize experimental errors. An ex-ample would be an experiment to test the effects of caffeine on learning that does not include a placebo control group. Such an experiment might produce data indicating improved learning in the group getting caffeine, but it also introduces the possibility that their improvement was due to the attention they were receiving and not the caffeine.

In studying psychology, you should become sensitive to the possibility of misinterpreting data about behavior. In a science, facts do not become facts simply because they are discovered by scientists but because they are supported by the operations used in the process of discovering them. If the operations are valid, the facts are also.

Scholars are finicky about their statements of facts; they want to know who said them, what each word refers to, and how the facts can be verified. Suppose we read that in 1890, 358,000 persons were enrolled in high schools in the United States and that 5,358,000 persons from 14 through 17 years of age lived in the United States. Most readers accept this and read on. But the specialist asks himself: Who did the study? Was it exactly 358,000 persons? Were all 5,358,000 persons counted, or were certain groups of people counted and the total estimated on the basis of some information related to those groups? How would you deter-mine if a school was a high school in 1890? Even today so-called high schools may encompass three to six grades. For that matter, semantics can be further stretched so that in speaking of someone who is 14 years old, different connotations might make him be 15, or even 13 years old.

Once the specialist has answered these questions, he knows whether to accept the statement and can then specify its meaning and accuracy better than he did on first reading. Thus he knows that the figures are specified to the nearest 1,000 so that, for example, 357,501 would have been recorded as 358,000.

What the specialist has done has been to specify the *operational* definition of terms in a statement alleged to be a fact. That is, he has been finding out what operations or acts are required to count how many persons were in high school and how many were from 14 through 17 years of age. Dealing with facts concretely is absolutely essential, otherwise one scholar would count one thing and another something else. Given concrete terms and facts, any controversy among scholars can only be about the relative importance of these facts (a question of value) or about what predictions may be based on them.

Our purpose in discussing this matter is to encourage you to carefully analyze what you read. However, do not think that every statement of presumed fact you read requires your careful analysis. Now, when you read "7% of American children of high school age were in high school in 1890," you realize the different operations that might have been used to yield that figure. In particular, you will notice that 7% is an overestimate obtained by dividing 358,000 by 5,358,000—even though some of the 358,000 surely weren't of high school age, i.e., from 14 through 17. Yet, unless this matter is your most serious intellectual concern of the moment, you are much better advised to accept the 7% figure rather than to seek a more definitive statement.

What Is Educational Psychology?

Because education is so closely associated with the study of learning, psychologists play a central role in our educational systems. In the United States, educational psychologists represent about 8% of all psychologists, and school psychologists, about 6% (see Table 1-1). This figure would undoubtedly be much larger if it included psychologists in other subfields who do research in a school setting—the clinical psychologist who studies emotional problems in the underachiever or the counseling and guidance specialist. Much of the research done in all the subfields of psychology has a direct relevance to problems of education.

Educational psychologists, like their colleagues in most other areas of psychology, are employed as professors in colleges and universities throughout the United States. Most school psychologists, on the other hand, are employed in public school systems (see Table 1-2). One of the characteristics of academic employment is the high value placed on research and publications. The educational psychologist has a large commitment both to research in education and to the application of research done in any area to the process of education.

The educational psychologist is, in many ways, an educational engineer concerned with the application of knowledge to practical problems of behavior. He uses the school classroom as his major laboratory and does research to find solutions to such problems as the relationship between cultural background and learning ability, why some children achieve better with one teacher than with another, or what factors influence the choice of a college.

Many educational psychologists believe that they should depend less on other areas of psychology for the principles being applied to education (6) and do more of their own theory development and systematic research. In a recent statement addressed to educational psychologists, Wittrock (19) emphasized that research in educational psychology needs to progress beyond the level of unrelated facts about instruction and teaching. As a summary of the present state of the art of teaching, he points out:

> Research in educational psychology has not progressed far beyond the development of an organized body of knowledge relevant to the understanding and the control of instruction and teaching. Infrequently have we designed our studies to build sequentially upon earlier findings or to produce useful knowledge about the cause and effect relations between instruction and individual differences on the one hand, and the multiple outcomes of instruction and teaching, on the other hand.

Wittrock believes that educational psychology has reached the stage in its development to afford more liberal and less restrictive conceptualizations of its role. The educational psychologist should think of himself as something more than a psychologist who applies psychological principles to education. Wittrock (19) underscores what many feel to be the future course of educational psychology and of the researchers engaged in it when he states:

> It is time for us to practice a liberal conceptualization of educational psychology as the scientific study of human behavior in educational settings. As scientists we should attempt to describe, understand, predict, and control behavior in education.

The topics of study in psychology that are relevant to education are representative of the whole spectrum of research activity in psychology. If the educational psychologist's major motive in research is an attempt to "describe, understand, predict, and control behavior in education," then what should he know in order to conceptualize the facts of psychology and build sequentially upon them for further research and theoretical development? A tempting answer is "Everything." But a more reasonable answer would be a list of some of the major areas in which the educational psychologist should have some competence:

1. The physiological structure of the organism, physical growth, and maturation. Man's behavior is limited by his physical structure. Behavior changes within the limits set by the physical systems of the body. The most important of these systems psychologically is the nervous system.

2. Learning as a fundamental process underlying behavioral change. Learning is central to education since education exists to promote learning. From the psychologist's standpoint, the study of education and of learning overlap to a great degree.

3. Motivation as an important factor in understanding behavior: the factors which determine the direction and strength of behavior. Motivation is directly connected with learning, since no learning takes place in the absence of motivation.

4. The development of personality: the relationship between behavior and the physical, emotional, cultural, and social stimuli which influence individuality.

5. The process of individual development viewed in its continuity over time. Emotional development, physical development, and social development, together with intellectual development, are considered in terms of their nature and course through time, and in terms of their interrelatedness.

6. The measurement and evaluation of behavior. If psychologists are to study behavior they must be able to express it quantitatively. Psychological testing is of tremendous importance to education as a means of obtaining some information about the uniqueness of both teacher and student.

All these broad topics are interrelated, so that trying to understand one without also considering the others would be extremely difficult. Other topics could be listed, too, either as part of those above, or as separate subjects. Some of what you will read will seem to have little, and some to have a great deal, of direct relationship to education. Do not be impatient for immediate answers to specific problems; psychology contains more general answers which point the way to specificity. Even with the problem of the moon illusion, not all the answers are in; nor are all the answers available about why Johnny can't read or why there are such differences in achievement between slum children and children from the suburbs. Not all that you read in this book will make teaching easier. In fact, some of it may make teaching more difficult, for you may become more sensitive to classroom problems than you were when you started your reading. To understand behavior in a way that permits you to begin to shape and control behavior—and this, after all, is the basic reason for education—psychological fact is indispensable. Whether the teacher directs the student through vigorous efforts to shape his behavior or whether the student directs himself is almost irrelevant. What is important is that successful education changes behavior in the direction of agreed upon objectives. It is the authors' hope that what you read here will help you to think about behavior more objectively and more logically as you develop a frame of reference that identifies you as a teacher.

Summary

Among the most important areas of applied psychology are classroom learning and classroom teaching. This textbook presents some of the principles of psychology relevant to learning and teaching.

The science of psychology is both an academic discipline and a technology. As a discipline, psychology is the scientific study of the behavior of man and of animals. As a technology, psychology is a means of changing behavior by applying the findings of psychological research. To say that psychologists attempt to be scientific is to say that they believe in:

1. Fact over "expert" opinion
2. Logic over intuition
3. Purity of research methods over speed of gaining knowledge

Psychological research has many purposes but its major goal is to contribute new knowledge. Many researchers engage in scientific investigations of various aspects of behavior in an attempt to describe and understand behavior. However, many psychologists seek to predict behavior and ultimately to develop techniques for its control. B. F. Skinner is representative of this group, and many of his ideas have influenced educational practices.

The educational psychologist is a psychologist trained to do research in the field of education. He not only designs and completes research on problems of educational practice, he also evaluates and applies relevant knowledge from other fields of psychology which may have value for educational practice. Although much of the research you will encounter in this textbook was done outside the context of the school, it is reported here because it is helpful in describing and understanding the behaviors involved in educational activity. Research projects also suggest how educational programs may be developed to shape behavior.

SUGGESTED READINGS

Berelson, B., & Steiner, G. A. *Human behavior, an inventory of scientific findings.* New York: Harcourt, Brace & World, 1964.

The authors have attempted to "select, condense, organize and translate" many of the findings of psychological research that, in their judgment, are sufficiently supportable as to constitute a "proper generality" in the behavioral sciences. Some psychologists may resent this attempt to distill their science with its accompanying suggestions of certainty; however, others have welcomed this approach as one way of beginning to develop systematic organization out of the factual knowledge in the behavioral sciences. The book is an excellent reference source for a quick tour of psychological knowledge.

Krumboltz, J. D. (Ed.) *Learning and the educational process.* Chicago: Rand McNally, 1965.

In June, 1964, a research conference was held at Stanford University on Learning and the Educational Process. This volume contains the papers presented. Although they were not written for the beginning undergraduate, the interested student can find much here which is helpful in understanding some present trends in educational learning.

Skinner, B. F. *Walden two.* New York: Macmillan, 1948.

A successful novel by a psychologist, *Walden Two* presents a defense of the controlled society. Mr. Frazier, the central character, is really B. F. Skinner presenting his views concerning a social system which could be shaped by the kinds of psychological techniques that have been found successful in the laboratory. He argues that such control could be directed toward the benefit of mankind. *Walden Two* presents a blueprint for change which seems to become less fanciful each year.

Kuhlen, R. G. (Ed.) *Studies in educational psychology.* New York: Random House (Blaisdell), 1968.

A recent collection of articles and research reports in educational psychology which presents topics studied by the educational psychologist. Many of the articles are timely studies that comment on relevant issues in learning and teaching today.

REFERENCES

1. Bloom, B. S., Englehart, M. D., Furst, E. J., Hill, W. H., & Krathrohl, D. R. *Taxonomy of educational objectives.* New York: Longmans, Green, 1956.
2. Boring, E. G. The moon illusion. *American Journal of Physics,* 1943, **11,** 55–60.
3. Bowles, J. W., Jr., & Pronko, H. H. Identification of cola beverages. II. A further study. *Journal of Applied Psychology,* 1948, **32,** 559–564.
4. Compton, B. Psychology's manpower: characteristics, employment, and earnings. *American Psychologist,* 1966, **21,** 224–229.
5. Davis, C. M. Self-selection of diet by newly weaned infants. *American Journal of Diseases of Childhood,* 1928, **36,** 651–679.
6. Haggard, E. A. The proper concern of educational psychologists. *American Psychologist,* 1954, **9,** 539–543.
7. Harris, T., Otto, W., & Barrett, T. C. Summary and review of investigations relating to reading July 1, 1965 to June 30, 1966. *Journal of Educational Research,* 1967, **60,** 290–320.
8. Holway, A. H., & Boring, E. G. The apparent size of the moon as a function of

the angle of regard: further experiments. *American Journal of Psychology,* 1940, **53**, 537–553.

9. Huxley, A. *Brave new world.* Garden City, N. Y. Garden City Publ. Co., 1932.
10. Kaufman, L., & Rock, I. The moon illusion, I. *Science,* 1962, **136**, 953–961.
11. Leibowitz, H., & Hartman, T. Magnitude of the moon illusion as a function of the age of the observer. *Science,* 1959, **136**, 569–570.
12. Mathis, C. Is theory necessary for educational research? *Psychology in the Schools,* 1965, **2**, 10–16.
13. Pfaffman, C., & Bare, J. K. Gustatory nerve discharges in normal and adrenalectomized rats. *Journal of Comparative and Physiological Psychology,* 1950, **43**, 320–324.
14. Pozdena, R. F. Eine methods zur experimentellen und konstruktiven bestionmeng der form des firmamentes. *Zeitschrift für Psychologische und Physiologische der Sinnesorganen,* 1909, **51**, 200–246.
15. Reimann, E. Die scheinbare vergroserung der sonne und des mondes am horizont. *Zeitschrift für Psychologische und Physiologische der Sinnesorganen,* 1902, **30**, 161–195.
16. Rock, I., & Kaufman, L. The moon illusion, II. *Science,* 1962, **136**, 1023–1031.
17. Skinner, B. F. *Walden two.* New York: Macmillan, 1948.
18. Taylor, D. W., & Boring, E. G. The moon illusion as a function of binocular regard. *American Journal of Psychology,* 1942, **55**, 189–201.
19. Wittrock, M. Focus on educational psychology. *Educational Psychologist,* 1967, **4** (March), 17.

2

THE TEACHER AND THE CLASS

How would you describe a school classroom? Would it be a large room with windows along one side, furnished with rows of desks and a blackboard?

There are several "typical" images of a classroom—each valid for its place and time—yet none describes more than the physical aspects of a room. The point is that regardless of the physical description of a classroom, much more is implicit in the term. In the context of this book, a school classroom is really the psychological atmosphere in which students and teachers interact and learn. The physical surroundings are part of this atmosphere, but certainly not all of it. Psychologically speaking, a classroom exists if teacher and students meet purposefully under a tree outside the school building. The important factors about the classroom are the teachers and students who come together for the purpose of learning.

The scientific frame of reference emphasizes two factors important in teaching. The first is to see behavior as made up of specific acts. Total behavior, all that a teacher and a student experience in a classroom, is made up of specific happenings. Many teachers become so overly concerned with the "total picture" that they fail to develop a sensitivity to specific behaviors. Just as the chemist studies a chemical compound by breaking it down into component parts and finding out how they relate to each other, so must the educator become aware of the component parts in a sequence of behavior and attempt to learn how they fit together. This cannot be done without becoming sensitive to the behavioral details of a classroom.

The second important factor is the need for the teacher to creatively test opinions about behavior. Many teachers arrive at conclusions about the causes of behavior that are not supported by the realities of the situation. To the question, "What causes behavior?" the answer often requires that a specific decision be made. One such decision that would test the teacher's opinion would be the referral of a child to the school nurse for a hearing or an eye examination. Or the opinions being tested might involve an elaborate experimental arrangement of grouping the children on the basis of intelligence or some other variable. Unless the teacher is willing to test his hypotheses, teaching becomes haphazard and inefficient. For teaching to be successful, the teacher must learn to regard behavior with a scientific attitude.

If behavior is the key to the psychological atmosphere of the classroom, then it is an atmosphere that is different from one situation to the next. Not only does the behavioral climate change constantly within a given classroom, change and difference are inevitable when comparing classrooms. Two facts are apparent from observational data about the classroom. For one thing, teachers are not always teaching the formal studies associated with school learning—such as reading and arithmetic—and students are not always engaged in the activity of learning associated with these formal aspects of education. Teachers engage in many activities which have little, if any, relation to teaching. In fact, a frequent complaint made by teachers is that they do not have enough time to help individual students learn because there are too many students in the classroom. Another common complaint is that teachers are expected to do many things, such as keeping records, which detract from their major role in helping students learn.

Pupils in the classroom are faced with many kinds of learning, both relevant and irrelevant when compared with the objectives of the formal curriculum of the school. Traditional research on classroom behavior has concentrated on the formal curriculum and the behavioral outcomes of learning defined in that context. The achievement levels of pupils in relation to their socioeconomic background represents one kind of research which deals with the functions of schooling in terms of knowledge gains. Recent attention has been directed toward the hidden curriculum in the classroom which includes many behavioral outcomes thought by some to be just as important to the later success of a pupil as his intellectual achievement.

In a perceptive analysis of the classroom, *Life in Classrooms,* Jackson (14) gives insight into various aspects of student existence in the elementary classroom. He points out that students are exposed to a hidden curriculum through learning situations consistently occurring in the classroom though not part of the recognized content of school activities. Becoming a member of a crowd, learning through indications of praise and reproof that one's actions are evaluated as good or bad and developing relationships to authority through interaction with the teacher and the institution are three major ways in which students are confronted with realities which occur consistently only in a classroom setting.

Many of the activities of the teacher are controlled by the crowded conditions of the classroom. Teachers do many things throughout a school day which are reactions to classes with so large a number of students that they cannot be dealt with individually. The teacher's role as traffic manager creates a common experience for students, that of delay. And one of the inevitable outcomes of delay is waiting, which Jackson feels is one of the major time consumers in the classroom. The teacher's activities in relating to the crowd of students also produces frustration in the many instances when the student wishes for some response from the teacher but the wish is bypassed or the interest allowed to diminish before attention can be given. Interruption is another feature of the crowded social conditions of the classroom which disrupts the continuity of learning. Social distraction is also present in the classroom where students are expected to behave as if they were alone but are surrounded by other students.

Although students are evaluated in many ways before they start school, the school itself soon becomes the major source of behavior evaluation. The teacher provides consistency in judging students' behaviors and is the one best able to make evaluative decisions. Both directly and indirectly, students soon learn to evaluate themselves by learning from the teacher what constitutes good and bad performance. The official school evaluation is usually represented by grades and by communications to parents. For the most part, these relate to the student's achievement of educational objectives. But students are also evaluated in terms of their adjustment to the school's expectations and the presence or absence of certain specific personality characteristics. Much of the nonacademic evaluation of the student comes from fellow students and is based on the values they have learned concerning acceptable or unacceptable and good or bad behavior.

In their relationship to parents, children learn to react to authority before starting school. Then, with the teacher as a power figure the experience is less intimate and less intense than the earlier relationship. In the interaction of teacher and student, students learn to follow directions of adults with whom they are less personally involved than they are with parents. The teacher's authority is more prescriptive than the restrictive expression characteristic of parents.

Learning to relate to crowded classrooms, teacher and peer evaluations, and authority represented in the teacher-student relationship instruct the student in patience, in tolerance of public assessments of one's strengths and weaknesses, and in developing habits of obedience and docility which are often necessary for adult adjustment.

Jackson (14) sums up the importance of these factors in the following statement:

> . . . the crowds, the praise, and the power that combine to give a distinctive flavor of classroom life collectively form a hidden curriculum which each student (and teacher) must master if he is to make his way satisfactorily through the school. The demands created by these features of classroom life may be contrasted with the academic demands—the "official" curriculum, so to speak—to which educators have paid the most attention.

The remainder of this chapter presents some of the factors influencing the environment known as a classroom, with emphasis on the teacher as its significant controller.

Teachers' Attitudes about Behavior

Some teachers' attitudes about present-day classroom behavior are reflected in the reports of studies on common types of misbehavior and the frequency of their occurrence. Cutts and Moseley (5) found that of 1000 boys and 1097 girls in the seventh grade, the types of misbehavior noticed most among the boys, in order of frequency, were talking, physical attack, undue activity, throwing things, and unexcused absence. The types of misbehavior among the girls, in order of frequency, were talking, chewing gum or eating candy, undue activity, physical attack, and immorality.

In another study Henning (13) asked 225 principals to list the behavior problems they viewed as most serious and most frequent. The most serious were reported as lying, being disrespectful of faculty supervision and authority, committing petty thievery, and congregating in lavatories and halls. The most frequently occurring misbehaviors were: congregating in lavatories and halls, running in corridors and on stairs, misbehaving in class, wasting school property, and displaying general rudeness and lack of consideration for others.

In 1928, E. K. Wickman (33) published his well-known study of teachers' attitudes about their students' behaviors. Two groups—teachers and mental hygienists—were asked to rate certain behaviors according to their seriousness as problems. The teachers tended to rate dishonesty, immorality, transgressions against authority, and aggressive personality traits as more serious than recessive and withdrawing personality traits. Mental hygienists, on the other hand, tended to rate the recessive and withdrawing traits as more serious behavior problems. The teachers were more disturbed by students who were rowdy and boisterous, and who disobeyed than they were by the students who made little contribution to classroom activity, either for better or worse.

Stauffer (27) reported an investigation which repeated the Wickman study but had some significant improvements in the experimental design. Wickman's data were of questionable validity because different instructions and different questionnaires were used for the teachers and the mental hygienists. Stauffer attempted to test for the effects of the differences in the two sets of instructions and to obtain data which would be objectively compared with the Wickman results. Stauffer also used different questionnaires—one for teachers and one for mental hygienists. The teachers also received an additional questionnaire, the one the mental hygienists filled out. The study showed that whether the two groups used the same questionnaires or different ones, they were in much greater agreement about what constitutes a serious behavior problem than were the two groups in Wickman's original study. Stauffer reported a high degree of correspondence between the responses of the teachers and the mental hygienists under conditions of both different directions and the same directions. Wickman reported almost no correspondence between the teachers' and the mental hygienist's rankings of behavior problems. Nervousness, sullenness, and resentfulness are considered serious behavior problems by teachers today, whereas these behaviors were not the kind considered important by teachers in 1928. Largely because psychology has become increasingly important in the preparation of teachers, today's teacher is more aware of recessive behaviors than was the teacher of forty years ago. However, like his earlier counterpart, today's teacher does not like aggressive behavior and transgressions against authority and considers such behaviors bad (15).

These investigations of teachers' attitudes toward the behavior of children, reported in the classic studies of Wickman (33) and Stauffer (27), have continued to stimulate psychologists' interest in classroom behavior as perceived by the teacher and others. A recent study (30) indicates that there are still differences between teachers' and mental health workers' attitudes about children's behavior problems. Teachers appear to be more concerned with problems of classroom management, sexual adjustment, and adherence to authority, while mental health professionals emphasize withdrawal behavior and behavior suggesting a deterioration of emotional and social adjustment.

The investigators tested a group of elementary school teachers and a group of clinical psychologists, giving each a list of items descriptive of children's behavior. The respondents were asked their opinions about whether the items represented normal or abnormal behavior for a child. The teachers and the psychologists differed significantly on 22% of the 295 items in the instrument. Of those items, 11% were in the area of behaviors indicating psychosomatic and physical disturbances, 32% in the area of aggressiveness, and 29% in the items relating to affect expression. Elementary teachers tended to evaluate behavior which could be described as regressive, aggressive, and emotional as more pathological than did the psychologists. Analyzed in terms of teaching experience, those who had been teaching longest had the greatest degree of agreement with the psychologists; teachers who were just beginning had the greatest degree of disagreement. For example, these are children's behaviors considered normal by experienced teachers, while less experienced teachers thought them indicative of abnormal behavior: cries or whimpers, plays with or fingers his mouth, has headache, coordination becomes poor at the slightest upset, becomes frightened in crowds, is afraid of being alone in wide open space, has difficulty expressing his thoughts, tells lies.

The authors (30) conclude that: "The present findings suggest that psychologists tend to be more acceptant, or at least more tolerant, of a greater variety of child behavior than teachers, and tend to regard a wider range of behavior as being normal."

The lack of greater agreement between psychologists and teachers concerning the behavior problems of children suggests that teachers may be resistent to change. Do teachers as a professional group tend to be rigid in their thinking and to compartmentalize their attitudes and ideas? Rabkin (21), in a study of the dogmatism of teachers, concludes that teachers are less dogmatic than other professional groups. The Rokeach Dogmatism Scale, a technique for evaluating dogmatism, was administered to 107 school teachers. A total score on the scale is indicative of the respondent's belief system indicating the extent to which he has an open or a closed mind about the content of the items on the scale. The sample tested consisted primarily of married, Protestant females with a median age of 27 and a median level of teaching experience of approximately 3 years. Such a sample, of course, is not representative of all groups of teachers. The data, however, do suggest that many younger female teachers in the elementary grades may be like these teachers studied by Rabkin. The scale scores indicated that the teachers scored lower in dogmaticism than did the groups reported by Rokeach (23) in his discussion of the scale. Rabkin (21) concluded from the analysis of the data that:

> . . . the tendency toward excessive dogmaticism or closed-mindedness is not a general characteristic of this group of present-day educators. Indeed, the results indicate a considerably lower degree of this rigid type of thinking as compared with various other college and noncollege groups. This is clearly not to say that there are *no* dogmatic teachers, just as one would hardly venture to deny the existence of prejudiced, hateful, anxious, frightened, or passive-aggressive teacher-types. What is suggested by these findings is that perhaps some of the criticism leveled at teachers, whether fledglings or veterans, for their conservatism and intense devotion to the status quo needs a good bit of tempering.

Perhaps the underlying difference between teachers and mental hygienists is a difference in roles rather than views. The very nature of his role makes the teacher object to pupils' behaviors that threaten that role. The mental hygienist cares less about immediate classroom management than about the children's long-range development. Certainly teachers know the importance of the total development of the individual, but they need to understand better the dynamics of behavior leading to it. Toward that end, researchers working in many disciplines are trying to relate sound principles of personality development to classroom dynamics. Their different points of view are due more to the perspectives of their varying roles than to a basic disagreement concerning what constitutes mental health in the classroom.

The Role Characteristics of the American Teacher

In any discussion of the teacher's attitudes toward behavior in the classroom it must be recognized that his role is one which society defines in a particular way. The way the teacher behaves and the rules society sets up for his behavior are of tremendous importance in a classroom. A good teacher can be successful with students who are barely educable; a bad teacher can fail with the most brilliant student in school. Whether or not a child learns in school will depend to a great extent on what the teacher does in the classroom.

Teaching has not always been so specialized a profession as it is today. In eighteenth-century Europe there were few schools, and teaching was considered a job for those unable to do anything else. It was common for the teacher to hold other jobs as well; in 1722, for example, country schoolmasters in Prussia had to be selected from those who were also tailors, weavers, blacksmiths, wheelrights, or carpenters—in 1738, the elementary teachers were granted the tailoring monopoly (4).

In colonial America the situation was somewhat better. Although academic qualifications for teachers ranged from just the ability to read to a college degree, the grammar schools throughout the colonies were for the most part staffed by competent teachers of "ability and learning" (7). Aside from a knowledge of subject matter the chief requisite for employment was the strength needed to whip and physically chastise the students. Teachers were also required to perform other duties, such as taking care of the church and participating in church services. Cubberley (4) reports on a contract made in 1682 in Flatbush, New York, which required the teacher to instruct the children in common prayers and in the catechism, to keep the church clean and ring the bell three times before sermons, to read the scripture before the sermon, to provide the water for baptisms, to give the funeral invocations, and to dig the graves.

But those conditions pertained almost three hundred years ago. Today, the typical teacher in the United States is not only thoroughly competent but far better prepared than her counterpart of a generation ago. The National Education Association (20) reported that in 1965, teaching in the United States was primarily a feminine occupation. Approximately 65% of the teachers were women, with 70% of them teaching in the elementary grades. High school teaching was more popular with men, with 78% of them in secondary education, compared with only 30% of the women.

From the data collected by the NEA, a description of the typical American teacher emerges. As of 1965, the male teacher was 35 years old, married, had a bachelor's degree and was working toward his master's. He had been teaching nearly ten years, with eight of those years in his present school system. He was employed in a high school, and he taught approximately 135 pupils in five classes a day.

The typical woman teacher in 1965 was 41 years old and married. Like her male counterpart, she held a bachelor's degree but was less likely to be pursuing a master's. She had taught about 13 years, nearly nine of them in the system where she was employed in 1965. She was an elementary teacher and had about 29 pupils in her class. Like the male teacher, she was active in community organizations including church, was an active voter in elections, and were she to choose a career would again choose teaching.

Although this describes the "typical" teacher, do not think that to be a successful teacher you must fit that description. Descriptions are based on averages—on sameness—not on the many possible differences. Also, descriptions say nothing about how a successful teacher will react when a student answers a question incorrectly or when he refuses to obey directions, for a teacher's reactions depend upon a multitude of factors. How does the teacher feel about the student? Does he like him? How does the teacher feel about himself? How does the school administration expect him to react, and what does society expect of him? And, very important, how does the child feel about him?

When the behavior of the teacher is examined, one thing is immediately apparent: The act of teaching cannot be divorced from other acts. The teacher does not become, when he enters the classroom, a person who is all-wise and all-powerful. Basically he is still subject to the same motivations that influence him outside the classroom. Probably because he plays a number of roles in his function as a teacher, it is thought that he should be somewhat superior to other people. He is expected to be someone children will want to emulate. Certainly it is right to expect him to be a moral person, but it is unrealistic to expect him to be anything other than a human being—with the imperfections being human entails.

Havighurst and Neugarten (11) point out that what a teacher is called upon to do in a school includes a number of different roles. In dealing with the school board the teacher plays the role of employee. He is also a subordinate to the principal, an advisee to the supervisor, and a colleague to other teachers. Sometimes the teacher is required to be a follower, sometimes a leader. In his relationship with students, however, the teacher's major role is directing learning and transmitting knowledge—a mediator of learning. Teachers tend to feel secure in this role, for most of the preparation for teaching emphasizes what is to be taught and how it is to be taught. To some extent success can be measured through testing and grading individual pupils, with the pupil's progress the criterion for success.

In a study designed to investigate the manner in which prospective teachers conceive of themselves in the role of teacher, data reported by Walberg (32) suggest that the beginning teacher tends to approach his role defensively, which makes him less willing to be intellectually free or experimental. The preference for neatness and control in presenting ideas in the classroom may be associated with a preference for children who, in the classroom, give expected responses to problems rather than answers that characterize creative response patterns.

A teacher is also a disciplinarian, a role which probably causes every teacher some concern. Although physical abuse is no longer a disciplinary measure, other forms have taken its place. Disciplinary problems confuse many teachers—and create conflict situations.

Discipline has many functions, and the teacher is faced with the problem of making choices concerning these functions nearly every teaching day. Mowrer's view (19) of some of the broader functions of discipline is that discipline is necessary for sound mental health. The basic function of discipline obviously is to protect children from the natural consequences of their actions. Learning by doing is not always practical because of the dangers involved in some behaviors. Also, because children are often unable to associate immediate behavior with much later consequences, discipline is needed to ensure a desired, or prevent an undesired, outcome. For instance, a child who rebels at attending school cannot foresee what his future—without schooling—might be. Disciplinary intervention is necessary. The parents' use of discipline induces a sensitivity in the child so that he learns to respond to the threat of punishment. Discipline is necessary to a productive personality, and is involved in learning to renounce immediate pleasures in anticipation of future rewards. The teaching process is related to all these facets of discipline.

Since the school-age child is away from home for part of the day, the teacher also becomes a parent substitute. Being a substitute parent, especially a substitute mother, influences the behavior of the elementary school teacher more than it does the behavior of teachers of older pupils; but no teacher completely escapes this function. Being a parent substitute may take the form of behaving in a manner the student would like to imitate—being an ideal person to be liked and respected—or it may place the teacher in the position of having to decide whether she will actually provide the physical love and comfort the child craves. Many unmarried women satisfy their own needs for love, security, and a family by functioning as a substitute parent in their teaching.

A teacher also acts as a judge in teaching. Being a disciplinarian involves judging the rightness or wrongness of behavior, and although the explicitness of this role varies, every teacher judges, accepts, or rejects behaviors which daily are encountered in teaching. The judging may not always be done overtly, but the very act of paying attention to behavior involves a judgment of that behavior.

The teacher is not only a judge and a disciplinarian in the classroom, but is expected to be both friend and confidante to his pupils. It is not easy to balance the authoritarian roles with the familiar without abdicating either one or the other.

Teachers also play a number of roles outside the classroom. A teacher is usually expected to participate in community affairs, and may reasonably be expected to sing in the church choir, teach a Sunday School class, work for the Red Cross, or do a stint as a census taker. However, participation in community affairs is usually limited to "safe" activities that carry little prestige. Community resistance is usually encountered if the teacher becomes too active in politics or too actively involved in a business on the side. For most teachers, the tendency is to participate some in community affairs, but not as leaders.

Even though the teacher is expected to participate in some aspects of community life, and to avoid participation in others, he is not necessarily expected to "sink roots" into the community. The teacher has been described as a "sociological stranger" (11)—a person who is *in* the community but not *of* it.

Many factors have contributed to the teacher's position of social isolation: (a) Teachers represent a group whose cultural interests generally differ from those found among others in a community. (b) Most people expect the teacher to remain socially neutral in order to be more objective in teaching. (c) The teacher is sometimes considered too idealistic to bother with social identifications in the community, outside of the school. (d) Traditionally, too, teachers have been a transient group. All these factors contribute to the teacher's social isolation in many communities.

The teacher, of course, is not able to act out all his roles with complete success. Most successful teachers are skillful in several roles and tend to emphasize those in which they feel more comfortable. Nevertheless, society's high expectations of the teacher may lead to conflicts and tensions. One investigator suggests that teaching is characterized by more possibilities of conflicts than other professions because of the contradictory roles the teacher is required to play (9). For example, people usually think of a teacher as someone who seeks the truth and communicates it; however, the successful teacher knows better than to take this role too literally. Another source of conflict may be due to the teacher's image as a traditionalist, one exercising a conservative influence, and the expectation that he also be a creative, imaginative individual and an innovator of ideas. Most teachers soon learn how far they can go in the different roles they must play, and this realization reduces much of the potential conflict. Regardless of how a teacher reacts at any given moment, his behavior is likely to be more appropriate if he is not bound by inflexible rules.

Some interesting insights about teachers' roles were obtained by comparing their views of themselves with the views of other professionals. Smith (26) studied the responses of 160 high school teachers and 173 nonteachers who were given a list of terms describing behaviors and asked to rate the concepts as either "typical high school teacher" or "ideal high school teacher." The nonteachers' concept of the ideal high school teacher made him more active, more aggressive, and more of a leader; the teacher group did not consider these characteristics desirable. The nonteacher group thought of the typical teacher as being less strong, less active, less flexible, less agressive, less democratic, and less of a leader than did the teacher group. The teacher group viewed the typical teacher as a close approximation of the ideal, whereas the nonteacher group thought the typical teacher lacking in a number of desirable characteristics. Smith summarized that teachers believed they should be seen and not heard, while nonteachers defined a more active role for the ideal teacher.

In a second study (26), a list of phrases from the writings of various educators describing a good teacher was used to test high school teachers and university students in a nonteaching curriculum. Both groups ranked the statements in the order that best described the ideal or superior high school teacher. The nonteacher group emphasized superior intelligence, creative imagination, aggressive drive, and social leadership. The teacher group emphasized a neat appearance, good organization, and the ability to discipline as being more indicative of the ideal teacher. Here again the teachers' concept of the ideal teacher was someone less imaginative and less aggressive than the nonteachers' ideal.

In a third study to further investigate the relationship between the real and the ideal self-concept of high school teachers, Smith (26) used the rating scale of the first study and asked those tested to rate themselves as they think they really are and as they would like to be. Ten groups of 17 persons were used. Group 1 consisted of teachers over age 40 with more than 15 years' teaching experience, and Group 2 was made up of teachers with less than 15 years' experience and under age 40. Groups 3 and 4 consisted of student teachers with either some teaching experience or with no initial experience. Groups 5 through 10 were made up of business administration students, barber college trainees, student nurses, registered nurses, construction workers, and factory workers. Everyone in each group rated himself both as he is and as he would like to be—each according to his own vocational frame of reference. The teachers who had the most experience and were over 40 years old showed the least discrepancy between self and ideal ratings. The largest discrepancy was found in both groups of student teachers. This difference between the experienced teachers and the student teachers might be attributed to the difference in age were it not for the fact that the student nurses rated themselves very much like the experienced teachers rated themselves— even though the mean age of the student nurses was 19 years and the mean age of the experienced teachers was 41 years. Smith (26) offers the following interpretation of his three studies:

> Perhaps the younger teacher is beginning to view his profession in terms of a more aggressive, active, leadership role in contemporary society. . . . The

major results of the three studies can be given a rather consistent interpretation. [Study I and study II] indicate that the nonteacher group wishes the
teacher to be more active, aggressive, and socially forceful, while the teacher
group seems to think of their role as a more passive, conforming, "seen and
not heard pattern." . . . [Study III] indicated that it is the older, more experienced teacher who views the teacher role as that of one who is "seen and
not heard."

These studies underscore the conflict and tension sometimes encountered in the teaching profession by the teacher who is not satisfied
with what is perceived to be the difference between "what is" and "what
ought to be." The increasing militancy of teachers who seek higher
salaries and a greater voice in what goes on in the classroom suggests that
the image of the teacher as active and aggressive may be more real than
ideal in many communities.

That self-perception in teachers is less than static is demonstrated by
research indicating that feedback between teacher and student acts as a
potent and influential factor. Gage (8) describes a research program
investigating the influence of information feedback from pupils to
teachers on the teachers' behavior, and the accuracy of the teachers'
perceptions of their pupils' perceptions. Each superintendent of schools
in Illinois was asked to provide the name of the first teacher in the
alphabetical list of all sixth-grade teachers in the superintendent's
district. One teacher in each district was sent a questionnaire containing
a section asking her to describe herself. She was also asked how she
thought her pupils would describe her. Then the teacher was asked
to administer a questionnaire to her students containing the same items.
The pupils were asked to describe their teacher on those items and were
also asked to describe "the best teacher you can imagine." The pupils'
responses were randomly divided into experimental and control groups.
The teachers of the pupils in the experimental group received a report
indicating where on the 12-item scale the median pupil had ranked the
teacher and where the median pupil had rated the "best imaginable"
teacher on the same twelve items. Similar reports were prepared for but
not given to the teachers in the control group until the experiment was
completed. About two months after the reports had been sent to the
teachers in the experimental groups, all teachers were again asked to
fill out the ratings on the scales and the students were asked to repeat
their performance.

The results confirmed that teachers who received feedback (the experimental group) seemed to change their perceptions in the direction
of pupils' "ideals" more than did teachers who had not received feedback
(the control group). Teachers in the experimental group were also more

accurate in predicting their pupils' ratings, perhaps because that group was told how their pupils rated them. Feedback of information from pupils to teachers did produce changes in the teachers' behavior and made them better able to perceive how their pupils saw them. The fact that the teachers changed in the direction of the ideals expressed by the pupils suggests that the results could have some implications for communication between teachers and students.

In a variation of the experiment described above, Daw and Gage (6) investigated the effects of feedback from teachers on the behavior of their principals. Using a design similar to the one discussed above, the investigators presented elementary school principals with information concerning how their teachers had rated them and how they had rated an ideal principal. Other principals rated in a similar way were not given this feedback information. The results of the study indicated that feedback was associated with changes in the principals' behavior. The application of feedback techniques in educational settings provides a possible way of making the behavior of teachers, principals, and other school personnel more effective.

Recent analyses of the teacher's role suggest that teaching is in transition, influenced basically by the introduction of technological advances in education and by the changes apparent in society's definition of the objectives of education. According to Lee (16), the transitional aspect of educational goals is characterized by at least three crucial trends. First, the basic purposes of schools have been moving more toward meeting broad national goals and away from serving the personal needs of individual students. Literacy is being emphasized more in relation to pressing political and social realities than to the students' need to satisfy their personal aims. Second, the broad commitment to psychosocial development as a dominant objective of education is being supplanted by a commitment to the cultivation of intellectual power. Understanding and skill in the basic disciplines are important, again in terms of their relationship to national rather than individual needs. Competence in the basic disciplines and preparation for college have taken precedence over the goals of personal adjustment and happy living. Third, the concept that education has a definite beginning and end is being supplanted by a concept of continuity of educational experience, with the teacher becoming a promoter of "lifelong learning" and the educational process concerned with the problem of learning how to learn.

The changes in the goals of education are accompanied by changes in the roles that students and teachers play in the educational setting. The concept of educating the whole child is being superseded by the view that the school has unique functions to perform which relate only to particular aspects of the learner's personality. In addition, the school has become increasingly concerned with different types of students and has shown interest in developing education programs to accommodate them. Although the goals of education are changing from those centered in individual needs and aims to those more nationalistically oriented, the time being devoted to individual students in schools is increasing, compared with the time traditionally given them.

The teacher's role is becoming that of a specialist in some field of learning. Consequently, less is expected of the teacher relative to the range and diversity of his functions, but more in terms of fitness to perform those functions which remain. The teacher is becoming less of a source of data and a dispenser of knowledge and more of a classroom catalyst who stimulates learning. Having become less didactic and more tutorial, the teacher is more a resource for learning than a source. As this role stabilizes, the teacher will become increasingly occupied with mobilizing materials for learning. These three characteristics—specialization, intellectualization, and continuity—mark the changing role of the teacher in the latter third of the twentieth century (16).

The Personality of the Teacher

Psychologists who study education have always been interested in the personality of the teacher. Are certain characteristics specific for success in the profession? How do unsuccessful teachers differ from successful ones? Do elementary teachers have personalities that are different from secondary teachers? These and many other questions have been used in studies of personality characteristics of teachers. Typical examples of such research are studies by Witty (34) and by Symonds (28).

Through a national radio program, "Quiz Kids," Witty solicited letters from students all over the United States, who were asked to write about "The Teacher Who Has Helped Me Most." Over 14,000 replies were received from second- to twelfth-grade pupils. The letters were analyzed to determine the predominant characteristics most often mentioned by the pupils. Being cooperative, having a democratic attitude, showing kindness and consideration, being patient, having wide interests, being fair and impartial, and having a sense of humor were the characteristics the pupils mentioned most often in association with the helpful teacher.

A follow-up study using 33,000 letters corroborated the results of the first study. In addition, a random sample of letters was selected and analyzed for negative characteristics. Those most frequently mentioned were intolerance, a bad temper, being unreasonable in demands made upon the pupil, being sarcastic and unfriendly, and having an unattractive appearance. These are the good and bad characteristics of teachers, but they would be applicable for almost any other professionals.

Symonds asked pupils questions such as, "Which of your teachers makes the work most interesting?" On the basis of the pupils' ratings a group of superior teachers and a group of inferior teachers were identified and their personality characteristics studied. Symonds' conclusions were that on the average the superior teachers liked children, the inferior teachers disliked them; the superior teachers were secure and self-assured, the inferior teachers were insecure and felt inferior and inadequate; finally, the superior teachers seemingly had well-integrated personality patterns while the inferior teachers seemed personally disorganized.

One should not conclude from this study that feelings of inferiority, inadequacy, or any of the negative characteristics mentioned will automatically cause a teacher to be inferior. Possibly these characteristics predispose the teacher toward failure; yet many fine teachers do have characteristics usually associated with poor teachers.

A very exhaustive investigation of the personal attributes of teachers is the Teacher Characteristics Study sponsored by the American Council on Education (25). During the study, more than 100 separate investigations involving more than 6000 teachers in approximately 1700 schools were completed. The study comprised three types of investigation. In one area of research, trained observers were used to see what patterns of teachers' classroom behaviors might be important. The second area was the development of tests of differences among teachers. The last area was the comparison of specific groups of teachers (e.g., elementary and secondary) on certain personal and social characteristics. These three general types of investigations were usually performed in sequence, so that the observations made in the classroom were used in designing the test instruments, which in turn were used to ascertain the personal and social characteristics of the different groups of teachers involved in the project.

Comparisons were made of the attitudes, educational viewpoints, verbal understanding, and emotional adjustment of the teachers in the sample. From the data collected, some answers can be made to the question, "What is a teacher like?"

The major testing instrument used in the Teacher Characteristics Study was a test booklet named the Teacher Characteristics Schedule which made it possible to score such characteristics as warmth, understanding, friendliness versus aloofness, and egocentricity. A number of observations are possible concerning the comparison of specific groups of teachers, using the scores on the testing instrument. A few are as follows:

1. More favorable attitudes were held by elementary teachers toward administrators, pupils, fellow-teachers, and nonadministrative workers than were held by secondary teachers.

2. Teachers who were judged superior by their principals had more favorable attitudes toward pupils and administrators than did the teachers judged unsatisfactory.

3. Women teachers in the secondary schools tended to express more favorable attitudes toward pupils than did their elementary counterparts. Among elementary teachers, however, men appeared to express more favorable attitudes than did the women.

4. Teachers who were judged warm, understanding, and stimulating by the classroom observers displayed more favorable attitudes toward pupils and administrators.

5. The way pupils behaved in class did not appear to be related to the attitudes of the teachers.

6. The educational views of secondary teachers tended to be traditional; the elementary teachers' viewpoints about education were more permissive. And among the secondary teachers, those in science and mathematics tended to be more traditional in their viewpoints than those in social studies and English.

7. Teachers considered warm and understanding by the classroom observers had more permissive educational viewpoints than teachers judged to be businesslike and systematic.

8. Secondary teachers scored higher on tests of verbal understanding than did elementary teachers.

9. At both the elementary and secondary levels, men appeared to be more emotionally stable than women.

10. Teachers 55 years of age or older tended to have a different cluster of characteristics than those expressed by the younger group.

11. The classroom behavior of male teachers in the elementary schools was less responsible, systematic, and businesslike than that of the women.

12. Differences between the sexes were more pronounced at the secondary level than at the elementary. Secondary women teachers exhibited more understanding, friendliness, and responsibleness in their classroom behavior than did their male counterparts.

13. At the elementary level, the married teachers were superior to those who had never married, for their classroom behavior was friendlier, more responsible, and also more businesslike. Married teachers held more stimulating classes, showed a favorable attitude toward their students, and had child-centered views on education.

14. At the secondary level, single teachers rated higher: they were more given to responsible, businesslike classroom behavior, had favorable attitudes toward democratic classroom practice and permissive educational viewpoints and showed better verbal understanding than did the married teachers. However, single teachers were less stable emotionally than married teachers.

15. Teachers who engaged in vocational activities tended to score higher on most of the characteristics measured.

16. Teachers who considered themselves to have been outstanding students in college tended to score higher on most of the favorable characteristics studied.

The findings just summarized (25) answer some questions about teachers' traits. A disappointing result is hidden in the list, however. Since the fifth point is that pupils' behavior in the classroom is unrelated to teacher attitudes, those attitudes may be less important than had been thought. New studies are surely needed to show what does affect pupils' classroom behavior.

Thelen (29) who has studied the classroom extensively as a social system (or as a microsociety with distinct similarities to the larger social world or macrosociety), feels that the major influence on the organization of the classroom is the personality of the teacher. In a summary of research on classroom organization he concluded that grouping students had very little effect on the overall outcomes of the learning experience of the classroom. He points out, however, that one conclusion does emerge from an analysis of the literature on grouping:

> We are forced to see that *the organizing principle of the classroom society is the personality of the teacher* and, therefore, the way to improve the classroom society through grouping is to fit students to the teacher in such a way that the educative tendencies within his personality will be most reinforced. Short of intensive clinical study of teachers and students, educational theory at present would offer no suggestions as to how to effect such matching.

There is enough evidence to suggest that the students' perceptions are influenced by the attitudes, values, and biases which are part of the individual teacher's personality. For example, one study reported that the distribution of rewards common to the elementary and secondary schools is also found at the college level. Middle- and upper-class students received proportionately more attention and higher grades than those below them socially (31), suggesting that the rewards used by teachers— the way a teacher grades, whom the teacher praises, and the degree to which the teacher accepts the pupils' behaviors—are influenced by the pupils' socioeconomic backgrounds. Teachers tend to favor those behaviors representing a "good" middle-class style of life. A second explanation should also be considered: On the average, students of high socioeconomic background perform better than do pupils of low socioeconomic background. In all probability, some of these differences are innate; others are the result of special opportunities afforded students of "good" families.

Most people tend to approve of those whose thinking and behavior are like their own. An analysis of the careers of a number of Chicago teachers suggests that careers are influenced by the movements made from school to school as teachers seek the most satisfactory place to work. The satisfaction, or lack of satisfaction, associated with a particular school usually depends on the teacher's finding the "right" kind of pupils, parents, principal, and colleagues (1). Obviously, the teacher's behavior is strongly influenced by his attitudes about the pupils he teaches and the people he works with. The Chicago teachers reported that their greatest teaching problems were in schools with a predominantly lower-class student body. This is understandable, for most teachers come from a middle-class family background and represent a middle-class morality, and also because lower-class students more often commit genuinely unacceptable behaviors (11).

Inevitably, teachers react subjectively to students. One study found a positive relationship between the personality ratings a teacher assigns a child and the grade the child receives in class. The more favorably the teacher viewed the child's personality, the higher the child's grade tended to be (24). Whether teachers assign good grades on the basis of the child's personality or whether the child's personality is more attractive because of superior performance is open to question. However, a child with an attractive personality usually does make good grades.

Ideally, the teacher should not allow the sex of the child to influence his feelings, but classroom observations show that boys receive more blame from teachers than do girls (17). Our society teaches us to expect more aggressive behavior from boys than from girls, and teachers, like everyone else, respond to this indoctrination. How much of this expectation is justified and how much is biased remains to be seen.

The problem of the teacher's own mental health and how it affects the ability to be a good teacher is obscured by divergent opinions about what a "good" teacher is like. Although the teacher is usually thought of as an emotionally stable person, emotional instability is not conclusive evidence that a person is unfit to teach (22). Certain types of behavior irritate the maladjusted teacher more than they do the emotionally stable one, just as some behaviors bother the stable rather than the unstable teacher; but this does not mean that emotional instability should automatically bar someone from the teaching profession (3). The teacher, like everyone else, is subject to frustrations and tensions that can produce a state of bad mental health, which may be reflected in the way he performs his job. Rarely, though, does it seriously affect his performance. Nonetheless, teaching would certainly be easier, and perhaps more productive, if all teachers were paragons of good mental health; but, then, so would any other professional activity.

An exhaustive survey of the literature on the personality of teachers was reported by Getzels and Jackson (10) in the recently published *Handbook of Research on Teaching*. Although their bibliography contains over 150 items, they conclude that very little is known about the personality of the teacher and its influence on teaching. According to these authors, much of the research on teachers has an almost universal application. To say that good teachers are friendly, sympathetic, and kind is to say that they are like everyone else who has a "good" personality. One of the most difficult problems still facing the researcher in this area is to set the criteria for defining a good or a successful teacher as opposed to a bad or unsuccessful one. Meanwhile, the researcher continues to be puzzled by contradictions found in those studies attempting to relate success in teaching to such variables as personality.

Learning in the Classroom and Effective Teaching

Classroom teaching would be easier to define if it could be conceptualized as either effective teaching or ineffective teaching. Unfortunately, some fifty years of research on teacher effectiveness has produced no criteria agreed on by educators and other concerned specialists. Mitzel (18), in a concise and perceptive review of approaches to such a study, points out that inadequate criteria, or standards, to be used in evaluating teacher behavior are responsible for the lack of success in defining effective teaching behaviorally. Empirically, teacher effectiveness has no meaning other than the criteria used to define successful teaching. These criteria should have four attributes in order to produce data that can contribute to our understanding of effective teacher behavior. These attributes are: (1) validity, (2) reliability, (3) freedom from bias, and (4) practicality.

Mitzel (18) classifies criteria for teacher effectiveness into three major groups. One is referred to as product criteria, the outcomes of teaching. Changes in behavior as a result of teaching—what the student learns— is the product. A second grouping consists of criteria associated with the process of teaching and focuses on the behavioral interactions between teacher and student as teaching takes place. The student encouraged by the teacher's acceptance of new ideas gets up to lead a class discussion; the teacher's own sense of security prompting him to invite dissenting opinions are examples of process criteria. The third group of criteria is called presage criteria. Presage criteria are peripheral to, or by-products of, other criteria. For example, the intelligence of the teacher is a presage criterion since students react not to the teacher's I.Q. but to the teacher's behavior, intelligence and personal adjustment.

For many years educators assumed that teachers who were effective in one dimension were also effective in others and that teachers judged effective by the criterion of greatest gains in student achievement would also demonstrate effectiveness in other criterion attributes. Actually interpreting effectiveness as a unitary trait is an oversimplified and somewhat naïve conceptualization of the problem. Success in teaching is multidimensional, and should be studied in terms of the interaction and interrelatedness of all its factors.

Although the tremendous and varied literature on the problem of effective teaching has failed to produce any specific criteria for distinguishing the outstanding teacher from the poor one there is evidence to suggest that agreement on the criteria, whatever they may be, is not so random as one might imagine. A recent study (12) reported a high consistency among ten methods used to identify outstanding elementary school teachers. However, it does not follow that the poor teacher could be agreed upon with the same degree of concordance.

The investigators used ten methods at ten elementary schools to determine which teachers were most outstanding. These methods were both objective and subjective; the objective data identified those teachers who were best trained, most experienced, highest paid, and had the highest rating. The subjective choices were made by principals, district administrators, peer teachers, nonteaching staff members, and informed parents. Consistency among all ten methods was at a highly significant level (statistical probability of .001) making it apparent that even such disparate methods—formal, objective procedures and informal, subjective judgments—can yield agreement. Educational psychologists would benefit by knowing what factors were significant in producing the agreement; however, the very fact of agreement is reassuring to those who must make pragmatic decisions in recognizing superior achievements in teaching.

In order to study teaching and classroom effectiveness in relation to learning, the researcher needs some concept, or model, of what he intends to investigate. Mitzel's description and classification of criteria for investigating success in teaching is a concept broad enough to cover the multidimensional aspects of teacher effectiveness. Learning in the classroom, however, involves more than just the teacher's effective behavior. Teacher effectiveness may be one aspect of the model, but it represents only one factor. One simple way to conceptualize school learning is to classify the variables related to it.

Carroll (2) points out that "the primary job of the educational psychologist is to develop and apply knowledge concerning why pupils succeed or fail in their learning at school, and to assist in the prevention and remediation of learning difficulties." A number of concepts have been used traditionally to organize data about behavior. Maturation, social development, and motivation are useful concepts, but they make little contribution toward developing a model of school learning, since they overlap and often lack the specificity needed in a model. According to Carroll:

> What is needed is a schematic design or conceptual model of factors affecting success in school learning and of the way they interact. Such a model should use a very small number of simplifying concepts, conceptually independent of

one another and referring to phenomena at the same level of discourse. It should suggest new and interesting research questions and aid in the solution of practical educational problems. With the aid of such a framework, the often conflicting results of different research studies might be seen to fall into a unified pattern.

Carroll's model is directed toward those tasks concerned with learning. The major organizational theme of the model is the assumption that a learner will succeed in "learning a given task to the extent that he spends the amount of time he *needs* to learn the task."

Time factors related to learning are (I) *time needed to learn* and (II) *time spent in learning.* Time needed depends on: (a) aptitude for the specific task to be learned, (b) the ability to understand instruction, and (c) the quality of the instruction. Variables associated with time spent are: (a) the time allowed for learning, and (b) perseverance, or the extended time the learner is willing to spend.

The five elements in the model can be classified another way, this time by relating them either to the student or to external conditions. Aptitude, the ability to understand instruction, and perseverance are the variables that are unique for each student. Opportunity (the time allowed for learning) and the quality of instruction are the external factors, influenced by the organization of the school and the effectiveness of the teacher.

Still another way of expressing these variables is as a function of time. *Aptitude* is the amount of time needed to learn a task—assuming optimal instructional conditions. *Perseverance* is the amount of time the learner is willing to devote to learning the task. *Opportunity* is the time allowed for learning. The *time needed* to learn is inversely related to the quality of the instruction and to the ability of the learner to understand instruction. The poorer the quality of teaching and the less the aptitude for learning the longer is the amount of time needed to learn. Carroll offers the following formula as a summary of the model:

Degree of learning (is a function of)

$$= f \frac{\text{time actually spent (aptitude, opportunity, perseverance)}}{\text{time needed (quality of instruction, ability to understand instruction)}}$$

The model suggested by Carroll is only one of a number of models that could logically be developed from an analysis of classroom learning. Each of the variables in this model could form the basis for an extensive research program on school learning. The need for broader conceptualization of research in educational psychology, which was discussed in Chapter 1, could be met through research programs built on variables related to each other through just such models. Questions about the validity of the model and about the interdependent nature of the variables would necessitate having basic data on school learning so the model can have empirical support. Carroll (2) emphasizes the contributions of a conceptual model such as this by stating:

> [the] model probably contains, at least at a superordinate level, every element required to account for an individual's success or failure in school learning [at least in the learning tasks to which the model applies]. The explication and refinement of these factors and the exploration of their interactions constitute a major task of educational psychology. Its other major task is to account for those types of school learning (e.g., attitudinal and emotional conditioning) to which the present model is not intended to apply and for which a separate model might well be constructed.

This model is again described in Chapter 3, when some of the implications of the model for learning are discussed.

Models for classroom learning are essential to the development of research programs which will, it is hoped, answer some of the basic problems of classroom learning, but the models themselves contain no answers. Obviously, there are no universal rules for understanding and explaining behavior. As long as a teacher realizes this, he places himself in a position of not being too disappointed when a particular child responds in a manner different from the prescribed textbook responses. The classroom is a unit within which a phenomenal range of behavior is not only possible but highly probable.

Summary

Teaching involves many skills and attitudes, expressed through the behavior of the teacher and influential in shaping the behavior of the learner. The role society expects the teacher to play is really a composite of many roles, some complementary and others contradictory.

Classrooms are psychological atmospheres in which teachers and students interact and learn. While the formal curricula of the school helps to organize the activities of education, the classroom has a second, "hidden," curricula that influences the behaviors of learners as much as do the reading and arithmetic lessons. The teacher and the classroom have a profound influence on shaping the behavior of the child in our society.

Teachers have individual, rather than prescribed, attitudes and values about behavior. They tend to agree, however, that pupil behavior is bad if it is disruptive or if it threatens the authority of the teacher. Teachers today are more sensitive to the students' psychological problems even if they are not expressed in aggressive and hostile behaviors.

Teaching styles show great diversity, partly because teachers find certain classroom roles more compatible than others and develop the more comfortable ones. Today the teacher's role no longer fits traditional definitions, for it is in a state of transition.

Teachers are seeking less diversity and more specificity in their teaching activities. As a result, teaching is increasingly being viewed as a professional activity requiring extensive preparation.

Although the role of the teacher is coming closer to being specifically defined, the attributes that contribute to effective teaching are not being identified with any certainty. The ingredients which, when put together, make a good teacher are still not specified. Perhaps the act of teaching is too complex to be reduced to a formula. Educational psychologists, however, continue to seek those factors related to good teaching, hoping to discover exactly how the teacher and the learner interact to produce changes of behavior in the learner. The model advanced by Carroll (2) attempts to do this by discussing the relationship between the time spent in learning in the classroom and the time actually needed.

We will know more about the teacher-learner relationship as researchers continue to examine the interrelatedness of learning and teaching, and as they seek interacting causes for the problems of classroom behavior.

SUGGESTED READINGS

Amidon, E. J., & Hough, J. B. (Eds.) *Interaction analysis: Theory, research and application.* Reading, Mass.: Addison-Wesley, 1967.

Interaction analysis is a technique for studying the instructional process in the classroom by analyzing the dynamics of classroom activities, particularly verbal interactions between teacher and learner. This collection of comments and studies involving interaction analysis gives an interesting view of the classroom and the many factors which relate to teacher-pupil activity.

Carroll, J. B. A model of school learning. *Teachers College Record,* 1963, **64,** 723–733.

Classroom learning is only just beginning to be approached by the educational researcher as a complex phenomenon involving many variables that are best understood through their interactions rather than as isolated factors. Professor Carroll defines some of these variables in his excellent article and presents a model that will interest beginning teachers.

Gordon, I. J. *Studying the child in the classroom.* New York: Wiley, 1966.

Gordon's very practical book deals with the task of becoming aware of the student by studying him. The emphasis is on the teacher and the information he needs about children in order to make instruction more effective. Gordon includes examples of techniques for developing information about student behavior.

Jackson, P. W. *Life in classrooms.* New York: Holt, Rinehart & Winston, 1968.

This small book contains a perceptive essay on the classroom as a social system, complete with a hidden curriculum that is as potent as the public curriculum in influencing change in student behavior. Professor Jackson's observations are based on his own classroom experiences. With great insight he discusses those classroom activities that are relevant to behavioral change and those that are not.

REFERENCES

1. Becker, H. S. The career of the Chicago public school teacher. *American Journal of Sociology,* 1952, **57,** 470–477.
2. Carroll, J. B. A model of school learning. *Teachers College Record,* 1963, **64,** 723–733.
3. Clark, E. J. The relationship between the personality traits of elementary school teachers and their evaluation of objectionable pupil behavior. *Journal of Educational Research,* 1951, **45,** 61–66.
4. Cubberley, E. P. *Readings in the history of education.* Boston: Houghton Mifflin, 1920.
5. Cutts, N. E., & Moseley, N. *Practical school discipline and mental hygiene.* Boston: Houghton Mifflin, 1941.
6. Daw, R. W., & Gage, N. L. Effect of feedback from teachers to principals. *Journal of Educational Psychology,* 1967, **58,** 181–188.
7. Elsbree, W. S. *The american teacher.* New York: American Book Co., 1939.
8. Gage, N. L. A method for "improving" teacher behavior. *Journal of Teacher Education,* 1963, **14,** 261–266.
9. Getzels, J. W., & Guba, E. G. The structure of roles and role conflict in the teaching situation. *Journal of Educational Sociology,* 1955, **29,** 30–40.
10. Getzels, J. W., & Jackson, P. W. The teachers' personality and characteristics. In N. Gage (Ed.), *Handbook of research on teaching.* Chicago: Rand McNally, 1963. Pp. 506–582.
11. Havighurst, R. J., & Neugarten, B. L. *Society and education.* Boston: Allyn Bacon, 1962.
12. Hawkins, E. E., & Stoops, E. Objective and subjective identification of outstanding elementary teachers. *Journal of Educational Research,* 1966, **59,** 344–346.
13. Henning, C. J. Discipline: are school practices changing? *Clearing House,* 1949, **23,** 267–273.
14. Jackson, P. W. *Life in classrooms.* New York: Holt, Rinehart & Winston, 1968.
15. Kaplan, L. The annoyances of elementary school teachers. *Journal of Educational Research,* 1952, **45,** 649–665.
16. Lee, G. C. The changing role of the teacher. In J. Goodlad (Ed.), *The changing American school. Sixty-fifth yearbook of the National Society for the Study of Education.* Part II. Chicago: University of Chicago Press, 1966. Pp. 9–31.
17. Meyer, W. J., & Thompson, G. G. Sex differences in the distribution of teacher approval and disapproval among sixth grade children. *Journal of Educational Psychology,* 1956, **47,** 385–396.

18. Mitzel, H. E. Teacher effectiveness. In C. Harris (Ed.), *Encyclopedia of educational research*. New York: Macmillan, 1960. Pp. 1481–1485.
19. Mowrer, O. H. Discipline and mental health. *Harvard Educational Review*, 1947, **17**, 284–296.
20. National Education Association. *Research Bulletin*, 1965 (October), **43**(3), 68.
21. Rabkin, L. Y. The dogmatism of teachers. *Journal of Teacher Education*, 1966, **17**, 47–49.
22. Retan, G. A. Emotional instability and teaching success. *Journal of Educational Research*. 1943, **37**, 135–141.
23. Rokeach, M. *The opened and closed mind*. New York: Basic Books, 1960.
24. Russell, I. L., & Thalman, W. A. Personality: does it influence teachers marks? *Journal of Educational Research*, 1955, **48**, 561–564.
25. Ryans, D. G. *Characteristics of teachers: their description, comparison, and appraisal*. Washington, D. C.: American Council on Education, 1960.
26. Smith, T. E. The image of high-school teachers: self and other, real and ideal (should teachers be seen and not heard?). *Journal of Educational Research*, 1965, **59**, 99–104.
27. Stauffer, G. A. Behavior problems of children as viewed by teachers and mental hygienists. *Mental Hygiene*, 1952, **34**, 271–285.
28. Symonds, P. M. Characteristics of the effective teacher based on pupil evaluations. *Journal of Experimental Education*, 1955, **23**, 289–310.
29. Thelen, H. A. Group interactional factors in learning. In E. Bower & W. Hollister (Eds.), *Behavioral science frontiers in education*. New York: Wiley, 1967. Pp. 257–287.
30. Tolar, A., Scarpetti, W. L., & Lane, P. A. Teachers' attitudes toward children's behavior revisited. *Journal of Educational Psychology*, 1967, **58**, 175–180.
31. Wade, D. E. Social class in a teachers college. *Journal of Educational Sociology*, 1954, **28**, 131–138.
32. Walberg, H. The structure of self-concept in prospective teachers. *Journal of Educational Research*, 1967, **61**, 84–87.
33. Wickman, E. K. *Children's behavior and teachers' attitudes*. New York: Commonwealth Fund, 1928.
34. Witty, P. A. The teacher who has helped me most. *Elementary English*, 1947. **24**, 345–354.

3

LEARNING: THE ACQUISITION
OF NEW RESPONSES

This chapter presents the principles of the learning process as an experimental psychologist might see them. Because the prospective teacher may be surprised to find this chapter emphasizing how animals learn, some comments about animal and human behavior seem appropriate. Animals clearly are capable of simple learning: Dogs are taught to come to their masters; elephants are taught circus tricks; pigeons and rats are taught many things in psychological laboratories. The biological kinship of animals and men suggests that part of man's learning process bears a similarity to that of the lower animals. Therefore, in finding out what goes on in organisms without the capacity for speech and writing, there will be indications that the simple processes thus observed do take place in humans as well. Some higher mental processes of humans, such as concept learning, will prove to be closely related to simpler processes. However, not all human learning is necessarily interpretable as the product of the elementary processes discovered in studies with animals.

A further advantage of studying animal behavior is that it has led to an emphasis upon analyzing behavior into specific acts. A naive person talking about teaching geography might say that one task of the teacher is to help children learn the names of the continents. However, an experienced teacher or a psychologist would know that this statement must be made more specific. At least three levels of activity are involved here:

(a) students learn to *recognize* the names of the continents as continent names, (b) students learn to *recall* the names of the continents when asked to name the seven continents, and (c) students learn which continent name belongs to which shape on a globe representing the earth. The latter process could be called *association* of names and maps of places.

Teachers of geography will normally want to accomplish more than teaching recognition, recall, and association of continent names and places. But once they know how to analyze learned behavior into specific processes such as these three, they will be able to express more clearly just what goals they do have. Also they may be able to discriminate between subject matter where recognition learning is all that is needed and other subject matter in which recall for a day will be sufficient or in which recall for a year will be essential. Then their teaching procedures can be geared to those needs. The process of analyzing the material to be learned and specifying exactly what is to be accomplished is called the process of *specifying behavioral objectives* (52), i.e., desired changes in student behavior.

When we speak of a change in behavior, we are often speaking of learning, one special kind of such change. *Learning is a relatively permanent change in behavior resulting from experience.* It may accompany changes such as those due to growth. But, for example, though high jumping is dependent on both body structure and skill, no one would call the improvement in high-jumping ability from 4 to 12 years of age an indicator of learning. Nor would one call a person's response of relief after taking an aspirin tablet an evidence of learning.

The improvement in high-jumping ability just mentioned is termed an effect of growth or maturation. The response to an aspirin tablet is a direct biochemical effect without mediation of a learning process. We could also note changes in effort put forth by a marathon runner during a race and attribute any reduction in speed from one mile to the next to *fatigue* rather than to learning: the change is not relatively permanent even though it results from experience, one condition of our definition of learning. A further distinction can be made between changes attributable to motivation and to learning: If someone offers to pay you $1 per hour to pick strawberries, and while you are picking them a friend says he has $40 he'll share with you on an all-day spree, you may stop picking strawberries because the motivation for picking is lower than the motivation for going with your friend. Though there are elements of learning in this process, your change in behavior is not relatively permanent—it reflects a temporary motivational condition rather than a learning by experience. However, if every day your friend came by and every day you left with him without a promise of money but received money each time you went with him, you would be learning to go with your friend because a relatively permanent response was being developed.

_____ **Acquiring Information or Developing Habits?**

Most people think of learning as the acquisition of information. This belief is consistent with the definition above, for acquiring a bit of information implies a change in behavior due to experience—if you have the information, you will be able to transmit it to others. Or will you? How many times have you said, "I know the answer, but I just can't explain it"? And a moment later, perhaps, you gave a good explanation, nonetheless. You can hardly think of learning, then, as the putting of scraps of information on small sheets of paper and dropping them into a bucket, to be retrieved as necessary.

A well-known psychologist, in a moment of levity, once formed a hypothesis somewhat like this idea of the bucket, however. His *pine plank hypothesis* states that information is stacked on a pine plank inside the head. As new information is placed on the plank, old information is pushed to the back of the plank, eventually to be pushed off the other end completely (and thus wholly forgotten) as new material crowds in. According to this preposterous theory, your difficulty in recalling an answer might mean that you have to search all over the pine plank for the information because it has been moved since you learned it. In actual fact machines now have memories and do have to search through those memories for certain information. A recent article on artificial intelligence (62) will give you some idea about the similar capabilities of these machines and human beings. You may be surprised to find that these machines (digital computers) can play checkers, solve algebraic story problems, and even "learn" in the sense defined at the beginning of this chapter.

Perhaps human beings are less efficiently built than digital computing machines. The machine memory either stores a unit of information or does not. But when you are trying to retrieve something from your memory, you not only have to "look for it," you have problems with its clarity—you may visualize it well enough to recognize it when told but not well enough to state it correctly by yourself. Therefore, psychologists distinguish between methods for testing memory by "recall" and by "recognition," whereas the machine could always be required to produce by recall.

But this incompleteness of human memory makes it scientifically inconvenient to focus upon the acquisition of information per se as learning. If a test for recognition shows an item to have been learned and a test for recall does not, it is more to the point to speak of learning to recognize that item than to speak of learning the item itself. Now the response said to be learned is reasonably specific; if necessary it can be made even more specific.

Even in this example, however, the emphasis is on acquiring information. Oddly enough, psychologists studying learning have stressed other processes more. Learning probably always includes some storage of information, but this storage is often a minor aspect of learning. What information do you acquire while tying your shoes? Precious little. But every time you do it, the responses involved are strengthened. The emphasis here is on changes in habit.

One reason for the psychologist's emphasis on aspects of learning other than the acquisition of information has been his interest in animal behavior. Animals can be taught to find their way through a complex maze in order to obtain food; this behavior can be thought of as the manifestation of acquired information about the maze. However, no sub-human animal appears to approach the information-storing capacity of man. Consequently, other aspects of animal behavior necessarily have received greater attention. Biologists have been most interested, perhaps, in largely unlearned behavior specific to certain species, such as the pouncing, swatting, and biting which cats will do even when raised in zoo incubators and deprived of a mother to copy (28). Psychologists have been more concerned with so-called *conditioning processes.* In conditioning, an animal learns to make a certain response whenever a certain stimulus appears (classical conditioning, or Skinner's type S); or he learns to make the response as a means of increasing the frequency with which he obtains food or some other desired stimulus (instrumental conditioning, or Skinner's type R).

Surely conditioning must be important in human beings as well as in animals. It would seem possible that information could be acquired passively just by listening to the radio or keeping one's eyes open while traveling. But what makes people go to lunch about noon, go surfing at the beach, or pay money to go to the movies? These responses depend much less upon what one knows than upon how one has been conditioned to act. If someone has been rewarded for surfing, he continues to surf; if not, he gives it up.

Teachers will recognize that much of their job is to condition children to make certain responses. It is not enough to give children information or even to teach them skills such as reading. For example, children rewarded for reading newspapers will probably continue to do so—and at the very least will have a basis for intelligent voting in adulthood.

The foregoing has been an overview of a very few of the problems which will concern us in the next three chapters. Though we will try to present a unified approach to learning, it will be evident that certain experiments reflect an interest in conditioning stemming from research with animals, while other studies reflect an interest in the acquisition of information stemming largely from what is called the *verbal learning* tradition of research with human beings.

It should be emphasized that the same fundamental processes operate to produce most data obtained in conditioning studies and in verbal learning studies; in fact, what is called *conditioning theory* is often applied to verbal learning studies or to other experiments emphasizing the acquisition of information. However, it should also be said that some investigators (5, 65) of the acquisition of information or of thought processes in general favor some form of *cognitive theory* (so named because it emphasizes cognition, i.e., knowledge and understanding), which will be discussed later in this book.

Most psychologists who use the rigorous scientific methods emphasized here are called *behaviorists*. It is their belief that psychological data consist solely of *observable* behavior. For example, a thought or a feeling cannot be part of the data of psychology because only the person experiencing it can observe it—though not objectively. The cognitive theorist must recognize that he is trying to study knowledge and understanding indirectly, since these are not observable behaviors.

_____ **Conditioning**

Skinner's investigations of animal behavior, first reported in 1930, clearly follow from the work done by E. L. Thorndike at Columbia University. Thorndike's Law of Effect specified the relationships to be anticipated between a stimulus and a response as a result of the consequences of the response. According to Thorndike (82), "When a modifiable connection between a situation and a response is made and is accompanied by or followed by a satisfying state of affairs, that connection's strength is increased. When made and accompanied or followed by an annoying state of affairs, its strength is decreased." Thorndike is saying that rewards expedite the learning of the rewarded behavior while punishments impede this learning. He later modified the Law of Effect because studies reported in 1932 indicated that punishment did not have the opposite effect of a reward on behavior. Reward was found to be the more effective factor in controlling the learning process.

Skinner further extended the principles involved in the Law of Effect. A dedicated behaviorist, Skinner calls his point of view *operant condi-*

tioning. He emphasizes that the kind of learning which is under the control of its consequences is the most relevant model for human learning. The tradition which is associated with the development of Skinner's operant conditioning model has been referred to historically in psychology as a subclass of S–R theory. This stimulus–response (S–R) orientation, in much that is written about learning, is influenced by several factors. For one thing, the S–R approach corresponds in many ways to what is known about the activity of the nervous system. Also, S–R theory anchors the events of learning to observations and measurements made in the external world. According to Hill (39):

> This emphasis on the objective environment . . . provides a basis for studying the manipulations that produce behavioral change. This makes the S–R approach well suited for studying the conditions under which learning occurs. These various factors help to explain why the S–R approach, despite some limitations, has remained popular with those psychologists interested in the experimental study and theoretical analysis of learning.*

There is another group of theorists, S–S (stimulus–stimulus) theorists, who also recognize conditioning processes, but have sometimes de-emphasized their applicability to all learning situations (86). They point instead to the learning of connections between stimuli (e.g., learning that a dog, one stimulus, may also bite, another stimulus). It should also be mentioned here that S–S theory is a form of *cognitive theory*, which was mentioned earlier.

Skinner makes no claim to theory in his approach to learning even though many students of conditioning do call themselves S–R theorists. Although there is lawfulness in operant conditioning, Skinner's conceptualization of learning emphasizes inductive statements which provide this lawfulness in the individual case rather than in any statistical sense. His interest is in the prediction of behavior in single individuals rather than in the behavior which is studied in terms of averages of groups or individuals.

Skinner (77) distinguishes between two types of behavior, which he calls respondent and operant. Responses caused, or elicited, by known stimuli are the *respondents.* He refers to a second type of response as *operants* since they are emitted responses which need not be associated with any known stimuli. These two types of responses, respondent and operant, are related to two types of conditioning, type S and type R. Type S conditioning is associated with respondent behavior because the *reinforcement* is related to the stimuli. The *classical conditioning ex-*periment of Ivan P. Pavlov (1849–1936) is of *type S* in which the *conditioned stimulus* (CS, a bell) is presented together with the *unconditioned*

stimulus (UCS, some food) and acquires the properties of the unconditioned stimulus to elicit the response (salivation), now called a
conditioned response. Skinner considers type S learning relatively unimportant in human behavior and feels that type R is of much more importance. In *type R conditioning*, or *operant conditioning* (also called
instrumental conditioning by many investigators), the reinforcement is
correlated with the response rather than with the stimuli. In operant or
type R conditioning, the crucial factor is that reward, or reinforcement,
is not possible unless the response is emitted. Reinforcement becomes
contingent upon the response in type R, whereas in type S, reinforcement is contingent upon the stimulus. The basic law of type R conditioning, according to Skinner (77), is as follows: "If the occurrence of
an operant is followed by presentation of a reinforcing stimulus, the
strength is increased." Although the term "stimulus" is used, it refers to
the rewarding, or reinforcing, situation. What gets strengthened is the
response, or operant, and not an S–R connection as in Thorndike's Law
of Effect.

The basic experiments that demonstrated the relationship between
operants and reinforcement were done with animals (white rats and
pigeons) which were placed in a box equipped with a lever which, if

Fig. 3-1. A Skinner box, used for the study of operant conditioning with rats. For
pigeon apparatus see Fig. 3-6. (Photograph courtesy of the Lafayette Instrument
Company.)

pressed, would deliver a pellet of food. The lever could be attached to a recording system which would produce a record of the number of times the lever was pressed as a function of time. This apparatus has since become known as the "Skinner Box" and is a standard piece of equipment in any learning laboratory in which operant conditioning is being investigated. Figure 3-1 pictures the Skinner Box. The apparatus can be adjusted to deliver food (reinforcement) every time the appropriate lever-pressing behavior occurs or it can deliver food only at appropriate intervals. Skinner has clearly demonstrated the potency of reinforcement in controlling behavior since the consequence of the reinforcement is an increase in the rate of the response. Thus Skinner clearly shows an empirical relationship between a response and the immediate reinforcing of that response which is stable and lawful with respect to the control of the rate at which the response is emitted. This increase in the rate of responding is, in fact, a measure of operant strength which is referred to in the law of type R conditioning given above. Figure 3-2 presents a diagram comparing types R and S.

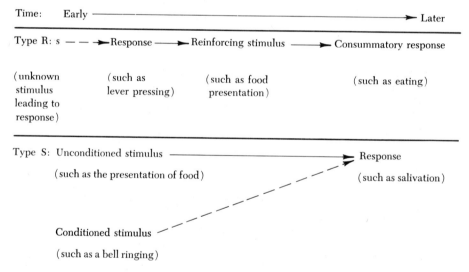

Fig. 3-2. Diagram and partial explanation of type R (operant or instrumental) and type S (respondent or classic) conditioning. In type S conditioning, the response is called an *unconditioned response* if it occurs following the unconditioned stimulus (solid arrow) but not following the conditioned stimulus alone. It is called a *conditioned response* if the conditioned and unconditioned stimuli have been repeatedly presented at about the same time and now the response will be made following the conditioned stimulus by itself (dashed arrow indicates that the conditioned stimulus has this effect).

A reinforcement may be either positive or negative. *A positive reinforcer increases the probability of the response when added to a situation. A negative reinforcer increases the probability of a response only when removed from a situation.* Food might act as a positive reinforcer while an electric shock would act as a negative reinforcer. In either instance, however, the reinforcement strengthens the probability of the response occurring again. Often reinforcers are further required to be events occurring shortly after the response to be strengthened. However, in classical conditioning the UCS is called a reinforcer because it strengthens the response. Note that UCS's occur whether or not the conditioned response is made.

Skinner and his associates (24) have extensively studied the effects of varying schedules of reinforcement on behavior. In order to maintain an acceptable rate of response, reinforcement does not need to accompany every desired response. Skinner distinguishes two major types of intermittent reinforcement which have been investigated in the laboratory. In a schedule of *interval reinforcement,* the reinforcing stimulus is presented at fixed or average intervals of time, such as following the first response after five minutes have elapsed since the immediately previous reinforcement. In a schedule of *ratio reinforcement,* the reinforcer, such as a piece of grain, is delivered after a fixed number of responses has been made. Skinner has shown that the rate of response can be maintained for extended periods of time without the reinforcer being present. In one instance he reports as many as 10,000 responses in a pigeon pecking at a key (a Plexiglas disk) for grain before the pigeon would stop responding.

The possibilities for controlling behavior through reinforcement are, according to Skinner, extensive. He refers to this process as the *shaping of behavior.* The shaping of behavior depends upon a process of analysis which permits the behavior to be broken down into its component parts. These parts are called *chained responses,* and the total pattern is conceptualized much as one might think of links in a chain. Examples of chained responses as units of behavior suggest that a careful analysis of behavior is necessary to determine the functional units necessary in a chain to make the behavior meaningful experimentally. Hilgard and Bower (36) present an elaboration of an illustration of chaining taken from a textbook by F. S. Keller and Schoenfeld (46). They discuss the behavior of a rat in a Skinner box by specifying the behavior in terms of six distinct operants as follows[*]:

---

[*] Reproduced by permission of Appleton-Century-Crofts, Educational Division, Meredith Corporation.

Operant number	Discriminative stimulus	Response of the rat
1	Bar location	Approach of rat to front of box
2	Visual bar	Rising on hind legs; placing paws on bar
3	Tactual bar	Pressing of bar; thus activating food–magazine
4	Apparatus noise	Lowering foreparts to food-tray
5	Visual pellet	Seizing of pellet by teeth and paws
6	Pellet in mouth	Chewing of pellet

The independence of these links in a chain of behavior can be tested experimentally. The *discriminative stimuli* acquire reinforcing properties and act to shape the behavior so that the well-conditioned rat appears to behave in a way which obscures the importance of the units themselves.

The concept of *successive approximations* in behavior is closely related to chaining and is central to the approach Skinner takes to the control of behavior. Skinner believes that behavior can be shaped by reinforcing those units of a behavioral chain which lead to a desired response. The experimenter would control the behavior of an experimental animal by successive approximations of the final response pattern, which would involve building in the operants necessary to reach the desired response.

The basic claim of Skinner's system is that the consequences of reinforcing operant behavior are increases in the rate of response. When a behavior leads to a reward or a reinforcement, it occurs more frequently.

The approach of B. F. Skinner to learning has had a profound effect on psychology and education. On the one hand, the simplicity of the approach with its lack of emphasis on many concepts, such as insight, which at one time were central to thinking about educational practice, has led some educators to overemphasize his technique for classroom instruction. On the other hand, Skinner has stimulated much serious thought about units and sequences of behavior which can lead to some more global goals of education. Skinner's approach to classroom learning demands that specific behavioral objectives be determined in order to know the direction that shaping must take. Operant conditioning has had application in the laboratory in the testing of drugs in experimental animals as well as in the office of the psychotherapist. The most widespread application, however, has been in the field of programmed instruction and in learning through the use of the teaching machine, to be discussed in Chapter 4.

_____ **Motivation and Learning**

A full treatment of motivation is deferred until Chapters 11 and 12 so that the topic may be presented near the related topic of personality. However, motivation is so closely related to learning that it is essential to mention it here as well. Motivation theorists often distinguish between *needs,* which are conditions of the organism in which certain substances such as food or water are required, and *drives,* which are consequences of those needs, such as tendencies to look for food. It is well known that a response such as pressing a bar to obtain food is more frequent when food drive is high than when it is low.

Skinner has not attempted to explain why this well-known fact is true, or even why reinforcements strengthen responses. However, Hull (41) has proposed the most commonly accepted hypothesis: Whenever a response made in a certain situation is followed by a reduction in level of some drive, the tendency for that response to be made in the situation is increased. Thus drive reduction following a response is a reinforcement of that response. The hypothesis just stated is the cornerstone of a drive–reduction theory of learning. It suggests, but does not logically demand, that all learning requires drive–reduction following the response to be learned. To accept this suggestion is to hold to a *strong theory of drive reduction,* strong in the sense that drive reduction has the strongest possible role in learning. To reject it is to hold to a *weak theory of drive reduction,* weak in the sense that drive reduction always facilitates learning but is not absolutely necessary before learning can take place.

We have just offered an explanation for the effects of some reinforcements, at least: They reduce the level of a drive and therefore strengthen the response preceding reinforcement. Now why do animals or people respond more frequently when the drive being reduced by the response is high than when it is low? Although other factors also operate, Hull indicates that a principal reason for this phenomenon is that rate of responding depends upon amount of learning (where learning cannot be directly observed but must be inferred from existing data and theory) and amount of drive, with drive having a multiplier effect so that a little learning leads to very frequent responding if drive is high enough. Note that both these explanations fail to give direct physiological descriptions of the mechanisms by which the effects are produced; however, they serve as useful preliminary descriptions of the way drive, reinforcement, learning, and rate of responding are related.

———————————————   **All–or–None Learning versus Gradual Learning**

The Problem

Most studies of learning report many observations made over many trials, minutes, or even years of experimentation. Estes (23) points out that we ought to look first at the effects of single events: one stimulus, one response, one reinforcement. From these effects we will get the information upon which to build a theory about long-term learning.

Consider what happens if you are a pupil and a teacher says that "John Brown" was hanged for leading an insurrection at Harper's Ferry just prior to the Civil War. Maybe you are looking out the window when Brown's name is mentioned. You cannot even repeat it immediately thereafter. You have not learned anything about it. Or perhaps you were not looking out the window. If asked immediately who led the insurrection, you say, "John Brown," and so have learned something in a single repetition. Perhaps, if not asked then but asked a day later, you respond, "John Brown," and have both learned and retained something for a day after only one repetition. Notice that if the name were "Browm" instead of "Brown," you would probably have said "Brown" exactly as you did before. You would still have learned, but incorrectly.

In the example given, unless you were looking out the window, you learned "John Brown," "John Browm," or something similar in a single stimulus presentation. This is called *one-trial learning* or *all–or–none learning*. Anything you can report back immediately after its occurrence has been learned, or perhaps mislearned, in a single trial. Some of your capacity for one-trial learning no doubt stems from previous experience. Yet in some sense the first experience of a speechless infant may also yield one trial learning, often retained as briefly as are the names of many people we meet.

It is possible to interpret the learning resulting from presentation of a single stimulus not followed immediately by an overt response as classical or instrumental conditioning. But such interpretation always seems forced—you end up assuming that responses were made which no one saw. Let us assume instead that the simplest form of learning is *one-stimulus learning*, a process by which mere presentation of a stimulus changes response propensities to be exhibited later. This is, of course, a form of learning closely allied to the storage of information concept we naively started with and will be most relevant to verbal learning experiments.

All–or–none learning exhibited by perfect performance after one trial is rare. A more common finding is that several trials are required before performance is perfect. This may mean that a little bit is learned every time a name or word to be remembered is heard (*incremental theory of learning*), or it may mean that the probability of learning on any one trial is small, but that when it is learned it will be all at once (all–or–none learning but not necessarily on trial 1). The former is an incremental theory because the learner acquires a little more (an increment) on each trial. Much research is being conducted to decide the circumstances under which each explanation is correct (15, 72).

One example of the controversy on this point concerns the shape of the learning curve for a conditioned eye blink response, indicated by anticipatory responding to the conditioned stimulus (CS) before the unconditioned stimulus (UCS) appeared. Those who believe that learning occurs a little at a time (incremental theorists) would predict a gradual learning curve for an individual learner and for a group of learners whose data are averaged. Figure 3-3 shows a gradual increase in the average probability of that response by 20 college psychology students (33). The UCS was a puff of air directed to the cornea of one eye. The CS was an increase in brightness of a milk-glass disk 10 centimeters in diameter. This CS appeared 400 milliseconds (i.e., 0.4 seconds) before the UCS. As Fig. 3-3 shows, there was learning with two CS's called + and − in that figure. (The discrimination learning section of this chapter will discuss these two conditioned stimuli further.)

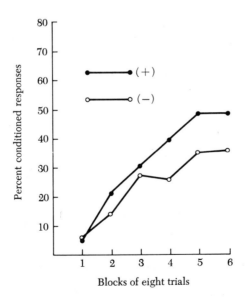

Fig. 3-3. Percentage frequency of conditioned responses to positive (+) and negative (−) conditioned stimuli. 400-millisecond interval between CS and UCS. From Fig. 1 of Hartman and Grant (33). Copyright 1962 by American Psychological Association and reproduced by permission.

Spence (79), an incremental theorist, reports that most individuals he studied showed gradual learning curves like the average curves of Fig. 3-3. This would suggest that individuals do learn a little at a time, just as the average curves would indicate. However, it is possible to be misled by averaging. Voeks (93), who subscribes to the *all–or–none theory*, found that half the individual learning curves were like those in Fig. 3-4. (Only about a fifth of the individual curves could be called gradual learning curves.) Yet when averaged for a group of 15 persons having similar curves but jumps on other trials than the trial 6 jump in Fig. 3-4, the curves lost their abrupt character. The average curves appeared to be consistent with *incremental theory* but the more important individual curves supported the *all–or–none* theory.

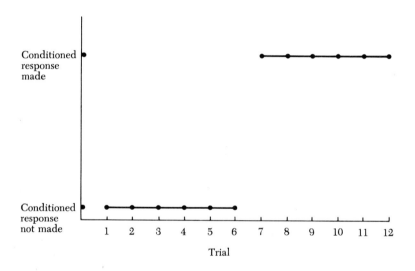

Fig. 3-4. All–or–none responding as found by Voeks (93). No conditioned response was made prior to trial 6. A conditioned response was made on every trial thereafter.

When rats are taught to press a lever to obtain food, average curves of performance often show gradual improvement. But graphs of data from a single rat may show results like those in Fig. 3-5. Apparently the third reinforcement has made a substantial difference in the individual's response rate. (Note that the total number of responses so far in the experiment is plotted for each time value of Fig. 3-5. This is called a *cumulative curve*.)

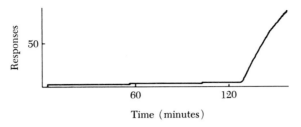

Fig. 3-5. A sudden increase in rate of response after 120 minutes in a lever box and three previous reinforcements. Figure 3 from Skinner (77). Reproduced by permission of Appleton-Century-Crofts, Educational Division, Meredith Corporation.

We may conclude that gradual improvement in average performance of a *group* is the uniform result of successive training trials. The question as to whether or when an *individual* demonstrates gradual rather than all–or–none learning has not yet been resolved. Even though the issue is not yet settled, the advocates of all–or–none theory deserve great credit for raising this important issue. It is particularly noteworthy that one of these advocates was sufficiently open-minded to be able to shift from a previous strongly held incremental position. Estes had founded the very influential field of *statistical learning theory,* a theory which uses advanced mathematics in generating predictions about behavior. After using incremental assumptions in that theory for several years, he became convinced that, for many experimental situations, if not all, an all–or–none process should be assumed instead. Because of its mathematical complexity, statistical learning theory is only briefly mentioned here. Interested readers are referred to Neimark and Estes (64) as a recent source of information on that topic.

_____ **Discrimination Learning**

Extinction

The procedure of withholding reinforcement even when a formerly reinforced response is made is called *extinction.* A customary effect of extinction is the cessation of response. For example, a rat which has repeatedly pressed a lever and been reinforced with food will gradually decrease its rate of response if food is no longer given. Some fluctuation should be expected in the use of this term. For certain scholars extinction is the withholding of reinforcement, as just defined. For others it is the consequent cessation of response. The next chapter will treat the effects of extinction quite fully; it is briefly discussed now because of its relevance to the next topic—*discrimination learning.*

The Discrimination Learning Paradigm

Discrimination is, in common parlance, the ability to distinguish between two or more objects, entities, or attributes, i.e., to tell them apart. By this usage, discrimination is a topic in the psychology of sensation and perception.

Discrimination learning, however, means more than this. The experimenter wants to teach someone to make a different overt response to one stimulus than to the other. To be concrete, consider a traffic light. Many children can tell the difference between red, amber, and green before they learn to go, proceed with caution, or stop when faced with

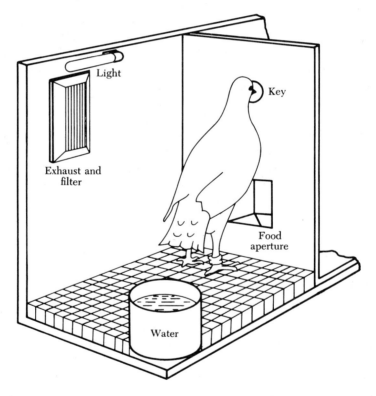

Fig. 3-6. A pigeon in an experimental box ready to respond to discriminative stimuli. Figure 1 from Ferster and Skinner (24). Reproduced by permission of Appleton-Century-Crofts, Educational Division, Meredith Corporation.

one of those colors. Learning to do as the lights direct is called *discrimination learning*. Usually it is not learning to discriminate between two stimuli but rather learning to respond appropriately to two or more already discriminable stimuli.

A standard discrimination apparatus is illustrated in Fig. 3-6. When the pigeon pecks the electrical key armature (made of frosted Plexiglas), food is given if the key is lighted with a red light from behind the aperture but not if it is lighted with a blue light. The red light, then, is positive (*a positive discriminative stimulus*). The blue light is negative (*a negative discriminative stimulus*). At first the pigeon pecks an equal amount under both conditions. However, the extinction procedure employed with the blue light leads to a decline and eventually almost complete elimination of the response to blue. Simultaneously, reinforcement of the response to red strengthens that response, and discrimination learning becomes complete.

A further example of a discrimination learning situation comes from the study by Hartman and Grant (33) on which Fig. 3-3 is based. The positive CS(+) of that study (an increase in brightness of a milk-glass disk) was always followed by the UCS, a reinforcement. The negative

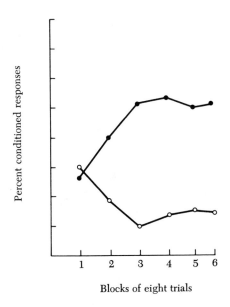

Blocks of eight trials

Fig. 3-7. Percentage frequency of conditioned responses to positive (●) and negative (○) conditioned stimuli. 1000-millisecond interval between CS and UCS. From Fig. 1 of Hartman and Grant (33). Copyright 1962 by American Psychological Association and reproduced by permission.

CS(−) of that study was never followed by reinforcement. Because the negative CS was very much like the positive CS, differing only in its location relative to the person being tested, it is not too surprising that Fig. 3-3 shows learning to both the positive and negative CS's or discriminative stimuli. However, Hartman and Grant found that discrimination learning, as evidenced by dropping out of the response to the negative CS, would occur if the time interval between the CS and UCS were increased to 1000 milliseconds, possibly because the added time allowed a perceptual discrimination to occur. Figure 3-7 shows the data for the 1000-millisecond condition.

An interesting side benefit of discrimination learning is that it enables us to test the sensory powers of subhuman organisms. The dark-adaptation curve of a pigeon was obtained by this general method by Blough (11), who trained the pigeon to press one key when no light was present and another key when a light was on and bright enough to be visible. As the pigeon spent more time in the dark, his eyes adapted to the darkness and he could perceive dimmer lights than he had seen before, as indicated by his responses to the two keys. Figure 3-8 shows how much this sensitivity to light changed in the first hour spent in darkness.

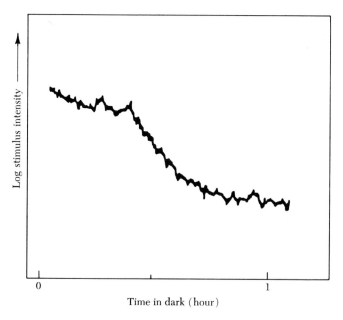

Fig. 3-8. The decline in visual threshold (smallest visible light intensity) of a pigeon during a period of dark adaptation. From Fig. 2 of Blough (11). Copyright 1958 by the Society for the Experimental Analysis of Behavior, Inc.

Paired-Associates Learning

Use of the properties of discrimination learning together with stimulus–stimulus (S–S) theory helps in understanding an area of verbal learning research called *paired-associates learning.* Two paired stimuli become known as belonging together, according to S–S theory. If you see PEAR BARK, you are learning to associate Pear and Bark.

Stimulus–response (S–R) theory is also relevant to paired-associates learning. Now, when you see PEAR and are asked to tell what goes with it, you will probably respond BARK. Then you may be presented with PEAR BARK again and find that you are correct. The word PEAR has served as a *positive discriminative stimulus* for you to say BARK. The PEAR BARK after you say PEAR has served as a reinforcement of S–R learning, the learning to connect a given response (R) to a specific stimulus (S).

Figure 3-9 shows a *memory drum,* an apparatus frequently used for teaching associations such as PEAR BARK. The memory drum is currently set to expose two blank spaces where the stimulus and response words will later appear. When the experiment begins, a cylinder or drum inside the memory drum apparatus will turn to where the first stimulus word is printed and stop there for the subject to view it. Then the drum will turn again to the next position, in which the original

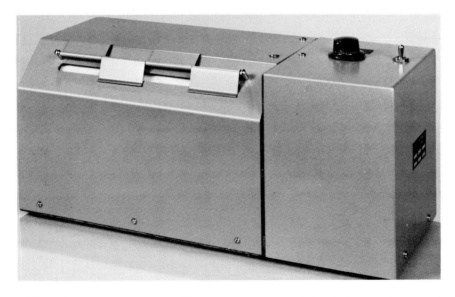

Fig. 3-9. A memory drum. (Photograph courtesy of the Lafayette Instrument Company.)

stimulus word and the first response word are both presented. The next movement of the drum will present the second stimulus word, and so on. By moving the flaps over the white paper drum, the experimenter can expose only one space instead of two, or he can increase the number of viewing spaces beyond two if desired. One space is normally used in *serial learning,* in which a list of items such as BROWN, RED, GREEN, YELLOW, BLACK, PURPLE is learned in a certain order—all items being response words.

Had you been in error on the PEAR BARK association and said BUTTER instead of BARK in response to PEAR, a subsequent presentation of PEAR BARK would be a nonconfirmation of your response. It could also be called a nonreinforcement of the BUTTER response because it does not strengthen that response. But unlike simpler examples of extinction, the correct answer was also given, permitting S–S learning of the pair. A double process seems to have occurred—extinction of incorrect S–R learning and reinforcement of S–S learning. Similarly, when the correct response is made, it may be that S–R learning and S–S learning are both occurring.

Some psychologists may find the use of the term *reinforcement* inappropriate in this instance because the response which was reinforced (BARK) was not actually made. However, there is ample precedent for this usage in verbal learning studies: Estes, Hopkins, and Crothers (23a) define reinforcement as "paired presentation of stimulus and response members of an item," regardless of what response was actually made prior to that presentation. Their definition is actually the standard definition for reinforcement in a classical conditioning experiment if *stimulus member* is equated with *conditioned stimulus* and *response member* with *unconditioned stimulus.*

This paired-associates learning is comparable to your studying with foreign language flash cards. On one side of a card you may have placed the "stimulus" word in German, on the other the "response" word in English. When you see the German stimulus side of the card, you try to give the English response word. After going through your set of cards once, you usually shuffle them before repeating. You do this because you want to be able to translate the German word in any context, not just when it is in a certain position in the list. Martin and Saltz (56), among others, have investigated this problem. A paired-associates list is sometimes learned faster without rearrangement between presentations, but responses are not necessarily correct on test trials with rearranged items. Standard research practice, therefore, is much like your procedure. Several different arrangements of the test are printed on the paper for the memory drum; the same arrangement is not used on any two successive trials.

Your memorizing procedure differs from the usual experimental procedure in that you eventually reverse your flash cards, letting English words be the "stimuli" and German words be the "responses." On the first trial after the reversal you are surprised by the amount you already know. You have not only learned to go from A to B but also to go from B to A, a reverse process. Jantz and Underwood (43), among others (21), have demonstrated this B–A effect in the laboratory. It is not a contradiction of earlier learning principles, but represents the effect of S–S pairing. The B–A learning is probably less than the A–B learning up to the time of reversing procedures because you were not responding overtly (i.e., out loud) with A to B, whereas you were responding overtly with B to A.

--- **Reinforcement**

Some Typical Reinforcements

Experimenters commonly provide reinforcements in distinct but small quantities. A reinforcement for a pigeon may be a kernel of corn or two seconds' access to grain following a desired response. A reinforcement for a child in a school experiment may be a small chocolate candy, again following the response to be strengthened. A reinforcement for a music student may be a small bust of Chopin, given for a good performance; a reinforcement in geography class may be a red "A" marked on a good test paper.

Some reinforcements have nutritive value but, being small, leave the organism in about the same state of need as before reinforcement. This is desirable in many cases. The state of need is intended to be a *controlled extraneous variable,* i.e., a variable whose effects are intended to be constant throughout the experiment because it is irrelevant or extraneous to the major purpose of the study. Increasing the size of the reinforcement has dramatic effects upon behavior.

Not all reinforcements are food or water, however. Monkeys may be reinforced by being allowed to look out a window of their cage. Rats may be allowed access to a wheel which spins when they climb inside it and make walking movements (an activity wheel).

Premack (71) believes that the wide variety of reinforcers just noted is best explained by some principle other than the satisfaction of bodily needs. Premack originally suggested that the stronger of two responses is necessarily reinforcing if the other response must be made first. Thus:

If a boy is more likely to *swing* than *eat* when given a choice, his rate of eating can be increased by requiring him to eat in order to swing.

If a boy is more likely to *eat* than *swing* when given a choice, his rate of swinging can be increased by requiring him to swing in order to eat.

From a teacher's standpoint this principle means that children can be taught to increase a desired response, such as reading, if that response is necessary for permission to engage in some more probable response (i.e., preferred response). It is important that the teacher know what is preferred, because the more probable response for one child may not be the more probable for another.

Premack also recognized that *response suppression* may be necessary for reinforcement to occur: Suppose eating is to be used as a reinforcement for studying, but a student already studies enough to "earn" all the food he normally eats. Then his amount of studying will not increase because an increase is not necessary. However, if the experimental condition required him to study twice as much for a given amount of food, this would suppress the eating response enough to force him to study more.

Eisenberger, Karpman, and Trattner (20) have shown that this response suppression principle can even be used to make a nonpreferred task a reinforcer for a preferred response. Among 21 college students who were originally more likely, but not ten times more likely, to turn a wheel than press a bar, 16 further increased their rate of wheel turning when told that they had to turn it ten times in order to press the bar. Their bar pressing had been suppressed because, though it was the nonpreferred response, they could not press as much as before without increasing the amount of their preferred activity. In school situations it may sometimes be possible to use a relatively unpopular response, such as doing arithmetic, as a reinforcer of a more popular response, such as recreational reading, provided that the unpopular response has some probability of occurrence.

Most of the reinforcements just discussed were used in instrumental conditioning. In classical conditioning the reinforcement (unconditioned stimulus) may be a tap to the kneecap, an electric shock, a puff of air to the eye, or the sight of food, among other things.

Real life reinforcements may be different from those in the laboratory. A complete dinner follows a hard afternoon's work—it is not presented "piecemeal" after small units of activity. Sometimes a reinforcement requires years of activity, as in the attainment of a college diploma. Lesser reinforcements, such as statements of approval by fellow students and professors, intervene before graduation.

The nearest laboratory parallel to these real life situations is ratio reinforcement with large amounts of reinforcement. Ratio reinforcement means that a certain number of responses has to be made before a reinforcement is given. For a pigeon this number might be 600 pecks of an illuminated key. For the college student there might also be 600 responses (many more by some methods of measuring responses) required to earn the reinforcement; however, there probably is more variety in the student's responses than in the pigeon's. For the pigeon a large amount of reinforcement might be eating from a food hopper for ten seconds; for the college student the large amount of reinforcement is receiving the college diploma, attention from friends and relatives on Commencement Day, and possibly gaining better employment than is possible without the diploma. Morse (63) has reported that B. F. Skinner and he have found a higher rate of key-pecking with a fixed ratio of 600 responses per reinforcement if the food hopper is available for 10 seconds than if it is available for 5 seconds. This confirms the commonsense presumption that large amounts of reward will be important when a large project must be accomplished prior to reinforcement. Consequently, it is presumed that instructors should try to provide specially large reinforcements in connection with large tasks. However, large assignments are problems to teachers and experimenters alike because of the possibility that the learner's response will drop out (extinguish) before the reinforcement occurs.

A second discrepancy from the usual laboratory procedure is the entwining of response and reinforcement in many life situations. Riding a tricycle *may* be reinforced by arrival at a candy store and subsequent food purchases; it usually is reinforced by something else. A foot pushes against a pedal, and the pedal turns—kinesthetic stimuli from this turning are among several reinforcements. Visual stimuli from the front wheel of the tricycle and changing visual cues as the whole tricycle moves are also reinforcing. These reinforcements occur continually: after one response, before another, and during all of them. Riding a tricycle is somewhat of a chained response, then, with one response linked to a reinforcement which links to the next response, and so on. But this is an oversimplification: In some sense it is more like a section of woven fence with an upper row of wire representing successive responses, a lower row representing successive stimuli, and vertical wires representing influences of stimuli on responses and vice versa.

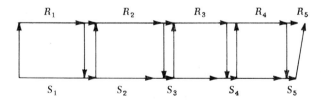

To use an old reinforcement in a new situation, allow a three-year-old child to open a shutter built over a glass window inserted in a wall of a suitable box. This response by itself may drop out quickly since little reinforcement is available. If, however, many of the cues from tricycling are presented through the window (a pedal goes up and down, a wheel turns around, etc.) the child may repeatedly open the shutter, showing that the stimuli inside the window are reinforcers. A thorough analysis of the situation would, of course, reveal other processes than those just discussed.

Secondary Reinforcers

Whereas, in paired-associates learning, the *stimulus words* act as discriminative stimuli for appropriate responding, the *response words* presented after the subject's responses serve as reinforcers. Reinforcement does not satisfy or reduce any bodily drive, as the strong theory of drive reduction would require, but conceivably it might reduce some stimulus associated with a state of anxiety, a need to achieve, or (indirectly) a need for food. Reinforcement effects provided in a paired-associates task, then, are clearly *acquired reinforcement effects*.

In their simplest form acquired reinforcement effects result from repeated presentation of a neutral stimulus immediately before a *primary reinforcer,* i.e., one which would be an effective reinforcer without special training. The former neutral stimulus is then called a *secondary reinforcer*. The phrase, "Have an ice cream cone," followed repeatedly by ice cream cone presentation, should make, "Have an ice cream cone," a secondary reinforcer. A person so trained could be taught a new response with that secondary reinforcer as the only reinforcer. Consider the following outline of an experiment to be used with children who have never seen an ice cream cone before.

Group	Day 1	Day 2
I	Secondary reinforcement training: Pairing "Have an ice cream cone" and cone presentation	"Have an ice cream cone" follows every occurrence of Response A
II	Nothing	Same as Group I

Response A could be any voluntary response the experimenter wishes to strengthen: tying a package when presented, turning a knob on a toy, adding 2 and 2, etc. If the Day 1 procedure for Group I was well planned, "Have an ice cream cone" would become an effective secondary reinforcer and Group I would show a higher average number of the Response A than Group II on Day 2 up to a point where extinction sets in because the primary reinforcement is not presented. This statement assumes that the assignment of subjects to the two groups was unbiased, of course. One would not take the oldest available children for Group I and the youngest for Group II; instead, the groups might be assigned randomly, perhaps by drawing names for one group from a hat and letting the remaining names in the hat represent the other group.

The general design just outlined has been used most frequently with rats as subjects, with a stimulus such as a tone as the secondary reinforcer, with food or water as the primary reinforcer, and with a simple act such as lever pressing as the response (22). Yet a similar method for demonstrating secondary reinforcement effects has also been performed with human subjects (40).

Perhaps most learning studies performed with human subjects use reinforcers other than primary ones and yet seem at least one stage removed from the secondary reinforcement training just discussed. A light shown to a student may be termed the sign of a correct response and treated as if it is a primary reinforcer. Similarly, typical paired-associates experiments may be thought of as using secondary reinforcers which were previously paired with primary reinforcers. [See Skinner (78) for a discussion of how words become reinforcers.]

Consider how this secondary reinforcement training may have built up. In learning the association PEAR BARK mentioned earlier, the learner says BARK and is reinforced by being able to read BARK on the memory drum. But this is reinforcing because parents and teachers had previously done two things—given verbal approval for correct guesses in games and classwork and given verbal approval for reading words correctly. This verbal approval, in turn, is a secondary reinforcer previously neutral in effect but now reinforcing because the words of approval were learned in childhood and also because those words were paired with food and with soothing tones of vocal expression. Counting links in the chain would cause one to call BARK a higher-order reinforcer, perhaps a fourth-order reinforcer. But there are so many branches in the chain and ambiguities in its structure that it seems unwise as well as unnecessary to attempt a specific numbering of its level.

A more critical question is why the printed word BARK can continue to function as a reinforcer when so many subsequent parts of the total chain are absent. Studies with animals show that repeated presentation of secondary reinforcers after a response without primary reinforcers leads to relatively fast abolition of the response (60). In a real life situation with human beings the same thing should happen if no primary reinforcement was paired with higher-order reinforcers. The answer to our critical question must be that such pairing does frequently occur. Spoken words of approval are continually paired with primary reinforcers; therefore, they maintain their reinforcing properties. Reading certain things frequently brings spoken words of approval and this causes that reading to be reinforcing. Even though extinction of higher-order reinforcers is frequently occurring, relearning also frequently takes place. As a consequence, almost any stimulus can maintain reinforcing properties almost indefinitely, even though direct links to primary reinforcement are absent.

The topic of secondary reinforcement can be seen to be very important to psychological theory and also to one's understanding of his own behavior. Objects such as money are good examples of secondary reinforcers. More involved analysis is required to recognize the receipt of letters or magazines as secondarily reinforcing, but it surely is. Accordingly, it is possible to recognize a major part of our pattern of daily activity as maintained through secondary reinforcement.

Behavior Modification: Reinforcement Principles in Human Behavior

Students of learning theory have been developing techniques of teaching or of treating emotionally disturbed persons, using the principles of conditioning. These techniques are often termed methods of *behavior*

TABLE 3-1

General Rules for Teachers Engaged in Behavior Modification with Children Having a Particular Set of Undesired Behaviors[a]

1. Make explicit rules as to what is expected of children for each period. (Remind of rules when needed.)
2. *Ignore* (do not attend to) behaviors which interfere with learning or teaching, unless a child is being hurt by another. Use punishment which seems appropriate, preferably withdrawal of some positive reinforcement.
3. Give *praise* and *attention* to behaviors which facilitate learning. Tell child what he is being praised for. Try to reinforce behaviors incompatible with those you wish to decrease.
   Examples of how to praise: "I like the way you're working quietly." "That's the way I like to see you work." "Good job, you are doing well."
   Transition period. "I see Johnny is ready to work." "I'm calling on you because you raised your hand." "I wish everyone were working as nicely as X," etc. Use variety and expression.
   In general, give praise for achievement, prosocial behavior and following the group rules.

[a] From Becker (7).

modification. One example of the use of such techniques comes from research by Becker, Madsen, Arnold, and Thomas (7), who wished to eliminate certain undesired behaviors in some or all of ten children they were studying in classroom situations. These undesired behaviors included such varied items as rocking in chairs, tapping pencils, biting, crying, conversing with other children when it was not permitted, ignoring the teacher's question or command, and sucking fingers or other objects. Table 3-1 presents the general instructions given to teachers as ways to eliminate undesired behaviors. In addition, special instructions were given for ways to help each individual child in the study.

Data were obtained by having one or two observers watch each child for 20 minutes a day recording each occurrence of an undesired behavior in the list developed by Becker *et al.* During the five weeks before behavior modification techniques were introduced, there was an average of 1.86 undesired responses per minute per child; during a nine-week period using the procedures of behavior modification, this rate dropped to 0.86 per minute. Certain children improved more than others, suggesting that even more individualization of treatment technique is desirable. These results and others obtained in similar studies make behavior modification techniques seem promising for use in the schools.

Effect of Amount of Reinforcement on Speed of Response

Some reinforcements have greater effects than others. A large amount of money would be expected to reinforce an act more strongly than a small one. Also one kind of food, ice cream, would be expected to be a stronger reinforcement than another, spinach. The layman would probably predict the effects just suggested, the former being an effect of reinforcement quantity and the second of reinforcement quality. However, it is up to the research psychologist to show whether these effects actually occur, and to what degree. Since effects of reinforcement quantity and quality are seldom studied with humans, we turn again to research with animals.

Figure 3-10 shows a classic result obtained by Crespi (16) when three groups of rats were trained to run through a long alley to obtain different amounts of laboratory food pellets. Animals given 256 pellets per trial ran substantially faster than the 64-pellet group members, who in turn were faster than the 16-pellet animals. These differences lasted only a brief time after the treatments of the groups were changed. Groups shifted from a large number of pellets to a small number soon began to run slower, as shown in the second part of Fig. 3-10.

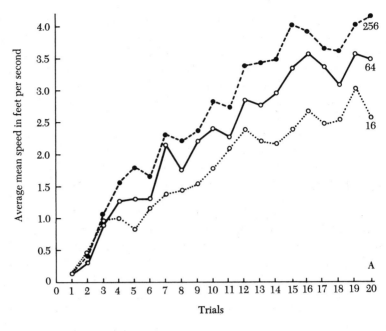

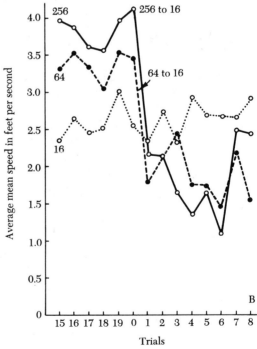

Fig. 3-10.

Studies like that of Crespi are often termed studies of *incentive motivation,* the "pulling power" of a reward. Hull (42) calls the theoretical concept which measures incentive motivation, K, and gives an equation to show the degree to which the value of K is larger with large amounts of reinforcement than with small. Reference to the topic of incentive motivation could be restricted to Chapter 11 (Motivation and Learning) but is made earlier because one aspect of it so clearly involves learning. Note that Hull's definition might be taken to imply an instantaneous change in K when a new reward magnitude is introduced. However, Crespi's data show that a transition phase occurs following a shift in reward. This gradual shift in reward must be termed a learning phenomenon because the animals involved required practice with the reward before they responded at the new level appropriate to the change in magnitude of the reward.

No doubt something like Crespi's results would hold for your speed in walking across campus to class provided something more palatable than rat food were offered you. The larger the reinforcement for getting there quickly, the faster you would travel.

Effect of Amount of Reinforcement on Quality of Performance

Increased amounts of reinforcement are highly effective in producing increased effort, as in running or in studying. However, the effect on accuracy is less substantial. To be sure, reinforcement must be larger for the correct choice than for the incorrect if learning is to occur. But in some discrimination tasks no change in percentage of correct responses occurs as the amount of reward for the correct choice increases. The usual result is that accuracy increases if the same group of animals is tested under all conditions; it does not change otherwise. This statement is confirmed by Fig. 3-11 comparing these effects for a *shift group,* monkeys tested under each of the conditions, and a *nonshift group,* monkeys divided into subgroups tested under different amounts of reward (76).

It may be that the failure of psychologists to study reinforcement magnitude effects in human verbal learning stems from an intuition that such effects will be no more substantial than they are in discrimination learning in animals. Nonetheless, it is desirable that this variable be investigated with verbal learning materials, for animal behavior and

---

Fig. 3-10. (A) Greater running speeds in groups having greater numbers of reward pellets per trial. Figure 2 of Crespi (16). (B) Shifts in running speeds following shifts in numbers of reward pellets. Figure 8 of Crespi (16). Reproduced by permission of University of Illinois Press.

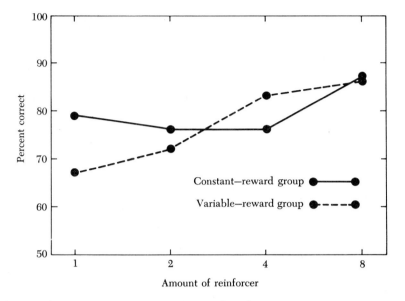

Fig. 3-11. Increases in amount of reward and consequent increases in percent correct responses, particularly for the same monkeys tested under all conditions of reward (shift or variable reward group). A modification of Fig. 1 from Schrier (76), provided by Schrier. Figure 1 copyright 1958 by American Psychological Association and reproduced by permission.

human behavior are not always comparable, particularly when language is involved.

Delay of Reinforcement

Unless language behavior is available to prolong its effects, a reinforcer must follow a response by a reasonably short interval if the response is to be strengthened. Otherwise a reinforcer could strengthen many responses at once, some of which had occurred days or even years before. Training a particular response might then become impossible because the reinforcement effects were so diffuse. Fortunately, this is not a problem. In a true experimental situation reinforcers must occur within 5 seconds or less after the response if they are to be effective. Figure 3-12 shows how the speed of learning depends (in a discrimination task) upon this delay interval, according to a study by Grice (29). With a near-zero delay that speed is high, but it declines very rapidly as the delay moves toward 5 seconds.

Figure 3-12 is applicable only if great care has been taken to prevent

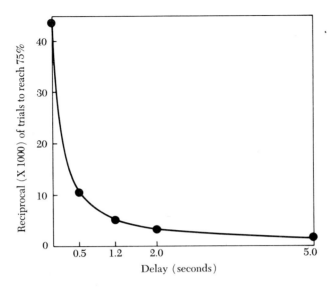

Fig. 3-12. Decline in speed of learning (1000 times the reciprocal of the number of trials to reach a level of 75% correct) with increased delay of reward. Figure 3 of Grice (29). Copyright 1948 by American Psychological Association and reproduced by permission.

secondary reinforcement from occurring during the delay period. Otherwise even a 20-minute delay may not retard learning (97).

Delay of Informative Feedback

Psychologists have sometimes concluded from studies with animals on delay of reinforcement that existing classroom procedures for children provide reinforcement (or *informative feedback*) much too late for efficient learning. However, Bilodeau and his coworkers (8, 9), among others, have provided convincing evidence that a delay of informative feedback for as long as 1 week does not impair learning of a motor task, provided that the total time interval between each pair of trials is held constant. Note that informative feedback is a special form of reinforcement in which *information* about the correct response is given, possibly even when an incorrect response has been made.

There is, to be sure, some evidence that increased delay of reinforcement slows down concept formation (18) or verbal learning (47) in humans. However, Denny, Allard, Hall, and Rokeach (18) have shown that using the same sort of control employed by Bilodeau eliminates the delay of reinforcement effect in concept formation tasks. Bourne and Bunderson (12) have extended that result, showing that delay between reinforcement and the next trial is the critical variable. Apparently a long interval after informative feedback is used by the learner as a time to rehearse the correct answer. The longer the postreinforcement interval, then, the greater the learning rate, regardless of the amount of delay in reinforcement. This suggests that teachers should allow their pupils a period of time after presenting each correct answer, before going to the next question in a learning task. Regardless of the laboratory evidence with animals or humans, however, the real benefit is found in the classroom. Lacking such evidence, the psychologist should not conclude that a laboratory method is scientific and should replace a classroom method. For example, Newman (66) once asked research workers in the field of learning the most effective way to present electrical information to students. On their recommendation he used a modified paired-associates method but found it inferior to self-directed study of a list of symbols and definitions.

With delay of reinforcement, even if it should have a large effect on classroom learning when secondary reinforcement is absent, there is still no reason to eliminate secondary reinforcement between the response and the "primary reinforcement," knowledge of results. Until research in the classroom proves otherwise, the introduction of immediate reinforcement by some device such as a teaching machine (see Chapter 4) will not, in the absence of other changes in procedure, lead to appreciably faster learning than before. In fact there is already some evidence (13) that immediate knowledge of results given by a teaching machine does not lead to superior performance.

Further evidence on delayed reinforcement is provided by Sturgis (80). She used what may be called a TRTT design, where a T refers to a 38-item multiple-choice test on the social sciences and R refers to providing the correct answers (reinforcements or informative feedback) to each question. An immediate reinforcement group received the correct answer to each question immediately after the response to that individual item, after which the next item was answered, the correct answer given, etc. The delayed reinforcement group was not told any correct answers until 24 hours after taking the first test. The second T occurred immediately after completion of the R stage in each group, but the third T was deferred until 7 days after the second test.

Sturgis found no effect of delay of reinforcement upon performance on the second test. Presumably this is because the students had so recently seen the correct answers that they were relying upon *short-term memory* (see Chapter 5), so that the time since the original test had little effect.

The results of the final test depend upon a feature of the research design which has not yet been mentioned: If students received informative feedback which included the complete question, identification of the correct answer, and all incorrect options, the 7-day delay condition led to superior performance to that of the no-delay condition. However, if only the question and the correct option were shown, there was no difference in performance under 7-day delay and no delay. This experiment goes even farther than those previously cited in denying the supposed benefits of immediate reinforcement, for Sturgis' findings suggest that delayed reinforcement is sometimes superior. One reason for this effect may be that the delayed reinforcement students are able to rehearse or think over the test between reinforcement and the next test— if they received a great deal of information (question, correct answer, and wrong answers) during the reinforcement phase, this rehearsal could be more profitable and superior performance following delayed reinforcement might result.

_____ **Latent Learning**

The effects of magnitude of reinforcement already noted are consistent with most theories of learning. Now consider a case which gives trouble: Let magnitude of reinforcement be zero in trials preceding the first standard training session (extinction before acquisition). Will these "non-reinforced" training trials facilitate later performance where food reinforcement is available? Blodgett (10) and many others have found that they do. This effect has been called "latent learning" since it did not appear at the time it was being developed. How should this be explained? A vast oversimplification of the situation gives three choices: (a) What is called S–R *reinforcement theory* states that some unknown small reinforcement was presented at the end of each trial where food was not given. This reinforcement was enough to produce learning later to be converted into performance by sizable food reinforcement. (b) What is called S–R *contiguity theory* states that learning took place simply because the correct response was sometimes made to each stimulus during the latent learning period. When a sizable reinforcement is given, this magnifies existing response tendencies and the learned response is exhibited. (c) What is called S–S *contiguity theory* says that relations between stimuli were learned without an overt response—in fanciful language Tolman (85) said that maps were being formed in the heads of the subjects in the experiment. Once food was provided, the learned stimulus relations were put into play.

Explanations (a) and (b) turn out to be almost equivalent—if the reinforcement required for learning is so small it cannot be identified, it need not be mentioned. Accordingly, the S–R contiguity position has been gaining importance recently. Reinforcement is thought less to be a basis for learning and more to be a basis for performance of tasks than in earlier years. The S–S contiguity argument while usable appears not to be necessary to the understanding of most latent learning studies. However, we mention one latent learning experiment which is particularly amenable to interpretation by S–S theory. Herb (35) rewarded rats for choosing each blind alley choice in a maze constructed by connecting 14 T-shaped sections together. (A blind alley is an arm of a T which does not lead to another T section or to a reward.) In a latent learning group, a food reward was not given the first 10 days; these animals made fewer and fewer blind alley choices from day to day as they learned to make the "correct" choices required to get to the end of the maze. But after reward was introduced on day 11, they rapidly increased their numbers of blind alley choices, quickly catching up with the performance of a control group which had always been rewarded for choosing blind alleys.

According to S–S theory, Herb's latent learning rats had been learning relations between stimuli early in the experiment, using this learning appropriately after food was introduced. The other theories under consideration imply that these rats were primarily learning correct choices (i.e., turns away from the blind alleys), not blind alley choices, for correct choices were increasing from trial to trial during that period. If an S–R explanation is to apply both to the Blodgett and the Herb findings, it must imply that both correct and incorrect habits were building up during the latent learning period, or else that some facilitating factor such as reduced excitability was resulting from handling by the experimenter during the latent learning period. We are inclined to apply the S–S theory here but admit that the other theories have not been disproved.

--- **Response Prompting**

The method of response prompting is a method in which the subject is told the correct answer before he makes it or is at least given a hint as to that answer. For example, a biology student might be shown: "Male ♂" and then be asked to give the appropriate symbol when shown "Male." This is unlike response confirmation in which the person is told after correctly responding that he was correct. Aiken and Lau (1) reviewed most existing studies on these two topics and found only three whose results showed better performance with response confirmation than with response prompting. Because of psychological theories which emphasize reinforcement (response confirmation) principles, teachers are already aware that response confirmation is important to learning. The Aiken and Lau article makes it plain that they should also use response prompting to improve classroom learning. Often it will be possible and desirable to use both techniques in the same learning situation, telling a student that, for example, the capitol of Illinois is Springfield, then asking, "What is the capitol of Illinois?" and saying, "Correct," if the student answers, "Springfield."

Stimulus Generalization

> Yesterday George Smith walked up to a stranger and slapped her repeatedly in the face, knocking her to the ground, and requiring her treatment in St. Luke's Hospital. Interviewed by reporters last night in City Jail, Smith said, "I'm sorry I did it. I made a mistake. I thought she was my wife."

The news item just paraphrased originally appeared in a metropolitan newspaper in the United States. A case of mistaken identity, it illustrates the fact that persons sometimes respond to one stimulus as if it were another. This phenomenon is called *stimulus generalization* in psychology. Consider an experimental demonstration of stimulus generalization:

Guttman and Kalish (31) trained six pigeons to peck a key in an apparatus like that shown in Fig. 3-6 and receive food. A green stimulus light from the back of the key served as a positive discriminative stimulus; no light from the key or in the box served as the negative discriminative stimulus. Variable intervals, averaging 1 minute in length, were required before a response to the positive stimulus would be reinforced. This schedule served to increase resistance to extinction, facilitating tests with other stimulus lights. (See the section on Partial Reinforcement in Chapter 5 for the discussion of this increased resistance to extinction.) During extinction the birds were tested for response to ten different wavelengths (hues) ranging from a blue-green to a yellow in addition to the positive discriminative stimulus. Three additional groups of pigeons were trained and tested with other wavelengths. Figure 3-13 presents the results of these tests. Notice that response during extinction was always greatest to the positive discriminative stimulus (or CS as Guttman and Kalish call it) with a relatively rapid decline for stimuli having other wavelengths. The response to these other stimuli is called *stimulus generalization*. Failure to respond to them would be called *complete discrimination;* responding as much to them as to the CS would be called *complete generalization.*

The Guttman–Kalish experiment demonstrates stimulus generalization

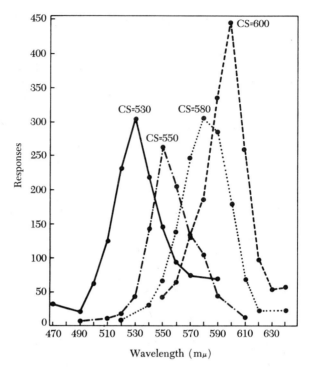

Fig. 3-13. Number of responses during extinction to stimuli of different wavelengths, as a function of the wavelength of the conditioned stimulus (CS). From upper section of Fig. 1, Guttman and Kalish (31). Copyright 1956 by American Psychological Association and reproduced by permission.

of an instrumental response. The phenomenon, however, was discovered in classical conditioning studies. Today its greatest significance is in the study of *transfer of training*, a topic related to both classical and instrumental conditioning. We deal with this topic below.

_____ **Transfer of Training**

Definition of Transfer of Training

Transfer of training is the use of responses in one situation which were developed in another. In its grossest sense, we are interested in the transfer of responses from one school subject (Latin) to another (English) or from a curriculum (liberal arts) to a career (medicine). Consider transfer of training studies by Thorndike (82a) showing some effect of instruction in certain courses upon performance in other courses. Thorndike's research led to a de-emphasis of certain courses such as Latin and Greek. These courses had been held essential under the doctrine of "Formal Discipline"; the doctrine that certain subjects served to strengthen desirable mental capacities and should therefore be studied even if they had no direct applicability to the student's life. Crowley (17) quotes an 1880 report by President Barnard of Columbia College to illustrate the attitude of advocates of formal discipline:

> Mental discipline, however, and not the acquisition of knowledge, having been the recognized and exclusive end of the early collegiate education, it followed as a necessary and inevitable consequence that the curriculum of study chosen for the purpose should be, as it was, extremely limited in range . . .
>
> In a certain sense, considering the object in view this was wise, for as in physical training, neither strength of limb, nor skill of hand, nor command of muscular movement can be acquired except on the condition of often repeated and long-continued practice of the same identical forms of exercise; so, in education, no increase of mental vigor, no sharpening of the faculties, no facility of wielding to purpose the intellectual energies will be secured, unless the subjects employed to provoke the mind to exertion are so few as to make it certain that such exertion shall be steady and continuous.

Restated to describe overt behavior rather than mental events, it becomes a doctrine that substantial transfer of training occurs from one subject to another. To understand Thorndike's problem in evaluating the doctrine of formal discipline, consider the following diagram of a standard experimental design for testing this hypothesis:

Group	Session 1	Session 2
Experimental	Training task A	Test task B
Control	None or unrelated activity	B

Here two groups are given different treatment in their first session but the same treatment in the second session. If the experimental group is superior to the control group on B, whatever that task or subject may be, *positive transfer of training* is said to have occurred. If the experimental group is inferior to the control group on B, *negative transfer of training* is said to have occurred, presumably because responses were learned on task A which interfere with performance of task B. The names of these groups are worth remembering, for research workers often call a group with special treatment the *experimental group,* and a group without that treatment the *control group.*

Reading some discussion of Thorndike's work might lead one to suppose that positive transfer of training never occurs and certainly not in the classroom. The truth is that Thorndike's research weakened the doctrine of formal discipline but not by disproving the existence of positive transfer of training. Positive transfer is found in most studies of the effect of one course upon another, if they are at all similar. But almost never does training in one subject, say Latin, improve performance in a second, say English, more than the same amount of instruction in the second. The percentage of efficiency,

$$\% \text{ Efficiency} = \frac{\text{Amount improved on B after practice with A}}{\text{Amount improved on B after practice with B}}$$

is less than 100%. In such cases, if the aim is to master task B, it, rather than task A, should be studied, regardless of the doctrine of formal discipline. Training for transfer will be most effective if we can train on one task and expect transfer to many different tasks. Usually, both tasks are important to the person, so that positive transfer becomes an added dividend of training on one task. Therefore, an understanding of positive transfer may greatly facilitate the work of the teacher.

Effects of Stimulus and Response Similarity upon Transfer

Our study of stimulus generalization tells us that the use of test stimuli like those of training will increase the strength of the old response to a new situation to a greater extent than if the test stimulus and training stimulus were dissimilar. This leads to the conclusion that a high degree of similarity among training task stimuli and test task stimuli leads to high positive transfer provided the responses involved are held constant. In classroom situations this could mean, for example, that neatness responses would transfer from one course to another if similar stimuli from teachers were provided.

However, if the stimuli remain the same for the two tasks, but new responses are desired in the test task, there will be a tendency to continue the old responses. Consequently, we conclude that negative transfer will result when distinctly different responses in training and test tasks, with stimuli the same in each task, are required. These two principles were propounded together by E. Gibson (27). Negative transfer can be a real problem in schools. Even on such a simple thing as the way a student's paper is to be headed, different teachers may require different responses and thus evoke negative transfer.

Young and Underwood (100) have shown that the positive transfer occurring with dissimilar stimuli and similar responses is due to *response differentiation* (learning to make specific responses, regardless of what they are paired with) during original learning. This is a modification of Gibson's theory; and Underwood (89) has found that many other modifications are necessary, perhaps so many as to make a complete new theory necessary.

Effects of Number of Trials during Training upon Transfer

In the foregoing discussion, stimulus and response similarity were discussed as if their effects were independent of all other variables. We must now qualify our earlier conclusions by noting that training of the original task well beyond apparently complete learning (that is, presenting many *overlearning trials*) can eliminate negative transfer even though new similar responses are being learned to old stimuli (55).

On the other hand, increasing the amount of original learning tends to increase positive transfer when similar stimuli and identical responses are used in the training and test tasks (54).

Transfer of Structure-Advanced Organizers

Though teachers sometimes have occasion to rely upon transfer between specific words, they have much more reason to be concerned about transfer from one part of a course to another, or even from one chapter to the next. Ausubel (3) has advanced the hypothesis that students who are beginning to learn a new topic use the first material they read as a scaffolding upon which to organize the rest of that topic. This is an efficient procedure if the early material is truly introductory, offering an outline of what is to follow. However, many authors seek to arouse interest by telling the life story of the inventor of the cotton gin, say, instead of by describing the basic process by which the cotton gin works. If the material to be learned later is a detailed analysis of that process, biographical information cannot prove an appropriate scaffolding, or as Ausubel calls it an *advanced organizer*. An advanced organizer, then, is introductory material at the beginning of a chapter or passage which provides structure for reading later material and thus facilitates learning of the later material.

Experimentation with advanced organizers has shown that although no test questions are answered within the organizer alone, studying it rather than less fundamental material leads to faster learning of later passages on the same topic. Two examples of this are the use of such an organizer prior to study of the metallurgical properties of carbon steel (3) and of quite a different organizer prior to study of Buddhism (4).

The degree to which an organizer is effective depends somewhat on the student's ability and his prior knowledge. Students with high learning ability or knowledge of material related to what is to be learned profit little or none from such organizers; their usefulness is greatest for slow learners or for students working in a field entirely new to them (4, 6).

Using the study of Buddhism as the principal learning task, Wittrock (96) found a hint of poorer original learning and found distinctly poorer retention of learning if students were instructed merely to understand and remember the material being studied. Superior performance was found for three groups of students instructed to note and remember (a) similarities, (b) differences, or (c) similarities and differences between the Judeo–Christian tradition and Buddhism.

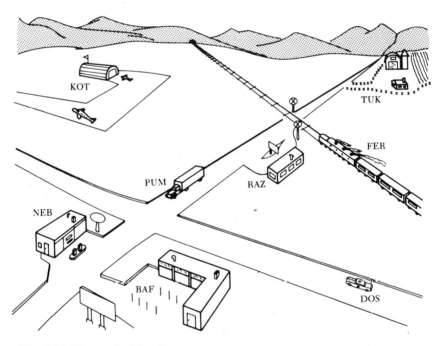

Fig. 3-14. Map studied by the cognitive structure group prior to learning sentences such as "KOT is a pilot." This map is Fig. 1 from Reynolds (73). Copyright 1966 by American Psychological Association and reproduced by permission.

A structural transfer much like that in advanced organizers has been demonstrated using a map suggested by Tolman's article on cognitive maps mentioned earlier. Reynolds (73, 74) hypothesized that three 30-second periods of studying the map shown in Fig. 3-14 would lead to rapid learning of sentences based on that map. In the 30 seconds, college men were instructed to memorize the three-letter nonsense syllables and their locations on the map. Following each study period they were asked to recall the syllables and write them in the proper position on a test map. Transfer was measured by determining whether these subjects, members of the so-called cognitive structure group, were superior to comparison groups in learning to fill in the blanks below, where the material in parentheses is the appropriate answer for each set of blanks:

KOT——(is a pilot)
NEB——(is a gas station attendant)
BAF——(is a shopkeeper)
PUM——(is a truckdriver)
DOS——(is a policeman)
RAZ——(is a cook)
FER——(is a brakeman)
TUK——(is a farmer)

The cognitive structure group (or experimental group) did learn this task more rapidly than the other groups did. The comparison groups, or control groups, were so treated that some of them would also have proved superior if the only benefit of studying the map derived from unstructured knowledge such as could be obtained by looking at a map without nonsense syllables on it and also by looking at the list of nonsense syllables without a map. Consequently, it appears that the manner of presentation was essential to the rapid learning shown by the cognitive structure group.

One particular group is of special interest to teachers: The S–R group (stimulus–response group) had the opportunity to memorize such associates as AIRSTRIP–KOT and to place them on a sheet of paper in the same position as they would have been on a map. However, this group never saw the map itself and consequently did not learn the final task as well as the cognitive structure group did. This result supports many educators' strong convictions that learners need to learn more than words in order to master school material. The S–R group had all the words available to make an easy transfer to such sentences as "KOT is a pilot," but their lack of real life experience (inspection of the map) prevented rapid learning.

The present paragraph should be recognized as a speculative extension of Reynolds' findings: Many students may have mastered material in textbooks but have learned only words (somewhat like the S–R group just described) because their life experiences have been too limited. For this reason, schoolteachers encourage children to establish school banks or stores as means of making their arithmetic training lifelike.

Our study of transfer has taken us close to the field of thinking and problem solving. When that topic is treated later in the chapter, the matter of transfer will again be discussed briefly.

Learning to Learn and Learning Sets

A variety of studies with both human beings and lower animals indicates that an ability to learn tasks of a certain type can be developed with practice on a variety of such tasks. This ability is called a *learning set or learning to learn*. It represents a transfer of a more general sort than that usually emphasized under the heading *transfer of training*.

Thune (84) has demonstrated that human subjects learn to learn paired-associates adjectives. Figure 3-15 shows a substantial improvement in performance from the first list learned on the first day of training to the first list learned on the fifth day of training. This improvement can be considered a measure of *learning to learn*. Furthermore, within any day there is a substantial improvement from the first list learned to the third list learned. Since most of that improvement is lost in the rest period before the next day's training, it will be called *warm-up effect* and considered a temporary effect only. Meyer and Miles (59) have confirmed the findings by Thune, relating them to the so-called *learning*

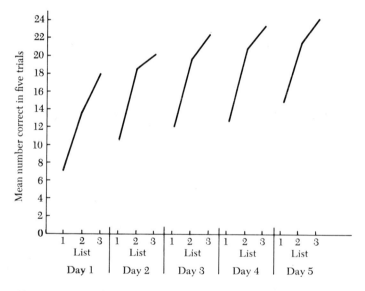

Fig. 3-15. Learning performance on three different lists per day for five days. Figure 33 from McGeoch and Irion (58), but based on the Thune experiment (84). Used by permission of David McKay Company, Inc.

sets of Harlow (32) who showed a regular improvement in learning rate by monkeys given 312 discrimination tasks to learn. With so many successive tasks to learn, each one requiring the monkey to choose which of two stimulus objects covered a filled food well, the monkeys eventually got to the stage where one incorrect trial on a task was sufficient to produce nearly perfect performance thereafter. For the last 56 tasks, 97% of the choices made on trial 2 were correct, compared with the 50% which would have been correct had nothing been learned on trial 1. The Harlow article reports that 17 human children from 2 to 5 years of age also developed learning sets with repeated training on these tasks.

A sidelight of this study was the finding that eight monkeys with extensive damage to half their brain cortex were able to develop learning sets, but not as effectively as normal monkeys could. Further tests showed, however, that brain-damaged monkeys with learning set training learned faster than did normal monkeys without such training.

Learning sets may specially facilitate the performance of the slowest human learners. In a study by Duncan (19) the best one-fourth of the learners were not improved as much over ten different tasks as the poorest one-fourth, partly because the former group were already near the upper limit of possible performance. This result is shown in Fig. 3-16.

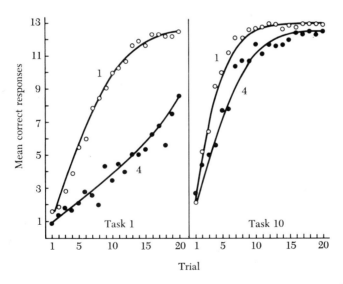

Fig. 3-16. Performance on tasks 1 and 10 of the persons in the top and bottom quarters of performance on task 1. Figure 5 from Duncan (19). Reproduced by permission of University of Illinois Press.

———————————————————————— **Several Aspects of Verbal Learning**

Difficulty of Learning as a Function of Task Length

Learning can be expected to become more difficult as the length of the task increases. Consider the problem of learning a so-called *serial list* of words or nonsense syllables, presented on a memory drum such as that of Fig. 3-9. A serial list differs from the paired associate task we have been previously discussing in this way: rather than learning what pairs to hook together, the subject must now learn a given number of items (perhaps 10) in a specific (serial) order. Thus one might memorize

DEC	MEV
JOX	GUL
PAQ	TOZ
BIR	HAJ
ZUP	KIF

in that order, learning to spell DEC out before it appeared on the drum, to spell out JOX while DEC appeared, PAQ while JOX appeared, and so on, with MEV being the "word" to follow ZUP.

The question arises whether a ten-item list should be twice as difficult to learn as a five-item list, more difficult than that, or somewhat less than twice as difficult. Most experiments on this topic indicate that difficulty (trials to learn to a criterion) more than doubles as the length of the list doubles. Figure 3-17 presents data from one of the earliest of those investigations supporting the conclusion just drawn.

Mnemonic Devices

Extrapolating the curve shown in Fig. 3-17 might lead to the conclusion that a very long list could hardly be learned at all. Under ordinary conditions this is no doubt true. However, work with mnemonic devices (cues for aiding memorizing) shows that long lists of meaningful words can be learned in only one trial. Miller, Galanter, and Pribram (61) discuss at some length a device which you may once have used:

First, you memorize so thoroughly that you think you could never forget it, the following:

One is a bun.	Six are sticks.
Two is a shoe.	Seven is heaven.
Three is a tree.	Eight is a gate.
Four is a door.	Nine is a line.
Five is a hive.	Ten is a hen.

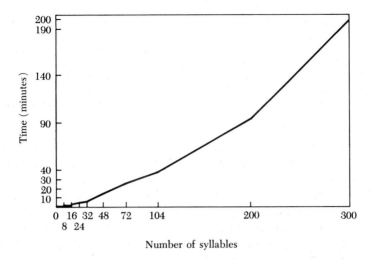

Fig. 3-17. The increase in time required to learn a list as the number of syllables in the list increases. From Fig. 52 of McGeoch and Irion (58). Used by permission of David McKay Company, Inc. Based on research by Lyon (51).

Then you have a friend make a list of ten common words, preferably nouns, and read each one to you with a few seconds' pause between. As he reads the first word, try to associate it with *bun:* if the word is *rabbit,* you might imagine a rabbit eating a bun. As he reads the second word, try to associate it with a shoe, and so on. With practice, you should later be able to say which is number 7, number 2, or any other number by recalling which word was associated with each cue word. For memorizing more than ten words, longer lists of cue words can be constructed and memorized. Miller, Galanter, and Pribram (61) go on to describe an experiment (94) in which subjects were given so much training in memorization that they eventually could, without even having cue word lists, listen to pairs of words for an hour or more at a time with a few seconds between pairs, associate each pair with a visual image, and after only one hearing of a list of 700 pairs give the second word of a pair in response to the first, from any part of the list, with 95% accuracy.

A less spectacular demonstration of improvement in memorization comes from a well-known study in which Woodrow (99) taught seven simple rules for memorization. Those seven rules were (in more modern language):

1. Study the whole passage to be learned and grasp its overall structure before learning individual parts.
2. As you study, test yourself by repeating aloud the poem or other material to be learned.

3. Make use of cues from the rhythm or grouping existing or producible in the text to be learned.

4. Pay attention to the meaning of what you are studying. Maybe you could even form a mental picture which symbolizes the meaning to be remembered.

5. Keep mentally alert and concentrate upon the learning task.

6. Have confidence in your ability to memorize.

7. Use associations between the material to be learned and other things you already know.

Students given almost three hours of practice and instruction with these rules improved an average of 36.1% in ability to memorize, compared to an average gain of 4.5% for students who practiced memorizing for almost three hours but were not told to use the rules above.

One warning should be given about any memory technique, however. Despite its potential usefulness, a method for memorizing cannot substitute for reasoning ability. Therefore schools quite properly emphasize learning to use knowledge intelligently, not simply learning to retain and repeat information on request. Some of the advantages and disadvantages of special memory techniques are given by Wood (98).

Effect of Degree of Meaningfulness upon Learning

In much experimentation on verbal learning, the stimuli are nonsense syllables such as JOQ, constructed to minimize the amount of learning prior to the experiment. Not even nonsense syllables are meaningless, however, just because they are not English words. KOW has a great deal of "meaning" to us, as does TER: the former because its pronunciation is like COW, the latter because it appears in many real words (89). Even words themselves vary in their subjective meaningfulness to us. Consequently, it has seemed wise to develop measures of meaningfulness so that experimenters can control meaningfulness in their experiments, sometimes holding it constant for all conditions and sometimes varying it and studying its effects (2, 67). By these standards, the list on p. 90 would have low meaningfulness.

The method of scaling meaningfulness varies from investigator to investigator. Noble defines the meaningfulness of a nonsense syllable or other set of letters as the average number of different associations it produces in persons tested by asking them to give all possible associations to each letter set presented. Most other definitions of meaningfulness are closely related to this one, and *association value* is often used as a synonym for meaningfulness.

It is interesting to ask what makes a word or syllable meaningful. Underwood (88) offers Table 3-2 as evidence that the more often a word is seen or heard the more meaningful it becomes. In brief it compares

60 words arranged by Noble (67) in their order of meaningfulness with their frequency of appearance in printed English according to the Thorndike–Lorge word count (83). As Table 3-2 shows, six of Noble's seven most meaningful words occur more than 100 times per million printed words. None of his 20 least meaningful words appears more than seven times per million.

Teachers can use this finding in their classrooms: A new word to children will have little meaning to children at first, but repeated use of it will make it meaningful. One would also expect the meaningfulness of words to increase with the vividness of the situation in which they are first encountered. Therefore, a teacher may want to give meaning to material about reproduction by letting a class care for an expectant mother cat, watch the reproductive process, and raise the kittens.

Meaningfulness is important because it is an aid to learning. Under-

TABLE 3-2

*Scaled Meaningfulness of Words and Frequency of Occurrence
in the English Language*[a]

Word[b]	T–L	Word	T–L	Word	T–L
1. kitchen	AA	21. region	A	41. argon	—
2. army	AA	22. quarter	AA	42. sequence	6
3. money	AA	23. leader	AA	43. pallor	2
4. dinner	AA	24. mallet	3	44. tankard	1
5. wagon	A	25. kennel	6	45. bodice	2
6. office	AA	26. keeper	23	46. vertex	—
7. heaven	AA	27. fatigue	19	47. rostrum	—
8. jelly	19	28. unit	29	48. ovum	—
9. jewel	41	29. effort	AA	49. tartan	1
10. insect	40	30. quarry	11	50. endive	—
11. village	AA	31. quota	3	51. jetsam	—
12. garment	40	32. yeomen	11	52. lichens	7
13. zebra	2	33. zenith	4	53. percent	—
14. captain	AA	34. ordeal	5	54. capstan	—
15. typhoon	—	35. pigment	4	55. lemur	—
16. youngster	21	36. naptha	1	56. nimbus	—
17. uncle	AA	37. pallet	2	57. carom	—
18. income	46	38. entrant	—	58. flotsam	—
19. zero	11	39. jitney	—	59. grapnel	—
20. hunger	37	40. rampart	4	60. stoma	—

[a] From B. J. Underwood, "Verbal learning in the educative processes," *Harvard Educational Review,* **29,** Spring 1959, p. 113. Copyright © 1959 by President and Fellows of Harvard College.

[b] The 60 words are from Noble (67); they are given in order of meaningfulness. The T–L column indicates the frequency of occurrence of that word in the Thorndike–Lorge count (83). AA is most frequent, such words occurring more than 100 times per million. A number refers to the actual frequency per million. A dash indicates that the word does not occur in the 20,000 most frequent words.

wood and Schulz (92) have shown that in laboratory learning this is usually true. However, there is one limitation worth noting: In a paired-associates list where the stimulus is presented and the proper response must be recalled, it is helpful to learning if the *response word* is highly meaningful but less important if the *stimulus word* is highly meaningful. Underwood and Schulz (92) conclude that there is three times as large an effect of response meaningfulness as of stimulus meaningfulness. This seems a reasonable result when one thinks about it. A meaningful response will be easy to recall because it has been used so often or with such intensity in the past. However, a stimulus word doesn't have to be recalled; all one has to do is look at it or listen to it being read and try to remember what should be related to it. An increase in stimulus meaningfulness may help to differentiate stimuli, but learning the associations will still be difficult unless the response words are meaningful and therefore easy to recall for the purpose of associating the appropriate stimulus and response words in pairs.

This emphasis upon different effects of stimulus and response meaningfulness takes us back to the discussion of analyzing behavior with which this chapter began. If a botany teacher wants students to be able to give both the Latin and English names for a plant, he will have to give more practice trials for the Latin names than for the English names because the former are less meaningful. However, if he merely wants students to be able to state the English name associated with each Latin name, this will be quickly learned because low meaningfulness of the stimulus does not greatly retard learning the response. Analysis of the exact behavior to be taught thus influences the teaching technique to be employed.

Incidental Learning

It is generally believed that paired-associates learning has two aspects, *response learning*, which tells the subjects what syllables or words to use, and *associative learning*, which tells them which response goes with each stimulus. High meaningfulness aids response learning but may not affect associative learning. To some extent each kind of learning can occur with or without instruction to learn. Without such instruction the learning is called *incidental learning*.

Under certain conditions incidental learning can be almost as fast as "intentional learning" (70, 75). This finding poses some difficulties for S–R learning theorists. They are committed to the proposition that making a response is necessary to learning, but the incidental learning situation requires fewer task-oriented overt responses than the intentional learning procedure. S–R theorists explain the matter by assuming that hidden responses such as subvocal repetitions of words with the tongue or larynx account for the incidental learning. S–S theorists are able simply to say that incidental learning follows from exposure to appropriate stimuli. Any superiority of the intentional learning group indicates an added increment due to responding overtly. Postman (69a) emphasizes that if instructions to an intentional learning group produce no change in what that group does (compared with the incidental learning group) there will be no difference between the groups in amount learned.

The incidental learning experiments have much importance to the classroom teacher. He must expect that anything the pupil observes— activity in the classroom, television programs in the home, fights on the playground—will produce learning of some degree and kind. Effective teaching requires that as much appropriate experience as possible be given the pupils. It is for this reason that summer tours to Washington, D. C., by high school classes can be justified educationally. Without doubt, instructions and self-instruction for intentional learning on such tours may be somewhat minimal for some pupils, the trip naturally having the appeal of sociability as well as education. However, much learning of an academic nature can result.

One word of warning should be made: Incidental learning in the laboratory is usually smaller when measured by an immediate recall test than when followed by intentional learning. What incidental learning procedures do best, then, is to facilitate later learning.

Much, then, of the educational effects of tours and other activities or project-oriented learning experiences may lie dormant unless followed by a more formal learning procedure. In some cases this dormant state may be adequate. Familiarization with a topic may be all that is desired. If not, the extra classroom time required to make the incidentally learned material available for immediate recall will be well spent.

Effects of Similarity within Parts of a List

The amount of similarity among different items of a serial list (called *intralist similarity*) is sometimes defined by the number of letters, particularly consonants, used twice, three times, or even more in the list. By this definition the illustrative serial list from p. 90 has *low intralist similarity* because only three consonants are used twice and none more than twice. The items of that list were earlier seen to have low meaningfulness, which should retard learning. What should be the effect of its low intralist similarity? Underwood and his co-workers (90, 91) have shown that low intralist similarity facilitates learning and high intralist similarity retards it. A naive reader would no doubt have predicted this finding, saying that high intralist similarity causes each syllable "to be confused" with the other, i.e., to interfere with the others. It is interesting to note that Underwood found a low meaningfulness, low intralist similarity, list to be about equally difficult for learning to a high meaningfulness, high intralist similarity list. Apparently the opposite effects of meaningfulness and intralist similarity just about balance each other out. Teachers therefore should take pains to use highly meaningful material with enough variety in each lesson that learning will not be retarded by this similarity effect.

_____ **Thinking and Problem Solving**

The Mediation Hypothesis

Psychologists from the time of J. B. Watson (95), the founder of behaviorism, have emphasized that the only accessible aspects of thinking are the responses which are written down, said, or in other ways made publicly observable. (In fact behaviorism may be defined as the belief that the only acceptable data of psychology are the observable behavior of animals and people.) Watson believed that thinking was largely composed of subvocal speech. In support of this view, he cited an anecdote that Laura Bridgman, a well-known, deaf-mute lady, dreamed with her hands moving in sign language, which was subsequently verified experimentally for deaf-mutes in general (57), using electrical potential changes in the finger muscles as indications of hand movements. Novikova (68) confirmed this finding and also showed that in a variety of tasks, such as mental pronunciation of a poem or mental arithmetic, persons who can speak commonly exhibited tongue movements during the tasks.

Regardless of the correctness of Watson's inference about the nature of thought, psychologists have followed his advice in studying the overt products of thought. As we shall see shortly, however, there has been a recent interest in *mediational processes*, which have much the character of thoughts themselves rather than of overt stimuli and responses.

Consider an example of a mediating response which is observable. Someone points to a tree near you and asks, "Is that a Jeffrey pine?" You may have learned to say, "This is a pine tree," when you see one, but other kinds of pine trees look like Jeffrey pines. Therefore, you delay a reply until you can sniff a twig of the tree. Only if it smells like vanilla, do you say, "Yes, it's a Jeffrey pine." Your sniffing response was a mediating response, in that it came between the question and answer and facilitated the answer.

Here is another example: A friend asks, "What is 28 times 7?" Not having memorized the answer, you calculate somewhat as follows (either out loud or to yourself), "7×8 is 56, so carry 5; 2×7 is 14; $14 + 5$ is 19. 19 followed by 6 is 196." Then you answer, "196." Whether the calculation was done aloud or to yourself, it was a set of mediating responses once again. Many psychologists would hesitate to admit it occurred if you had said it to yourself. They point out rightly that we can only find out what the mediating response was by asking you to introspect, and that the information you give may not be correct. Furthermore, there seems to be something philosophically unsatisfying about having a mediating response which can be identified so poorly by electrical recording apparatus that no one but the person making the response can know what it was.

Nonetheless, psychologists are now beginning to accept these unobservable mediating responses as well as the observable ones. Lachman (50), a thoroughly behavioristic psychologist in training and outlook, explicitly equates mediating responses with subvocal saying of words, without committing himself as to what such subvocal speech may actually be.

No matter what that subvocal speech may be, teachers should encourage subvocal mediating responses as well as observable ones. Fluornoy (25) has demonstrated that instruction to practice "mental arithmetic," accompanied by time periods for that practice, leads to subsequent improved performance in sixth-grade arithmetic and other school subjects. This "mental arithmetic" has the status, of course, of mediated responses. Some of those responses are probably non-speech responses—hand, arm, and even leg movements. However, Fluornoy, other writers such as Perry (69), as well as the present authors, believe it advisable, from a pedagogic view, at least, to consider them largely subvocal speech and to give instructions in "mental arithmetic" which encourage that behavior, even though it is unobserved outside the pupil himself.

A Representative Experiment on Problem Solving

Now we refer to a classic experiment on thinking, or problem solving, to be more specific. Maier (53) gave students the task of finding a way to simultaneously grasp two strings suspended from the ceiling of a room. As Fig. 3-18 shows, the distance between strings was too great for them to be able to hold one string with one arm and reach over to the other

Fig. 3-18. The Maier string problem—to tie two distant strings together. The pendulum motion of the weight attached to one string enables the subject to reach both strings at once. Figure based on Fig. 12.9 of Kendler (48). Reproduced by permission of Appleton-Century-Crofts, Educational Division, Meredith Corporation. Based on research by Maier (53).

string with the other arm. Various objects were left in the room, however, and the experimenter intimated that they could be used in the solution. Eventually (though often with help) most subjects found that they could do the task by making a pendulum with one string tied to a pair of pliers, swinging it so that it could be reached with one hand while the other hand pulled the second string toward the first.

In Maier's experiment an appropriate mediating response would have been to say aloud or covertly, "If I had a method of getting one string into pendulum motion, then I could reach the other and grab the first." When Maier questioned his successful subjects, 7 out of the 23 who required hints before solution reported that seeing the experimenter pull one string in swaying motion made them think of a device for increasing its sway. Most of the other successful subjects had not "consciously" made such a mediating response, but had stumbled on the correct solution.

Do not let the Maier experiment lead you to think that a mediating response must be verbal, however. It may also be a glance in a certain direction, such as looking at a traffic light before crossing a street. Lower animals such as rats may have mediating responses even though they do not have speech in the sense we know it.

In many cases mediating responses are inferred to have occurred even though they were not observed directly, no verbal report was given about them by the subjects after the experiment, and their exact nature is not known.

Reversal versus Nonreversal Shifts as
Related to Mediational Responses

Research by Kendler and Kendler (49) suggests that one kind of discrimination learning is easier than another if mediating responses are available, and that certain species and animals at certain ages find that such learning is indeed easier.

The original learning task used by the Kendlers may be oversimplified to mean that in selecting one of a pair of objects the subject learns to choose a big object rather than a little one when the former is black (A) and the latter is white (B) or when the former is white (C) and the latter is black (D).

(A)   (B)   (C)   (D)

Thus the choice must be made on the basis of size (the relevant difference) even though there is always also a difference in brightness (the irrelevant difference) as well.

The critical question from the Kendlers' point of view is whether subjects trained first on size discrimination will later find it easier to reverse that response or to learn a differential response to brightness. *Reversal shift training* would mean doing the opposite of the old correct response: choosing a small object (B or D) rather than a big one (A or

C) irrespective of color. *Nonreversal shift learning* would mean respond-ing to the previously irrelevant cue and choosing a black object (A or D) rather than a white one (B or C) irrespective of size.

The Kendlers assumed that a mediating response during the original learning amounted to a covert response to size. Reversal learning would be easy for a subject with this mediating response: The subject would still respond to size (perhaps by scanning the outline of each test object visually) and would just reverse the overt choice previously made. Non-reversal shift learning would be harder because the old mediating re-sponse as well as the overt choice would have to be modified. Therefore animals with the ability to make mediating responses should show faster reversal shift learning than nonreversal shift learning. The Kendlers also present an argument to the effect that the reverse is true for animals that cannot make mediating responses. The Kendlers go on to cite evidence that human adults, who have well-developed language and, therefore, mediating responses available, do learn reversal shifts more easily than nonreversal shifts. Correspondingly rats and nursery-school children learn the nonreversal shifts easier, presumably because they do not have mediating responses available. A clever consequence of this argument is the Kendlers' prediction that older children will be more likely to make mediating responses than younger ones, and the older a child is, the more likely he is to choose a reversal shift rather than a nonreversal shift in later learning. Figure 3-19 shows the result of an experiment testing and confirming that prediction.

Wolff (97a), in an exhaustive review of shift learning studies, found evidence to support the prediction of faster reversal than nonreversal shifts in adults; however, he concluded that the prediction of faster non-reversal shifts than reversal shifts in young children was not confirmed by the bulk of the evidence available.

Transfer of Mediating Responses in Complex Problems

The last section demonstrated that mediation facilitates a particular kind of positive transfer. Gestalt psychologists (psychologists emphasiz-ing the importance of the total situation or *gestalt*) have long argued that thinking processes taught in the schools should emphasize meaning-ful relations (and consequently, no doubt, mediating responses as well). One of them, Katona (45), has designed a card trick to illustrate his theme, arguing that when it is learned by an "understanding" method it will be better remembered and more positive transfer will occur to related card tricks than if a rote memorization method is used.

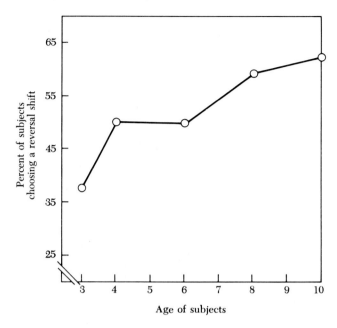

Fig. 3-19. The increased percentage of children responding in a reversal shift manner with increased age. Figure 5 from Kendler and Kendler (49). Copyright 1962 by American Psychological Association and reproduced by permission.

Consider, for example, the trick of stacking a set of eight playing cards, four red and four black, so that if you place the top one face up on a table, it will be red, the second from the top being placed on the bottom of the stack, the third being placed face up on a table and being black, the fourth being placed on the bottom of the stack, and so on until all cards are on the table in R–B–R–B–R–B–R–B order where R refers to red and B to black, of course. Members of a rote memorization group would simply memorize the following order: R–R–B–R–R–B–B–B in which the cards would have to be stacked. Members of an understanding group would use a plan to solve the problem which would apply to other related problems as well. At least five understanding methods have been employed experimentally (37). This is the one originally proposed by Katona:

Make a row of eight question marks to indicate the unknown cards. In the second row replace the first question mark by an R, leave a question mark in the second position because it represents a card to be placed on the bottom of the deck, replace the third by a B, leave the fourth, replace the fifth by an R, and so on. In successive rows decide below each remaining question mark whether it should be repeated or replaced by an R or B. At length you will obtain the following tabulation:

1.	?	?	?	?	?	?	?	?
2.	R	?	B	?	R	?	B	?
3.		R		?		B		?
4.				R				?
5.								B

Summarizing the tabulation by pulling down the R or B for each column yields

6.	R	R	B	R	R	B	B	B

just as for the rote memorization condition.

Hilgard, Irvine, and Whipple (38) have verified Katona's earlier finding that training with this understanding method leads to greater positive transfer to related problems than does training with a rote memorization method. Consider a new task such as stacking three red cards and three black cards so that they would come out R–B–R–B–R–B when laid out on the table as before. Only 3 out of 30 members of the memorization group could do the new task on the first try, but 16 of 30 members of the understanding group could do so. Similar results occurred when the transfer task was to arrange four red cards and four black cards so that they would eventually come out R–B–R–B–R–B even though two cards rather than one card were placed on the bottom of the pack following each placement of a card on the table. You may want to try to solve each of these new problems for yourself by Katona's method.

Katona's conclusion that the understanding method was learned more slowly than the rote memorization one was verified by Hilgard, Irvine, and Whipple; however, his conclusion that retention is also superior for the understanding method was largely contradicted by the more carefully executed Hilgard, Irvine, and Whipple experiment.

What can be concluded from this research? One should not necessarily decry rote memorization methods. Repetition (rote) is required to learn how to write down the six-row tabulation just presented. Thus, understanding methods are also rote methods. The important question is, "*What should be learned?*" We conclude that general principles should be learned wherever possible. The method of the six-row tabulation has taken more time for learning than memorizing R–R–B–R–R–B–B–B but is by definition applicable to other tricks than the one first used. School teachers can vastly improve their teaching if they keep this point in mind, for students are much more likely to want to learn material if they can see that it has many uses than if they think of it as an isolated set of facts appropriate only to a situation in which they are not particularly interested. This emphasis upon teaching principles rather than specific items without generality is not only attractive to students, it also makes sense to intellectual leaders. The reasons for this are two: (a) knowledge of principles is essential to understanding of an area of scholarship, and (b) with the great current increase in amount of published information in a subject, individuals cannot read fast enough or memorize quickly enough to know the factual information in anything more than a very small subspecialty of their area of interest. Therefore, they must focus as much as possible upon learning principles which summarize the state of knowledge in a field they wish to understand.

Educational psychologists have made much the same point as Katona by telling teachers to "teach for transfer." They point out that pupils may develop neatness in an arithmetic class which is not transferred to any other course or situation because no one has encouraged them to use their learning from one situation in new ones. However, specific attempts to teach geometry in a way that fosters critical thinking in other courses have been successful (87). A further educational experiment on transfer (34) shows that children given practice in shooting an air rifle at an underwater target learn less quickly than those also given instruction concerning the relevant principle that light rays bend on leaving the water, making the apparent position of the object differ from its actual position. It would seem that mediating responses such as subvocal saying, "The target must be a little to the right of where it appears," may be occurring and facilitating performance in the "principles learning" condition.

Transposition

Transposition is a form of stimulus generalization or transfer in which a stimulus responded to positively during training will not evoke a positive response during the transfer test period. Though transposition does occur among animals, we are most interested in transposition by humans, since there may be some way to use this fact about humans in the classroom. In one example of a transposition task, children may be asked under which of the following boxes a reward will be found:

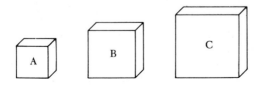

The same box (C), the largest of the three, always has the reward under it. A standard test for transposition in the above situation is to present the formerly correct box (C) together with box B plus a larger box which had not previously been presented:

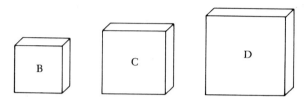

Young children will typically choose the formerly correct box (C) on the test trial with boxes B, C, and D; older children and adults will select the largest of the new boxes (D) possibly because older persons use mediation processes and say to themselves, "The reward is under the largest box."

An alternative procedure devised by Jensen (44) used boxes A, B, and C during training, with the reward consistently under box C, followed by a test trial involving presentation of three identical-sized (though the size was unspecified) boxes with a picture of one animal on each box. The pictures were the same size, but the sizes of the animals (horse, mouse, and elephant) obviously differ in real life. Most kindergarten and first-grade children who were tested appeared to choose a box at random; however, most third- and fourth-grade children tested chose the box with the elephant picture, thus apparently employing a mediating response of "largest" which had been developed during training.

Discovery Methods and Learning by Rules

Teachers are often advised to let class members develop new ideas for themselves rather than learn them from the teacher. This is hard for a teacher to do; he often feels that an answer is obvious and will be remembered once the pupil is told that answer. However, experience proves that we do not learn everything we hear.

It is not clear that in cognitive (intellectual) processes the discovery of knowledge is necessarily the best way for children to proceed. One advocate of a discovery process found that physics students required considerable prompting before they could make sensible inquiries into their topic (81). Nonetheless, there is enough evidence to suggest that teachers should consider letting children find their own solutions to certain problems. One such task, though an unlikely one for most classrooms, is breaking simple letter codes (30). Thus TABBIR might be a cryptogram meaning RABBIT. Some students (rule group) were taught a rule for solving such cryptograms: Exchange the first and last letters of the word. Other students (example groups) learned the same principle by trial and error on successive words coded by that principle. The rule group also had experience solving cryptograms by the rule taught them. One example group later was taught the rule; another was not. To complicate the experiment further, all students learned how to solve two kinds of cryptograms formed with different rules and were tested for retention of those tasks and for transfer to cryptograms using different kinds of rules. The outcome was that the rule group was best in retention of the solutions originally learned. However, the example group, which was never explicitly taught a rule, proved superior in transferring cryptographic skills to a new type of problem. Apparently the example group profited from attempted solution, from failure, and from techniques developed in the process of that failure. To the extent that this experiment is representative of problem-solving tasks in life, it would seem that teachers might well emphasize learning by trial and error because of its greater transfer to new situations.

A related experiment also serves to de-emphasize the purely logical approach to problem solving. Gagné and Smith (26) tried to find out if telling subjects to look for a logical solution to a mechanical puzzle would facilitate performance on various versions of that puzzle. Such instruction had no effect of any consequence. However, when the subjects were instructed to say aloud why they made each move, this procedure produced dramatic improvement when compared with other instructions. A clinical psychologist might think of this experiment as showing the effects of therapy (talking about one's problems) in a purely intellectual situation.

--- **A Model of School Learning**

Most of this chapter has been devoted to the principles of learning as studied in research laboratories where basic learning processes, not teaching techniques or principles, are of major interest. This coverage is important, but you as future teachers are interested in the overall instructional problem, not simply in separate learning processes. Let us return to the model (or theory) of school learning developed by Carroll (14), presented in Chapter 2, and fit the foregoing material to it. You will notice that this model talks not only about learning processes per se but also about aptitude, teaching technique, and motivation as well. This is important because the teacher is interested in an overall educational result rather than in knowing the effect of some single variable such as magnitude of reinforcement, for example.

Carroll begins his article by defining a learning task: "The learner's task of going from ignorance of some specified fact or concept to knowledge or understanding of it, or of proceeding from incapability of performing some specified act to capability of performing it, is a learning task." He distinguishes between narrowly defined tasks such as learning to spell all the words on page 20 of a spelling book and broadly defined tasks such as learning to read printed English. Another useful distinction is made between learning to do such things as spelling correctly and learning feelings of brotherhood among all people. He says that the first process is operant behavior (instrumental conditioning) and the second respondent behavior (classical conditioning). Most of Carroll's discussion pertains to the instrumental side of learning though he recognizes the importance of teaching desirable attitudes as well.

According to this model, the number of learning tasks accomplished or the degree of learning within a task depends upon five basic variables, including three which emphasize the importance of time spent in learning. Consider the time factors first:

1. Success in learning any task depends in part upon one's *aptitude* for learning that task. The reason Carroll calls aptitude a time variable is that one could measure aptitude by how long a person takes to learn the task. (Chapter 14 describes more common methods of measuring intellectual aptitude.) Educators know that aptitudes vary widely from one child to another; consequently, a major decision in the school must be made as to whether each child will be allowed the time he needs to learn a task or whether a fixed amount of time will be provided for everyone.

2. As implied above, the amount learned will also depend upon the *amount of time the teacher allows for learning*. This variable corresponds to the experimental variable, number of trials, discussed earlier in this chapter, indicating that learning generally increases with number of trials.

3. In some cases an adequate amount of time will be allowed for learning, but the student does not use the available time for studying. Our third variable, then, is *willingness to spend the available time in learning*. Carroll says that this willingness is related to one's willingness to withstand discomfort and to face failure. A student who does not very much wish to learn will not study when he has a slight cold or a headache. A student who is afraid he might fail even though he tries hard to learn an assignment may choose not to try. Part of the teacher's

task is to motivate the student in such a way that he will be able to withstand discomfort and that he will risk occasional failure for the purpose of learning. Point 3 is almost more important than point 2 because allowing time for learning is useless without a willingness to spend time learning; a person who is willing to spend such time may even find it outside of school if inadequate time is provided in school. An even more important laboratory variable than number of trials, then, is number of responses. We have already emphasized in this chapter that many tasks should be overlearned, i.e., studied or practiced for several trials after a perfect performance is first attained. This will require both adequate time for overlearning and adequate willingness to spend that time.

The two remaining factors in school learning depend less obviously upon time:

4. *The ability to understand instruction* has some relation to aptitude for learning. However, it depends upon specific training to a greater extent than does intelligence. Children should be taught how to listen to instruction, how to use dictionaries and other reference works, and even how to read examination questions before answering them.

5. The *quality of instruction* is the effectiveness with which the teacher gives instructions or information, organizes the materials presented for learning, ensures that the students actually read or hear those materials rather than merely possess them, and induces students to spend time learning. Though quality of instruction depends a great deal upon the performance of the teacher, it also is affected by the materials he chooses or is required to use—textbooks, workbooks, films, and invited speakers, for example. Quality of instruction is affected by the teacher's use of the learning principles discussed earlier in the chapter; it also depends on the application of many principles about aptitude, motivation, and other aspects of behavior.

_____ **Summary**

1. Learning is defined as a relatively permanent change in behavior due to experience.

2. The study of learning teaches one to analyze complex learning tasks—such as the study of literature—into specific acts. Once this has been done, a teacher can more easily state the goals of a course by specifying the *behavioral objectives* or specific responses to be strengthened by the course.

3. Much of learning consists of the acquisition of information. How-

ever, some desirable behavior, such as good citizenship, is not assured simply by teaching the facts. Therefore, research on changes in response choices or vigor of response in animals has as much relevance for teachers as does research on humans involving memory processes.

4. B. F. Skinner discovered much of the fundamental information about type R or operant conditioning (also called instrumental conditioning). In this form of conditioning a response may be made spontaneously by a person or an animal, without any obvious evoking stimulus. When that response is followed by a reinforcement, such as food for a hungry organism, the response is strengthened and will be more likely to occur the next time the person is in the same situation under which the response was made.

5. Ivan P. Pavlov discovered the classical conditioning process, also called Pavlovian conditioning in his honor, and termed type S conditioning by Skinner. Classical conditioning consists of repeatedly presenting an unconditioned stimulus (UCS), i.e., a stimulus which already evokes a response the experimenter wants to employ, and a conditioned stimulus (CS) which does not originally evoke that response. After several trials in which the CS and UCS are presented either simultaneously or with the CS slightly preceding the UCS, conditioning is demonstrated if presentation of the CS alone leads to the response originally made only to the UCS. That response is now called a conditioned response.

6. There is considerable controversy over whether an individual learns gradually (incremental learning) or instantaneously (all–or–none learning). We can conclude that gradual improvement in average performance is an almost universal finding. Such gradual average curves often mislead readers to believe that individual learning curves were gradual when they may not have been.

7. Positive reinforcement is any event following a response which strengthens that response. (In classical conditioning and some verbal learning experiments the response does not always precede the reinforcement.) There are several different schedules of reinforcement, such as ratio reinforcement in which a certain number of responses has to be made before a reinforcement is given.

8. Extinction is withholding reinforcement when a formerly reinforced response is made. The usual effect of extinction is weakening of the response.

9. Secondary reinforcers acquire their power through paired association with a primary reinforcer. The primary reinforcer is reinforcing without special training, but a secondary reinforcer is a neutral stimulus until it is associated with a primary reinforcer. Thereupon it also becomes reinforcing. Repeated presentation of a secondary reinforcer after a

response without primary reinforcement leads to a reduction of the secondary reinforcing properties, and the secondary reinforcer becomes a neutral stimulus again. Objects such as money are examples of secondary reinforcers.

10. Increases in the quantity and quality of reinforcements lead to increased speed of response. However, they do not necessarily affect the quality of performance, as measured by proportion of errors.

11. With animals, if the reinforcement is to be maximally effective, it is mandatory that a reinforcer follow a response by only a short interval. For humans, a delay of knowledge of results for as long as one week does not impair learning of a motor task provided that the time intervals between each successive trial remain constant. Similarly, in human concept or classroom learning a relatively long delay of reinforcement does not impede learning.

12. Latent learning is learning that is not demonstrated at the time it is developed. Three possible explanations of latent learning are: (1) A small reinforcement present at the end of each latent learning trial is too small to produce immediate improvement in performance but does produce learning which is demonstrable as soon as reinforcement magnitude is increased (stimulus–response reinforcement theory). (2) Correct responses are made during the latent learning period and thus are learned. However, they will not be made with vigor or with high frequency until the reinforcement conditions are changed to make such responses useful (stimulus–response contiguity theory). (3) The relationships between stimuli, such as the geography of a maze and the location of a food receptacle, are learned through sensory and central nervous system processes rather than response processes. This occurs during the latent learning period; overt responses such as going through the maze without error will occur as soon as reinforcement is increased (stimulus–stimulus contiguity theory).

13. Though earlier research emphasized the great importance of reinforcement or confirmation of correct responses after they are made, the best current information is that humans profit more from prompting, i.e., being told the correct answer before studying it or being given clues to the correct response.

14. Transfer of training is using responses in one situation which were learned in another. Where transfer is beneficial to performance of a new task, it is called positive transfer. Where detrimental, it is called negative transfer. Transfer of training experiments have been used to support the proposition that certain academic subjects should be studied, not for their direct benefits, but for their help in learning other topics. However, transfer effects are normally less than the effect of direct training on the

desired skill. Therefore, one should not study Latin as a basis for learning French; it is more efficient to spend that time on French if there is no other reason to study Latin.

15. Transposition, like transfer of training, is dependent upon the similarity between two situations. However, in transposition experiments persons fail to respond to stimulus values which were formerly positive. Thus in the test situation one might choose the largest of a set of stimulus objects because one thinks that large stimuli are always correct, even though a slightly smaller stimulus is presented in the test situation and that stimulus had been the largest one available on previous trials.

16. Experimentation with so-called advanced organizers shows that studying quite general introductory material before the actual content to be mastered will facilitate the learning of the ultimate task.

17. Mnemonic devices are often used to facilitate verbal learning, thus longer and longer lists can be remembered through association of words with other words or objects. However, improved memory ability cannot substitute for reasoning ability.

18. Meaningfulness of a word is defined in terms of the number of associations to that word which are produced by instructions to recall related words. More meaningful words are those with high numbers of associations. The more meaningful a set of material is, the more quickly it will be learned. Vividness of a word in a list to be learned will also facilitate learning that word.

19. Anything a person observes will produce some learning. If his observations are controlled to some extent, as in school, this incidental learning may be guided as a means of increasing his total useful knowledge.

20. Mediating responses, observable and unobservable, facilitate human learning. It is desirable for teachers to encourage subvocal mediation (such as solving mathematics problems mentally) as well as audible mediation in which students explain how they are trying to solve a problem.

21. Research on Katona's "understanding method" of learning suggests that teachers should attempt to teach for understanding and transfer rather than for memorization of techniques which cannot be transferred to new situations.

22. Carroll has developed a model of school learning emphasizing five basic variables determining the number of learning tasks accomplished or the degree of learning within each task: (1) aptitude for learning, (2) amount of time allowed, (3) willingness to spend time in learning, (4) ability to understand instructions, and (5) quality of instruction.

SUGGESTED READINGS

McConnell, J. Learning theory. In R. A. Baker (Ed.), *Psychology in the wry*. Princeton, N. J. Van Nostrand, 1963. Pp. 66–81.

This is part of a very funny book about psychology, a story supposedly by and about a human captured by invaders from outer space who place him in a Skinner box, maze, and similar apparatuses where he consciously demonstrates the laws of learning.

Skinner, B. F. How to teach animals. Reprint from *Scientific American*, 1951 (December), 5 pp. Available from Freeman, San Francisco, California.

Specific advice on training animals and human babies.

REFERENCES

1. Aiken, E. G., & Lau, A. W. Response prompting and response confirmation. *Psychological Bulletin*, 1967, **68**, 330–341.
2. Archer, E. J. Re-evaluation of the meaningfulness of all possible CVC trigrams. *Psychological Monographs*, 1960, **74**(10, Whole No. 497).
3. Ausubel, D. P. The use of advanced organizers in the learning and retention of meaningful verbal material. *Journal of Educational Psychology*, 1960, **51**, 267–272.
4. Ausubel, D. P. *The psychology of meaningful verbal learning*. New York: Grune & Stratton, 1963.
5. Ausubel, D. P. *Educational psychology. A cognitive view*. New York: Holt, Rinehart & Winston, 1968.
6. Ausubel, D. P., & Youssef, M. Role of discriminability in meaningful parallel learning. *Journal of Educational Psychology*, 1963, **54**, 85, 331–336.
7. Becker, W. C., Madsen, C. H., Jr., Arnold, C. R., & Thomas, D. R. The contingent use of teacher attention and praise in reducing classroom behavior problems. *Journal of Special Education*, 1967, **1**, 287–307.
8. Bilodeau, E. A., & Bilodeau, I. M. Variation of temporal intervals among critical events in five studies of knowledge of results. *Journal of Experimental Psychology*, 1958, **55**, 603–612.
9. Bilodeau, E. A., & Ryan, F. J. A test for interaction of delay of knowledge of results and two types of interpolated activity. *Journal of Experimental Psychology*, 1960, **59**, 414–419.
10. Blodgett, H. C. The effect of the introduction of reward upon the maze performance of rats. *University of California Publications in Psychology*, 1929, **4**, 113–134.
11. Blough, D. S. A method for obtaining psychophysical thresholds from the pigeon. *Journal of the Experimental Analysis of Behavior*, 1958, **1**, 33–43.
12. Bourne, L. E., Jr., & Bunderson, C. V. Effects of delay of informative feedback and length of postfeedback interval on concept identification. *Journal of Experimental Psychology*, 1963, **65**, 1–5.

13. Brackbill, Y., Wagner, J. E., & Wilson, D. Feedback delay and the teaching machine. *Psychology in the Schools,* 1964, **1,** 148–156.
14. Carroll, J. B. A model of school learning. *Teachers College Record,* 1963, **64,** 723–733.
15. Cotton, J. W., Sloss, J. M., Taplin, J. R., and Nielsen, A. E. A comparison of a Hullian paired associate learning model with other models appropriate to an $R^N T^5$ design with $1:1$ pairing of stimuli and responses. *Journal of Mathematical Psychology,* 1968, **5,** 442–462.
16. Crespi, L. P. Quantitative variation of incentive and performance in the white rat. *American Journal of Psychology,* 1942, **55,** 467–517.
17. Crowley, W. H. Freedom and discipline. *Educational Record,* 1944, **25,** 5–22.
18. Denny, M. R., Allard, M., Hall, E., & Rokeach, M. Supplementary report: delay of knowledge of results, knowledge of task, and intertrial interval. *Journal of Experimental Psychology,* 1960, **60,** 327.
19. Duncan, C. P. Description of learning to learn in human subjects. *American Journal of Psychology,* 1960, **73,** 108–114.
20. Eisenberger, R., Karpman, M., & Trattner, J. What is the necessary and sufficient condition for reinforcement in the contingency situation? *Journal of Experimental Psychology,* 1967, **74,** 342–350.
21. Ekstrand, B. R. Backward associations. *Psychological Bulletin,* 1966, **65,** 50–64.
22. Estes, W. K. Discriminative conditioning. II. Effects of a Pavlovian conditioned stimulus upon a subsequently established operant response. *Journal of Experimental Psychology,* 1948, **38,** 173–177.
23. Estes, W. K. Learning theory and the new mental chemistry. *Psychological Review,* 1960, **67,** 207–223.
23a. Estes, W. K., Hopkins, B. L., & Crothers, E. J. All-or-none and conservation effects in the learning and retention of paired associates. *Journal of Experimental Psychology,* 1960, **60,** 329–339.
24. Ferster, C., & Skinner, B. F. *Schedules of reinforcement.* New York: Appleton-Century-Crofts, 1957.
25. Fluornoy, M. F. The effectiveness of instruction in mental arithmetic. *Elementary School Journal,* 1954, **55,** 148–153.
26. Gagné, R. M., & Smith, E. C., Jr. A study of the effects of verbalization on problem solving. *Journal of Experimental Psychology,* 1962, **63,** 12–18.
27. Gibson, E. J. A systematic application of the concepts of generalization and differentiation to verbal learning. *Psychological Review,* 1940, **47,** 196–229.
28. Glickman, S. E., & Schiff, B. B. A biological theory of reinforcement. *Psychological Review,* 1967, **74,** 81–109.
29. Grice, G. R. The relation of secondary reinforcement to delayed reward in visual discrimination learning. *Journal of Experimental Psychology,* 1948, **38,** 1–16.
30. Guthrie, J. T. Expository instruction versus a discovery method. *Journal of Educational Psychology,* 1967, **58,** 45–49.
31. Guttman, N., & Kalish, H. I. Discriminability and stimulus generalization. *Journal of Experimental Psychology,* 1956, **51,** 79–88.
32. Harlow, H. F. The formation of learning sets. *Psychological Review,* 1949, **56,** 51–65
33. Hartman, T. F., & Grant, D. A. Differential eyelid conditioning as a function of the CS-UCS interval. *Journal of Experimental Psychology,* 1962, **64,** 131–136.

34. Hendrickson, G., & Schroeder, W. H. Transfer of training in learning to hit a submerged target. *Journal of Educational Psychology,* 1941, **32**, 205–213.

35. Herb, F. H. Latent learning—non-reward followed by food in blinds. *Journal of Comparative Psychology,* 1940, **29**, 247–256.

36. Hilgard, E. R., & Bower, G. *Theories of Learning.* New York: Appleton-Century-Crofts, 1966. P. 129.

37. Hilgard, E. R., Edgren, R. D., & Irvine, R. P. Errors in transfer following learning with understanding: Further studies with Katona's card-trick experiments. *Journal of Experimental Psychology,* 1954, **47**, 457–464.

38. Hilgard, E. R., Irvine, R. P., & Whipple, J. E. Rote memorization, understanding, and transfer: An extension of Katona's card-trick experiments. *Journal of Experimental Psychology,* 1953, **46**, 288–292.

39. Hill, W. F. Contemporary developments within stimulus-response learning theory. In E. Hilgard (Ed.), *Theories of learning and instruction. Sixty-third yearbook of the National Society for the Study of Education. Part I.* Chicago: University of Chicago Press, 1964. P. 27.

40. Hubbard, W. A. Secondary reinforcement of a simple discrimination in human beings. *Journal of Experimental Psychology,* 1951, **41**, 233–241.

41. Hull, C. L. *Principles of behavior.* New York: Appleton-Century-Crofts, 1943.

42. Hull, C. L. *Essentials of behavior.* New Haven, Conn.: Institute of Human Behavior, 1951.

43. Jantz, E., & Underwood, B. J. R-S learning as a function of meaningfulness and degree of S-R learning. *Journal of Experimental Psychology,* 1958, **56**, 174–179.

44. Jensen, A. R. Verbal mediation and educational potential. *Psychology in the Schools,* 1966, **3**, 105–109.

45. Katona, G. *Organizing and memorizing.* New York: Columbia University Press, 1940.

46. Keller, F. S., & Schoenfeld, W. N. *Principles of psychology.* New York: Appleton-Century-Crofts, 1950.

47. Keller, L., Thomson, W. J., Tweedy, J. R., & Atkinson, R. C. Effects of reinforcement intervals in paired-associate learning. *Journal of Experimental Psychology,* 1967, **73**, 268–277.

48. Kendler, H. H. *Basic psychology.* (2nd ed.) New York: Appleton-Century-Crofts, 1968.

49. Kendler, H. H., & Kendler, T. S. Vertical and horizontal processes in problem solving. *Psychological Review,* 1962, **69**, 1–16.

50. Lachman, R. *A theory of thinking: Application of the laws of transfer and of operant verbal conditioning.* Unpublished manuscript, 1960.

51. Lyon, D. O. *Memory and the learning process.* Baltimore: Warwick & York, 1917.

52. Mager, R. F. *Preparing instructional objectives.* Palo Alto, Calif.: Fearon, 1962.

53. Maier, N. R. F. Reasoning in humans: II. The solution of a problem and its appearance in consciousness. *Journal of Comparative Psychology,* 1931, **12**, 181–194.

54. Mandler, G. Transfer of training as a function of degree of response overlearning. *Journal of Experimental Psychology,* 1954, **47**, 411–417.

55. Mandler, G., & Heinemann, S. H. Effect of overlearning of a verbal response on transfer of training. *Journal of Experimental Psychology,* 1956, **52**, 39–46.

56. Martin, C. J., & Saltz, E. Serial versus random presentation of paired associates. *Journal of Experimental Psychology,* 1963, **65,** 609–615.
57. Max, L. W. An experimental study of the motor theory of consciousness: III. Action-current responses in deaf-mutes during sleep, sensory stimulation, and dreams. *Journal of Comparative Psychology,* 1935, **19,** 469–486.
58. McGeoch, J. A., & Irion, A. L. *The psychology of human learning.* (2nd ed.) New York: Longmans, Green, 1952.
59. Meyer, D. R., & Miles, R. C. Intra-list –inter-list relations in verbal learning. *Journal of Experimental Psychology,* 1953, **45,** 109–115.
60. Miles, R. C. Secondary reinforcement stimulation throughout a series of spontaneous recoveries. *Journal of Comparative and Physiological Psychology,* 1956, **49,** 496–498.
61. Miller, G. A., Galanter, E., & Pribram, K. H. *Plans and the structure of behavior.* New York: Holt, 1960.
62. Minsky, M. L. Artificial intelligence. *Scientific American,* 1966 (September), **215,** 247–260.
63. Morse, W. H. Intermittent reinforcement. In W. K. Honig (Ed.), *Operant behavior: Areas of research and application.* New York: Appleton-Century-Crofts, 1966. Pp. 52–108.
64. Neimark, E. D., & Estes, W. K. *Stimulus sampling theory.* San Francisco: Holden-Day, 1967.
65. Neisser, U. *Cognitive psychology.* New York: Appleton-Century-Crofts, 1967.
66. Newman, S. W. Student vs. instructor design of study method. *Journal of Educational Psychology,* 1957, **48,** 328–333.
67. Noble, C. E. An analysis of meaning. *Psychological Review,* 1952, **59,** 421–430.
68. Novikova, L. A. Electrophysiological investigation of speech. In N. O'Connor (Ed.), *Recent soviet psychology.* New York: Liveright, 1961. Pp. 210–226.
69. Perry, H. W. The relative efficiency of actual and imaginary practice in five selected tasks. *Archives of Psychology,* 1939, No. 243.
69a. Postman, L. Short-term memory and incidental learning. In A. W. Melton (Ed.), *Categories of human learning.* New York: Academic Press, 1964. Pp. 145–201.
70. Postman, L., & Adams, P. A. Studies in incidental learning. *Journal of Experimental Psychology,* 1956, **51,** 329–333.
71. Premack, D. Reinforcement theory. In D. Levine (Ed.), *Nebraska symposium on motivation.* Lincoln: University of Nebraska Press, 1965. Pp. 123–180.
72. Restle, F. Significance of all-or-none learning. *Psychological Bulletin,* 1965, **64,** 313–325.
73. Reynolds, J. H. Cognitive transfer in verbal learning. *Journal of Educational Psychology,* 1966, **57,** 382–388.
74. Reynolds, J. H. Cognitive transfer in verbal learning: II. Transfer effects after prefamiliarization with integrated versus partially integrated verbal-perceptual structures. *Journal of Educational Psychology,* 1968, **59,** 133–138.
75. Saltzman, I. J. Comparisons of incidental and intentional learning with different orienting tasks. *American Journal of Psychology,* 1956, **64,** 274–277.
76. Schrier, A. M. Comparison of two methods of investigating the effect of amount of reward on performance. *Journal of Comparative and Physiological Psychology,* 1958, **51,** 725–731.
77. Skinner, B. F. *Behavior of organisms.* New York: Appleton-Century, 1938. P. 21.
78. Skinner, B. F. *Verbal behavior.* New York: Appleton-Century-Crofts, 1957. Pp. 53–54.
79. Spence, K. W. *Behavior theory and conditioning.* New Haven, Conn.: Yale University Press, 1956.

80. Sturgis, P. T. Verbal retention as a function of the informativeness and delay of informative feedback. *Journal of Educational Psychology,* 1969, **60**, 11–14.
81. Suchman, J. R. Building skills for autonomous discovery. *Merrill-Palmer Quarterly,* 1961, **7**, 147–169.
82. Thorndike, E. L. *Educational psychology.* Vol. 2. *Psychology of learning.* New York: Teachers College, Columbia University, Bureau of Publications, 1921. P. 4.
82a. Thorndike, E. L. Mental discipline in high school studies. *Journal of Educational Psychology,* 1924, **15**, 1–22, 83–98.
83. Thorndike, E. L., & Lorge, I. *The teachers' word book of 30,000 words.* New York: Teachers College, Columbia University, Bureau of Publications, 1944.
84. Thune, L. E. Warm-up effect as a function of level of practice in verbal learning. *American Psychologist,* 1950, **5**, 251. (Abstract)
85. Tolman, E. C. Cognitive maps in rats and men. *Psychological Review,* 1948, **55**, 189–208.
86. Tolman, E. C. Principles of purposive behavior. In S. Koch (Ed.), *Psychology: A study of a science.* Vol. 2. New York: McGraw-Hill, 1959. Pp. 92–157.
87. Ulmer, G. Teaching geometry to cultivate reflective thinking: an experimental study with 1239 high school pupils. *Journal of Experimental Education,* 1939, **8**, 18–25.
88. Underwood, B. J. Verbal learning in the educative processes. *Harvard Educational Review,* 1959, **29**, 107–117.
89. Underwood, B. J. An evaluation of the Gibson theory of verbal learning. In C. N. Cofer (Ed.), *Verbal learning and verbal behavior.* New York: McGraw-Hill, 1961. Pp. 197–217.
90. Underwood, B. J., & Richardson, J. Studies of distributed practice: XVIII. The influence of meaningfulness and intralist similarity of serial nonsense lists. *Journal of Experimental Psychology,* 1958, **56**, 213–219.
91. Underwood, B. J., & Schulz, R. W. The influence of intralist similarity with lists of low meaningfulness. *Journal of Experimental Psychology,* 1959, **58**, 106–110.
92. Underwood, B. J., & Schulz, R. W. *Meaningfulness and verbal learning.* Chicago: Lippincott, 1960. P. 293.
93. Voeks, V. W. Acquisition of S-R connections. *Journal of Experimental Psychology,* 1954, **47**, 137–147.
94. Wallace, W. H., Turner, S. H., & Perkins, C. C. Preliminary studies of human information storage. Signal Corps Project No. 132C, Institute for Cooperative Research, University of Pennsylvania, 1957.
95. Watson, J. B. *Behaviorism.* (Rev. ed.) New York: Norton, 1930.
96. Wittrock, M. C. Effects of certain sets upon complex verbal learning. *Journal of Educational Psychology,* 1963, **54**, 85–88.
97. Wolfe, J. B. The effect of delayed reward upon learning in the white rat. *Journal of Comparative Psychology,* 1934, **17**, 1–21.
97a. Wolff, J. L. Concept-shift and discrimination-reversal learning in humans. *Psychological Bulletin,* 1967, **68**, 369–408.
98. Wood, G. Mnemonic systems in recall. *Journal of Educational Psychology,* 1967, **58**, No. 6, Pt. 2, 27 pp.
99. Woodrow, H. The effect of type of training upon transference. *Journal of Educational Psychology,* 1927, **18**, 159–172.
100. Young, R. K., & Underwood, B. J. Transfer in verbal materials with dissimilar stimuli and response similarity varied. *Journal of Experimental Psychology,* 1954, **47**, 153–159.

4

LEARNING AND THE TECHNOLOGY
OF EDUCATION

The future historian assessing the educational developments of the latter half of the twentieth century will undoubtedly be impressed by what appears to be the trend in education today: Technology is moving into the classroom. The teaching machine and the computer are part of the new educational technology, as are films and television; listening-and-study techniques utilizing tape recorders are being used for individualized instruction in all fields.

The impetus spurring the use of a technology of instruction came in the 1940's, when the Armed Services was faced with the problem of training men—quickly—to perform specific skills. The generalized approaches to education prevalent in the public schools could not be adapted to provide the kind of education needed to train soldiers, within a specific time, to attain a definite level of effectiveness in certain skills, for example, in operating a radarscope. The Armed Services turned to psychologists to help solve such problems. From their research, the psychologists were able to distinguish education from the more specific demands of training, and were stimulated to investigate the nature of the objectives in both educational and training practices.

Paralleling these activities for the Armed Services, educational psychologists were developing theories and points of view on which to base their conceptualizations of the learning process in terms of training approaches to learning. The psychologist most responsible for the development of a technology of education is B. F. Skinner.

Automated Instruction and Programmed Learning

Skinner's application of operant conditioning to programmed instruction dates from about 1954. Later, in an article in *Science* (31), Skinner called for a reassessment of the teaching function in present-day schools. He pointed out that the demands for education cannot be met simply by training more teachers, that education must become more efficient in the one activity which is central to education—learning. Skinner advanced the concept of the teaching machine as one item in the technology of education which could increase efficiency.

Skinner was not the first to recognize the possibilities of a machine that could teach. During the 1920's, at Ohio State University, Sidney Pressey designed several machines which were useful in testing for information. One of Pressey's machines could be used in taking a multiple-choice test. The device was simple for a student to operate: He pressed a button representing his first choice of answers; if the response was correct, the device moved on to the next question. If the response was incorrect, the machine recorded the error. The student was free to record choices until he got the correct one. Pressey predicted that because the machine provided test results immediately it would become an instructional tool in the classroom. The student could learn at his own pace and would not be hindered by the need to adapt his behavior to the pace of the teacher.

The instructional revolution Pressey envisioned for the 1920's did not come to pass. Instead, his contributions were largely forgotten until Skinner promoted an interest in teaching machines in the 1950's, and both the Pressey and the Skinner points of view became the basis for this phase of the technological revolution in education. Although both Pressey and Skinner advocated using the teaching machine as an instructional device, only Pressey believed it should be used to supplement regular classroom instruction. Skinner, on the other hand, would not use automated instruction devices to supplement regular instruction but to take the place of much of the usual teacher activity.

The Programming of Instruction

The automated instruction device, such as the teaching machine, and the learning sequence, or program, are complementary parts of the technological package. Alone, the device is impotent; with a properly conceived series of incremental learning steps covering what is to be learned, it becomes a powerful tool. The series of steps, or increments, in the learning sequence is referred to as the program. The term program, or programmed instruction, when applied to classroom learning generally indicates the Skinnerian approach. The program's means of increasing the response rate depends less on the method of presentation than on the order of the programmed events and the presence or absence of reinforcements. A good program—good in the sense that particular response rates are increased—can be presented through the different media of books, films, TV, as well as through specially built machines.

Stolurow (33), in a major review of the literature on automated instruction, suggests that recent developments in the field of programmed instruction have precipitated a major reexamination of the instructional process aimed at promoting more efficiency in learning. Attempts to improve learning efficiency, however, have usually been sidetracked by issues peripheral to the instructional process, such as the number of children in the classroom or the length of the school year. By substituting an automated instructional device for the usual teacher-pupil confrontation, the learner, the device, and the program create a learning situation that can be adjusted and controlled as needed. Most teachers, regardless of their skill in interpersonal relations, do not impart information in the systematic, measured way programmed instruction does.

What is a program of instruction? In its simplest form, it is a series of logically related items which represent the intrinsic elements of some specific content, such as algebra or introductory psychology. An efficient program which proceeds in a direct manner toward accomplishing specific informational learning might have the following attributes, according to Schramm (28):

1. An ordered sequence of items, logical and explicit in content
2. Little possibility of error
3. A record of a constructed response to each item
4. Reinforcement in the form of immediate knowledge of results

Agreement among authorities on the most effective techniques to use in constructing a program is not unanimous. One author, Fry (7), considers the following principles sound ones involving most of the requisite points for developing the program:

1. Specific goals to be accomplished *must* be decided on beforehand. These goals or objectives should be specific enough to permit analysis of some of the operants involved in their attainment. A program usually involves a series of small stepwise goals in learning certain items of information.

2. The subject matter to be learned is divided into small steps or increments. Step size depends on the difficulty of the content and the skill of the learner. Usually a trial-and-error procedure is necessary to determine the proper step size for the person or persons using the program.

3. These units or steps, usually called frames, may vary in length from several sentences to several paragraphs. In most programs a significant majority of the frames require some type of active response from the learner. The response to be made can involve a number of modes; for example, the response might be the selection of a correct term from a multiple choice or it might involve writing a word or a phrase in an appropriate space. Skinner's point of view emphasizes the need for an active response. If the learner is to be reinforced, he must *do* something.

4. To be effective the program must contain some provision for the feedback of information so that the learner can judge the correctness or incorrectness of his response. Immediate knowledge of the correct responses is the central reinforcement in programmed learning. This immediate knowledge is rewarding if the answer given by the learner is correct, or it leads to the correct answer by providing some basis for the learner to correct his error.

5. The units, frames, or "chains" in the program are logically ordered so that the learner progresses from the simple to the complex. Each unit builds on the knowledge acquired from exposure to previous frames. This principle of programming parallels Skinner's idea of shaping behavior through a process of careful, successive approximations of the total learning expected of the program.

6. Writing a program is an exercise in trial and error. The program must be tested in a number of different learning situations to find out if the step size between frames is too large or too small, if the information is arranged in an order that is logical to the learner, if the provisions for reinforcement are adequate, and if the language is understandable to the learner. The major criterion for the success of any program is whether the response rate of the learner is increased with respect to the objective of the program.

Programmed learning is an individualized learning experience because the learner proceeds at his own pace and sets his own limits on exposure time. Individualizing the learning experience through programmed instruction procedures can be further increased by employing a number of different strategies in the organization of the program itself. Almost all programs include items the learner responds to by writing an answer to a question or by making a choice from a number of alternatives.

Programs can also be organized so that they are developed in either a "linear" mode or a "branching" mode. Combinations of these two modes are also possible.

The linear program is a step-by-step arrangement of material from which the learner benefits most when he proceeds in a first-to-last order— or in linear progression.

The branching program offers alternative instructional pathways, depending on the learners' level of competence. It also permits the learner to assess the degree of correctness of his answers. Based upon this assessment, the learner may be instructed to skip portions of the program, to repeat portions, or to shift to alernate subprograms to improve his knowledge of information that is essential to his progress in the total program. Probably the most widely used branching technique at present is the "scrambled-book" approach of Crowder (4). In this approach a minimally correct response leads to a branch containing information to correct the error.

Programmed Instruction and the Learner

Automated instruction and programmed learning deal with the machine and the program. The basic question, though, is, does the learner learn with programmed instructional technology and, if he does, is the learning significantly better than what he learns through exposure to traditional methods? Stolurow's (33) review of the research on this point concludes that programmed instruction is effective for teaching, and that students learn by using teaching machines and other automated instructional devices. There is no evidence, however, to indicate conclusively that the amount learned with the programmed approach is significantly superior to that learned with other approaches. Some studies have reported phenomenal gains while others have reported low gains or no gains at all.

Programmed instruction is not limited to a certain kind of learner, for its use has been successful with the gifted and with the mentally retarded. Evidence in support of the programmed approach has been obtained from many different experimental populations representing the whole range of abilities. Stolurow's review does not go beyond 1961; however, evidence accumulated since then further validates his conclusions. That all gains in learning through programs and teaching machines are not significantly superior to gains employing other methods is not to be construed as criticism of the programmed approach. Many variables operate to control learning; and the programmed approach, while controlling some of these, does not control them all. The effectiveness of the program employed may vary along with the learner's motivation. The important fact about programmed learning is that it can be effective.

Schramm's (28) summation of research on programmed instruction relates research to the program's variables. He offers the following conclusions:

1. Research comparing logically sequenced programs with random-order programs do not provide data consistently in support of the logical sequence. The contradictory results may be due to brevity of the programs used in the studies. Research by Gagné and others, however, does support the concept of a logic for program design.

2. Most research is supportive of programs with short steps (requiring a larger number of frames to attain a particular learning objective). Step size, however, should not be so small as to bore the learner.

3. The question of whether the learner should actually write his response to programmed items (i.e., the learner constructs the response) has been answered by a number of studies which conclude that there is no significant difference in learning due to either the overt or covert response.

Holland (15) states that the overt response is important if the items are so prepared that writing the response becomes a necessary operation in mastering the material. Otherwise, differences between overt and covert responses do not seem to be important.

4. Many studies concur that immediate knowledge of results is reinforcing. Several studies also support the idea that knowledge of results plus an explanation is more reinforcing than knowledge of results alone.

The discussion in Chapter 3 of delay of reinforcement indicated, however, the lack of conclusive data to show that the more immediate the reinforcement, the greater the amount of learning. Programs for automated instruction devices tend to favor immediate knowledge of results as a more potent reinforcer than delayed feedback. A recent study by More (22a) suggests that, with verbal materials learned in the classroom, the principle of immediate feedback of correct responses should be replaced by a principle emphasizing an optimal feedback-delay interval. More gave his eighth grade subjects an article to read and tested them on its contents. They learned of their results, and the correct answers, after one of four different periods of delay (no delay, 2½ hours, 1 day, 4 days). The subjects were then tested again immediately after receiving feedback or 3 days after receiving feedback. Within those groups who had been tested immediately after being given feedback, the group having no delay in feedback scored significantly lower on the retest than the groups having a 2½ hour, 1 day, or 4 day delay in feedback. Within those groups who were retested 3 days after feedback, the groups having 2½ hours and 1 day of delayed feedback scored significantly higher on the retest than the immediate feedback group or the 4 day delayed group. More concludes that:

> The implications to education are for those teachers who make a great effort to return graded tests to students as quickly as possible. The results of the present study suggest that it may be beneficial to wait about a day before returning tests. A much more important implication is in the use of programmed learning, in which considerable time, thought, and expense often go into providing immediate feedback. The results of the present study suggest that this effort may not only be ineffective, but may actually inhibit retention learning.

Schramm (28) points out that the experimental literature on self-pacing in programmed learning gives little support to the idea that the student who is able to set his own pace on a teaching machine learns more than the student who must accommodate himself to an imposed pace. Programmed materials on television and film seem to be used as effectively as in a teaching machine, although the pacing of television and film cannot be controlled by the learner.

Certain subjects, such as mathematics, particularly lend themselves to programming. Programmed instruction of factual content is much easier to construct than those involving conceptual learning. Most programs now available were constructed to teach specific facts.

A major dimension of programmed instruction to be investigated is the influence of motivation on automated instruction, especially that involving the teaching machine. Some psychologists feel that the machine itself should produce a high degree of motivation because the learner becomes involved with a new instructional medium. The actual manipulation of the machine may itself be rewarding. Higher motivation should keep the learner at the machine for a longer time than he might normally devote to reading a book or to listening to a teacher. One study (16) suggests that regardless of the mode (programmed book or teaching machine), the critical variable may be the amount of time spent in learning. Motivation, of course, helps determine the amount of time spent in learning.

The use of programmed instruction in the schools has elicited favorable comment—and some criticism. Some of the factors in support of the automated rather than the traditional approach are (21):

1. Programmed instruction impels the learner to participate directly in the learning situation so that he learns directly rather than vicariously.

2. The use of teaching machines and programmed learning should relieve the teacher of those tasks best done by machine—for example,

teaching factual content—thus freeing the teacher to spend time on those classroom activities that only the teacher can perform.

3. Programmed instruction allows the learner to set his own pace and determine his own rate of speed.

4. Programmed instruction induces individualized learning at its maximum.

5. The anxiety that sometimes results from the interaction of teacher and student, and which may interfere with learning, is minimized by programmed learning.

6. The knowledge programmed for automated instruction is more logically and better organized than the teacher can usually manage to do.

7. The information supplied programs is constant, in contrast to the variations caused by repetition of the same content by teachers.

8. Programmed instruction is learner-centered. The learning situation is controlled by the student, not by the teacher or the scheduling demands of the school.

9. Cheating becomes less important in the programmed approach, for the student who looks ahead to find the answer is only ensuring reinforcement at the proper time.

Those critical of the programmed approach to learning usually offer the following observations (21):

1. Learning through the programmed approach becomes an automatic operation that minimizes much of the subtle and incidental nature of the learning experience.

2. Novelty of response and spontaneity of expression are highly restricted by the programmed approach. Since the teaching machine usually rewards only one correct response, there is no place for imaginative or unusual responses.

3. Programmed instruction emphasizes recall and recognition of information as major goals in education. Goals involving appreciation and understanding become difficult, if not impossible, to program.

4. Each learner's progress through a program, by use of a teaching machine, depends upon how well he can read. If he cannot read well, he may miss critical elements in the program.

5. The success of programmed instruction depends upon the effectiveness of the program. A poor program may be more harmful than none at all.

6. Automated instruction lacks the elements of emotion, feeling, and desire.

7. Well-engineered teaching machines are too expensive to use with large numbers of students.

8. Teaching machines encourage rigidity in educational practice. The automated approach makes no provision for inquiry, insight, emergence, critical thinking, intuition, and abstraction as parts of the learning process.

9. Teaching machines will destroy education's commitment to humanistic goals.

Sechrest and Strowig (29) present some compelling justifications for the use of teaching machines and programmed instruction either as a supplement to or as a replacement for traditional classroom methods. They point out that the programmed approach makes it possible for the individual student to learn while being independent of the demands of the formal educational system. They offer the following observation about the formal system of education in existence today:

> The current rate of change in every aspect of our environments demands persons who recognize that their education is not complete at the time of graduation and who are prepared to continue to study so that they may remain competent, expert and in good contact with our civilization. Unfortunately, it often seems to be the case that our educational system is organized to convey to students the impression that education is something that does and can only occur within the confines of a classroom and in the presence of a teacher, and that education consists of something akin to the fulfillment of a military obligation or a prison sentence; when one's time is done and the discharge papers completed, education ceases.

These authors argue that teaching machines will not suppress individual differences by controlling the students' responses but that the diversity of programs available and the use of programmed learning as an adjunct to other methods of instruction should, in fact, increase the diversity of students' responses. Certainly the teaching machine should release the teacher to spend more time on individualized instruction and to do so in a more creative fashion. The only impediment to such a development is the inability of the teacher to handle individualized instruction as creatively as would be needed. Some teachers are able to teach only the content—which a teaching machine can also do. Such teachers, because they cannot conceptualize and solve learning problems demanding a creative approach, prefer the old dependable method and have little use for the bonus of added time.

What is the future of programmed instruction in education? Lange (17) quotes an authority whose conclusion is that programmed instruction is moving quietly in the direction of becoming a mature technology. An examination of the history of new technologies suggests that technological development tends to progress through three stages or phases in its evolution toward maturity. First, there is an acceleration resulting from the initial overenthusiasm about the possibilities of the technological advancement. The second phase is generally one of disillusionment, brought about by the development's failure to fulfill the original optimistic expectations. The third phase is a gradual but solid growth toward maturity as the development is accepted on its own terms and experimentation provides additional data concerning the new technology's usefulness.

A number of the basic issues in programmed instruction are in need of Wittrock's type of conceptualization discussed in Chapter 1. For example, step size in programming should be investigated in specific contexts and adjusted according to the difficulty of the material to be learned, the different abilities of the learners, and the length of time the program is employed. Skinner's early insistence on small steps, which minimize error, may have been a carryover from his work in animal research. Recent data suggest that the variables involved in programming for practical school learning are far more complex (24).

Payne, Krathwohl, and Gordon (25) investigated the complexities of logical vs. scrambled programmed instruction because earlier data did not support the assumption that sequence is crucial to effective learning. The Payne *et al.* study investigated the effect of item-scrambling in which the demands of the program for logical sequencing was the independent variable. Logical and scrambled forms of three programs covering elementary measurement and statistical concepts were used. Subjects were tested immediately and again after a two-week period for retention of items learned. There were no significant differences between the immediate or the delayed test reactions, nor was there for the degree to which the content of the programs depended on sequence of items. To learn why these data were consistent with other studies but not with logical expectations, the experimenters monitored students as they proceeded through the programs. Payne and his associates (25) concluded that the students mentally sorted out and rearranged items from memory so that knowledge and principles were built into the programs inductively through an approximation of a discovery method of learning. These investigators summarize their study by stating:

> The evidence seems to bear testimony to the flexibility and adaptability of the college student. Possibly students with less ability would not have the capacity to bridge the gaps between items in a scrambled program. This study and the literature seem to suggest that in general we have not usually bracketed nor found a way to describe with any generality the limits of adaptability of the college student's mind with respect to programmed instruction.

A summary of the uses of programmed instruction (18) indicates that it is involved in a greater variety of learning situations than is warranted by our present knowledge of the art of programmed learning. This gap between basic knowledge and the development of hardware should grow smaller as research analyzes the multitude of variables relating to the outcomes of learning through programmed media.

Defining Objectives in Learning

One important factor in any consideration of learning is the goal to be achieved. The psychologists' interest in the concept of training as a way of learning—in contrast to the broader concept of education—has been a stimulus to redefining objectives in learning. The psychologists' success in developing training techniques for the military has brought training into focus for consideration as a method in any type of learning activity. Programmed instruction contains much that could be called training.

Several factors distinguish training from education. Training involves highly specific objectives, such as how to repair a watch or navigate a boat, whereas education usually involves broader objectives that can be defined in humanistic terms, such as becoming a good citizen, developing responsibility, or learning to relate maturely to others. Training implies a certain behavioral uniformity that can be measured and specified; for example, the number of errors made in assembling a rifle while blindfolded. Education, on the other hand, usually refers to individual differences and to the realization of the individual's potential through the educational process. Schools in the United States utilize both education and training, but some psychologists feel that more would be accomplished if the principles of training were applied more frequently to learning in the classroom. Robert M. Gagné (9), a psychologist vitally interested in applying training procedures to instruction, defines training as "the set of conditions employed to increase the level of performance of some human function by means of learning."

Training and education both deal with learning, but differ basically in purpose. Crawford (3) makes the following distinction:

1. Training involves learning in which the needs of a *particular* system, such as the military, are met.

2. Education involves learning which attempts to prepare people for *many* systems of society.

3. Training involves a definite program of instruction which is designed to prepare the learner to perform on a particular job within a system.

4. Education does not usually involve the definition of a specific job to be performed.

5. A training program is evaluated in terms of what it contributes to the output of a particular system.

6. The worth of education is generally evaluated in terms of individual growth and development.

Interest in the training model as a way of adding specificity to learning in education has made it necessary to define the objectives of education in terms of behaviors that can be handled as goals of training. In a recent book on teaching, Skinner (32) points out that the first step in designing instruction is to define the terminal behavior, or what the student is to do as a result of having been taught. He states that terms such as "adapting," "adjusting," or "surviving" do not describe behaviors—nor do terms which refer to mental or cognitive processes. Unless terminal objectives can be specified as behaviors, it is impossible to determine the reinforcement contingencies needed to accomplish those terminal objectives.

Robert F. Mager (20) has delineated the process of defining objectives in education through the format of a programmed book, *Preparing Instructional Objectives*. He points out that the educator should be able to identify those instructional objectives stated in terms of performance, to identify the portion of an objective that determines an acceptable performance at a minimum level, and to distinguish between performances involved in the evaluation of the objective and those that are not.

The teacher's basic skills should be the ability to identify behavioral and nonbehavioral objectives and to determine what aspects of performance are relevant to the attainment of the objective. Mager suggests that much of our confusion about educational goals comes from using words that have many possible interpretations. For an objective to be specific it should be stated in language that itself is specific, that is, open to few interpretations other than the intended one. Mager gives the following examples of words open to many, and to fewer, interpretations:

Words Open to Many Interpretations	Words Open to Fewer Interpretations
to know	to write
to understand	to recite
to *really* understand	to identify
to appreciate	to differentiate
to *fully* appreciate	to solve
to grasp the significance of	to construct
to enjoy	to list
to believe	to compare
to have faith in	to contrast

The words open to fewer interpretations are those associated with specific behaviors. Teaching becomes less haphazard and learning more efficient in proportion to the specificity of educational objectives, which then provide for measurable behavioral outcomes as part of the learning.

Learning: Theory and Application

The emphasis on a technology of education in the schools today derives much from Skinner and his views about learning. However, other theoretical interpretations of learning are also involved, for teaching machines, programming, and training are not tied to any one theoretical formulation. These approaches have in common a formulation that emphasizes a pragmatic approach to learning. One of the current trends in the study of learning is a synthesizing of viewpoints, which emphasizes that a number of different types of learning are possible in human beings. Gagné (8) identifies eight types of learning, each of them associated with the names of individuals important in the development of theoretical formulations in learning:

1. Signal learning—Learning to respond to a signal in a general and diffuse way. This type of learning involves the classical conditioned response of Pavlov in which the responses are general, diffuse, and emotional with an "involuntary" character.

2. Stimulus-response learning—A much more specific type of response learning than Type 1 above. The individual learns a connection between a stimulus and a response as described by Thorndike, or he learns an operant as defined by Skinner. A precise response is made to a stimulus through a process involving discrimination.

3. Chaining—Learning that involves connecting previously learned responses, as described by Skinner. The major prerequisites for chaining are that the individual links must have been learned previously and a contiguous relationship must exist between the response links for the chain to form.

4. Verbal association—Learning verbal response chains.

5. Multiple discrimination—Learning which involves any number of responses to differing stimuli (such as the teacher who learns the names of all her students). Multiple-discrimination learning differs from Type 2 in that learning new chains involving many responses and stimuli introduces the phenomenon of interference, which involves forgetting.

6. Concept learning—Learning that involves a common response to different stimuli sharing the attributes of some common classification (e.g., the concept of warmth—heat—from different stimuli, which share the characteristics of emitting heat). Language plays a major role in this type of learning.

7. Principle learning—A principle is a chain of two or more concepts

that represent a relationship between the concepts. This type of learning is similar to Type 3, except that concepts, rather than singular responses, are involved.

8. Problem solving—Principles acquired by human beings provide a basis for thinking, which permits combining principles into new and novel higher order principles. This process of combining old principles into new ones allows the human being to solve problems, or to "think through," a new principle.

Gagné arranges these eight types of learning in a hierarchial order, from simple to complex, to indicate that the simpler forms of learning are necessary for the mastery of the more complex forms. While these eight types have their own rules, the student of learning will recognize the dominance of the stimulus-response approach, especially in the simpler types, with Thorndike and Skinner among the psychologists most often associated with this position. Gagné's hierarchical approach is already proving useful in the analysis of learning involved in various areas of the school curriculum. An analysis of several of these areas in terms of the hierarchical model is presented in his book, *The Conditions of Learning.*

Teachers frequently ask, "What do we know that is practical from all the different approaches to learning?" By answering in relation to military training, Hilgard (12) offers some generalizations about learning in relationship to training and instruction with which he feels the majority of learning theorists would agree:

1. The capacities of the learner are very important. More intelligent people can learn things which less intelligent people cannot learn. Older children learn more readily than younger ones.

2. The learner who is motivated learns more readily than the one who is not motivated.

3. Motivation made excessive by pain or intense anxiety may be accompanied by distracting emotional states, which interfere with learning.

4. Learning accompanied by reward is usually preferable to learning accompanied by punishment. Learning motivated by success is preferable to learning motivated by failure.

5. Intrinsic motivation is preferable to extrinsic motivation.

6. A backlog of success is helpful in increasing the learner's tolerance to failure. Failure is better tolerated by the person who has been successful in the past than by the person who has not been.

7. Experience in goal-setting is essential to setting realistic goals in learning. Realistic goal-setting is associated with more satisfactory improvement than is unrealistic goal-setting.

8. The learners' personality may affect his ability to learn from a particular teacher.

9. Learning in which the learner actively participates is preferable to learning which he passively receives.

10. Learning that is meaningful and involves tasks understood by the learner is more efficient than learning that is not meaningful.

11. Repetitive practice is essential to overlearning skills involving memorization.

12. Learning is aided by knowledge of results, i.e., by an awareness of mistakes, correct responses, and the nature of a good performance.

13. Transfer of learning is enhanced if the learner is able to discover for himself the principles governing the transfer and if he can apply these principles in a variety of tasks.

14. Distributed recalls are better for learning material that must be remembered for a long time.

Future studies by psychologists will probably synthesize various theories about learning so that similarities leading to specific generalizations can be advanced for practical use in learning situations. The differences in concept and theory can then be isolated for further investigation.

Computer-Assisted Instruction

The technological revolution in education introduced the computer into the instructional system of the school, where it provides information quickly for the teacher or controls the learning situation directly by coordinating some type of teaching machine. The computer, a complex mechanism, is essentially an arrangement of electrical circuits that provide for the input and output of information—usually in the form of numbers. The computer's circuits provide for the retention of information, or for memory, so that the information can be called for and then returned in the arrangement prescribed by the program used. The computer program, in the form of directions given the circuits of the computer, is really the rules governing the handling of the information which is received and/or stored in the computer. The computer is like the human brain in that the human brain involves a processing of information through input and output pathways combined with a memory system.

Computers have revolutionized the processing of information in every phase of our society. From income-tax returns to moon landings, the computer-based information system is the source of accurate information, almost instantly available. The computer is also making record-keeping—

whether it be for public or private affairs—potentially a matter of general knowledge. This country's space program would be impossible to achieve without the computer to handle with split-second precision the millions of calculations necessary to solve orbital and re-entry problems for space vehicles. (See Fig. 4-1.)

Computers have not been used in education to nearly the extent they are being used in business, but this situation is changing. The university has been the computer's major consumer for use in education, and will undoubtedly continue to be.

In a recent article, Patrick Suppes (34) points out that the function envisioned for computers in education lies in their use in classroom instruction. Suppes has this to say about the desirability of computer-based instruction:

> The computer makes the individualization of instruction easier because it can be programmed to follow each student's history of learning successes and

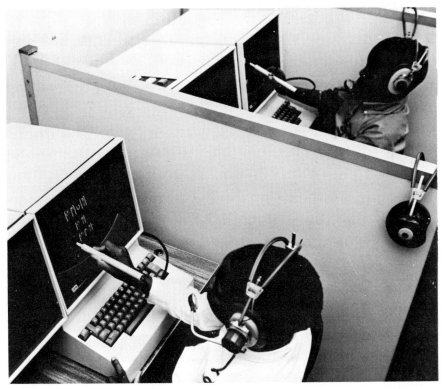

Fig. 4-1. The IBM 1500 Instrumental System. (Photograph courtesy International Business Machines Corporation.)

failures and to use his past performance as a basis for selecting the new problems and new concepts to which he should be exposed next. With modern information-storage devices it is possible to store both a large body of curriculum material and the past histories of many students working in the curriculum. . . . A computer . . . can provide daily information about how students are performing on each part of the curriculum as it is presented, making it possible to evaluate not only individual pages but also individual exercises. The use of computers will have important consequences for all students in the immediate future.

Projects are currently under way at a number of university centers throughout the country to study the dimensions of computer-based instruction. The one Suppes is engaged in at Stanford University is typical. The Stanford studies involve elementary pupils who have access to a visual device much like a television screen, where visual displays from the computer can be projected for the student as part of the instructional program. There is also a typewriter keyboard with which the learner responds to visual displays. The apparatus can also be equipped with a light pen for the student to respond with by touching the pen directly to the visual screen. A sound device presents spoken messages to the student. These three elements—the visual device, the keyboard, and the sound transmitter—constitute the basic elements of the system at one end; the computer is the basic element at the other end.

Responses made by the learner can lead to an infinite variety of instructional presentations, which are stored in the computer memory. These presentations can be programmed by the computer for individual variation, based on past responses of the learner, and tutorial cues can be introduced through the sound system at appropriate positions in the program. The possible combinations of individual systems of instruction are limited only by the information stored in the computer's memory and the programming of responses from the learner. The use of computer-based instruction as one type of automated teaching in schools will undoubtedly increase tremendously as the cost of equipment decreases and curriculum content designed for such instruction becomes available.

Lange (17) believes that Computer-Assisted Instruction will become one of the major thrusts in educational development in the decade ahead. Computer use in the instructional program has the advantage of individualizing the conditions of learning and at the same time implementing the need for mass education. In addition, the computer can introduce a research dimension to instruction which has been lacking. In a recent survey of activities in Computer-Assisted Instruction, Filep (6) offers the following observation about the current state of knowledge about CAI:

1. CAI is not only a tool to control drill and practice; instructional paradigms involving complex problem-solving strategies can be individualized by CAI.

2. CAI is capable of self-pacing, integrating instructional sequences with earlier responses and past information, interacting, diagnosing learning weaknesses, and incorporating different media for instructional sequences.

3. A successful CAI program requires that personnel act as a team; school administrators would need to examine their personnel policies in order to effectively use a CAI approach to instruction.

4. A centralized computer source could accommodate several school systems through time-sharing.

5. The development of CAI hardware is proceeding steadily but slowly. Present costs must decrease if CAI is to become available to all school systems desiring CAI capability.

Recent reviews of the state of the art with respect to Computer Assisted Instruction (1, 2) point out that the problems associated with CAI have produced much speculative comment but little experimental research. Atkinson (1), in reporting on a CAI program in reading developed at Stanford University, distinguishes between three types of CAI systems:

1. At the simplest level are the drill-and-practice systems in which problems are presented in a fixed, linear pattern. Decisions are not programmed as part of the time given to the instructional sequence, and the program cannot be modified subsequent to monitoring the student's response history.

2. At an intermediate level of complexity is the tutorial type of CAI program. In this program the student interacts with an instructional system that has a fixed capacity to react to his response history and to alter the linear progression of the instruction by branching into alternate modes of instruction. These changes are triggered by information given to the system through single responses or combinations of responses made by the student. A tutorial program format allows certain flexibility for each student, a flexibility limited by the responses prescribed by the program.

3. The most sophisticated CAI system is a dialogue program in which the student's range of possible interactions is almost unlimited, permitting him to construct natural-language responses and to initiate questions not restricted by limiting rules built into the program. A true dialogue system would give the student the power to control the sequences of events comprising the elements of instruction in the program. Unfortunately, dialogue programs are difficult to construct and are available only in experimental form.

The CAI reading program Atkinson (1) describes is a tutorial program involving the same type of system utilized by Suppes (34) at Stanford in the field of elementary mathematics. The CAI reading program, in operation for several years, has accumulated sufficient data to permit some general conclusions about its effectiveness. Atkinson (1) reports that test data obtained from an experimental group, which received reading instruction through the use of the program, and a control group, which received reading instruction in the traditional way, indicated that the experimental group performed significantly better on almost all of the measures. Although their posttest scores were significantly different, performance of the two groups was similar before the experimental group started the CAI reading program. Atkinson feels that CAI has a future in education, not only as an instructional system, but also as a research tool that could bring together the psychologist who has isolated learning theory from instruction and the educator whose concern has been instruction but not learning theory.

Technology and Innovations in the Curriculum

The development of a technology of education can have two meanings (19). In one sense, technology refers to tools and hardware, such as teaching machines, which are used to instruct. All the equipment, especially electronic equipment, used in instruction pertains to this meaning of technology. In another sense, technology in education refers more broadly to the basic application of knowledge to specific problems. In this manner, technology is a form of educational engineering in which the basic sciences, particularly the behavioral sciences, relate to education in much the same way physics or mathematics might relate to mechanical engineering. One of the persistent problems facing education as it moves toward involvement with technology is the development of the software, or the materials, that can be used by, or can supplement, the hardware. Curriculum demands are being analyzed anew. Subject matter traditionally represented by such curriculum titles as reading, mathematics, science, and social studies will remain, but the approaches to knowledge in these areas are rapidly changing. These curriculum areas have become increasingly important, for the new tools, the hardware of education, demand that the materials, i.e., the software, be designed so that media and materials form a complementary technology. This broad definition of technology includes media design, innovation in curriculum and materials, and educational engineering—and gives new significance to some recent developments in the major curriculum areas in education.

Reading

Probably no other curriculum area has been so much researched as the teaching of reading. The history of reading instruction is marked by the dominance of one or another method: the phonics approach or the one relying on learning words as "wholes." A recent summary of re-search in the field suggests that the thinking about reading has moved away from an either-or position to one acknowledging that children are different and learn in different ways; that the best method of instruction for one person may not be the best for another. The processes involved in learning to read, both psychological and physiological, are much more complex than had previously been thought (27). There now seems to be no empirical support for the assertion that one method exists which is best for all children learning to read.

Learning to read involves learning to recognize and identify symbols and learning the meanings for the symbols. An examination of any set of readers commonly used in public schools shows that those used for beginning reading instruction place a great deal of emphasis on recogni-tion. Teaching recognition generally proceeds from the simple tasks of recognizing letters, syllables, and words to the more complex tasks involved in recognizing phrases and simple sentences. Obtaining the meaning from the printed symbol is the next step. Most series of texts used for reading instruction follow a form of programming in which repetition of symbols, first in isolation and gradually in some meaningful context, parallels a process of increasing the complexity of symbol com-binations. In the early grades actual reading is interspersed with exercises and lessons involving ways to "unlock" the sound of a word and identify meanings from the context in which a word appears. Spelling usually accompanies reading instruction in the early grades.

Compared with methods of thirty years ago, reading instruction in today's schools has not radically changed; what is new is the emphasis on the use of different methods in combination and the use of teaching aids to support the child's interest. Subscribing to a trend, a number of pub-lishing firms in the United States concentrate almost exclusively on age-graded reading series, from pre-primer to high school level, accompanied by supportive aids, exercises, and lessons.

In an effort to combat the stereotyping often found in these series, some publishers are introducing reading series that use pictures and situations that the atypical child would find meaningful and understandable. Thus many culturally deprived children—often from minority groups—are taught to learn meaning by recognizing familiar sights and situations. This innovation is a further example of the premise that the best approach is that which best fits the demands of a specific learning situation.

One of the most discussed issues in reading instruction during the past ten years has been whether teaching phonics is necessary for reading. Most research supports the use of a phonics approach. With the phonics approach, children learn the sound of single letters or groups of letters, which are used as auditory cues in recognizing words. Most teachers use a phonics approach in some form or another, although it may not always be given the name "phonics."

To review all the research and discuss all the issues pertaining to teaching reading would require much more space than can be given here. Briefly some of the major issues are:

1. *Readiness:* Since reading is the first major skill the school offers the child, research has been dominated by the question of how to determine when a child is ready to begin learning to read. A study by Morphett and Washburne (23) concluded that a mental age of 6.5 is the optimum time to begin reading instruction. Since a mental age of 6.5 and a chronological age of 6.5 equals an I.Q. of 100, which is considered average, a chronological age of 6.5 has become the standard in most school situations. However, since many schools have programs which bring the child to school before the age of six, this is becoming less important, and in many instances these younger children are successfully exposed to beginning reading instruction. Perhaps it is time that educators realized that a mental age of 6.5 occurs before the chronological age of 6.5 in many children who begin kindergarten programs.

Green and Simmons (10), in a summary of research concerning chronological age and school entrance, suggest that the magic age of six years as a basis of entrance into the first grade may not have so defensible a relationship to maturation. The assumption that the older the child the more ready he is to learn may overlook the advantages an earlier start at learning may give the child, even though he may achieve less when compared with the older child.

Durkin (5) studied the effects of an early start in reading on the child's later achievement in formal reading instruction in school. When Durkin started her study in 1958 she acknowledged that many teachers felt that early reading instruction in the home could be deterimental; children who began reading too early would be bored later, or, if they learned from someone not trained to teach reading they would develop problems which would lead to confusion when they encountered reading instruction in the school. Durkin found that these predictions were unfounded. In the groups she studied, the early readers "maintained their lead in achievement over classmates of the same mental age who did not begin to read until the first grade." These children continued to be ahead of their classmates even after six years of formal school instruction.

Technological advances in education are providing techniques and aids that individualize reading instruction so that all children are no longer treated as an "average" child. The emphasis on single factors, such as mental age, in determining readiness has frequently been criticized (36). Research on readiness in all areas of instruction suggests that readiness is a compound of psychological and physiological factors, with the weight of each factor creating a different balance in each individual.

2. *The Physiology of Reading:* The visual process in reading was once thought to involve a continuous scanning of lines by the eyes. When research was first done on this topic, however, it was discovered that the eye movements of good readers proceed along the lines of print in a rapid series between fixations. Each fixation allows the reader to recognize units of words before moving on to the next fixation. When the eye movements reach the end of a line, a rapid movement focuses their return to a point close to the beginning of the next line. This point defines the first fixation for the new line of print. At times, the eye movements may travel backward and fixate at a point behind the point of greatest progress. These backward movements, or regressions, appear to be more characteristic of poor readers, although they appear in the eye movements of all readers. Remedial programs that attempt

to increase reading speed usually concentrate on decreasing the number of fixations and regressions. Some programs emphasize attempts to read "down" the page with one fixation per line. Variations in fixations and regressions correlate with the type of material being read, so that fewer fixations and regressions occur with material easily scanned and understood than with difficult material. Research has shown that the fixation pattern in reading is generally constant regardless of the language or culture. The implication is that the basic mental processes involved in reading are the same in every culture.

Many authorities have emphasized the relationship of early eye movement habits to later difficulties in reading. The correlation between visual defects during the child's early years and later reading difficulties is obvious. Most schools provide some type of visual screening for defects in their beginning health programs.

Some research suggests a relationship between imperceptible movements in the vocal apparatus and reading, although not all authorities agree that reading is accompanied by this subvocal speech. Those who hold the view that reading is accompanied by silent movements of the vocal apparatus theorize that meaning and language are so closely related in the mind that recognizing meaning in reading cannot occur without some vocal movement. Many research studies have also shown that hearing and reading are related, and that the better readers generally rank higher in auditory acuity than do the poor ones.

3. *Speed in Perception:* One problem that has interested the researcher has been the investigation of factors related to the speed in perceiving words that are read; that is, in recognizing the word. In one study, Thurstone (35) found that speed of perception is related to the reader's reaction time, his speed of judgment (his readiness in making a choice), the time required to obtain closure (his ability to fill in details and persist in maintaining a configuration of words against distraction), and his ability to maintain and manipulate two or more configurations at the same time. Another study, done by Postman and Rosenzweig (26) suggested that the speed of recognition depends upon the frequency of the reader's use of the word in the past.

Other investigators have introduced data which suggest that the presence of emotionally toned words, the incidence of long words, and the frequency of least preferred words are related to a decrease in the speed of word perception.

4. *Developmental Factors and Reading:* Many studies have been made of the relationships between growth, development, and reading. Perhaps the most valid fact to emerge from these numerous data concerns the relationship between the reader's mental ability and his progress in reading. More intelligent persons tend to read better than those who are less intelligent. This conclusion is based on correlational evidence and does not imply a cause and effect relationship. By definition, reading speed and comprehension are usually included in the measurement of intelligence. Reading ability is an efficient predictor of general intelligence. As might be expected, the correlations between reading ability and intelligence tend to be higher when verbal aspects of intelligence are involved. Research on the social and emotional aspects of development in relation to the reading process support the conclusion that emotional and social immaturity are associated with poor reading ability—the issue of cause and effect here being as obscure as in the relationship between mental ability and reading level.

Much that is being developed to individualize the teaching of reading suggests that many children will be teaching themselves to read through the use of machine-based instructional programs or programmed texts within the next ten years. The age at which a child is considered ready to learn to read has been severely challenged during the past decade. Evidence indicates that children as young as three or four can learn to recognize symbols and deal with reading skills at a recognition level even though their life experience has not equipped them for the full meaning of the symbols involved. Present-day exposure to communication media such as television prepares a child for the meaning of reading to a greater degree than was possible before. During the years ahead the educator will be challenged to teach reading to the child who comes from a social background where reading is not something of value. The Head Start programs of the Federal government have made inroads on this problem. Another challenge will undoubtedly be to teach youths and adults who have not learned to read as they should have from their first exposures to reading instruction in the primary grades. No other skill is so closely associated with economic opportunity and vocational advancement as reading. The person who does not read does not learn; and learning is essential at all levels of life in a society that requires all persons to have the ability to adapt to the new skills which a changing technology will undoubtedly require of us all during our lifetime.

Mathematics Instruction

No other curriculum innovation in public education has received the attention and publicity that accompanied the introduction of the "new math" into the classroom. For many years, educators had been aware of the need for a new approach to teaching mathematics to better prepare students for the increasing importance of mathematics in our culture. In 1955, the College Entrance Examination Board appointed a commission to make recommendations concerning a revision of the mathematics curriculum for the high school. The executive director of the commission pointed out that the content of mathematics courses had changed little in the past three hundred years, yet mathematics as a discipline had changed significantly. In 1958 the commission reported that the curriculum should be exposed to major surgery which would delete obsolete material. What was left should be regrouped for learning and new concepts should be added. Sharp (30) sums up the specific changes as follows:

> Specifically, the report gave the axe to most of solid geometry and to a portion of the traditional course in trigonometry, especially the extensive work in logarithms—a rapid calculating device of the seventeenth century, replaced now by electronic computers. They favored the addition of classes in probability, a subject that deals with the application of mathematics to events in which luck plays a role, and in modern (abstract) algebra.

The commission's report stimulated interest in research projects to evaluate and develop these changes in the mathematics area. Both the University of Illinois and the University of Maryland became involved in these activities. The National Science Foundation in 1958 and 1959 sponsored the organization of the School Mathematics Study Group, which represented a cross-section of the mathematics profession, and helped to initiate the writing of appropriate text materials for this new approach to instruction. These text materials eventually reached the level of fourth-grade work in mathematics.

The basic concept needed to approach an understanding of the new mathematics is the concept of a set. A set is a group of things that are alike in some way. Three fundamental operations called union, intersection, and complementation govern their relationships. Concepts in arithmetic such as addition, subtraction, multiplication, and division take on a new meaning when defined in terms of sets. A recent book by Lola May and Ruth Moss, *New Math For Adults Only*, (22) lucidly explains the basic elements of this new approach.

Much attention has been given not only to the content of the curriculum in mathematics but to the teaching methods employed in presenting this curriculum. One author (11) distinguishes between telling methods and heuristic methods. The telling methods involve the introduction of the item of knowledge to be taught, clarification of this knowledge, justifying the knowledge, introducing problems involving the item of knowledge, and making a transition to the next item. Heuristic methods are of two types, the inductive and the deductive. The inductive method involves the presentation of instances of the information to be taught, the presentation of evidence, and the stating by the student of the inferences gained from the steps above. The deductive method emphasizes the use of rules and principles in combination with drill and recitation involving specific instances of these principles so that the relationship between the general principle and the specific application is apparent.

There is no conclusive evidence that any one method of instruction in mathematics is significantly better than another, or that the content of one mathematics curriculum is significantly better, from an instructional point of view, than another. One thing is certain, however; the changes taking place in mathematics instruction in both the elementary and the high school are extensive and are stimulated by the support of a technology which fits mathematics instruction better, perhaps, than it does any other curriculum area. The new approach to math has stimulated thought and examination by teachers of mathematics, whether or not they are involved in teaching the new curriculum. The development of the new curriculum in mathematics could serve as a model for what should be accomplished in other curriculum areas.

Instruction in Other Areas

The fields of reading and mathematics are by no means the only curricula where major changes are taking place. Science education has undertaken a quiet revolution, especially in the field of physics, in developing new approaches to the vast knowledge contributed to the culture each day. One strong stimulus to producing change in the high school science curriculum has been the demands made by colleges for students who are better prepared in such fields as chemistry, biology, and physics. The field of social studies has also been influenced by the university to make changes in social studies curricula. The area of social studies has always been more sensitive to the demands of the local community than other areas of study have been, for the social studies deal in ideas and information involving people in a more personal fashion than do fields such as mathematics or chemistry. Usually, the more progressive the community, the more innovative the social studies curriculum can be. In many school systems, the social studies now include extensive study of contemporary social and political systems; whereas a decade ago, the emphasis was on historical studies and factual learning. One major goal of the social studies is to help students become aware of the social, political, and economic realities around them. This goal is difficult to implement in communities dominated by traditionally conservative attitudes. One of the problems encountered when attempting to change the social studies curricula is the need to accept the fact that the American heritage does not stop with World War I but also includes events in the lives of today's students. The new curricula must not be limited to a study of the past in isolation, but must encompass a study of the present, and sometimes the future, in terms of a relationship to the past.

The study of English is also undergoing subtle change in public schools, both apart from, and in relation to, other fields of instruction. The use of language as a communications skill is receiving more attention—often combined with instruction in the social studies and the sciences—and more attention is being given to composition and the use of language in expressing ideas. Curriculum revision in English and in the social studies is being supported by the Federal government through curriculum centers at major universities, funded to stimulate innovations in instruction in these fields.

The change taking place in education is more rapid in some classrooms than in others; however, no school is the same today as it was ten years ago. The recent support given by the Federal government to local school districts for improvements in their educational programs has resulted in the introduction of materials, aids, electronic devices, films, television, and many other techniques that vary the instructional pattern and introduce more efficient ways of teaching. The new technology has also given the teacher more time to spend with individual students in situations where a close personal confrontation is still the best method of teaching. Teaching is in many ways still an art, but it is becoming more of a science every day, largely through the improvements associated with its accompanying technology.

Science, Technology, and Education

We live in an age dominated by science and the scientific answer. The development of a technology of education is one aspect of the scientific invasion of the classroom. But the scientific solution to classroom activity—as either the best or most productive approach—should not be accepted without knowing what it means. Our culture today singles out the scientist and the scientific result as the ultimate in authority. Thus it is the scientist who is often called upon to contribute to the mainstream of cultural development rather than the leaders of other professional groups.

The development of a scientific basis for educational practice parallels the development of a science in other applications. Traditionally, applied science has been distinguished from pure science as less exact and more restricted by the need for an immediate solution to some problem. Although the stereotyped image of the scientist pursuing problems of no practical value is no longer valid, the scientific community, however, does tend to separate those scientists who engage in basic research without regard for immediate application and those who are more committed to apply their own and the research of others to practical activity. The educational psychologist is less active in the field of basic research and more active in the application of psychological knowledge to classroom activity.

Activities in the field of psychology today attest to a rapprochement between basic and applied psychology in which the roles of both are interactive and less independent than past conceptualization has emphasized. The field of education provides an outstanding example of these interacting forces of psychology. Hilgard and Bower (14) discuss this interaction in relation to the study of learning, distinguishing between basic science research on the one hand and technological research and development on the other. Three degrees of relevance are projected for basic research in learning as follows:

A. Basic science research
  1. Research that is not directly relevant, such as conditioning studies with laboratory animals.
  2. Research on relevant topics and/or relevant subjects, such as human verbal learning.
  3. Research on topics relevant to school activities, such as reading mathematics, etc.

Research on the application and technological development of results such as the above involves three steps:

B. Technological research and development
  1. Developments in a laboratory or special classroom, such as a language laboratory, involving programmed instruction or other approaches to learning.
  2. Expansion to typical classroom activity where the results of laboratory use are tested in a larger instructional setting.
  3. Adoption for use as an ongoing part of the instructional program, with the teacher trained in the use of new developments.

To be effective, these steps cannot involve isolated psychologists who work apart from their colleagues. To be sure, the basic–applied differences remain as a functional commitment, but communication between the basic and applied cultures reinforces the interaction between the two. Fortunately, psychology appears to be moving in the direction of greater communication across the lines of professional commitment. While this is the result of psychologists understanding their profession better, it is also the result of better means of communication between basic and applied researchers.

The role of pure, or basic, science was in the past overshadowed by applied developments, especially in industry and the military. That balance has now changed to the extent that Hilgard (13) has been prompted to point out that application has a unique and special place in scientific pursuits. He states:

> The strong emphasis these days upon the importance of pure science is an attempt to restore balance, but it must not be permitted to degrade the importance of applied science. The applications of science require the same high order of abilities, and the same concern for objectivity, that characterizes pure science.

The cult of pure science, in which a particular bit of research is valued primarily because of its remoteness from application, is beginning to disappear in psychology, although some of this attitude is still apparent.

The major scientific emphasis in education has been in the development of a technology of instruction. If science were to continue to make its contributions to education solely through technological developments, it would be reasonable to anticipate that educational activities would be limited to those types of learning the technology supports best. The challenge to educational psychology is to expand the scientific basis for education so that it can include a wider range of possible behaviors.

In the field of psychology, as in other sciences, there is a preoccupation with the structure of the discipline rather than with the data of the discipline. As was pointed out in Chapter 1, this tendency to confuse science with the package it comes in can lead to accepting the word of an authoritative speaker instead of examining the validity of the data spoken about. The emergence of a scientific basis for educational practice has been retarded by a lack of data coupled, in many instances, with an abundance of opinion. This direction is now changing to emphasize the importance of fact over opinion. It is hoped that the future will witness the expansion of educational technology and its accompanying developments in learning to include much that is still part of the art of education. Some educators have referred to education as a combination of the art of teaching and the science of learning. This balance is swinging toward casting the teacher's role into one of interaction with students, a role best supported by the technology of instruction. Whether the teacher will continue to be the best advocate of those types of activity science cannot handle at present, or whether the teacher will become the electronics expert whose role is totally submerged beneath the dominance of technology remains to be seen. Certainly the role of the teacher in the classroom is changing so rapidly that traditional models of teacher preparation are becoming outdated.

The teacher who is prepared to do only what a machine can do better will have no place in the future of education. In many communities the school of the future has already arrived. Whether such schools will be staffed by teachers who have a productive role in the educational process depends upon how well the scientific basis of education is developed to indicate what science can accomplish in a classroom as well as what it can not accomplish.

Summary

Education in America is in the midst of a technological explosion which could either provide a process for individualizing learning in the classroom or put a constraint on the flexibility and variety of goals education has traditionally represented. The teacher's use of technology will determine the direction technological support will ultimately take. One of the major challenges facing the teacher today is learning to use available technology for effective and creative instruction.

This technological revolution was accelerated by Harvard professor B. F. Skinner through his articulate advocacy of the teaching machine and programmed learning as an instructional device and a method that could provide learning activities that give the learner maximum opportunity to pace his own learning and control his own instruction. Skinner feels that programming creates a logical and orderly organization of the curriculum, which reflects the intrinsic sequence of content within a body of knowledge. Supporters of this view envision the use of technological support for teaching as a way of relieving the teacher of those instructional tasks a machine can do as well as or better than a human can, thus giving him time for the more personal tasks in education revolving around student-teacher confrontations. Automated instruction and programmed learning have produced new ideas about instruction which are beginning to influence the way resources for instruction should be organized.

The type of teaching machine used by Skinner is being supplanted by technological systems involving computers and instructional terminals that allow the learner to interact with the information system stored in the computer. This new system may consist of a linear program, which presents questions and requires answers, or it may consist of branching programs, which direct the student to various sets of items, based on his error rates within a set of items. Computer Assisted Instruction is only now beginning to be used in regular classroom instruction for it is prohibitively expensive. Its potential, however, remains enormous, so that as its cost decreases an increase in the use of CAI systems is quite probable.

The use of technology in instruction has stimulated a rethinking of many of the traditional content areas in schools. The types of inputs needed for the computer in a program on elementary mathematics may not be the same as those required for a textbook on elementary mathematics. The logic demanded by programming necessitates an analysis by the teacher of content fields in a way that has not been required before. New ways of organizing the content of mathematics and other fields of study in education are emerging from the demands of technology in instruction.

One result of the technological explosion in education has been more frequent analysis of educational outcomes, i.e., expected pupil behaviors, which can be measured and evaluated. For individualization in learning to be effective, reliable and valid techniques of evaluating performance objectives need to be introduced. The emphasis in education on training models for the analysis of the educational task represents a trend toward a more systematic analysis of the educational process and a more specific approach to defining the goals of education.

Technology has brought science into the process of education and has helped to define the teacher–learner relationship in a way that is amenable to experimental study. Some who criticize the technological invasion of the classroom say that machines dehumanize the educational process and make of teaching a nonhuman science rather than the humanized art it once was.

While many abuses of technology in education do take place in individual instances of use, the future of the instructional process in the classroom will include a more frequent involvement of technology and will witness a more efficient accomplishment of learning objectives. The present problem of education is not the presence of a technology for learning but rather the misuse of this technology because the teacher has not yet defined his most effective role in relationship to the technology. As teachers improve their skills in using technology, the technology will become more effective.

SUGGESTED READINGS

Gage, N. L. (Ed.) *Handbook of research on teaching.* Chicago: Rand McNally, 1963.

This handbook, sponsored by the American Educational Research Association, represents a collection of original articles summarizing research on teaching. The contributors have presented one of the most comprehensive views of teaching available anywhere in the literature. Prospective teachers who would wish to study some of the experimental literature on teaching will find in the *Handbook of Research on Teaching* many chapters to help them develop a frame of reference about teaching.

Glaser, R. (Ed.) *Teaching machines and programed learning.* Vol. II. Washington, D. C.: National Educational Association, Department of Audiovisual Instruction, 1965.

Prof. Glaser has edited a second volume of original articles dealing with various aspects of programing and automated learning. Volume I appeared in 1960. The book was sponsored by the Department of Audiovisual Instruction of the National Educational Association and is meant for teachers who have an interest in learning about many of the current issues relating to technological support for instruction. Articles on the technology involved in the use of teaching machines, their application to subject matter and the dimensions of their use in instruction are included.

Hilgard, E. R. (Ed.) *Theories of learning and instruction, the sixty-third yearbook of the National Society for the Study of Education.* Part I. Chicago: University of Chicago Press, 1964.

The National Society for the Study of Education sponsored this volume as part of its yearbook series which appear each year and represent, for the most part, scholarly commentary on contemporary issues in education. This volume contains articles by many of the psychologists cited in this chapter. Rather than survey research studies, the authors comment upon, and interpret, research trends in education which are relevant to learning and instruction.

Oettinger, A. G. *Run, computer, run; the mythology of educational innovation.* Cambridge, Mass.: Harvard University Press, 1969.

For those students who may be seeking a critique of computer assisted instruction, and automated instruction generally, Professor Oettinger provides the "other side of the coin" to the optimistic comments usually presented. He feels that the exploitation of technology is contributing to a myth about instructional efficiency which is not supported. This exploitation and misuse leads to self-delusions about technology which obscure the services which a technology can perform in an educational system.

REFERENCES

1. Atkinson, R. C. Computerized instruction and the learning process. *American Psychologist,* 1968, **23,** 225–239.
2. Atkinson, R. C., & Wilson, H. A. Computer-assisted instruction. *Science,* 1968, **162,** 73–77.
3. Crawford, M. P. Concepts of training. In R. Gagné (Ed.), *Psychological principles in systems development.* New York: Holt, Rinehart & Winston, 1965. Pp. 301–342.
4. Crowder, N. Automatic tutoring by means of intrinsic programming. In E. Galanter (Ed.), *Automatic teaching: The state of the art.* New York: Wiley, 1959.
5. Durkin, D. *Children who read early.* New York: Teachers College, Columbia University, Bureau of Publications, 1966.
6. Filep, R. T. What we know, so far, about computer-assisted instruction. *Nations Schools,* 1967, **80**(4), 62–63.
7. Fry, E. *Teaching machines and programmed instruction.* New York: McGraw-Hill, 1963.
8. Gagné, R. M. *The conditions of learning.* New York: Holt, Rinehart & Winston, 1965.
9. Gagné, R. M., & Fleishman, E. A. *Psychology and human performance.* New York: Holt, Rinehart & Winston, 1959. P. 394.
10. Green, D. R., & Simmons, S. V. Chronological age and school entrance. *Elementary School Journal,* 1962, **63**(1), 41–47.
11. Henderson, K. B. Research on teaching secondary school mathematics. In N. Gage (Ed.), *Handbook of research on teaching.* Chicago: Rand McNally, 1963. Pp. 1007–1030.

12. Hilgard, E. R. Theories of human learning and problems of training. Symposium on psychology of learning basic to military training problems. Department of Defense, Panel on Training and Training Devices, Committee on Human Resources, Research and Development Board, Washington, D. C., 1953.
13. Hilgard, E. R. Learning theory and its applications. *New teaching aids for the American classroom.* Palo Alto, Calif.: Institute for Communication Research, Stanford University, 1960.
14. Hilgard, E. R., & Bower, G. H. *Theories of learning.* New York: Appleton-Century-Crofts, 1966.
15. Holland, J. G. Research on programing variables. In R. Glaser (Ed.), *Teaching machines and programed learning.* Vol. II. Washington, D. C.: National Education Association, 1965. Pp. 66–117.
16. Hunt, W. A., & Mathis, B. C. A study of programmed instruction in an introductory psychology class. *Psychology in the Schools,* 1966, 3, 140–143.
17. Lange, P. C. Future developments. In P. Lange (Ed.), *Programmed instruction, the sixty-sixth yearbook of the National Society for the Study of Education.* Chicago: University of Chicago Press, 1967. Pp. 284–325.
18. Leib, J. W., Cusack, J., Hughes, D., Pilette, S., Werther, J., & Kintz, B. L. Teaching machines and programmed instruction: areas of application. *Psychological Bulletin,* 1967, **67**, 12–26.
19. Lumsdaine, A. A. Educational technology, programmed learning, and instructional science. In E. Hilgard (Ed.), *Theories of learning and instruction, the sixty-third yearbook of the National Society for the Study of Education.* Chicago: University of Chicago Press, 1964. Pp. 371–401.
20. Mager, R. F. *Preparing instructional objectives.* Palo Alto, Calif.: Fearon, 1962. P. 11.
21. Mathis, B. C. Programmed instruction in university education. *Journal of Dental Education,* 1964, **28**, 82–89.
22. May, L., & Moss, R. *New math for adults only.* New York: Harcourt, Brace & World, 1966.
22a. More, A. J. Delay of feedback and the acquisition and retention of verbal materials in the classroom. *Journal of Educational Psychology,* 1969, **60**, 339–342.
23. Morphett, M. C., & Washburne, C. When should children begin to read? *Elementary School Journal,* 1931, **31**, 496–503.
24. Mouly, G. J. *Psychology for effective teaching.* New York: Holt, Rinehart & Winston, 1968.
25. Payne, D. A., Krathwohl, D. R., & Gordon, J. The effect of sequence on programmed instruction. *American Educational Research Journal,* 1967, **4**, 125–132.
26. Postman, L., & Rosenzweig, M. R. Perceptual recognition of words. *Journal of Speech and Hearing Disorders,* 1957, **22**, 245–253.
27. Russell, D. H., & Fea, H. R. Research on teaching reading. In N. Gage (Ed.), *Handbook of research on teaching.* Chicago: Rand McNally, 1963. Pp. 865–928.
28. Schramm, W. *The research on programmed instruction, an annotated bibliography.* Bulletin No. 35. Washington, D. C.: U. S. Office of Education, 1964.
29. Sechrest, L., & Strowig, R. W. Teaching machines and the individual learner. *Educational Theory,* 1962, **12**, 157–169.
30. Sharp, E. The new math. *Saturday Review,* 1963, **64**(3), 65–67.
31. Skinner, B. F. Teaching machines. *Science,* 1958, **128**, 969–977.
32. Skinner, B. F. *The technology of teaching.* New York: Appleton-Century-Crofts, 1968.

33. Stolurow, L. M. *Teaching by machine.* Cooperative Research Monograph No. 6. Washington, D. C.: U. S. Office of Education, 1961.

34. Suppes, P. The use of computors in education. *Scientific American,* 1966, **215**(3), 206–223.

35. Thurstone, L. L. *A factorial study of perception.* Chicago: University of Chicago Press, 1944.

36. Tyler, F. T. Issues related to readiness to learn. In E. R. Hilgard (Ed.), *Theories of learning and instruction, the sixty-third yearbook of the National Society for the Study of Education.* Part 1. Chicago: University of Chicago Press, 1964. Pp. 210–239.

5

FORGETTING AND EXTINCTION:
THE ELIMINATION OF BEHAVIOR

This chapter describes the changes in old behavior occurring as time passes, new materials are learned, and old responses are nonreinforced. *Forgetting* is defined as a decrement in potential behavior during a time when the response was not evoked. For example, forgetting has occurred if you cannot remember today what an instructor told you yesterday. *Extinction* was defined in Chapter 3 as the nonreinforcement of a previously reinforced response. Extinction typically leads to a response decrement. Some investigators also refer to the decrement itself as extinction. A classroom example of extinction would be that teachers and other students stop paying attention to a certain student's misbehavior whenever it occurs. If the student has been reinforced by the attention, this extinction procedure should decrease his misconduct.

_____ **Forgetting**

Forgetting as a Function of Time since Learning

Forgetting is usually defined as losing information previously possessed. Occasionally, forgetting has to do with a skill, as in a game like tennis where information is not the essential ingredient. Forgetting is also a matter of degree: One may have forgotten the names of half the chemical elements but still remember the others. It is also common to find that forgotten material is relearned faster than original material is learned. In addition, everyone has sometimes experienced the *recovery* of a name that had originally been forgotten.

The section on forgetting in this chapter will be devoted to adding to the knowledge derived from personal experience, the findings of experiments on the topic. The reader is referred to an interesting article on forgetting by B. J. Underwood (78) for a general introduction to this topic. As an example of forgetting the simplest responses, Fig. 5-1 shows the average number of trials required for a rat to relearn to press a Skinner box lever from one to eleven weeks following original learning. About 60 trials were required for original learning, compared with from 16 to 25 trials for relearning, as shown in Fig. 5-1, indicating that the rats exhibited forgetting, but not complete forgetting. Note that forgetting increases with increased time between learning and relearning. It is interesting, too, that in rats, retention improves if learning is delayed until the animal is nearly mature. Campbell and Campbell (13) found that rats conditioned to fear at the age of 100 days showed nearly perfect

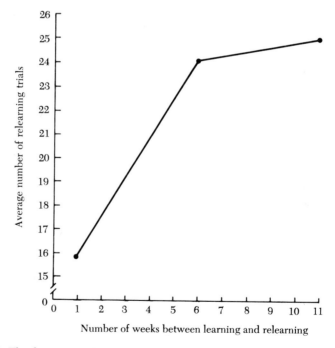

Fig. 5-1. The forgetting of a lever-pressing response, as indicated by an increasing number of trials required for relearning. [Based on Table 3 of Goodman (25). Copyright 1953 by American Psychological Association and reproduced by permission.]

retention 42 days later, whereas rats conditioned at the age of 18 days had lost most of the conditioned fear response 21 days later. To the extent that this phenomenon also holds with human beings, it suggests that much learning in childhood is most efficient if delayed until the child is fairly mature. (See Chapter 15, for an example of the problems encountered in teaching French to American children in primary grades.)

Curves comparable to those in Fig. 5-1 have been demonstrated for human beings ever since the work of Ebbinghaus (21). The course of this forgetting can be indicated by plotting Krueger's data (39) on the percentage of individual words recalled after various lengths of time between learning such a list and testing. These lengths of time are called *forgetting intervals* or *retention intervals,* depending on whether you feel optimistic or pessimistic. Figure 5-2 shows these percentages for subjects previously trained to a criterion of all correct responses in one trial.

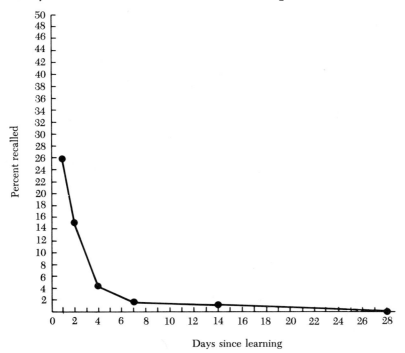

Fig. 5-2. Amounts recalled after various retention intervals. [Based on Table 2 of Krueger (39). Copyright 1929 by American Psychological Association, and reproduced by permission.]

This graph makes it clear that, in man, retention of words decreases or forgetting of words increases with time, just as forgetting of lever pressing increases in the rat. The measure of retention in this case is the number of words correctly anticipated on the first test trial, divided by 12, the number of words originally learned. It should be remarked that Krueger found much less retention after one day than would be expected under optimal conditions. (See *proactive inhibition* later in this chapter.)

Teachers often ask, Why teach material to children if it is to be forgotten anyway? What can be done to prevent or retard forgetting? Several possibilities are that: (a) particularly thorough learning will minimize forgetting; (b) certain arrangements of training conditions will minimize forgetting; (c) forgetting is not permanent, and study time is not completely wasted even though some tests indicate almost complete forgetting; and (d) more meaningful material will be better remembered. We consider these possibilities in turn.

Effects of Completeness of Learning upon Forgetting

Forgetting is generally reduced by *overlearning,* that is, practice beyond the stage at which the task first can be performed without error. Perhaps overlearning, though an accepted word in psychology, is a misnomer. Repeating the German list of prepositions, *an, auf, hinter, in, neben, über, unter, vor, zwischen,* until they can be said in sequence once from memory without error, is, no doubt, learning to a minimal criterion. Repeating them half again as many times as required by that criterion of learning is possibly enough to produce the amount of learning ordinarily desirable, but psychologists call this 150% learning or 50% overlearning. Correspondingly, training with as many trials beyond the criterion as before it is called 200% learning or 100% overlearning. In the study summarized in Fig. 5-2, Krueger (39) compared forgetting of words in persons trained to criterion to 100% learning, 150% learning, and 200% learning, with several different forgetting intervals between training and testing. Figure 5-2 gives only the results for the group when trained to criterion, but it can be completed as follows:

Pencil in a curve, starting at 49% for 1 day, having much the same shape as that already given in Fig. 5-2, but falling more gradually. You have now shown how forgetting proceeds after 100% overlearning (200% learning). If you draw another curve, using dotted lines, and make this curve come nearer to the first penciled curve than to the original curve, you will have approximated the course of retention after 50% overlearning (150% learning). This implies that the 50% overlearning procedure has substantially reduced forgetting, compared with the 100% learning condition, but that 100% overlearning does not reduce forgetting much beyond that for the 50% overlearning condition. Evidently overlearning is a good idea, but it will have less effect beyond 50%.

Penciling in additional curves on Fig. 5-2 has helped you learn the effects of overlearning. At the end of this chapter, the actual results of the entire experiment are given.

Although overlearning reduces forgetting, as measured by the number of words not recalled on a later test, forgetting was almost complete (100% forgotten) in all groups of Krueger's study after 28 days. Thus overlearning is useful in rote memorization, but not very long-lasting.

The data on relearning indicate that forgetting is less when measured by other criteria, such as speed of relearning, than by the recall measure just discussed. But the possibility remains that underlearning may reduce forgetting.

A person who has practiced until he can correctly repeat five words—once—from a ten-word list normally remembers fewer total words a day later than a person who has learned to repeat all ten correctly, for he has *underlearned* the list. Can he remember a higher percentage of those learned than the other person can?

Underwood (75) compared retention of ten pairs of adjectives for two groups of subjects (among others) who had been trained until they were correct on five and ten items, respectively, their training being without rest intervals between trials.

A day later the former group recalled an average of 1.50 items and the latter an average of 4.58. Thus, the former group retained 30% of its original criterion and the latter group 45.8%. Furthermore, although the group with partial training had fewer learning trials than the fully trained group (about 4.9 and 14 trials, respectively), the partially trained group retained less per learning trial than the other. Both on an absolute and on a percentage basis, then, retention was better following more thorough training.

So far, there has been the implicit assumption that overlearning studies *with school material* would demonstrate greater retention for overlearned material than for material learned only to a criterion of perfect performance on one trial. In actual fact there is almost no direct evidence to corroborate or refute that assumption. One could argue that review of material before an examination or at least after original learning is an overlearning procedure, differing from laboratory studies only in that the overlearning does not immediately follow original learning; we will consider research on such review later in this chapter. Convincing experimental evidence on overlearning in the classroom has not been abundant, but there is an eminently sensible passage from Stroud [(70), by permission from David McKay Co., Inc.]

In a very general sense there probably is some degree of overlearning in connection with the prosecution of all courses of study, as the pupil actually makes use of previously learned information in attacking new learning situations. For various reasons this form of overlearning has much to recommend it.

It avoids monotony, it provides for practice in a useful situation, and conditions for the operation of the "reinforcing mechanism" are favorable. Attempts to "overpower" the learner by sheer dint of enforced repetition are likely to be relatively unproductive and uninteresting. In endorsing overlearning we need not likewise commit ourselves to laborious drill; and by the same token, we need not fail to take advantage of overlearning because of our disaffection for excessive drill.

General Effects of Massing and Distribution of Practice

Massed and *distributed* conditions should be defined, for they are the central terms of the next few paragraphs. A *massed* condition, or *massing of practice*, occurs when little rest is allowed within the practice period. In verbal learning studies, presenting one word or syllable at a time, two variables largely define the degree of massing: the rate at which successive syllables are presented (once every 2 seconds, 3 seconds, or whatever) and the *intertrial interval*, the amount of time elapsing between the end of one presentation of the complete list and the beginning of the next trial or presentation of the complete list. Intertrial interval is more commonly used than *presentation rate* to control massing.

Massed conditions are matters of degree. The opposite of a massed condition is a *distributed* condition, or *distribution of practice*. In some experiments a comparison is made between learning or retention following a highly massed condition (e.g., a syllable presented every 2 seconds, and a 6 second rest at the end of a trial) and a highly distributed condition (e.g., a syllable presented every 2 seconds and a 2-minute rest between trials). It is more common to compare three or more degrees of massing in the same study.

The effects of massing upon acquisition are presented here rather than in the preceding chapter because the theoretical variables which are most commonly used to explain them are closely associated with extinction and forgetting processes. Highly massed training conditions often hinder acquisition of a motor (muscular) response such as sorting playing cards as fast as you can. A concrete example of this retardation is given in the section on *reminiscence* to follow. A layman's interpretation of this retardation is that the subjects "tire" without adequate rest between trials, thus retarding improvement in performance. This notion, cleansed of its subjective connotation, was advocated in Hull's theory (32) under the name *reactive inhibition*. This inhibition was assumed to build up with continued muscular effort. When it became large, it counteracted the positive effects of practice and thus led to poor performance. Reactive inhibition is assumed to disappear gradually during rest periods and therefore not to handicap performance during distributed learning.

Despite the large effects seen in the task just mentioned, distribution of practice seems not to affect the learning rate of verbal lists substantially, particularly if this rate is measured in terms of time spent learning rather than total number of trials. Highly distributed practice usually requires fewer trials for the learning of a list; but, since a longer total time per trial is involved, the total time spent is approximately constant (16).

The memorization of *connected discourse* (such as a poem or prose paragraph) or of the content of connected discourse probably is facilitated by distribution of practice, particularly distribution with a day or more between trials. Table 5-1 presents evidence from Bumstead (12) based on his own memorization of passages from "Paradise Lost," showing a decline in the amount of study time required to memorize a passage as a function of time between study sessions. Table 5-1 also shows that an even greater facilitation is produced by learning short passages at one time. Note, however, that the elapsed time required for learning increases rapidly with increases in the time interval between trials and with decreases in the amount of material studied at one time.

One way to combat this problem of increased elapsed time while preserving the advantages of distribution of practice or shortened units for learning is to diversify study materials. The school day with its several different class sessions applies this principle well: If all of one day were spent studying one long assignment in one subject and all the next day were spent on some other subject, less would be learned per day than is learned with the present method of studying as many as six subjects in a single day. Bumstead's research would also suggest that

TABLE 5-1

Effect of Distribution of Practice and Memorizing Short or Long Passages (from "Paradise Lost") upon Total Study Time and Elapsed Time to Learn[a]

	Fifty lines studied all at once		Fifty lines studied five lines at a time	
Time between study sessions	Study time required (min)	Elapsed time required (days)	Estimated study time[b] (min)	Estimated elapsed time required[b] (days)
0	170	1	60	10
1 hour	140	4	40	20
2 days	48	32	20	170
7–8 days	46	98	20	490

[a] Based on Table 1 of Bumstead (12).

[b] Estimated by multiplying the time required for five lines by ten.

several different topics should be presented within any one class hour, for his five-line tasks sometimes took only 2 minutes to learn and were very efficiently learned.

Reminiscence

In the case of certain tasks, massing of practice and underlearning combine to yield an interesting facilitation of performance after a rest interval. A test for forgetting may show that more is remembered than apparently had been learned! This paradoxical result is called *reminiscence.*

To be specific, let us say that you were correct on six out of twelve items under massed conditions for the last trial of a session and after a 2-minute rest were correct on eight out of twelve. You appear to have improved, or reminisced, by two items because of the rest period. However, notice that practice on the last trial before rest could have produced part or all of this effect. Consequently, a comparison is needed to show what would have happened on a test trial immediately after the last training trial. We can summarize an appropriate experimental design for this comparison as follows:

As in Chapter 3, group I of Table 5-2 is the control group. Each of the other groups can be considered an experimental group, or a group given a special treatment whose effect is to be studied. In the testing session *reminiscence* is defined as any superiority of an experimental group over the control group. One experimental group is all that must be used. However, since reminiscence might appear with one rest interval and not with another, it is reasonable to use several experimental groups.

Designs very much like that of Table 5-2 have occasionally shown reminiscence in verbal learning following massed training (59). However, early reports of sizable reminiscence of verbal tasks after rest periods as long as a day have been discredited. It is now generally conceded that the only spectacular demonstrations of reminiscence come from studies of so-called *motor learning.*

TABLE 5-2
Possible Design of a Reminiscence Study

Group	Training	Testing
I	To a fixed criterion of learning	Immediately
II	To a fixed criterion of learning	Two minutes later
III	To a fixed criterion of learning	Ten minutes later
IV	To a fixed criterion of learning	One day later

One motor learning task which yields reminiscence effects is inverted alphabet printing. The subject must print capital letters upside down, beginning from the right-hand side of the page:

Z ⅄ X ʍ Λ Ո ⊥ S Ꮮ Ò Ԁ O N W ⊤ Ʞ ſ I H Ɔ Ⅎ Ǝ ᗡ Ɔ ᗺ ∀

With a 40-second rest between half-minute trials (highly distributed practice), subjects average about 38 letters printed on the twentieth trial. However, if no rest is given following trials, they average only 23 letters on the twentieth trial. A 5-minute rest after the twentieth trial produces a sizable gain in performance for highly massed groups, as Fig. 5-3 shows (57). An average gain of almost seven letters occurs after rest (experimental group). But in some instances the groups given no additional rest before their twenty-first trial (control group) also showed average gains. Therefore, the difference between gains of experimental and control groups for each degree of distribution is the amount of reminiscence. Examination of Fig. 5-3 with this point in mind shows that

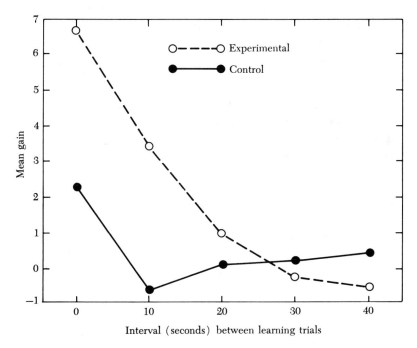

Fig. 5-3. Inverted letter printing for groups given rest (experimental groups) and no rest (control groups) after varying degrees of massing during training. [Figure 2 of Pubols (57). Copyright 1960 by American Psychological Association, and reproduced by permission.]

reminiscence declines steadily as distribution during training increases. Since control group gains are greater than experimental group gains with the 30- and 40-second distribution conditions, it appears that forgetting rather than reminiscence occurs for those conditions.

One point of experimental design is apropos now. Table 5-2 represented the design of a reminiscence study in which amount of rest was varied and massing was held constant. Figure 5-3 showed the results of a reminiscence study in which amount of massing or distribution was varied and the rest interval was constant for all experimental groups. With each design there are enough control groups available to test for reminiscence. Therefore, both are "good designs." One is used to answer one question: How does reminiscence change with changes in rest interval? The other is used to answer another question: How does reminiscence change with distribution of practice?

Other Effects of Distributed Practice

Even though reminiscence fails to occur under some distributed practice conditions, retention may still be better following distributed practice than following massed practice. Gordon (26) found that a class which heard the Athenian Oath read aloud six times in succession with only 30 seconds between readings remembered less on a retest 4 weeks later than a class treated the same way but with a 3-day rest between the first three readings and the next three. Since the two groups had similar scores on a test immediately after the six readings, the difference was in retention rather than in original learning.

Experimenters find it difficult to prevent students from rehearsing learned material on the days between various stages of experiments like the one just described. For that reason much retention research has employed short intervals between learning and final testing or short distribution of practice intervals. In a study of memory for a single numeral presented in a list of numerals appearing once per second or four times per second, Waugh and Norman (81) found no difference in retention, a contradiction of the Gordon experiment just cited. Underwood, Keppel, and Schulz (79) found that the amount of interference from previous associations controlled whether retention of paired associates was improved or unaffected by increased distribution of practice in a situation using relatively short distribution intervals. Increased interference led to more positive effects of increased distribution. More research is needed to determine if this principle holds with learning materials like those used by Gordon.

Meaningfulness and Retention

It is commonly believed that more meaningful material is easier to remember than is the less meaningful. A connected story should be remembered better than a long list of randomly arranged letters. If it is better remembered *immediately after a single reading*, it is because of a principle discussed in Chapter 3: Highly meaningful material is learned more rapidly than less meaningful material. One repetition of a story gives more learning than one repetition of the random letter list. If more training were given with the letters than with the story, thus equalizing the amount of learning, later tests for forgetting the two types of material might show no difference. This is what was found in a study by Underwood and Richardson (80) using syllables with very high association value and syllables with very low associative value and showing equal retention of equally learned material. (*Association value* refers to the number of associations which a syllable calls forth from a person.) In a much different context, it is supported by the Hilgard, Irvine, and Whipple (31) study on learning by understanding rather than by rote mentioned in Chapter 3. It was stated there that the learning by understanding method of doing the Katona card trick problem led to greater positive transfer of training to new problems than did the rote learning method. The former method may be called a learning of meaningful material, since the earlier discussion emphasized that different, more meaningful responses were learned with it than with the latter method. But Hilgard, Irvine, and Whipple report no difference in retention with these two groups, indicating another situation in which retention is unaffected by meaningfulness.

Pressey, Robinson, and Horrocks [(56), p. 281] have summarized some evidence in Fig. 5-4 that retention of connected discourse or other highly meaningful material is greater than it is for the isolated words represented in Fig. 5-2 earlier in the chapter. Figure 5-4 shows a relatively slow decline in memory of *observed material* (the contents of an orange–yellow sheet of cardboard, on which were attached two photographs, a red and white label, a white button, a one-cent postage stamp, and a penny) and a more rapid decline, at least in the first 30 days, of memory for six stanzas of poetry and of memory of the content of interesting factual prose. The latter material was tested by multiple-choice items, making the experiment much like a classroom study. The material presented in Fig. 5-4 makes it reasonable to hope for substantial retention of learned meaningful material which is either connected discourse or a pool of information such as the collage described above. None of

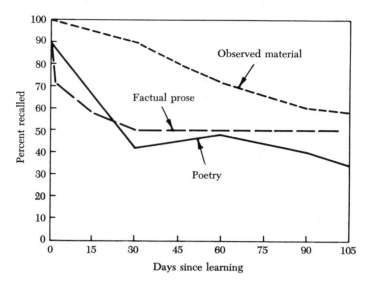

Fig. 5-4. Amounts of meaningful material recalled after various retention intervals. [Figure 9.2 from Pressey, Robinson, and Horrocks (56), p. 281. Data originally reported by Dietze and Janes (18), McGeoch and Whitely (44), and Whitely and McGeoch (83).]

the three curves goes as low in 105 days as occurred in the first day for the curve in Fig. 5-2.

Retention of Classroom Learning

Based on laboratory research on retention of meaningful material, there is no reason to expect different amounts of retention of different subjects, such as arithmetic and reading, unless one of two things happens. If one topic is better learned originally than the other, more should be remembered of the better learned one. Also, if one topic is used during the retention interval, retention test performance will be better on that topic than on one which is not used or otherwise rehearsed or practiced. These expectations are generally confirmed in studies of the permanence of school learning. Sterrett and Davis (69) have reviewed several articles on the retention of elementary, secondary, and college subjects over a summer or longer. They report substantial losses of material learned, even in a summer. At the elementary level some studies show reading skills decline over the summer; other show either no change or an increase. Arithmetic typically shows a loss over the summer. It seems reasonable to interpret the difference as being due to the fact that the students read during the summer but do not do arithmetic. Little forgetting of principles, as contrasted to facts, is reported—perhaps because the principles were overlearned originally.

Sterrett and Davis report up to 94% loss in college science learning over a 1-year retention period. However, Smeltz (63) found only 32% forgetting of high school chemistry over the same length of time. One reason for substantial retention in Smeltz's study was that two-thirds of the students studied physics during the year following chemistry. Those students retained more chemistry than did the others, presumably because of transfer between physics and chemistry instruction. For persons not taking related subjects later (e.g., those girls who study mathematics or science only because it is required), retention should be particularly poor.

Sometimes an investigator concludes that students who want to remember what they learned in school will retain it better than those who do not. Evidence for this conclusion might come from a comparison of students taking mathematics as preparation for college and those taking it for some other reason. Or such evidence might result from an experiment in which students in one group are asked to learn a subject with the intention of remembering it well. Both kinds of studies require precautions, however, in order to assure that learning was equal for two groups prior to the retention period. Ausubel, Schpoont, and Cukier (6) have taken such precautions in an experiment on the learning of a 1400-word passage about the history of opiate addiction. In that experiment, two groups had the same instructions and performed equally well until the end of learning, whereupon one group was advised to expect a retest (though without an effect upon course grades) after 14 days, and to try to remember the material learned. The other group was not given this advice. Since the two groups showed equal retention in the retest after two weeks, this experiment suggests that intent to remember is not important after original learning has occurred unless opportunity to rehearse is also given.

One should also beware of concluding that the proportion of learned material which is retained depends upon the intelligence of the student. It is true that more intelligent persons have better memory of a list of digits immediately after they are spoken aloud (35). However, Klausmeier and Check (37) and Klausmeier and Goodwin (38) report that, in general, retention percentage over a period of weeks does not depend upon intelligence.

It is worth emphasizing that the important goal for the teacher is to have a large amount of each subject actually learned by each child. Less capable or less interested children will learn less than the others. However, all will forget about the same amount. What is forgotten will be substantial, but it can be reduced by frequent review, by overlearning, and by subsequent teaching of related material.

There is experimental evidence that various forms of review facilitate classroom performance. Spitzer (68) has shown that taking a test on a topic previously studied (with students not being given answers to the test items before the experiment ends) improves later performance on this same test. Stroud and Johnson (71), among others, have shown that another method of review, rereading of previously studied material, will facilitate retention of classroom reading. Stroud and Johnson's findings on the effect of the time at which the review is given [interpreted in the light of later research by Ausubel (5)] may be taken to show that a review given immediately or shortly before testing leads to better performance than a review given some days before testing. This, perhaps, explains in part the students' tendencies to "cram" on the night before an examination. Taken together, the Stroud and Johnson and the Ausubel studies give little indication that the time between original learning and review affects performance, so long as the time between review and later testing is held constant.

Even though forgetting seems undesirable, it is inevitable. Gagné (see Chapter 4) advocates teaching foundation skills in mathematics as a basis for studying more complicated mathematics, so that one learns to identify and draw a line segment before one learns to identify and draw a triangle. The former task is called a *learning set* or a *subordinate task*. Although it would seem that subordinate tasks would be strengthened during learning of the tasks they are subordinate to, Gagné and Bassler (23) found that over a retention interval of 9 weeks the ultimate tasks were not forgotten, whereas the subordinate tasks learned prior to the ultimate tasks showed substantial forgetting. The reason for this seems to be that not all of the subordinate task is really needed for the final task. Identifying a line segment really is not a prerequisite to identifying and drawing a triangle, even though it is a closely related task. To some extent, then, students will forget nonessential tasks and remember only what is required for the mastery of new material.

Different Measures of Forgetting

The forgetting curves presented earlier in this chapter make it appear that very little effect of learning exists after a month has passed. However, forgetting should not be thought of as the elimination of all traces of past experience.

The method of measuring forgetting may itself control the amount of forgetting found. Consider the retention of serial lists; for example, suppose the *method of recognition* is used. A list of 24 syllables or words might be presented, from which the subject of the experiment must select the 12 syllables or words actually employed in the learning phase of the experiment. Better performances could be expected on this recognition measure than on a test asking the subject to repeat all syllables or words in proper sequence just before each appeared on a memory drum. The measure of the latter performance on the first relearning trial is called the *recall* measure or *anticipation* measure. The measure of performance over the number of trials required for complete relearning is called the *relearning* measure of retention, and should be about intermediate between the recognition and relearning measures in percentage retained. Postman and Rau (54) have generally confirmed these predictions for words and for nonsense syllables. Figure 5-5 shows their results for retention tests 20 minutes, 1 day, and 2 days following training. Note that a method not previously mentioned, *free recall* (the subject writes down as many items as he can remember, regardless of order in the list), gives greater retention than relearning and less than *recognition.*

The curves in Fig. 5-5 and other curves like them have been interpreted in the past to mean that the use of identical training procedures for all groups leads to different retention, depending on the method of measure-

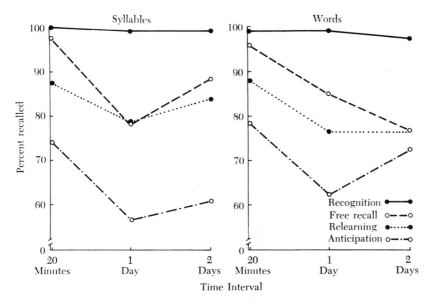

Fig. 5-5. Retention curves for nonsense syllables and words as a function of the method of measurement. [Figure 4 from Postman and Rau (54). Reprinted by permission of The Regents of the University of California.]

ment, and that it is easier to retain material for the purpose of recognition than for other criteria of response. The first conclusion seems sound. However, the second, which looks almost like a logical corollary of the first, has been vigorously questioned by Bahrick and Bahrick (9, 10). They argue that learning by recognition, for example, is quicker than learning by recall. Consequently the recognition condition leads to better test performance because of better learning rather than better recall.

Savings in Relearning from Previous Learning

Relearning proceeds more rapidly than original learning. One might think of forgetting as the burying of a memory. The first recall trial after a long retention interval may show little effect of original learning. But each successive relearning trial unearths a little more learned material so that forgetting seems less and less permanent as relearning proceeds. As a consequence of this process, a substantial saving is demonstrated in relearning, compared with original learning. Figure 5-5, for example, showed 87% retention of nonsense syllables after 20 minutes, as measured by relearning. This means that 87% fewer trials were required for relearning than for original learning.

Figure 5-6 presents an idealized comparison of learning and relearning curves following different retention intervals. The vertical distance between a relearning curve and the original learning curve for any trial number may be considered the advantage due to memory at that stage. A 30-day retention interval yields a substantial advantage at trial 3 though none at trial 1. Teachers faced with students who have massive memory losses after a summer vacation (or even after three years of not studying a subject) should help their students review old material, knowing that the forgotten material can be reinstated rapidly.

Means of Maximizing Recall

In addition to the procedure of overlearning discussed earlier, a variety of means of maximizing recall exist: First, allow enough time to recall the material. Michotte and Portych (46) have reported that the speed of giving a correct response is much greater for recently learned items than for items learned some time ago, as follows.

Time of test	Speed of response (seconds)
Immediately after learning	1.5
One day after learning	2.4
One week after learning	3.0

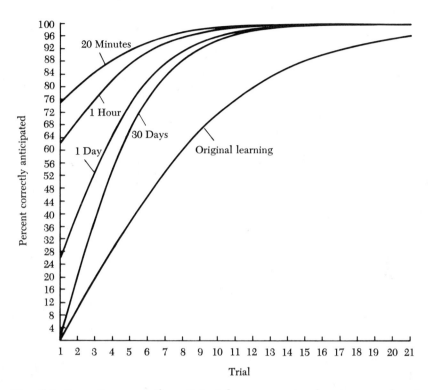

Fig. 5-6. Proportion correctly anticipated on successive learning or relearning trials, as a function of retention interval prior to relearning. (An idealized curve.)

Poorly remembered items take longer to recall, and allowing adequate time between items in relearning trials will facilitate recall. This conclusion is indirectly supported by research by Simley (62), showing that speed of response increases with amount of training.

Second, a "warming-up" activity prior to recall or relearning may improve performance. This is not a rehearsal of the material to be recalled but practice in an activity having the same tempo. Thus Irion and Wham (33) report that naming digits prior to a retention test with nonsense syllables facilitated performance on the syllables. Though Irion has found similar results in other studies, contradictory results from Rockway and Duncan (60) leave the usefulness of the procedure in some doubt.

Third, a forgotten response may be evoked by the presentation of stimuli once associated with the response to be made. For example, if you cannot think of the name of a person you knew in elementary school any other way, go back to the school and walk around, letting the stimuli there bring back the memory you seek. Woodworth and Schlosberg (84) illustrate this process by describing an experiment reported by Ohms:

> Nonsense words were studied and later tested by paired associates. When a word failed of recall, it was spoken to [the subject] through a poor telephone or visually exposed for only a small fraction of a second. The auditory or visual presentation was not good enough to enable [the subject] to understand nonsense words, but he could often understand one when the stimulus for its recall had just been given. If a name is "on the tip of your tongue" and someone pronounces it indistinctly to you, that extra push may be enough to bring the name up above the threshold of recall. The response is in such a condition of readiness that it can be evoked by an otherwise inadequate stimulus.

A fourth method of maximizing recall over very short periods of time is somewhat similar to the above. Suppose the following eight letters were shown to you all at once for only 0.05 second.

X   M   R   J
P   N   K   P

Immediately afterward, if asked to recall the letters in each row, you may be correct on only four of the eight. Your immediate-memory span is only four, then, or 50%. However, G. Sperling (65) has shown that approximately six of those letters are "available" under ideal recall conditions. Suppose that *after presentation* of the eight letters you are told which ones to recall. If a tone signal after presentation of

X   M   R   J
P   N   K   P

indicates that you should recite the letters seen on the *first line,* you will recall three of them, on the average. If a different tone is presented, indicating that you should recite the letters seen on the *second line,* you will recall three. Thus a total of six were retained long enough for a partial report to be made on a single row selected after stimulus presentation. This method of reducing forgetting is simply the limitation of the amount of material to be recalled. Its theoretical basis comes from studies of short-term memory like Sperling's, showing that a great deal of information is learned when presented, but that much of it is lost in the first few seconds thereafter. (Short-term memory is discussed more fully later in this chapter.)

A fifth way to maximize recall, one considered particularly important by psychologists, is to learn by distributed practice. In reminiscence studies, research indicated that learning connected discourse, motor skills, or certain lists of disconnected items proceeds more quickly with distributed practice than with massed practice. However, this superiority disappears in a serial list or paired-associates list unless there is interference between items in the list or between response items in the paired associates listed to be learned (77). Therefore, learning by distributed practice may not always facilitate learning. (Similar evidence regarding retention was also presented earlier in the chapter.)

Finally, the sixth and most important key to maximal recall: Avoid interference between the responses learned and others related to them. The simultaneous study of two foreign languages is an example of what to avoid. Certainly English–German and English–Spanish flash cards should not be used to study both languages on the same evening! Otherwise there may be confusion about whether to respond *la casa* (Spanish)

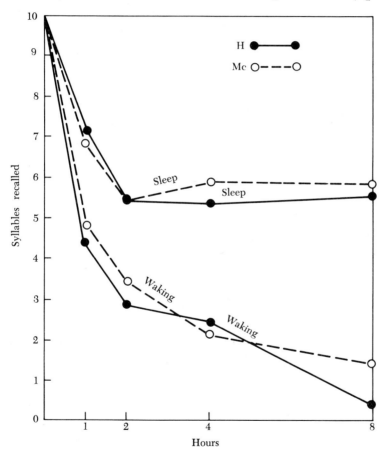

Fig. 5-7. Number of syllables remembered after 0 to 8 hours asleep or awake by persons H and Mc. [Figure 2 from Dallenbach (17a), a modification of Fig. 1 from Jenkins and Dallenbach (34). Reproduced by permission of University of Illinois Press.]

or *das Haus* (German) when encountering a flash card reading *house*. However, possibilities for interference are all around—and not all of them can be avoided. So simple a thing as being awake can produce interference, for Jenkins and Dallenbach (34) found much greater retention of nonsense syllables by two subjects who spent the retention interval sleeping than when they spent it awake. (Figure 5-7 shows how large an effect this was.)

Interference Theory: Proactive and Retroactive Inhibition

The Jenkins and Dallenbach study could be called a study of *negative transfer:* Activities of the waking state have transferred negative effects to the retention test task. By custom, however, psychologists refer to this particular result as *retroactive inhibition* rather than as negative transfer. Actually, retroactive inhibition is a special kind of negative transfer. Being awake between learning and recall inhibits the recall, termed retroactive because it is presumed to have *acted back* on the physiological trace of an earlier behavior, the original learning.

Proactive inhibition may also occur. If one task preceding a second one retards either the learning or subsequent recall of the second task, the inhibition is forward or *proactive*. We all probably suffer from a great deal of proactive inhibition: Every time a set of nonsense syllables or words is learned makes it harder to remember the next set learned. Underwood (76) estimates that forgetting is only about 25% in 24 hours rather than the 75% (25% retention) shown in Fig. 5-2, provided proactive inhibition from previous learning in the laboratory is eliminated by using naive subjects without previous experience of this kind. Figure 5-2 would be very different, then, if based on data from naive subjects.

Whereas forgetting was once attributed largely to retroactive inhibition, Underwood's estimate makes proactive inhibition appear the more important contributor to forgetting. Underwood points out that the activity which students engage in between learning and retention tests in the laboratory should not really produce much retroactive inhibition: "Even if we agree with some educators that much of what we teach our students in college is nonsense, it does not seem to be the kind of learning that would interfere with nonsense syllables."

This raises a question: What is "interfering"? The Jenkins and Dallenbach study shows that just being awake is interfering. If you must be awake between learning and testing, you should avoid situations similar to the learning one, and particularly avoid making different responses to stimuli similar to the test stimuli. Don't, for example, confuse two subjects such as English grammar and psychology by studying punctuation in a psychology book just before a psychology test. Thus preventing retroactive inhibition depends on principles like those involved in avoiding negative transfer. The same is true of proactive inhibition; but there is a further problem: Early learning may have positive transfer value or it may produce proactive inhibition. Again, proactive inhibition is a specific kind of negative transfer. The terms retroactive and proactive inhibition are most often used in connection with verbal learning; negative transfer is more often used to refer to decrements in other skills. However, all negative transfer is either retroactive or proactive inhibition.

A principal subsidiary to avoiding interference between learned responses is counteracting interference by added practice. If either proactive or retroactive inhibition is expected between two school subjects such as German and French, the interference between them can be neutralized by repeated and alternative practice of each subject. It is not enough, however, to study just anything in German for an hour, switch to French for an hour, and then go to some new topic in German for the next hour, etc. Instead, it will be necessary to review each topic in German at least once after the study of French has intervened. This procedure is much like successive acquisitions and extinctions, to be discussed later in the chapter. Relearning German each time presumably causes extinction of some French responses, which in turn are relearned when French is restudied, and so on.

The possibility of positive transfer should also be remembered by the teacher. *Proactive facilitation,* one form of positive transfer, occurs if knowledge of earlier material facilitates the later learning of something else. In certain subjects such as mathematics and physics, proactive facilitation is particularly likely because the material to be learned has a hierarchical structure in which advanced material can hardly be understood unless the elementary concepts have been mastered. There were hints of proactive facilitation of this kind in the description of Gagné's hierarchical theory of learning. (See Chapter 4.) Teachers will find that proactive facilitation can be produced in nonhierarchical subjects as well. The teacher who begins a new topic by reviewing old material or life experiences of the pupils in such a way that they see a logical connection between the old and the new is likely to produce proactive facilitation. (Note that the *advanced organizers* discussed in Chapter 3 have an effect very similar to this.)

Studies on retroactive and proactive inhibition and facilitation of classroom learning have not been done as frequently as research on those factors in the learning of nonsense syllables or single words. Recent work by Ausubel, Stager, and Gaite (7) suggests, however, that retroactive inhibition may be less a problem in classroom learning than research on nonsense syllables had suggested. Though traditional verbal learning studies have indicated that high similarity between the original task and the interpolated task (more specifically, high similarity between questions on the two tasks and dissimilarity on the answers), produces retroactive inhibition, Ausubel and his co-workers found that interpolated learning about Buddhism facilitated retention of earlier material about Zen Buddhism.

One reason for the finding just noted is that the learning and testing procedure used in the Ausubel study was different from that of traditional laboratory studies. Ausubel's subjects spent most of a Monday–Wednesday–Friday sequence of classes reading experimental material, and were tested on the succeeding Monday with a multiple-choice examination. In contrast, a representative retroactive inhibition experiment by Postman and Stark (55) employed ten-item paired-associates lists of single letters as stimuli and four-letter adjectives as responses. Original learning, second task learning, and retesting on the original task were all conducted in a single session for each person. Postman and Stark found retroactive inhibition in most of their experimental groups which had to recall the responses to be made. However, in a phase of their experiment somewhat like Ausubel's study in that it used multiple-choice questions to facilitate performance on the letter (stimulus) and adjective (response) task, Postman and Stark found no retroactive inhibition except in one group: That group was designed to produce maximum interference by using a second-stage task with the same stimuli and responses as in the first task but with different pairings ("S-mute" and "B-tall" might originally have been two pairs; later "S-tall" and "B-mute" might have been the pairs). This suggests that Ausubel's findings resulted in part from the use of multiple-choice tests, eliminating inhibition thereby. The actual facilitation may have come from some experimental difference other than those noted above or it may have resulted from rehearsal and clarification of original learning on Zen Buddhism during the learning of other Buddhism material, as Ausubel and his associates suggest.

There are many apparent contradictions between verbal learning studies employing lists of words or nonsense syllables and those employing connected discourse. The latter studies are potentially more valuable to teachers; however, the former tend to be more recent and more carefully conducted. In trying to apply verbal learning findings in the classroom it will be necessary to evaluate the similarity of the experimental task to the classroom task; it may also be necessary to ask how well controlled the study was and therefore how valid its conclusions are.

Immediate (Short-Term) Memory

Heretofore in this chapter we have been largely concerned with memory over a period of hours since learning a group of correct responses. Such studies necessarily involve repeated training trials and usually lead to overlearning some responses while bringing the others up to criterion. Now let us consider studies of learning and retention of a single item such as a telephone number (30) or the combination "CBL." Peterson and Peterson (52) have devised a method in which the experimenter spells a three-letter syllable and immediately speaks a three-digit number whereupon the subject may count backwards by threes or fours from this number (309, 306, 303, . . . , for example). The rate of counting is set by a metronome, so the amount of time and activity spent in counting is easily controlled. A red light is turned on to signal the subject to say the syllable presented just before the number. Peterson and Peterson found that a long recall interval (time spent hearing the number and counting) resulted in much forgetting whereas in a short interval there was little forgetting. Figure 5-8, which shows part of the results of that study, makes it plain that forgetting of individual items presented only once is very rapid. After a recall interval of only 18 seconds there is less than one chance in ten that an item will be recalled correctly by the criterion used.

With these materials, immediate (short-term) memory based on a single exposure of stimuli seems to be transitory, lasting for only a few seconds. Peterson and Peterson have also shown that immediate memory can be substantially improved, however, if the stimulus to be learned is repeated by the subject once or more than once before the usual recall interval is begun. Thus practice has an effect on short-term memory as well as on memory in more traditional experimental situations.

The Peterson and Peterson experiment might lead one to think that no kind of material is retained well for as long as 18 seconds. Murdock (48), who confirmed their findings for consonant syllables, found that memory for a single word is excellent (nearly 90% chance of correct recall) after an 18-second recall interval. Thus immediate memory is stronger for items which are already known in their grouped form (words) than for ones which do not yet belong together (consonant syllables).

Waugh and Norman (81) have found evidence that passage of time alone is not an adequate explanation of forgetting in short-term memory experiments. Forgetting curves such as Fig. 5-8 may be presumed to result from an increased number of words spoken or observed by the learner as time passes between learning and testing.

A popularized presentation of material on the topic of short-term

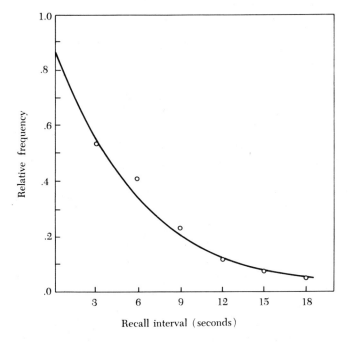

Fig. 5-8. Frequency of correct recalls as a function of recall interval. (Only those recalls which took no longer than average for the experiment, 2.83 seconds, are included.) [Figure 3 from Peterson and Peterson (52). Copyright 1959 by American Psychological Association, and reproduced by permission.]

memory was recently published in *Scientific American* (51), and is recommended as supplementary reading.

Two-Process Theory

Although laymen tend to think of forgetting as an inactive process in which the neural record or *trace* of something previously learned simply decays or fades away, the interference theory of forgetting has been dominant in psychology until very recently. However, the short-term memory data recently obtained have led a number of psychologists to feel that just after exposure to a stimulus a memory trace is indeed formed and that this trace decays rapidly as time passes *or new stimuli occur*. The present section takes this new point of view, in the sophisticated form we call *two-process* theory.

There are two kinds of memory processes, short term and long term. If a stimulus is perceived, it is placed in short-term memory and can be recalled as long as it stays in short-term memory. If it receives attention or is rehearsed by the learner, it may be shifted into long-term memory and therefore more or less permanently retained. (Probably interference theory is most applicable to the forgetting of material in long-term memory though some theorists de-emphasize interference factors even there.) Without rehearsal or attention, an item's trace in short-term memory decays and is lost completely. The reason that intervening stimuli produce decay of short-term memory is that successive stimuli have to "line up" to receive attention. If there are too many of them or if the attention mechanism works too slowly, the early stimuli will be forgotten before they can be rehearsed (49).

An interesting analysis of long- and short-term processes in memory comes from Atkinson and Shiffrin (4) and Shiffrin and Atkinson (61). They hypothesize that human memory resembles the system developed in high-speed digital computers to store information and permit its recovery and use at a later time. Such computers take in information through their *sensory register* (corresponding to human sense organs), storing information briefly in a region called a *buffer* in the *short-term store* which is intermediate between the input of the computer and the permanent storage area. If information is needed only for use in getting an answer, that information can be discarded from the computer's buffer after the desired answer is obtained. An oversimplified example of a case in which this would be true is the following: We know the amount learned by each of 50 children in grade 1, 50 children in grade 2, and 50 children in grade 3. We want to compute the average amount learned in each grade, but only for the purpose of averaging the three grade averages to yield an overall average. When the three grade averages are computed, they are placed in the buffer for just long enough to get them ready for the final computation. Then they might be discarded (forgotten) and the overall average placed in the permanent storage area until it is needed. When needed, the permanently stored information is called back to the buffer, from which it can be printed out on paper for examination.

When human beings memorize something, according to Atkinson and his co-workers, they employ a buffer system and a permanent storage device in the brain. Furthermore, they summarize their information or *encode* it, as would be said of the computer. Rather than store what you heard at public school the last time you attended, you might store the fact that you heard the repeating of the Pledge of Allegiance. Since you already know the Pledge, there is no need to store it again. This encoding process helps to enlarge your effective memory or that of the computer because it prevents unnecessary duplication in the storage area.

In a computer, the recall of information from the buffer may be much faster (about 250 billionths of a second rather than 1/200th of a second) than it is from permanent memory, just as you may recall something which you have very recently experienced more quickly than a trivial event of some years ago. In some cases the computer may not be able to recall some item from its permanent memory, usually because certain equipment is not hooked up at the time the recall is desired. This inaccessibility of information is a problem for people, too. The forgetting studies mentioned already in this book make it sound as if the material originally learned has been lost forever. However, much of the forgotten material may actually be in some permanent storage place, but hard to get back. Tulving and Pearlstone (73) have shown, however, that the accessibility of material can be increased after it is apparently forgotten if subjects are told how many cases of each of several kinds of words were originally learned. Similarly, Hart (29) has shown that people who are asked such questions as "What is the capital city of New Mexico?" may not be able to answer the question immediately though they think they know it. They later show that they do know it by marking the correct answer when given a choice between Albuquerque, Santa Fe, Los Alamos, and Carlsbad. This suggests that their storage system is adequate, but that their system for retrieval or finding what they know is defective. In a sense, the brain is like a library with plenty of books but a poor card catalog.

Brown and McNeill (11), in discussing the "tip of the tongue" phenomenon observed by Hart (and also observed in Ohms' experiment mentioned earlier in this chapter) have suggested that people act as if they did have a card catalogue with several cards indexing the definition of each word to be remembered but with certain crucial features of the word appearing on only a very few cards, making recall difficult.

A good deal of attention has been given to theories which emphasize two kinds of memory processes, short term and long term. It is probable that such theories will be increasingly prominent in the future. Nonetheless, interference theorists argue strongly that there is a great deal of similarity between the processes which take place in short- and long-term memory studies and that the ideal theory should be valid for both situations (45, 53).

Extinction

Comparison of Extinction and Forgetting

In what sense is extinction similar to the procedure under which forgetting occurs? It is typical of both to produce a decrement in performance, but extinction appears to involve suppression rather than elimination of responses, such as occurs in forgetting. The rat stops pressing the lever during extinction, but the lever-pressing response is not forgotten (i.e., not unavailable); rather, it is that the rat has learned to inhibit lever pressing. But a forgotten response cannot be made even when the appropriate stimulus is presented.

Spontaneous Recovery and Interference Theory

Many psychologists think extinction has an interfering effect like that of retroactive inhibition, and emphasize the interference between responses learned in extinction and the responses to be extinguished. Wendt (82) pointed out many years ago how monkeys inhibit previously learned responses, not by inactivity but by substitution of other behavior.

Miller and Stevenson (47) have recorded the presence of agitated, "nervous" behavior in the rat, such as rapid dashing to and fro or vigorous cleaning of the whiskers, which occurs during extinction. Figure 5-9 shows how a rating of amount of agitation increases during extinction of a rat's running response. Note that this rating closely parallels the increased time required to run the length of the experimental apparatus as extinction proceeds.

In discussing massing effects, it was noted that Hull's theory of extinction (32) points to the suppression of the response due to fatigue or *reactive inhibition*. Reactive inhibition is a good explanation of *spontaneous recovery*, the fact that, with the passage of time after extinction, responses regain strength. For example, bar-pressing responses in the

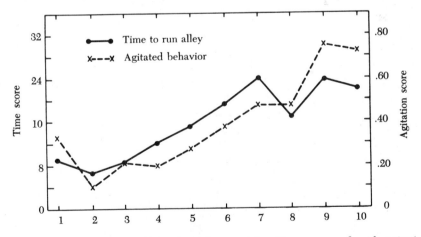

Fig. 5-9. Time required to run through a straight alley, compared with agitation scores, on successive days of extinction. [Figure 2 from N. E. Miller and S. S. Stevenson, "Agitated behavior of rats during experimental extinction and a curve of spontaneous recovery," *Journal of Comparative Psychology*, **21**, 205–231. © 1936, The Williams & Wilkins Co., Baltimore, Maryland.]

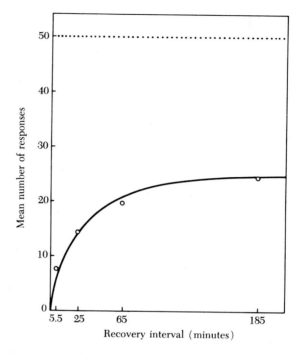

Fig. 5-10. Average number of responses after different spontaneous recovery intervals following extinction. Notice that number of responses never reached the dotted line representing complete recovery. [A portion of Fig. 3 of Ellson (22). Copyright 1938 by American Psychological Association, and reproduced by permission.]

albino rat were very few in a test only 5½ minutes after extinction. However, the responses more than doubled in a test 185 minutes after extinction. Figure 5-10 shows the trend of spontaneous recovery for four different recovery intervals used by Ellson (22).

Findings consistent with Ellson's have been obtained with several experimental situations and species of subjects, including children who worked for peanuts as a reward (8).

A further hypothesis which follows from the assumption of reactive inhibition is that responses requiring large amounts of effort should therefore generate large amounts of reactive inhibition, making extinction effects occur more quickly. This prediction has frequently been verified, though not uniformly so (15).

The fact that spontaneous recovery, as shown in Fig. 5-10, never became complete indicates that reactive inhibition is not the sole reason for the response decrement accompanying extinction or that it does not ever completely dissipate. That effect of extinction not due to reactive inhibition is presumably due to interference.

Interference theory has been suggested as an explanation for both extinction effects and forgetting. This does not imply that extinction and forgetting are equivalent processes. Forgotten responses cannot be retrieved without retraining or special cues; extinguished responses recover rather than disappear with the passage of time. Note, too, that there are no serious advocates of a decay theory of extinction: extinction clearly demands the nonreinforced occurrence of a response, not simply the passage of time.

Successive Acquisitions and Extinctions

A second factor producing extinction has been discussed by Zeaman (85) and by Dufort and Kimble (20). Extinction is the extreme case of reducing amount of reinforcement; its effects are greater than those of small reductions in amount. Reacquisition, then, becomes an exaggerated case of increasing the amount of reinforcement. These results can be interpreted theoretically as follows: If the reinforcer (e.g., food) is an incentive to the organism and the organism makes a response to obtain the reinforcer, then changing the amount of reinforcement (or incentive) presumably changes the amount of motivation produced by that incentive. Consequently, increasing or decreasing the amount of reinforcement (even in the extremes of shifting it to zero—extinction—or increasing it from zero—reacquisition) changes what has previously been called incentive motivation, i.e., Hull's K concept mentioned in Chapter 3.

This interpretation of extinction and reacquisition effects as attributable to incentive motivation changes is like a commonsense notion that extinction effects occur because the subject doesn't *expect* reinforcement of responses, whereas reacquisition occurs when the subject does expect reinforcement. Tolman's theory of behavior, an S–S theory as defined in Chapter 3, has such a commonsense orientation. Tolman (72) defined "expectation" indirectly in the following discussion:

> Thus if . . . a change be made from a "good" reward to a "poor" one, or *vice versa,* it seems obvious that this change can induce a corresponding change in behavior only after the new reward has had a chance to be experienced one or more times—only after, that is, it has had a chance to induce a new cognitive expectation. The rats must have experienced the new "better" or "worse" reward for one or more times, before their behavior can change so as to become appropriate to it. They must have had a chance to build up a "cognitive expectation" for this new reward with its greater or less satisfactoriness for the given demand.

Despite the difference in outlook between S–R theorists like Hull and S–S theorists like Tolman, the similarity between the hypotheses of incentive magnitude effects and of expectation makes it seem that the theories themselves can come closer together.

Figure 5-11 illustrates how successive acquisitions and extinctions proceed in the T-maze. The smooth curves included in the graph are based on equations which state a theory of successive acquisitions and extinctions with mathematical precision. The upward and downward shifts in incentive magnitude assumed above largely, though not completely, control the shape of these smooth curves.

One puzzling aspect of Fig. 5-11 is apparent to the careful observer. Though one group of animals (AEEAE) had 40 trials of extinction while another (AAAAE) was receiving 40 acquisition trials, the two groups seem to have learned equal amounts: On trials 61 to 80 a shift from zero reinforcement to the usual reinforcement amount for acquisition produces a rapid increase in running speeds for the AEEAE group to the level of the always-reinforced group.

This puzzle can be resolved in several ways. One of the simplest seems almost paradoxical. Assume, with Spence (64), that learning (increase of *habit strength*) occurs on every trial in which a response is executed, even if the response is reinforced very little or not at all. Then the group receiving extinction trials is learning the response of running even during extinction. Once reacquisition begins, that learning manifests itself by a rapid improvement in performance, so that no difference remains which can be attributed to the previous extinction trials.

The hypothesis just stated turns out to be the S–R contiguity argument used in Chapter 3 to interpret most latent learning phenomena. Closer examination of Fig. 5-11 justifies this; except for the reinforcements during the first 20 trials of the experiment, Fig. 5-11 could depict a latent learning study, too. Thus, successive acquisitions and extinctions can be closely related in procedure and theory to latent learning experiments.

Partial Reinforcement Effects

Razran (58) and Lauer and Estes (40) call attention to the similarity between the procedure of successive acquisitions and extinctions and *partial reinforcement*. This term sounds like a reference to small-sized reinforcements, half a banana instead of a whole one, perhaps. Actually it concerns something else. To partially reinforce is to give reinforcement only part of the times on which the response is made. When reinforcement is given following every response, the procedure is called *continuous reinforcement*.

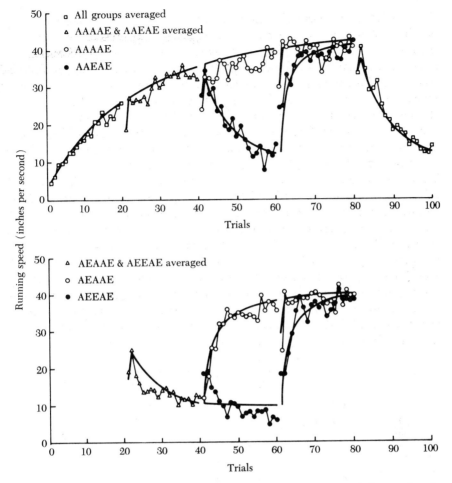

Fig. 5-11. Successive acquisitions and extinctions of running behavior by the white rat. (Each A represents a 20-trial block of acquisition trials; each E a 20-trial block of extinction trials.) [Figure 1 from Cotton and Jensen (17). Copyright 1963 by American Psychological Association, and reproduced by permission.]

Several different means of partial reinforcement have been used. For example, to repeat material in Chapter 3: (a) *Ratio reinforcement:* A certain number (*n*) of responses may be required before each reinforcement. This is like piecework in the factory or on a farm: "Pick eight boxes of strawberries and receive 25 cents." (b) *Fixed interval reinforcement:* A certain amount of time may be required to pass before a response—if made—will be rewarded. This is like a time lock on a bank safe. "Work the combination 10 hours from now, and the safe will open." (The opening of the safe, of course, is the reinforcement.) (c)

Variable ratio or variable interval reinforcement: Randomly varying numbers of responses may have to occur or intervals may have to pass before reinforcement is presented. This is like a Las Vegas gambling house. Note that in all these cases of partial reinforcement, acquisition trials (reinforcement) are followed by extinction trials (nonreinforcement), though not necessarily in as regular an order as in the traditional studies of successive acquisitions and extinctions already mentioned.

Some partial reinforcement studies have actually been done with gambling devices. Lewis and Duncan (42) obtained a commercial slot machine from their local sheriff's office after a raid on a gambling den. They remodeled it for their own purposes, arranging that 0, 12½, 25, 37½, 50, 75, or 100% of the times a slug was placed in it, a nickel would be credited to the person in the experiment. After eight such trials for each person, extinction was begun: The machine never paid off again. Like other partial reinforcement studies, this experiment gave a somewhat paradoxical result. As Fig. 5-12 shows, fewer extinction trials were made by persons who had always been reinforced for pulling the lever (continuous reinforcement) than by persons in any other group. Partial reinforcement seems to make responses more resistant to extinction than would otherwise occur. This general effect of partial reinforcement has been observed in many studies with animals and humans (41)

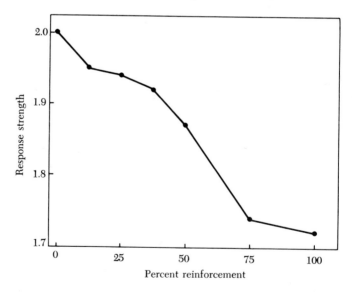

Fig. 5-12. Slot machine responses during extinction as influenced by percent reinforcement. [Figure 1 from Lewis and Duncan (42). Copyright 1956 by the American Psychological Association, and reproduced by permission.]

in a great number of different experimental situations. It is the more surprising because partial reinforcement usually results in poorer performance during the acquisition phase than does continuous reinforcement. Poorer performance during that phase could easily be explained as due to the successive acquisition and extinction process going on then.

Explanations of partial reinforcement effects during extinction have often been proposed. No explanation of the superiority of partial reinforcement groups during extinction seems wholly satisfactory, but perhaps the most popular one is the *discrimination hypothesis*. This hypothesis states that a change in procedure from reinforcement on every trial to extinction is abrupt, easy to discriminate, and therefore quickly followed by a reduction in responding. However, a change from partial reinforcement to extinction is less abrupt because extinction trials are included in the partial reinforcement procedure. Consequently, the procedural change is difficult to discriminate, and the immediate reduction in responding is not so great.

Frustration and Partial Reinforcement

An alternative to the discrimination hypothesis is to suggest that clear understanding of *frustration* will help explain the superiority of partial reinforcement groups to continuous reinforcement groups. Generally, frustration refers to a feeling of being thwarted or prevented from doing something desired. Experimental psychologists seldom use *feeling* as a technical term, but their meaning is much the same, although largely restricted to frustrations of one certain type: failure to reinforce a response that has previously been reinforced sets up an emotional response within the person or animal. The emotional response cannot be observed directly, but its effects may be observed.

Amsel (1) has cited evidence that what he calls a *frustrative event*— the absence of or delay of a rewarding event in a situation where it had been present previously—can cause an increase in effort (the *frustration effect*) which makes it reasonable to think an emotional response (*frustration*) has taken place. If a straight alley is so constructed that a goal box is interposed between its first and second halves and a second goal box is placed at the end of the second half, a frustrative event would be to omit a reward in the first goal box following a training series in which food was given in that goal box. A test for frustration effect is whether the animals trained to run through the two halves of the goal box in sequence have different running speeds for the second half on trials in which reward was given in the first goal box than they do on trials in which it was not. Amsel and Roussel (3) have shown that they do: Second half runway speeds are faster on trials when reward has been omitted in the first half of the runway than when it has been provided. Amsel interprets this to mean that frustrating events produce an emotional response—frustration—as expected, *and* that its effect is to increase the amount of effort made by the frustrated organism. Because of a similarity between these effects and those that make the organism hungrier (increasing the *food drive,* as it is called in Chapter 11) the emotional response is called *frustration drive* by Amsel.

Studies of frustration drive are important in their own right, but can they explain the superior resistance to extinction by partial reinforcement groups? Amsel (2) suggests that a mediating response (see Chapter 3) of anticipatory frustration is built up on nonrewarded trials following earlier rewards. The normal effect of this mediating response is to cause a weakening of the running response on the next trial. Continued nonreinforcement, then, would lead to traditional extinction effects. However, in partial reinforcement situations, reinforcement of a trial also leads to mediated responses for strengthened running on the next trial. The conflict between tendencies for faster and slower running leads to great variability in speed for animals having partial reinforcement.

Amsel says that continued partial reinforcement leads the animals to run fast on most trials, but does not explain why this is true. At any rate, the mediating response of anticipatory frustration is conditioned to running. Finally, when a series of extinction trials is begun, a partial reinforcement group runs faster on the average than a continuous reinforcement group because the former group has been conditioned to run fast in the presence of anticipatory frustration and the other has not.

The interpretation just given of partial reinforcement is confirmed by Capaldi and Senko's (14) research: After 120 trials, of which 33% randomly selected trials were reinforced, rats ran faster on trials following nonreinforcement than following reinforcement. After switching to an alternating pattern of reinforced and nonreinforced trials, these animals ran distinctly faster after the nonreinforced trials, as frustration drive theory would predict. Similar findings in an alternation condition have been reported by Tyler, Wortz, and Bitterman (74), lending further support to the frustration interpretation. The frustration drive is considered further in Chapter 11.

Some Principles of Response Elimination, with Hints for Classroom Application

Guthrie (27) has presented several principles which may be used to eliminate undesired behavior. To the extent that they prove sound, they may be useful substitutes for punishment or for simple extinction of undesired classroom behavior. First, if a child is emotional, or is fearful of some new situation, the crucial stimulus can be presented at low intensity until the child adapts to that situation, and then be gradually increased until the child can accept the full situation. Thus Jones (36) taught a baby not to fear a rabbit in a cage: During the baby's eating time the caged rabbit was kept in view of the baby, at first at a great distance, then gradually closer each day as the baby showed less fear. This general method is called the *method of toleration.* It may also be used to adapt children or beginners to the water when they are learning to swim.

Now consider the problem of boisterous behavior when a teacher leaves a classroom unattended. The conditioned stimulus (CS) for boisterousness may be the teacher's saying, "I have to go to the audio-visual storeroom and will be back in 10 minutes." Guthrie's toleration method applied to this situation would be to present a stimulus less likely to evoke the students' noisy behavior. The teacher might leave the room for half a minute several times during the first six weeks, then for a minute at a time during the next six weeks, and gradually increase the length of time the students are left alone and responsible for themselves as the year continues. It may be necessary to remind students of the behavior expected of them during the teacher's absence, particularly at first; in some cases it may be necessary to express disapproval after the teacher returns.

Some teachers may not believe it worthwhile to train students to be quiet in their absence. These teachers would like to employ Guthrie's second method of response suppression, which is to physically prevent a response in the presence of its CS. But how can children be physically restrained from misbehaving after the teacher announces he is leaving the room? Unable to answer this question, some teachers may simply remain in the classroom to prevent disorder. In some cases this may eventually transfer to quiet behavior in the teacher's absence. However, much misbehavior is insensitive to modification by simple learning processes but is dependent instead on cues provided by the overall social situation. Thus the student who is a "problem" in high school in May might be quite restrained in college in September because of the differences in the overall high school and college environments.

Still a third Guthrian principle may be worth the teacher's consideration. To eliminate one response in a certain situation, find a way to evoke an even stronger one. If a 6-year-old boy repeatedly disturbs a TV lesson by playing with the loudness, brightness, and other controls, drastic action would be to give him a complex camera to adjust while the program is in session. For a time, at least, the response of playing with the camera will probably be stronger than the response of playing with the TV controls. The child may not learn as much as he should from the TV program, but neither will he hinder other class members from learning. Later, if the response to the camera weakens, a new substitute response can be produced.

Effect of Habit Reversal upon Learning Sets

In Chapter 3 it was seen that an ability to learn can be developed through training on a long series of somewhat related learning tasks. The learning–how–to–learn leads to the formation of *learning sets,* as reflected in the discussion of Harlow's research (28). The development of learning sets that are so strong that one error can lead to uniformly correct performance thereafter can also result from a long series of habit reversal tasks. Harlow reported on eight monkeys that received 112 additional discrimination tasks; in each task training on the original problem was followed by eight reversal trials in which the previously correct object was now incorrect and the previously incorrect object had to be chosen if food were to be found. After about 70 such reversal tasks, the monkeys showed almost perfect performance on trial 2 of each reversal. This learning set seemed even stronger than the original one. Similar results were obtained with children.

Dufort, Guttman, and Kimble (19) have shown that rats can also learn a reversal learning set so that they can change from one response to its reverse after a single nonreinforcement of the old response.

The reason for such rapid reversal learning is not entirely clear. Dufort, Guttman, and Kimble cited evidence that complete learning of each successive habit was necessary to this phenomenon. They also predicted, and many investigators (see 43, 50, 66, 67) proved, that *overlearning* of the first task facilitated habit reversal. However, there have recently been enough studies that fail to confirm the overlearning effect to make Gardner (24) suppose it to be spurious. Pending clarification of this issue, it would be premature to look for practical applications of the phenomenon.

─── **Summary**

1. Forgetting (of rote materials at least) is greatly reduced by overlearning. Overlearning is produced by practice beyond the point at which

the task is first successfully mastered. One hundred percent overlearning is achieved if as many trials are given after first reaching the criterion of learning as were given in order to reach that criterion.

2. Massing and distribution of practice can differentially affect the rate of learning motor skills, but appear to have no substantial effects on learning verbal lists except when there is a great deal of interference between the previous learning and the present task. Massed practice occurs when little rest is allowed between parts of the practice period; highly distributed practice might allow as much as a day between trials. Massed practice customarily hinders the learning of a motor response. Massed practice also increases the number of trials required to learn connected discourse such as a poem.

3. Reminiscence is a paradoxical phenomenon in which more is recalled on a test trial than was apparently learned originally. Reminiscence is most likely to appear after a rest period if massed practice had been previously employed and the task was one for which massing led to poorer performance during training than distributed practice would have done.

4. Highly meaningful material is sometimes thought to be more easily remembered. Meaningful lists are easier to learn; but, when once learned to the same criterion, meaningful and nonsense lists are usually equally well retained.

5. Retention of classroom material can be increased by later use of the material learned. One study showed only 32% forgetting of high school chemistry material over a year, partly because most of the students studied physics following their chemistry course. Transfer between physics and chemistry apparently increased the amount of retention.

6. Motivation to learn may affect the amount originally learned. However, unless the more highly motivated students review or rehearse old material more than the unmotivated students do, there is no reason to believe that motivation will affect the percentage of learned material which is retained.

7. Intelligence level affects rate of learning but does not affect amount remembered once it has been learned.

8. Relearning occurs more rapidly than original learning. Therefore, realizing that much material taught a year before has been forgotten, the teacher can reinstate the old material rapidly by reviewing it with his students.

9. Interference with present learning due to previous learning is called proactive inhibition. Interference with prior learning by subsequent learning is called retroactive inhibition.

10. A nonsense syllable heard only once has a forgetting curve which

drops to almost zero recall within 18 seconds. This is called short-term memory in contrast to long-term memory studies in which well-learned lists of syllables are at least partially retained for several days.

11. Many investigators of short-term memory assume that forgetting shortly after exposure to a stimulus results from the decay of a memory trace. Interference theorists assume that similar interfering processes account for forgetting in both short- and long-term memory studies.

12. Extinction is an extreme case of reduction in magnitude of reinforcement and has similar effects. Reacquisition following extinction may also be viewed as a special case of increasing reinforcement magnitude.

13. Some time after extinction, a response regains some of its strength without further reinforcement. This is called spontaneous recovery.

14. Partial reinforcement is reinforcement provided for only a fraction of the total number of occasions on which the response is made. Under most partial reinforcement schedules the response appears weaker during acquisition than if reinforcement were always given. However, during extinction the reverse is true.

15. Guthrie's methods for response elimination may have some application in school situations: (a) The toleration method involves presenting stimuli at intensities too low to evoke the undesirable response, increasing the intensity on successive trials as the person becomes less likely to respond to it. (b) Physical prevention of the undesired response in the presence of its conditioned stimulus may be useful. (c) In a situation where an undesirable response is likely, it may be possible to present a stimulus for some other response so that the second response will replace the first.

Appendix to Chapter 5

The augmented figure summarizing data from all three groups of the Krueger study of the effects of overlearning upon forgetting is shown on the facing page (Fig. 5-13).

SUGGESTED READINGS

Asimov, I. And it will serve us right. *Psychology Today*, 1969, **2**(11), 38–41, 64.

A comparison of computers to science-fiction robots, with the warning that the robot-computer may replace man.

Deutsch, J. A. Neural basis of memory. *Psychology Today*, 1968, **1**(12), 56–61.

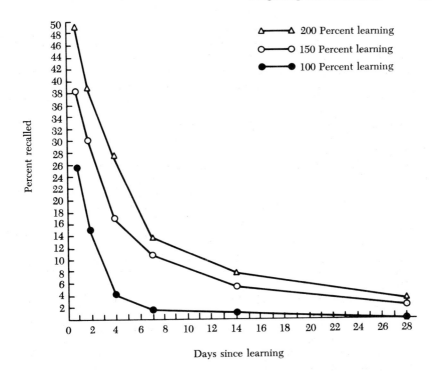

Fig. 5-13. (Fig. 5-2 completed.) Amounts recalled after different degrees of learning and various retention intervals. [Based on Table 2 of Krueger (39). Copyright 1929 by the American Psychological Association, and reproduced by permission.]

This paper shows how certain drugs injected into rats can either facilitate or retard recall of a previously learned task.

Hall, M. H. An interview with "Mr. Behaviorist"—B. F. Skinner. *Psychology Today,* 1967, 1(5), 20–23, 68–71.

This article is a fascinating window into the mind of a very important behavioristic psychologist.

REFERENCES

1. Amsel, A. The role of frustrative nonreward in noncontinuous reward situations. *Psychological Bulletin,* 1958, **55,** 102–119.
2. Amsel, A. Frustrative nonreward in partial reinforcement and discrimination learning: some recent history and a theoretical extension. *Psychological Review,* 1962, **69,** 306–328.

3. Amsel, A., & Roussel, J. Motivational properties of frustration: I. Effect on a running response of the addition of frustration to the motivational complex. *Journal of Experimental Psychology,* 1952, **43,** 363–368.

4. Atkinson, R. C., & Shiffrin, R. M. Human memory: a proposed system and its control processes. In K. W. Spence & J. T. Spence (Eds.), *The psychology of learning and motivation: Advances in research and theory.* Vol. 2. New York: Academic Press, 1968.

5. Ausubel, D. P. Early versus delayed review in meaningful learning. *Psychology in the Schools,* 1966, **3,** 195–198.

6. Ausubel, D. P., Schpoont, S. H., & Cukier, L. The influence of intention on the retention of school materials. *Journal of Educational Psychology,* 1957, **48,** 87–92.

7. Ausubel, D. P., Stager, M., & Gaite, A. J. H. Retroactive facilitation in meaningful verbal learning. *Journal of Educational Psychology,* 1968, **59,** 250–255.

8. Baer, D. M. Effect of withdrawal of positive reinforcement on an extinguishing response in young children. *Child Development,* 1961, **32,** 67–74.

9. Bahrick, H. P. Retention curves—facts or artifacts? *Psychological Bulletin,* 1964, **61,** 188–194.

10. Bahrick, H. P., & Bahrick, B. O. A re-examination of interrelations among measures of retention. *Quarterly Journal of Experimental Psychology,* 1964, **16,** 318–324.

11. Brown, R., & McNeill, D. The "tip of the tongue" phenomenon. *Journal of Verbal Learning and Verbal Behavior,* 1966, **5,** 325–337.

12. Bumstead, A. P. Distribution of effort in memorizing prose and poetry. *American Journal of Psychology,* 1940, **53,** 423–427.

13. Campbell, B. A., & Campbell, E. H. Retention and extinction of learned fear in infant and adult rats. *Journal of Comparative and Physiological Psychology,* 1962, **55,** 1–8.

14. Capaldi, E. J., & Senko, M. G. Acquisition and transfer in partial reinforcement. *Journal of Experimental Psychology,* 1962, **63,** 155–159.

15. Capehart, J., Viney, W., & Hulicka, I. M. The effect of effort upon extinction. *Journal of Comparative and Physiological Psychology,* 1958, **51,** 505–507.

16. Cooper, E. H., & Pantle, A. J. The total-time hypothesis in verbal learning. *Psychological Bulletin,* 1967, **68,** 221–234.

17. Cotton, J. W., & Jensen, G. D. Successive acquisitions and extinctions in the T-maze. *Journal of Experimental Psychology,* 1963, **65,** 546–551.

17a. Dallenbach, K. M. Tables vs. graphs as means of presenting experimental results. *American Journal of Psychology,* 1963, **76,** 700–702.

18. Dietze, A. G., & Janes, H. E. Factual memory of secondary school pupils for a short article which they had read a single time. *Journal of Educational Psychology,* 1931, **22,** 667–676.

19. Dufort, R. H., Guttman, N., & Kimble, G. A. One-trial discrimination reversal learning in the white rat. *Journal of Comparative and Physiological Psychology,* 1954, **47,** 248–249.

20. Dufort, R. H., & Kimble, G. A. Changes in response strength with changes in amount of reinforcement. *Journal of Experimental Psychology,* 1956, **51,** 185–191.

21. Ebbinghaus, H. *Über das Gedächtnis.* 1885. Duncker & Humblot. (Translated by H. A. Ruger & C. E. Bussenius as *Memory: A contribution to experimental psychology.* Columbia University College of Education Reprints, No. 3. New York: Teachers College, Columbia University, Bureau of Publications, 1913.)

22. Ellson, D. G. Quantitative studies of the interaction of simple habits. I. Re-

covery from specific and generalized effects of extinction. *Journal of Experimental Psychology,* 1938, **23**, 339–358.

23. Gagné, R. M., & Bassler, O. C. Study of retention of some topics of elementary nonmetric geometry. *Journal of Educational Psychology,* 1963, **54**, 123–131.

24. Gardner, R. A. On box score methodology as illustrated by three reviews of overtraining reversal effects. *Psychological Bulletin,* 1966, **66**, 416–418.

25. Goodman, R. W. An experimental investigation of extinction as a measure of retention. *Journal of Comparative and Physiological Psychology,* 1953, **46**, 194–199.

26. Gordon, K. Class results with spaced and unspaced memorizing. *Journal of Experimental Psychology,* 1925, **8**, 337–343.

27. Guthrie, E. R. *The psychology of human conflict.* New York: Harper, 1938.

28. Harlow, H. F. The formation of learning sets. *Psychological Review,* 1949, **56**, 51–65.

29. Hart, J. T. Second-try recall, recognition, and the memory-monitoring process. *Journal of Experimental Psychology,* 1967, **58**, 193–197.

30. Heron, A. Immediate memory in dialing performance with and without simple rehearsal. *Quarterly Journal of Experimental Psychology,* 1962, **14**, 94–103.

31. Hilgard, E. R., Irvine, R. P., & Whipple, J. E. Rote memorization, understanding, and transfer: an extension of Katona's card-trick experiments. *Journal of Experimental Psychology,* 1953, **46**, 288–292.

32. Hull, C. L. *Principles of behavior. An introduction to behavior theory.* New York: Appleton-Century-Crofts, 1943.

33. Irion, A. L., & Wham, D. S. Recovery from retention loss as a function of amount of pre-recall warming up. *Journal of Experimental Psychology,* 1951, **41**, 242–246.

34. Jenkins, J. G., & Dallenbach, K. M. Oblivescence during sleep and waking. *American Journal of Psychology,* 1924, **35**, 605–612.

35. Jensen, A. R. *Individual differences in learning: Interference factor.* Berkeley: Institute of Human Learning, University of California, 1964. (Report of Cooperative Research Project No. 1867, U. S. Office of Education.)

36. Jones, M. C. The elimination of children's fears. *Journal of Experimental Psychology,* 1924, **7**, 382–390.

37. Klausmeier, H. J., & Check, J. Retention and transfer in children of low, average, and high intelligence. *Journal of Educational Research,* 1962, **55**, 319–322.

38. Klausmeier, H. J., & Goodwin, W. *Learning and human abilities.* (2nd ed.) New York: Harper & Row, 1966.

39. Krueger, W. C. F. The effect of overlearning on retention. *Journal of Experimental Psychology,* 1929, **12**, 71–78.

40. Lauer, D., & Estes, W. K. Successive acquisitions and extinctions of a jumping habit in relation to schedule of reinforcement. *Journal of Comparative and Physiological Psychology,* 1955, **48**, 8–13.

41. Lewis, D. J. Partial reinforcement: A selective review of the literature since 1950. *Psychological Bulletin,* 1960, **57**, 1–28.

42. Lewis, D. J., & Duncan, C. P. Effect of different percentages of money reward on extinction of a lever pulling response. *Journal of Experimental Psychology,* 1956, **52**, 23–27.

43. Mackintosh, N. J. Selective attention in animal discrimination learning. *Psychological Bulletin,* 1965, **64**, 124–150.

44. McGeoch, J. A., & Whitely, P. L. The recall of observed material. *Journal of Educational Psychology,* 1926, **17,** 419–425.
45. Melton, A. W. Implications of short-term memory for a general theory of memory. *Journal of Verbal Learning and Verbal Behavior,* 1963, **2,** 1–21.
46. Michotte, A., & Portych, T. Derixieme étude sur la mémoire logique. La reproduction aprés des intervalles de differentes longuers. *Etudes Psychologie,* 1914, **1,** 237–264. [As reported in R. S. Woodworth & H. Schlosberg *Experimental psychology.* (Rev. ed.) New York: Holt, 1954. P. 720.]
47. Miller, N. E., & Stevenson, S. S. Agitated behavior of rats during experimental extinction and a curve of spontaneous recovery. *Journal of Comparative Psychology,* 1936, **21,** 205–231.
48. Murdock, B. B., Jr. The retention of individual items. *Journal of Experimental Psychology,* 1961, **62,** 618–625.
49. Norman, D. A. *Memory and attention. An introduction to human information processing.* New York: Wiley, 1969. Pp. 148–156.
50. Paul, C. Effects of overlearning upon single habit reversal in rats. *Psychological Bulletin,* 1965, **63,** 65–72.
51. Peterson, L. R. Short-term memory. *Scientific American,* 1966, **215,** 90–95.
52. Peterson, L. R., & Peterson, M. J. Short-term retention of individual verbal items. *Journal of Experimental Psychology,* 1959, **58,** 193–198.
53. Postman, L. Short-term memory and incidental learning. In A. W. Melton (Ed.), *Categories of human learning.* New York: Academic Press, 1964. Pp. 145–201.
54. Postman, L., & Rau, L. Retention as a function of the method of measurement. *University of California Publications in Psychology,* 1957, **8,** 217–270.
55. Postman, L., & Stark, K. Role of response availability in transfer and interference. *Journal of Experimental Psychology,* 1969, **79,** 168–177.
56. Pressey, S. L., Robinson, F. P., & Horrocks, J. E. *Psychology in education.* New York: Harper, 1959.
57. Pubols, B. H., Jr. Reminiscence in motor learning as a function of prerest distribution of practice. *Journal of Experimental Psychology,* 1960, **60,** 155–161.
58. Razran, G. Partial reinforcement of salivary CR's in adult human subjects: Preliminary study. *Psychological Reports,* 1955, **1,** 409–416.
59. Riley, D. A. The influence of amount of prerest learning on reminiscence effects in paired-associate learning. *Journal of Experimental Psychology,* 1957, **54,** 8–14.
60. Rockway, M. R., & Duncan, C. P. Pre-recall warming-up in verbal retention. *Journal of Experimental Psychology,* 1952, **43,** 305–312.
61. Shiffrin, R. M., & Atkinson, R. C. Storage and retrieval processes in long-term memory. *Psychological Review,* 1969, **76,** 179–193.
62. Simley, O. A. The relation of subliminal to supraliminal learning. *Archives of Psychology,* 1933, No. 146.
63. Smeltz, J. R. Study of the retention of learnings in high school chemistry for a period of one year. *Science Education,* 1966, **50,** 359–370.
64. Spence, K. W. *Behavior theory and conditioning.* New Haven, Conn.: Yale University Press, 1956.
65. Sperling, G. The information available in brief visual presentations. *Psychological Monographs,* 1960, **74**(11, Whole No. 498).
66. Sperling, S. E. Reversal learning and resistance to extinction: A review of the rat literature. *Psychological Bulletin,* 1965, **63,** 281–287.
67. Sperling, S. E. Reversal learning and resistance to extinction: A supplementary report. *Psychological Bulletin,* 1965, **64,** 310–312.

68. Spitzer, H. F. Studies in retention. *Journal of Educational Psychology,* 1939, **30,** 641–656.
69. Sterrett, M. D., & Davis, R. A. The permanence of school learning: A review of studies. *Educational Administration and Supervision,* 1954, **40,** 449–460.
70. Stroud, J. B. *Psychology in education.* (Rev. ed.) New York: Longmans, Green, 1956.
71. Stroud, J. B., & Johnson, E. The temporal position of reviews. *Journal of Educational Research,* 1942, **35,** 618–622.
72. Tolman, E. C. *Purposive behavior in animals and men.* New York: Appleton-Century, 1932. P. 71.
73. Tulving, E., & Pearlstone, Z. Availability versus accessibility of information in memory for words. *Journal of Verbal Learning and Verbal Behavior,* 1966, **5,** 381–391.
74. Tyler, D. W., Wortz, E. C., & Bitterman, M. E. The effect of random and alternating partial reinforcement on resistance to extinction in the rat. *American Journal of Psychology,* 1953, **66,** 57–65.
75. Underwood, B. J. Studies of distributed practice: XII. Retention following varying degrees of original learning. *Journal of Experimental Psychology,* 1954, **47,** 294–300.
76. Underwood, B. J. Interference and forgetting. *Psychological Review,* 1957, **64,** 49–60.
77. Underwood, B. J. Ten years of massed practice on distributed practice. *Psychological Review,* 1961, **68,** 229–247.
78. Underwood, B. J. Forgetting. *Scientific American,* 1964, **210,** 91–99.
79. Underwood, B. J., Keppel, G., & Schulz, R. W. Studies of distributed practice: XXII. Some conditions which enhance retention. *Journal of Experimental Psychology,* 1962, **64,** 355–363.
80. Underwood, B. J., & Richardson, J. The influence of meaningfulness, intralist similarity, and serial position on retention. *Journal of Experimental Psychology,* 1956, **52,** 119–126.
81. Waugh, N. C., & Norman, D. A. Primary memory. *Psychological Review,* 1965, **72,** 89–104.
82. Wendt, G. R. An interpretation of inhibition of conditioned reflexes as competition between reaction systems. *Psychological Review,* 1936, **43,** 258–281.
83. Whitely, P. L., & McGeoch, J. The curve of retention for poetry. *Journal of Educational Psychology,* 1928, **19,** 471–479.
84. Woodworth, R. S., & Schlosberg, H. *Experimental psychology.* (Rev. ed.) New York: Holt, 1954. P. 70.
85. Zeaman, D. Response latency as a function of the amount of reinforcement. *Journal of Experimental Psychology,* 1949, **39,** 466–483.

6

THINKING AND CONCEPT FORMATION

How human beings think is the theme of most of psychology. Thinking calls upon—activates—the thinker's nervous system, intelligence, social attitudes and habits, and developmental patterns—some of the areas of research in psychology. Historically, psychology began as a discipline concerned with thinking, or consciousness. Philosophers speculated about mental content; one, John Locke, felt that the mind was blank at birth and that mental content was accumulated with experience. Thinking was a process of associating the impressions and awarenesses experienced; it was also a process of reflecting on experiences through the use of memory. Locke's view is similar to the contemporary attitude that man's mind is analogous to a machine that receives stimuli, records them, and responds. From Locke's model, thinking and reacting would be difficult to separate conceptually, since one would be dependent upon the other.

A different view of the mind was held by philosophers like René Descartes. Descartes believed that man's mind existed and was not the entire creation of experience.

Two theories about the thought processes, or mental content, have prevailed in psychology. One has been that thought is dependent upon a multitude of simple associations, mental content then being created by the formation and expression of these associations. The opposing theory is that thinking is basically different from the activity involving the association of stimuli and responses. The association point of view has some-times been referred to as a uni-process theory; its counterpart, with thinking a deliberate and unique process, has been called a dual process theory (21). The seventeenth-century philosophers, Locke and Descartes, were early exponents of these two theories about thought and thinking.

René Descartes

Descartes (1596–1650) lived a generation earlier than Locke (1632–1704). Descartes' concept of the mind was rooted in his serious concern that man's mind or soul existed as a basic element in man's dual nature (8). The term "Cartesian dualism" is often used as a kind of shorthand to describe Descartes concept of man being constituted of matter or body (extended substance) and mind or soul (unextended substance). The two substances interacted to influence behavior—the mind on the body and vice versa—but the interaction did not clarify the basic nature of extended and unextended substance as separate aspects of man's nature. The body, or extended substance, operated much like a machine, its behavior the result of reflexlike activity typical of the overt response patterns associated with a behaving person. Unextended substance, or the soul—mind, was responsible for the kind of mental behavior asso-ciated with willing and perceiving. Unextended substance was responsi-ble for much of what are now termed the higher mental processes.

Integral to Descartes' concept of mind was his belief in innate ideas, ideas that did not depend on experience to exist. This concept of innate ideas as an element of mental organization implied that the basic postu-lates of all knowledge were inherent in the mind itself (18). For Descartes, two such ideas were God and self. Eby (18) describes the educational implications of Descartes theory:

> He (Descartes) believed that all primary ideas are innate, and that the growth of knowledge consists merely in drawing out their implications. The true method of science, therefore, is deductive in its procedure. The funda-mental process of learning is rational, constructive thinking. After (Descartes) all the great educational reformers demanded that knowledge must possess those qualities of certainty, clearness, and positiveness which characterize rational thinking. . . . Even more significant than this change of attitude, however, was the radical antagonism between the Cartesian theory of innate ideas and the principle of sense perception as the origin of knowledge. This deep-seated difference was to appear later as the dominant problem of both philosophy and education.

Descartes' views can be traced through psychology as they later influenced Kant, the Gestalt psychologists, and present-day existentialists in psychology. The concept that man's mind is an entity apart from his physical nature can be found in many contemporary postures offered to explain the human being as distinct from the animal in the world. Descartes had little to say about the working of the mind, but he did suggest that the answer to the organization of the thought process was not to be found in a persistent scrutiny of man's reflexes. Although it is opposed by many psychologists for its inadequacy as a basis for a science of behavior, dualism is nonetheless present in many forms in psychology—and will continue to be present in psychological theory until unitary theories emerge to account for a wider range of human behavior than is now explained by most theoretical constructs in psychology.

John Locke

The source of knowledge, according to Locke's philosophy, was the senses. For him, mind was a system of associations involving ideas—the units of the mind. Mental content consisted of these units, or ideas, which were derived from experience. To illustrate how this worked, Locke offered his tabula rasa concept. The tabula rasa was a wax tablet that could record impressions made by a stylus. Symbols and words could be etched on the tabula rasa, just as ideas can be recorded on the brain. Impressions are made on the brain through the mechanism of the senses' transmitting stimuli to the brain. These sense impressions, or images, are the simple ideas which form the basis for mental activity. In this analogy, the mind appears like a passive and receptive receiver of sense data. However, the senses contribute only one source of knowledge; the other source is generated from reflections of past experiences. This reflective activity provides ideas to be added to mental content and thus augments it.

The ideas, or elements, of mental content form associations with each other that group into concepts, abstractions, and principles. This, Locke's concept of mind, was particularly opposed to Descartes' belief in innate ideas. Locke could see no basis for the origin of ideas other than through sense transmission or reflection. These two sources of mental content, sensation and reflection, formed the foundation of a theory of association of ideas that is still present in the psychological views of learning theorists such as Thorndike, Hull, and Skinner.

Contemporary Views of Thinking

Contemporary contributions to theories of thinking have been made by many present day psychologists. A recent report on experimental studies in thinking (17) presents research in problem solving, mental set, information and language processes, concept learning, induction, and verbal mediation, to cite only a few of the areas of experimentation associated with the problem of thinking.

One theorist whose work will be considered in more detail in Chapter 10 is Jean Piaget. Piaget's studies of mental processes in both children and adults were accomplished through observation and inquiry rather than from experimentation; nevertheless, his writings have greatly influenced the field of child development. Piaget's contributions about childhood thinking come, for the most part, from his observations on the development of intelligence in children. Rowland and McGuire (29) report on Piaget's identification of a number of major themes, one of which emphasized a continuous and progressive change in children's thinking and behavior which marked specific stages of development in a fixed order of sequence. (See Chapter 10.) Piaget also stressed the relationship of thought to action and the logical aspects of children's thinking when viewed within the framework of the child's developmental level.

Piaget has described those developmental stages as relatively constant and invariant in their sequence. These stages, however, should not be thought of as occurring within fixed periods of time. To impose a cognitive structure before the child has reached a readiness for it would lead only to verbal learning and not to mental growth (29). Readiness appears to play an important role in mental growth and, like the stages of development, is not related to specific intervals of time. According to Piaget (27), conceptual thinking, as a first step to the development of logical thought in the child, begins when perceptual development first starts at the infancy end of the sensorimotor stage.

The development of the conceptual system takes place in the child independent of perceptual and sensorimotor adaptations to reality. Although the developmental systems represented in the child by perception and conceptual activity interact, they do not become the same system. The acquisition of conceptual thought is influenced greatly by the eventual appearance of a relationship between the memory of past experiences and present thinking, which allows previous knowledge to have an effect on thought. According to Baldwin (3):

> The first step in cognitive representation is the mental image. Out of this beginning a variety of representative schema gradually develop. . . . The child's concepts begin as piecemeal acquisitions that are not coherently organized. Thus, he does not behave consistently, particularly when he must integrate temporally separate events. Before the final development of coherent logical structures, there is a more concrete intuitive stage where the child's

imagery becomes quite serviceable for picturing and predicting the effects of various changes; but even at best this stage results in only a limited predictability.

The conceptual system is distinguished from the sensorimotor system and the perceptual system in that conceptual thought can integrate information which has spatial or temporal attributes more effectively than can the other two systems. Piaget believes that the relationship between intelligence and thinking begins toward the conclusion of the sensorimotor stage, when the child reflects the influence of imagery in imagination and play. His entrance into a preoperational level of intelligence is characterized by egocentric thought processes that make little distinction between reality and imagination. For such a child, a cloud is alive because it moves; dolls should obey when given a command; parents are omnipotent because they create and control. The preoperational child's thinking makes no distinction between the real and the imagined world.

The older child who shifts from a preoperational intelligence to one that is concretely operational expresses a more adultlike pattern of thinking, for he is able to utilize the thinking of others as part of his conceptual process. He is also less egocentric and so can relate objects with ideas about objects. Piaget believes that the preoperational child, whose behavior depends to a great degree on perception, focuses on single rather than multiple dimensions of problems. The concretely operational child depends less on perception and more on reasoning and analysis; thus he can deal more effectively with the potential of response rather than with just the actuality.

The child who is formally operational in his intellectual activity can project a wide range of possibilities in advance of actual exposure to problems. The dimensions of adult thought, capable of abstraction, anticipation, symbolic representation, and empathy, exemplify the formally operational intelligence.

A recent book by the contemporary theorist Daniel Berlyne (5), *Structure and Direction in Thinking*, shows Piaget's influence in the analysis of thinking in terms of motivational states and behaviors relating to the organization of thought. Berlyne's emphasis on the relationship between motivation, curiosity, conflict, and reinforcement in learning has helped to make exploratory behavior and curiosity subjects for study in experimental investigations of the learning process.

Berlyne believes that conflict is a necessary condition for learning since it leads to a type of behavior which he calls epistemic and which represents the activities necessary for building up knowledge (7). This might include such activities as thinking, observing, asking questions, or imitation. Conflict becomes the arousal condition for the drive which motivates exploratory behavior. Epistemic curiosity is the motivating condition which makes for epistemic behavior. Epistemic curiosity has its origins in conceptual conflict due to discrepancies in thoughts, beliefs or attitudes (6).

Berlyne (6) has identified several types of conceptual conflicts:

1. *Surprise*, which involves a phenomenon contrary to the observer's beliefs—and therefore unexpected. For example, students uninstructed in the expansion properties of metals might be shown a metal ball just large enough to go through a ring. After it is heated, the ball sits on top of the ring. Here the conflict is due to the students' surprise, which in turn creates an epistemic curiosity to motivate and direct further thinking about the problem. The initial conflict is reduced when, through instruction or discovery, the reality of the situation is established.

2. *Doubt* is a conflict between a tendency to believe and the tendency to disbelieve.

3. *Perplexity* occurs when a problem has a number of logical routes to solution but only one correct one—and that one is not known to the person so confronted.

4. *Bafflement* is the conflict that occurs when a situation involves irreconcilable demands. For example, the middle of a desert would not be the place to chart one's location.

5. *Contradiction* is the conflict resulting from seeming incompatible information, i.e., information too limited or incomplete to verify fact. For example, children who learn how plants make use of chlorophyll and sunlight in photosynthesis in order to exist find a contradiction when introduced to fungi, which exist without chlorophyll and sunlight. This conceptual conflict is resolved, and becomes reinforcing, when the children learn more about plant life and discover that the rules of life for green plants may not be the rules of life for other plants.

Reducing a conceptual conflict is achieved by direct thinking to acquire and/or reject information relevant to the conflict-producing problem. Conceptual conflict acts as a motivational stimulus, initiating and preserving thinking. It also introduces cues for variations in the direction of thinking.

Another important contemporary theorist is Jerome Bruner. Bruner's writings on thinking, concept formation, and education have been widely accepted by those who differ with the traditional views held by John Locke. Bruner's contributions to psychology are many, but they cluster around establishing a conceptual framework for thinking that could be useful in defining learning and instruction. An early major work (12), *A Study of Thinking*, summarizes his formulations concerning thinking. From research done at the Center for Cognitive Studies at Harvard University, Bruner developed a frame of reference for cognition that establishes learning and categorization as its basic elements (30). Bruner's two types of categorizing in thinking are identity categories, which emphasize the common attributes of stimuli, and equivalence categories, which emphasize the manner in which stimuli share commonality because of some equivalent attribute. Categorization in thinking is a reflection of the thinker's culture influenced by such factors as language and life style.

In a major statement of his position, Bruner (10) distinguished between three basic information processing models representing cognitive organization in man:

1. *Enactive representation,* a process of representing past events through motor responses.

2. *Iconic representation,* in which percepts and images are organized in a selective fashion to represent events.

3. *Symbolic representation,* in which information processing takes place by means of a symbol system, such as a language, with the environment being represented by features of the symbol system.

The transformation from enactive representation of information in thought to symbolic representation is a developmental one, and involves the uses of language by the child in learning to represent reality with verbal symbols. Verbal symbols give range to childrens' imagery and enable them to integrate experience into a longer sequence than that involved in their immediate memory of events.

Bruner's most recent writings about education have been directed toward developing a theory of instruction to parallel what is already known about learning. His recent statement (11), *Toward a Theory of Instruction,* is based on the belief that children are innately curious and enjoy learning if it is organized appropriately. Bruner believes that most children are capable of learning much more at earlier ages than has been realized. The following ideas are basic to his theory of instruction:

1. Education is the process of reorganizing experience.

2. Knowing is a process of intellectual activity, not its product. This process should involve the student, not as a retainer of knowledge, but as a participant in the process of discovery.

3. Learning is intrinsically rewarding. External reinforcement may control specific acts of behavior, but reinforcement does not nourish the intellect.

4. Subject matter reflects a way of thinking about a body of knowledge or a discipline.

5. The preparation of teachers should emphasize conjecture, inquiry, and problem solving so that they will be prepared to teach discovery processes in the classroom.

6. The teaching of understandings begins with the teacher's understanding.

Bruner feels that education has become too mechanistic, emphasizing as it does retention and factual knowledge rather than problem solving and discovery. If education neglects man's unique cognitive skills it can not recognize man's potential as a thinking human being.

These, then, are some of the historical and contemporary theories about thinking and cognition. Although problem solving was introduced in Chapter 3, let us consider this area again as a specific aspect of thinking.

Problem Solving

Problem solving in human beings has been of concern to twentieth-century experimental psychologists, but the rate of the research has been low compared with some other topics in psychology, and the research does not lend itself to a systematic organization (17). One obstacle has been a suitable operational definition for thinking and problem solving. Duncan (16), in a review of problem-solving studies, states that:

> The defining characteristics (in thinking and problem solving research) most frequently mentioned are the integration and organization of past experience when the definition refers to all of thinking, and the dimension of discovery of correct response when reference is made to problem solving specifically. Problem solving is considered to be fairly high on the discovery dimension, as one way of distinguishing it from conditioning and rote learning which are presumed to involve relatively little response discovery.

Consider two classic problems usually cited as examples of problem solving. In one, a chimpanzee is placed in a cage with a bunch of bananas suspended over his head. In the cage are two sticks, one with a connector on one end so that the other stick can be fitted to it to make one long pole. The problem the chimpanzee faces is getting a banana to eat. He cannot reach the overhead bunch, and each stick is too short to be of help. If he solves the problem, he will have discovered that the sticks fit together and can be used as a pole to hit the bananas, and thus knock some of them down. In another problem situation a person is placed in a room that has two strings suspended from the ceiling, several feet apart. The problem for the subject is to tie the strings together although they are too far apart to reach one while holding the other. The subject is given a screw driver or a pair of scissors to use in solving the problem. The solution is to use the implement to weight one string and swing the string back and forth while holding the other string. The solution involves discovering this use for the implement. The illustration and explanation of the Maier two-string problem (see Chapter 3) is the prototype for problems of this type.

Very often problems are difficult to solve because they involve a novel conceptualization—and past experience becomes a hindrance. Such experience predetermines the particular response to a situation. The readiness to respond in a certain way is known as a *set*. Not everyone faced with the problem of the two strings (above) would think of using the screw driver or scissors as a weight on one string because these tools are usually associated with other activities. But many familiar objects have a variety of uses other than their most common ones. An interesting game to play, one which demonstrates the difficulty of overcoming set, is to list as many uses for an object as you can think of. The game really becomes interesting when there is a time limit on it. For example, a brick can be used as a building material or a door stop, but it can also be used as a bed warmer or a support for shelves.

Each person's approach to solving most problems is conditioned by the types of sets he brings to their solution. Past attitudes, experiences, and memories influence the formation of sets that predetermine responses. Sets can also be established by instructions. For instance someone instructed to speedily complete a test may do just that—at the expense of accuracy.

Sets usually increase the probability that certain responses will occur in a problem-solving episode. (By the same token, they also decrease the probability that other responses will occur.) The concept of set has wide application in psychological experimentation aside from research on problem solving. For example, Wittrock (39) reports on an experiment in which student teachers were told that their final grades in educational psychology and in student teaching were dependent upon the amount of gain shown by pupils in their classes. Analysis of pretest and posttest information revealed that those who had been instructed to teach for gain; i.e., those whose instructions provided a set for pupil gain, earned significantly higher grades than did those student teachers who had not been given the instructional set. Wittrock (39) points out that sets can be developed either by appropriately reinforcing trial and error performance, or by giving verbal instructions that are sufficiently motivational.

Here is a common puzzle problem, which gives an example of the persistence of set in problem solving. Below are nine dots arranged in three rows of three dots each.

The problem is to connect the dots by using only four straight lines without lifting the pencil from the paper or retracing a line. Most persons approach the problem by testing hypotheses which conceive of the dots as points on and within a box, with the four lines to be drawn projected within the box rather than beyond the dots. In other words, it is generally thought that the usable space is contained within the dots rather than within and around the dots. The solution to the problem is:

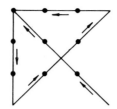

People usually tend to persist in sets that have proved successful and have been reinforced by success. Most everyday problems do not require novel or unique responses for their solution. In fact, because of the commonality of many of our problems, we develop standard hypotheses which we tend to test first. The persistent recurrence of hypotheses become sets for that particular kind of solution. (See Chapter 3 for a discussion indicating that sets can be learned for particular tasks.)

One type of set common to all behavior is *functional fixedness*. Functional fixedness is the inability to use an object in a unique or unfamiliar way; i.e., the inability to see uses for objects other than those which were intended. This type of set is an instance of a fixed association that is difficult to overcome, especially if the objects in question are often used. Each successful use of an object in a usual way reinforces the set for its future use in the same way.

Our knowledge of how problem solving takes place is very incomplete. Duncan (16) concludes his survey of research on problem solving by stating that few, if any, variables found in experiments demonstrate sufficient stability to be used to support any principles of problem solving with any degree of certainty. The influence of sets is well established, as is the relationship between the organization of the elements in a problem and the solution to the problem. Individual differences in problem solving is well established; in fact, the ability to solve problems is reflected in many tests of intelligence. There is much evidence that, at least with intelligent responses, solutions to problems are not just the result of much trial and error behavior. Problem solving seems to involve a new insight into the nature of the problem together with a shift in the way the problem is perceived (31).

Creativity and Problem Solving

The creative person is often described as one whose ability to present unique and unusual solutions to problems or to employ different methods in solving problems sets him apart from most other people. Getzels and Jackson (19) studied two groups of students, one high in intelligence but low in creativity and the other high in creativity but lower in intelligence, and found that the two groups approached problem-solving situations differently. Educators have tended to define giftedness and creativity in terms of level of intelligence. The Getzels and Jackson study indicates that creativity and intelligence may not be so closely related—contrary to a belief often advanced to define creativity. According to Getzels and Jackson (19):

> The members of the high IQ group possess the demonstrated ability to perform with excellence in the type of problem-solving tasks common to the conventional intelligence test. They do not apparently possess the ability to perform with the same excellence on the type of cognitive tasks included in the "creativity" instruments. They may be able to define the word "homunculus" with ease or to supply quickly the "unique" missing digit in a number series, but they have less facility with problems requiring them to think of several novel uses for a stereotyped object like a brick or a new ending to a familiar fable.
>
> The reverse is true for the members of the high creative group. They do not do as well as the high IQ subjects on the intelligence test problems. But their performance is very striking indeed on tasks calling for inventiveness and originality.

Barron (4) reported a study done at the University of California in which the characteristics of creative painters, writers, physicians, physicists, biologists, economists, and anthropologists were assessed through many different testing methods. His conclusions about the creative artist, and to a lesser extent about the creative scientist, indicate that:

1. The creative person is especially observant and values accuracy in observation.
2. The creative person usually seeks to call attention to the unobserved by expressing part–truths about phenomena.
3. The creative person perceives things as others do, but he also perceives them as others do not.
4. His thinking is more independent and acute than that of others.
5. The creative person values correct perception highly.
6. His thinking is capable of involving many ideas at one time and of synthesizing them in a more unique and unusual way than can the noncreative person.
7. He expends a great deal of energy in thought.
8. The creative person tends to seek tension and conflict, especially in the cognitive area, because of the reinforcement derived from its release.
9. His thinking reveals a use of imagination and fantasy indicative of a greater than usual expression of the unconscious.
10. The creative person has a very broad and flexible awareness of self and so can tolerate contradictory or ambiguous traits better than most noncreative persons can.
11. The creative person is less inhibited by the demands of the unconscious and

is more willing to allow unconscious impulses to be considered at a conscious level than are most other people.

It is necessary to find out much more about the dimensions of creativity. Certainly the creative individual brings to his behavior an originality and refreshing newness not found in the behavior of others, but the causes of this originality are not known. Certainly educators would profit from knowing whether creativity can be taught. If being creative is nothing more than thinking differently and productively, then it should be possible to discover strategies for teaching creativity as a skill. But if creative behavior begins early in the developmental relationships between parents and children, intervention at the public school level may be too late. In his studies of intelligence Guilford (20) indicates that the conceptualizations presently involved in assessing intellectual abilities are too narrow and that the intelligence tests used in schools neglect many important abilities which contribute to problem solving and creative performance. Unless these factors are identified and diagnosed, the educational system will not be able to provide the intervention necessary to change them. The development of instructional strategies for problem-solving behaviors remains one of the unfulfilled challenges to education.

Concept Learning

One aspect of the study of thinking involves a kind of learning that is of fundamental importance in human behavior. This special type of learning is called concept learning. What distinguishes it from other types of learning is that it has a different outcome. An individual who has learned a concept is able to make the appropriate response to stimuli he has never before experienced. To illustrate what is involved in concept learning, examine the designs in Fig. 6-1 and the appropriate responses. After going over the figures carefully, the student will probably be able to give the appropriate "name" to each of the designs; i.e., he will have learned to associate the response with the stimulus. Now look at the new set of designs given in Fig. 6-2. If the student has learned the concept involved, he will be able to make a better than chance score in naming

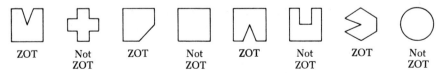

| ZOT | Not ZOT | ZOT | Not ZOT | ZOT | Not ZOT | ZOT | Not ZOT |

Fig. 6-1. Examples of ZOT and Not-ZOT figures from which the concept of "ZOTness" can be learned.

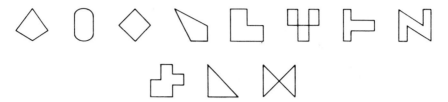

Fig. 6-2. Test figures for the concept ZOT.

each of the designs in Fig. 6-2 even though they were not seen before in this context.

Concept, then, means that within a group of heterogeneous stimuli some of the stimuli are recognizably similar to each other and different from the rest. A concept is learned when one distinguishes the commonality in stimuli—even if the group of stimuli is unfamiliar. The latter point should be emphasized; i.e., the capacity for identifying new examples of the concept, because otherwise only ordinary paired associate learning may have occurred. Certainly, in the task given above it would be very simple for most people to make the appropriate response to a particular figure and yet not be aware of any special way in which the figures are similar to or different from each other. Such learning would only be like learning to say one nonsense syllable after being shown another. Another example would be found in teaching children the concept of honesty. One way to do so is to give examples of behavior that can be labeled honest or not honest. The danger here is that children will learn to give the right response and yet not be able to identify new examples of behavior as honest or dishonest. When children have learned the concept of honesty, they will be able to recognize appropriate new examples.

Concepts are often conveniently labeled; i.e., there is a handy verbal definition of the similarity among a set of stimuli. For example, the word "triangle" is a convenient label for the knowledge that enables us to see the similarity in the row of visual stimuli in Fig. 6-3. However, psychologists believe that it is the pattern of responses that identifies a concept and not the label. Thus, Rensch, a German investigator, has been able to show that elephants can be trained to distinguish various geometric figures and then discriminate successfully patterns never before encountered. Figure 6-4 presents the stimuli used by Rensch (28)

Fig. 6-3. Examples of the concept triangle.

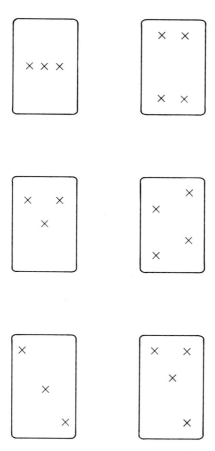

Fig. 6-4. Stimulus figures for a number concept learned by an elephant. The elephant was originally trained to discriminate between the two top cards: The XXX card was positive and its choice rewarded by a piece of bread; the XXXX card was negative and its choice went unrewarded. Without further training the elephant was able to make the correct choices from cards similar to the four lower cards. [From "The Intelligence of Elephants" by B. Rensch (28). Copyright 1957 by Scientific American, Inc. All rights reserved.]

in his experiment together with a brief explanation of the study. The elephant probably operates without a verbal label, but a concept exists nonetheless. Often we are forced to infer the existence or nature of a concept from the pattern of choices an individual makes, without knowing what special label he might be using—or if, indeed, he is using one at all.

Human beings with their highly developed verbal skills often use verbal labels or symbols for concepts, and the labels may be of some help in making the correct pattern of choices in identifying examples of a concept. However, the relationship between the capacity to verbalize a concept (the ability to recite the correct definition) and the ability to make the correct identifications is by no means a perfect one. The usual procedure in research on concept learning is for the experimenter to ask subjects to identify examples of the concept to be learned (e.g., "Tell me, is this a DAG or not a DAG?"), but usually the subjects are also asked to give a verbal statement of the concept if they can. Subjects are often able to make correct identifications before they can give a definition (24, 35). It is also true that people can sometimes give the correct definition without being able to make as many correct identifications as might be expected (33). It becomes evident that the concept "label" is just that, a convenient tag, and that knowing it does not ensure correct performance. We will return to this point shortly when we discuss the teaching of concepts.

Stimulus Generalization and Concepts

What happens if a dog that has been trained to salivate when he hears a given tone (i.e., when a conditioned response has been established) hears a new tone, one close to the training stimulus? There will probably be a salivary response—the two stimuli, the original and the new, being equivalent to some degree—and observers will conclude that stimulus generalization has occurred. Note the similarity to concept learning: A subject is trained to make a particular response to certain stimuli, and then he is tested for stimuli close to the ones on which he was trained. To the extent that the stimuli are equivalent, the same response could be expected to occur.

When a concept is learned what happens is that a group of stimuli is sampled, from which the subject learns to make a special response to certain stimuli and a different response to other stimuli. Concept learning is very much akin to the situation in which an animal is trained to respond to a particular stimulus and to all other stimuli that are close enough to it to be regarded as equivalent. The principal difference is that in conditioning experiments it is not usually intended to produce equivalence of stimuli, whereas it is in concept learning. However, if the subject cannot perceive the similarity of the stimuli, concept learning cannot occur.

Concept learning usually takes place, as does other learning, in a setting of reinforcements for particular responses. Thus, a small child may initially make the response "doggie" to nearly any animal; but the adults around him, impatient with such inaccuracy, will immediately begin to administer appropriate reinforcements. "Yes, nice doggie" or

"No, not a doggie. A horsie." As the universe of dogs is sampled, the pattern of reinforcements will be differentiated for various characteristics of animals, and gradually the concept "dog" will be developed, with several defining characteristics. Soon the child will be able to correctly identify specimens he has never before seen; i.e., he will respond to stimuli whose values lie adjacent to previously observed (and reinforced) stimuli.

It seems unlikely that in most concept-learning situations the learner waits passively for the stimulus and the correct answer. Actually, the learner is likely to form hypotheses, or ideas, about the nature of the concept, and his hypotheses will then lead toward biases in his responses (9). If evidence proves a hypothesis is correct, it will be strengthened; if it is not, it will be weakened. For example, if the child decides that dogs have four legs, and then, when a cat passes by, he learns it is not a dog, his hypothesis is weakened and may be destroyed. However, if it is a dog that next appears, the child's hypothesis works and may be strengthened even if it is wrong or, as in this case, incomplete. Concept learning often involves eliminating all but the correct hypothesis.

A concept may involve only one attribute of a stimulus, such as "red things," or "redness," or it may involve several attributes at once, such as "soft, spherical red things." The concepts that we are most familiar with involve conjunctions of attributes (12). A *conjunctive* concept requires the joint presence of several defining attributes or characteristics. Thus, the conjunctive concept "university" is comprised of several attributes: professors, laboratories, libraries, a graduate school. Taken separately, none of these attributes is sufficient. There are, however, certain important concepts that are *disjunctive;* i.e., one or more of a group of certain critical attributes identifies the concept. An obvious example of a disjunction is the concept of "ill." Any or all of these signs suggest illness: elevated temperature, prolonged pain, high white blood count. Many more disjunctions or partial disjunctions are also familiar: (a) a "good job" pays a high salary and/or permits a good deal of personal freedom; (b) "real estate" consists of land and/or buildings; (c) a "ball" is a pitch thrown outside the vertical and/or horizontal boundaries of the strike zone. Although disjunctions are common, there is evidence that they are more difficult to learn than conjunctions (12, 38). However, Haygood and Bourne (23) show that efficiency in solving any kind of concept problem improves with practice.

Still another kind of concept is the *relational* concept, which is defined by the relationship between two or more attributes of a complex stimulus. For example, the concept "fat man" is relational because here the relationship involves height and weight, and a fat man is heavier than he is tall. The concept "pretentious" is probably relational, for pretentiousness depends on the relationship of several aspects of an object. It might be pretentious for a plumber to drive a Cadillac, but it would not be pretentious for a bank president to do so. Very little is known about learning relational concepts, but it is clear that they are common and constitute a potentially important learning problem.

It is easy to construct concept learning situations in the laboratory, where concepts can be studied with highly simplified materials and limited by definite, consistent relationships. Real life is not so simple, and many of the concepts we must learn involve less than certain relationships between stimulus attributes and concept. For example, if asked to identify a dog from the indistinct silhouette of an animal on a screen, size would be a clue, and within a certain range of sizes the shadow could, indeed, be of a dog. However, either extreme in size would make identification much less certain. Another example: If a man speaks German fluently, is it absolutely certain that he is a German? To speak fluent German makes it only a probability that the speaker is German. It is more difficult to learn concepts for which the relationships of attributes are less than certain (9).

A vast amount of learning is conceptual; i.e., it involves learning an idea or principle that can be applied in situations not previously encountered. It is important to understand, then, what facilitates or retards such learning.

Efficient Learning of Concepts

Some kinds of concepts are more difficult to learn than others; and even among concepts of the same general kind—e.g., conjunctive concepts—there are variations in difficulty. For the most part, these variations reflect differences in how the concepts are learned rather than differences inherent in the concepts themselves. For example, learning an "easy" concept can be made difficult if a misleading or inconsistent reinforcement is given. (The person who is told that it is all right to keep the extra change the store clerk mistakenly gives him can only have a confused concept of honesty.)

It should be apparent that a concept cannot be learned if the subject cannot distinguish among the stimuli he is shown. To teach a child the concept of "square" as opposed to "rectangle," the examples used must not only be clearly distinguishable, they must also be within the discriminative power of the child. However, even if the child can discriminate, he will acquire concepts more easily if the stimuli values are striking than if they are slight (1, 32). Concepts of widely disparate stimuli values are probably easier to learn because the stimulus dimension is more salient, more demanding of attention. Note, however, that the stimuli in concept learning are complex, that is, they have more than just critical attributes. Obviously, a concept of size would be more easily learned if the size differences were marked; but what would happen if the concept to be learned was based not on size but on color? Concepts can be made easier to learn if the critical aspects of the stimuli are more outstanding and the irrelevant aspects less so.

A concept of more complex stimuli, i.e., more dimensions on which they differ, may be difficult to learn. Experiments by Archer, Bourne, and Brown (2) show clearly that the more distracting aspects a stimulus has, the more difficult a concept becomes. For example, if the squares and rectangles the small child is learning to distinguish are different in size, the concept would have a specifiable level of difficulty. If color is added to the stimulus, the concept would be more difficult; and if the examples are placed in different positions on a page, the concept would be even more difficult. In fact, the difficulty of the concept would increase out of proportion to the number of distracting elements added, producing a curve like that in Fig. 6-5.

Every concept has two qualities—a positive and a negative. A positive example is one that is in fact an example of the concept. A negative example is one that the concept is not. Thus a square is a positive example of the concept "square," while a rectangle is a negative example. Can we learn from both positive and negative examples? To a great

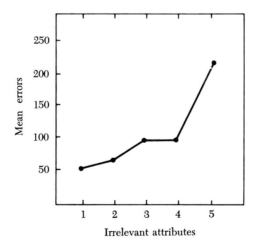

Fig. 6-5. The relationship between the number of errors made in identifying a concept and the extent of irrelevant attributes associated with the concept. [From Archer, Bourne, and Brown (2).]

extent, the answer is yes. Knowing what a concept is not is potentially helpful. However, evidence suggests that people do not learn as well from negative information (33, 36). We seem to have a strong preference for positive information and a rather marked tendency to ignore negative information even when it can be helpful. Therefore, the engineering of efficient concept learning demands a preponderance of positive information and the careful introduction of negative information.

A concept can be taught by selecting a few good examples and presenting them repeatedly. Or numerous examples of the concept could be chosen to be presented frequently. Would one procedure be more effective than the other? For one thing, it is apparent that using a small number of instances over and over incurs a risk of poor sampling—especially with a complex concept, for the instances selected may not be representative. Moreover, if only a few examples are given repeatedly, it is possibile that the subject will learn the correct concept name by rote before he learns the concept. On the other hand, presenting a great number of examples only once might be confusing because the subject has no opportunity to study the instances and to note their critical characteristics. It would seem, then, that a combination of the two methods— i.e., to present a moderate number of instances of the concept with some repetition—would be the most effective way to teach concepts, a conclusion that is consistent with research evidence (14, 34).

But surely the task can be simplified: Why not teach just the principle and dispense with the repeated examples? If a student is to learn the concept of "red squares" as distinguished from other geometric, colored figures, why not just tell him, "The idea is 'red squares' "? Or, to explain "dog" to a child, why not say, "Dogs are four-legged animals, usually about 12 to 30 inches high, with hairy pelts,"? This is a common way of teaching concepts, and it obviously saves much time and effort. However, a good many years ago Hull (24) showed that teaching difficult concepts requires that the subjects be exposed to the actual instances. More recent research (33) confirms Hull's findings and shows that even with simple concepts the stated principle does not teach so effectively as does exposure to both principle and examples. It may be that a verbal statement becomes really meaningful only when the phenomena, or the choices, to which it refers are clear. Although it may be possible for someone to recite a definition perfectly, such ability is no assurance of comprehension. Similarly, on tests of moral judgment, the answers of both delinquent and nondelinquent boys are basically alike (22); it is their behaviors that are different. To summarize: Concepts are more easily learned when: (a) the relevant aspects of the stimuli are salient and the irrelevant aspects are less sharp; (b) the number of irrelevant aspects of the stimuli are minimized; (c) positive examples are employed; (d) a moderate number of examples are given with opportunity for repetition, and (e) both verbal definitions and examples are given to the subject for study.

Concept Attainment in the Classroom

Because classroom conditions do not often permit the type of controls on learning that are found in the experimental laboratory, the procedures for teaching concepts in a classroom setting vary. Teachers often combine different methods designed to make teaching easier while affording students the maximum opportunity to learn. Both laboratory research and analytical analysis have contributed some insights into the problem of teaching concepts in the classroom. One author, Carroll (15), argues that the inductive approaches typical of the laboratory do not parallel the deductive, verbally oriented types of teaching generally found in the classroom and in textbook materials. According to Carroll, concepts are rarely taught in the classroom by a discovery method involving an inductive exposure to a series of positive and negative instances. Instead, teachers generally follow a more deductive method, which may involve elements of discovery but usually depends upon verbal descriptions of the concept together with the statement of a rule or a definition. It is Carroll's feeling that laboratory experiments, to be more relevant to classroom demands, should involve a greater examination of verbalization and deduction in concept learning.

Most classroom teaching involves both deductive and inductive procedures (15). A definition of a concept is composed of elements critical to the total understanding of that concept, but current data do not suggest how these elements should be organized and presented to the student. Experimental data are needed to prescribe the order in which the attributes of a concept should be presented to enhance learning. Haygood and Bourne (23) have investigated the attributes of concepts and the rules used in learning concepts. They concluded that concept attainment can be analyzed by studying the relevant attributes of the concept important to its attainment. Their study of the rules used in learning concepts and the attributes of the concepts suggest that rules and attributes represent two separate problems in learning concepts.

When inductive procedures are used in the classroom they are usually associated with the discovery method of concept attainment, in accord with the laboratory paradigm of presenting positive and negative instances of the concept to be learned. Earlier in the chapter, it was pointed out that presenting more positive than negative instances made concept learning easier (33). Feedback from the experimenter during a concept attainment experiment has a motivational effect on the hypotheses emitted by subjects in determining the rule or principle involved in concept attainment (37). Misinterpretation of the experimenter's negative feedback as punishment for wrong responses rather than as a cue to the information needed to attain the concept tends to inhibit the formation of hypotheses (13). These results of laboratory research on concept attainment have direct relevance for classroom activity, but only in instances where teaching a concept involves this discovery approach. In a classroom, the use of positive or negative instances usually goes much beyond their use in the laboratory (15). Inductive procedures may be valuable in the classroom in that they give the learner opportunities to evaluate his retention and understanding of concept attributes first learned through deduction. (See Chapter 3 for a further discussion of discovery methods.)

Johnson and Stratton (25) evaluated five methods of teaching concepts in the classroom. Of these, four methods generally used by teachers were identified: (a) classifying the concept, (b) defining the concept, (c) using the concept in a sentence, and (d) giving a synonym for the concept. These four methods, together with a mixed method, which combined aspects of the four, were tested in teaching the concepts. The test evaluated the four single methods equally effective while the mixed method was judged best. Johnson and Stratton (25) concluded that the results support the practical efforts of teachers and textbook writers who combine several different methods in teaching and presenting concepts.

An analytical summary of some generalizations and principles supported by research data about teaching concepts is presented by Klausmeier and Goodwin (26):

1. An essential prerequisite to giving objects and events a conceptual identity is the ability to recognize and remember likenesses and differences among these objects and events. Teaching should emphasize the attributes of the concept to be learned.

2. In order to communicate about a concept, some verbalization about the attributes of the concept is necessary. Teaching should emphasize the correct language for the concept to be learned.

3. The manner in which one experiences instances of a concept is related to the stability of the cognitive organization of the concept. Teaching should provide for proper and logical sequences of introductory experiences with a concept.

4. The retention of a stable cognitive organization for a concept is related to the inclusion of such factors as experimentation and productive thinking involving the concept. Teaching should provide for student discovery in concept learning.

5. The successful extention of learned concepts to new learning situations helps to insure the permanence of the concept. Teaching should include a wide range of application possibilities for a concept which is to be learned.

6. Learning to evaluate concepts which have been attained is essential for independence in concept attainment. Teaching should stress the independent evaluation of learned concepts.

Much of classroom learning involves conceptual problems—and learning attributes and rules associated with concepts is essential to solving problems involving concepts. Concepts play a critical role in the structure of a language. Bourne (9) suggests that the capacities for conceptual and verbal behavior develop in a parallel fashion, with important interactions between the two. He points out, too, that research on concept attainment and research on verbal behavior need to be examined as a single process rather than as two discrete avenues of investigation in psychology.

Some educational psychologists feel that to produce solutions to classroom problems, research must bring together theories of learning with models of instruction. Future research on concept attainment, if it is to contribute useful data to educational practice, must begin to reflect experimentation on teaching concepts as well as on learning them.

_____ **Summary**

Thinking has been a subject of study for psychologists since the establishment of psychology as an experimental discipline. Before that, speculation about the nature of consciousness, mental content, and thought had been the work of philosophers. Two in particular, René Descartes and John Locke, led the two major trends in the speculative analysis of thinking. Descartes emphasized man's dual nature and the difference between rational and reflexive mental processes. Locke, on the other hand, felt that mental content was unified and resulted from experience "etching" itself on the mind.

Experimental psychology reflects Locke's beliefs rather than Descartes', and tends to study thinking, or cognition, as a process that results from, and is motivated by, the interaction between man and his surroundings. Jean Piaget, D. E. Berlyne, and Jerome Bruner represent the views of several contemporary psychologists who theorize about thinking and its development. Piaget observed children and young people and developed a theory of cognitive development emphasizing stages of development and the nature of the transitions made from one stage to the next. Berlyne emphasizes the relationship between conflict and epistemic curiosity and exploratory behavior. Bruner has studied cognitive growth in terms of the process of thinking and the way in which it develops through both formal and informal education.

One function of thought is to solve problems—and many factors in problem solving can be studied experimentally. For example, the concept of *set* has been studied extensively. Set is a particular way of thinking about a problem, based on past experience with similar problems. Sets can help solve problems easily if their solutions call for strategies that have been successful before. Sets can also impede problem solving if the problem requires a novel or unique solution.

The ability to depart from the standard behaviors in approaching problems is characteristic of the creative person who seeks solutions involving new and different response patterns. Creativity has recently been the subject of extensive study, but it is still not known if creativity is a trait that can not be taught or a characteristic that responds to suitable instructional techniques.

Teaching concepts is a major classroom activity. Learning a concept involves recognizing similarities and differences between sets of stimuli; if concept learning has taken place the learner is able to identify new examples (i.e., examples other than those used in the original learning) of the concept. Teachers use both inductive and deductive procedures in teaching concepts in the classroom. Other classroom techniques for concept learning, which are often used interchangeably, are giving specific examples or giving definitions. In teaching concepts the teacher should try to emphasize the attributes of the concept to be learned, the correct language involved, and specific relevant introductory experiences in the use of the concept.

Many psychologists feel that a discovery approach to concept learning is better than the traditional didactic approach in which the teacher tells about the concept. Allowing the student to discover the correct meaning of a concept through guided explorations creates more potent reinforcement than the weak reinforcement usually found in instances where the student is a passive participant in the learning process.

_____ **SUGGESTED READINGS**

Barron, F. *Creative person and creative process.* New York: Holt, Rinehart & Winston, 1969.

Much of Professor Barron's time has been spent at the Institute of Personality Assessment and Research at the University of California studying the creative person. Students interested in the creative process as it emerges from the study of creative people will find much in this book to interest them.

Bruner, J. S. *Toward a theory of instruction.* New York: Norton, 1966.

Over the past decade Professor Bruner has given much attention to the problems of education and learning. The chapters in this book are his essays on several of the attributes of the educational process.

Piaget, J., & Inhelder, B. *The psychology of the child*. New York: Basic Books, 1969.

This small volume presents the latest and most authoritative summary of Piaget's views about the development of thinking and behavior in children. Piaget's intuitive methodology does not involve much experimental data, and this book helps project the logic of his conclusions.

Shulman, L. S., & Keislar, E. R. *Learning by discovery, a critical appraisal*. Chicago: Rand McNally, 1966.

These papers were first presented at a conference sponsored by the U. S. Office of Education and Stanford University. The topics provide broad coverage of the important issues involved in a discovery approach to learning.

REFERENCES

1. Archer, E. J. Concept identification as a function of obviousness of relevant and irrelevant information. *Journal of Experimental Psychology*, 1962, **63**, 616–620.
2. Archer, E. J., Bourne, L. E., & Brown, F. C. Concept identification as a function of irrelevant information and instructions. *Journal of Experimental Psychology*, 1955, **49**, 153–164.
3. Baldwin, A. L. *Theories of child development*. New York: Wiley, 1967. P. 248.
4. Barron, F. The psychology of imagination. *Scientific American*, 1958, **199**(4), 151–166.
5. Berlyne, D. E. *Structure and direction in thinking*. New York: Wiley, 1965.
6. Berlyne, D. E. Curiosity and education. In J. D. Krumboltz (Ed.), *Learning and the educational process*. Chicago: Rand McNally, 1965. Pp. 67–89.
7. Berlyne, D. E. Conflict and arousal. *Scientific American*, 1966, **215**(2), 82–87.
8. Boring, E. G. *A history of experimental psychology*. New York: Appleton-Century-Crofts, 1950.
9. Bourne, L. E. Concept attainment. Paper presented at the symposium on Verbal behavior theory and its relation to general S-R theory. University of Kentucky, Lexington, 1966.
10. Bruner, J. S. The course of cognitive growth. *American Psychologist*, 1964, **19**, 1–15.
11. Bruner, J. S. *Toward a theory of instruction*. New York: Norton, 1966.
12. Bruner, J. S., Goodnow, J. J., & Austin, G. A. *A study of thinking*. New York: Wiley, 1956.
13. Byers, J. L. Hypothesis behavior in concept attainment. *Journal of Educational Psychology*, 1965, **56**, 337–342.
14. Callantine, M. F., & Warren, J. M. Learning sets in human concept formation. *Psychological Reports*, 1955, **1**, 363–367.
15. Carroll, J. B. Words, meanings and concepts. *Harvard Educational Review*, 1964, **34**, 178–202.

16. Duncan, C. P. Recent research on problem solving. *Psychological Bulletin,* 1959, **56,** 397–429.
17. Duncan, C. P. (Ed.) *Thinking: Current experimental studies.* Philadelphia: Lippincott, 1967.
18. Eby, F. *The development of modern education.* Englewood Cliffs, N. J.: Prentice-Hall, 1952. P. 162.
19. Getzels, J. W., & Jackson, P. W. *Creativity and intelligence.* New York: Wiley, 1962. P. 21.
20. Guilford, J. P. Intelligence has three facets. *Science,* 1968, **160,** 615–620.
21. Harlow, H. H. Thinking. In H. Helson (Ed.), *Theoretical foundations of psychology.* Princeton, N. J.: Van Nostrand, 1951.
22. Hartshorne, H., & May, M. *Testing knowledge of right and wrong.* Chicago: Religious Education Association, 1927.
23. Haygood, R. C., & Bourne, L. E. Attribute and rule learning aspects of conceptual behavior. *Psychological Review,* 1965, **72,** 175–195.
24. Hull, C. L. Quantitative aspects of the evolution of concepts. *Psychological Monographs,* 1920, No. 123.
25. Johnson, D. M., & Stratton, R. P. Evaluation of five methods of teaching concepts. *Journal of Educational Psychology,* 1966, **57,** 48–53.
26. Klausmeier, H. J., & Goodwin, W. *Learning and human abilities.* New York: Harper & Row, 1966. P. 243.
27. Piaget, J., & Inhelder, B. *The psychology of the child.* New York: Basic Books, 1969.
28. Rensch, B. The intelligence of elephants. *Scientific American,* 1957, **196**(2), 44–49.
29. Rowland, T., & McGuire, C. The development of intelligent behavior. I: Jean Piaget. *Psychology in the Schools,* 1968, **5,** 47–52.
30. Rowland, T., & McGuire, C. The development of intelligent behavior. IV: Jerome S. Bruner. *Psychology in the Schools,* 1968, **5,** 317–329.
31. Scheerer, M. Problem-solving. *Scientific American,* 1963, **208**(4), 118–128.
32. Sechrest, L., & Kaas, J. S. Concept difficulty as a function of stimulus similarity. *Journal of Educational Psychology,* 1965, **56,** 327–333.
33. Sechrest, L., & Wallace, J. Assimilation and utilization of information in concept attainment under varying conditions of information presentation. *Journal of Educational Psychology,* 1962, **53,** 157–164.
34. Shore, E., & Sechrest, L. Concept attainment as a function of the number of positive instances presented. *Journal of Educational Psychology,* 1961, **52,** 303–307.
35. Smoke, K. L. An objective study of concept formation. *Psychological Monographs,* 1932, No. 191.
36. Smoke, K. L. Negative instances in concept learning. *Journal of Experimental Psychology,* 1933, **16,** 583–588.
37. Wallace, J. Concept dominance, type of feedback, and intensity of feedback as related to concept attainment. *Journal of Educational Psychology,* 1964, **55,** 159–166.
38. Wallace, J., & Sechrest, L. Relative difficulty of conjunctive and disjunctive concepts. *Journal of Psychological Studies,* 1961, **12,** 97–104.
39. Wittrock, M. C. Set applied to student teaching. *Journal of Educational Psychology,* 1962, **53,** 175–180.

7

THE PHYSICAL BASIS OF BEHAVIOR

Many people feel that psychology is the study of man's mind and not his body, failing to see their very close relationship. Because any study of human behavior must include some consideration of man's physical nature, the psychologist's study of the mind gains perspective from his study of the physical functions that parallel mental activity. There are other justifications for the psychologist's interest in the physical properties of the human organism:

1. All behavior, as viewed by the psychologist, involves some physical activity of the organism. The activity may be complex, such as the functional changes that take place under severe stress, or it may be so subtle that only the most sensitive measuring instruments can detect it. But, always, to exist is to function physically.

2. All behavior takes place within the limits set by the physical properties of the organism. Because of his excellent physical apparatus, particularly his nervous system, man is a superior animal. Still, man's body imposes limitations on his behavior that only a drastic rearrangement of physiology could overcome. Man sometimes compensates for this deficiency by using his superior nervous system—for example, man has invented ways to travel through the air, although he is not physically equipped to fly. Even though man has overcome many of the limiting factors inherent in his organic structure, he is still limited and controlled by them.

3. That the physical status of the organism influences the psychological being has been clearly demonstrated. For example, personality can be profoundly altered by damage to the central nervous system. Changes in the endocrine system can upset the hormonal balance and produce behavioral changes. The behavioral pattern known as involutional melancholia, which sometimes affects women during menopause, is an example. This pattern usually subsides after the hormone irregularities associated with menopause disappear.

4. Conversely, psychological factors can influence the physical functioning of the organism. A person placed under conditions of extreme psychological stress over a prolonged period may undergo physical changes that can cause permanent damage.

Psychologists have always been aware that a relationship exists between our bodies and our behavior, but they have not agreed on the nature of this relationship. However, because more is known about the functioning of the central nervous system, especially the brain and its control of behavior, psychologists are much closer to agreement than they were 50 years ago. Each year the contributions from the field of neurology suggest that mental phenomena and neurological processes are identical; that is, mental phenomena can be explained in terms of underlying neural activity. The possibility is strong that researchers may one day discover a complete identity of mental phenomena and neural activity (21).

─────────────────────────────   **The Physical Organization of Behavior**

Once the importance of the relationship between the functions of the body and behavior is acknowledged, how does the psychologist approach the study of man's physical apparatus? As in the other sciences, classification is the first step. The psychologist classifies the various functions of the body into a descriptive system that enables him to talk about behavior in physical terms. This descriptive system is analogous to a machine that takes in directions and puts out responses. The most important parts of this mechanism are the central nervous system (CNS) and the peripheral nervous system (PNS), which form a basis for the functioning of other important parts of the mechanism such as the special senses (vision, hearing, taste, smell), muscles, and glands. The central nervous system is an extremely complex network of nerve fibers comprising the brain and spinal cord while the peripheral nervous system is composed of all those nerve fibers which channel impulses into and from the cranial and spinal nerves. Central nervous system fibers are part of the brain and spinal cord; peripheral nervous system fibers are outside the brain and spinal cord.

These components of the physical mechanism can also be classified into either *receptor* functions or *effector* functions. The receptors are made up of specialized nerve cells which receive stimulation from some source such as the rods and cones in the retinea of the eye. The effectors are composed of specialized nerve cells, such as those found in muscles and glands, which respond to the stimulation provided by the receptors.

The Neuron

Since the complicated network of nerve pathways in the body serve to connect receptors with effectors, let us consider some of the properties of these pathways. As with all living matter, the fundamental unit of construction is the cell. Nerve cells are called neurons, and they have many of the characteristics of other cells of the body (cytoplasm, nuclei, Golgi bodies, etc.). The neuron's special function is to conduct the nerve impulses, a function that makes the neuron unique. To speak of "the nerve cell" is somewhat misleading, for there is a greater variety of different types of nerve cells in the human body than there are in all the other types of tissues taken together (15).

There are many different classes and types of neurons so far identified, varying greatly in shape and size. However, neurons have several attributes in common: They all consist of three parts—the cell body, the dendrites, and the axon. Figure 7-1 is an example of one type of neuron, a motor neuron of the spinal cord. Neurons vary tremendously in size, but none can be seen with the naked eye. Fulton (10a) gives some indication of the relative size of the parts of the neuron:

> One need consider but a single example: a motoneuron originating in the sacral spinal cord of man which supplies by its axon muscle fibers of some small muscle of the foot. If one were to visualize the cell body of such a motoneuron to be about the size of a tennis ball then, keeping other parts commensurate, the axon would be little less than a mile in length and no more than half an inch in diameter. The dendrites of such a motoneuron might be splayed out in the space equivalent to an average living room.

Nerve pathways are made up of neurons arranged in series, with contact effected by the dendrite of one neuron with the axon of another. This functional contact of axon with dendrite is referred to as the synapse. The dendrite receives activity from cells around it and conducts the activity to the cell body. Activity to other neurons is transmitted by the axon. The axon conducts in either direction if it is stimulated. A nerve impulse, however, can cross the synapse in only one direction, from axon to dendrite (39).

The Myelin Sheath

One feature of the nervous system is its color. A neuron appears gray; however, many nerve fibers are covered with a myelin sheath, which is white. As long as the axons and dendrites remain within the gray matter they are simply extentions of the cell body, but as soon as they enter the white matter they become myelinated by being encased within the white,

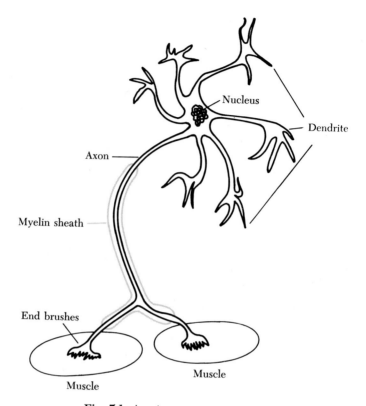

Fig. 7-1. A primary motor neuron.

fat-like substance called myelin. Figure 7-1 shows a myelinated neuron with the position of the myelin as indicated on the axon.

Myelin is considered extremely important in the development of early behaviors, because nerve fibers in the various conducting pathways of the nervous system do not function until they grow to the point of becoming myelinated. It is thought that myelin makes them functional. Sensory nerve fibers usually become myelinated first, starting between the fourth and fifth month of fetal development. Most of the motor pathways do not become myelinated until about the second month after birth, and myelination is usually not complete until after the second year of life. Nerve fibers in association pathways of the nervous system myelinate at even later ages. The pattern and extent of myelination parallels the developing behavior patterns in the infant. However, not all neurons are myelinated. A tremendous amount of activity in the nervous system, particularly in the brain, takes place over nonmyelinated pathways.

Nevertheless, in those portions of the nervous system associated with white matter, myelin appears to be necessary for successful functioning.

The Nerve Impulse

Anything that causes a change in the environment of neural tissue can also cause a nerve fiber to react. Specifically, a nerve fiber can be stimulated by electrical means, by changes in temperature, by chemical processes, and by mechanical means. Any stimulus which initiates activity in the nervous system must have certain characteristics. One of these is *strength*. Because a certain minimal intensity or strength is required, not all stimuli can initiate activity. However, a stimulus below minimal value for excitation does affect the nerve. These inadequate stimuli can summate so that an immediately proceeding stimulus of lower intensity than that originally required can set off a response. This property of the nervous system is referred to as the summation of inadequate stimuli.

Another characteristic of stimuli necessary to elicit neural activity is the *duration* of the stimulus. Usually the stronger the stimulus the less the amount of time needed for the stimulus to excite the nerve fiber. For example, if an electric current is used as a stimulus, the amount of time needed to excite a nerve fiber shortens as the strength of the current increases.

As soon as an adequate stimulus excites a nerve to respond, the impulse becomes self-propagating; that is, it continues under its own power until it terminates. The energy for this transmission is taken from the nerve fiber over which the impulse passes. The following analogy illustrates the manner in which a nerve impulse is carried along a fiber (3):

> The impulse resembles a spark traveling actively along a train of gunpowder rather than a wave transmitted passively through air or water . . . if a section of the powder fuse is dampened in advance of the spark, the latter becomes less intense as it passes through the dampened section, and travels more slowly. Upon reaching a succeeding dry portion the spark flares up again to its previous intensity and velocity, and, so long as the powder remains dry, is transmitted without change to the end of the fuse. In a comparable way, if the activity of a segment of nerve is depressed by treatment in a chamber with a narcotic (alcohol or ether vapor) the impulse undergoes a reduction in amplitude and velocity in its passage through the narcotized region, but upon reaching the untreated nerve beyond, regains its original value, and is transmitted unchanged to the termination of the nerve.

The origin of the slight electrical discharge which constitutes the energy of the nervous system is not fully understood by the neurologist. The present theory of the origin of the electrical discharge is based on the knowledge that an adequate stimulus applied to a nerve fiber causes sodium to enter the interior of the fiber at a rapid rate, causing the polarization of the fiber to be reversed so that the external surface becomes negative to the interior. Depolarization, as it is called, spreads rapidly along the fiber without being influenced by the stimulus. As the impulse subsides, the entry of sodium is slowed down, and potassium begins to leave the fiber, which brings about the original polarity that existed in the fiber prior to the impulse. After the return to original polarity, sodium concentration is restored, and potassium slowly builds up in the interior of the fiber (11). In the inactive fiber, sodium is about 10 times more concentrated outside the cells than in them, and potassium is about 20 to 50 times more concentrated inside the cell than outside it.

The "All-or-None" Principle of Nerve Conduction

If a stimulus is capable of exciting a nerve fiber the fiber responds to the maximum of its ability. Any increase or decrease in the strength of the stimulus does not correspondingly affect the response in the fiber. In other words, the nerve fiber's response is its maximum, regardless of the strength of the stimulus. This is known as the "all-or-none" principle of neural conduction. Not all nerve fibers respond to the same level of stimulus intensity because some fibers are more easily excited than others; nevertheless, once the fiber is excited, it responds at its maximum level. This action potential of a nerve cell can be compared with a digital computer in which each component can be in only one of two possible states.

The decision the neuron makes concerning activation depends on a graded type of activity which differs from the all-or-none activity evident after the discharge threshold of the cell has been reached and the discharge occurs. When nerve cells are stimulated small changes occur in the electrical potential of the membrane of the cell—the amount of these changes being proportional to the characteristics of the stimulating activity. According to Thompson (39):

> . . . the size of the graded potential varies in a continuous fashion. If the change in the graded potential is sufficiently large, the *spike discharge threshold* of the cell is reached and an all-or-none spiked discharge travels down the axon. However, if the graded potential does not reach spike discharge threshold, *no activity* is conducted down the axon. The occurance of these graded potentials in the nerve cell body can be likened to a decision-making process. The neuron considers all incoming activity, and depending upon the amount and kind of this activity, "decides" to fire or not to fire. These graded potentials have often been compared to the operation of an *analogue* computer, which processes signals that vary continuously in amplitude.

The Synapse

A synapse is a junction between neurons—where the axon of one neuron makes a functional contact with the dendrites of another. The synapse plays an important role in facilitating and inhibiting nerve impulses. Facilitation takes place when nerve impulses arrive at the synapse from different sources simultaneously, thus increasing the strength of the impulse. Conversely, some types of neural activity are inhibited at the synapse. For example, a stimulus applied a certain interval after another stimulus may be ineffective because it occurs during a refractory period. Synaptic junctions in the nervous system are basic decision points where much of the magnification and braking effects necessary for adequate functioning of the nervous system take place (12).

One of the major questions in the study of the physiology of the nervous system is how the nerve impulse is transmitted across the synapse. One theory emphasizes the electrical events associated with this transmission, while another emphasizes the chemical mediation of the impulse. The chemical theory is supported by evidence suggesting that synaptic transmission occurs when small amounts of a chemical substance are released between dendrites and axons (39). But these many questions, and probably their answers, only indicate the enormity of the problems faced by the neurologist in his quest to unravel the mysteries of the nerve impulse. Continued research should bring new knowledge to and more basic understanding of the processes involved.

This discussion of the organization of the nervous system—its most basic unit, the neuron, and the transmission and conduction of the nerve impulse—leads to a consideration of more complex units of organization within the nervous system, the sense receptors.

The Eye

The visual system is responsible for what people usually consider their most important sense. It is also the most thoroughly researched of the human senses. Visual perception is made possible by the activities of the eye as the receptor for sensations and through its translation of light rays into neural impulses which are transmitted to the visual area of the brain. The eye can be compared with a camera: The light-sensitive film or plate corresponds to the retina in the eye, which contains the nerve endings that are sensitive to light (see Fig. 7-2). Light is admitted to the interior of the eye through the cornea, which is transparent, then through the pupil, and finally through the lens. The lens is controlled by muscular tissue so that its curvature can be changed to alter the focus of the light rays on the retina, which contains the nerve endings that are

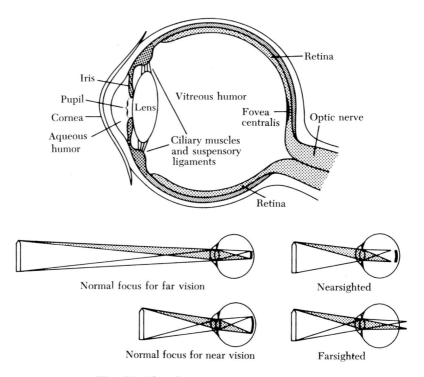

Fig. 7-2. The physical structure of the eye.

activated when stimulated. The size of the pupil, which is regulated by muscular tissue, controls the amount of light admitted through the lens; the changes in curvature of the lens control the focus of the light on the retina. The greater the degree of focus at a point on the retina, under conditions of adequate light and attention, the clearer the visual image.

The retina is made up of layers of neurons and cells which are activated by the stimulation of light admitted through the pupil and lens. The most sensitive area of the retina is the fovea, which is located directly behind the lens. Direct vision usually produces a focus of light rays on or in the vicinity of the fovea. The point on the retina where the nerve fibers leave the retina and enter the optic nerve is known as the blind spot, since there are no light-sensitive receptors available for stimulation there. The optic nerve enters the eyeball at a slightly different location in each eye so that stimulation reaching the blind spot in one eye would not impinge on the blind spot in the other eye.

Impulses that reach the retina are received first by the sensory neurons and in turn are transmitted to the bipolar nerve cells, then to the ganglion cells, and from there to the optic nerve. The sensory cells are composed of rods and cones. Cones are more frequent in the central portion of the retina, while the rods increase in frequency on the periphery of the retina. The most widely accepted theory about the functioning of the rods and cones is the Duplicity Theory, which was advanced toward the end of the nineteenth century (26). The theory assumes that the cones are more sensitive to conditions of high illumination and the rods more sensitive to conditions of low illumination. The rods mediate visual perception dominated by lack of color; the cones are central to the mediation of color vision. Full color vision, which is maximal at the center of the visual field and diminishes away from the central area of the eye, is associated with the greater stimulus energy of daylight. Night vision improves progressively toward the periphery of the retina and is related to a low level of stimulus intensity. These factors distinguish night vision from daylight vision (4):

1. In night vision all color qualities disappear except black, gray and white.
2. The grays and whites that remain are slightly tinted with blue.
3. At night the whitest colors appear for stimuli that create yellow-green under normal intensities.
4. The fovea, which is the central area of the retina, is blind at night.

A chemical substance, rhodopsin, has been associated with the activity of the rods. The chemical activity of the cones is not nearly so well understood, although a substance called iodopsin has been found in the cones of some animals. If the eyes have been in total darkness for some time, their sensitivity is greatly increased. The energy needed to stimulate the dark-adapted eye is about a thousand times less than the energy needed to stimulate the light-adapted eye.

Clarity of vision is influenced by many factors. The most common problem is the eye's inability to focus light rays at a point on the retina because of imperfections in the curvature of the lens. Factors less often involved are interference at the level of the retina or interference in the transmission of the neural impulse to the visual portion of the brain. Astigmatism, a common visual defect, can be caused by an imperfection in the shape of the cornea that cannot be fully compensated for by the lens. Astigmatism can also be caused by the lens itself if the lens cannot accommodate properly to focus light at a point on the retina. The distortions of astigmatism may be horizontal, vertical, or diagonal, and can usually be corrected through the use of glasses. Nearsightedness results from a focus of light rays by the lens slightly in front of the retina. Farsightedness results from a focus slightly to the rear of the retina. Cross eye is the result of a disequilibrium in the strengths of the rectus muscles in one eye or in both eyes which causes an improper focus of the image on the retina. Visual problems that result from factors affecting light stimuli before they impinge on the retina can usually be corrected by wearing glasses.

The Ear

The stimulus that initiates hearing is a pressure wave in the air which causes a fluctuation of the ear drum. The translation of this pressure stimulus into sound is accomplished by a complex series of mechanical and neurological events culminating in the perception of sound in the auditory centers of the brain. The hearing mechanism comprises the outer ear, the middle ear, and the inner ear (see Fig. 7-3). The outer ear consists of the fold of skin known as the pinna and the ear canal down to the eardrum. The eardrum is a thin membrane at the end of the auditory canal attached to the hammer in the middle ear. The middle ear is a small cavity within the temporal bone that connects with the interior of the nose and throat through the eustachian tube, which in turn helps to equalize the air pressure in the middle ear. The three small bones in the middle ear—known as the hammer (malleus), the anvil (incus), and the stirrup (stapes)—form a bridge between the outer and the inner ear. The hammer is attached to the eardrum, the stirrup to one of the two openings into the inner ear, the oval window. The other opening, the round window, absorbs the pressure existing within the inner ear as a result of the force of the stirrup on the oval window. Within the temporal bone are a series of openings containing the semicircular canals and the cochlea. The semicircular canals are involved in the sense of balance. The cochlea is the part of the inner ear associated with hearing and

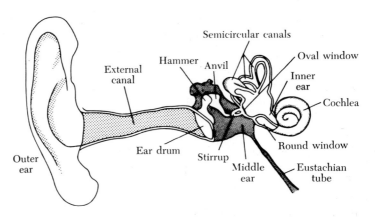

Fig. 7-3. The physical structure of the ear.

contains the nerve endings that provide the neurological basis for hearing. The cochlea is like a snail shell—it has three full turns. The main canal is subdivided into three openings, or smaller canals. The cochlear duct, a smaller canal on the outer side of the cochlea, is next to a larger canal, the scala vestibuli; both are above the largest canal, the scala tympani. The scala vestibuli and the scala tympani are connected through a small opening at the tip of the cochlea called the helicotrema. The auditory nerve travels through the center of the cochlea and emerges into the canals of the cochlea on the basilar membrane. This membrane partitions the scala vestibuli from the scala tympani and the cochlear duct from the scala tympani. Resting on the basilar membrane is the organ of Corti containing the nerve fibers which are the beginnings of the neurological transmission system to the auditory centers of the brain.

The activity of the outer and middle ear can be explained by physical principles which relate to the translation of sound waves in the air into movement of the stirrup. The cochlea receives the movement of the stirrup through pressure waves in the fluid that fills the cochlea. These pressure waves stimulate the hairlike nerve endings on the organ of Corti which sets up the electrochemical message that is translated into sound in the brain. Loudness of sound is related to the number of nerve fibers that are fired at any one time, thus controlling the number of impulses reaching the brain. Pitch is related to distance along the basilar membrane, which thickens as it progresses through the cochlea. Although a major portion of the membrane may be affected by a sound wave, one point along the membrane receives a maximum deflection. High frequencies tend to affect the thinner portions of the basilar membrane near the base of the cochlea; low frequencies affect the thicker portions of the membrane.

The semicircular canals occupying the inner ear along with the cochlea help maintain the body's equilibrium. These canals are small fluid-filled membranous tubes containing small hair cells much like those of the organ of Corti. The hair cells are stimulated by the pressure on the surrounding fluid. The three canals on either side of the head each occupy a different plane in space. When the head is moved in any direction the fluid in one or more of the canals stimulate the nerve endings in the hair cells.

It is evident from Fig. 7-4 that the connection of visual pathways with the visual area of the brain is different from the connection of auditory pathways with the brain. If the optic nerve in front of the optic chiasma is destroyed, blindness in that eye results. If the destruction is at a point beyond the optic chiasma partial blindness in both eyes is the result. This is referred to as *hemianopia,* or blindness in half of the visual field

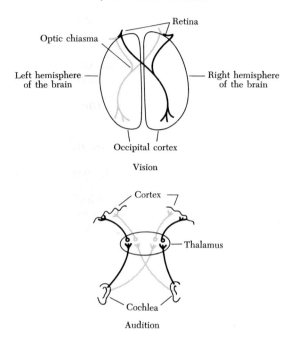

The connection of the visual and auditory pathways from
the eye and the ear to the brain

Retina

Optic chiasma

Left hemisphere
of the brain

Right hemisphere
of the brain

Occipital cortex

Vision

Cortex

Thalamus

Cochlea

Audition

Fig. 7-4. The connection of the visual and auditory pathways from the eye and
the ear to the brain.

of each eye. The destruction of an auditory nerve on one side leads to
deafness on that side, but a unilateral lesion in one of the auditory pathways in the brain does not lead to deafness since these fibers represent
both cochleae.

Taste and Smell

The receptors for taste are located in the mouth on the tongue and
palate, and on the pharynx and larynx. The receptors for smell, or
olfaction, are located in the upper part of the nose on each side of the
nasal cavity. Usually, taste is perceived through a combination of stimuli
from taste and olfactory receptors. The receptors for the sense of taste
are spindle-shaped cells located in groups called taste buds. The receptors for olfaction are nerve cells in the mucous membrane lining the
upper nasal passages. Taste has four primary qualities: saline, sour,
bitter, and sweet, but these basic qualities can combine to give a multitude of different taste sensations. Not all the taste buds on the tongue

are sensitive to all four qualities. The tip of the tongue is most sensitive to sweet, the sides to sour, the tip and sides to saline, and the back to bitter. Sensitivity to bitter is the most pronounced. The sensitivity to taste qualities vary greatly from one person to another. Some few persons have a disability known as "taste blindness" for a substance called PTC (phenyl-thio-car-bamide). Some find this substance quite bitter, others find it tasteless. This taste deficiency appears to be an inherited characteristic. A commonly observed phenomenon is that sensitivity to taste changes as one grows older. Children have more taste buds and a lower threshold of excitation than adults do. Taste sensitivity is also affected by the temperature of the solution being tasted. Extremely hot or cold substances tend to inhibit the activity of the taste buds. As with other sensory experiences, prolonged exposure to a particular taste leads to a sensory adaptation, so that the fourth piece of sweet candy usually tastes less sweet than the first.

The fundamental qualities of odor are not so well established as are those of taste. Most authorities accept Henning's theory of olfaction, which classifies six basic qualities of smell (4):

1. Fragrant—the odor of violets
2. Ethereal—the odor of oranges
3. Spicy—the odor of cloves
4. Resinous—the odor of balsam
5. Burnt—the odor of tar
6. Putrid—the odor of decaying matter

As with taste, sensitivity to odor is tremendously variable, differing not only from one person to another, but for each person at different times. Loss of sensitivity to smell—anosmia—can be either partial or complete. Probably the most common cause of anosmia is temporary inflammation in the membrane containing the receptors for smell. Adaptation occurs when there is prolonged exposure to an odor; with the passage of time the perception of the odor becomes weaker. Although the sequence of stimulation for both taste and smell is known, the mechanisms of stimulation by food or minute vapors in the air are not known, especially those concerning the transition from a sensation to the perception of a taste or an odor.

Somesthesis

Somesthesis refers to the feelings associated with the skin of the body and concerns, for the most part, the receptors for pressure, pain, warmth, and cold. Somesthesis also refers to the feeling of motion, or kinesthesis, which originates as a sensation from the sensory nerves in those parts of the body associated with movement. The skin contains many nerve endings, unevenly distributed throughout the layers of the skin. Pressure sensitivity, for example, can easily be mapped across the surface of the skin to yield a pattern of sensitivity with identifiable areas of high sensitivity and low sensitivity. The types and variations of nerve endings in the skin and muscle are complex. Pressure, or touch, is thought to correlate with the presence of a type of nerve ending called the Meissner corpuscle. Pain sensitivity seems to correlate with the presence of free nerve endings—the parts of the body most sensitive to pain are the cornea of the eye and the inner reaches of the external auditory canal, which have only free nerve endings. The identification of the receptors for warmth and cold have been made only tenuously, on the basis of uncertain evidence. The classic theory suggests that cold is associated with a type of nerve ending known as the Krause end bulb while sensitivity for warmth correlates with the presence of another type of corpuscle called the Ruffini cylinder. Further intensive research is needed, for much remains to be learned about the skin senses and their activities, which seem both complex and interrelated.

_____ **The Central Nervous System**

The Spinal Cord

The brain and the spinal cord constitute what is classically described as the central nervous system, and are basic to understanding the relationship between the nervous system and behavior. Although the brain is one of the most complex and interesting structures of the human organism, only the barest of facts and descriptive information are presented here, for to do otherwise would necessitate excluding other areas of importance in behavior. The student interested in the neurological basis of behavior, and in pursuing the subject further than the outline presented here, should supplement his reading with books that deal exclusively with the subject.

The structure of the spinal cord is much simpler than that of the brain. The spinal cord's major function is to conduct impulses to and from the brain and the peripheral nerve pathways. In addition, the spinal cord plays a mediating role in initiating and supporting some complex reflexive behaviors.

The Brain

The classification for the parts of the brain most frequently used (26) divides the brain into the hindbrain, the midbrain, and the forebrain

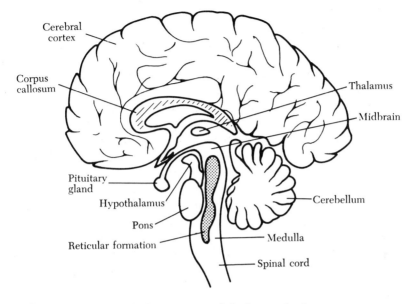

Cerebral cortex

Corpus callosum

Thalamus

Midbrain

Pituitary gland

Hypothalamus

Pons

Reticular formation

Cerebellum

Medulla

Spinal cord

Fig. 7-5. Cross section of the human brain.

(see Fig. 7-5). The *hindbrain* is composed of the medulla, the cerebellum, and the pons. The medulla links the spinal cord to the brain and is the entrance and exit for most of the cranial nerves. The medulla also contains the neurological centers for the control of breathing, cardiac activity, blood pressure, and gastrointestinal functions. Since these functions are associated with the medulla, it is sometimes called the vital center of the brain.

Contained in the *cerebellum* are collections of nerve fibers linking the cerebellum with the pons, the spinal cord, the sensory mechanisms controlling equilibrium, and the cerebral cortex. The cerebellum functions to coordinate impulses involved in the movement of muscles and plays a major role in motor coordination. Research on the evolution of the brain indicates that the cerebellum was the first structure of the nervous system with the special function of coordinating sensory and motor impulses. The major change in the cerebellum in mammals is the appearance of a part of the cerebellum, the neocerebellum, which is associated with impulses coming from, and going to, the cortex. In experimental animals when the cerebellum is removed there is a severe disturbance in muscular coordination. The loss of coordination, to remain permanent, must usually be accompanied by the removal of large areas in the cortex. Such research suggests that the cerebellum does not operate independent of other higher centers that are involved in sensory and motor activity (36).

The *pons* functions as an associative system of nerve fibers which supports the functions of the medulla and the cerebellum. In addition, the pons contains the nuclei of the trigeminal nerve, which is associated with sensations of movement of the face and mouth.

The *midbrain* is primarily a connecting link between the forebrain and the hindbrain. The midbrain conducts impulses between higher and lower centers of the nervous system; it is also associated with visual and auditory stimulation. One structure which has interested psychologists in recent years is the reticular system which is found principally within the hindbrain and extends into the midbrain and hypothalamus. The reticular formation has been identified as a central arousal system for cortical activity (27). This brain formation and the functions associated with it have been named the reticular activating system, or RAS. The reticular system is a small nerve network which appears to be associated with the arousal of the cortex. Reticular response to sensory stimulation is basically the same regardless of the source of the stimulus. The arousal of the cortex is global rather than specific for discrete parts of the cortex. The RAS alerts the cortex to an attentive, wakeful state so that specific centers of the cortex can identify appropriate stimuli when they are received.

The RAS seems to act selectively in its sensitivity to particular stimuli, for the intensity of the stimulus needed to activate the system varies (10). Consciousness is made possible by the RAS. The RAS is stimulated by sensory nerves and by impulses from parts of the cortex. The RAS appears to provide a basic ingredient necessary for higher mental processes by arousing attention in the organism.

The *forebrain* is of great interest to psychologists because support by the CNS for such behavioral patterns as those seen in emotion, motivation, and thinking appears to be mediated at this level. The thalamus and the hypothalamus are two structures important to behavior found at this level of the brain. The thalamus is a central relay point in the brain consisting of many neuclei connected with each other and with the hindbrain, the midbrain, the spinal cord, and the cortex. The activities of the cerebellum and the frontal lobes that control the movements of muscles are coordinated in the thalamus, the seat of the major relay stations between most forms of sensory activity and the cortex.

The *hypothalamus* is associated with the activity of the autonomic nervous system, but does not produce autonomic responses (fluctuation in blood pressure, rise in heartbeat, contraction of the pupil, etc.). Instead, the hypothalamus integrates these response patterns into coordinated activity that adjusts the internal environment. The body's internal environment is formed by the chemical, temperature, and sensory conditions that create an environment for its organs and systems. The hypothalamus is also associated with the neurological basis of emotional behavior. Bard (1), in a classic study, demonstrated the focal role of the hypothalamus in the organization of emotional responses in dogs and cats. Later investigations indicate the role the lower brain centers play in emotional response; however, the hypothalamus remains a critical structure in the sequence of neurological events that parallel emotional responses. Bard studied rage responses in dogs and cats before and after the removal of brain tissue. Removing tissue from the cerebral cortex had the effect of lowering the threshold for rage responses, causing the animals to respond with rage to stimuli that had previously evoked only mild interest. The cortex apparently acts to smooth, inhibit, and restrain the subcortical mechanisms that mediate rage. This complete rage response, however, could be obtained in the experimental animals who had cortical tissue missing only so long as the hypothalamus was intact. Bard concluded that the hypothalamus is central to the organization of the response elements that constitute rage behavior by integrating these elements into a total somatic pattern of rage. Numerous later studies have shown that emotional responses can be elicited by stimulating the hypothalamus (26).

Recent statements about the neurology of emotions emphasize its complexity. Pribram (32) views an emotion as the expression of a relationship between perceiving and acting. Emotion becomes the bridge between the information-processing aspects of the nervous system and its control mechanisms, images, and neural programs. Emotions become neural programs which become active when disequilibrium is present (33). Emotion is not the simple result of hypothalamic stimulation which Bard's research suggested, although the hypothalamus is a basic neural structure in the expression of Pribram's neural programs. A further discussion of the physiology of emotion is presented in Chapter 13.

The *cerebral cortex* is the structure of the brain that most distinguishes man from the lower orders of animals. The cortex is a much larger area of tissue than might be judged from its dimensions, for the fissures or folds are wrinkles in the tissue that appear as the brain grows, and which help to accommodate the surface of the brain to the skull. The brain is divided by a deep longitudinal fissure into two approximately equal hemispheres. These hemispheres are joined principally by fibers passing through the corpus callosum. The cortex has several major fissures aside from the one that separates the hemispheres. One fissure cutting laterally across both hemispheres is the Fissure of Rolando (see Fig. 7-6). Another is the Fissure of Sylvius.

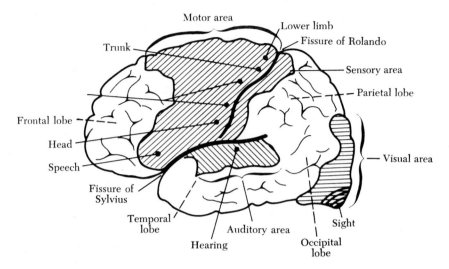

Fig. 7-6. The location of important areas of the cerebrum.

Below the cortex are nerve fibers that lead from other parts of the brain and the spinal cord, and which link different parts of the cortex. These fibers are myelinated and appear white on exposure; hence this interior portion of the cerebrum is referred to as the white matter of the brain. The two cerebral hemispheres of the cerebrum comprise approximately 70% of the entire nervous system. Most of the characteristics that distinguish human behavior from animal behavior—memory, associations, and meaningfulness—seem to be mediated by the cortex. Certainly the association and mixing of sensory impulses is a cortical function as is the process of attributing meaning to sensory impulses. Figure 7-6 presents the location of some of the more important areas of the cortex and their relationship to specific activity. The occipital lobes at the back of the cerebrum are related to vision. Those visual cues which lead to interpretations of color, form, size, and distance are mediated in the visual centers of the brain. Injury to this area of the brain can cause blindness.

The *temporal lobes* have been the subject of much investigation since a report by Kluver and Bucy (19). They found that removal of the temporal lobes in monkeys produced striking visual disturbances that made the animals unable to recognize familiar objects or to perform normally on visual tasks. Most research today indicates that the temporal lobes are involved in the mediation of visual habits and learned visual discriminations as well as audition and taste. Animals who have had their temporal lobes removed can learn new visual habits, but the extent and speed of relearning depends on the amount of tissue lost.

The *frontal lobes* are associated with some of the most complex processes of human behavior. Judgment, reason, will, and complex emotional responses are mediated at the level of the frontal lobes. Severing the nerve fibers in the prefrontal area of the cortex is a technique used in treating severe mental disorders characterized by emotional depressions and extensive anxiety. The operation first used in this procedure was called a leucotomy. Today the term "lobotomy" is frequently used to indicate a severing of nerve fibers in the cortex for therapeutic reasons. The operation is successful in many cases, but the change in behavior is not always in the desired direction. An operation that relieves inhibitions and anxieties to too great a degree can turn the individual into as much of a social problem as he may have been before the operation.

One of the most important aspects of the cortex is its involvement in the motor functions of the body. Studies show that the amount of brain surface associated with specific somatic and motor functions is not proportional to the size of the area of the body involved but is instead related to the extent that area is used. For example, the area involved with the hands and fingers is larger than that for the feet and toes because the hands and fingers are used more in human behavior (14). The projection area of the brain associated with the activity of the lips occupies more of the somatic sensory area than that related to the rest of the head. These projection areas for somatic and motor functions on the cortex become an index of the experience of the organism, since the extent of the use of specific somatic and motor behaviors can be judged from the size of the projection area given to those specific functions. For example, the projection area for the snout of the pig dominates that of all other somatic areas.

One of the major problems encountered in investigating the activity of the brain has been the need for techniques that indicate this activity without damaging the subject while data are being obtained. The use of the electroencephalograph (EEG), which records the electrical activity of the brain, has increased during the past thirty years and is now one of the major sources of information about the activity of the brain. Another problem the researcher has faced is how to interpret the recordings of brain waves, once obtained. The recent use of computers in the process of averaging data, which permits the analysis of long-term observations, signals another advance in understanding the activities of the brain (5). The typical brain wave pattern is obtained by taping electrodes to the head of the subject, who is at rest in a darkened room with his eyes closed. This pattern consists of one set of waves known as alpha waves, which register as deflections occurring on the electroencephalogram at the rate of 10 to 12 times a second.

A second set of waves, called beta waves, can sometimes be observed superimposed on the alpha waves. The beta waves consist of smaller and faster deflections, when compared with the alpha waves. A third set of waves, called delta waves, can sometimes be observed in the normal subject, but only when he is asleep. Variations in the appearance and activity of these brain waves can be observed and measured in association with different types of sensory input and output. The patterns from one individual to another are similar enough to permit the electroencephalogram to become a diagnostic tool in some types of brain damage, such as the central nervous system dysfunction associated with epilepsy.

_____ **The Autonomic Nervous System**

The autonomic nervous system, a part of the peripheral nervous system, is distinguished by the functions it performs in relation to the expression of emotion. Autonomic fibers are not set apart as a separate nervous system, but are found in the smooth muscles of the viscera, the heart, and the glands. These fibers are linked through the spinal nerves to the central nervous system, which is sometimes referred to as the visceral nervous system because of its crucial relationship to the functioning of the viscera.

The autonomic nervous system is divided into two parts, the sympathetic and the parasympathetic. It was once thought that the sympathetic branch was associated with feelings of unpleasantness and the parasympathetic branch with feelings of pleasantness. This distinction is now considered an oversimplification since some parasympathetic activities, such as crying, are not pleasurable. The sympathetic branch mobilizes or effects activity in the body, and it is that activity which prepares the body for maximum efforts. The parasympathetic branch, on the other hand, soothes or calms body activity. In general, the activities of the sympathetic branch of the autonomic nervous system are antagonistic to those of the parasympathetic branch. For example, the rate of heart beat is inhibited by parasympathetic stimulation and accelerated by sympathetic stimulation. The activities of the sympathetic branch have been described as an emergency system that physiologically prepares one to meet some threat. Digestive functions are inhibited and the blood supply is directed toward the voluntary muscles. The heart pumps faster and thus supplys more blood to the muscles. Blood sugar is secreted by the liver and breathing increases, thus insuring a greater supply of oxygen. Table 7-1 summarizes the functions of the autonomic nervous system in relation to the organs of the body served by it.

TABLE 7-1
The Functions of the Autonomic Nervous System[a]

Organ	Sympathetic function	Parasympathetic function
Heart	Rate increased	Rate decreased
Surface arteries	Dilated; more blood	Constricted; less blood
Visceral arteries	Constricted; less blood	Dilated; more blood
Pupil of eye	Dilated; more light	Contracted; less light
Sweat glands	Sweat secreted	
Hair on skin	Hairs erected	
Adrenal glands	Adrenalin secreted	
Liver	Sugar liberated into blood	Insulin liberated, blood sugar reduced
Salivary glands	Salivation stopped	Salivation increased
Stomach	Contraction and secretion stopped	Contraction and secretion increased
Intestines	Contraction and secretion stopped	Contraction and secretion increased
Rectum	Defecation inhibited	Feces expelled
Bladder	Urination inhibited	Urine expelled
Genital organs	Seminal vesicles contracted	Erection induced

[a] Adapted from Hunt (18a).

The changes in the autonomic nervous system and the endocrine glands caused by prolonged anxiety, stress, and other emotions may be responsible for actual physical damage to the body. For example, prolonged anxiety, with its concomitant increased heart rate and blood pressure, may cause actual physical damage. The physical disorders that have their origins in autonomic changes are known as psychosomatic disorders ("psycho"—mind, "soma"—body). Autonomic involvement in stomach ulcers is a common observation; however, not all stomach ulcers are psychosomatic. The autonomic nervous system is profoundly influenced by the cortex and the hypothalamus center, and vice versa, so that any emotional response has some autonomic involvement.

_____ **The Central Nervous System and Behavior**

Psychologists have long sought explanations for the relationships between the functioning of the central nervous system, especially the brain, and behavior. Lashley (20) was one of the early pioneers in this area of research. In a series of experiments with rats to assess the influence of cerebral destruction on behavior in learning and retaining maze habits, Lashley concluded that the capacity to form maze habits is reduced by destruction of cerebral tissue in proportion to the amount of tissue loss. Given a certain amount of cortical destruction, the animal's retardation in learning a complex problem was greater than it was in learning a simple one. Destroying cerebral tissue in the animals used by Lashley affected their ability to retain information as well as the ability to learn.

Lashley also reported from data obtained in his experiments that the loss in learning ability appeared unrelated to the location of the cortical lesion. Many investigators interpreted this to mean that all parts of a rat's cortex are involved in the process of learning; that is, the parts of the rat's cortex are equipotential with respect to behavior in a maze. This conclusion has not been fully supported by further research. Studies of electrical stimulation of an animal's brain, to be discussed later in this chapter, indicate that the stimulation acts as a reinforcer in certain portions of the brain and as a punishment when applied to other portions. It would be wrong to conclude, however, that the brain operates in a manner to integrate relatively isolated centers having discrete functions. The brain's function in behavior is much more complex than this, and is only beginning to be understood. This statement on the complexity of brain functioning is taken from a summary of research on the brain and behavior (22):

> . . . total extirpation of a particular cortical center in an animal leads to only an initial loss of the corresponding function; the disturbed function is gradually recovered and, if any isolated part of the cerebral cortex is subsequently extirpated, it does not cause the secondary loss of this disturbed function. It was concluded from these findings that the cerebral cortex does not consist of separate, isolated centers and that the recovery of a function must not be attributed to transfer of the function to a new, vicarious center but rather, to a structural reorganization into a new, dynamic system widely dispersed in the cerebral cortex and lower formations.

Luria's (22) excellent and detailed interpretation of research on higher cortical functions in man and their relationship to behavior and intellectual processes summarizes evidence relating brain lesions to behavior. The major conclusions of his observations are:

1. The idea of localization of mental functions in the brain, in which these functions are thought to be related to rigidly demarcated areas of the brain, and the notion that higher mental processes and the biological functions of the brain are unrelated represent concepts that are not supported by the evidence on the relation between brain lesions and behavior.

2. Disturbances in the neurological process induced by brain damage generally produce symptoms in which the higher levels of organization of the mental process appear to suffer most and are accompanied by a corresponding depression of various forms of mental activity.

3. The location of the brain lesion is important in relation to the behavior that is disturbed. For example, patients with a lesion in the frontal region of the cortex usually demonstrate an inability to analyze a problem in a systematic manner and to perceive the important connections within it. On the other hand, patients with lesions in the parietal or occipital regions of the brain may be unable to solve a problem if its solution requires the identification of visual signs and spatial organization. However, these patients display an organizational strategy in problem solving which is usually absent in the patient with a frontal lesion.

4. The concept of absolute dominance of one hemisphere of the brain with respect to all mental functions is not entirely supportable by evidence relating cortical functioning and behavior. Many persons show only partial or unequal dominance of a hemisphere when different mental functions are considered.

Luria (23) sums up his dominant point of view concerning the organization of the cortex as follows:

> . . . the cerebral cortex is a highly differentiated system of zones, working together, on which complex forms of behavioral processes are based. The higher psychological functions, which are in fact complex functional systems, may be disturbed by lesions in any link in this collectively working dynamic complex, but each of these disturbances exhibits specific features and may help to reveal the role of a particular area of the cerebral cortex in the structure of the particular functional system.

The complexity of the functional systems mediated by the cortex is further supported by the suggestion of McCleary and Moore (24) that the vertical rather than the horizontal organization of the brain is the more important in relating brain functions to behavior. Damage at any of the vertical points in the complex circuits of the central nervous system may be more disruptive of a specific function than damage which isolates the function horizontally.

Luria (22, 23) presents a wealth of evidence in support of his concept that man's cortical functions are far more complex and diversified than neurologists traditionally assert. For example, a local lesion of the cortex in the external portions of the left temporal region is associated primarily with a deterioration in the ability to understand speech. Luria points out that such a lesion is also accompanied by disturbances in the ability to analyze speech sounds, deterioration in writing and in the ability to repeat and memorize words, and a disturbance of the intellectual functions associated with these abilities. Orientation in space, ability to ascertain direction, and the ability to carry out arithmetical operations are not disturbed. Lesions of the parieto-occipital regions are classically associated with loss of orientation in space. According to Luria, such lesions also produce disturbances in the concept of numbers and arithmetical operations and in logico-grammatical structures. Left undisturbed are such functions as hearing and understanding speech, and the perception and reproduction of musical melodies. These examples not only indicate the dynamic organization of the cortex; they also illustrate the basic observation that lesions in different parts of the brain give rise to different symptoms that usually have a functional relationship indicative of a cerebral system that is less than discretely localized in its functions.

The work of Sperry (37, 38) has attracted considerable attention because it suggests many possibilities for future research on learning and perception in which a subject's experiences can be directed to one or the other hemisphere of the brain separately. Sperry has directed his efforts to a study of the corpus callosum, the bundle of nerve fibers connecting one hemisphere of the brain with the other. Each of these cerebral hemispheres is a mirror image of the other. The left hemisphere is associated with sensory input from the right side of the body, and the right hemisphere with sensory input from the left side of the body, although the association of each hemisphere with the opposite body side is not absolute. The corpus callosum functions to transfer learning from one hemisphere to the other. The importance of the corpus callosum in learning is evident when these fibers are severed in an experimental animal. The "split-brain" animal when presented with learning problems, demonstrates little, if any, deterioration in the ability to learn, indicating that each cerebral hemisphere has the capacity to function as a separate and independent brain. The only detrimental effect of the split-brain operation is that it prevents coordination of responses on the two sides of the body.

In a series of experiments with a tactual discrimination problem, Sperry used a pedal-pressing apparatus to teach "split-brain" cats to use their paws to make opposite discriminations without negative transfer from one paw to the other, and to make positive discriminations without one paw's being facilitated by learning involving the other paw. Intact cats would have found the negative problem difficult because "first paw" learning would have interfered with "second paw" learning, while the problem of similar discriminations would have been influenced by positive transfer.

Neurologists have long known that activity in nerve circuits involves chemical reactions in the nervous system, particularly in the region of the synapse. Fisher (9) has reported a number of experiments in which the injection of specific chemical substances into localized regions of the brain result in behavior associated with drives such as hunger and thirst. In one attempt at chemical stimulation, testosterone injected into experimental animals at a point in front of the hypothalamus and at the level of the optic tracts produced maternal behavior. The same hormone injected to one side of the hypothalamus produced male sexual activity—even in female animals. Chemicals other than testosterone failed to produce either response. Further investigations of the relationship of chemicals to behavior have produced the findings that noradrenalin and acetycholine, substances associated with the transmission of nerve impulses, can stimulate eating and drinking in animals when injected into a site just above the hypothalamus. Fisher concludes from his studies that drive-oriented behavior (see Chapter 11) can be stimulated and sustained by chemical intervention and that certain brain cells can be stimulated selectively by specific chemicals.

The effects of experience on the anatomical and chemical structure of the brain have been the subject of a series of studies reported by Rosenzweig (34). Two groups of animals (rats) were assigned after weaning to either an enriched environment or to an impoverished environment. At the end of 80 days the brains of the animals were examined both anatomically and chemically. The brains of the animals exposed to the enriched condition were greater in weight than were the brains of their impoverished littermates. This weight difference was more pronounced when brain weight was compared with body weight, since the enriched animals were about 7% less in body weight than their counterparts. The chemical analysis of the brains of the animals revealed that those from the enriched environment showed a slightly greater activity of the enzyme acetylcholinesterase, which is important at the synapse where acetylcholine is the chemical transmitter for the nerve impulse. In addition, the cortex of the enriched rats showed increased activity of another enzyme group, cholinesterase. Histological studies of the brains of the experimental animals showed that the ratio of glia to neurons was higher in the enriched animals than in the impoverished animals. The exact function of the glia are not known, but they are thought to act as a support to the nerve cell and its activity.

Studies of simple conditioned responses in animals and their relationship to ribonucleic acid (RNA) have been reported by Sechrest and Wallace (35). From an extensive review of this research they concluded that RNA, which is involved in the production of proteins involved in a number of the body's reactions, facilitates learning simple conditioned responses. They report on several studies (7, 40) in which planaria were conditioned to respond to light with a contraction of the body by pairing the light with electric shock. The planarian is a small flatworm that is able to regenerate parts that have been cut away. When the planaria were cut in half and allowed to regenerate, both halves of the worms exhibited evidence of the conditioned response. Since RNA is involved in the regeneration process in worms, this manifestation of retention may be associated with the role RNA plays in memory. McConnell (25) also reported that when planaria that had been conditioned were eaten by untrained cannibal planaria, the untrained planaria exhibited evidence of the transfer of the conditioned response.

Brain Stimulation and Learning

One of the major areas of study in learning is the motive or drive that initiates a learning experience. The role reward and punishment play as motives in learning has been studied during the last decade at the level of the neurophysiology involved. Delgado, Roberts, and Miller (8) were the first to show that stimulation of the brain can have punishing effects in a learning situation. Olds and Milner (31) contributed the initial data on the role of brain stimulation as a rewarding mechanism in behavior. Olds (30) relates that during a research program investigating the reticular centers in the rat, an electrode was implanted, quite by accident, in a structure near the rat's septum. The electrical stimulation seemed to have the effect of a potent reward on the behavior of the animal. Successive stimulations while the animal was at a specific location in a T maze caused him to spend more time there. The specific choices made by the rat in the maze could also be controlled by the presence or absence of stimulation. If the animal can control the stimulation by pressing a bar, he will respond up to 5,000 times an hour in seeking intracranial stimulation. Hungry rats will withstand a greater amount of pain (electric shock) to seek intracranial stimulation than they will withstand to seek food. Olds has hypothesized that electrical stimulation in the portion of the brain where the rewarding effects seem greatest must excite nerve cells related to the satisfaction of basic drive states such as hunger, sex, and thirst (29).

The investigation of specific reward and punishment centers in the brain is only beginning to reach a stage where theoretical speculation is supportable by data. At present, it appears that reward sites in the rat are widely distributed throughout the subcortex. Hilgard and Bower (18) report generalizations that can be made about the features of electrical stimulation of the brain:

1. Self-stimulation involves behavior that does not satiate, contrary to the behavior associated with eating or drinking. Animals may stimulate their brain for hours, sometimes stopping only from exhaustion.

2. Despite a high response rate, the behavior associated with electrical stimulation usually extinguishes very rapidly after the stimulation is stopped.

3. In some learning situations, such as those involving discrete trials, behavior is

poor if the intertrial interval is long. The animal sometimes has to be "primed" by the experimenter before he will again seek self-stimulation.

4. The reward effect of stimulation at some points in the rat's brain appears to be associated with other motivational systems.

Much research remains to be done before these and other features of brain stimulation can be fully understood in relation to behavior and learning. The investigations being reported with increasing regularity suggest a breakthrough in the study of the neurophysiology of learning.

These facts and observations about man's nervous system rest on the premise that man's links with physical and psychological reality are his senses and his nervous system. Without the nervous system, behavior would be impossible. The relationship between nervous system activity and behavior, however, is not a simple and direct one in the sense that a certain neurological input always produces the same response, for the stimuli producing sensations are variously perceived. Some of the elements involved in the integration of sensations into the complex interpretation of reality—which we call perception—will be briefly discussed.

Sensation and Perception

A description and understanding of how the senses function does not fully explain how the organism apprehends and reacts to whatever stimulates the senses. Psychologists have long been interested in the ability possessed by humans and most animals to incorporate past knowledge and meaning with sensory data to develop a relationship to, or an experience of, reality. This process of adding meaning and interpretation to sensations is called perception, and it involves the activity of the total organism and not just a specific sensory sector.

Some psychologists emphasize neurological correlates in the study of perception and seek data to define perception as essentially an integrating state within the nervous system that incorporates memory, past experience, and prior knowledge. Other psychologists emphasize the behavioral correlates to perception and interpret perception as one kind of learning. Still another point of view is held by psychologists who define perception in terms of both the neurological and the psychological. Psychologists who place the events of conscious experience in a central position are sometimes called phenomenologists; others who define perception in terms of the stimulus energies which are translated into sensations and judgmental responses are sometimes referred to as behaviorists.

The tradition in psychology has been to regard perception as a combination of sensory and imaginal components. No less a figure than

Wilhelm Wundt, generally considered the "father" of experimental psychology, recognized that perception is more than the simple summation of sense data (16). More recently, Helson (17) advanced a general theory of perception called adaptation–level theory, which attempts to develop a mathematically based theory of perceptual behavior. A–L theory is based on the assumption that experience is ordered by the organism in an individual way—the differing dimensions for the ordering depending on the individual involved—even though identical stimuli may be the source of experience from one individual to another. The creation of this order is a result of the constellation of all forces impinging on the organism from both within and without. One characteristic of this patterning in perceptual behavior is that neutral levels of functioning are established. These neutral regions represent the organism's level of indifference to the stimuli involved in any instance of perceptual behavior. Helson's theory of perceptual behavior is based on pooling three sources of stimuli, or factors, that have been found important in establishing an adaptation-level in psychophysical studies: (a) the immediate stimuli to which the organism is attending; (b) all other immediate stimuli that form a background stimulus pattern; and (c) the effects of previous stimuli that form residual patterns from past experience. This process of pooling the immediate, background, and residual stimulus factors forms the basis for a quantification of the adaptation process in simple judgmental behaviors.

The study of perception as a relationship between stimulus and response has long asked the question of whether this relationship has basic innate qualities. If individuals respond to stimuli that call for discriminations or judgments in a uniform way without having learned these discriminatory responses, then there is a reasonable basis for the hypothesis that such behavior is innate. No conclusive answer to this problem has been contributed to the literature on perception. One series of studies, however, suggests strongly that certain discriminatory responses are innate. Gibson and Walk (13) report data relating to the ability to discriminate height in human infants. The researchers used a runway extending over the edge of a drop down to a lower level. Glass was placed at a point on the runway to keep the subjects from falling over the edge. These "visual cliff" experiments involved infants from 6 to 14 months old. A significant number of the 36 infants crawled off the runway on the side where there was a shallow drop. Only three infants crawled off the runway on to the glass. Gibson and Walk concluded that even at this early age infants were capable of discriminating vertical distance. This evidence, together with that of other experimenters who tested the discriminatory ability of rats reared in total darkness, strongly suggests that some aspects of perceptual ability are innate.

TABLE 7-2
The Constancies of Perception[a]

Near stimulus: variable	Object situation: variable	Property of object: constant
Retinal image size	Distance of object from eye	Size of perceived object
Shape of retinal image	Angle at which object is viewed	Shape of perceived object
Intensity of light entering the eye	Surface illumination	Brightness of object surface
Spectral composition of light	Color of illuminant	Perceived color of object
Intensity of sound waves entering ear	Distance of wave source	Loudness of sound at source

[a] Adapted from Table XV in Newman (28).

One problem central to the study of perception is the question of object constancy. Objects in the physical world do not change their shape, size, or mass; nevertheless, the sensations we receive as indications of these objects vary as we move about. It is the point of view, not the objects, that changes. However, when given adequate clues of light and distance, our judgments are consistent with the objects. Each instance of constancy (size, shape, brightness, color, etc.) represents the operation of two systems, one involving stimulus properties that are constantly changing, and the other, stimulus properties that are constant. Table 7-2 explains some of the more common perceptual constancies by presenting the variable and the constant stimulus situations. The first two columns list the variable stimuli which integrate to produce the constant given in the third column. Unless we can perceive objects as constant even under variable conditions of observation, the world of experience would become chaotic and confusing. The habitual judgments which we make subconsciously would become difficult beyond belief.

Newman's (28) summary of generalizations about the perceptual process was made from past investigations:

1. The selectivity of perception depends on what we pay attention to as stimuli. Selectivity, or attention, is governed by intensity, novelty, repetition, intention, motivation, and patterning: Those stimuli which are more intense are usually attended to first; those stimuli which are novel or new tend to be perceived in place of older stimuli; a repeated stimulus is selected over one that is not repeated; a stimulus that corresponds to a predetermined mental set is more potent than one which does not; the motivational system of the individual selects stimuli that correspond to momentary needs; and the configuration of a total number of stimuli into a pattern perceived according to the above rubrics is selected over a pattern that does not attract attention.

2. The organization of stimuli influences attention and perception. If attention is

paid to various objects, the tendency is to group together those which are similar. It is also usual to group together things that are near as opposed to those that are far. Symmetrically grouped stimuli tend to be perceived as a unit, in contrast to stimuli that are not symmetrically related. Stimuli seen as having a common movement tend to be grouped together. The parts of an object perceived in motion maintain their relationship to each other.

The organization of stimuli influences our selection of the realities of the world which we perceive and do not perceive. Obviously, not all the rules given here always apply in every situation. The degree of motivation, for example, can mask the intensity and novelty of a situation. For example, a mother can usually be awakened by the soft cry of her child but not be bothered by the louder noises of automobiles passing by on the street. Also, the repetition of a stimulus is attention-getting until we become used to it. It is possible to sleep in a room with a blinking sign outside the window after adapting to its repetitiveness and losing awareness of its presence.

The basic organizing factor in perception, which appears to be innate, is the ability to group stimuli into figure–ground relationships. The object, or figure, is well defined and appears separate from the background, or ground. Sometimes stimulus figures are reversible so that figure and ground can be interchanged in the perception. The illustration below is one such arrangement which may be perceived either as a vase or as a pair of twins looking at each other.

Recent studies of perception point out that need and value may influence or distort judgment. As the stimulus situation becomes more ambiguous or the individual's motives become stronger, the stimuli are perceived as the person wants to perceive them, not necessarily as they actually are. For example, subjects who are hungry tend to see more food objects in neutral stimulus pictures than do subjects who are not hungry. In a classic study, Bruner and Goodman (6) found that young children from poor family backgrounds overestimate the size of coins in comparison to their estimates of the size of discs patterned after the coins. Children from wealthy family backgrounds are more accurate in their judgment of coin sizes. The degree to which perception is distorted by past experience is not known, but such distortion is more prevalent in unusual and ambiguous situations.

Most of our daily perceptions are relatively accurate and correct, even though our view of the world does not always correspond to the facts of physical reality. A major factor in distortion is that in some situations we perceive what we wish to perceive, and do not attend to stimuli that go counter to our needs of the moment. When the physical world and the motivational system of the individual are not congruent, the tendency is to behave in a way that will change the real world to conform with our motives. If this is impossible, the discrepancy is usually reduced by the changes we make in our perception of reality (2).

Summary

Behavior is not possible without the involvement of the nervous system. The relationship between neurology and behavior makes any understanding of human performance incomplete without some knowledge of the nervous system, especially the brain and its involvement in much that is called the higher mental processes. A knowledge of neural processes begins with an understanding of the activity of the neuron and the nerve impulse, its transmission across synaptic junctions to the complex involvement of affector and effector networks in the spinal cord and brain, and in the peripheral nervous system.

It has been the tradition in psychology to emphasize the senses as the contacts between physical reality and behavior. The concept of the stimulus and the response in psychology gives the sensory elements of the organism a central place in the mediation of behavior. Vision and audition are man's two most important senses involved in the learning of responses. Most of the changes in behavior that are brought about by practice are based on visual and auditory stimuli.

The central nervous system in man, especially the cortex, is involved in nearly all of the response systems that distinguish humans from subhumans. The brain is a complex network of interacting systems that can be identified in relation to their involvement in specific behavioral response patterns. The neurological basis for reward in learning is beginning to be identified in experimental animals, which suggests a neurological basis for the control of certain behaviors.

The relationship between the brain and behavior involves not only the interconnective network of neural pathways in the nervous system but also the basic chemical reactions that are crucial in determining the brain's capacity to react in specific ways. The study of the biochemical nature of neurological activity has been of increasing interest to researchers because of the possibility that nutritional deficiencies in early childhood may alter the normal development of the structure of the brain.

The relationship between physical reality and subjective interpretations of the signals of reality is of great interest to psychologists in their study of how man perceives the world around him. The lack of a one-to-one correspondence between our sensations and the interpretation, or the perception, we have of them has led psychologists to study extensively the influence of learned values and attitudes on behavior. Past experience affects our interpretation of immediate stimulation in many different ways. In general, it causes us to include, and exclude, the elements of any sense experience we might find compatible, or incompatible, with our past reactions.

Although the teacher in the classroom has little, if any, opportunity for direct neurological intervention in helping students learn, a knowledge of neurological processes in learning will help to establish a more complete frame of reference concerning the way learning takes place. Not all learning problems are the result of insufficient skill and practice. Some are the result of basic flaws in the nervous system which are not affected by practice. Educators are becoming more aware of the interaction between learning and the nervous system, so that today, children with a neurological problem can be given the special attention they require.

***

SUGGESTED READINGS

Hilgard, E. R., & Bower, G. H. Neurophysiology of learning. In *Theories of learning.* New York: Appleton-Century-Crofts, 1966. Ch. 13, pp. 426–479.

This textbook is one of the psychologist's basic sources of information about learning. In the chapter indicated above, the authors present a comprehensive view of the relationship between neurophysiology and learning. The student who wishes to go beyond an introductory presentation of the topic should consult this reference.

Luria, A. R. *Human brain and psychological processes.* New York: Harper & Row, 1966.

Professor Luria is an outstanding Soviet neurologist who has studied the patterns of brain involvement and behavioral deficit. This book summarizes his points of view, which have only recently become available in this country in an English translation.

Miller, G. A., Galanter, E., & Pribram, K. H. *Plans and the structure of behavior.* New York: Holt, Rinehart & Winston, 1960.

The authors' information-processing model for behavior contains some interesting observations concerning the relationship between the nervous system and the information-processing system described by TOTE.

Thompson, R. F. *Foundations of physiological psychology.* New York: Harper & Row, 1967.

This textbook is a comprehensive and up-to-date account of the physiological basis for behavior. The beginning student will find Professor Thompson's account of the nervous system and behavior worthy of his serious attention.

--- **REFERENCES**

1. Bard, P. A diencephalic mechanism for the expression of rage with special reference to the sympathetic nervous system. *American Journal of Physiology,* 1928, **84,** 490–515.
2. Berelson, B., & Steiner, G. A. *Human behavior, an inventory of scientific findings.* New York: Harcourt, Brace & World, 1964.
3. Best, C. H., & Taylor, N. B. *The physiological basis of medical practice.* Baltimore: Williams & Wilkins, 1955. Pp. 919–920.
4. Boring, E. G., Langfeld, H. S., & Weld, H. P. (Eds.) *Foundations of psychology.* New York: Wiley, 1948. P. 357.
5. Brazier, M. A. The analysis of brain waves. *Scientific American,* 1962, **206**(6), 142–153.
6. Bruner, J. S., & Goodman, C. C. Value and need as organizing factors in perception. *Journal of Abnormal and Social Psychology,* 1947, **42,** 33–44.
7. Corning, W. C., & John, E. R. Effect of ribonuclease on retention of conditioned response in regenerated planaria. *Science,* 1961, **134,** 1363–1365.
8. Delgado, J. M., Roberts, W. W., & Miller, N. E. Learning motivated by electrical stimulation of the brain. *American Journal of Physiology,* 1954, **179,** 587–593.
9. Fisher, A. E. Chemical stimulation of the brain. *Scientific American,* 1964, **210**(6), 60–68.
10. French, J. D. The reticular formation. *Scientific American,* 1957, **196**(5), 54–60.
10a. Fulton, J. F. (Ed.). *A textbook of physiology,* 17th edition, Philadelphia: Saunders, 1955. Pp. 1–2.
11. Gardner, E. *Fundamentals of neurology.* Philadelphia: Saunders, 1963.
12. Gerard, R. W. Brains and behavior. *Human Biology,* 1959, **31,** 14–20.
13. Gibson, E. J., & Walk, R. D. The visual cliff. *Scientific American,* 1960, **202**(4), 64–71.
14. Gray, G. W. The great ravelled knot. *Scientific American,* 1948, **179**(4), 27–39.
15. Hamburger, V. The life history of the nerve cell. *American Scientist,* 1957, **45,** 263–277.
16. Helson, H. *Theoretical foundations of psychology.* New York: Van Nostrand, 1951.
17. Helson, H. *Adaptation-level theory.* New York: Harper & Row, 1964.

18. Hilgard, E. R., & Bower, G. H. *Theories of learning.* New York: Appleton-Century-Crofts, 1966. Pp. 426–479.
18a. Hunt, W. A. Feeling and emotion. In E. G. Boring, H. S. Langfeld, & H. P. Weld (Eds.), *Foundations of psychology.* New York: Wiley, 1948. P. 95.
19. Kluver, H., & Bucy, P. C. Preliminary analysis of functions of the temporal lobes of monkeys. *A.M.A. Archives of Neurology and Psychiatry,* 1939, **42**, 979–1000.
20. Lashley, K. S. *Brain mechanisms and intelligence.* Chicago: University of Chicago Press, 1929.
21. Lashley, K. S. Cerebral organization and behavior. In H. Solomon, S. Cobb, & W. Penfield (Eds.), *The brain and human behavior.* Baltimore: Williams & Wilkins, 1958.
22. Luria, A. R. *Higher cortical functions in man.* New York: Basic Books, 1966. P. 29.
23. Luria, A. R. *Human brain and psychological processes.* New York: Harper & Row, 1966. P. 49.
24. McCleary, R. A., & Moore, R. Y. *Subcortical mechanisms of behavior.* New York: Basic Books, 1965.
25. McConnell, J. V. Memory transfer through cannibalism in planarians. *Journal of Neuropsychiatry,* 1962, **3**, 542–548.
26. Morgan, C. T. *Physiological psychology.* New York: McGraw-Hill, 1965.
27. Moruzzi, G., & Magoun, H. W. Brain stem reticular formation and activation of the EEG. *Electroencephalography and Clinical Neurophysiology,* 1949, **1**, 455–473.
28. Newman, E. B. Perception. In E. Boring, H. Langfeld, & H. Weld (Eds.), *Foundations of psychology.* New York: Wiley, 1948. P. 236.
29. Olds, J. Pleasure centers in the brain. *Scientific American,* 1956, **195**(4), 105–116.
30. Olds, J. Self stimulation of the brain. *Science,* 1958, **127**, 315–324.
31. Olds, J., & Milner, P. Positive reinforcement produced by electrical stimulation of septal area and other regions of rat brain. *Journal of Comparative and Physiological Psychology,* 1954, **47**, 419–427.
32. Pribram, K. H. The new neurology and the biology of emotion. *American Psychologist,* 1967, **22**, 830–838.
33. Pribram, K. H. Feelings as monitors. Paper presented at the Third International Symposium on Feelings and Emotions, Loyola University, Chicago, 1968.
34. Rosenzweig, M. R. Environmental complexity, cerebral change, and behavior. *American Psychologist,* 1966, **21**, 321–332.
35. Sechrest, L., & Wallace, J. *Psychology and human problems.* Columbus: Merrill, 1967.
36. Snider, R. S. The cerebellum. *Scientific American,* 1958(August), **199**(2), 84–90.
37. Sperry, R. W. Cerebral organization and behavior. *Science,* 1961, **133**, 1749–1757.
38. Sperry, R. W. The great cerebral commissure. *Scientific American,* January, 1964 (January), **210**, 42–52.
39. Thompson, R. F. *Foundations of physiological psychology.* New York: Harper & Row, 1967. P. 165.
40. Thompson, R., & McConnell, J. V. Classical conditioning in the planarian, dugesia dorotocephala. *Journal of Comparative and Physiological Psychology,* 1955, **48**, 65–68.

8

EDUCATION AND THE ATYPICAL CHILD

Only since World War II has the public school consistently acknowledged a responsibility to the exceptional child. Today most public schools can teach the child who has a neurological, physical, or emotional problem that can best be handled in a special instructional situation. Special education, as distinguished from regular classroom teaching, is available to the "exceptional child," a term now used to include the exceptionally gifted child as well as the child with some disability.

Most teacher preparation programs include some information about the atypical child; however, the physical and emotional factors in learning need to be particularly stressed for teachers of special education classes. Most teachers tend to conceptualize learning problems in terms of the psychology involved and to attempt remedial measures on that basis. It is true that behavior represents a complicated interaction between the physical and the psychological. Nevertheless, teachers in both regular and special education classrooms do encounter difficulties in learning in students whose behaviors stem from a physical, rather than a psychological, problem.

The concern for the exceptional child developed from a number of changes in society's attitudes about the individual who is "different." The school child who is physically different is no longer pitied or rejected. Such changes in attitude parallel changes in attitudes concerning the purpose and function of education. Larger populations increase the number of school-age children—among them, an increasing number with disabilities. Legislation has been enacted to keep children in school for a longer time than was once required. These changes call for special attention to be given to the unique instructional demands that are made on the school system. By 1948, 41 states had recognized the problems of the exceptional child and had enacted legislation authorizing support at the local level for the atypical child. [As early as 1817, The American School for the Deaf had been established in Hartford, Connecticut (4).] Today, every state in the United States has provided some legislation for special education.

At one time, only the child with a hearing deficiency or visual impairment was given special attention by the school. Today, however, the exceptional child is broadly defined as one whose physical, social, or mental characteristics would interfere with his profiting from a conventional educational program. The field of special education concerns those persons who are physically handicapped, blind or partially sighted, deaf or hard-of-hearing, mentally retarded, emotionally disturbed, or who have speech defects or some other special health problem. The gifted child is also a concern of special education since the typical classroom situation may in itself be a handicap to the development of his special talents.

Incidence of Exceptional Children and Youth

A survey completed by the Office of Education in 1958 indicated that over 882,000 exceptional children and youth were enrolled in special education programs in the public schools of the United States (19). Table 8-1 shows the distribution of these pupils according to the most applicable category of exceptionality. (To maintain an unduplicated count, the table does not reflect the incidence of disability.)

Between 1948 and 1958, enrollment in special education programs in the public schools rose 132%—three times the rate of increase for regular elementary and secondary enrollments. Table 8-1 indicates that in 1958 the two major categories of handicapping conditions were speech impairments and mental retardation. Although these two areas of exceptionality showed significant increases during the ten-year period leading to 1958, the greatest expansion took place in programs for the blind, which increased fivefold. A doubling of the number of children and youth classified as mentally retarded and as gifted, as well as those in need of speech correction, took place during this decade.

The 1958 survey found that programs for the partially sighted and the hard-of-hearing had not developed at a pace fast enough to accommodate all who required special programs in these areas. No significant changes

TABLE 8-1

Special Education Enrollments in Local Public School Systems[a]

Area of exceptionality	Number of pupils[b]
Blind	2,844
Partially seeing	8,598
Deaf	6,424
Hard of hearing	13,113
Speech impaired	486,944
Crippled	29,311
Special health problems	23,077
Socially and emotionally maladjusted	28,260
Mentally retarded (upper range)	201,406
Mentally retarded (middle range)	16,779
Gifted	52,269
Other	13,041

[a] Based on a survey of public school systems in urban communities of over 2500 or more in population. From 5041 questionnaires mailed, 97% were returned in completed form. These data are reported in Mackie and Robbins (19).

[b] Total number, 882,066.

were noted in the enrollment of children who were crippled or who had special health problems. Table 8-2 summarizes the increases in public school enrollments in the categories discussed above and presented in Table 8-1. A comparison of Tables 8-1 and 8-2 shows the relationship between percentage gains and gains in absolute numbers.

Special education programs vary throughout the nation, but several arrangements seem to dominate. The self-contained classroom in which the student benefits from the program on a full-time basis is found in most schools. This type of program arrangement, particularly for the deaf, the mentally retarded, and the gifted, is increasing as the number of qualified special education teachers increases. Another plan is the combination of part-time involvement in the special education program combined with instruction in the regular classroom. Many educators feel that this arrangement is best for the exceptional student whose handi-capping condition permits, since it provides the special instruction needed and also exposes the student to as normal a situation as is possible in his relations with other students. One of the major goals of special education is to teach the exceptional child to live an efficient and produc-tive life in a world inhabited by both handicapped and nonhandicapped individuals. Many educators feel that the exceptional child needs to be placed in situations where he must come to terms with the nonexceptional portion of the world to which he will be exposed after the school years.

TABLE 8-2

Increases in Special Education Enrollments during the Decade 1948–1958[a]

	0	100	200	300	400
Blind					
Partially seeing					
Deaf					
Hard of hearing					
Speech impairment					
Crippled and special health problems	No increase				
Socially and emotionally maladjusted					
Mentally retarded					
Mentally gifted					

Increase in total enrollment of public elementary and secondary day schools

[a] From Mackie and Robbins (19).

Special education arrangements also include instruction for a small number of children and youth who are confined to hospitals or nursing homes because of the nature or severity of their handicap.

Home visitations is another program arrangement available to the student whose problem keeps him from school for an extended period of time, or whose handicapping condition is such that he must remain at home. Such students are instructed at home by a visiting teacher.

Much more research is needed to increase our understanding of the relationship between behavior and handicapping conditions. Fortunately, each year funds become increasingly available for research on the atypical child.

The need for special education for the exceptional child will increase, if only because of the increase in the number of children of school age having disabling conditions. While medical science is making great strides in erasing some of these problems—polio, for example—research is making it possible for children with nonreversable handicapping conditions to benefit from a school experience—either in a regular or in a special education classroom. There are many specific impairments and disabilities that delineate the student's need for special education.

Sight is the major pathway to learning. The person with normal sight receives more sensations to be interpreted in the brain through the visual sense pathways than through the other senses. Disturbances in vision can occur from interference with the normal projection of a visual image on the retina, from the transmission of retinal stimulation over the optic nerve, or from the interpretation of these sensations in the visual area of the cortex and from there to other association centers in the brain. No absolute definition exists to define the amount of visual defect; however, persons with visual handicaps are usually classified as being either partially sighted or blind. The partially sighted are persons whose visual acuity is between 20/70 and 20/200 in the better eye after maximum correction. This group also includes children in special education programs who, because of some disease or difficulty, must have special care. The legal definition of blindness specifies a visual acuity of 20/200 or less in the better eye after maximum correction. Blindness also constitutes a visual field restricted to less than 20 degrees in the widest diameter (12). Blindness is not necessarily the total loss of sight, according to the legal definition. Many children in special education programs who are classified as blind may engage in some activities requiring partial sight.

The children served by special education programs for the blind do not represent all the children with visual problems in the schools. Many children are handicapped by visual problems that could easily be corrected by glasses or proper therapy. As part of the school health program many school systems now have mandatory eye examinations. In 1952, the National Society for the Prevention of Blindness estimated that approximately 7.5 million children were in need of eye care (18). This number has undoubtedly increased since then, even though methods of detection have improved. In one study, 27% of first- and sixth-graders had eye conditions requiring some attention by a physician (18).

The child who is blind has a greater adjustment problem than the partially sighted child has. Where special education programs are available, the blind child is usually not involved in learning situations in the regular classroom. Unless it is the school's policy to include blind children in the regular classroom as part of their adjustment, regular classroom teachers usually do not become involved in special instructional programs. The problems attendant on placing the blind child in a regular classroom have been the subject of extensive comments and attention. Unfortunately, no clear-cut answer to these problems has emerged. One author, Norris (23), concluded from a five-year study of blind children who participated in a regular nursery school program that integrated experiences are important for the development of the blind child; however, counseling for parents is an important adjunct to making this type of experience a success.

How does the blind person perceive objects and obstacles? Some recent research on the perception of obstacles demonstrates that auditory cues, especially pitch, enable the blind to perceive obstacles. In one study Cotzin and Dallenbach (7) used both blind and normal subjects in controlled situations to determine the auditory dimensions involved in the perception of obstacles. Previous research on the problem of "facial vision" had shown that aural stimulation by sound waves reflected from the obstacle was necessary. Cotzin and Dallenbach concluded that changes in the pitch of the sound being reflected are necessary for the obstacle to be perceived by the blind person. Changes in loudness alone are not sufficient. High frequencies are better than low frequencies, with a frequency below 8000 being insufficient to produce the necessary pitch change. A high tone of a single frequency is sufficient to support the perception. Continuous sounds are as effective as intermittent sounds.

Ammons, Worchel, and Dallenbach (1) experimented to determine whether the results of the earlier laboratory investigations could be replicated under the uncontrolled conditions of normal outdoor life. They also wanted to know if the ability to perceive obstacles through the use of aural cues (changes in pitch) could be learned by persons possessing normal vision and hearing. They concluded that the ability could be learned by persons who were blindfolded and who possessed normal hearing. They also concluded that less efficient cues, such as those based on other dimensions of sound, temperature, wind pressure, and odor, could be used in perceiving obstacles.

The psychological adjustment of the blind person has been the subject of considerable comment by authorities concerned with the education of the blind. Little controlled experimentation in this area has been done, however. Some authorities feel that blindness effects changes in the perception of social relationships, or prevents these relationships from developing normally. Chevigny (5) and others point out that (a) the blind usually do not achieve satisfactory social adjustments, (b) they appear to have some emotional problems in making new social contacts, (c) they have few close personal friends, and (d) they appear to withdraw into a fantasy life to a greater degree than sighted persons do. Whether this is the result of the particular isolation of the blind or the result of basic personality differences has not been determined. One major problem for the blind child, as for children with other handicapping conditions, is his parents' adjustment to the disability. Education for the parents is important, for without their support, any kind of educational program will be difficult for the blind child.

Very little research has been done on the child who is diagnosed as partially sighted, but no evidence exists to indicate that deviations in visual acuity result in personality problems beyond those expected of a normal population. Kerby (17a) studied over 7000 partially sighted children and found that their visual problems could be classified as follows:

1. Refractive errors (myopia, hyperopia, astigmatism), 49%
2. Developmental anomolies (cataract, albinism), 22%
3. Defects of muscle function (strabismus, nystagmus), 18%
4. Other diseases or defects (general diseases, infections, traumas, tumors), 11%

The relationship between visual acuity and learning is basic to what a child perceives as instructive in any classroom situation. If a child cannot see with a normal degree of acuity, he will not utilize his abilities to the extent that might be expected of children with no visual problems. Kelley (17) has listed a number of common symptoms of visual defects that are sometimes treated as purely psychological problems by the classroom teacher. These are:

1. Achievement in school which does not fully represent a child's true ability
2. Visual behaviors, including manipulation of reading materials, that are anomalous
3. School behavior that is not desirable
4. Atypical reading distance as evidenced by holding reading materials either too far from or too close to the eyes

Other manifestations are a lack of interest in and motivation for learning tasks which involve some type of visual accommodation and concentration, such as reading; nervous symptoms which tend to increase after tasks involving visual concentration; and rubbing the eyes, frequent blinking, watering of the eyes, together with an abnormally short attention span.

The classroom teacher should always consider the possibility that physical problems may be responsible for any learning difficulty the student has. Although behavioral symptoms may be present in all instances of inability to learn, these symptoms are not always the cause. Sometimes underlying physical problems can be the basic cause of the atypical behavior. All children with learning problems should be examined both physically and psychologically. Spache (27) gives ten symptoms of visual difficulty that are frequently misinterpreted:

1. Facial contortions and forward thrusting of head
2. Facial contortions and tilting of head

3. Facial contortions and tension during close work
4. Forward thrusting of head and holding book close to face
5. Tension while looking at distant objects
6. Posture that may indicate strain
7. Excessive head movements while reading
8. Frequent rubbing of eyes
9. Avoidance of close work
10. Tendency to lose place in reading

When these symptoms are frequent, repetitive, or severe, the teacher should recommend that the child be examined by a physician.

-- **Auditory Problems**

Hearing is the second most important sense to the learner. Actually, most learning takes place through the combined use of seeing and hearing. Accurate estimates are not available on children of school age who have some degree of hearing loss, for many children have a hearing loss that was never diagnosed. One study made in 1952 estimated a prevalence rate of hearing disability among school children of about 5% (18). In 1952, approximately 1.3 million children were thought to be in need of further observation to determine the extent of the hearing loss. Data from standard school health screening programs suggest that about 3.5% of elementary school children have hearing defects severe enough to be discovered by standard screening techniques.

There is no exact line of demarcation that separates persons who are hard of hearing from those who are deaf. For educational purposes, carefully administered hearing tests are relied on to assess aural acuity. The following levels of acuity loss have been suggested as guides for placement in school programs (18):

1. Slight losses of 20 decibels or less in the better ear
2. Moderate losses of 25 to 55 decibels in the better ear
3. Marked losses of 60 to 75 decibels in the better ear
4. Profound losses of 70 to 75 decibels or more

The first two categories constitute the population of the hard-of-hearing; the latter two categories define those who are considered deaf.

Three major types of hearing impairment have been identified (26). These are classified according to the location of the blockage in the auditory system. *Conduction deafness* refers to any condition that interferes with the passage of sound waves through the external or middle ear and into the cochlea. This type of impairment may be caused by adhesions that affect the ability of the tiny bones in the middle ear to conduct, changes in the structure of the eardrum that interfere with its elasticity, growth of new bone in the middle ear, and infections which allow the collection of fluid in the middle ear.

The hearing aid is a device that provides a conduction bypass of the middle ear through the bone surrounding the middle ear. The hearing aid does not provide an exact replication of sound; however, modern electronic techniques have helped to make the hearing aid acceptable to many persons who have a permanent conduction hearing problem.

Nerve deafness is the second major type of hearing impairment. Nerve deafness is usually caused by a degeneration of the nerve cells of the inner ear, where sound waves become nerve impulses. Damage to the auditory nerve can also be responsible for nerve deafness. Prolonged exposure to loud sounds can either temporarily or permanently damage the hair cells in the cochlea, depending on the intensity, pitch, and duration of the sounds. Persons whose jobs expose them to prolonged loud sounds usually show a loss of auditory acuity over the years. Nerve deafness can not be corrected since the degeneration in the neural portion of the auditory system is not reversible. The degenerative process, however, can be arrested if the cause is identified and if treatment is available for the problem which underlies the atrophy of the nerve cells.

The third type of deafness is *central deafness*. Central deafness is a rare disorder of the auditory pathways, caused by interference with nerve impulses going from the auditory nerve to the cortex. Central deafness is infrequently mentioned, and most deafness is attributed to conduction problems, neural damage, or a combination of both. Central deafness is associated with loss of speech and also with psychogenic disorders that do not involve physical deterioration of the cortical auditory centers.

Recent improvements in educational programs for the deaf and hard-of-hearing have helped accelerate their progress in mastering the fundamentals of education. The deaf child's stay in elementary programs has been shortened by as much as four or five years through a number of recent advances: early detection of hearing problems, the practice of starting the young deaf child in a preschool program as early as possible, better preparation of teachers for the deaf and hard-of-hearing, and the improvement of the technology of education for the deaf, which includes more sensitive identification devices as well as self-instruction techniques. The earlier the identification of hearing loss takes place, the more time the child has to progress through the curriculum.

Some controversy still exists as to whether the deaf child should be given instruction which emphasizes the use of speech, since the speech pattern of the deaf is always somewhat artificial. Some authorities feel that learning to speak and to read lips is not worth the amount of time and effort in terms of the benefits the deaf person derives. However, most instructional programs for the deaf emphasize the oral method, and many improvements have been made in techniques and in the design of supportive devices which aid the teacher in helping the deaf person acquire a spoken vocabulary.

The intellectual potential of the deaf child has been the subject of some study. Meyerson (20) reports that conflicting results appear in the literature about studies dealing with the performance of the deaf child on an individual performance test of intelligence and on group non-verbal and nonlanguage tests of intelligence. Some investigators report that the I.Q. of the deaf child is lower than average, while some studies provide data indicating that the I.Q. is not different. Even though the I.Q. of the deaf child may not be different from that of the child who has normal hearing, the instructional techniques necessary to help the deaf child use his intelligence in a learning situation are drastically different. Investigators seem to agree, however, that the intelligence score of the hard-of-hearing is slightly lower, significantly, than the score of normal hearing subjects when verbal tests are used.

Despite the arguments about the intelligence of the deaf or the hard-of-hearing child, the deaf child may be considered educationally re-tarded when compared with the child with normal hearing unless the deaf child has been given the type of educational program that would minimize the causes of this retardation. To a lesser degree, the same is true of the child who is hard-of-hearing. While this retardation, or lagging behind, is less during the early elementary years, it becomes progressively greater with increased age. Educational retardation is most evident in the verbal skills involving understanding the meaning of words and phrases. Lesser deficiencies are noted in spelling and arithmetic.

Compared with children with normal hearing, the deaf child is less well adjusted. Hard-of-hearing children obtain scores on personality tests, however, which are quite similar to the scores of normal children. But some deaf children do have a relatively rigid personality structure which does not allow for adaptability and flexibility in behavior that is not highly goal oriented. It would be wrong to conclude, however, that deafness or significant loss of hearing results in alterations of the personality and in a low I.Q. Personality and I.Q. deviations in the deaf and hard-of-hearing child could be due to a factor that eludes identification. One study of the socioeconomic status of a group of public school children with diagnosed hearing defects found that the majority of these children were underprivileged in almost every sense of the word, suggesting that in some children the home environment might have some relation to hearing loss (11).

Most children who are diagnosed as deaf are educated in special schools or special classrooms by teachers who are prepared to handle the problems deafness presents. The deaf child may spend some time in the regular classroom—primarily for social contacts with normally hearing children—but his presence in the classroom will usually not involve any attempts at instruction unless he is thoroughly able to communicate through speech and lip reading. The child the regular classroom teacher sees more frequently is the child who is hard-of-hearing. As with visual problems, hearing defects can produce behaviors that seem unrelated to the hearing loss unless the teacher is able to perceive the possibilities of physical causality for behavioral deviations. Sometimes just moving a child with a hearing or visual problem from the back of the classroom to the front can tremendously increase his ability to comprehend. Most children learn evasive behavior very early to "cover up" for a physical problem that interferes with their ability to relate and respond to a classroom situation. Most teachers are aware that education involves providing for individual differences. Not all teachers are aware, however, of the ramifications of a concept of individual differences when it involves physical handicaps and their relationship to learning disability.

Speech Impairment

Many teachers underestimate the effects of substandard speech habits on the child with a speech problem. Children who do not articulate properly can be the object of rejection by both parents and peers. The child whose speech is "different" can have severe adjustment problems in school. Oral communication is one of the most basic methods of maintaining contact with other persons. Speech impairments involve such conditions as stuttering, cleft palate, or other obvious signs of defects in the speech mechanisms. Many children whose signs of speech impairment are less obvious are handicapped, nonetheless, by the way they use their voice. Loudness, pitch, rate of speech, and quality are all related to the attractiveness of an individual's speech pattern. Departure from the normal in any of these factors can produce a speech pattern which is unpleasant.

Speech patterns are extremely important in teaching. The teacher whose ability to communicate is hampered by annoying speech habits is not effective in the classroom. Teachers should listen to themselves critically and be willing to discuss any speech problems with a speech therapist who is familiar with the demands of the classroom.

Disorders of speech may result from physiological defects such as cleft palate or nasal obstructions or they may result from psychogenic problems. Sometimes a physical problem becomes a psychological problem after the physiological problem is removed. Karlin (16) has examined a wide range of speech and language disorders and has produced the following classifications:

1. Delayed speech, characterized by retardation in the acquisition and use of words
2. Articulatory disorders, characterized by distortion, omission, and substitution in sounds
3. Voice disorders, characterized by the absence of voice or by an abnormal production associated with the intensity, pitch, or melody of the sound produced
4. Cluttering, associated with rapid speech and with slurring and distortion of sounds
5. Stuttering, characterized by a disorganization of the rhythmic flow of speech
6. Aphasia, indicates disorders of linguistic symbolization

The relationship of defective speech to other communication skills has been established. Children with speech defects have more difficulty in reading, especially in oral reading. The stutterer is, on the average, a grade below normal in comprehension and two grades below normal in rate of reading. The relationship between speech defects and poor spelling ability has been well documented. This is especially true of those persons who attempt to spell a word as it sounds when the sound they produce is consistently defective. Children with speech problems are, on the average, somewhat retarded in their overall school progress, and the retardation becomes progressively more severe unless some corrective measures are imposed.

Teachers should be aware of the characteristics generally associated with defective speech. A pupil may be considered to have a speech problem if the sounds he makes are not readily audible or intelligible, if they are vocally unpleasant, or if he is visually unsightly when he is producing sounds; if there is obvious labor in the production of sounds, or if they are lacking in typical rhythm and stress; and if the speech is linguistically deficient and inappropriate to the speaker in terms of age, sex, and development (10).

Boys outnumber girls among the school age population with speech problems. Children with speech defects are somewhat lower in measurable intelligence than the average for the general population. Speech defects are more common among mentally deficient children than among the general population.

Some speech problems are not reversible, that is, they cannot be removed completely through therapy, but many of the less severe problems do respond to therapy. Articulation problems can usually be dealt with successfully through a consistent program of therapy. Speech defects that result from brain damage and show no improvement for an extended period are difficult, if not impossible, to correct. But even with this type of problem speech therapy can help to sensitize the person to his problem so that he can minimize the defect. Speech defects caused by cleft palate can usually be corrected by surgical alleviation of the basic anatomical condition. This is also true for speech defects that result from nasal and throat obstructions or improperly aligned teeth. Those individuals who must have the larynx removed can learn to use esophageal speech. Although it is limited in loudness and pitch, this type of speech does not limit communication.

Motor Impairments and Special Health Problems

Motor handicaps include many conditions that interfere with the normal activity of muscles, bones, joints, and with the functions controlled by the affected areas. A motor impairment may be the result of a neurological or an orthopedic problem or a combination of both. The term "motor handicap" is used to cover a range of conditions, often crippling. At one time poliomyelitis was the major contributor to crippling conditions among children. Today, polio has been controlled by vaccines and cerebral palsy emerges as the major crippler of children. It is also the chief concern in the field of special education for children with motor handicaps.

Cerebral Palsy

Cerebral palsy is considered a congenital defect, since about 90% of its incidence is due to neurological problems in the central nervous system that were present at birth or occurred very shortly thereafter. Cerebral palsy is used as a classification to describe any condition that indicates damage to the portion of the brain that mediates the coordination or control of the muscles. The incidence of cerebral palsy in the general population is difficult to estimate. One study estimates that cerebral palsy, in some degree, is found in about 300 to 350 per 100,000 persons (12).

The types of cerebral palsy are referred to either by the neurological syndromes or by the orthopedic manifestations. The neurological basis for cerebral palsy appears to be damage to the motor area of the brain. The cerebral palsy child differs from the usual brain-injured child in that his physical symptoms, usually of a crippling nature, are of major importance. Although a neurological classification is frequently used in research and for clinical practice, most literature on cerebral palsy refers to the orthopedic aspects and accentuates differences in motor functions. One such classification has been developed by Phelps (24), using six terms:

1. Flaccid paralysis—the muscle is flabby and lifeless
2. Spastic paralysis—the muscle is hyperactive and has a tendency to contract to a greater degree than normal muscle
3. Athetosis—involves an involuntary movement or series of movements in a muscle
4. Ataxia—no control over the size or direction of an initiated voluntary motion
5. Tremors—usually classified as coarse or fine and rapid or slow. In muscle tissue, tremors may be voluntary or involuntary
6. Rigidity—a sustained, involuntary condition of loss of elasticity and contractibility in muscle

Based on this classification, spasticity, athetosis, and ataxia in that order account for the largest number of cases of cerebral palsy. One report found that 46% of cerebral palsy cases in the sample studied were classified as spastic and 26% were classified as athetoid (13).

Many studies have attempted to answer the question of the relationship between cerebral palsy and intelligence. Some studies indicate that as many as two-thirds of the cerebral palsied are borderline or mentally retarded. Conclusions concerning the intelligence of the child with cerebral palsy are difficult to make because the nature of the condition precludes testing with the usual methods, or certainly makes it difficult. It would be wrong to conclude that all persons with cerebral palsy are dull normal or mentally retarded, for many cerebral palsied children show remarkable ability when given the special attention needed.

The brain damage responsible for cerebral palsy may be due to a number of factors. It was once thought that the excessive use of forceps during delivery was responsible. This is now one of a number of possible known causes, which include brain damage that can take place before birth as well as mechanical injury at birth. Cerebral palsy appears to be more common among premature babies than among full-term infants. Hypoxemia, or lack of oxygen, in blood feeding the brain is considered a major cause. Prolonged lack of oxygen can cause extensive brain damage. Cerebral hemorrhage is another major cause of brain damage in the child with cerebral palsy. Rh-factor incompatability and toxic conditions affecting the mother are also related to cerebral palsy. Any condition that could conceivably result in damage to the motor area of the brain, either before, at, or after birth, could be counted in the etiology of cerebral palsy.

Other Crippling Conditions

Although most of the research on motor disability has been done on the child with cerebral palsy, other crippling conditions contribute to motor disability. Many authorities in the field of special education now include conditions other than motor disability under the classification "crippling." For example, heart disease, diabetes, leukemia, cancer, and other diseases that are usually prolonged are now thought of as crippling conditions. Children thus afflicted require special attention in the classroom. Educators are becoming aware that any child whose physical or emotional health deviates from the normal is a potential candidate for a special education classroom for part of or all the instructional program within the school.

Very little is known about the characteristics of some kinds of handicapped children, but what is known suggests that the disabled child must be viewed in terms of his disability's effects on both his psychological and his physical well-being. One investigator found, in comparing sentence-completion test data of 264 physically handicapped children and the responses from a group of nonhandicapped children, that the self-perception of children with orthopedic, cardiac, and neurological handicaps includes more fears and feelings of guilt than does the self-perception of the nonhandicapped children (8).

Cardiac problems in children are usually related to rheumatic fever or congenital defects. The child with a heart problem may frequently appear more neurotic and dependent than normal children do. Personality problems in children with heart defects tend to increase as the severity and longevity of the problems increase. Such children may be placed in a regular class, but it is usually necessary to restrict their activities.

Several studies have been made of the problems of the diabetic child. In one study, 57 diabetic children were given a battery of psychological tests, from which the authors concluded that (a) the children were of average intelligence; (b) they tended to turn their aggressions outward; (c) they evidenced high rates of anxiety and tension; and (d) their general pattern of socialization was different from that of normal children of the same age (15). Although there are not many diabetic children of school age, their problem is important because caring for, or accommodating, the illness becomes a central issue in the life of the child.

Epilepsy

Now that drug therapy has proved successful in controlling seizures in many patients, epilepsy is no longer talked about in whispers, nor is it regarded with the fear and mystery that hampered understanding of the condition. Epilepsy is usually diagnosed by the presence of overt seizures. The physician usually supplements these diagnostic signs with evidence from an electroencephalogram. The brain wave pattern of the person with epilepsy usually shows abnormal variations, although this is not true of all epileptics. The most common cause of epilepsy in young children is a cerebral birth injury. There is evidence, too, that heredity may play a role in epilepsy. In many instances the specific cause of the seizures cannot be determined.

Four major clinical types of epilepsy are generally recognized (13):

1. Grand mal—the convulsive type in which the person usually falls, with muscles tightened and twitching. He usually loses consciousness for a few minutes

2. Petit mal—momentary loss of consciousness without the convulsive behavior exhibited in grand mal

3. Psychomotor—mild psychomotor seizures resemble petit mal; severe seizures resemble grand mal. The person usually appears to be conscious. Amnesia is the outstanding characteristic of psychomotor seizures

4. Jacksonian—a modified grand mal type in which consciousness is retained during the first part of the seizure

Contrary to popular opinion there is no research evidence that personality and intellectual deviations accompany epilepsy. Some studies have shown that epileptics who are institutionalized have a lower average intelligence than do persons who do not have epilepsy—but this could be due to the depressing effects of institutionalization. Other studies indicate that the intelligence of the epileptic in society does not deviate significantly from that of the nonepileptic. Intellectual deficit as a result of the underlying neurological damage may be present, but in these instances the lower intelligence and the epilepsy show only correlational relationships, not that of cause and effect. The more severe the seizures the greater the likelihood of personality problems arising as a result of the epilepsy; however, this does not mean that an "epileptic personality" is either present or identifiable in all cases of this disability. The child who occasionally experiences seizures at school is inevitably singled out by his classmates as someone who is different. For this reason, the mental health of the epileptic child should be of concern to both parents and teacher. The epileptic child whose seizures are not severe enough for him to be institutionalized can usually adjust quite well to a regular classroom situation if the teacher understands the relationship between stress and seizures that prevails in most cases. The epileptic student is someone with a specific disorder which can be controlled with proper medical attention and with the understanding and support of the parents and the school personnel.

_____ **General Health Problems**

Fortunately, only a small percentage of children have permanent ill health. Many children at some time during their school careers do have health problems severe enough to seriously affect their ability to learn. One study of the findings of periodic health examinations of 1056 first-grade children reported that 21% of those examined had conditions that adversely affected their health. These conditions did not vary significantly by sex or socioeconomic status (28). This same study reported that adverse orthopedic conditions were found in 4.8% of the sample (for the most part these were pronated feet and extremely flat arches usually accompanied by knock-knees), allergic problems in 3.9% (asthma, eczema, and other allergic diseases), emotional disorders in 3.4% of the children (with such symptoms as enuresis, tics, extreme aggression, hostility, and anxiety), ear, nose, and throat problems in 3.2% (mostly chronically infected adenoids and tonsils), nutritional disorders in 2.4%, and cardiac disease in 0.9%.

Another study of the illness experience of a group of 126 normal children over an 18-year period produced the following data (2):

1. Colds and upper-respiratory infections were experienced by the total sample and accounted for the majority of disabilities reported
2. Gastrointestinal disturbances and allergy were important in infancy and in adolescence. Gastrointestinal disturbances were the most frequent illness reported before the first birthday
3. Communicable diseases such as measles, chicken pox, mumps, etc., occurred at all ages, with peak incidence during the elementary school years
4. A small number of children and youth had accidents and surgery every year. The surgical rate showed a gradual decline and the accident rate a gradual increase up to the middle of adolescence
5. Symptoms attributable to the neurological and endocrine systems increased during adolescence
6. Accidents were more frequent among the boys and endocrine symptoms more frequent among the girls

These data clearly suggest that the regular classroom teacher will see many health problems which could adversely affect the behavior of the students involved. Teachers should not underestimate the relationship between physical health and learning. Children who do not feel well do not learn effectively.

_____   **Mental Retardation**

A tremendous amount of research on the problem of mental retardation in children has been stimulated by the public's awareness and concern, particularly during the past fifteen years. Mental retardation is a term broadly used to indicate any type of intellectual deficit. In most instances this deficit is measured in terms of an intelligence quotient. (See Chapter 14 for a discussion of I.Q.) An I.Q. below 75 or 80 is usually considered indicative of mental retardation. For educational purposes the following classifications are generally accepted in discussing subnormal I.Q.'s:

1. I.Q., 0–35; totally dependent, custodial, mentally handicapped
2. I.Q., 35–55; trainable, mentally handicapped
3. I.Q., 55–75; educable, mentally handicapped
4. I.Q., 75–90; slow learners

Since intelligence is a continuous function in man, establishing arbitrary points on an I.Q. scale has many dangers. The amount of error always present to some degree in the measurement of intelligence would be a strong argument against this type of classification. However, classifications must be made to determine educational programs for the mentally handicapped and to establish a legal basis for financial support for special education programs. Many states have acknowledged the need for competently handled I.Q. examinations by establishing standards for psychologists and psychometrists who administer the intelligence tests.

Children classified as slow learners should be able to function at a normal level of competence, though they will require more time and effort for learning than will the child with an average I.Q. The educable mentally handicapped child should be able to demonstrate competence in skills usually associated with instruction at the elementary school level. This means they should attain a level of education that allows them to perform in a literate manner. However, the trainable mentally handicapped child should not be expected to progress much beyond the level of third grade skills. A level of education necessary for literacy is usually not possible for these children, but they can be trained to develop some skills in the area of oral communication, self-care, and socialization. They will usually require a dependent environment for most of their lives. The custodial mentally handicapped child cannot be expected to acquire any skills which will lead to independent behavior, and he will usually require life-long custodial or institutional care.

It is difficult to estimate the incidence of mental retardation with accuracy. The National Association for Retarded Children estimates that wherever the subpopulation is large enough to reflect the characteristics of the population at large the incidence of intellectual deficit is 3%.

One problem that has interested researchers in the area of mental retardation is the relative importance of congenital as opposed to environmental factors in causing mental deficiency. Some types of deficit are so closely associated with certain conditions that they are accepted as congenital (mongolism, cretinism, micro- and hydrocephalus). Congenital factors appear to be more evident in the severely retarded, while environmental factors are more often suspected as a primary cause of less severe deficits. As with any question concerning a congenital characteristic versus a characteristic shaped by the environment, it is difficult, if not impossible, to obtain conclusive evidence because the two influences are interrelated. Most behavioral scientists tend to emphasize the influence of postnatal deprivation (i.e., social and cultural stimuli) that acts to depress the intellectual capacity of the retarded person. The medical emphasis, however, tends to accentuate congenital factors.

Very little is known about the effect of mental retardation on the socialization patterns of the mentally retarded child. Sociometric studies suggest that in a regular classroom the mentally handicapped child is usually socially segregated in a physically integrated environment. The child's social rejection appears to be based on his deviant personality traits rather than on his poor ability. Several studies have reported that educable mentally retarded adults usually make social adjustments which are no better or worse than those made by persons of normal intelligence (9). However, the mentally retarded adult has a more difficult time in finding employment than his normal counterpart does during periods when unemployment is high.

Specialists in the field of special education do not agree on what constitutes the best type of educational program for the mentally retarded pupil. Some feel that such a child should be placed in a special classroom, supervised by a teacher who is especially prepared for this kind of work. Others feel that the mentally retarded child should be kept in a regular classroom whenever possible. Johnson (14), in a review of research on the use of special classes in the education of the mentally handicapped, concluded that "the reported research to date does not support the subjective evaluations of teachers and their contention that the education for mentally handicapped children in special classes is superior to that provided these children in the regular classes." The studies cited by Johnson agree consistently that mentally handicapped children enrolled in special classes show a significantly lower level of achievement in comparison to mentally handicapped children who remain in regular classes. Children in special classes for the mentally handicapped learn motor skills at the same rate as do those who are in regular classes. The only area in which the special class may prove a possible advantage is in personal and social development. The lack of peer acceptance for the mentally handicapped child in the regular class-room is countered by evidence of peer acceptance in special classes for the mentally handicapped, thus giving the special class a probable advantage in this facet of development.

Johnson feels that preparation programs for teachers of the mentally handicapped have too often emphasized the child's disability rather than his ability. Most programs tend to accentuate the creation of good mental health in the mentally retarded child rather than emphasize learning and achievement. Such a shift of emphasis diminishes the child's need to progress. Johnson concludes that the mentally retarded child, whether in a regular or a special classroom, should be given some reason to learn by the introduction of realistic stress as a motivation. The mentally handicapped child should be placed in learning situations that require him to exert some effort for a satisfactory conclusion. The teacher needs to understand each child and his ability to perform so that learning goals can be set at a level slightly above this ability but not so far above it to be demoralizing. As each learning task is successfully completed the teacher should set the goal of the next activity at a higher level. In this manner the child should improve his performance incrementally from day to day.

The mentally retarded child is capable of learning. True, this capability is limited by the severity of the retardation; however, the educable and the trainable mentally handicapped can be taught skills and understand-ings which will help them toward an effective personal, social, and economic adjustment as an adult. Teachers too often conclude that intellectual deficit precludes the possibility of learning and achievement. Actually, the mentally retarded can perform many useful functions in society if taught the skills necessary for useful performance.

_____ **Psychoneurological Learning Disability**

Different from the child with gross deficit of physical or neurological functioning is the child whose learning disability is related to a minimal brain dysfunction. Unlike the child with cerebral palsy whose neuro-logical impairment is extensive and whose impairment of motor functions is visible, the child with minimal brain dysfunction is characterized primarily by difficulty in learning. The mentally retarded child usually has some brain damage, but his primary characteristic is an intellectual deficit. Myklebust (21), who has studied the brain-damaged child extensively, defines the characteristics of minimal brain damage as follows:

> In the population with minimal brain damage, it is the fact of adequate motor function, average to high intelligence, adequate hearing and vision, and adequate emotional adjustment together with a specific deficiency in ability to learn that constitutes the basis for homogeneity.

The child with this type of learning disability usually suffers from more information being delivered to the central nervous system (CNS) by the senses than the child is neurologically capable of handling. This overloading of the CNS is in contrast to the deprivation that characterizes the child whose senses underload the CNS, as is typical in blindness and deafness. The child whose disability is related to inadequate input of stimulation (peripheral disorders of the nervous system; sensory deprivation) does not get the amount of stimulation to the brain which the normal child has in a learning situation. The child who is deprived of input pathways must be given a special type of education that takes advantage of the remaining input channels. The child with a CNS disability (brain damage, minimal brain dysfunction, cerebral palsy) receives a normal input of stimuli if no damage is present in the sensory receptors, but the CNS disability does not permit the brain to utilize this stimulation adequately. Such a child must be given an educational program that controls the quantity and quality of input until the child has demonstrated an ability to tolerate and profit from normal stimulation in learning.

Myklebust and Johnson (22) suggest using the term "psychoneurological learning disability" to characterize the child who has been labeled "brain damaged," "perceptually handicapped," or "neurophrenic," since this new term implies the homogeneous nature of the learning problems related to minimal CNS impairment.

In a recent study, Boshes and Myklebust (3) investigated the subtle nature of the relationship between minimal brain dysfunction and behavior. Their research was conducted with 85 children, from 7 to 18 years old, whose difficulty in school was described, for the most part, as an inability to learn to read and write. All the children studied had an I.Q. of 90 or above. Based on the findings of extensive neurological examination, the sample was subdivided into three groups—negative, suspect, and positive—describing the suspected presence of neurological dysfunction based on clinical examinations. Data were also collected from each subject on 21 behavioral characteristics, which included scores on the subtests of the Wechsler Intelligence Scale for Children. A comparison of group averages on the behavioral characteristics revealed no significant differences, suggesting the influence of factors other than neurological disability.

A further analysis of the data indicated that the relationships between certain behavioral signs and the results of the neurological examination tended to increase as the neurological signs became more evident. From this evidence the investigators concluded that neurological integrity is more closely related to behavior than had heretofore been suggested. This relationship is a subtle and complex one. The absence of a significant difference in the mean behavioral scores of children who have different neurological classifications does not mean an absence of differences in the ways they learn. Individuals may be equal in ability but different in the ways they perceive and interpret reality. The three behavioral indices showing the greatest trend relationship with neurological deficit were spelling, social maturity, and auditory blending. These behaviors might provide a clue to techniques that would be useful in further study of the child with a minimal brain dysfunction.

Most of the recent research on the child with a psychoneurological learning disability makes the point that this type of impairment may be responsible for many learning disorders that had once been considered psychological in origin. Minimal brain dysfunction can be present in learning disabilities that are manifest in various combinations of impairment of conceptualization, perception, memory, language, and control of attention, impulse, and motor function (6). Any of these learning problems, when seen in children who appear normal in intelligence and in emotional adjustment, may be rationalized by the teacher through any of a number of hypotheses about the cause. The persistence of a learning disability in any child is ample reason for having the child undergo a thorough neurological examination. However, unless the teacher is aware of the continuing nature of the disability and is willing to call it to the attention of the child's parents and those in the school system who would recommend and arrange for such an examination, the opportunity to help the child is missed. Perhaps at some future time a thorough neurological examination will be routinely given to all children at the time they enter school.

The Emotionally Disturbed Child

Although emotional problems in children and youth are considered handicapping conditions, they are not always due to physical or neurological impairment. However, emotional problems are often associated with physical disability. The emotionally disturbed child is encountered frequently enough in the regular classroom to warrant a discussion of this type of disability, whether or not physical pathology is involved.

Education for the emotionally disturbed child is probably the least advanced of special education programs for children and youth. Although there are strong social pressures to initiate such programs, there is also a serious lack of the basic knowledge needed to classify and place children in such programs. Most classification and placement of the emotionally disturbed child, according to Quay (25), is done on the basis of impressions rather than data. Usually, the children who are unable to adjust to regular class instruction and are not classifiable in a more specific category of exceptionality are labeled emotionally disturbed. The nomenclature for adult emotional disturbances is not applicable to most of the problems of children. Methods of distinguishing types of emotional disturbance and the need to define these types in terms of their relationship to the learning process is a pressing problem in special education.

The recurring symptoms in children with an emotional problem can be classified into two major patterns. One pattern is characterized by acting-out behavior, and children who behave in such a manner are usually looked upon by the teacher as a conduct problem. The other pattern is characterized by withdrawal behavior and is usually referred to as a personality problem. Quay distinguishes three types of programs usually established in schools to deal with these patterns of emotional disturbance. One he labels the "holding action" practice in which an attempt is made "to exert a minimum of achievement and performance demands while waiting either for some form of therapy to deal with the emotional disturbance or for the coming of the age at which the child can leave school." Another practice is to consider education as a therapy for the child instead of a process of instruction. A theory of psychotherapy tends to dominate this approach. The last type of practice Quay discusses is one that emphasizes achievement and instruction rather than therapy. Not all educational programs fit into one of these three classifications, but the majority of programs do fit to a great degree.

The child with a personality problem usually has a great deal of anxiety about education, and may learn additional anxieties incidental to classroom situations that would not affect the normal child. Quay believes that it is most important to avoid unpleasant and fear-producing stimuli in working with this type of child. However, some children with a conduct problem need to learn some fear and avoidance reactions so that impulse behavior can be controlled. The psychopathic child, particularly, needs to develop some internalized restraints on behavior.

Other children with conduct disorders may either be neurotic or may display behavior appropriate to a social context that is not acceptable in the social system of the school. The neurotic child's behavior may be an acting out of anxiety rather than an internalizing of it. The child may regret his actions, but be unable to control them because of the strong feelings of unhappiness which motivate them. The child whose conduct is appropriate to his own subculture but not to that of the school is not necessarily emotionally disturbed. He may only need to learn to distinguish between the choices of behavior that are appropriate to his own world and to school. Not all children who deviate behaviorally are sick. Some are expressing behaviors that may appear different in contexts other than the one in which the behavior was learned. The solution to the problem is education rather than therapy.

Summary

Tremendous advances have been made in recent years in education for the atypical child. These advances were based on a concern for the individual learner. Concern for individuality costs money, however, and only recently has there been the financial participation at local, state, and national levels sufficient to begin to support the special education programs needed. There is a continuing need for more research on the various handicapping conditions and their relationship to special education efforts. Many programs are haphazardly developed because basic knowledge is lacking about the conditions being served. Screening procedures are becoming more thorough in many school systems, so that more children who need special education programs now get them early enough for the program to do some good. Public education in this country will undoubtedly make great strides in the field of special education for the atypical child.

The problems exhibited by the learner who may be in need of a special education program range from physical disabilities (such as loss of vision and loss of auditory acuity) to emotional disturbances. Attention has recently been given to the child with a psychoneurological learning disability that results from the inability of the brain to handle stimulation in a normal manner. Recent research suggests that the number of children who exhibit learning problems because of a neurological deficit is larger than had been previously imagined. Teachers tend to look for solutions to learning disabilities in the learner's past educational history rather than in a history of his behavior, which might indicate a neurological problem. Fortunately, the physical problems that can influence learning are being given more attention each day. The field of special education alerts teachers to the importance of considering both the physical and the psychological organization of the learner.

SUGGESTED READINGS

Bettelheim, B. *Love is not enough.* Glencoe, Ill.: Free Press, 1950.

Professor Bettelheim's association with the Orthogenic School at the University of Chicago is the subject of this early description of the treatment of emotionally disturbed children in that facility. Many of the activities of the staff in their relationships with the children were considered quite advanced when this book was written. The Orthogenic School has long been known for a type of therapeutic experience for the emotionally disturbed child that many other facilities have adopted.

Farber, B. *Mental retardation: Its social context and social consequences.* Boston: Houghton Mifflin, 1968.

Professor Farber discusses mental retardation from the viewpoint of its social significance. He regards the mentally retarded person as a social phenomenon in our culture. As such, he treats the occurrence of mental retardation in society by emphasizing its sociological perspective rather than its psychological relevance. Many of the major problems associated with mental retardation will be solved by changes in individual value systems rather than through increases in institutional efficiency.

Myklebust, H. R. (Ed.) *Progress in learning disabilities.* Vol. 1. New York: Grune & Stratton, 1968.

This book is a collection of original articles dealing with various aspects of learning disabilities. The articles emphasize the neurological basis of many types of learning disabilities and present discussions of developmental views of learning problems. Teachers should become familiar with the problem of learning disability in the classroom, for the trend in education toward the individualization of instruction gives the classroom teacher more responsibility in helping the learner pace his own instruction.

Smith, R. M. *Clinical teaching: Methods of instruction for the retarded.* New York: McGraw-Hill, 1968.

Many practical problems of providing instruction for the retarded are discussed here. Professor Smith feels that the special education teacher should become much more of a diagnostician in determining what the special learning problems of the retarded are. Clinical teaching depends for its success on the development of this increased sophistication in teachers who work with retarded children.

── REFERENCES

1. Ammons, C. H., Worchel, P., & Dallenbach, K. M. Facial vision: the perception of obstacles out of doors by blind-folded and blind-folded, deafened subjects. *American Journal of Psychology,* 1953, **66**, 519–535.
2. Bayer, L. M., & Snyder, M. M. Illness experience of a group of normal children. *Child Development,* 1950, **21**, 93–120.
3. Boshes, B., & Myklebust, H. R. A neurological and behavioral study of children with learning disorders. *Neurology,* 1964, **14**, 7–12.
4. Cain, L. Special education. In C. Harris (Ed.), *Encyclopedia of educational research.* New York: Macmillan, 1960. Pp. 1324–1330.
5. Chevigny, H. *The adjustment of the blind.* New Haven, Conn.: Yale University Press, 1950.
6. Clements, S. D. *Minimal brain dysfunction in children.* Publ. No. 1415. Washington, D. C.: Public Health Service, 1966.
7. Cotzin, M., & Dallenbach, K. M. Facial vision: the role of pitch and loudness in the perception of obstacles by the blind. *American Journal of Psychology,* 1950, **63**, 485–515.
8. Cruickshank, W. M. The relation of physical disability to fear and guilt feelings. *Child Development,* 1951, **22**, 291–298.
9. Dunn, L. M. Mentally retarded children. In C. Harris (Ed.), *Encyclopedia of educational research.* New York: Macmillan, 1960. Pp. 835–848.
10. Eisenson, J. The nature of defective speech. In W. Cruickshank (Ed.), *Psychology of exceptional children and youth.* Englewood Cliffs, N. J.: Prentice-Hall, 1955. Pp. 184–213.
11. Fiedler, M. F. A study of the socio-economic status of a group of public school children with hearing defects. *Child Development,* 1951, **22**, 193–198.
12. Fouracre, M. H. Physically handicapped children. In C. Harris (Ed.), *Encyclopedia of educational research.* New York: Macmillan, 1960. Pp. 995–1008.
13. Garrison, K. C., & Force, D. G. *The psychology of exceptional children.* New York: Ronald Press, 1965. P. 410.
14. Johnson, G. O. Special education for the mentally handicapped. *Exceptional Children,* 1962, **29**, 62–69.
15. Johonnsen, D. E., and Bennett, E. M. The personality of diabetic children. *Journal of Genetic Psychology,* 1955, **87**, 175–185.
16. Karlin, I. Speech and language handicapped children. *Journal of Disabled Children,* 1958, **95**, 370–376.
17. Kelley, D. J. Using children's school atypicalities to indicate ocular defects. *Journal of Educational Research,* 1954, **47**, 455–465.
17a. Kerby, C. E. A report on visual handicaps of partially seeing children. *Exceptional Children,* 1952, **18**, 137–142.
18. Lesser, A. J., & Hunt, E. P. The nation's handicapped children. *American Journal of Public Health,* 1954, **55**, 166–170.
19. Mackie, R. P., & Robbins, P. P. *Exceptional children and youth: A chart book of special education enrollments in public day schools of the United States.* Publ. No. OE–35109. Washington, D. C.: U. S. Office of Education, 1959.
20. Meyerson, L. A psychology of impaired hearing. In W. Cruickshank (Ed.), *Psychology of exceptional children and youth.* Englewood Cliffs, N. J.: Prentice-Hall, 1955. Pp. 120–183.

21. Myklebust, H. R. Learning disorders: psychoneurological disturbances in childhood. *Rehabilitation Literature*, 1964, **25**, 354–360.
22. Myklebust, H. R., & Johnson, D. J. *Learning disabilities; educational principles and procedures.* New York: Grune & Stratton, 1967. P. 354.
23. Norris, M. What affects blind children's development. *Children*, 1956, **3**, 123–129.
24. Phelps, W. M. Description and differentiation of types of cerebral palsy. *Nervous Child*, 1949, **8**, 107–127.
25. Quay, H. Some basic considerations in the education of emotionally disturbed children. *Exceptional Children*, 1963, **30**, 27–31.
26. Ruch, T. C., Patton, H. D., Woodbury, J. W., & Towe, A. L. *Neurophysiology.* Philadelphia: Saunders, 1961.
27. Spache, G. D. Facts about vision significant to the classroom teacher. *Claremont College Reading Conference, Twenty-First Yearbook.* Claremont, Calif.: Claremont College, 1956. Pp. 65–74.
28. Yankauer, A., & Lawrence, R. A. A study of periodic school medical examinations. *American Journal of Public Health*, 1955, **45**, 71–78.

9

NORMATIVE AND BIOLOGICAL STUDIES OF CHILD DEVELOPMENT

Discussions in earlier chapters have shown that psychology is dependent on physiology. Nowhere is this more true than in the study of the psychology of child development. The child's growth in height and weight is physiologically determined. His ability to follow moving objects with his eyes depends on a certain preceding period of growth and presumably on attaining muscular maturity and neural control over those muscles. Development of his vocabulary, toilet habits, play behavior will all be influenced by training; nonetheless, his bodily development always limits the possible changes training can produce.

The physiological limitations upon children's behavior are most evident in infancy: Great changes in behavior or potential behavior occur within a few months of birth, and they seem relatively independent of extra training or of special limitations on the experiences of early life. This chapter will present normative research findings; i.e., evidence of the average physical and behavioral development of children of various ages. It should be emphasized that knowledge of typical growth or behavior patterns at any age is only one sort of knowledge about children. It is even more important to know the conditions producing personality or intellectual differences among individuals and the degree to which training or special experience modifies their behavior.

_____   **Behavioral Development during the First Year of Life**

Responses Available at Birth

Psychologists who study children know that behavior can occur even before birth. Such behavior is not a transmission of thoughts from mother to child, as old wives' tales report, but the movement of the fetus inside the womb occurring as an unlearned response to a loud noise. Fetal movement may also be a learned response, as shown in an experiment with a vibrator applied to the mother's abdomen just before the noise (66).

Since learning can occur so early in life, perhaps no response is really unlearned. Maybe the fetal movement in response to a loud noise was also learned. But many responses, that one included, seem to be unlearned. Usually the simplest such responses to specific stimuli are called *unconditioned reflexes*. Startle responses to loud sounds, pupil contraction in bright light, and blinking when objects approach very near the eye are typically called unconditioned reflexes. The more complex, largely unlearned sets of responses such as nest building or singing by birds are called *instinctive*.

Normative Data

Gesell and Thompson (30) chose for their normative research families whose parents were in the middle of the occupational scale for the country. For the 107 families studied, the average occupational rating of the fathers of girls was equivalent to that of an electrical repairman. The corresponding rating for the fathers of boys was slightly lower, that of a forest ranger, according to the rating scale they employed. These average occupational ratings were very near the average of all gainfully employed men in the United States. Gesell and Thompson also sought to avoid extremes in this sample so did not study any children with major physical or psychological handicaps and excluded very low and very high occupational groups from the study. Because of the occupational restrictions, these data probably are better indicators of average development than of the range or spread of normal development. Nonetheless, only if growth rate depended very much on the parents' occupations could a great increase in spread be expected from a study of other occupational groups.

This research obtained five types of records:

1. A stenographic record (or, for some infants under 16 weeks of age, motion

pictures) was taken of responses to specific standardized situations intended to evoke "motor, visual, auditory, adaptive, vocal, and social responses" (30).

Here is an abbreviated account of one of these situations, presented to infants from 40 to 56 weeks in age.

> The child is sitting on crib platform; right crib panel is completely raised; left one, lowered. Procedure: (a) With somewhat playful approach, place the child squarely in front of the mirror while the curtain is still drawn before it. (b) When he is looking forward toward the curtain, raise it promptly but not too abruptly. Remain in position ready to lend support to the child if he loses his balance, and observe inconspicuously his response to the mirror image. (c) Allow the child full postural freedom, permitting him to stand if he desires (30).

These standardized situations, making up a *behavior examination*, were very carefully planned and executed as the description above indicates. Whether done in the Yale Child Clinic or in the home, the examining room was always arranged in the same way, if possible, with the mother, the examiner, the keeper of records, and the infant in fixed positions in the room and all necessary equipment in specified places. All concerned in the examination took well-defined sanitary precautions, and rules for gaining and keeping good relations with the infants were listed and followed by all concerned.

> 2. A second record was a listing of the times of day at which the baby usually slept, ate, played, and so on. This is called a *behavior day record*.
> 3. In the process of obtaining the behavior day record, an interviewer gained added information about the infant's behavior at home. This usually pertained to his developing skills as revealed in the home situation.
> 4. Physical measurements were taken to establish typical size of various body parts, weight, and dental development at different ages.
> 5. A history of the prenatal period, the birth, early development, and health was also taken, serving in part as a basis for excluding children with physical abnormalities.

Gesell's Findings for Infants under One Year

These five kinds of records picture the development of infants of 4 weeks to 56 weeks of age. (This summary presents the earliest age at which 50% or more of the children attained each behavior. Obviously, no child is typical on every trait or even on most of them.)

Four Weeks. The infant may be able to hold his head in midposition while lying supine but is more likely to turn it to one side or the other. He does not fix his eyes on a dangling ring until it is placed in the direct line of vision, and he follows it with his eyes no more than 45 degrees in either direction. If the handle of a rattle is touched to his hand, the hand either clenches or opens. No vocalization or prelanguage behavior appears except perhaps for small throaty noises.

Twelve Weeks. The infant still is most likely to hold his head to one side or other when supine. When he is sitting, supported, the head is held bobbingly erect or perhaps set forward. When a dangling ring is placed at the midline of his body, he looks at it and follows it if it is moved slowly from side to side. When a rattle is touched to his hand, the hand opens at once. He will hold the rattle in one hand for a period of time. While lying supine he smiles at the examiner.

Twenty Weeks. When sitting supported, the infant holds his head steadily erect. When put in standing position he extends his legs repeatedly and supports a large fraction of his weight for a moment at least. He grasps a dangling ring promptly when it is presented in the midline. He brings the dangling ring to his mouth. He turns his head to the sound of a voice or a ringing bell, but not necessarily in the correct direction.

Twenty-eight Weeks. While supine he may lift his head forward as if trying to sit up. When placed in a standing position, he supports a large proportion of his weight for more than a moment. When sitting unsupported, he is momentarily erect but tends to lean forward. He will now look at the string as well as the ring dangling from it. He can transfer a rattle, dangling ring, cube, spoon, and bell from one hand to the other. Toys and his foot are frequently placed in his mouth. Four weeks from now he will say "da" or perhaps say it or another short syllable twice, as "da da" or "ma ma."

Thirty-six Weeks. If supported at each side of the trunk under the arms, he stands on his toes. When in a sitting position he can lean forward actively rather than passively and return to his original position. Though he approaches and grasps a bell with the right hand, he is more likely to grasp the spoon with the left hand though the bell and spoon were each placed in a standard position not favoring either hand. He can pull the string to obtain the ring. The child responds appropriately to "Where is the ———?" or "Bye-bye." In four weeks he will be able to roll over from the supine to the prone position, or the reverse, and be able to go to the sitting position from either reclining position.

Forty-four Weeks. The infant is able to creep. With slight help he can pull himself from a sitting position to a standing position. After the examiner marks a sheet of paper with a crayon, he will do the same. He picks up a bell by the top of its handle; the bell is one of the few test objects he continues to put in his mouth. He will now release an object if the examiner says, "Give it to me," and grasps it.

Fifty-two Weeks. He is able to walk with support of one or both hands. He can now hold a cube in one hand while using the other to grasp a second cube. He can manipulate a bottle so that a pellet falls out. He looks at his mirror picture of himself and talks to it. He now uses two or more words.

In four weeks he will be able to stand alone, at least momentarily.

A Comparison of Infant Humans and Infant Chimpanzees

Man's similarities to other animals have been emphasized by biologists, and observations of primate behavior confirms these similarities. However, precise comparisons were impossible until psychological work with other animals became widespread. Riesen and Kinder (59) published a book comparing the children studied by Gesell and Thompson to baby chimpanzees given the same postural tests. Up to the age of one year, when the chimpanzee study stopped, the chimpanzees attained most skills earlier than the humans, sometimes as much as 34 weeks earlier. Figure 9-1 shows the ages at which ten of the test items were attained by each species. Here the chimpanzees, in addition to developing more

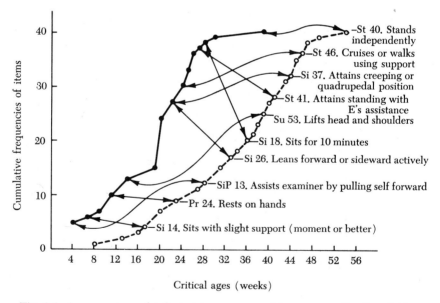

Fig. 9-1. A comparison of infant chimpanzees and humans on Gesell and Thompson, developmental items. The *critical age* is the age at which 50% or more of a group first passed an item. Cumulative frequency is the total number of items which have reached the critical age. The left curve is for chimpanzees; the right for humans. Only 10 (the 4th, 8th, 12th, etc.) of the 40 items summarized are specifically labeled, with an arrowed line connecting the two curves at the points appropriate to each item. [Figure 7 from Riesen and Kinder (59).]

rapidly than humans, acquired developmental skills in an order different from humans. The chimpanzee, for example, has as his fourth skill the ability to assist the examiner by pulling himself forward; the human has this as his twelfth skill on a list of forty. However, the human infant has as his twentieth skill the ability to sit for 10 minutes; this is the thirty-second skill for the chimpanzee. Riesen and Kinder conclude from their study that similar physiological processes control the development of postural skills in the two species being compared. These studies show the many differences between human babies and other infants but they also indicate that much animal behavior is similar to human behavior. More than anything else, this knowledge may help teachers to appreciate the fact that it is incorrect to expect a specific type of behavior at an age that is too early for it to occur naturally. Training obviously influences the course of development, but age limits that influence.

_____ **Children's Behavior One Year and Over**

Gesell and his co-workers continued to examine infant behavior after 1938 and extended their work to cover all ages before maturity. Several of their books on these studies are cited at the end of this chapter.

Gesell's later books sometimes give more subjective interpretations of behavior than those in *The Psychology of Early Growth*. For example, one description (27) of the 3-year-old child begins: "Three is a delightful age. Infancy superannuates at Two and gives way to a higher estate. The transition is not abrupt but is evident in many quaint anticipations of maturity, serious for the child, amusing to us. Psychologically Three has more affinities with 4 year oldness than with 2 year oldness."

Gesell's research with older children and young people is quite different from that with infants. The motor tests of infancy are, of course, too easy for adolescents; and more difficult motor tasks seem less important than other descriptions of a youth's developmental state. The 14-year-old is described in great detail with respect to health, tensional outlets, vision, physical development, sex awareness, eating, sleeping, and bathing, clothes and care of his room. Money, work, emotions, the growing self, interpersonal relationships, philosophical outlook are among other things discussed.

Gesell's later studies are less concerned with obtaining representative children than were his early investigations. Thus in *Youth: The Years from Ten to Sixteen* (29), 52% of the youngsters studied were reported to have fathers in professional occupations, in contrast to 6.2% in the urban population of the United States. The characteristics reported in that book are clearly typical of persons from "superior homes" and do not necessarily apply to a cross section of American youth. These studies are more useful as general descriptions than as scientific data, for unlike *The Psychology of Early Growth,* later books rarely document statements, nor do they tell whether a behavior is characteristic of almost all or only of a bare majority of persons of that age. Gesell's observations were apparently very carefully made, and his findings usually conform to our everyday opinions as well as to the conclusions of other scholars. Furthermore, his advice has the wisdom of long experience with children. It is regrettable, though, that his conclusions are presented without supporting evidence.

A brief description of Gesell's reports on typical development at various ages over 1 year follows. It is interesting to note that cyclic tendencies are reported, with appetite increasing and decreasing and increasing again from year to year, as does emotionality. It is important to remember that no child is exactly or even very closely like the composite picture given for a specific age. Some 10-year-old boys may seem more like 9-year-olds, others more like 11-year-olds. Most 10-year-old boys probably seem a mixture of all three descriptions.

Children from 18 Months through Four Years of Age

This section is based on *The First Five Years of Life* (27).

Eighteen Months. This child walks with a stiff, flat gait. He can seat himself on a child's chair, can creep downstairs and walk upstairs. He can roll a ball and can turn a page (or, more probably, several pages) of a book. He can pile two or three blocks vertically. He has about a 10-word speaking vocabulary and is giving up baby talk. When he is nonconforming with parents, they may suspect that he is afraid of a change in routine and is not simply aggressive. He is just beginning to get some control of his sphincters.

Twenty-four Months. He has enough balance to be able to run and to kick a ball. He can build a tower of six blocks; he can cut paper with scissors. The 2-year-old can identify many objects in pictures and perhaps a few letters of the alphabet if encouraged to learn them. He is just learning to use the words "I," "you," and "me." It may be easier for him to use his own name rather than "I" as the subject of a sentence. He can now form a negative judgment: "A knife is not a fork." He helps to dress and undress himself. If taken up in the night once, he can sleep without wetting the bed. Though toilet training is not complete, he shows signs of guilt about accidents. He seems to have some confusion of himself with others so that he may start leading a younger child out of a room and keep talking as if the infant were still with him even if the infant fails to follow. He may be a great dawdler at mealtimes or when parents expect a great deal of him.

Three Years. This youngster may not need so much activity as the 2-year-old does. The 3-year-old may choose to extract a ball repeatedly from a puzzle box rather than remove it once and then play ball with it. He runs smoothly, can make sudden stops and turn sharp corners. He can fold a piece of paper lengthwise and crosswise but not diagonally. He can copy a circle which is already drawn but may need to watch the drawing of a cross involving only two lines before he can copy it. He uses sentences effectively, responds appropriately to prepositions, and can execute fairly complex commands. The 3-year-old is more cooperative than he was at two, will bargain or take suggestions. He is increasingly interested in playing with other children. Now he sleeps through the night without wetting the bed. He can take himself to the toilet during the daytime pretty well also.

Four Years. Now he can do a running broad jump and a standing broad jump, but he can't skip. He can poke a knitting needle through a small hole and can fold along a diagonal of a rectangular sheet of paper; however, he can't copy a diamond-shaped figure. The 4-year-old asks many questions and takes the answers very literally although he does create metaphors in his own speech. His thinking is like free association; if he is asked, "What scratches?" he may say, "A cat scratches. I had a cat, but it ran away. When I looked for it, I saw lots of things." At this age a child may have a reputation for making alibis or even for telling untruths. There is some possibility that he doesn't yet know what is true and what is fiction. He can now dress and undress with very little help except for lacing his shoes.

Children from Five through Ten Years of Age

This section is drawn from the information in *The Child from Five to Ten*, Gesell and Ilg (28).

Five Years. Now he is self-assured, conforming, and may even enjoy separation from home because of his experiences in kindergarten. He has a capacity for friendship and also plays with imaginary companions, as he may have done at four. He can skip smoothly, can do little dances and physical exercises with training, and can brush his teeth and comb his hair. He can draw a recognizable man, can help in washing dishes, and can rearrange two diagonally cut halves of a card to form the original rectangle. He likes to finish what he has started. A 5-year-old makes definitions in terms of use: "A horse is to ride." He can use complex sentences with hypothetical and conditional clauses. He knows his right hand from his left but can't tell which of his mother's hands is which. He can tell his name and address if lost. He can be motivated to do something by appealing to a motive of rivalry with other youngsters.

Six Years. This is a very active age and an emotional one, possibly because of entry into the first grade. Tree climbing and wrestling are popular. Stomach upsets are common. Tantrums may reach a peak at 5½ or 6 years of age. Fathers may begin expecting boys of this age to be men and to fear they are sissies if they resist minor medical attention such as splinter removal. It is wise not to force these youngsters' compliance when they are strongly opposed to an adult's request. Six-year-olds are often big eaters, especially at bedtime. Their table manners and control of utensils may be poor. Boys especially may resist bathing or thorough washing. School work cannot be very academic and still keep the 6-year-old's interest. These children need to associate their reading and other subject matter with creative activity and physical movement related to everyday life. At this age a child may appear to read when in fact he has simply memorized what is before him in a book. He may have a real problem of taking things which do not belong to him. He may be indulging in some sex play or exhibitionism and likely is interested in marriage and amused by bathroom topics of conversation.

Seven Years. The 7-year-old is pensive and reflective. He can read a clock and may be able to tie his shoelaces tightly but yet not do it well very often. He may desire a close personal relationship with his teacher. He may be a perfectionist about schoolwork and cover up failure by alibis. Now if he lies, he seems concerned about the wrongness of so doing. He is more cooperative than he was a year ago. Boys may be more careful in playing in trees than they were a year earlier. They may also enjoy batting a ball, with the accompanying development of skill in an indirect orientation to a game. If he cries, he cries less from pain or fear and more because of hurt feelings. Boys may tend to withdraw from unpleasant situations rather than rush into physical combat as they did in earlier years. The 7-year-old may be developing minor love affairs with opposite-sexed children of his age.

Eight Years. At this age he may be "money mad" (if a boy) and is certainly interested in money and private possessions. Along with this interest in and understanding of private property comes less tendency to take things from others. His writing of words and sentences is beginning to be reasonably uniform in spacing and slant, and he draws human figures with some sense of body proportions. Ravenously hungry, he may have poor table manners at home but surprisingly good ones at a restaurant or at some friend's house. He is more reckless than he was a year ago, and bicycle accidents are definitely a threat to be considered by parents and teachers. Girls of this age may be interested in specific information about the origins of babies and about menstruation. Girls may especially enjoy school. There is likely to be more talk at home about school by the child of this age than before, but the teacher is less important than before, with other students becoming a central fact in the school experience. The 8-year-old may have developed a substantial interest in religion by now. He also has come to take death for granted.

Nine Years. The 9-year-old seems self-motivated and reasonable. His interest in religion and in fairy stories is decreasing. He likes reading and may be ready to practice on a musical instrument without continual pressure from his parents. He may not go to pieces as much at school when life is difficult as he would have done a year ago, but teachers find this year a difficult one because 9-year-olds want to be independent and resent any decisions which seem unfair to them. These children may particularly like or dislike arithmetic. At 9, children may easily be so vigorous that they overdo recess, games, or physical work and then require time to calm down or regain their strength. They are now old enough to cut meat well with a knife. Their eating is more temperate, with good eaters eating less and poor eaters eating more than they did in previous years. Boys may restrict themselves to a single close friend at a time; girls more often have larger friendship groups.

Ten Years. Now, except for girlish spats with their best friends, these children get along well with siblings, parents, and friends. Boys and girls generally have separate activities and friendships though there are exceptions. These children are happy, casual, even ready to ask advice when needed. Boys are now less likely to cry than girls. Ten-year-olds seem less tense than they were at 9 but may nonetheless bite their fingernails or play with their hair as means of tension release. They may have given up toy guns and paper dolls in favor of bicycles and outdoor games. They may be positively opposed to washing or bathing. Similarly they may strongly prefer to wear old clothes or play clothes. In contrast to earlier years, the father may be specially important to these children. School may be very popular. The children may particularly want their teachers to be friendly to every student, not just to oneself or one's friends. At this age a child may love to memorize material but have trouble combining or connecting two or more facts. Girls are already beginning to show signs of sexual maturity; they are a little more rounded in body and may have a slight projection of their nipples and a little light downy pubic hair. Boys are showing less physical changes but may be peeking at girls who are dressing or may be learning "four letter Anglo-Saxon words" and bawdy limericks.

Youth from 11 through 16 Years of Age

Eleven Years. The 11-year-old is self-assertive, argumentative, even rude. He is likely to have more quarrels with siblings and rebellions against his parents than he did a year earlier. By now the girls are typically showing a conelike breast development and some pubic hair. Boys may be exhibiting extra fat over the hips and chest and a heavier bone development than before. Some 11-year-old boys have a little downy pubic hair and larger genitalia. Many of them will have experienced erections and perhaps half have masturbated. Eleven-year-olds may hate work and resist household duties. However, they are becoming more systematic in their spending of money. They may be motivated by academic competition between whole classes or schools. These children have a great deal of curiosity in school and out but are still largely fact-oriented rather than intellectually reflective. One of the principal attractions of school is that it is a place to see friends. Eleven-year-olds may be very critical of school policy and of their teachers. Elevens need to be listened to when they complain. They may want teachers to be firm, not treating students like babies but not talking over their heads either. The ethical view these youngsters hold is that fairness is a central value. At this age a conflict begins to arise between the teachings of parents and those of the peer group, the friends with whom the 11-year-old associates.

Twelve Years. Now the child is friendly, outgoing, cooperative, and ready to please. Expressions of anger are better controlled than before but may still be a problem. Boys may enjoy sports but overexert to the point of collapse. Girls will probably menstruate before they are 13. Boys know about ejaculation but probably haven't experienced it. Girls are paying more attention to clothing and desire glamorous, adult-looking clothing. Boys may want to look sharp but not at the expense of giving up tennis shoes, even on dress occasions. Twelve-year-olds can disrupt a classroom but respond well to a firm and well-informed teacher. In contrast to earlier years, boys may be more interested in school work than in girls; the girls use school as a place to catch up on the social news in some cases. Twelves may actually ask for homework on occasions when it is not assigned. They enjoy light adult reading. Boys enjoy science and science fiction; girls take an interest in home economics.

Thirteen Years. At this age a person may seem to do more thinking about choices, wishes, etc., than he had before. He may withdraw from close relationships with parents and seem moody some of the time. Though he has an increasing interest in the approval of other people, he is more selective in his choice of friends than he was before. This youth may be better controlled emotionally but may compensate with feelings of sadness. Though girls are filling out in the breasts and hips, they may appear more slender than before because of slimming down in the face, neck, and shoulders. Boys are beginning to show darkened hair over the lip. Thirteen-year-olds are more interested in school than are 12-year-olds and are less boisterous in the halls at school. They may be quite critical of the school principal, a sign of broadening awareness of authority and some rejection of it.

Fourteen Years. More outgoing and friendly than at 13, the 14-year-old enjoys a variety of friends and tends to run in groups. He may have occasional outbursts of temper, but they are verbal rather than physical and the expression of feeling tends to make the underlying anger temporary. Girls have now developed enough to look more like young adults than like children. Boys are exhibiting a deepened voice and have fairly dense pubic hair and hair on their forearms and calves. Ejaculation has begun, and the first nocturnal emission may have occurred just before 14. At this age the choice of clothes is good and care of clothes is improving. These youth may sometimes clean and press their own clothes. They are definitely capable of working for money, and they are dependable in performing chores about the home. They take real interest in student organizations and school elections. Smoking may have begun for some of these youngsters. Drinking is also being discussed.

Fifteen Years. Fifteen-year-olds may seem apathetic and even rebellious. They seem to want privacy from adult inquiries. Boys seem especially hesitant to discuss personal problems with an interviewer (possibly because the interviewer was female). At 15, young people seem to have increasing degrees of self-awareness. They have a loyalty to home, school, and church but may nonetheless seem to be resigning from their own families because of their need for independence. They especially enjoy spontaneous gatherings of groups of boys and girls of their own age. By now boys have some hair on their chest. They probably have facial hair on the sides of their chin and near their ears. The 15-year-old may be a good worker for employers away from home. He is beginning to think about his career, but he isn't likely to be planning for marriage because he doesn't want to be tied down. All the girls are contemplating marriage, however. There are a good many conflicts between teachers and students of this age. Potential dropouts would profit from a combined work–study program in which they attend school half a day and work on a job in the "real world" the other half of the day. Fifteens enjoy panel discussions and guest speakers in class. They seem to need definite assignments for their courses but are sometimes capable of selecting those assignments themselves. By now most boys and girls have experimented with smoking.

Sixteen Years. Whereas the 15-year-old was striving for independence, the 16-year-old has a sense of being independent. This is accompanied by a wholesome self-assurance so that he is not touchy, covers up hurt feelings when they exist, and in general has his emotions pretty well controlled. Sixteens can even see other people's points of view and assess their motivations. There is less parent–child tension and teacher–student tension than there was a year earlier. However, they do not wish direct and unasked for advice from others. Multiple friendships and companionships on a nonromantic basis are common. Boys tend to cultivate friendships on the basis of mutual interests. Girls are more likely to have a few very intense friendships with other girls. Boys now shave about once a week. They are increasingly interested in girls. Kissing and petting are common, with boys having problems of self-control of sexual activity but the 16-year-old girls developing effective strategies for distracting boys from heavy petting. Masturbation is the most common producer of ejaculation, with nocturnal emission increasing in frequency. There is a strong interest in one's future career, education, and marriage, though marriage continues to be of substantially more interest to girls than to boys. At 16 the main worries are about school. Boys and girls both have a drive to excel academically. They do not think of achievement in terms of competition with others, but rather in terms of living up to their own potential. At this age special attention should be given to students who are maturing slowly in intellectual ability but who are trying to keep up with college preparatory courses and having a difficult time of it.

———   An Application of Gesell's Techniques to Classroom Procedures

Two of Gesell's co-workers have recently published a book (35) designed to help kindergarten and primary grade teachers ensure that their pupils are not placed at a more advanced level than the children's developmental status suits them for (see also ref. 36). Ilg and Ames believe that some kindergarten children (perhaps 16%) are not ready for kindergarten when they enter it and that even more children (perhaps 45%) have some readiness and may or may not prove appropriately placed in kindergarten. These authors believe that many school children who seem either disruptive or unmotivated are actually too immature for kindergarten or the particular grade to which they are assigned. If such children are shifted to a lower grade or delayed a year before entering kindergarten, they may be expected to adjust better to the school environment. In some cases a lack of readiness may be a lack of intellectual readiness, but in others the child involved has developed far enough intellectually but is emotionally immature or physically under-developed. Ilg and Ames recommend that, if chronological age alone is the criterion for admission to kindergarten, children be 5 years old by September 1. This would make kindergarteners somewhat older, on the average, than they are in most schools. (Only nine states now require children to be 6 before October 1 in order to enter the first grade.) However, Ilg and Ames feel that no arbitrary age level can be assigned which is appropriate to all children. Therefore, they have prepared a developmental examination using items much like those originally employed in establishing the Gesell norms. This examination is used, together with a test of vision and visual skills and two tests of personality, as a measure of the maturity of each child. School systems in various parts of the United States are now employing these tests as screening devices to determine which children are ready for kindergarten and which are not. Other views on the readiness of children for various school experiences are discussed later in this chapter.

_____ **Typical Growth Patterns**

While examining the details of physical growth, it should be kept in mind that many kinds of change are involved in growth. Seven have been listed by McCandless (41), who relied upon a classification originally developed by Meredith (44):

1. Changes in kind—such as changes from cartilage to bone
2. Changes in number—such as the change from 48 or more teeth at age five (when deciduous and permanent teeth are both present) to about 28 teeth at age 15
3. Changes in size—such as the increase in height from birth to maturity
4. Changes in shape—such as the change from a fetus shape in which the head is as long as the rest of the body to a man's shape in which the head is a small fraction of total body length
5. Changes in position—such as the big toe being widely separated from other toes at birth but moving closer to them in early life
6. Changes in pigmentation—such as the shift from dark hair at birth to lighter hair in early childhood and darker hair in later childhood
7. Changes in texture—such as the loss of elasticity in the skin as people move from maturity toward old age

Height

Physical growth is most commonly assessed by measures of height and weight though a host of other characteristics are also used. Figure 9-2 presents the average height, age by age, obtained in a careful sample from the general population of Canadian civilians outside institutional homes. Several points are worth noticing in this figure. First, though other data show that boys and girls begin postnatal life with very similar average heights of about 18 inches (13), they reach very different average heights at maturity (about 68 and 63 inches, respectively). Second, there is a period at 12 and 13 years when girls exceed boys in average height, reflecting the fact that girls begin the period of pre-adolescent and adolescent rapid growth earlier than do boys. Third, neglecting that period of spurting growth, the amount of growth in height tends to decline slightly from year to year.

This third tendency is more easily recognized if growth per year rather than total height is plotted. Because different persons have their periods of maximum growth at different ages, the average gains in

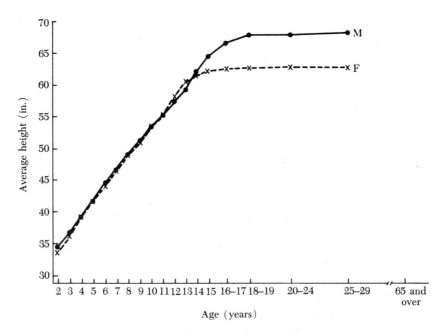

Fig. 9-2. Average height of male and female Canadians by age. [Reprinted from "The Canadian weight-height survey," *Human Biology,* 1956, **28,** 177–187, by L. B. Pett & G. F. Ogilvie, by permission of the Wayne State University Press. Data for ages 30 to 64 are omitted to conserve space.]

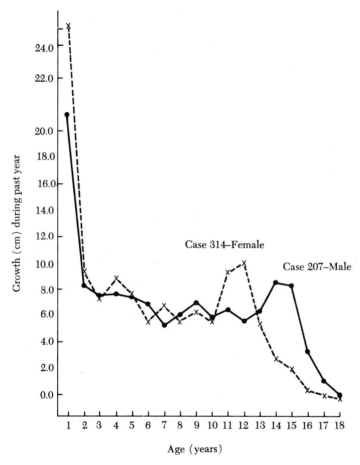

Fig. 9-3. Yearly growth in height by a boy and girl studied from birth to the age of 18 years. [Based on data from Tuddenham and Snyder (71, p. 235 and p. 308).]

height for Canadian boys and girls mirror individual growth curves rather poorly. Figure 9-3, showing year by year growth in height, is not based on the data of Fig. 9-2. It presents instead a single study of the growth curves of a boy and girl who had been measured repeatedly over a period of 18 years. As expected, the girl's growth spurt precedes that of the boy. In other respects, the two growth curves are very similar. Other children would show somewhat different characteristics, of course.

In addition to the growth of individuals, there may be progressive changes in height from generation to generation. Meredith's (43, 45) summary of a number of studies indicates that the height of both white and Negro Americans of all ages up to 20 years has been progressively

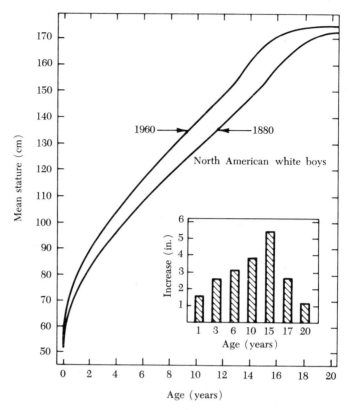

Fig. 9-4. Mean stature of North American white boys at birth (0) and at intervening years up to 20 years of age, based on data of 1880 and of 1960. [Figure 1 from Meredith (45). Inset shows differences between the main curves at several ages.]

increasing since at least 1880. Figure 9-4 compares the mean heights of North American white boys in 1880 and 1960, as a function of their ages. Note that although 20-year-olds in 1960 were about 2.9 centimeters taller than their counterparts in 1880, the most striking change in 80 years was an earlier attainment of maximum height. Thus at some ages the boys studied in 1960 were over 12 centimeters taller than their counterparts of 1880 even though their final heights differed only slightly. Meredith emphasizes that the reason for greater height in recent years is unknown even though factors such as improved nutrition or improved medical care are often suggested as causes.

A Note on Research Methods: Cross-Sectional and Longitudinal Studies

The data of Figs. 9-2 and 9-3 come from excellent studies epitomizing two very different research methods. Figure 9-2, based on the Canadian height–weight survey, compares the heights of different people at various age levels. Figure 9-3, based on the so-called Guidance Study of the University of California, compares the growths in height of the same individuals from year to year.

Comparison of different people at various ages is called a *cross-sectional study*. The advantage of this method is that a research project can be completed shortly after it is started, without waiting for the subjects studied to grow up. Consequently it is more feasible to study a large number of persons and estimate a statistical average for an entire country, as in the data of Fig. 9-2, if a cross-sectional sample is used.

Comparison of the same people at different age brackets is called a *longitudinal study*. The advantage of this method is that it shows the actual change in people from year to year. One might try to infer such changes from cross-sectional data. But consider such difficulties as this: If we assume from Fig. 9-2 that the average male has a height of 62.2 inches at age 14 and 68.3 at age 27, with a growth increase of 6.1 inches, it may be that this underestimates the growth in 13 years because present 27-year-olds have a shorter mature height than do present 14-year-olds. (This problem, in fact, occurred in the study by Meredith, Fig. 4.) Therefore, the longitudinal method seems the more accurate means of determining actual changes in people from year to year. Fortunately, at least ten longitudinal studies of many characteristics of children are now in progress or have recently been completed (37).

Even the longitudinal method can be misleading, however, if a measurement at one age tends to affect the results of a later measurement of the same person. Measuring a boy of 14 would not affect his height at 27, but measuring his intelligence at 14 might affect his intelligence score at 15 if the same test questions were asked each year. Many other test responses may be thus affected (63).

Weight

Figure 9-5 shows the average weights obtained in the Canadian study. As with heights, men reach a greater average level than do women. The second characteristic of the height curves is also present here: girls of 12 and 13 exceed boys of those ages in average weight. But the trend of weight growth is different from that for height. From 2 until 12 for girls and until 14 for boys, average weight gains tend to increase annually. Thereafter, the amount gained per year tends to decrease.

Again, there are advantages in examining the growth curves for individual children. Figure 9-6 shows the growth trends in weight of the two persons previously represented in Fig. 9-3. As expected, the girl

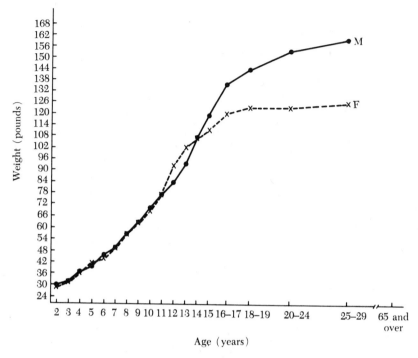

Fig. 9-5. Average weight of male and female Canadians by age. [From Table 1 of Pett and Ogilvie (53). Data for ages 30 to 64 are omitted to conserve space.]

reaches her period of peak growth before the boy, with a general decline on either side of that period. Data for the first year of life, not available from the Canadian study, may surprise the nontechnical reader: The change in weight in the first year is much larger than in other years of early childhood. In fact it is over 70% as large as the change in the year of peak gain early in adolescence. One reason for this rapid early growth is that prenatal growth depends upon the intrauterine environment, whereas the first year following birth is a time for separating the growth curves of children with genetic tendencies toward large size from those with tendencies toward small size.

Height and Weight at Two and at Maturity

A widely known "rule" says that a child of 2 has reached half his mature height and one-fifth of his mature weight. The Tuddenham and Snyder study on which Figs. 9-3 and 9-6 are based supports this rule reasonably well. The greatest average height for boys was attained at 18

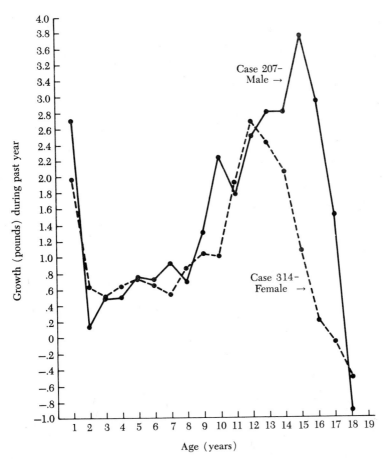

Fig. 9-6. Yearly growth in weight by a boy and girl studied from birth to the age of 18 years. [Based on data from Tuddenham and Snyder (71, p. 235 and p. 308).]

and was 2.0 times that at age 2; the greatest average height for girls was also attained at 18 and was 1.9 times that at 2. The greatest average weight for boys was attained at 18 and was 5.2 times that at 2; the greatest average weight for girls was attained at 17 and was 4.7 times that at 2. Unlike heights, these are not the greatest average weights to be expected during the course of life. We can nonetheless call them mature weights because skeletal maturity had been reached or almost reached by the age of 18 (71).

Bloom (8) has used Tuddenham and Snyder's data to support the so-called overlap hypothesis. In substance, the *overlap hypothesis* states that the older a child is the better his mature height can be predicted because height is cumulative, always building on what is already present. Predicting his mature height from his 2-year-old height is possible because there is a great degree of overlap between heights attained by 2 and what will be attained at skeletal maturity.

───────────────   **Psychological Consequences of Different Growth Rates**

The expression *skeletal maturity* refers to a measure of maturity in terms of bone development. X-ray pictures can be taken of the hand and knee in order to see if cartilage in certain areas is hardening into bones as a child grows up. Skeletal age is the age at which the average person reaches a particular stage in bone development. When this process of ossification is complete, skeletal maturity has been reached. Figure 9-7 shows how marked these changes really are: X-rays of the same hand at ages 3 months, 4 years, 6 months, and 11 years and 9 months show almost no wrist bones and large spaces between bones at finger joints at the earliest age but much more bone structure at later ages.

Children are often termed *early maturing* or *late maturing* on the basis of measurements taken from X-ray pictures such as these. The differences in physical and psychological characteristics of early and late maturing people are significant in education. Understanding these differences may help the prospective teacher understand himself; it will also help him understand his pupils, particularly those in junior and senior high school. The findings presented here were previously summarized by Eichorn (22).

Though some of the studies Eichorn discusses compared extreme groups with the greatest skeletal age and the least skeletal age for any given chronological age, it should be emphasized that skeletal age and most other measures of development have intermediate values as well.

On the physical side, early maturers (EM's) begin their adolescent growth spurt at a younger age than do late maturers (LM's). EM's also show earlier development of secondary sexual characteristics, characteristics that differentiate the sexes but are not necessary for biological reproduction.

There is a difference between the EM and LM groups in their development of primary sexual characteristics such as sperm production and ovulation, but this matter has not been intensively studied. Shock (65) reports that the average age of first menstruation (the *menarche*) is 11.5 years for EM girls and 14.75 for LM girls. He does not report a corresponding reproductive measure for boys but gives an average age of

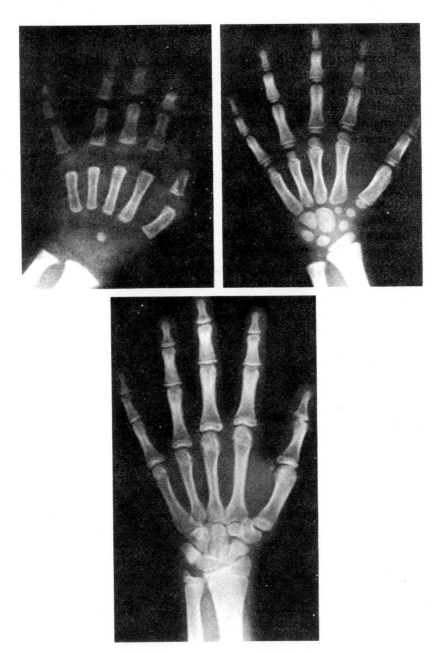

Fig. 9-7. X-ray photographs showing stages in the development of the bones of a girl's hand and wrist at (left) age 3 months, (right) 4 years, 6 months, and (bottom) age 11 years, 9 months. [Figure 3.2 from Stott (67).]

maximum growth in body (stem) length of 13.5 years for EM boys and of 16.0 for LM boys. A further characteristic of EM boys is that they have a more attractive physique during the six years from grades 6 through 12 than do the LM's. No difference in attractiveness between EM and LM girls has been found.

Corresponding differences appear in the behavior of EM and LM boys. During those six years, the LM's seem to compensate for their physical handicaps by being more generally active, expressive, and sociable. They are also more bossy and more tense than the EM's. In some ways their personality seems to fit the stereotype of short men—they call attention to themselves in various ways since they might otherwise not be noticed. Among boys a substantially higher proportion of EM's than LM's become outstanding high school athletes, are elected to important student offices, or are frequently mentioned in the student newspaper. To some extent these differences persist in adult life. As men the EM's have substantially more social life than the LM's, are more dominant, and are more likely to hold positions in which they supervise the work of others. A woman's degree of social participation appears not to depend upon her rate of maturation but rather upon the occupational status of her husband.

As in the case of social participation just mentioned, females do not necessarily show the same EM and LM differences in behavior as men. LM girls, like LM boys, are more expressive and more active. Unlike the LM boys, the LM girls are frequently mentioned in their high school newspapers. Various studies give inconsistent results about emotional adjustment of EM and LM girls. There is some indication that in the sixth grade prestige is associated with LM's but that in succeeding grades it is associated with the EM girls.

These findings may help teachers to recognize that certain personality characteristics of certain adolescents reflect their relative physical development. Some later maturing children may benefit from special counseling or from being in classes and social activities in which other LM's predominate. A brief form of counseling in which differences in rate of development are explained may reduce young peoples' anxieties about their own self-worth.

Changes in Body Proportion

Height and weight changes with age are known to everyone; the change in body proportions (e.g., relative head size) is less obvious. Figure 9-8 shows how greatly these proportions change in the human male from 2 months after conception until the age of 25. The head of

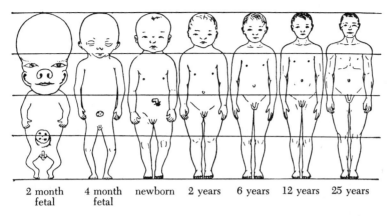

| 2 month | 4 month | newborn | 2 years | 6 years | 12 years | 25 years |
| fetal | fetal | | | | | |

Fig. 9-8. Body proportions in the human male at various stages of pre- and post-natal life. All figures drawn to the same height to facilitate comparison. [Figure VII–11, p. 152 from Patten (52).]

the 2-month fetus is 50% of the total length; at 25 years it is about 15%. Nearly the reverse occurs for leg length. Lesser changes such as the deepening of the chest during adolescence are apparent but not emphasized in Fig. 9-8. With the increased length of arms and legs comes the possibility of using one's muscles to control the environment.

Other Aspects of Growth

Babies generally have more rounded bodies than older children do. Thus Thompson (69, p. 307) summarizes physical development in childhood in these words, "The lower limbs grow rapidly in proportion to stem length. . . . Neither shoulder breadth nor pelvic breadth increases as rapidly as trunk length, but the pelvis broadens more rapidly than the shoulders. The total configurational change is a longer-legged, longer-bodied, and more rectilinear and flatter-bodied child."

A distinction should be made between the period of time immediately preceding puberty, which is called pubescence, and the point of time at which reproduction is first possible, called puberty. Adolescence is the period from puberty to maturity; it is sometimes considered to end at the age of 21 with the attainment of full legal rights of adulthood. However, viewed as a period of growing up, adolescence continues until a person assumes responsibility for his own support or until he reaches skeletal maturity, depending upon whether economic or physical maturity is the defining characteristic of adulthood.

————————————————————————— Muscular Development and Activity

At the biological level there is much evidence to suggest that development follows two "geographical" principles: cephalocaudal and proximo-distal. The *cephalocaudal* (head to tail) principle states that the head and its associated functions will start developing first and lead other parts of the body during most of maturation, letting successively posterior segments of the body follow in turn. The *proximo-distal* (near to far) principle states that units near the brain or spinal cord will develop before those farther from it.

The cephalocaudal principle was illustrated in its morphological aspects in Fig. 9-8, showing how large a proportion of human body length is devoted to the head and how this proportion decreases with age up through adulthood. The behavioral parallel to this is that the newborn infant gains quick control of his eyes and facial muscles but more slowly develops the ability to sit up, roll over, or stand.

The proximo-distal principle finds some morphological support in the progressive increase in relative length of arms and legs with increased age, as shown in Fig. 9-8. The principle is also supported by the fact that fine muscle skills, such as drawing, which use the fingers (distal parts) appear more slowly than large muscle skills using the arms and shoulders (proximal parts). Exceptions to this principle are also available; yet both principles have usefulness in summarizing growth trends in children. The latter has had impact on educational theory ever since kindergarten teachers have insisted that all toys requiring manipulative skill have oversize parts so that fine muscle skills would not be overtaxed (47).

So many studies of motor development in young children (e.g., the Gesell research previously discussed) now exist that a great deal is known about it: the sequence in which new skills such as walking, rolling over, and lifting the head customarily appear; the typical ages at which these responses appear (the *norms* for those responses); and, occasionally, the variability about the norm for a certain response. Less is understood about the muscular and neural mechanisms by which a response appears at a given age for the typical child.

A third proposed principle of development—less universally accepted—is the principle of development of specific movements from mass activity. According to this principle, newborn babies tend to move their whole bodies (mass activity) if they move anything. As they develop, movement of a restricted part of the body (specific movements) becomes the norm. This principle is probably an oversimplification of the situation. However, an experiment by Curti (15) illustrates the merit in this notion. The experimenter studied the process by which a 4-month-old baby learns to grasp a rattle with its hand. Early in training the baby not only reached for the rattle with its hand, it also kicked as many as 70 times with its feet in a 1-minute trial. After 14 such trials, however, the number of kicks per trial had decreased almost to zero. Thus at least one form of diffuse activity had markedly decreased as a specialized act had developed.

An Example of Developmental Norms with an Indication of Variability

Figure 9-9 summarizes Aldrich and Norval's data for 12 responses typically found in the first year of life (1).

A specific response like *pull up* occurs at about 8.7 months. This information alone is helpful in gauging the progress of infants. But it is not enough to recognize that a baby is slower than average, average, or faster than average in learning to pull himself up to a standing position. What constitutes unusually slow progress, suggesting a need for special examinations, or unusually rapid progress, suggesting that the baby will require play materials a little advanced for his age? No "true" standard for *unusual* exists, so we live by relative standards. A convenient one is represented by the 95% zone in Fig. 9-9: The horizontal distance between

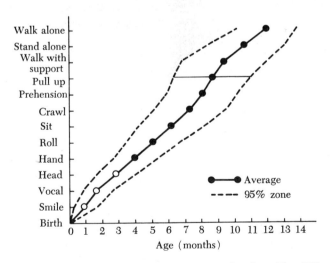

Fig. 9-9. Average age at which various responses develop. The 95% zone gives upper and lower boundaries within which 95% of infants first exhibit certain responses. [Figure 1 from Aldrich and Norval (1), with horizontal line opposite *Pull up* inserted by the present authors.]

dotted lines represents the age span including the middle 95% of children at the time they first made the response. For example, *pull up* has a horizontal line drawn across its 95% zone to show that it extends from about 6 months to about 11 months. This shows the wide variability in the age when *pull up* may appear and makes it clear that there is no cause for alarm if a child's response comes a month later than the average response. Note that there is less variability in the ages when responses appear for the less mature tasks; a month's retardation in smiling might be a matter of concern because this is a very early response.

Though Fig. 9-9 deals with the behavior of infants, the basic principle is applicable to elementary and secondary school children as well. The range of ages at which a task is first performed should increase with the maturation level required for the task. Correspondingly, a wide variation may be expected in the performance of a task which is acquired after infancy. Thus Suppes (68) found that even gifted first graders differed greatly in mathematics performance. When he gave them a 4-week accelerated mathematics program, the fastest working child completed approximately 3400 problems while the slowest child was completing only about 2200 problems. Teachers should be conscious of these differences in ability and should individualize instruction so that each pupil can work at his own level without becoming discouraged because of the impossibility of keeping up with others or being bored by being held back by slower students.

Children's Sleep

Children sharply reduce their daily requirement of sleep as they grow older. Early estimates of the amount of sleep needed were based on theory, not on a thorough knowledge of the actual sleeping habits of growing children. However, recent recommendations increasingly conform to the observed average hours of sleep at different ages. Although what is typical is not necessarily healthful, a knowledge of the average amount of sleep at different ages seems an indispensable ingredient in judging how much is necessary.

A newborn baby sleeps about 20 hours a day (55); the 1-year-old child, about 13; the 5-year-old, about 11½ hours; and the adult, 8 hours or less. It is well to remember that there is sometimes a large day-to-day fluctuation in the same person's sleeping habits and that there is a corresponding fluctuation from person to person.

Two fairly old studies are available which, when combined, cover the range from birth to 20 years of age. Figure 9-10 shows the mean hours of sleep reported in Minnesota for children of both sexes combined up to

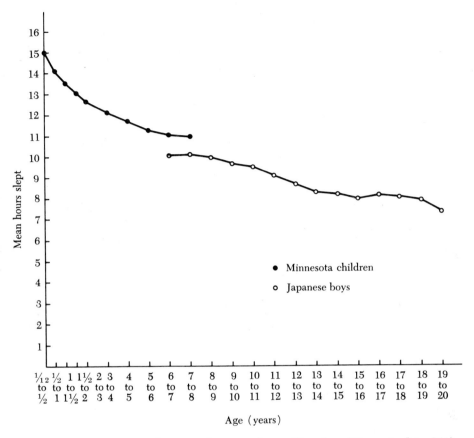

Fig. 9-10. Mean hours slept as a function of age. [Based on Minnesota data (74) and Japanese data (31).]

the age of 8 years (74); it also shows such data for Japanese boys from 6 to 20 years (31).

The Japanese data continue the Minnesota trend but at a level almost an hour below it. Interestingly, the Minnesota study showed no noteworthy differences between boys and girls, whereas the level for Japanese girls (not shown in Fig. 9-10) is generally about 30 minutes less than that for Japanese boys.

_____ **Effects of Impoverishment of the Environment**

Professor Dennis and his wife (20) in raising a set of twins, have shown that excellent physical care devoid of the special personal attentions usually considered essential to a baby's development can produce almost all the abilities other babies develop in their first year of life. What the Dennises did was this: They reared fraternal twin girls (whose own parents couldn't care for them) from the age of 1 month to the age of 14 months without ever rewarding or punishing a specific act and without even talking to or smiling at the children until they were 26 weeks old. The reason for this mechanical, almost unfriendly treatment was that the experimenters wanted to know whether social behavior such as smiling, laughing, and babbling would appear in the babies without encouragement or training by others. Although the girls were kept in a bare nursery room throughout the year's experiment, except for a very special test situation and a three months' stay in a summer cabin with a similar nursery, and despite the social barrenness of their experience, they spontaneously developed the habit of smiling and "talking" to their guardians when they entered the room. In the sixteenth week the girl named Del first gave an unmistakable laugh. In the twenty-first week the twin named Rey first gave an unmistakable laugh.

Dennis and Dennis (19) also studied the effects of restricted experience in a natural situation. They found that mothers in two of the Hopi Indian villages in Arizona, New Oraibi and Upper Moencopi, no longer kept their newborn infants tightly bound on a cradle board. Since cradling was still done in the other Hopi villages it was possible to find out the effects cradling had upon the age of walking.

If restricting a baby's movements in early life tends to retard walking, the cradled babies should surely be late walkers. Here is the Dennises' description of the use of the cradle board:

> In order to place the infant on the board, the child, naked or wearing a shirt or diaper, is put on a cotton blanket which lies on the board. The infant's arms are extended by his sides and the right side of the blanket is pulled right over the right arm and is put between the left arm and the left side and tucked under the infant's body. The left side of the blanket is then pulled firmly over the left arm and tucked under the right side of the child. The part of the blanket which extends beyond the feet is folded back under the infant's legs and buttocks. The infant, thus wrapped, is tied to the board by strips of cloth which encircle the baby and the board. The wrapping includes the legs which are thus fastened so that they can be flexed only to a slight degree. The infant is so firmly wrapped and tied that he cannot turn his body and cannot release his hands from the bindings. Only the head which rests on a small pillow or pad of folded cloth is relatively free to move. A piece of thin cloth is placed over the face guard in order to darken the face of the child and to exclude the flies. The cradle, with the infant upon it, lies upon the floor or upon a bed. It is never placed vertically, and is seldom carried about.
>
> The infant is thus bound to the board on the first day of life and for the

first three months he spends nearly all of his hours in this position. Although he is taken off one or more times daily, either for bathing or for replacing soiled cloths, these operations do not consume many minutes and he is returned to the board when they are completed. The infant nurses while tied to the board, the cradle with the child attached being held to the mother's breast. He sleeps on the board at night as well as by day.

Despite this continual restriction of movement for three months and a decreasing amount of cradling thereafter until the age of about 9 months, walking was not delayed. Mothers of 63 Hopi children raised on a cradle board reported an average age of 15 months for the first one or two unaided steps to occur. The same average was reported by mothers of 42 Hopi children who had not been cradled.

It is interesting that although both the cradled and uncradled Hopi children learned to walk at about the same time, both groups learned about one month later than any previously studied group had.

A few striking examples of extreme environmental impoverishment have occurred outside the laboratory. The known cases of children who have been found in a wild state or who were kept in isolation (for example, in a closet) by parents have not—with rare exceptions— attained normal social and intellectual development even after years in relatively normal surroundings. Many of these children seem mentally defective (18). A famous psychiatrist, Dr. Bruno Bettelheim (7), suggests that some of the children may be of normal intelligence but autistic (pathologically self-centered) because of the extreme emotional crisis of being completely alone for a period of time, however short it actually was.

The potential differences between the effects of mental deficiency and of developmental and emotional reactions to isolation are exemplified in two instances of illegitimate children raised as almost complete prisoners by their mothers. One, with the pseudonym Anna, was discovered at the age of almost 6 after about 5½ years of isolation (16). Anna learned in the next 2 years to walk, understand simple commands, feed herself, and exercise some control over elimination. About 3 years after being found, she had developed speech about equal to that of a 2-year-old. When she died at the age of 10, she still was much retarded. Because her mother had an I.Q. of only 50, it seems likely that her retardation was not due to her years of isolation.

In contrast, Isabelle was discovered at the age of 6½ after spending all her life isolated with her deaf mute mother (40). She was given very intensive speech and general intellectual training almost immediately thereafter, even though she was so retarded she seemed totally uneducable to some authorities. Two years later, she was of normal intelligence and was functioning normally in social situations. Isabelle's early deficiencies seem more akin to the autistic syndrome described by Bettelheim; Anna's, to mental deficiency.

A common form of impoverished environment is raising infants in a hospital or an orphanage for a few weeks or longer. If the institution has very few staff workers [one worker per six children in a hospital studied by Schaffer (62)], less attention will be paid the infants than if they were at home: they will be picked up, talked to, cuddled, and played with less than they would be at home. Children in such institutions typically show less maturity by Gesell norms or similar tests than do children raised in their own homes. Rheingold (57) has provided clear evidence that having a single person actively "mother" four 6-month-old babies 7½ hours a day for 8 weeks will increase the social responsiveness to the experimenter but not to someone else. There is also some research evidence that increasing the amount of social stimulation (62), increasing the amount of stroking the baby's skin (12), and increasing the amount of playing with the baby (61) can increase the maturity of hospitalized infants. Unfortunately, it is difficult to do research of this kind in a fully scientific manner without being unfair to the children involved. Consequently there are problems of interpretation in these studies—Sayegh and Dennis (61) note, for example, that their results are affected by Junior Red Cross workers dropping in and handling all the babies without this being part of the experimental plan. Such problems make it necessary to be cautious about drawing conclusions.

Restriction of Experience in Young Animals

It is important to know if skills can be developed through growth alone—without any practice. Carmichael (10) tested animals by the following procedure: Eggs of frogs (*Rana sylvatica*) and salamanders (*Amblystoma punctatum*) were kept in covered glass dishes filled with tap water until they had grown into embryos. Then half of the embryos were placed in an anesthetizing solution (3 or 4 parts of Chloretone per 10,000 parts of water was found best) to prevent any movement during their later growth. The remaining embryos were allowed to continue growing in plain tap water. When the unanesthetized frogs and salamanders had developed enough to begin swimming, the anesthetized frogs and salamanders were placed in plain tap water, too. Within 5 to 28 minutes, they were all swimming; by 30 minutes their swimming was well coordinated. The experiment proved that when the frogs and salamanders matured enough they could swim even if swimming had not been practiced. (In this instance, practice had been prevented by the immobilizing effect of the anesthesia.)

Carmichael (11) made a further experiment. He placed the group of unanesthetized salamanders in the Chloretone solution and found that it took them the same time to recover from the anesthesia—and to swim— as it had taken the first anesthetized group. He proved that these animals require essentially no practice before beginning to swim. Growth is the only prerequisite to their swimming.

Not all acts are as independent of training as was the swimming of the salamander. Many studies show that visual behavior depends greatly upon previous experience. To test this, kittens were raised in complete darkness for the first six weeks of their life, longer than the period their eyes would normally remain closed. Then, some of the kittens were permitted periods of relatively normal visual experience and others had some visual stimulation, but only when physically restrained so they could not reach out to touch anything they saw. The question was, what then happens to the kittens?

Riesen and Aarons (58) answered this question with a study somewhat more complex than just suggested, for the purpose of showing the effect of visual experience upon movement discrimination and intensity discrimination. Those kittens with a background of relatively normal experience (either living permanently in a cage with normal laboratory lighting or living in the dark 23 hours a day and playing in a lighted exercise pen 1 hour a day) learned to distinguish between a moving and a nonmoving stimulus pattern. Those kittens with restricted experience (either given 1 hour of light stimulation per day through a white mask while their bodies were restrained in a holder to minimize movement, or given 1 hour of light stimulation daily, without a mask to hide pattern stimuli but while restrained in a holder) did not learn the movement discrimination.

The kittens were said to have distinguished between a moving and a nonmoving stimulus pattern if they were 90% correct in choosing between a door on which a moving stimulus pattern appeared and a door on which the same pattern appeared but in a constant position. The kitten made these choices by pushing a door and finding either that food was available behind it (the correct door) or that it was locked (the incorrect door).

The kittens with restricted visual experience completely failed to learn the movement response, making it reasonable to assume that they were retarded but not incapable of learning. Yet three of these kittens showed no learning in 4000 trials, even though the unrestricted animals had learned the criterion in no more than 1709 trials. Riesen and Aarons call this finding an example of "the more general phenomenon of intellectual deficit after perceptual deprivation." That is, a permanent limitation on learning ability is now thought to result from early restrictions of perceptual experience. The implication of this finding for teachers is: A kindergarten or first-grade child without normal breadth of sensory and intellectual experience may be permanently handicapped in classroom situations. Very possibly he may benefit more immediately from trips, motion pictures, and class discussion than from exposure to such stimuli as books. This has been, in part, the philosophy underlying the widely acclaimed, but now unfortunately defunct Higher Horizons Program for children in schools located in the less privileged areas of New York City (39, 75).

The studies just mentioned include examples of withholding stimuli that are the normal biological concomitants of life. Since smiling in humans and swimming in salamanders developed readily without the usual opportunities for practicing these skills, they seem the products of growth rather than of learning. Riesen and Aarons' findings indicate, however, that the combination of visual perception and effective action cannot occur without a sizable history of experience with ordinary visual cues.

Research like that of Riesen and Aarons has led to the formulation of what is called the *principle of critical periods* (17, 64). Depending on the species involved, there are certain ages (critical periods) in which certain skills can be developed. If the skill, such as a puppy's learning to be friendly with humans, is not acquired then, it may be impossible thereafter. (The time before learning is possible is called the *latent period*.) A striking example of a response and its associated critical period is the duck's tendency to follow the mother duck. At the age of about 6 hours, if there is no mother duck to follow, the duckling will learn to follow a moving human being or a moving duck decoy. This age–specific learning of a following response is called *imprinting* and has been widely studied. The interested reader is referred to representative articles on imprinting by Hess (32) and by Klopfer (38).

One might suppose that a true critical period, excluding the possibility of learning a particular response after that period ends, implies some physiological change in the absence of a certain kind of stimulation or learning. Two such possibilities are relevant to the Riesen and Aarons experiment: Rasch, Swift, Riesen, and Chow (55a) found that cats, rats, and chimpanzees reared in total darkness for several months (36 months for cats) thereafter showed significant lowering of RNA (ribonucleic acid) levels in their retinal cells. Wiesel and Hubel (74a) found that two kittens who had been allowed to see only with their left eyes up to the age of 3 months showed atrophy in the lateral geniculate body of the brain but only for cells receiving stimulation from the right eye. These two experiments indicate that both the brain and the sense organs may be damaged by lack of normal experiences.

Effects of Delayed Schooling

It is not difficult to predict the effect on humans of withholding intellectual stimuli. It is common knowledge that children in a nonliterate society grow up illiterate—unless, of course, they come under outside influence. Similarly, in an American community the average artistic achievement of school children is usually much below that of Japanese school children. The reason is obvious: The Japanese child is trained more thoroughly in art and is expected to become more proficient than the American child is.

This is not to say that a cultural skill will not be acquired if formal instruction is lacking. Informal contact with cultural material is common to most societies. Thus Altus (2) found some Mexican–American men who had learned to read Spanish without formal instruction (but not without help from others) although in the 2 to 3 years they had attended American public schools they had not learned to read English.

A further example of the benefits of informal instruction is given by Morphett and Washburn (49), who apparently produced beneficial effects by withholding all direct instruction in reading, writing, and arithmetic during the first grade and a half of school. Informal learning during this period was not sufficient to make this group of children perform as well on standard achievement tests at the end of the second grade as did a comparable (control) group of children trained more traditionally. However, in both the third grade and the eighth grade the experimental children were more eager to learn academic material and in other ways were better suited personally for school life than were the control children. It is possible that the children's personal characteristics may be one of the results of withholding academic instruction and may in turn be responsible for their slightly superior ratings on the Stanford Achievement test at the end of the third grade and thereafter. By the end of the seventh grade the experimental children were an average of six-tenths of a grade ahead of the control children on this test.

Morphett and Washburn (48) claimed that reading instruction could not usefully begin until a child reached the intelligence level (or mental age) of an average 6½-year-old. Although this conclusion was widely accepted for a number of years, it cannot be justified by existing research.

Gates (25) found that four different groups of first-grade pupils yielded very different results, with the minimum mental age for effective reading instruction being 5.0 with one group and as high as 6.5 to 7.0 years for another, the ages presumably changing with the quality of instruction offered.

The Morphett and Washburn conclusion is also shaken by Durkin's (21) study of children who had learned to read before entering the first grade. In Oakland, California, and in New York City, there were 205 such children out of 9568 first graders who were checked for reading ability on beginning the first grade. The early readers, defined as having the ability to identify at least 18 words from a pre-primer list of 37 words, included a number of children with mental ages below 6 years. While it is true that the children who were more advanced mentally were the most rapid in further reading development, the overall findings suggest that average or better than average reading progress was possible for the early readers, even for those with low mental ages at school entrance. Evidence for the practicality of systematic reading instruction before the chronological age of 6 will be given in the next section of this chapter.

Sax and Ottina (60) reported that delaying arithmetic instruction until the fifth grade led to the students' superior understanding of arithmetic concepts and equal computational ability in the seventh and eighth grades, compared with students of the same intelligence who studied arithmetic throughout elementary school. This study would be more convincing if it were a true experiment, with children initially assigned to two matched groups and given equivalent instruction in all topics other than arithmetic. Since the ideal research design was not used, it seems reasonable that the delayed arithmetic group's superior understanding may have come from superior instruction outside arithmetic—particularly since that group studied at the University of California (Los Angeles) elementary school and the other group did not. Nonetheless, this study and a more anecdotal pair of reports by Benezet (4, 5) do suggest that delayed instruction in arithmetic can be compensated for later.

A better case has been made for a delay in arithmetic instruction than for a delay in reading. In neither case, however, is there a clear comparison of the amount of learning per year at various ages. Consider the data on teaching a foreign language: A group of private schools has an extensive testing program which enabled it to report that children who had studied French for two years, including grade 7, showed no greater median French achievement than children who had studied it in grade 9 only (50, Table 9). Assuming equivalent language aptitude and amount of French instruction per year in the two groups, it may be unreasonable to offer two years of French classes beginning at grade 7 rather than grade 9. However, if the time can be spared for four years of French instruction before grade 10, it would seem likely that study of French throughout grades 6, 7, 8, and 9 would bring greater skill than a single year at grade 9.

Effects of Unusually Early Training

Very different from institutional treatment of infants is the mothering provided by Ugandan parents who have not yet adopted European or American child rearing patterns. Ugandan babies are never left by their mothers. The baby rides on his mother's back, possibly having skin-to-skin contact there, sleeps with his mother, eats on demand at any time, and generally is deprived of nothing he seems to ask for, until the time of weaning. Geber (26) found that infants raised in this manner were generally precocious. Figure 9-11 shows a 5-month-old child from that study holding herself upright and taking the round block out of its hole in a testing board (called a *form board*), the latter being a task first performed by 61% of children at 8 months, according to Gesell and Thompson (30). Geber further reports that Ugandan children who were being raised like Europeans, spending their early infancy sleeping on cots and being fed at regular intervals, were less precocious after the first month of life than were the traditionally raised children. Some of the precocity of Ugandan children appears immediately after birth; it may be physically determined. However, Geber believes that this precocity reflects special prenatal care associated with the mothers' enthusiasm for childbearing and childrearing. (Note the contrast between the precocity found by Geber and the slow development reported by Dennis and Dennis (19) with Hopi infants.)

Now consider some experimental rather than natural evidence on the effects of unusually early training or attention. Three examples will be presented: (a) training a motor skill, (b) toilet training, and (c) teaching reading and writing.

Motor Skill. Hicks (33) studied the maturational effects on throwing a ball. The ball was tossed at a target 4 feet in diameter moving for 8 feet at right angles to a child and coming as close as 5 feet to him. Figure 9-12 shows that four practice groups of different ages that were given ten practice throws per week for 8 weeks between a pretest and retest series of ten throws improved little more or no more than did the control groups which did not receive practice in those eight weeks.

Toilet Training. Another skill learned in early life is voluntary control

Fig. 9-11. A five-month-old Ugandan girl who can hold herself upright and take the round block out of its hole in a form board (normally accomplished at 32 weeks). [Figure 4 from Geber (26).]

of urination. Does training in toilet habits speed or retard gaining this control? One way of answering this question is to compare identical twins, one of whom receives toilet training at an early age and one of whom does not. For her research, McGraw (42) used two sets of identical boy twins. Peter Dalton (a pseudonym) was given toilet training from the age of 23 days on through 470 days, whereas his twin, Charles, began training at 430 days—when Peter had reached the level of approximately 40% successes—and continued to 470 days of age. Hugh Putney received training from the age of 41 days to 800 days. His twin, Hilton, was given no toilet training until the age of 2 years (730 days). Training then continued to 800 days. Figure 9-13 shows the percentage of successes for each boy at different ages. Note that during the first year the trend of each twin receiving training is to decline in the proportion of successes. The immediate effect of toilet training in the first year, then, seems to be detrimental. Note that Charles Dalton has only about 10% fewer successes in the period from 430 to 470 days than does his brother; evi-

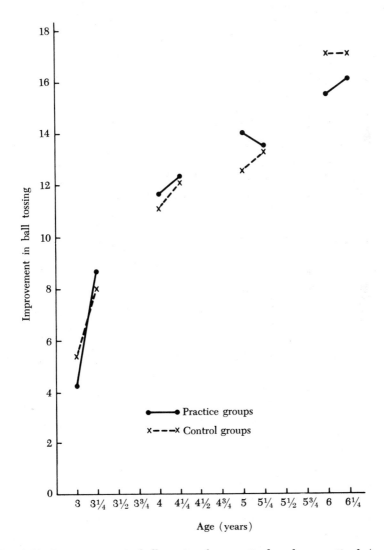

Fig. 9-12. Improvement in ball tossing for practiced and unpracticed (control) groups of various ages. [Data points taken from Tables 2 and 3 of Hicks (33). Copyright 1930 by the Society for Research in Child Development, Inc., and reproduced by permission.]

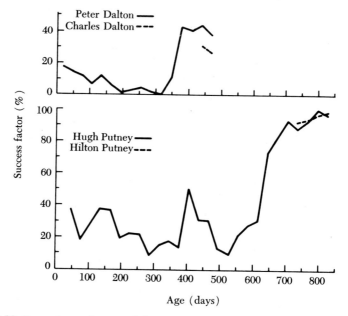

Fig. 9-13. Percentage of successful urinations with and without early toilet training in two sets of twins. [Figure 3 from McGraw (42).]

dently by 430 days of age maturation alone has produced almost as much readiness for training as did maturation plus more than 400 days of early training.

"Maturation alone" does not imply just the passage of time; something more is required. With the passage of time there is surely some physiological growth. In the twin experiments, the untrained twin had many experiences, directly related or unrelated to sphincter control, which may have influenced his later performance. Presumably he saw his brother being taken to the toilet, and this may have made him more cooperative when his own training began.

The curves for the Putney brothers show a similar effect at a later stage of training. Hilton Putney's performance is not retarded, compared with his brother's, once his training begins. The level of success is much higher for the Putneys than at the time the study of the Dalton brothers stopped, again showing the beneficial effects of increased age.

Wherever the effects of training seem limited unless a person has reached a given age, it may be that some part of the body has not developed sufficiently to permit learning the desired habit. McGraw found two types of physiological studies relevant to the problem of toilet training. One type indicates that no part of the *cortex* (see Chapter 7) of the brain is functioning appreciably in a newborn baby. The second type of study showed that infants of from 2 to 6 months had the same pattern of rhythmic contraction of the *detrusor urinae* (fibers of the muscular coat of the bladder) during urination as do adults with lesions in the supranuclear area of the cortex, suggesting that this area does not function in infants up to the age of 6 months, thus preventing voluntary control of urination. An interesting secondary finding by McGraw is that there is no rhythm or typical time for urination in infants under the age of 800 days. This is not to say that other reasons for regular training do not exist; McGraw placed the twins on the training chamber once per hour during the day. It is also worth noting that there was no trend toward less frequent urination nor were greater amounts voided per urination as the children became older. Again this contradicts common belief.

Reading. A spectacular demonstration of the effects of early training upon ability to read and write has been reported by O. K. Moore (47a), Moore and Anderson (47b), Pines (54), and Time Magazine (70). Moore uses a special typewriter as an instructional device for children in the age range from 2 to 6 years. This computer-connected typewriter is so constructed that when a symbol such as "A" is typed by the child, that letter is spoken by a soft voice from a previously made recording and the letter is also shown on the typewriter's paper. In order to ensure that the child will learn to type meaningful material, Moore arranged that sometimes all keys but one are inoperative, with a red arrow being pointed at that key in order to encourage the child to type it. Successive unlocking of the proper series of letters can lead the learner to type any word the experimenter desires. The recorded voice speaks the word typed also; this encourages the construction of other words by the child. With this training device children of 3 can learn to read, to type, to make up stories, and to type those stories. The learning process takes about a year but involves much more learning than is usual for a child of 3. It should be noted that there is nothing magical about the American system of beginning formal reading instruction at the age of 6. Though it is rare to find that reading instruction is begun at 2 as Moore has done, in Scotland reading instruction is begun at 5 when compulsory education begins (73, p. 1172).

Another exciting piece of research on preschool training comes from Bereiter and Engelmann (6), who worked with 15 black children, about 4½ years old, whose older brothers and sisters were having difficulty in learning at school. Instead of emphasizing how to play with others or providing broad cultural enrichment experiences, as is customary in nursery school or kindergarten, Bereiter and Engelmann decided to give these children a great deal of formal instruction in ordinary speech and in numerical and reading or prereading skills. The researchers believed that such an intensive program would enable these children to enter the first grade with equal skills and thus an equal chance for future academic success, compared with other pupils.

Bereiter and Engelmann (6) established 15 minimum goals for these children. The first goal is presented here as an illustration:

"Ability to use both affirmative and *not* statements in reply to the question 'What is this?' 'This is a ball. This is not a book.'"

Children in this experiment spent 2 hours a day at the preschool for 5 days a week throughout the academic year. There were three 15- to 20-minute classes per day in basic language skills, reading, and arithmetic, each with a different teacher. The remaining hour included 10 minutes of unstructured activity at the beginning of the day, 30 minutes for toilet, juice, and music after the first class and 20 minutes for semi-structured "expressive activity" after the second class.

The result of 9 months of this instruction was to raise these children's intelligence test scores from below average to average and to bring 11 children up to or above the beginning first-grade level in reading. In arithmetic 11 were at or above the beginning second-grade level. In spelling, which was not taught by Bereiter and Engelmann, the children's averages were at the middle of kindergarten level. Even more important than the children's test progress was their improvement in oral English; they had begun to use well constructed sentences and to discuss things rather than to merely express wants and feelings. Further research is needed to prove the effectiveness of the Bereiter and Engelmann method. However, at least one other preschool using that technique has had similarly favorable results (56).

Long continued, well controlled studies of unusually early or extensive instruction in certain skills are rarely conducted by psychologists, so it is necessary to turn to real life records of such instruction even though such records leave doubt as to the factors controlling the results. John Stuart Mill (1806–1873), distinguished English philosopher, political theorist, and statesman, was educated at home by his father, James Mill. The scope of his early training is partly shown by this quotation from his autobiography (46):

> I have no remembrance of the time when I began to learn Greek. I have been told that it was when I was three years old. My earliest recollection on the subject is that of committing to memory what my father termed vocables, being lists of common Greek words, with their signification in English, which he wrote out for me on cards. Of grammar, until some years later, I learnt no more than the inflexion of the nouns and verbs, but, after a course of

vocables, proceeded at once to translation; and I faintly remember going through Aesop's Fables, the first Greek book which I read. The Anabasis, which I remember better, was the second. I learnt no Latin until my eighth year. At that time I had read, under my father's tuition, a number of Greek prose authors, among whom I remember the whole of Herodotus, and of Xenophon's Cyropaedia and Memorials of Socrates; some of the lives of the philosophers by Diogenes Laertius; part of Lucian, and Iocrates Ad Demonicum and Ad Nicoclem. I also read in 1813, the first six dialogues (in the common arrangement) of Plato, from the Euthyphron to the Theatetus inclusive: which last dialogue, I venture to think, would have been better omitted, as it was totally impossible that I should understand it. But my father, in all his teaching, demanded of me not only the utmost that I could do, but much that I could by no possibility have done.

An extraordinary first 7½ years. Mill may not have known much Greek at three, for a letter from his father to Jeremy Bentham when John was over 3 years, 1 month, of age makes it plain that he did not even read English at that age (51). Yet we have seen that Moore has taught reading to 3-year-olds, and there are reports that Bentham and Emerson were reading at the age of 3. Mill may indeed have been right in his report. Now what did Mill think were the results of his very extensive home education, proceeding, beyond the record above, until he was fourteen?

If I had been by nature extremely quick of apprehension, or had possessed a very accurate and retentive memory, or were of a remarkably active and energetic character, the trial would not be conclusive; but in all these natural gifts I am rather below than above par; what I could do, could assuredly be done by any boy or girl of average capacity and healthy physical constitution: and if I have accomplished anything, I owe it, among other fortunate circumstances, to the fact that through early training bestowed on me by my father, I started, I may fairly say, with an advantage of a quarter of a century over my contemporaries (46).

Curiously, John Stuart Mill felt that many of his attainments were due to his education and none to any innate superiorities. Psychologists have disagreed on this point; one said that Mill had had more unusual intellectual gifts (judging by his estimated I.Q.) during the first 17 years of his life than had any other eminent man since the year 1450 (14). The truth seems to be that Mill would surely have scored very high on an I.Q. test had one existed in his youth, but also that some of his superiority undoubtedly rested in his unusual educational background.

_____   **A Modern Assessment of Readiness**

Discussions of child development often refer to questions about readiness to learn some particular task such as reading. Bruner (9) asserts,

"We begin with the hypothesis that any subject can be taught in some intellectually honest form to any child at any stage of development." On the contrary, Tyler (72) says, "There can be little disagreement with the notion that pupils learn most effectively and efficiently when instruction is introduced at an appropriate time—neither too early nor too late but, rather, when they are ready."

Evidence of slow learning or of emotional problems in young children is usually considered evidence that they are not ready for that learning experience. Some child psychologists, such as Ilg and Ames (35), seem to think of readiness as something that develops automatically with age, just as a flower unfolds from its bud, and object to early instruction such as that of Bereiter and Engelmann (6), feeling that artificial attempts to hasten development simply distort the maturational process without genuinely hastening learning. Though much is owed to psychologists who have determined the ages at which given responses usually appear, the concept of readiness as unmodifiable by training does a great disservice to education. It is much better to attempt to modify readiness and perhaps fail in some cases than to dogmatically assume that it is impossible and not try to find out the facts of the matter.

Tyler (72) points out instruction of various kinds has often been postponed in the schools because of the view that maturation cannot be forced and that certain topics are almost impossible to learn at certain ages. A well-balanced view of readiness is held by Gagné (24) who says, "Within limitations imposed by growth, behavioral development results from the cumulative effects of learning." Both growth and learning are important to Gagné, but readiness can be developed if one knows the skills which define readiness. For example, judging equalities and inequalities of volumes of liquids in rectangular containers depends upon knowledge of concepts of liquids and lengths of straight lines. These concepts do not develop just because a child grows. They can either be taught directly by a parent or teacher as a means of inducing readiness, or they can be learned in the course of ordinary life, in which case readiness may come later.

———————————————— **A Summary of the Comparative Effects of Age and Experience upon Development**

General Notions

Some principles about the development of behavior should be stated, even though these principles may be vague and unproved in some cases. References to investigations discussed in the past few pages will partly support these generalizations, but they by no means establish them beyond doubt. The conclusions and figures illustrating them are similar to, but not identical with, material presented earlier by Baldwin (3, pp. 389–390).

Three general propositions seem true, both for tasks which develop universally in man and those which require special training:

1. At any age the performance of any act has some limit beyond which the performer cannot pass. This limit is often called the *physiological limit*. Customarily this limit increases with age (improved performance is possible), at least until the end of adolescence.

2. At every age most people perform slightly below their own physiological limit. This level may be called the *norm* for people of their ability at their age.

3. Most tasks will be done poorly or not at all for a few minutes, hours, days, or even years after birth, regardless of the amount of training or experience offered in situations where the tasks could be performed. This period before a response can develop appreciably is called its *latent period*.

Behavior Largely Dependent on Age for Its Development

Without saying that a certain response develops without any learning, it can be said that many responses are nearly universal at certain ages, even in widely different cultures, while others are present only if repeated contact with certain stimuli are present. The first group of responses, which includes walking, eating, babbling, and to some degree sexual behavior, may be characterized in three ways from their curves of development:

1. A small difference is to be expected between the physiological maximum for the response and the level of actual performance. This is true even if special training is not provided.

2. If performance of the response is actively prevented (by a parent or an experimenter, for example), beginning during the latent period and continuing for some time after its close, the response may nonetheless appear at normal strength for the individual's age once the prevention ceases. This principle was illustrated in the Carmichael study of swimming in salamanders.

3. If, however, the response is prevented too long, freedom to make the response may be followed by only partial development of the desired response strength (the critical periods hypothesis), as if permanent physiological damage to the organism had resulted. This phenomenon was exhibited in Riesen and Aarons' kittens which could not learn move-

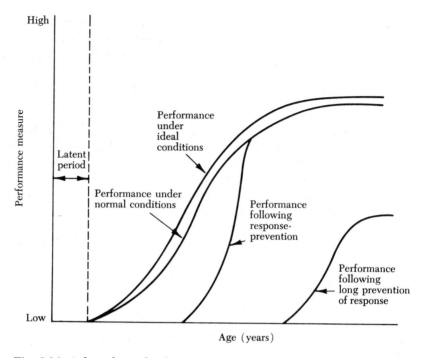

Fig. 9-14. A hypothesized relation between performance and age in a response largely dependent on age for its development, showing the effects of response prevention as well as depicting the latent period, performance under ideal conditions, and actual performance under normal conditions.

ment discriminations, apparently because of long deprivation of visual pattern cues. Though indications were that three months of physical restriction did not retard walking in Hopi children, extended periods of neglect or inactivity, as evidenced in some orphanages, could be expected to produce retardation in walking also.

Figure 9-14 presents an idealized representation of the course of development of a response largely dependent on age, showing the implications of the three generalizations just stated. The response in question might be considered locomotion (creeping, walking, and running) and the measure of performance as the speed of locomotion.

Behavior Largely Dependent on Training

When we turn to a response like piano-playing, the heavy dependence upon training is obvious. Again three principles may be stated to describe the development of such acts with age:

1. A large difference is to be expected between any person's physiological maximum and actual performance of the response unless optimal conditions of practice, training, and motivation are present.

2. If experience with the task in question is retarded past the end of the latent period, introduction of practice will not produce instantaneous achievement of the person's normal performance level for his current age. Rather, the acquisition of the desired response will be gradual, showing its dependence on practice. However, much research evidence shows that learning is often faster at advanced ages, so that a delay before initial practice may be followed by more nearly instantaneous improvement than a short delay.

3. Preventing experience in a certain act for many years is unlikely to prevent later learning of the behavior when training is given, except insofar as physical disabilities in old age preclude the act, or other competing habits have been established which retard learning of the new

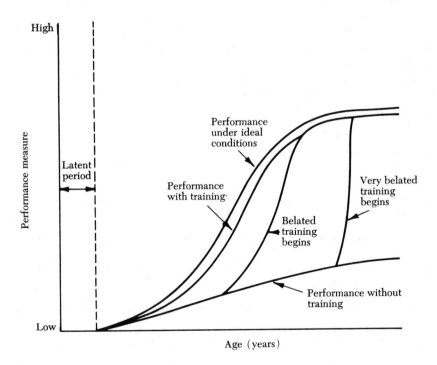

Fig. 9-15. A hypothesized relation between performance and age in a response largely dependent upon training for its development, showing the effects of beginning training at the end of the latent period or thereafter and showing performance under ideal conditions as well.

behavior. The old saying, "You can't teach an old dog new tricks," is probably wrong.

Figure 9-15 above illustrates how learned behavior may develop with age and how the three principles just stated would apply. This figure represents a guess at the general trend of performance for all sorts of tasks, but it may be useful to think of something specific as the performance measure on the graph.

Though a distinction has been made just now between behavior that is largely dependent on age and behavior that is largely dependent on experience, recent thinking on developmental processes focuses on the interaction of experience and physiological structure and maturation as crucial in all tasks (34).

A further warning should be made about responses said to depend primarily on age: Unless age increases without any accompanying activity by the child (or better yet, without any activity or any sensory experience), one cannot conclude that training was not important. Fowler (23) has emphasized that Americans stress the value of sensory–motor experience in child rearing, making it likely that a child who is not given special training has nonetheless received a great deal of training related to almost any task which might be given to an experimental group. Therefore, experience may be more important in skills such as learning to walk than existing experimental data might suggest.

SUGGESTED READINGS

Calderone, M. S. The development of healthy sexuality. *Education Digest,* 1966 (December), **32**, 28–31.

A discussion of a broadly conceived education on sexuality at various age levels.

Hammond, R. A., & Forsythe, H. Should *any* child skip kindergarten? *Instructor,* 1969(May), **78**, 60.

Pro and con arguments on a subject closely related to theories of child development.

Scott, J. P. A time to learn. *Psychology Today,* 1969(March), **2**, 46–48, 66–67.

How social attachments and other behavior patterns are most easily formed at certain ages. For example, in young dogs attraction to strangers is greatest at 5 weeks of age, whereas fear of strangers begins at 5 weeks and lasts at least until 12 weeks.

REFERENCES

1. Aldrich, C. A., & Norval, M. A. A developmental graph for the first year of life. *Journal of Pediatrics,* 1946, **29,** 304–308.
2. Altus, W. D. The American Mexican: The survival of a culture. *Journal of Social Psychology,* 1949, **29,** 211–220.
3. Baldwin, A. L. *Behavior and development in childhood.* New York: Holt, Rinehart & Winston, 1955. Pp. 389–390.
4. Benezet, L. P. The story of an experiment. *Journal of the National Education Association,* 1935, **24,** 241–244, 301–303.
5. Benezet, L. P. The story of an experiment. *Journal of the National Education Association,* 1936, **25,** 7–8.
6. Bereiter, C., & Engelmann, S. *Teaching disadvantaged children in the preschool.* Englewood Cliffs, N. J.: Prentice-Hall, 1966. Pp. 48–49.
7. Bettelheim, B. Feral children and autistic children. *American Journal of Sociology,* 1959, **64,** 455–467.
8. Bloom, B. S. *Stability and change in human characteristics.* New York: Wiley, 1964.
9. Bruner, J. S. *The process of education.* Cambridge, Mass.: Harvard University Press, 1960. Pp. 9, 32.
10. Carmichael, L. The development of behavior in vertebrates experimentally removed from the influence of external stimulation. *Psychological Review,* 1926, **33,** 51–58.
11. Carmichael, L. A further study of the development of behavior in vertebrates experimentally removed from the influence of external stimulation. *Psychological Review,* 1927, **34,** 34–47.
12. Casler, L. The effects of extra tactile stimulation on a group of institutionalized infants. *Genetic Psychology Monographs,* 1965, **71,** 137–175.
13. Cole, L. *Psychology of adolescence.* (4th ed.) New York: Rinehart, 1954. P. 7.
14. Cox, C. M. Genetic studies of genius, Vol. 2, *The early mental traits of three hundred geniuses.* Stanford, Calif.: Stanford University Press, 1926.
15. Curti, M. W. *Child psychology.* New York: Longmans, Green, 1930. Pp. 168–171.
16. Davis, K. Final note on a case of extreme isolation. *American Journal of Sociology,* 1947, **52,** 432–437.
17. Denenberg, V. H. Critical periods, stimulus input, and emotional reactivity: A theory of infantile stimulation. *Psychological Review,* 1964, **71,** 335–351.
18. Dennis, W. A further analysis of reports of wild children. *Child Development,* 1951, **22,** 153–158.
19. Dennis, W., & Dennis, M. G. The effect of cradling practices upon the onset of walking in Hopi children. *Journal of Genetic Psychology,* 1940, **56,** 77–86.
20. Dennis, W., & Dennis, M. G. Development under controlled environmental conditions. In W. Dennis (Ed.), *Readings in child psychology.* New York: Prentice-Hall, 1951. Pp. 104–131.
21. Durkin, D. *Children who read early. Two longitudinal studies.* New York: Teachers College, Columbia University, Bureau of Publications, 1966.
22. Eichorn, D. H. Biological correlates of behavior. In H. W. Stevenson (Ed.),

Child psychology. Sixty-second yearbook of the National Society for the Study of Education. Part 1. Chicago: University of Chicago Press, 1963. Pp. 4–61.

23. Fowler, W. Cognitive learning in infancy and early childhood. *Psychological Bulletin,* 1962, **59,** 116–152.

24. Gagné, R. M. Contributions of learning to human development. *Psychological Review,* 1968, **75,** 177–191.

25. Gates, A. I. The necesary mental age for beginning reading. *Elementary School Journal,* 1937, **37,** 497–508.

26. Geber, M. The psychomotor development of African children in the first year, and the influence of maternal behavior. *Journal of Social Psychology,* 1958, **47,** 185–195.

27. Gesell, A., Halverson, H. M., Thompson, H., Ilg, F. L., Castner, B. M., Ames, L. B., & Amatruda, C. S. *The first five years of life, a guide to the study of the preschool child.* New York: Harper, 1940. P. 40.

28. Gesell, A., & Ilg, F. L. (in collaboration with L. B. Ames and G. E. Bullis). *The child from five to ten.* New York: Harper, 1946.

29. Gesell, A., Ilg, F. L., & Ames, L. B. *Youth: The years from ten to sixteen.* New York: Harper, 1956.

30. Gesell, A., & Thompson, H. (assisted by C. Strunk). *The psychology of early growth.* New York: Macmillan, 1938. Pp. 8, 52.

31. Hayashi, Y. On the sleeping hours of school children of 6 to 20 years. *Jido Jatshi (Child's Journal),* 1925, p. 296. (As reported in *Psychological Abstracts,* 1927, **1,** 439.)

32. Hess, E. H. Imprinting in birds. *Science,* 1964, **146,** 1128–1139.

33. Hicks, J. A. The acquisition of motor skills in young children. *Child Development,* 1930, **1,** 90–105.

34. Hunt, J. McV. *Intelligence and experience.* New York: Ronald Press, 1961. Pp. 41–42.

35. Ilg, F. L., & Ames, L. B. *School readiness. Behavior tests used at the Gesell Institute.* New York: Harper & Row, 1964.

36. Ilg, F. L., Ames, L. B., & Apell, R. J. School readiness as evaluated by Gesell developmental, visual, and projective tests. *Genetic Psychology Monographs,* 1965, **71,** 61–91.

37. Kagan, J. American longitudinal research on psychological development. *Child Development,* 1964, **35,** 1–32.

38. Klopfer, P. H. Stimulus preferences and imprinting. *Science,* 1967, **156,** 1394–1396.

39. Landers, J. *Higher Horizons: Progress report.* New York: Board of Education, 1963.

40. Mason, M. K. Learning to speak after six and one-half years of silence. *Journal of Speech Disorders,* 1942, **7,** 295–304.

41. McCandless, B. R. *Children. Behavior and development.* (2nd ed.) New York: Holt, Rinehart & Winston, 1967.

42. McGraw, M. B. Neural maturation as exemplified in achievement of bladder control. *Journal of Pediatrics,* 1940, **16,** 580–590.

43. Meredith, H. V. Stature and weight of private school children in two successive decades. *American Journal of Physical Anthropology,* 1941, **28,** 1–40.

44. Meredith, H. V. A descriptive concept of physical development. In D. B. Harris (Ed.), *The concept of development.* Minneapolis: University of Minnesota Press, 1957. Pp. 109–122.

45. Meredith, H. V. Change in the stature and body weight of North American boys during the last 80 years. *Advances in child development and behavior,* 1963, **1,** 69–114.

46. Mill, J. S. *Autobiography.* (3rd ed.) London: Longmans, Green, Reader, and Dyer, 1874. Pp. 5–6, 30–31.

47. Montessori, M. *The Montessori method.* (4th ed.) New York: Frederick A. Stokes, 1912.

47a. Moore, O. K. The preschool child learns to read and write in the autotelic responsive environment. In Y. Brackbill & G. G. Thompson (Eds.), *Behavior in infancy and early childhood.* New York: Free Press, 1967. Pp. 340–352.

47b. Moore, O. K., & Anderson, A. R. *Early reading and writing,* 16 mm. film in color. Guilford, Conn.: Basic Education Council, 1960.

48. Morphett, M. V., & Washburn, C. When should children begin to read? *Elementary School Journal,* 1931, **31,** 496–503.

49. Morphett, M. V., & Washburn, C. Postponing formal instruction: A seven year case study. *Official report,* American Educational Research Association, Washington, D. C., 1940. Pp. 168–172.

50. 1944 achievement testing program in independent schools and supplementary studies. *Educational Records Bulletin,* 1944, No. 40.

51. Packe, M. S. J. *The life of John Stuart Mill.* New York: Macmillan, 1954.

52. Patten, B. M. *Human embryology.* (3rd ed.) New York: McGraw-Hill, 1968.

53. Pett, L. B., & Ogilvie, G. F. The Canadian weight-height survey. *Human Biology,* 1956, **28,** 177–187.

54. Pines, M. How three-year-olds teach themselves to read—and love it. *Harper's,* 1963(May), **226,** 58–64.

55. Pratt, K. C. The neonate. In L. Carmichael (Ed.), *Manual of child psychology.* (2nd ed.) New York: Wiley, 1954. Pp. 215–291.

55a. Rasch, E., Swift, H., Riesen, A. H., & Chow, K. L. Altered structure and composition of retinal cells in dark-reared mammals. *Experimental Cell Research,* 1961, **25,** 348–363.

56. Reidford, P., & Berzonsky, M. Field test of an academically oriented preschool. *Elementary School Journal,* 1969, **69,** 271–276.

57. Rheingold, H. L. The modification of social responsiveness in institutional babies. *Monographs of the Society for Research in Child Development,* 1956, **21** (2, Whole No. 63).

58. Riesen, A. H., & Aarons, L. Visual movement and intensity discrimination in cats after early deprivation of pattern vision. *Journal of Comparative and Physiological Psychology,* 1959, **52,** 142–149.

59. Riesen, A. H., & Kinder, E. F. *Postural development of infant chimpanzees.* New Haven, Conn.: Yale University Press, 1952.

60. Sax, G., & Ottina, J. R. The arithmetic achievement of pupils differing in school experience. *California Journal of Educational Research,* 1958, **9,** 15–19.

61. Sayegh, Y., & Dennis, W. The effect of supplementary experiences upon the behavioral development of infants in institutions. *Child Development,* 1965, **36,** 81–90.

62. Schaffer, H. R. Changes in developmental quotient under two conditions of maternal separation. *British Journal of Social and Clinical Psychology,* 1965, **4,** 39–46.

63. Schaie, K. W. A general model for the study of developmental problems. *Psychological Bulletin,* 1965, **64**, 92–107.
64. Scott, J. P. Critical periods in behavior development. *Science,* 1962, **138**, 949–958.
65. Shock, N. W. Basal blood pressure and pulse rate in adolescents. *American Journal of Diseases of Children,* 1944, **68**, 16–22.
66. Spelt, D. K. The conditioning of the human fetus in utero. *Journal of Experimental Psychology,* 1948, **38**, 338–346.
67. Stott, L. H. *Child development. An individual longitudinal approach.* New York: Holt, Rinehart & Winston, 1967.
68. Suppes, P. Modern learning theory and the elementary-school curriculum. *American Educational Research Journal,* 1964, **1**, 79–93.
69. Thompson, H. Physical growth. In L. Carmichael (Ed.), *Manual of child psychology.* (2nd ed.) New York: Wiley, 1954. Pp. 292–334.
70. *Time.* O.K.'s children. 1960, **76**(19). 103.
71. Tuddenham, R. D., & Snyder, M. M. *Physical growth of California boys and girls from birth to eighteen years.* Berkeley: University of California Press, 1954. Pp. 198, 235, 308.
72. Tyler, F. T. Issues related to readiness to learn. In E. R. Hilgard (Ed.), *Theories of learning and instruction. Sixty-third yearbook of the National Society for the Study of Education.* Part 1. Chicago: University of Chicago Press, 1964. Pp. 210–239.
73. UNESCO. *World survey of education. III. Secondary education.* New York: International Documents Service, Columbia University Press, 1961. P. 1172.
74. University of Minnesota Institute of Child Welfare. *The sleep of young children.* Circular No. 4. Minneapolis: UMICW, 1930.
74a. Wiesel, T. N., & Hubel, D. H. Effects of visual deprivation on morphology and physiology of cells in the cat's lateral geniculate body. *Journal of Neurophysiology,* 1963, **26**, 978–993.
75. Wrightstone, J. W., Forland, G., Frankel, E., Lewis, B., Turner, R., & Bolger, P. *Evaluation of the Higher Horizons Program for underprivileged children.* New York: Board of Education, cooperative research project no. 1124, 1965.

10

PSYCHOLOGICAL PROCESSES OF DEVELOPMENT

<hr>

_____ **Development of Language Behavior**

Use of oral and written language sets man apart from all other living species. Many species have some capacity for speech sounds. Figure 10-1 shows a picture of Viki, a chimpanzee, being helped to say "Mama," one of three words she learned to speak. Chimpanzees do not spontaneously make a wide enough variety of sounds to permit them to develop a large speaking vocabulary. Nonetheless, it seemed possible to Gardner and Gardner (23) that the chimpanzee brain was well enough developed to permit communication if appropriate methods could be found. As Kellogg (40a) notes, several investigators have observed a number of hand and arm movements in chimpanzees, some of these movements serving the same purpose that gestures do in humans. Because of this gesturing, Gardner and Gardner decided to try to teach a young female chimpanzee some elements of the American sign language, which is used by deaf persons.

The chimpanzee Washoe, named after the county in Nevada where the University of Nevada is located and the Gardners' research is conducted, was estimated to be between 9 and 15 months old when experimentation with her began. Since then, Washoe has been exposed daily to the use of sign language by human beings communicating with each

Fig. 10-1. Moving the lips of Viki, a home-raised chimpanzee, to form an M, as in "Mama." Photograph from Hayes (31).

other or with her. Oral language is never used with Washoe lest she pay attention to it and not to the hand signs. Sign language instruction has been very successful; within 3 years Washoe had learned to use over 90 signs and to make sequences of signs approximating sentences (22–24). For example, Washoe has learned individual signs for "please," "out," and "go." When she is confined to her house trailer on a winter day, she may combine these signs to say, "please out go"—poor grammar, but not bad for a chimpanzee.

Washoe is also being given discrimination training and testing in which boxes are used for presenting one object at a time in random order to determine how consistently she can properly identify the objects. One virtue of this method is that the errors Washoe makes provide clues to her perceptual and thought processes. For example, when a toy dog or toy cow is presented, Washoe should make the sign for "dog" or for "cow." If she makes a nonsense response, either she hasn't learned or wasn't paying attention on that trial. However, sometimes she makes the sign for "baby," indicating that she is responding to the size of the figure, not to its form.

Even more interesting than the sign language of a chimpanzee is the linguistic capacity of human beings. Osgood (53) tape recorded a baby's verbal activity for 10 minutes a week, and was able to report that by the end of its first 2 months the infant had made all the separate speech sounds recognized by linguists as basic to human language. The baby babbled the sounds of all languages and began to omit certain sounds only when outside stimulation provided special rewards just for the English sounds. Even though all sounds may occur in early infancy [but see contradictory data mentioned later in this section (44, 48)], the relative frequency of their occurrence changes as the infant grows up. The type–token ratio is a convenient index of this change. In any set of 100 speech sounds (called *tokens*) there are some duplications; the number of different sounds is the number of *types*. The *type–token* ratio, then, is the ratio of the number of types to the number of tokens. (The type–token ratio is reported in percents, thus the ratio in decimal form is multiplied by 100%.) As speech becomes diversified, this ratio increases. Figure 10-2 shows that this ratio increases in every 2-month period during the first year for a fixed token size. (The ratio decreases with larger token size because the tokens reflect increased talking with a consequent duplication of vocabulary used.) The characteristic increase with age continues beyond infancy. For 100-word written samples Chotlos (11) has shown that it increases from 58.6 for children aged 149 months and under attending fourth grade or above, to 64.0 for children 150 to 179 months of age, with no significant increase for older children up through the twelfth grade.

Not only does the diversity of separate sounds increase, but they become arranged into words. Typically, the 8-month-old child uses no words appropriately from a standard list and the 10-month-old child uses one such word. At the end of the first, and second through sixth years of life, the child can use 3, 272, 896, 1540, 2072, and 2565 words, respectively (68). These are underestimates because the test list was selected from a relatively short basic list rather than from an unabridged dictionary.

Lynip (48) implies that almost all existing research findings on infant speech sounds are undependable. Lynip recorded voice samples of an infant for 56 weeks, beginning with her birth cry, and then analyzed these records with a sound spectrograph (a machine indicating the relative strengths of different sound frequencies in a sound), and found that the infant did not produce a single vowel or consonant sound comparable to adult vowels or consonants until about the end of the first year. Even at that time the sound only approximated the equivalent adult sound. Since this infant didn't make the same physical sounds an adult did, Lynip believes that phoneticists' discriminations of the vowel and consonant sounds of infants are in error.

Winitz (79) stated that sound spectrographs for any given vowel are known to shift toward higher frequencies as one turns from data for men

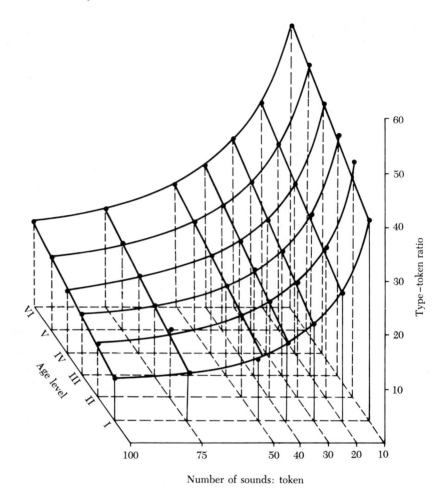

Fig. 10-2. The type–token ratio (number of different speech sounds divided by total number of sounds made) as a function of number of sounds and age level. Age levels refer to the first two months of life (I), the second two months (II), etc. Graph 3 from Chen and Irwin (10).

to those for women or to those for children. Thus, even an older child does not make the same physical vowel sound an adult makes. Winitz showed that infants with a mean age of 11½ months make vowel sounds further shifted from the low frequencies and somewhat more variable than they make at later ages. However, Lenneberg (44) concludes that spectrographic evidence gives little basis for identifying speech sounds in the first four months of life with any particular English vowels.

M. K. Smith (69) estimated the vocabulary size of school children ranging from 6 to 19 years by administering the Seashore–Eckerson

English Recognition Vocabulary Test (63) to pupils in 12 grades of one school and 8 grades of another. Though the part of the test measuring basic vocabulary (recognition of words printed as separate entries along the margin of a dictionary rather than as related words in the discussion of the original entry) included only 158 words, the score obtained is useful in estimating overall vocabulary. This is true because the test was devised by randomly sampling the 158 words from the complete list of basic words in the Funk and Wagnalls two-volume *New Standard Dictionary of the English Language*. [*Random sampling* is a procedure of selecting a certain number (call it *n*) of members of a set in such a way that every possible group of *n* from that set has an equal chance of being chosen. In this study $n = 158$ and the set is all the basic words in the dictionary.] Consequently a correct answer on a basic word was taken as an indication that many words in the full dictionary were known.

But what does it mean to "know" a word? Many criteria have been used, of which M. K. Smith mentions three: "(a) recognition of the commonest meaning of a word, (b) definition in the subject's own words, (c) use of the word in a sentence or citing an illustration." Criterion (a) was used by M. K. Smith, and it should be remembered that other criteria would give different results. Thus, (b) and (c), being apparently more difficult to satisfy, would yield lower estimates of the vocabulary size. Though the procedure employed in giving the English Recognition Vocabulary Test was slightly changed for different age ranges of children, it included four-choice questions throughout. For example, knowledge of the word "adhesive" was tested by allowing the child to choose a possible synonym from the words "slippery," "rough," "fatty," and "sticky." Obviously a child who knew the meanings of no words in the test might be correct occasionally because of a fortunate guess, and so the scores obtained were reduced enough to correct for this guessing effect.

Figure 10-3 shows the increase in estimated basic vocabulary with increased age. At age 6 the median vocabulary size was about 16,000 words whereas at the age of 17 it was about 47,000 words. (The *median* is the score in a set of scores which is exactly in the middle when the scores are arranged in order from highest to lowest. To say that the median vocabulary at age 6 is 16,000 words is to say that 16,000 was the middle value of all those obtained for 6-year-olds.) A decline at ages 18 and 19 results because older children still in high school typically have been delayed in graduating because of academic difficulties. They might therefore be expected to be below average in vocabulary for their age. Templin (72) has repeated M. K. Smith's study for ages 6, 7, and 8, showing reasonably consistent results for the two studies.

Figure 10-3 is also instructive in showing the great *range* of knowledge

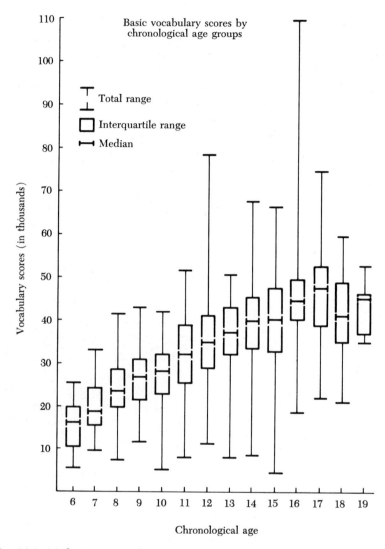

Fig. 10-3. Median size, total range, and interquartile range of recognition vo-cabulary of school children as a function of age. Figure 3 from M. K. Smith (69).

within each age group. (Range is used in statistics to mean the difference between the highest and lowest scores in a set.) The upright and inverted T's for each age group show the highest and lowest vocabulary sizes, respectively. Note that even at age 16 the smallest size vocabulary was not large enough to compare favorably with the median for 6-year-olds.

The indications of range are somewhat erratic from age to age because a single very precocious or very retarded child can affect it so much. A somewhat more stable measure of variability within age groups is also given in Fig. 10-3. The *interquartile range,* the vertical distance between the top and bottom of each double rectangle in the graph, is generally about 10,000 to 16,000 words. (The interquartile range is the distance between the score at the bottom of the highest 25% of the scores and the score at the top of the lowest 25%.) Because of this variability within age groups, teachers in any grade must expect that some children will find certain portions of reading material and spoken comments almost unintelligible while others will find it easily understandable. Some vocabulary deficiencies may be overcome through the use of selected textbook materials and also with broadening experiences ("show and tell" times for youngsters to describe their toys, hobbies, and trips; tours of points of interest near the community by the class). Nonetheless, in most classes, the pupils' vocabulary will persist in spanning a broad range and the teacher must learn to communicate with all the students simultaneously, and also to apportion time to individuals or to small groups.

Concurrent with vocabulary growth, increased age and education bring improved use of various parts of speech. This grammatical improvement is closely parallel to a change in word association habits. When asked to respond to a stimulus word such as "table," adults tend to give a response belonging to the same part of speech, such as "chair." However, children frequently give a word such as "eat," which is of a different class. Figure 10-4, based on research by Brown and Berko (7) shows that the percentage of homogeneous responses to nonsense syllables (using a grammatical structure appropriate to the usage previously given each syllable by the experimenter) increases from grade 1 to grade 3 and beyond that to adulthood. Figure 10-4 confirms the statement just made concerning responses (free associations) to stimulus words: Homogeneous responses or responses belonging to the same part of speech (count noun, mass noun, adjective, transitive verb, intransitive verb, or adverb) as the stimulus words are more frequent for older children than for younger ones and are most frequent for adults.

Brown and Fraser (8), among many others, point out that children reveal the grammatical rules they have learned by the mistakes they make. A small boy who says, "I digged in the yard," or "I saw some sheeps," or "Johnny hurt hisself," is using rules of grammatical construction which he has learned are applicable in very similar situations. Cofer (12) likens the development of syntactical rules in children to the process of concept formation. Just as in concept formation, the grammatical rule may be used before it can be stated by the child. The variables which affect concept formation, such as number of trials and number of dif-

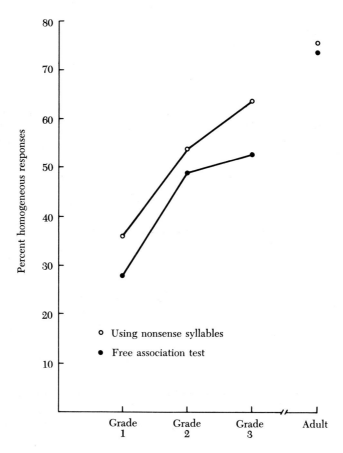

Fig. 10-4. Percent homogeneous (by part of speech) responses in using nonsense syllables and making free associations as a function of grade or age. Based on data from Brown and Berko (7). Copyright 1960 by the Society for Research in Child Development, Inc., and reproduced by permission.

ferent examples of a given concept (or application of a grammatical rule), may be expected to influence language development in general.

_____ **The Thought Processes of Children**

Thought processes are, of course, closely bound up with language behavior. However, intelligent behavior without use of words appears early in infancy. A sign of what adults would call intellectual puzzlement is the 1-year-old shown in Fig. 10-5 crawling behind a mirror, "looking" for the person seen in it (25). The infant fails to find the person in the mirror; yet the search seems reasonable in the light of previous experience.

Among children old enough to talk there are substantial effects of age upon learning. Berlyne (4) has summarized Soviet research by Ivanov–

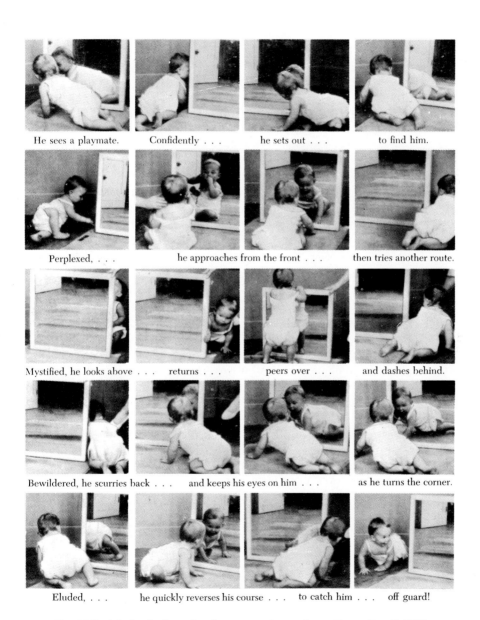

| He sees a playmate. | Confidently . . . | he sets out . . . | to find him. |

| Perplexed, . . . | he approaches from the front . . . | | then tries another route. |

| Mystified, he looks above . . . | returns . . . | peers over . . . | and dashes behind. |

| Bewildered, he scurries back . . . | and keeps his eyes on him . . . | | as he turns the corner. |

| Eluded, . . . | he quickly reverses his course . . . | to catch him . . . | off guard! |

Fig. 10-5. A baby looking for the person in a mirror. From Gesell (25).

Smolenski, by Paramanova, and by Luria using the so-called "verbal method" to teach children that, for example, when a green light is turned on, a rubber bulb held in the child's hand should be pressed whereas if a red light is turned on the bulb should not be pressed. Early in training the experimenter may say "Press," or "Don't press," when or shortly after the light is turned on. Later in training the experimenter merely tells the child after each light if what he did was correct. Children of 5 to 6 years learn this primitive "thinking" task, as Berlyne terms it, very quickly and maintain it well, perhaps because they are able to verbalize which response to each stimulus is correct. Three-year-old children, however, learn more slowly and are inconsistent in making appropriate responses.

Russian experimenters interpret the 3-year-old's performances to be like that of the lower animals and to be essentially conditioned responding. They speak of such behavior as being controlled by the *first signal system,* a hypothesized part of the nervous system. They further hypothesize a *second signal system* to control verbal and symbolic behavior, it being presumed operative in the 5- to 6-year-old children who learned the "Press" or "Don't press" discrimination so well. Thus to the Russians it seems that fully human powers of thought depend on a different neurological system or subsystem than that required for simple learning.

Just as the second signal system is alleged to facilitate complex learning by permitting learning of a simple symbolic representation of the overall task, so may normal growth in a child lead to simpler ways of thinking through abstraction. Bruner and Olver (9) have stated, "The development of intelligence, given intervening opportunity for problem solving in the life of the growing organism, moves in the direction of reducing the strain of information processing by the growth of strategies of grouping that encode information [in simpler form, with connections to previous groupings, and with a maximum possibility for using old groupings as bases for forming new groups]."* (Bracketed material is a paraphrasing of a complicated conclusion to the sentence being quoted.) These authors were referring to ways grade school children solve such problems as answering the following: "How are *BANANA, PEACH, POTATO, MEAT, MILK, WATER, AIR,* and *GERMS* alike?"

A child answering this question might say that the eight things mentioned are all present on earth. Bruner and Olver would say the child has used a very simple form of grouping—*Superordinate grouping*—in which a single attribute (presence on earth) forms the basis for saying that they are all similar. However, if the child said, "*BANANA* and *PEACH* are alike in being fruit, *PEACH* and *POTATO* are each spelled

* Copyright 1963 by the Society for Research in Child Development, Inc., and reproduced by permission.

with an initial P, *POTATO* and *MEAT* are eaten together, *MEAT* and *MILK* are both from animals, *MILK* and *WATER* are both liquids, *WATER* and *AIR* both contain oxygen, *AIR* and *GERMS* are hard to obtain in five pound quantities," this would be a much more complicated form of grouping—*Edge matching*—so-called because it finds a point of contact between, or relates, two things at a time. Bruner and Olver found five different complex forms of grouping, including the one just mentioned. The simple grouping *superordinate grouping* was used much more frequently by fourth grade children than by first grade children and somewhat more frequently by sixth grade children than by fourth grade children. The reverse effect occurred for complex forms of grouping: they were least frequent for sixth graders and most frequent for first graders.

The finding just reported is one argument in favor of Bruner and Olver's principle that the development of intelligence leads to simpler forms of grouping. Another one comes from analogy: In motor skills a great deal of waste motion is involved before the task is well learned. Afterward, however, the response is much simpler.

Other aspects of thinking may depend on piecemeal learning of very simple discriminations essential to effective attainment of goals. The young baby learning to pick up rattles may try to pick up a butterfly painted on the crib mattress, only learning to discriminate three-dimensional objects from two-dimensional pictures as repeated experience makes it plain that objects provide different visual cues from those of surfaces. Gibson and Walk (26) have demonstrated this kind of effect with a subhuman species: Young rats are helped in learning to select a triangle rather than a circle to get food if they have had cut-out triangles and circles hung on the walls of their cages for their whole life preceding testing. However, if the triangle and circles were presented as two-dimensional pictures painted on a food door rather than as cut-outs, the symbols had no three-dimensional properties and did not facilitate later learning.

———————— Piaget's Theory of Cognitive Development in Children

Many of the separate experiments on the intellectual development of children would be easier to remember and fit together if we knew a theory of cognitive development which stated general principles about that topic. Perhaps the most influential such theory is that of Jean Piaget, a famous child psychologist who has done most of his work in Geneva, Switzerland. His theory emphasizes that different kinds of intellectual processes are possible to or typical of a person at different stages in life. Piaget's theory employs quite different terms than the stimulus–response (S–R) learning theory which received primary emphasis earlier in this book. Berlyne (3) has suggested that, despite these differences in terminology, there is much in common between the two theories, with Piaget simply adding some concepts to those already existing in S–R theory. Some of the interrelations between the theories will be noted in the discussion below.

The Sensory–Motor, Preverbal Stage: The First Eighteen Months of Life

In the preverbal stage, the first of four stages described by Piaget (58), the infant learns to discriminate between different kinds of things and events. Thus he distinguishes between edible and inedible objects, eating the one and not the other. This may be called the development of *meaning*, but language requires that meaning be conveyed from person to person, which is done imperfectly and inefficiently by mere acceptance or refusal of food. One-year-old infants typically have a speaking vocabulary of two or more words and are able to respond appropriately to some simple questions or requests from an adult. Another kind of behavior is also developing—representational behavior or communication with one's self. Thoughts expressed in words but not verbalized can not be understood except in ourselves, although sometimes it is possible to be aware of another person's internal thinking from his lip movements. Wallach (76) describes some of Piaget's research in which the representation used is muscular but not yet verbal. At almost 18 months of age,

> One of Piaget's daughters already has had practice with turning over a matchbox in order to shake out a desired chain when the drawer of the box is rather fully pulled out and with poking in her index finger and extracting the chain when the drawer of the box is only partly pulled out. Now Piaget returns the chain to the matchbox and closes the drawer even farther. The child first tries to insert her finger into the slit, to no avail. She then interrupts this activity, observes the slit with great attention, and, a number of times in succession, gradually opens her mouth from a narrow to a wide aperture. Following several representations of this graduated opening of her mouth, she returns to the box and, without hesitation, pulls the drawer open farther and extracts the chain. . . . It appears that gradually widening the aperture of her mouth served to represent the "pullable" property of the drawer, and this representational response, in turn, functioned as a tool of discovery, since the drawer had never been pulled before.°

One comment about research technique: Psychologists are usually dissatisfied with reports like this, for details of procedure and response are omitted, as are photographic or other detailed recordings. Mouly

---

° Copyright © 1963 by the University of Chicago Press.

(51) called attention to weaknesses of this kind in Piaget's research, particularly in his earliest studies. For this reason the foregoing quotation should be regarded as only a tentative description of representational behavior in a young child. Whether it would occur again in other children of the same age and general experience is quite unknown.

It can only be said, then, that Piaget's daughter seems to have been making a mediating response in representing the changes in position of the drawer by the movements of her mouth. Later on, her mediating responses may have included muscular activities of this sort but no doubt became increasingly internalized as subvocal thought.

The Stage of Preoperational Representation: Eighteen Months to Six Years

To understand this stage it is first necessary to know what Piaget means by an *operation*. Piaget feels that knowledge depends not on making a mental photograph of reality but on being able to modify objects or events. For instance, one learns about rectangles by rotating them or by cutting one into two triangles. This modification can be called a *transformation;* the learner needs to develop the ability to make transformations and to understand what the nature or structure of these transformations is. Piaget also emphasizes that operations quickly become internal in the sense that one does not always have to perform a physical, external operation to understand it. Classroom teachers and Piaget would agree that a balance between internal and external operations is important, with some students having more need than others to physically manipulate the materials they are studying.

In the preoperational stage a child is able to talk and to form simple concepts of such things as the quantity of a liquid. But he has limited understanding of operations, particularly of the reversibility of operations. An adult who watches water being poured from a tall narrow glass into a short broad glass knows that this operation could be reversed to return the water to the tall narrow glass—and he knows that the amount of water is the same regardless of the glass in which it is held. However, a preoperational child will judge that there is more water in one glass than there is when it is contained in the other glass.

Piaget uses the term *conservation of amount of matter* to refer to a recognition that an amount of water or other substance is unchanged by changing its shape. He also studied conservation of weight, conservation of number, and conservation of volume as they are demonstrated by children's judgments in response to operations on stimulus materials.

A fascinating inversion of abilities for intellectual functioning has been discussed by Piaget (59) and by its discoverers, Mehler and Bever (50). The two researchers found that 2-year-old children were better able to tell which of two rows of balls had the larger number of balls than were 4-year-old children. If one row contained four balls quite widely spaced and the other contained six balls which were crowded together to make a shorter line, the 2-year-olds usually chose the short line with more balls. However, the 4-year-olds frequently chose the other line, apparently because it was longer. An explanation for the superior performance of the 2-year-olds is still being developed. Mehler and Bever seem to say that the perceptual processes which enable the 2-year-olds to make a correct judgment in this instance do not work in other situations; therefore, the child modifies his behavior by combining the perceptual processes and logical judgment. In the early stage of such combining, he actually loses some skills, but this is necessary to make greater progress and enter the stage of concrete operations.

The Stage of Concrete Operations: Seven to Eleven Years

The stage of concrete operations is one in which operations such as those just described above are performed. However, these operations are concrete in the sense that even when performed internally they refer primarily to physical or concrete objects rather than to hypothetical or logical entities. Inhelder and Piaget (35) illustrate the use of concrete operations by describing how an 8-year-old learns what variable controls the frequency of the oscillation of a pendulum. The child changes the length of the string and notices that a short distance from pendulum weight to the other end of the pendulum causes a faster oscillation. He also varies the amount of weight and, if his observations are carefully made, learns that this variable does not affect the oscillations. Early in his stage of concrete operations a boy may not yet realize that when he varies the weight to see its effect, he must hold other variables such as the length of the string constant in order to be sure which factor controls the behavior he observes.

The Stage of Formal Operations: Twelve to Fifteen Years

The stage of formal operations is one in which youngsters are able to use the notions of formal logic to reason through problems without direct experimentation and without necessarily having received training in logic. Inhelder and Piaget emphasize the importance of being able to list all possible combinations of events of some kind as basic to this sort of reasoning. Thus the boy in the pendulum example above would later have been able to list all four possible combinations of long versus short string and heavy versus light weight: long string–heavy weight, long string–light weight, short string–heavy weight, and short string–light weight prior to investigating the effects of these two variables.

Some Research on Piaget's Theory of Cognitive Development

Piaget and Inhelder (60, Chapter 3) used bead patterns as stimuli for the investigation of the stage of preoperational representation. Their procedure is to determine at what age (actually about 3 to 4½ years) children can first select a single bead which matches the color of one presented by the experimenter as a standard, at what age (5½ to 7 years) they can first select seven appropriately colored beads to form a straight-line pattern comparable to a standard one placed nearby, and at what ages other similar tasks can first be performed. This task bears a resemblance to intelligence testing procedures (see Chapter 14); it is also similar to Gesell's procedures for determining characteristic activities at different ages. However, Piaget and Inhelder are more interested in a theory of cognitive processes than was Gesell, who studied almost all aspects of behavior and was a theorist only in that he seemed to think of development as an automatic process occurring with the passage of time, even independent of the child's experiences during that time. Piaget's work differs from intelligence testing primarily in being less statistical and less standardized.

Braine (5) confirmed Piaget and Inhelder's finding for the seven-beads pattern, reporting that 67% of children in the range from 5 years, 9 months, to 6 years 5 months, performed the task correctly. If a three-bead pattern were the crucial task, it could be said that the concept of ordering is established by the age of 4 years, 3 months, to 4 years, 11 months, because half the children in that age bracket were able to copy the three-bead pattern. Once task complexity is fixed, Piaget's dictum that the concept of ordering appears at a definite age can be accepted. Piaget recognized this problem and seems to have chosen a relatively difficult standard, among all that he worked with, to define mastery of this concept.

The stage of preoperational representation is one in which many concepts other than ordering are coming to fruition. Figure 10-6 presents evidence from Braine's (5) work that a measurement task develops at almost exactly the same time as the ordering task (defined by the three-bead pattern) just discussed. This measurement task required children who had previously demonstrated the ability to distinguish between

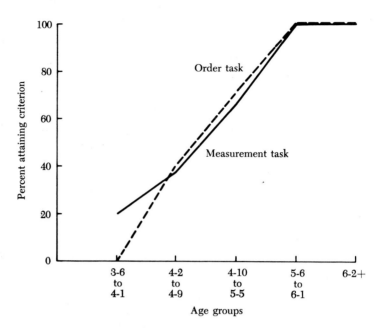

Fig. 10-6. A comparison of number of subjects at different age levels who could copy a 3-bead pattern (order task) or infer the relative heights of two uprights from a comparison of each with a measuring rod (measurement task). [Figure 7 from Braine (5). Copyright 1959 by American Psychological Association, and reproduced by permission.]

two uprights of obviously different heights to use inferential processes to discriminate between nearly equal heights. This discrimination was performed by noting that a measuring rod placed beside each upright separately was slightly taller than one and slightly shorter than the other. Though this measuring task and the ordering task seem quite different logically, they must have great psychological similarity, for not only does Fig. 10-6 show great similarity in growth of the two skills, but Braine's article states that children are almost always consistent in accomplishing either both tasks or neither.

In addition to these two tasks, a variety of behavior changes from ages 5 to 7 have been summarized by White (77). Table 10-1 presents some of these changes, together with references to Piaget's work on those topics. White concludes that the period from 5 to 7 years may be a time in which children add to their previous ability to learn by association (such as the paired-associates learning of Chapter 3), a higher level, cognitive mode of functioning characterized by the ability to use language in reasoning, as noted in Table 10-1. This second level process is very much like the second signal system Russian psychologists assume occurs in 5- to 6-year-olds.

Piaget's research emphasizes stages of development rather than the process by which children move from one stage to another. The process of movement is of interest to learning theorists, who tend to believe that this process can be slowed down or speeded up as a function of the experiences provided each child. Smedslund (66, 67) has presented evidence that special training may produce apparent conservation of weight but that this is not a true speeding up of development because the conservation is less permanent than when attained without special instruction. One method which Smedslund used to teach conservation of weight is called *external reinforcement*. This method provides knowledge of results (informative feedback) following a change in the shape of a ball of modeling clay into a sausage shape or some other shape. The child is first shown two equal balls of clay, and the experimenter learns that the child indeed sees them as being of equal weight. After one ball is changed in shape, the child is asked whether the ball or the sausage is heavier, or whether they are equal in weight. Then external reinforcement is provided by placing each object on a different pan of a balance scale and showing the child that the weights are equal. This is called external reinforcement because the child is presented external evidence of conservation rather than depending upon social reinforcement, i.e., being told by the experimenter that the two quantities are equal.

Smedslund (67) showed that if, following the training procedure just described, the experimenter cheated by surreptitiously taking away a piece of the ball being changed in shape, thus preventing the scale from

TABLE 10-1
Some Developments at Age Seven Reported by Piaget[a]

1926	
(a) Conversations indicating collaboration in action between two children	
(b) Conversations indicating collaboration in abstract thought	
(c) Genuine argument	Piaget (54)
(d) Avoidance of self-contradiction	
1959	
(e) Sharp increase in use of "because" and "since"	
(f) Use of "but" and "then" in logical sense	Piaget (55)
(g) Introspectiveness begins	
1960	
(h) Names treated as separate from things they represent	Piaget (56)
(i) Genuine physical explanations appear	
(j) Genuine awareness of need for causal agent	Piaget (57)

[a] Table IV from White (77).

balancing, all of the children previously trained to believe in conservation of weight would reverse their opinions (an extinction process, in learning theory terms). However, when such a trick was played on children who believed in conservation of weight prior to the experiment, almost half resisted the conclusion apparently forced by the demonstration. The resisters said that some clay must have been lost on the floor or hidden by the experimenter. Smedslund feels that this experiment is evidence that conventional learning procedures are not adequate to produce permanent beliefs in conservation. Though the experimental evidence on this point is still incomplete, he agrees with Piaget that the child develops his logical structure by an internal process called *equilibration,* which does depend on experience but not on direct reinforcement of the kind just discussed. For example, Smedslund would like to believe that practice in adding pieces of clay to an existing piece or taking clay away from an existing piece teaches the concept of conservation even though it does not give evidence on the effect of changing shape. This is said to instigate an equilibration process in which behavior becomes more stable, consistent, and complete. Furthermore, this practice of adding clay and removing clay causes the child to think about the nature of matter and to resolve questions in his own mind by reasoning rather than simply by observing. The authors of this book feel that equilibration theory has the virtue of emphasizing the child's use of rational processes in addition to observation. However, Smedslund's experiments by no means settle the issue; it seems very possible that extended periods of external reinforcement would produce a belief in conservation which would be so strong that it could not be eliminated by trickery. Rather than minimize the contribution of learning to the natural development of such concepts as conservation, we would emphasize that real life provides a wide variety of experiences which either by transfer or by direct reinforcement lead to the concepts Piaget has discovered develop at different ages.

Even though the stages of cognitive growth are difficult to modify, they do depend upon the experiences children undergo. In particular, a person's belief system about some natural event depends on the training given in his particular culture. Kohlberg (41) has shown that beliefs about dreams develop quite differently in the United States from those held by the Atayal aborigines, a Malaysian group in Formosa. Presumably because the Atayal culture is one in which dreams are believed to be real, most concepts about dreams develop later in the Atayal than in Americans, with the order of development also differing in the two cultures. American children of about 4 years, 10 months, have reached the conclusion that dreams are not real; by 6 years, 5 months, they have concluded that the dream is a thought. Eight-year-old Atayal children believe that dreams are not real; by 11, Atayal children have concluded that a dream is a thought; from 11 to 16 the Atayal view of dreams regresses from interpreting them as thoughts to interpreting them as coming from within but having some independent status. This regression seems to represent the effect of parental instruction as a counterbalance to the life experiences which previously had moved the children's beliefs toward a more "scientific" interpretation.

Application of Piaget's Theory to Teaching

Hooper (34) has presented a philosophy for the application of Piaget's theory in education; it is Hooper's article that is the basis of the next few paragraphs. First of all, theory and research within the Piagetian tradition tells something about readiness. We should not expect to work at the level of formal operations when a child is still at a preoperational stage and has not developed the notions of conservation. Nor, within a stage of development, should difficult tasks be taught before less difficult ones. In most of the curriculum (presumably excluding some aspects of aesthetic appreciation and physical education), the instructional emphasis should be on concepts and logical analysis rather than on isolated facts. Karplus and Thier (40) in describing the work of the *Science Curriculum Improvement Study*, which has been much influenced by Piaget's theory, emphasize that (for elementary school science) these concepts should not come in great part from books or lectures. Instead, concepts should be developed through experience with laboratory materials and through genuine discussion among pupils and with teachers, not "discussion" aimed at luring correct answers from children that the children are not yet ready to conceptualize for themselves. [This objection to guided discussion sounds plausible and in extreme cases is almost surely correct. However, Sigel, Roeper, and Hooper (65) present a verbatim transcript of a guided training session on properties of fruit, used as a means of teaching multiple attributes of objects. This sort of training over a 5-week period led to a substantial increase in the number of 5-year-olds who exhibited the concept of conservation of substance, weight, or volume. Teachers should therefore realize that both free and guided discussion are of value.]

Science instruction may aim directly at the development of concepts which Piaget has emphasized. Thus Fig. 10-7 shows children from the *Science Curriculum Improvement Study* learning about conservation of volume in a school science laboratory. Mathematics instruction can also be focused upon Piagetian stages, as illustrated in the work of Dienes

Fig. 10-7. Elementary school science students learning about conservation of volume in liquids. From Karplus and Thier (40).

(14), Lamon (43), and Lovell (47). This approach may emphasize the logical order in which Piaget conceives that number concepts should develop; but, as Wohlwill (80) points out, the final decision as to the order in which different concepts are presented depends upon the actual order of difficulty of those concepts. In either case, however, the result of a Piagetian emphasis is to structure mathematics teaching in psychological order, orienting it to the characteristics of children rather than to a mathematician's conception of a natural order for presentation.

Hooper has presented a stimulating analysis of ways that social science teaching can be influenced by Piaget. [The basic points were first made by Flavell (19a) and have also been discussed by Sigel (64).] Hooper (34) states, "The failure to derive any generalities or common threads from traditional narrative history is the most common failing of secondary pupils and college students." If this statement has any truth in it, history courses need to be revamped to help students look for guiding principles in human history. Not only in history, but also in social science in general, Hooper and Sigel believe that students need to develop four basic concepts (34):

1. The fundamental uncertainty of historical predictions of outcomes—the possibility of calculated guesses greater than chance
    The conception of outcomes as the results of stable identifiable determinants plus fortuitous determinants

2. Governmental tables of organization, authority relations, and related classifications of the hierarchical type
3. Causal structure of historical or political outcomes
   The notions of positive, negative, and neutral events in the context of
   that outcome
   Concepts of multidetermination of historical and political outcomes
   Concept of causes continuously operating across extended time periods
4. The possibility of across-instance generalizations about historical or political processes, for example, common causal patterns involved in any revolution, or any political process resulting in a new congressional law

These four concepts are intended to help students cope with the complexities of human affairs. They simultaneously emphasize that historical
events are not accidental but are caused and that the causes are multiple,
probabilistic, and hard to identify. Each concept has its counterpart in a
Piagetian concept which children are presumed to develop without
necessarily applying it to social science. For example, 2 above, relating
to government tables of organization, is an example of an ability to
classify items in multileveled systems, as when a biology student
classifies an organism into its phylum, genus, and species, as well as
other categories. Though a professional social scientist may look for a
somewhat neater set of principles, such as a physicist might employ,
these four concepts can help the student make sense of what otherwise
would be a multitude of unrelated facts.

The Perry Preschool Project in Ypsilanti, Michigan, has successfully
applied Piagetian concepts in teaching black children who have not
shown the cognitive development common to middleclass white homes.
Preschool instruction following traditional procedures that emphasize
social adjustment and unstructured experience with a variety of cultural
materials was less successful in the Perry Preschool Project; therefore,
a shift was made to direct instruction in basic cognitive skills. Sonquist
and Kamii (70) tell how three levels of symbolization were improved by
the teachers in this project. An *index*, according to Piaget, is a part of
an object or something representative, like a footprint, coming directly
from the object. Children were taught to recognize objects from their
indices by such procedures as the *mystery bag game:*

A teacher puts an object such as a toy duck in the bag and asks a
child to identify it by reaching into the bag and feeling its configuration.
The child, of course, is not given an opportunity to watch the duck
being placed in the bag.

A higher level representation of an object, a *symbol*, as Piaget would
call it, may be a picture, a model, or some other device such as a plain
wooden block which a child may choose to call a train, for example.
Children in the Perry Preschool Project are taught the use of symbols by

such activities as molding clay into the shape of a particular object or by pasting shapes together to represent people and animals.

The third level, the *sign,* is a word used to represent an object. Children in the project are continually given words to represent objects, but the words are used in a way to connect the objects with the nonverbal stimuli which have been associated with those objects. As the children's cognitive skills increase, less emphasis on nonverbal activity is necessary. Then it becomes possible to teach advanced concepts, such as *grouping,* in which it is not possible to point to an object when defining the word. Thus, children can be taught to put all of the plates in the cupboard and all of the cups on the table, or some of each in each place. If verbal skills have been well developed, these instructions can be given without indices or symbols, words being enough to communicate the task to the children.

Hodges and Spicker (32) and Kohlberg (42) both indicate that a substantial improvement in tested intelligence occurred among Perry Preschool Project children given special treatment. Thus, this project, like the Bereiter and Engelmann (2) study discussed in Chapter 9, provides evidence that new teaching procedures can appreciably enhance intellectual performance by preschool children. Weikart (76a) explicitly reports a sizable gain during the first Perry Preschool year in which Piagetian methods were used. The present authors have not seen a report on the permanence of the gain following Piagetian training. With earlier methods, however, the Perry Project found nonsignificant differences between experimental and control groups in all reported intelligence tests (following special preschool training) at the end of kindergarten, first, or second grade (32, 76a). This impermanence of gain has been common to many programs intended to give certain children a head start in school.

One may question to what extent even the temporary improvement just noted is due to specifically Piagetian principles. Bereiter and Engelmann did not invoke those principles, and yet were successful in raising their children's intelligence and achievement test scores, apparently because linguistic and arithmetic skills were so strongly emphasized. Kohlberg (41) is doubtful that this improvement was fundamental in the sense that Piagetian stages were reached faster than without the training. Kohlberg suspects that the learning was mechanical and did not indicate understanding of the concepts involved. However, Sullivan (71) points out that Piaget has been criticized for de-emphasizing the importance of verbal instruction in schooling, particularly in the light of the fact that deaf children more frequently appear to have intellectual retardation than do blind children, who would not be deprived of verbal stimulation. Sullivan also emphasizes that there is a faddism associated with Piaget's theory, leading some educators to accept Piaget's conclusions without carefully examining the evidence for them. Sullivan (71) goes so far as to say, "The author can only conclude that Piaget maintains his popularity because he reflects favorably a particular point of view about education. For education in the 1960's, Piaget is the psychological arm for the proponents of discovery–learning methods." (See Chapter 3 for a discussion of *discovery–learning*.) The present authors would conclude that classroom teachers will have to ignore some of the arguments about interpreting findings by Bereiter and Engelmann or from the Perry Preschool Project, but it seems permissible to use the teaching techniques of either project until further research evidence makes it apparent that one is definitely superior to the other in a specific way. Some evidence on this point appears in Chapter 14.

Development of Emotional Responses in the Young

A natural question is, Do any emotions exist at birth? Bridges (6) studied 60 infants over a period of several months, concluding that a newborn baby has only one emotion, diffuse excitement. By 3 months of age he has two: distress and delight. By the fifth month anger and disgust are differentiated from distress. Fear shows up at about the seventh month, elation and affection become distinguishable from delight between the tenth and twelfth months.

The many physical and behavioral similarities between monkeys and people lead us to expect that much of what we learn about monkeys will also be true of human beings—or will at least suggest processes to investigate in humans. Using monkeys for research has several valid reasons. First, young monkeys do form close relations with their mothers and do play with "friends" and fight with "enemies" just as young children do. Second, it would be improper to modify the normal rearing of humans as much as can reasonably be done with monkeys. To completely deprive an infant monkey of contact with members of his own species for a few months is more acceptable than to do the same with human babies. It is also easier to maintain a controlled environment and make frequent behavior records with monkeys than with humans.

The third, and final, reason for studying monkey behavior is that it is very important to learn the extent to which personality can be affected by nonverbal processes. We are accustomed to thinking that our friendships and family relationships are substantially influenced by what we say and have said to us. However, human beings are also influenced by nonverbal communication (61): by expressions and movements of the eyes, cheeks, and mouth; by handshakes, caresses, pushes, shoves; by

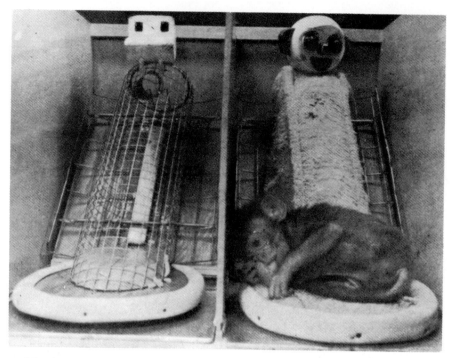

Fig. 10-8. A wire mother and a cloth mother with an infant monkey lying on the latter. Figure 1 from Harlow and Zimmerman (29).

approaches to and withdrawals from a person, etc. It is important to study the effects of nonverbal stimuli upon human beings; it is also necessary to see how these stimuli affect animal behavior. When certain kinds of infantile experiences in monkeys can be shown to affect their later mating and maternal behavior, it is reasonable to wonder if humans are equally affected by the same nonverbal stimuli. Harlow's studies of emotion in the monkey may help us to understand human behavior as well.

Harlow and Zimmerman (29) have studied the development of "love" in infant macaque monkeys raised without their mothers or other monkey companions. Eight infant monkeys had two mother–substitutes each, a wire dress dummy and a second dummy of wood covered with terry cloth. Figure 10-8 shows one such monkey lying at the foot of the terry cloth "mother."

To test whether emotional attachments develop with age and specific experiences, Harlow and Zimmerman fed four monkeys from milk bottles installed in the upper part of a wire dummy and four from bottles installed in the upper part of a terry cloth dummy. In each case the amount of time spent by the monkey on each of its two "mothers" was measured. As Fig. 10-9 indicates, the monkeys spent substantially more time on the cloth mothers, even if they had been fed by wire mothers. The tendency to lie on or cling to the cloth mother increased in the first 25 days of life but declined slightly in the subsequent 140 days.

What do these findings tell about the origin of love? The trend in the first 25 days suggests either that the monkeys learned to go to the cloth mother (love her?) or that maturation increased that tendency. Because secondary reinforcement comes from the place one is fed, learning theory might have predicted that infants fed by wire mothers would have preferred the wire mothers, but this was not true. Apparently cloth is innately more attractive than wire to the monkey. Or to say this in the terminology of learning theory, cloth is more reinforcing than wire.

The preference for the cloth mother is more than a preference for a soft, warm place to lie, according to Harlow and Zimmerman. Four of the eight monkeys preferred the cloth mother to a gauze-covered heated pad which was also available up to 18 hours a day. Very possibly the shape as well as the softness of the cloth mother was attractive to the infant monkeys. The affection of the infants for their substitute mothers

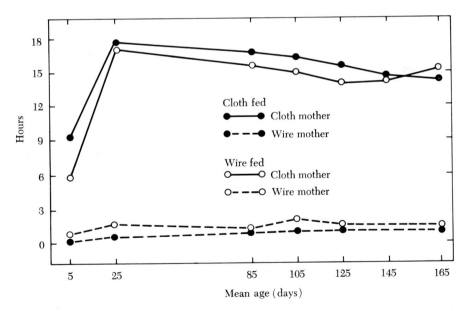

Fig. 10-9. Time spent on cloth and wire mothers. Figure 3 from Harlow and Zimmerman (29).

is also demonstrated by their strong response to fear-producing stimuli—when a mobile toy bear, for example, was presented, the monkeys usually went to their cloth mother after which their signs of terror were relieved. This was true even if they had been fed on the wire mother. Consequently, it seems that the cloth mothers, by virtue of their construction and of the infants' experience with them, became attractive both in a positive sense and as a refuge from fearsome stimuli.

An unexpected result of Harlow's research was that a later study showed that monkeys raised with both cloth and wire mothers, with wire mothers only, or alone in a wire cage were sexually unresponsive in maturity. Harlow, Harlow, Dodsworth, and Arling (28) report that about two-thirds of all the female monkeys they raised in these conditions consistently rejected sexual intercourse, apparently because they had not developed normal "friendship patterns" with other monkeys during infancy and early life. In this study 20 females eventually gave birth following either voluntary or involuntary insemination. Eight of these mothers were clearly abusive to their first-born infants. Four infants were actually killed by their mothers, and another infant had to be permanently removed from the mother before the age of 3 weeks to save its life. In addition, seven mothers were classified as indifferent to their first offspring, being unable to nurse the baby consistently and punishing the baby frequently.

Harlow *et al.* offer some evidence that separation from the mother does not necessarily lead an infant monkey to be an inadequate mother later in life. That evidence is slight since it depends only upon four cases: There were no abusive mothers among four who had social deprivation early in life but were raised in cages containing monkeys of their own age beginning sometime between 7 and 12 months after birth.

Despite the poor sexual and maternal behavior of the female monkeys studied (Harlow *et al.* say almost nothing about the effects of infant experience upon male monkeys), eventual improvement seems common. The females came to be more sexually receptive as they increased in age, but they never became as responsive as females raised in natural conditions. Another sign of improved social adjustment with age is that none of nine second-born or third-born infants of these motherless monkeys were abused by their mothers. Only one was even treated indifferently.

From these two studies, the evidence is that Harlow and Zimmerman's subjects showed some development of affection for a soft cloth mother kept in the cage with an infant monkey and a wire mother. However, Harlow *et al.* found just as much disturbance in sexual responsiveness and maternal behavior for females who had been raised in the presence of a cloth mother and a wire mother as for those who had been raised in a bare cage or with only a wire mother. This may be merely a proof of the obvious—that mechanical devices cannot substitute for mothering by an adult of one's own species. However, it is very important that Harlow made the obvious generality more specific. In experimentally showing the importance of infant experience upon adult sexual and maternal behavior he reached the same general conclusions that students of human personality have been forced to reach by nonexperimental research. Harlow's research is of great importance because of its simultaneous relevance to learning, motivation, and personality theory.

The development of emotional behavior had actually been studied for several decades previous to Harlow's work. For example, M. C. Jones (37) in 1924 followed up previous research findings showing that fear could be conditioned. She trained a baby named Peter not to fear a rabbit by presenting it at a great distance from the baby while he was eating and bringing it slightly closer each day until the child showed no fear at a very close distance. This is the toleration method mentioned earlier in Chapter 5.

Quite possibly many fear responses are learned and unlearned in the manner just described. In other instances the connection is more remote. The child learns to talk of dangers without having great fear responses, but this verbalization is sufficient to keep him out of the street when cars approach. Perhaps other fears simply develop.

Some emotional behavior could be called a pattern of living rather than a temporary event, such as crying or laughing. Some children respond to intellectual tasks with very quick responses, others with slow responses. Kagan has called these two types of children impulsive and reflective children. His description (39) of these two personality types, studied in the Fels Institute of Antioch College, is as follows:

> First, the reflective child demonstrates higher standards for mastery of intellectual tasks and greater persistence with such tasks during the early school years. He chooses more difficult tasks to work on (hard puzzles, various kinds of handcrafts) and works on them for a longer period of time. Second, the reflective child has a strong tendency to avoid peer group interaction and to be initially phobic in a strange social situation with peers or adults. The reflective child typically stands on the sidelines the first few days at the Fels nursery school and watches the group vigilantly before joining them. The reflective child often withdraws from peer group interaction and retreats to solitary, sedentary tasks. The impulsive child, on the other hand, typically enters the nursery school or day camp situation with zeal and appears to enjoy active social participation. Finally, the reflective child of three to five years of age shows a strong avoidance of activities that are physically dangerous. He is reluctant to climb high on gym apparatus, to walk a narrow plank, or to ride a tricycle fast. When the peer group becomes "wild," the reflective child is likely to withdraw to a quiet corner. These differences obtain for both boys and girls and suggest that the reflective child avoids "risky" situations that are potential sources of physical harm or social rejection.

You may have noticed a similarity between the description of reflective and impulsive children and everyday definitions of introverted and extroverted children, respectively. One major difference between the two classification systems should be mentioned, however. Introversion and extroversion are typically measured by observing how much a person prefers social contact to solitary activity. In contrast, reflective and impulsive children are identified by the way they solve intellectual problems. Following this identification of types, Kagan studied how the two groups behave at work and play, and discovered that the impulsive children act like extroverts and the reflective children act like introverts.

To determine which children are impulsive and which reflective (some children are a little of both and do not receive our attention here), Kagan found children who were relatively fast in responding and relatively inaccurate on two different tests. He called such children impulsive. Youngsters who were relatively slow in responding and relatively accurate were called reflective. What the children had to do is shown in Fig. 10-10, which gives two sample items from one test, the Matching Familiar Figures Test. The top item consists of seven pictures of a teddy bear sitting in a chair. The task is to select the one of the six bottom teddy bear pictures which is identical to the top one. The corresponding task holds for the seven tree pictures also. Almost anyone faced with this task, particularly if instructed to do it quickly, will be tempted not to do a thorough job of examining the pictures but rather to give the first apparently plausible answer one considers. Kagan found that younger children were more impulsive in this sense. First graders answered each question in an average of 11 or 12 seconds whereas third graders took an average of about 21 seconds. The number of errors also decreased from the first to the third grade, but not so sharply as the increase in time taken.

Although the children within any age group who were both relatively slow to respond and relatively accurate were called reflective, it would be wrong to infer that reflective children are more intelligent and impulsive children less intelligent than average. There may be a very slight tendency in that direction but not enough to be of practical importance. What is important to the teacher is the realization that there are reflective and impulsive children and teachers. Teachers should resist the tendency to expect their pupils to respond at the tempo which seems natural to the teacher. Instead, teachers should accept the pattern of behavior that seems natural for each child, taking care not to rush children into thoughtless answers nor to correct wrong answers in a way that might inhibit future response in class.

There are several topics related to the emotional development of

Fig. 10-10. Two sample items from the Matching Familiar Figures Test. Figure 1 from Kagan (39). The top teddy bear picture is like one of the other six below it. The tree pictures have a similar pairing.

children which could be added to this section but will appear in the chapter on personality (Chapter 13) instead. Material such as the effects of different kinds of parental discipline could be discussed either here or in Chapter 13; one reason it has seemed appropriate to delay such discussion is that the major theories of personality have a good deal to say about the effects of different child-rearing methods.

Sex Differences

Just as the preadolescent growth spurt occurs sooner in girls than in boys, so does puberty: Sixty-five percent of girls have had their first menstrual period before they are fourteen; only 30% of boys are clearly postpubescent by then, although another 24% are in the pubescent period at 13 (13). It is well known that girls of 12 and 13 exhibit more mature interests than do boys of the same age.

Though girls have the maturational lead, the superior strength and vital capacity of boys consistently appears even before adolescence: H. E. Jones (36) found that at 6 years of age boys have over 20% more vital capacity than do girls. Terman and Tyler (74) report that right-hand grip strength at 7 years is 10% superior for boys compared with girls. This strength superiority is accompanied, however, by a surprising inferiority in survival. Scheinfeld (62) emphasized that boys have a higher infant death rate than girls do and that they continue this tendency at all ages.

What behavioral differences exist between the sexes? Many are so obvious they require no research verification; some reported here are self-evident. Grown-ups, of either sex, tend to rate girls more intelligent, better behaved, and less neurotic than boys. This could mean that girls *are* all of these good things. However, among girls and boys of equal intelligence (as measured by standard tests) girls are still *rated* superior in intelligence. Apparently a "halo effect" is operating: Girls are clearly less noisy than boys and perhaps work more consistently within the limits of their intellectual ability. Teachers who rate their behavior may find them superior in these two traits and expect them to be superior in others.

Sometimes "halo effects" may be prevented by having machines measure the traits. If a hand dynamometer says that a boy exerts a grip strength of 20 pounds, "halo effect" has not tempered the measurement—though it may occasionally lead to an error in recording that measurement. But machines for measuring personality traits are rare, and human judgment is often essential to the measurement. What do the least halo-infected ratings of boys and girls show?

Even preschool boys are more often judged to grab toys and attack others than are girls (30). In contrast, when children are asked questions regarding their own personalities, girls are generally more likely to score high on the trait of anxiety than boys. Sometimes this difference is greater than chance but not always (27). These two findings conform to the everyday notion that girls are more emotional than boys but less overtly aggressive.

Conceivably the greater anxiety expressed by girls can be explained by what McCandless (49) calls the "admission phenomenon": A readiness to admit negative things about oneself could be stronger in girls than in boys regardless of the true number of anxiety symptoms each experiences. Correspondingly, some children of either sex might appear more anxious than they really are because the admission phenomenon leads them to admit difficulties that other children would deny. McCandless presents some evidence that those persons who are best adjusted personally are also the most willing to make damaging admissions about themselves.

Certain personality traits are so vaguely defined that psychologists find it difficult to make firm conclusions about them. Hattwick (30) points out that some specific traits may be called aggressive by one scholar but not by another. A person who considers that ignoring requests is aggressive might say that boys are more aggressive than girls; a person who feels that ignoring requests is introvertive might say that boys are more introverted than girls. Except where traits have been definitively classified into groups, findings are most sensibly reported for specific items such as "ignoring requests" or for scores from specific tests such as the Children's Manifest Anxiety Scale rather than for something like aggressiveness, which is not defined by a test but by an appeal to common sense.

Inquiries about sex differences in intellectual activity reveal a wealth of studies that suggest female superiority in language activities even before school age. In some instances a biased sampling may have been responsible: The girls were actually more intelligent than the boys. Studies of very young boys and girls of equal average intelligence typically show results like those of Winitz (78), who found that among kindergarten children seven of twelve measures of verbalization, articulation, vocabulary, or fluency favored girls, with only two of these seven being greater than chance superiorities and none of the five others being statistically significant in favor of boys. ("Greater than chance" or "statistically significant," means that an effect appears real rather than accidental. A more technical definition of statistical significance is given in any statistics text but is too lengthy to be included here.) Kindergarten boys and girls customarily differ in language ability, but the differences are relatively small. At school age and up to college age the differences in favor of the girls on reading comprehension and language are generally somewhat larger. Note also that boys are much more likely to become stutterers than are girls.

In contrast to their ability in language skills, boys are generally superior to girls in mathematics and science by the time they reach high school (19).

Among the first group of National Merit Scholars, for example, men scored 42 points higher, on the average, than women did on the mathematics section of the College Entrance Examination Board exams; women scored 16 points higher on the verbal section (33). Correspondingly, 73% of the male National Merit Scholars planned careers in science; only 36% of the females did. Interestingly, the first group of National Merit Scholars comprised 402 men and only 154 women, which suggests that distinguished academic prowess may be more common in males. (Possibly the selection process for these awards favors students strong in science.) Similar results have been reported in the Science Talent Search contests (15). The boys' general superiority in science probably does not exist in the early grades, although measurement of science achievement at such ages is not easy. It is possible that the differences in achievement between the sexes arise with maturity and experience— including the encouragement customarily given to boys to develop scientific interests.

As everyone who has ever bought a book for a child knows, the reading interests of boys and girls differ sharply. These differences are not marked up to the age of about 9 years (73). Then, for the next six years, at least, sex is the greatest single determiner of interest differences in reading. The boy–girl differences in reading preference are greater than those between Finnish and American school children (20). The differences are also greater than those between 10-year-old boys or girls and 15-year-old boys or girls and greater than between boys or girls of average or somewhat below average intelligence and those of superior intelligence (75). Boys prefer adventure stories, science, invention, and generally stories that feature male heroes. Girls prefer romantic fiction, home life stories, and stories about vocations for girls. Interestingly, girls often enjoy stories generally preferred by boys; the reverse is less often true (52). In our male-centered culture, it seems that girls may copy boys' behavior, but not vice versa.

These great differences in the reading interests of boys and girls point up one disadvantage of coeducational schools: the curricula necessarily reflect a compromise between materials more or less ideal for girls and those better for boys. Usually the literature studied—particularly the poetry— satisfies the girls' interests better than the boys'. It may be wise to allow interest groups of just boys or just girls to choose classroom reading materials for which they have a genuine preference.

The differences in intellectual interests of boys and girls are closely paralleled by similar differences in information. Figure 10-11 shows that high school boys know more about mechanics and are more interested in the subject than are girls. Correspondingly, high school girls know more about clerical work and are more interested in it than are boys. What may be the most extensive study of high school students' aptitudes, achievements, personalities, and interests was begun by John C. Flanagan in 1960. Called Project Talent, the study investigated about 5% of all ninth, tenth, eleventh, and twelfth graders in American high schools.

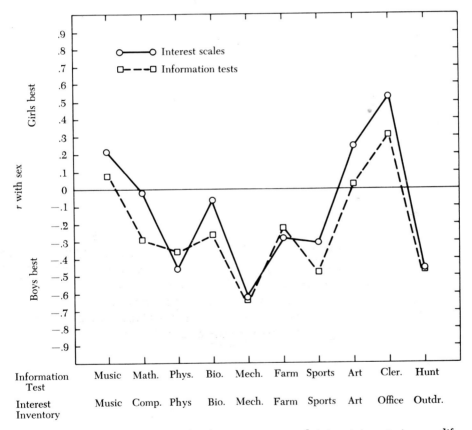

Fig. 10-11. The similarity of information tests and interest inventories on different topics reflects sex differences in high school students. The term "*r*" refers to the correlation coefficient, a measurement discussed in Chapter 14. Figure 8-4 from Flanagan (19).

Flanagan and his associates (19) theorize that the reason for the similarity between interests and knowledge shown in Fig. 10-11 is that people tend to learn and remember more about the things in which they are interested. It is also true that learning a new topic can create an interest in that area if the learning experience is pleasant and the topic relevant.

High School Interests and Activities

The primary concern of the teacher must be with the individual learner, not just with the differences in the interests of boys and girls. The teacher who is aware of the individual interests of his students is in a better position to counsel, communicate effectively, and build warm personal relationships. Unfortunately, many junior high and high school teachers get only a superficial impression of their students, for classes are large and each group spends only a small part of the day with each teacher. Because it is so difficult to know all the students as individuals, it is important to at least know the typical interests of youngsters of that particular age level.

Teachers who are only a few years removed from high school themselves remember many of their own experiences and attitudes, and also those of their contemporaries. Later, even though he is in constant contact with young people, the teacher of many years' experience often loses perspective about his students. If the teacher's view of his students becomes so narrow that he sees only the academic side of their lives, he may make false comparisons beginning with, "When I was in high school. . . ." For this reason, every experienced teacher should occasionally review the changing attitudes and interests of students. Jones (38) had the wisdom to question ninth graders in 1953 and 1959 in the junior high school where a similar investigation had been made in 1935. She presents evidence that from 1935 to 1953 there had been very little change in the socioeconomic classification of the parents for the groups studied, and that the students of both generations had equivalent intelligence scores. The most outstanding difference in the young people of the 1950's was their greater social sophistication, reflected by the girls in a greater tendency to go to dances, read love stories, and use lipstick, and evidenced by the boys in their attitudes toward most of the activities in which girls had been changing.

It is interesting that the social sophistication and increased heterosexual interests of today's students are not accompanied by increased frivolity and lessened interest in studies. Jones found a significant increase in the proportions of both boys and girls who, in filling out a questionnaire about their activities that week, reported that they had studied, had taken care of children, had read something about science, had talked about church and religion, and had talked about school activities. Jones emphasizes that although the junior high school students she studied were more responsible and socialized, they were not just more conformist to adult standards than were students of the earlier generation. In the 1950's more students than in the 1930's approved of disagreeing with their parents and saying exactly what they thought. Students also rejected the idea of always doing what is expected. The students' combination of seriousness and independence has enabled them to think independently, to look at issues, to take sides. Their activities may range from wearing freedom buttons in support of the civil rights movement or antiwar armbands (21) to boycotting certain nonintegrated schools. In Los Angeles some predominantly Mexican–American and black high schools were boycotted by students who demanded many changes, including teaching more about the cultural heritage of minority groups and hiring more members of minority groups as principals and vice-principals (45).

In the foreseeable future there may be increasing numbers of demonstrations and other signs of student independence, some violent, many challenging the traditional controls exercised by American schools. Appropriate responses to such problems will of course have to be made for each situation, based on the facts of the case. It is most important that teachers and school administrators study the psychology of students' thinking—the only possible preparation for the times when issues of this kind arise.

An example of the way psychological research reveals the interests and feelings of high school students is the findings by Lott and Lott (46) comparing white and black students judged to be leaders on the basis of their intelligence, the students' lists of outstanding seniors, and the teachers' lists of outstanding seniors. Table 10-2 shows that the leisure activities of the two groups are very similar. Apparently dating is less common among the black leaders than among the white. Most other differences were relatively small. However, on one particular attitude the two groups differed radically—and in a predictable way. When asked to suggest one of two most wished for changes to be made in the United States only 20% of the white student leaders suggested ending discrimination or segregation, whereas 71% of the black student leaders suggested it.

Although Lott and Lott found great similarity between black and white leaders it should not be assumed that there are few differences in

TABLE 10-2

Negro and White Student Leaders in Kentucky High Schools:
Report of Free Time Activities[a]

Response categories	Negro leaders ($N = 28$)		White leaders ($N = 30$)	
	Fre-quencies	Pro-portions	Fre-quencies	Pro-portions
Listen to music (radio–records)	27	0.96	27	0.90
Visit with friends	25	0.89	25	0.83
Read books	21	0.75	21	0.70
Participate in sports	18	0.64	20	0.67
Creative activity (e.g., draw, practice musical instrument)	17	0.61	22	0.73
Movies	18	0.64	18	0.60
Television	16	0.57	12	0.40
Parties—socials	12	0.43	8	0.27
Help at home—in neighborhood	6	0.21	10	0.33
Read magazines	8	0.28	7	0.23
Church activity	4	0.14	8	0.27
Commercial recreation (e.g., bowling, skating)	7	0.25	7	0.23
Solitary activity (e.g., driving, walking)	11	0.39	5	0.17
Dating	3	0.11	12	0.40
Miscellaneous	9	0.32	13	0.43

[a] Table 4.14 from Lott and Lott (46).

interests or activities of different ethnic or socioeconomic groups among persons other than leaders. Since many ethnic groups differ also in socioeconomic status and educational attainments, usually because of discrimination against them, an examination of groups with different educational histories will point up their other differences. The studies of Flanagan and Cooley (18) show a great many differences in the activities and interests of eleventh-grade students who, two years later, entered trade school, technical school, armed forces school, junior college, four-year college, or who had no post-highschool education. Figure 10-12 shows that the boys in this study could easily be grouped according to two interest dimensions. Those who attended junior college and four-year college were less interested in mechanical–technical topics than were the others. Boys who went to technical schools seemed to have some mechanical–technical interests but also ranked high on the second dimension, which involved an interest in social service and artistic activities and a disinterest in literary–linguistic activities, computation, and hunting and fishing. In this phase of Project Talent, Flanagan and

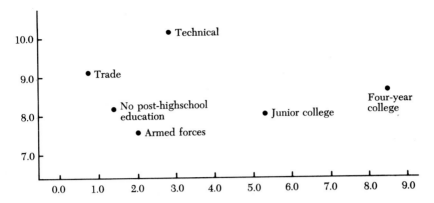

Fig. 10-12. Separation of six, very large groups of 11th grade boys who later entered different types of post-high school instruction, as a function of two types of interest categories. Scores along the horizontal axis decrease with increases in mechanical–technical interests but increase with increases in physical science interests and sales interest. Scores along the vertical axis decrease with increases in literary–linguistic, computational and hunting–fishing interests but increase with increases in social service and artistic interests. Figure 5-3 from Flanagan and Cooley (18).

Cooley report a number of indications that eleventh graders who subsequently went on to college were more interested in academic activities and less interested in dating, social life, and auto-repairing than were those who did not go on to college. It becomes apparent that economic necessity affects the degree of academic interest for most people: the noncollege-bound students also did more chores in their homes and were more likely to work 16 or more hours a week for pay during the school year. Presumably, if these students are to live at all comfortably, much of their extracurricular work is necessary; as a consequence, the time and energy available for studying is necessarily reduced.

It would seem reasonable to expect, then, that a person with intellectual ability would be more likely to attend college if he comes from a high- or moderate-income home than if he comes from a low-income home. Many studies confirm this expectation. Table 10-3 shows Flanagan and Cooley's evidence on this point, for girls. Girls rated in the lowest quarter regarding ability had little probability of going to college, but the probability increases consistently with increases in socioeconomic level. This holds true for girls of every ability level; the probability of the lowest socioeconomic quarter's entering college is much less than one-half the probability for the quarter of students in the highest socioeconomic bracket. Though not as striking, similar results were obtained with the boys.

Teachers are in a position to encourage students from low-income

TABLE 10-3
*Probability of a Girl Entering College as a Function of Her
Eleventh-Grade Ability and Socioeconomic Status[a]*

| | Socioeconomic quarter | | | |
| | Low | | | High |
Ability quarter	1	2	3	4
Low 1	0.07	0.07	0.05	0.20
2	0.08	0.09	0.20	0.33
3	0.18	0.23	0.36	0.55
High 4	0.34	0.67	0.67	0.82

[a] Table 5-4 from Flanagan and Cooley (18).

homes to go on to college or to continue with other post-high school instruction. Table 10-3 shows that even the ablest youngsters need such encouragement; and teachers are probably most aware of the loss to society when a student ranking in the highest quarter of intellectual ability group does not go on to college. However, other students also merit special attention and support—and their likelihood of entering college should be no smaller than that of persons of similar ability but with higher incomes. Today, the percentage of persons entering college is steadily increasing. Flanagan and Cooley (17) report that only 45.5% of the nation's eleventh graders of 1960 had not entered college or other post-high school training by the summer of 1962. A total of 31% had entered a college offering a bachelor's degree, and 7.5% had entered a junior college or community college. Others will no doubt attend college later.

It is important that teachers realize that high school students are likely to change their vocational goals from year to year. Flanagan and Cooley (18) show that a year after high school graduation, 68.6% of the boys have changed their choice of occupation from the one preferred in the twelfth grade. Even greater changes occur during the earlier school years, with 83.2% having changed from their ninth grade choices, for example. Girls' percentages of changes in preferred occupations range from 58.2 to 73.9 during the same period. These revised choices indicate that high school instruction cannot be profitably focused on a single occupation for each student. However, high school can be effective by providing some basic preparation for everyone's later profession. Flanagan and Cooley (18) distinguish between six kinds of careers. Three are scientific or technological; one, such as an engineering aide or a medical technician, does not require college training. The other two categories of scientific–technological work are oriented toward physical science and biological or medical science and do require college work. Three other kinds of careers are nontechnological and again include one area of non-college- and two areas of college-requiring jobs. An office worker, for example, need not have a college background. However, there is a business classification of positions, which includes lawyers and some accountants and salesmen, where college training would be essential or at least helpful. There is also a nonbusiness (humanities) classification including positions such as social scientist or clergyman for which college preparation would be essential.

If six different curricula were established in each large high school, one for each of the broad occupational groups just discussed, the students' preparation for later entry into their chosen occupations would be greatly facilitated, provided the number of changes across broad categories were much smaller than the percentages given above for specific occupations. For the five-year period from the ninth grade to a year after graduation from high school, changes from one of the six categories to another is 58%, lower than the percentages for specific jobs but nonetheless too high to warrant a rigid bracketing of students into six curricular areas. It is worth noting that fewer people entered the noncollege occupations than was expected from their ninth grade plans. Counselors should remember this fact, especially in working with members of minority groups who often feel they have been discouraged from attempting to enter occupations that demand college training.

Because it is so difficult to predict what kind of curriculum would be appropriate for each high school student, no simple separation of students into six or even eight basic programs of study could be satisfactory. Combinations of required courses and elective courses within college preparatory or other curricula seems most desirable. Flanagan (16) has gone farther than other educators have in individualizing the curriculum, suggesting that learning tasks be selected for a year in advance by a computer programmed for each student's aptitudes, interests, and background. The computer would indicate the basic subjects to be learned, but the teacher and the student would together select the specific teaching–learning units to be followed. Instead of competing with other students taking exactly the same course and examinations, each student would be given material which he can learn almost perfectly, so that success rather than frequent error would become characteristic of homework and examination performance. Flanagan is already experimenting with this curricular and instructional procedure in 14 school districts in California and the eastern part of the United States. This experiment has been criticized for minimizing group experience in school and for decreasing the pupils' opportunity to select their own study materials in libraries and laboratories (1). However, it is too early to evaluate the Flanagan technique; only after it has been used for a few years can its success be measured.

-- **Summary**

1. Language diversity increases with the user's age. Such diversity can be measured by the type–token ratio, 100% times the number of different speech sounds used (called types) divided by the total number of sounds emitted (called tokens). Correspondingly, a child's vocabulary increases from about three words at the age of 1 year to about 47,000 at the age of 17.

2. In learning to speak and to think, children make grammatical errors that are logical in that they are consistent. Children also exhibit intelligent behavior before they can talk—for example, in looking for a person behind a mirror. However, up to the age of 5 or 6 their performance on many tasks resembles that of lower animals, apparently because of deficiencies in their verbal behavior, as controlled by the so-called second signal system.

3. Piaget believes that the cognitive behavior of children goes through four stages: the preverbal stage (first 18 months of life), the stage of preoperational representation (18 months to 6 years), the stage of concrete operations (7 to 11 years), and the stage of formal operations (12 to 15 years). In this first stage the child learns a few words and develops differential responses to different kinds of things. In the second stage he learns such concepts as amount of water but does not understand that the operation of pouring water from one glass to a glass of a different size leaves the total quantity of water unchanged. In the third stage the child understands that certain operations do leave certain properties unchanged or invariant. In the fourth stage he is able to supplement experimentation by logical analysis of physical processes.

4. Piaget's theory has been applied at several levels of school with several different subject matters. One of the most interesting applications has been in the Perry Preschool Project in Michigan, which at least temporarily improved the tested intelligence of young children by providing cognitive training designed to improve their effectiveness in nonverbal and verbal representation of objects and relations.

5. Harlow demonstrated that infant monkeys raised with a terry cloth dummy as a substitute mother respond to that dummy somewhat as they would to a real monkey. However, female monkeys reared in this manner

are often completely unresponsive sexually in adulthood and if impregnated will usually be abusive or indifferent to their first-born young.

6. Teachers will find that they or their individual pupils have a characteristically impulsive or characteristically reflective personality which affects the way they react in social groups, engage in sports, and perform intellectual tasks. It may be important to adapt one's teaching practices to the temperament of each individual child insofar as individual treatment is possible.

7. Superior strength of boys compared with girls is accompanied by a lower survival rate of boys at every age. Girls are typically more capable verbally and boys more capable mathematically. Perhaps because girls are less disruptive in class, teachers tend to rate them as more intelligent than boys whose intelligence scores are actually equal to the girls'.

8. High school students are more socially sophisticated and more interested in dating than were students of the 1930's. However, they are also more concerned with their studies and are more serious minded. Furthermore, today's students are frequently independent in their thinking and increasingly likely to protest school conditions of which they disapprove.

9. The interests of high school boys differ substantially as a function of the type of later education they will obtain (college, trade school, technical school, etc.). When academic ability is held constant, children from high socioeconomic-level families are much more likely to enter college than are children from low socioeconomic backgrounds.

10. Occupational plans of high school students are not very stable. In the year following high school graduation 68.6% of boys change the specific occupation they wish to enter. There is some indication that students who originally plan not to attend college later enter an occupation that has more prestige than the one expected in high school.

—————————————————————————————— SUGGESTED READINGS

Bettelheim, B. How can elementary schools help boys learn to become men? *Instructor,* 1969(March), **78,** 61–62.

An argument in favor of letting boys take grown-up responsibilities whenever possible.

Elkind, D. Giant in the nursery: Jean Piaget. *Education Digest,* 1968(October), **34,** 19–23.

A description of Piaget's theory and of his personality.

Hockett, C. F. The origin of speech. *Scientific American,* 1960(September), **203,** 89–96.

Thirteen "design features" characterizing speech are defined, and different species and forms of communication are compared for possessing or lacking each feature.

─── **REFERENCES**

1. Anonymous. Flanagan . . . a consultant comments. *Phi Delta Kappan,* 1967, **49,** 32–33.
2. Bereiter, C., & Engelmann, S. *Teaching disadvantaged children in the preschool.* Englewood Cliffs, N. J.: Prentice-Hall, 1966.
3. Berlyne, D. E. Comments on relations between Piaget's theory and S-R theory. *Monographs of the Society for Research in Child Development,* 1962, **27,** 127–130.
4. Berlyne, D. E. Soviet research on intellectual processes in children. *Monographs of the Society for Research in Child Development,* 1963, **28,** 165–183.
5. Braine, M. S. D. The ontogeny of certain logical operations: Piaget's formulation examined by nonverbal methods. *Psychological Monographs,* 1959, **73,** No. 5.
6. Bridges, K. M. B. Emotional development in early infancy. *Child Development,* 1932, **3,** 324–341.
7. Brown, R., & Berko, J. Word association and the acquisition of grammar. *Child Development,* 1960, **31,** 1–14.
8. Brown, R., & Fraser, C. The acquisition of syntax. In C. N. Cofer & B. S. Musgrave (Eds.), *Verbal behavior and learning: Problems and processes.* New York: McGraw-Hill, 1963. Pp. 158–197.
9. Bruner, J. S., & Olver, R. R. Development of equivalence transformations in children. *Monographs of the Society for Research in Child Development,* 1963, **28,** 125–141.
10. Chen, H. P., & Irwin, O. C. The type-token ratio applied to infant speech sounds. *Journal of Speech Disorders,* 1946, **11,** 126–130.
11. Chotlos, J. W. A statistical and comparative analysis of individual written language samples. Unpublished doctoral dissertation, State University of Iowa, 1942.
12. Cofer, C. N. Comments on the paper by Brown and Fraser. In C. N. Cofer & B. S. Musgrave (Eds.), *Verbal behavior and learning: Problems and processes.* New York: McGraw-Hill, 1963. Pp. 197–201.
13. Cole, L. *Psychology of adolescence.* (4th ed.) New York: Rinehart, 1954. Pp. 69–70.
14. Dienes, Z. P. *Mathematics in the primary school.* Rev. ed. Melbourne: Macmillan, 1966.
15. Edgerton, H. A., & Britt, S. H. Technical aspects of the fourth annual science talent search. *Educational and Psychological Measurement,* 1947, **7,** 3–21.
16. Flanagan, J. C. Functional education for the seventies. *Phi Delta Kappan,* 1967, **49,** 27–32.
17. Flanagan, J. C., & Cooley, W. W. *Project Talent. Identification, development, and utilization of human talents. Report of the eleventh grade follow-up study.* Pittsburgh: University of Pittsburgh, 1965. P. 3/2.

18. Flanagan, J. C., & Cooley, W. W. *Project Talent. One year follow-up studies.* Pittsburgh: University of Pittsburgh, 1966. Pp. 177, 183.
19. Flanagan, J. C., Davis, F. B., Dailey, J. T., Shaycoft, M. F., Orr, D. B., Goldberg, I., & Neyman, C. A., Jr. *Project Talent. The identification, development, and utilization of human talents.* Pittsburgh: University of Pittsburgh, 1964. Pp. 3/2–3/3.
19a. Flavell, J. Unpublished outline mentioned in Hooper (34, p. 426).
20. Gaier, E. L., & Collier, M. J. Latency stage story preferences of American and Finnish children. *Child Development,* 1960, **31,** 431–451.
21. Garber, L. O. Legal outlook: More 1968 clashes over student rights. *Nation's Schools,* 1968, **81,** 74, 78.
22. Gardner, R. A., & Gardner, B. T. Signs that Washoe uses. Mimeographed paper, University of Nevada, 1968.
23. Gardner, R. A., & Gardner, B. T. Teaching sign language to a chimpanzee. *Science,* 1969, **165,** 664–672.
24. Gardner, R. A., & Gardner, B. T. Personal communication, July 1969.
25. Gesell, A. *How a baby grows. A story in pictures.* New York: Harper, 1945. P. 37.
26. Gibson, E. J., & Walk, R. D. The effect of prolonged exposure to visually presented patterns on learning to discriminate them. *Journal of Comparative and Physiological Psychology,* 1956, **49,** 239–241.
27. Hafner, A. J. & Kaplan, A. M. Children's manifest anxiety and intelligence. *Child Development,* 1959, **30,** 269–271.
28. Harlow, H. F., Harlow, M. K., Dodsworth, R. O., & Arling, G. L. Maternal behavior of rhesus monkeys deprived of mothering and peer associations in infancy. *Proceedings of the American Philosophical Society,* 1966, **110,** 58–66.
29. Harlow, H. F., & Zimmerman, R. R. Affectional responses in the infant monkey. *Science,* 1959, **130,** 421–432.
30. Hattwick, L. A. Sex differences in behavior of nursery school children. *Child Development,* 1937, **8,** 343–355.
31. Hayes, C. *The ape in our house.* London: Victor Gollancz, 1952. P. 152c.
32. Hodges, W. L., & Spicker, H. H. The effects of preschool experiences on culturally deprived children. In W. W. Hartup & N. L. Smothergill (Eds.), *The young child: Reviews of research.* Washington, D. C.: National Association for the Education of Young Children, 1967. Pp. 262–289.
33. Holland, J. L., & Stalnaker, R. C. Descriptive study of talented high school seniors: National Merit Scholars. *National Association of Secondary School Principals Bulletin,* 1958, **42,** No. 236, 9–21.
34. Hooper, F. H. Piagetian research and education. In I. E. Sigel & F. H. Hooper (Eds.), *Logical thinking in children. Research based on Piaget's theory.* New York: Holt, Rinehart & Winston, 1968. Pp. 423–434.
35. Inhelder, B., & Piaget, J. *The growth of logical thinking from childhood to adolescence.* New York: Basic Books, 1958.
36. Jones, H. E. The vital capacity of children. *Archives of Diseases in Childhood,* 1955, **30,** 445–448.
37. Jones, M. C. A laboratory study of fear: The case of Peter. *Pedagogical Seminary,* 1924, **31,** 308–315.
38. Jones, M. C. A comparison of the attitudes and interests of ninth grade students over two decades. *Journal of Educational Psychology,* 1960, **51,** 175–186.
39. Kagan, J. Impulsive and reflective children: The significance of conceptual

tempo. In J. D. Krumboltz (Ed.), *Learning and the educational process.* Chicago: Rand McNally, 1965. Pp. 133–161.

40. Karplus, R., & Thier, H. D. *A new look at elementary school science. Science Curriculum Improvement Study.* Chicago: Rand McNally, 1967. P. 27.

40a. Kellogg, W. N. Communication and language in the home-raised chimpanzee. *Science,* 1968, **162**, 423–427.

41. Kohlberg, L. Early education: A cognitive-developmental view. *Child Development,* 1968, **39**, 1013–1062.

42. Kohlberg, L. Montessori with the culturally disadvantaged: A cognitive-developmental interpretation and some research findings. In R. D. Hess & R. M. Bear (Eds.), *Early education, current theory, research, and action.* Chicago: Aldine, 1968. Pp. 105–118.

43. Lamon, W. An experimental study of the levels of learning an abstract structure by elementary school children. Part one. Research design. *Journal of Structural Learning,* 1969, **4**, 27–51.

44. Lenneberg, E. H. Speech as a motor skill with special reference to nonaphasic disorders. *Monographs of the Society for Research in Child Development,* 1964, **92**, 115–127.

45. Los Angeles Times. Venice High youths, police clash. *Los Angeles Times,* March 13, 1968, p. 1 & p. 3.

46. Lott, A. J., & Lott, B. E. *Negro and white youth. A psychological study in a border-state community.* New York: Holt, Rinehart & Winston, 1963.

47. Lovell, K. Concepts in mathematics. In H. J. Klausmeier & C. W. Harris (Eds.), *Analyses of concept learning.* New York: Academic Press, 1966. Pp. 207–222.

48. Lynip, A. W. The use of magnetic devices in the collection and analysis of the preverbal utterances of an infant. *Genetic Psychology Monographs,* 1951, **44**, 221–262.

49. McCandless, B. R. *Children—behavior and development.* (2nd ed.) New York: Holt, Rinehart & Winston, 1967. Pp. 266–269.

50. Mehler, J., & Bever, T. G. Reply. *Science,* 1968, **162**, 979–981.

51. Mouly, G. J. *Psychology for effective teaching.* (2nd ed.) New York: Holt, Rinehart & Winston, 1968. Pp. 248–249, 478–479.

52. Norvell, G. W. *The reading interests of young people.* Boston: Heath, 1951. P. 53.

53. Osgood, C. E. *Method and theory in experimental psychology.* New York: Oxford University Press, 1953. P. 684.

54. Piaget, J. *The Language and thought of the child.* New York: Harcourt Brace, 1926.

55. Piaget, J. *Judgment and reasoning in the child.* Paterson, N. J.: Littlefield, Adams, 1959.

56. Piaget, J. *The child's conception of the world.* Paterson, N. J.: Littlefield, Adams, 1960.

57. Piaget, J. *The child's conception of physical causality.* Paterson, N. J.: Littlefield, Adams, 1960.

58. Piaget, J. Development and learning. In R. E. Ripple & V. N. Rockcastle (Eds.), *Piaget rediscovered. A report of the Conference on Cognitive Studies and Curriculum Development.* Ithaca, N. Y.: Cornell University, 1964. Pp. 7–20.

59. Piaget, J. Quantification, conservation, and nativism. *Science,* 1968, **162**, 976–979.

60. Piaget, J., & Inhelder, B. *The child's conception of space.* London: Routledge & Kegan, Paul, 1956.

61. Ruesch, J., & Kees, W. *Nonverbal communication. Notes on the visual percep-*

tion of human relations. Berkeley: University of California Press, 1961.

62. Scheinfeld, A. *Women and men.* New York: Harcourt Brace, 1944. Pp. 58–71.

63. Seashore, R. H., & Eckerson, L. D. The measurement of individual differences in general English vocabularies. *Journal of Educational Psychology,* 1940, **31,** 14–38.

64. Sigel, I. Concepts, structure, and learning. In I. Morrissett (Ed.), *Concepts and structure in the new social science curricula.* New York: Holt, Rinehart & Winston, 1967. Pp. 79–85.

65. Sigel, I. E., Roeper, A., & Hooper, F. H. A training procedure for acquisition of Piaget's conservation of quantity: A pilot study and its replication. *British Journal of Educational Psychology,* 1966, **36,** 301–311.

66. Smedslund, J. The acquisition of conservation of substance and weight in children. II. External reinforcement of conservation of weight and of the operations of addition and subtraction. *Scandinavian Journal of Psychology,* 1961, **2,** 71–84.

67. Smedslund, J. The acquisition of conservation of substance and weight in children. III. Extinction of conservation of weight acquired "normally" and by means of empirical controls on a balance. *Scandinavian Journal of Psychology,* 1961, **2,** 85–87.

68. Smith, M. E. An investigation of the development of the sentence and the extent of vocabulary in young children. *University of Iowa Studies in Child Welfare,* 1926, **3,** No. 5.

69. Smith, M. K. Measurement of the size of general English vocabulary through the elementary grades and high school. *Genetic Psychology Monographs,* 1941, **24,** 311–345.

70. Sonquist, H. D., & Kamii, C. K. Applying some Piagetian concepts in the classroom for the disadvantaged. *Young Children,* 1967, **22,** 231–246.

71. Sullivan, E. V. Piaget and the school curriculum. *Ontario Institute for Studies in Education Bulletin,* 1967, No. 2, 38 pp.

72. Templin, M. C. *Certain language skills in children.* Minneapolis: University of Minnesota Press, 1957. Pp. 108–114.

73. Terman, L. M., & Lima, M. *Children's reading.* New York: Appleton, 1926. P. 68.

74. Terman, L. M., & Tyler, L. Psychological sex differences. In L. Carmichael (Ed.), *Manual of child psychology.* (2nd ed.) New York: Wiley, 1954. Pp. 1064–1114.

75. Thorndike, R. L. *A comparative study of children's reading interests.* New York: Teachers College, Columbia University, Bureau of Publications, 1941.

76. Wallach, M. A. Research on children's thinking. In H. W. Stevenson (Ed.), *Child psychology. Sixty-second yearbook of the National Society for the Study of Education.* Part I. Chicago: University of Chicago Press, 1963. Pp. 236–276.

76a. Weikart, D. P. Preschool programs: Preliminary findings. *Journal of Special Education,* 1967, **1,** 163–181.

77. White, S. H. Evidence for a hierarchical arrangement of learning processes. *Advances in Child Development and Behavior,* 1965, **2,** 187–220.

78. Winitz, H. Language skills of male and female kindergarten children. *Journal of Speech and Hearing Research,* 1959, **2,** 377–386.

79. Winitz, H. Spectrographic investigation of infant vowels. *Journal of Genetic Psychology,* 1960, **96,** 171–181.

80. Wohlwill, J. F. A study of the development of the number concept by scalogram analysis. *Journal of Genetic Psychology,* 1960, **97,** 345–377.

11

MOTIVATION AND LEARNING THEORY

This chapter treats the needs of the body and their psychological effects. A *need* is a bodily state. The need for food is produced by passage of time without eating and leads in extreme cases to starvation. But this need has no direct psychological impact; it is just an imbalance on a chemical ledger sheet. Needs commonly lead to acts that are *motivated:* The hungry child looks in the refrigerator for food; the starving adult rummages through garbage pails; the food-deprived animal presses a lever and receives food as a reward. In every instance the need for food has motivated the response. *Motivation,* then, is an inferred state which energizes and directs the individual's activities.

If each need were motivating and if each motivation stemmed from a bodily need, the theory of motivation would be relatively simple. This is not the case, as can be seen from the following examples.

1. Man requires oxygen to live. Yet it is not oxygen deficiency that motivates him to seek oxygen. Rather his motivation is to breathe something that smells "neutral." In high altitudes an aviator may be unmotivated because what he breathes has no distinctive smell, but he may be in mortal danger because there is not enough oxygen in the air.

2. Chimpanzees seem motivated to manipulate mechanical objects even though this doesn't directly satisfy bodily needs. Welker (129) has shown that chimps do this manipulation most frequently after being deprived of it and gradually reduce their activity with continual opportunity. With further deprivation, the manipulating drive is reinstated.

(*Drive* is a tendency to perform a class of related acts such as manipulation, or eating, or drinking without special training. *The strength of a drive* depends on the degree of deprivation.) No bodily need is consistently diminished by manipulating these objects, so far as is known. It seems evident, then, that motivations include more than the effects of need. This is not to say that a manipulatory drive is not useful; it may sometimes help a chimpanzee to escape from his cage and thus, indirectly, to obtain food. But the indirectness of physiological significance makes it a *general drive* in Morgan and King's terminology (99), rather than a *physiological drive* like hunger.

What is a drive? Is it the motivated behavior itself? Or is it some characteristic of the body inferred to be present because of the motivated behavior? The latter is usually judged the better answer. One early attempt to pin this concept down was the *local theory of hunger and thirst*. According to Cannon (23) who postulated this theory, hunger consisted of the sensory impulses present during contraction of the empty stomach. This conclusion was largely supported by a study by Cannon and Washburn (24) in which they measured pressure changes within the stomach. The method of measurement is fascinating enough to be discussed in some detail.

Washburn first accustomed himself to the presence of a rubber tube in his esophagus. Almost every day for several weeks he inserted the tube through his mouth, down the esophagus, and into the stomach, keeping it there for 2 or 3 hours at a time. With a rubber balloon connected to the lower end of the tube before insertion, Washburn was able to use the balloon to measure stomach contractions. On test days he went to the laboratory in the early afternoon, having eaten little or nothing since the previous day, inserted the tube and balloon, and then had the balloon blown up moderately. A gauge connected to the tube indicated pressure changes in the balloon, which were automatically recorded on a graph, together with Washburn's notations of hunger pangs. Figure 11-1 shows that stomach contractions slightly preceded each report of hunger pangs, whereas the record of respiration was independent of contractions and hunger.

The stomach contractions Cannon and Washburn discovered were long considered the physical basis for hunger feelings in man. More recently, however, R. C. Davis, Garafolo, and Kveim (32) seem to have disproved the hypothesis that stomach contractions increase as the time since eating increases. They found more electrical voltage changes on the surface of the abdomen in recently fed persons than in persons who had fasted for 8 hours, indicating that the stomach contracts more after eating than before eating. Why, then, did Cannon and Washburn observe stomach

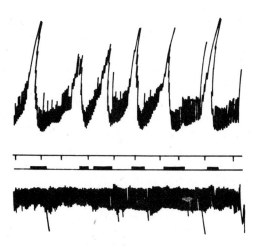

Fig. 11-1. One-half the original size. The top record represents infragastric pressure (the small oscillations are due to respiration, the large to contractions of the stomach); the second record is time in minutes (ten minutes); the third record is the subject's report of hunger pangs; the lowest record is respiration. From Cannon and Washburn (24).

contractions following food deprivation? Davis and his associates answered this question by comparing electrical measurements on the abdomen before and during the time an inflated ballon was in the stomach. Electrical activity (average size of voltage change) increased greatly when the balloon was in the stomach. Since electrical activity closely parallels pressure changes in the balloon (and therefore in the stomach wall), it seems that the balloon, not hunger, produces stomach contractions. Furthermore, in nine persons out of ten studied, Davis *et al.* generally found little correspondence between reported stomach pangs and electrical activity or pressure changes in the balloon. This point seems a contradiction rather than a reinterpretation of previous findings.

Obviously, there are reasons to doubt the local theories regarding hunger. Yet it is important to know where a drive originates because psychologists believe that physiological events evoke drive. A helpful clue to the nature of hunger comes from studies showing that food taken into the stomach by mouth reduces hunger (measured by future eating) more than does food placed directly in the stomach (12). This suggests that stimulation in the mouth and pharynx during eating partially reduces hunger and activates a "shut-off" mechanism in the brain. No one knows what this mechanism really is, but its effects can be observed. Grossman (49) points to gastrointestinal stimulation and possible stimulation from nutrients in the blood and tissues as activators of "shut-off" mechanisms. Similarly, the theory that thirst is local, which presumes that thirst is a direct consequence of dryness in the throat and mouth, requires revision. The evidence is that thirst can be reduced by placing water directly into the stomach (3) even though the procedure does not directly reduce dryness in the throat and mouth.

Although the physiological manifestations of a drive may pose an important question, the psychologist must ask other questions as well. What is the general effect of motivation on behavior? If the tendency to make a response is increased whenever that response is followed by a reduction in drive level, drive reduction theory (see Chapter 5) indicates that one of the best established responses of all should be eating. It is. It might also be expected that if the food taken did not reach the stomach, eating would stop. Hull and co-workers (65) found this to be true. An operated dog, with his esophagus so divided that food eaten would not go to the stomach, nonetheless ate 5000 cubic centimeters of gruel in a test period. Kept alive by later insertion of gruel in the part of the esophagus leading to the stomach, after eight test periods the dog learned not to eat at all with the mouth since the food eaten was not reaching the stomach.

This also suggests a more obvious result: The amount eaten should be less for briefly deprived organisms than for highly deprived ones. Figure 11-2 shows how the amount of food eaten by white rats increases with increased time since the last feeding.

As food deprivation increases from 0 to 0.5, 1, 2, 6, 12, and 23.5 hours,

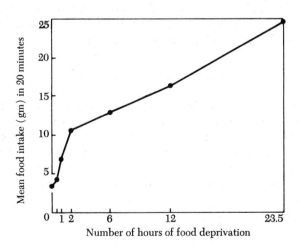

Fig. 11-2. Food eaten by female albino rats as a function of the amount of time since the last feeding. [Figure 4 from Horenstein (63). Copyright 1951 by American Psychological Association, and reproduced by permission.]

the average food intake (in mixture with water) increases from 4 to 24 grams. The upward trend of food intake with increased deprivation conforms to expectations; the exact shape of the curve would probably be different for another species or under radically different test procedures.

Just as the tendency to eat increases with deprivation, so does the tendency to select certain foods. Servicemen deprived of fresh milk during their military careers develop strong cravings for it. On the other hand, a person given angel food cake for dessert every day eventually stops accepting it. P. T. Young (132) used this principle to change rats' relative liking of two foods, cane sugar and wheat, by prefeeding the animals on the better liked one, cane sugar, before offering them a choice. The rats developed a consistent preference for wheat, even without reaching satiety on the sugar.

Sometimes the reason for changing food preferences is that a physiological need for a specific food exists. Sometimes, however, a specific food need does exist, but no preference for substances containing that food is shown (51). In other situations no specific need seems to exist; to refuse an excess of angel food cake is, perhaps, to admit boredom.

Psychologists often think that motivation arises primarily from deprivation states. In many food selection situations, this is true. However, food preferences also come from eating. Twenty-four hours of food deprivation may make both an Arab and an American hungry, but only the Arab is likely to accept sheep eyes as a means of reducing that hunger. Obviously, personal experience with foods accounts for the differences in eating patterns of various national groups. Far too little research has been done on the ways these patterns develop.

Hunger Affects Effortful Behavior in the Rat

Performance in a specific task should also depend on the length of the deprivation period. Figure 11-3 is an example of this. It shows that the time required for a rat to run through an eight-foot-long straight alley (or box, also called a runway) is greatest under 0 hours of food deprivation; the time gradually becomes shorter as deprivation is increased to as much as 22 hours. Figure 11-3 also shows that this effect is much reduced if data are not included for trials on which the animal let other activities compete with running (e.g., scratching himself or turning back in the wrong direction). Cicala (28) and R. A. King (70) each found similar results but with less reduction of the basic motivational effect due to competing activities. Champion (25) has shown that extra training of the competing responses can reduce or even reverse the relation of competing responses to motivated behavior.

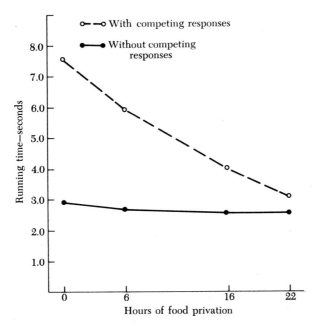

Fig. 11-3. Time required for running through a straight alley as a function of the amount of time since the last feeding and depending on competing responses such as scratching one's self. Figure 2 from Cotton (31).

The animals whose behavior is reported in Fig. 11-3 had been very highly trained in the running task before the test data were gathered. Thus it appears that the performance of well-trained animals depends quite noticeably on the level of deprivation during testing. Does performance during original training also depend on deprivation level? Zaretsky (134), like many other investigators, has shown that it does: Running times for animals trained under a 22-hour food deprivation are consistently less during training than those for animals trained under 1½-hour deprivation.

It is less obvious from the drive–reduction theory of learning whether drive effects from training should be permanent. Estes (39) concludes that the effect of deprivation during training is relatively temporary—in test periods designed to equalize deprivation during testing and still give no advantage to any group because of abrupt shifts between training and testing conditions, little or no residual effect of the training deprivation level remains.

Deprivation has thus been shown to affect running behavior at the time the deprivation is operative, with some possibility of a residual effect afterward. Similar results have been obtained with other responses, such as pressing a lever to obtain food or water. In general, psychologists have come to expect these effects with vigor responses, responses requiring energy output but not necessarily requiring a difficult selection from among alternative responses.

The weak theory of drive reduction in learning implies that an act followed by drive reduction will be strengthened. Does this imply there are more correct performances of a discrimination task when deprivation is high than when it is low? Theorists usually say, "No." Under conditions of high deprivation the organism is no more likely to select a correct response than under low deprivation and will learn it no more definitely either. Put in everyday terms, the theorists' prediction is that a small boy sent to the grocery store by his mother will go faster when hungry but choose his direction no more accurately than when not hungry.

Evidence on this question has been summarized by Brown (16), who says, ". . . the weight of evidence points to the conclusion that selection of the correct side [in a two-choice situation] is unrelated to time of food deprivation." (The bracketed phrase was inserted by the present authors.) Brown's conclusion presumes the following situation:

If two groups of animals, one trained under high deprivation (22 hours) and one under low deprivation (0 hours), have been forced to make 50% of their choices to the correct side and 50% to the incorrect side, the two groups will exhibit equal discrimination between sides even though different drive levels were present during training. This equality can be demonstrated in test procedures in which neither choice is rewarded. The probability of making a formerly rewarded response will be the same for each group, and it will take approximately the same average number of trials for members of each group to extinguish its tendency for one response over the other. Teel (126) has done such a study, and Brown relies upon Teel's work, among others, to prove his point.

Does the evidence from Teel's findings mean that students need not be motivated in order to learn? To some extent this is true; learning can occur with low motivation or perhaps even none at all, if the correct response is somehow made to occur. The import of motivational research on choice behavior is to show that high motivation will cause students to be more active [verified for rats, at least (16)] and that appropriate reward will then evoke the correct responses to be repeated. Indirectly, then, high motivation facilitates learning.

Though increased drive does not directly improve learning, teachers should note Clayton's (29) and Logan and Wagner's conclusion (80) that large differences in reward for correct and incorrect choices do facilitate learning. Taken together, the effects of drive and reward tell us that teachers can facilitate learning by increasing their students' drive and rewarding them for learning. A direct application of these findings from animals might be considered coercive when used with children: The teacher withholds food or some other desired commodity, such as praise, until the drive for that commodity is quite high. Thereupon the child is given the opportunity to learn and to be rewarded more highly for correct responses than for incorrect ones. This model of school motivation is most evident when course credit is withheld until term papers or other assignments have been completed. So long as teachers have the power to use grades and course credit as a motivational device, school work will be elicited in this way. (Chapter 12 discusses this and other methods of motivating students.)

Reading about the effects of food deprivation on performance in the laboratory may make one wonder whether children study harder just before lunch, when food drive is high, or after lunch, when it is low. If food were being given only as a reward to those who accomplish a certain task in their studies, then studying should indeed increase just before lunch. However, food drive and reward are not usually employed in school. Therefore, any effect of lunchtime would be indirect. Hull's theory (64) implies that the hunger drive just before lunch (an *irrelevant drive* since food is not the reward) would add to any other drive being rewarded by study, with the result that students would work somewhat harder immediately before lunch than they would immediately afterward. In discussing the topic of fear later in this chapter, it will be seen that different drive effects can be added together.

Thirst Drive

Deprivation of water has effects much like those associated with deprivation of food, with regard both to intake after deprivation and acquisition and maintenance of responses leading to the desired reward (33, 119).

Sexual Drive—Its Biological Aspects

Sexual motivation, too, is related to the period of deprivation. Schwarz (112) has shown how in the male rat the number of copulations increases with the increase of deprivation of access to a sexual partner since previous complete sexual exhaustion. Sexual activity, however, obviously depends more on hormonal processes and learning than do hunger and thirst effects. These distinctions are made not to minimize the physiological effects of hunger and thirst but to point up the particular characteristics of sexual behavior.

As is well known, though Kinsey, Pomeroy, and Martin (71) found great evidence of sexual play in preadolescent humans, even in the very young, the complete sexual act is delayed until adolescence, in both humans and other animals. In the 105-day-old male rat, for example, Larsson (76) showed that intromission (insertion of the penis into the vagina) occurred repeatedly when a sexual partner was first made available but ejaculation failed to occur for 2 out of 22 males. By the end of two additional tests, spaced 10 days apart, all males ejaculated. All animals tested for the first time at 138 days performed the full sexual response in that session. The delay in sexual activity until puberty depends on the maturation of the sexual organs and the resultant secretion of estrogen and progesterone in the female and testosterone in the male.

In some vertebrates a second physiological factor is that female sexual receptivity depends on reproductive cycles or periods between ovulations. In the female guinea pig, for example, the average period from one ovulation to the next is a little more than 16 days (133). During that 16-day period there is only an 8-hour interval in which the animal is in sexual heat or *estrus*. This period of sexual receptivity, the only time the female will permit the male to copulate with her, has a definite relation to the period of ovulation or ovule production: Ovulation occurs within an hour and a half after estrus ends.

As Fig. 11-4 shows, estrus is also dependent on the time of day. Relatively few female guinea pigs are sexually receptive except in the night hours.

Returning to an earlier topic, it should be noted that although deprivation can increase sexual activity, sexual activity can also increase sexual activity. [Some of the evidence for this statement is questionable. For example, Kinsey *et al.* (71) report that couples who have engaged in intercourse before marriage are more likely to be successful in bringing the wife to orgasm in early married life than those who have not. This effect is almost surely a reflection of differences between the two groups of people as well as of their different premarital sexual experience: In experimentally controlled situations, where comparable groups of sexually naive male animals are allowed different amounts of sexual experience before testing, it has been shown that initially unresponsive animals increase their speed and frequency of copulation with experience but that experience has no effect upon initially responsive animals (103).] Masters and Johnson (87), in experiments with humans, found that repeated sexual activity in the laboratory situation results in greater responsiveness by men and women who previously had some difficulty in reaching orgasms.

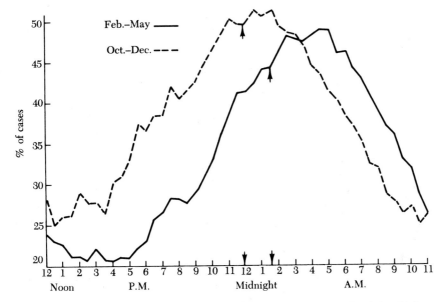

Fig. 11-4. Percentage of female guinea pigs found in heat at each of the 24 hours of the day during any one reproductive cycle. Figure 1 from W. C. Young *et al.* (133).

Michael (95) provides evidence that the sexual receptivity induced by estrogen is mediated by brain activity. He found that implanting solid estrogen in the hypothalamus (see Chapter 7), and nowhere else, of ovariectomized cats led to sexual receptivity for 50 to 60 days. Use of a certain chemical to trace the implanted estrogen as it moved from the place of injection showed that certain neural cells of the hypothalamus had a particular affinity for the estrogen, suggesting that those cells are part of the neural system controlling sexual expression.

Sexual deprivation, direct sexual experience, hormonal activity, and brain stimulation modify or affect sexual activity to some degree in some species. Harlow (55) has termed the tendency of young male monkeys to chase and threaten young female monkeys, even before puberty, a mechanism for ensuring continuing the species:

> Analysis of this behavior shows that males threaten other males and females but that females are innately blessed with better manners; in particular, little girl monkeys do not threaten little boy monkeys. . . . I am convinced that these data have almost total generality to man. Several months ago I was present at a school picnic attended by 25 second graders and their parents. While the parents sat and the girls stood around or skipped about hand in hand, 13 boys tackled and wrestled, chased and retreated. No little

girl chased any little boy, but some little boys chased some little girls. Human beings have been here for two million years, and they'll probably be here two million more.*

Harlow believes that part of this chasing behavior is learned, for his unmothered male monkeys described in Chapter 10 didn't chase the females. Nonetheless, in both humans and animals, particular stimuli also attract males to females. A long list of stimuli would include body shape, plumage, coquetry, odors. Most men find perfume attractive, but so also do animals as low as the cockroach. The female American cockroach emits a specific odorous substance that normally attracts males to her. Roth and Willis (107) have found that male cockroaches presented with the attractant substance alone will move their antennae, search for the source of the odor, flutter their wings, and usually exhibit protrusion of the abdomen, all as if the female cockroach were present and emitting the attractant. [Work at the Quartermaster Research and Engineering Center in Natick, Massachusetts (130) has led to the chemical isolation of the attractant substance and may soon lead to its synthetic production.]

Human Sexual Drive

In the section above, the sexual behavior of humans and of lower animals was described together to emphasize the biological basis of sexual activity. In human sexual behavior social factors are also important. Ehrmann (38) lists the three major influences on heterosexual behavior in our society; one factor (married or not married) is social, the other two (male versus female and the aging process) are biological. Although there are wide variations in the types of acceptable sexual activities permitted in various cultures before and after marriage (41), and the incidence of premarital coitus among Americans is substantial, particularly for men (105), it is marriage that gives full social sanction for a couple to engage in sexual intercourse. This sanction is highly correlated with the occurrence of intercourse.

Ehrmann (38) points out that men not only engage in more premarital intercourse, petting, and other premarital sexual activity than do women, but that they also tend to de-emphasize the role of affection in sexual expression. A man may or may not be in love with the woman with whom he is sexually involved; a woman is much less likely to be sexually involved if she is not also in love with the man—or at least fond of him. While both men and women are affected by parental and societal admonitions to inhibit sexual activity outside of marriage, women seem to accept such restraints more than men do. However, the double

* Copyright 1962 by American Psychological Association, and reproduced by permission.

standard in the United States has weakened during the twentieth century; the overall increase in premarital sex experience has been most marked for women (38). Reiss (105) believes that Americans will continue to modify the double standard of sexual behavior and will make affection the basis for decision about physical intimacy before marriage. Reiss believes that the trend of "permissiveness with affection," a policy of accepting coitus as right for both men and women when accompanied by affection, will eventually become dominant. This trend represents a move away from what he calls body-centered to person-centered sexual activity, with the emphasis on the person with whom one shares sexual activity rather than on the sensory experience itself.

Two other social factors deserve special emphasis. Kinsey, Pomeroy, Martin, and Gebhard (72) call attention to the close relationship between religious practice and sexual activity. In the three major faiths, the most devout (i.e., most regular in attending church services or other religious observances) are less sexually active before marriage. Education, too, influences sexual activity. Ehrmann (38) has summarized research by the Kinsey group and other investigators on the effect of educational level. College-educated males are less likely than noncollege males to have had intercourse before marriage. At any given age, however, unmarried college women are as likely to have had intercourse as are unmarried noncollege women. Because they marry later, college women have an overall higher probability of coitus before marriage. College level males and females have more similar sexual experience than do noncollege males and females. It should also be emphasized that intercourse is relatively less frequent among college students compared with noncollege students of the same age, whereas masturbation, petting to climax (for women), and nocturnal emission (for men) are relatively more frequent.

Much of the material just discussed focuses on factual information rather than on appropriate behavior. *Sex and the College Student* (50), written for administrators dealing with college students, may also be of interest to the students since it attempts to look at these questions from the standpoint of mature persons examining the college scene.

Activity Drive

Hill (59) has shown that increased periods of confinement without opportunity to move around led to increased amounts of running in an activity wheel like that shown in Fig. 11-5. Research by Kagan and Berkun (67) indicates that longer periods of confinement also led to faster lever pressing rates where each lever press releases an activity wheel for a minute of running. In general, then, activity deprivation has similar consquences to that of food deprivation.

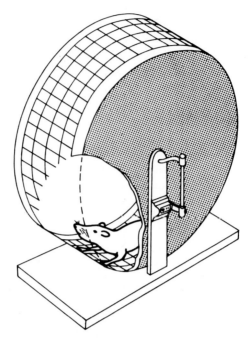

Fig. 11-5. Revolving activity wheel and automatic counter. The rat exercises by running inside the wheel, thus making the wheel turn. Figure 1 from Harlow (53).

Curiosity Drive

Recent studies (56, 57) have shown that the amount of interest a person has in what he is viewing may be indicated by the change in size of his pupils. When brightness of illumination is held constant, women's eyes dilate more than men's do when shown pictures of babies; men's dilate more than women's when shown pictures of pin-up girls. In the two photographs shown in Fig. 11-6 below, the girl on the left looks more interested than the girl on the right; at least, her pupils are more dilated. Hess found that when he showed each of these photographs to men, the men reacted with twice as large a pupillary dilation to the left picture as to the right one, even though most of them couldn't tell the experimenter in what way the two photographs differed. Apparently a young lady who looks interested in what is going on is also more interesting.

Experiments by Butler (18, 19), and Butler and Harlow (20) demonstrate that a rhesus monkey will learn and repeatedly execute a response to a certain color even if the only reinforcement is the opportunity to look outside of his confining cell for a few seconds. Figure 11-7 shows two views of the cell, one with a monkey looking out a cage aperture after pushing against the correctly colored door rather than the other door available to him. Figure 11-8, presenting the number of responses per hour as a function of previous hours in the cage without visual exploration, shows results much like the effects of food deprivation on running behavior. Apparently, visual stimulation has the same general effect as does stimulation associated with physiological drives such as hunger.

Whereas Butler emphasizes that deprivation of visual stimuli increases curiosity drive, other investigators have shown the corollary that repetition of visual stimuli satiates the organism, just as eating too much of any food satiates the hungry human. Some curiosity may remain for other stimuli just as hunger for other foods may continue.

The early evidence for *stimulus satiation,* as it is now called, was thought to indicate quite a different phenomenon. Zeaman and House (135) found, for example, that rats which were forced to turn to the right in a T-shaped maze, when they reached the junction between the two straight parts of the T, tended to go to the left if given freedom to choose their direction on the next trial. This tendency, called an *alternation tendency,* increased when the number of forced trials to the right increased. This fact is all the more surprising because the rats were always fed at the end of the maze to which they were forced to go.

Fig. 11-6. Identical pictures of the same young lady, except that the left one has been retouched to enlarge the pupils of her eyes. See text for discussion. From Hess (56). Photograph property of Camera Clix, Inc.

Zeaman and House attributed the alternation tendency to *reactive inhibition,* a concept previously suggested by Hull (64). Reactive inhibition is a fatigue-like state which is assumed to build up with repeated acts requiring muscular effort. In the T-maze situation it would be assumed to be specific to each direction of turning: The rat which has been forced to turn right several times would have considerable reactive inhibition for right turns but little or none for left turns, because he had not been turning left recently. Therefore, on a free choice, he would turn left according to Zeaman and House.

Though Zeaman and House's results are consistent with the reactive inhibition explanation, they could equally well be used to support *stimulus satiation* theory: If rats are forced to turn right several times, the stimuli on the right lose their power to satisfy the curiosity drive.

Fig. 11-7. Visual exploration apparatus (two views). [Figure 2 from Butler and Harlow (20). Copyright 1954 by the American Psychological Association, and reproduced by permission.]

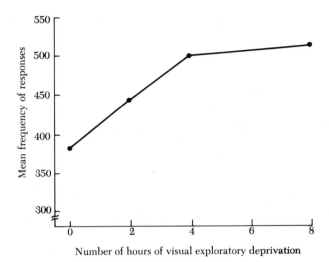

Fig. 11-8. Mean frequency of responses as a function of duration of deprivation. [Figure 1 from Butler (19). Copyright 1957 by the American Psychological Association, and reproduced by permission.]

Therefore, the rats turn left and get slightly different stimuli when given a free choice.

A critical test between these two theories would be one in which stimulus satiation would lead the animal to turn right, whereas reactive inhibition would lead him to turn left. Glanzer (45) performed a convincing experiment of this kind using the cross-shaped maze shown in Fig. 11-9. Sometimes the rats were placed in the chamber marked S and the door marked n was kept closed. Then a left choice took an animal to a black box marked B. A right choice took him to a white box marked W. Sometimes the rats were placed in the chamber marked N and the door marked s was kept closed. Then, of course, a left choice took an animal to the white box and a right choice took him to the black box. Glanzer found that on the days in which the first trial began at S and the second trial began at N, 83% of the rats chose black one time and white the other. This suggests that stimulus satiation was occurring. Note that this result implies that these 83% turned right on both trials or turned left on both trials. Therefore, it contradicts the theory that reactive inhibition associated with certain muscle acts involved in turning to the right produces alternation tendencies.

Stimulus satiation, when conceived as the opposite of curiosity drive, seems an acceptable explanation of alternation behavior. A complete treatment of this topic would require many pages; the remarks above tend to oversimplify the situation (35, 46). Though human tendencies

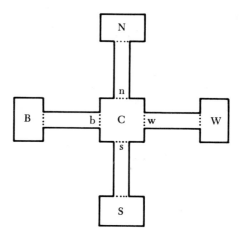

Fig. 11-9. Cross-shaped maze used in evaluating stimulus satiation theory versus reactive inhibition theory. Broken lines indicate doors. [A slightly modified Fig. 1 from Glanzer (45). Copyright 1953 by American Psychological Association, and reproduced by permission.]

to alternate choices in maze situations have also been studied, the more interesting aspects of their search for novelty are related to real life situations. Acker and McReynolds (1) compared four personality tests that measure originality, seeking change, etc., with items such as, "Every time I go out to eat, I like to go to a different restaurant," or "Because I become bored easily, I need plenty of excitement, stimulation, and fun." Affirmative responses to the items just mentioned would indicate a drive for novelty or a curiosity drive. Acker and McReynolds found that persons who had high scores on one test tended to have high scores on the other three. There was very little predictability from scores on these tests to performance in a maze or on a test of ability to be original in interpreting designs.

Other Drives

In addition to those drives already mentioned, several other states born of deprivation may be called drives. They include drives for air, for optimal temperature surrounding the organism, and probably for association with other members of the same species. Gewirtz and Baer (44) even found that 20 minutes of social isolation could increase the reinforcing value of praise from an adult to a child; nursery school children could be taught a correct choice more quickly if approval followed the choice and if the child had been previously isolated. Psychologists call something a drive if, and only if, increased deprivation of the defining substance or activity leads to increased intake of the substance or increased performance of the activity for some range of deprivation values. This definition does not imply that a drive corresponds to something necessary for survival—it may or may not be necessary, depending on the drive. As B. F. Skinner has informally remarked, any activity sought by an organism may be called a drive: If keeping paper away from an infant leads to an increase in paper crinkling when paper is made available to him, it is acceptable to refer to a paper-crinkling drive even though its usefulness to the infant is not obvious. The criterion for the existence of a drive, then, is that increased deprivation leads to increased performance of the activity in question.

From this reasoning, many of the most involved human activities could be interpreted as drives of some kind. This is not to say that an endless list of drives should be made. Usually, different hunger drives need not be distinguished, but occasionally it will be important to speak of a salt drive because salt alone has been withheld. Correspondingly, though Montgomery (98) found that rats placed in a maze shaped like a Y learned to choose that area of the Y which provided room to move in and several blocks to walk between, it is not necessarily appropriate to conclude that the rats had an exploratory drive. Even if it should be shown that depriving rats of the opportunity of such exploration increased the future likelihood of that choice in the Y maze, it might be preferable to say that a combination of activity and visual curiosity drives accounted for Montgomery's findings. Similar interpretations may often be necessary in order to simplify theories of motivational behavior.

Pathological Changes in Food or Water Intake

Disease or surgical removal of certain parts of the body may markedly modify the intake of certain substances. Nonfunction of the adrenal glands for either of these reasons produces a marked increase in salt intake—so that an organism is said to have an increased salt drive. Similarly, destruction of a certain part of the hypothalamus of a rat's brain has been found to cause unusually large amounts of food intake (58), making it seem that the hunger drive has been increased. Miller, Bailey, and Stevenson (97) have found, however, that large intakes are not necessarily accompanied by other usual consequences of deprivation. Figure 11-10 shows that operated animals ate more than control animals did unless quinine was placed in their food. With quinine they ate less. Correspondingly, the operated animals less often pressed a lever for food, ran more slowly, and pulled less hard when restrained from approaching food. Apparently this surgery modified food intake without increasing "willingness" to expend effort or accept unpleasant

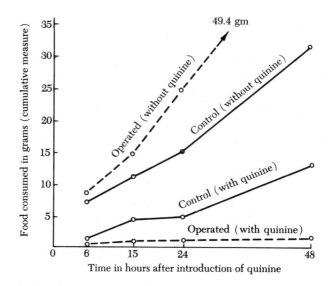

Fig. 11-10. Effect of a bitter taste on food consumption of rats with a certain part of the hypothalamus destroyed. Figure 3 from Miller *et al.* (97).

tastes to obtain food. Since this operation does not yield conventional hunger or thirst effects, it is appropriate not to speak of increased hunger or thirst but only of increased intake as a result of the operation.

Pain Stimulus Removal Drives

There are many drives that involve obtaining specific objects or activities, such as food or visual exploration. But some drives are drives away from certain stimuli. A drive for pain removal is one: When painful stimuli impinge on the person from the outside, he moves away from them. If painful stimuli arise inside himself, he takes medication to remove the pain stimulus.

Intensity of pain removal drives may be defined as equal to the intensity of the pain stimulus, all other factors being equal. Just as increased intensity of the hunger drive generally produces increased vigor of response, so does increased intensity of electric shock or some other painful stimulus. Figure 11-11 illustrates this point by showing the differences in running speed between groups of animals receiving 200, 300, and 400 volts, respectively, throughout their runs through an electrified straight alley to a "safe" goal box.

The reinforcement of response in painful situations is, of course, the removal of the pain stimuli. One rarely speaks of magnitude of reinforcement in these cases because customarily it equals the amount of shock, making drive level and magnitude of reinforcement equal. However, Campbell and Kraeling (22) have found that animals running to escape from high shock intensities to lower ones will run fastest for the greatest reductions (magnitudes of reinforcement). Consequently, it appears that magnitude of reinforcement effects with pain removal are comparable to those with hunger.

It should be emphasized that, though pain removal effects depend largely upon the amount of stimulation producing the pain, situational factors may control the response to pain. Melzack (94) has concluded that the degree of pain subjectively experienced depends on the "meaning" a person attaches to the situation. He quotes a World War II anesthesiologist who found that only one out of three wounded soldiers appeared to be suffering from enough pain to request morphine whereas 80% of civilian surgery patients with similar tissue injury asked for

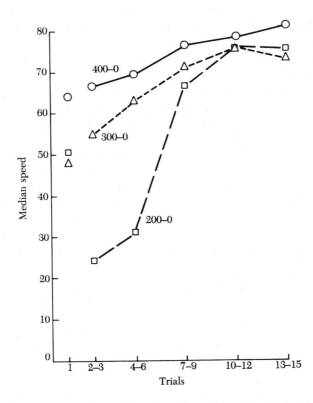

Fig. 11-11. Running speeds as they depend on intensity of electric shock and amount of practice. A number such as 400–0 gives the voltage from which the subjects were running and the zero voltage to which they were running. [Figure 3 from Campbell and Kraeling (22). Copyright 1953 by American Psychological Association, and reproduced by permission.]

morphine to kill the pain. The surgeon interpreted this difference as due to the soldiers' viewing their wounds as favorable—an escape from even more serious calamity—and the civilians' viewing surgery as unfavorable—involving unexpected bodily malfunction and portending possible death.

Frustration Drive

In Chapter 5 frustration drive was used to explain partial reinforcement effects. We must now look at frustration in the context of motivation in general.

A dictionary definition of *frustrate* is "to keep (someone) from doing or achieving something; baffle the efforts or hopes of" (42). Psychologists may frustrate humans by preventing them from completing a puzzle, or rats by preventing them from completing a run through a straight alley. Frustration may also be accomplished by removing the customary food reward from an apparatus.

To frustrate, then, is to do something to an organism which prevents certain customary responses. In so far as frustration has other effects than that of prevention, they may possibly be *states* of the organism like hunger drive. These states are *frustration drive states.* Reduction of such a frustration drive may be considered a reinforcement analogous to removal of electrical shock.

What is the evidence that frustration produces a state called frustration drive? Marzocco (84) has shown that extinction of a lever pressing response not only leads to a reduced response rate but also has an effect possibly attributable to frustration drive. As Fig. 11-12 shows, the amount of force applied to the lever increased substantially (frustration effect) on Trial 5, the first trial after reward was omitted. Continued nonreinforcement led to less force per trial, suggesting that frustration drive declines as extinction continues.

Marzocco takes pains to point out that the increased force of response may result from some mechanism other than frustration drive. For example, it could be that the animals learned much earlier in life, or even in the beginning of the lever pressing experiment, that making a forceful response may lead to reinforcement after a weaker one fails. (You, yourselves, have learned that, if no one answers the door after your first ring, a more pronounced depression of the doorbell button may be effective.) In some other frustration drive studies this objection is less convincing, however. Haner and Brown (52) showed with children that a response quite unlike the rewarded one also increased in magnitude after frustration by interruption of the task. Furthermore, this frustration effect was

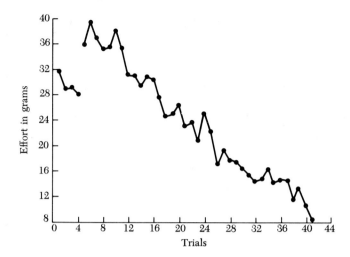

Fig. 11-12. Frustration drive indicated by increased effort expended in lever pressing due to nonreinforcement beginning on Trial 4. Effort expended finally drops below original level because extinction eventually eliminates all lever pressing. Figure 1 from Marzocco (84).

greatest when the interruption came just before the task would have been completed. Lambert and Solomon (75) have shown that the greatest frustration effect with rats also comes when blocking occurs just before the goal.

We have seen from Marzocco's experiment that the frustration effect eventually disappears with continued nonreinforcement. Using a two-stage straight alley or runway with a chamber following the first and second halves, Holder, Marx, Holder, and Collier (62) have shown that if the rats are delayed in the chamber following the first half, they will run faster in the second half than will undelayed rats. (Food reward was given in the chamber following the second half to all animals.) The delay may be considered a frustration whose effect was to produce partial extinction in the first half of the runway; this also occurs in Skinner boxes with nonreward. Thus frustration weakens those responses it follows; however, the fact that the rats run faster in the second half of the runway indicates that frustration induces a frustration drive which strengthens responses following its introduction. Amsel (5, 6) has reported on several experiments by himself and his associates which delineate these two types of effects. More recently, Peckman and Amsel (102) have shown that frustration drive is higher in a shift from continuous to partial reinforcement if the reinforcement magnitude is high than if it is low.

If frustrative events do produce a drive, it should be possible to use escape from frustration stimuli as a reinforcement in the same way that escape from pain can be used. Adelman and Maatsch (2) have done this. Ten animals were trained to run through a straight alley for food found in a goal box. Then extinction was begun, a frustrating procedure, and after each run the animals were allowed to escape the frustrative stimuli in the goal box by jumping or climbing onto a ledge on top of it. The frustrated animals learned to make the jumping response faster than did two control groups of animals, one of which was given food reward for jumping onto the ledge. A final test of the three groups showed even more striking effects of frustration. A day later, each animal was placed in the goal box, and was returned there shortly after each jump-out. The control groups stopped jumping onto the ledge (extinguished), but the frustrated group showed no decline in that response after 100 returns to the goal box. The frustration seems strong and permanent in this study, with effects that persisted for at least a 24-hour period.

_____ **Secondary Drives**

In contrast to the drives heretofore considered, which are primary or largely unlearned, the secondary drives require learning, or experience, before they can be manifested.

Conditioned Fear Drive

Miller (96) studied the conditioned fear drive in this way: He placed a rat in the white half of a black and white box (depicted in Fig. 11-13) with a separating wall and door. The animal was shocked continuously until it ran through the open door to the black section. After ten escapes of this kind, the animal was tested without shock. It ran from white to black, nonetheless. After five such trials, the door was closed and testing continued. The animal now could not go to the black box without turning a wheel to open the door. This he did, and escaped as before. Because the animal, and others like it, learned to turn the wheel, it is thought that an acquired and thus a secondary drive was the motivation for learning in the absence of the primary drive of shock. This secondary drive is called *conditioned fear* for obvious reasons.

Perhaps fear in everyday life is also a secondary drive. But two things with the same name may be very different. The person who appears fearful, jumpy, and anxious in some situations may be responding to stimuli previously conditioned as fear stimuli. On the other hand, there

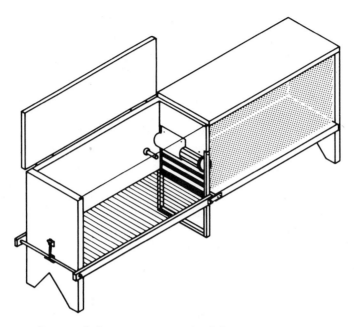

Fig. 11-13. "Acquired drive apparatus. The left compartment is painted white, the right one black. A shock may be administered through the grid which is the floor of the white compartment. When the animal is placed on the grid which is pivoted at the inside end, it moves down slightly making a contact that starts an electric timer. When the animal performs the correct response, turning the wheel or pressing the bar as the case may be, he stops the clock and actuates a [device] which allows the door, painted with horizontal black and white stripes, to drop. The [experimenter] can also cause the door to drop by pressing a button. The dimensions of each compartment are $18 \times 6 \times 8\frac{1}{2}$ in." [Figure 1 from Miller (96). Copyright 1948 by American Psychological Association, and reproduced by permission.]

may be no fear stimuli, and the person's fear may be internally generated.

It is possible to educate an organism to work as if motivated by a formerly neutral stimulus. It is generally believed that people are motivated by money, grades in school, fear of future catastrophes, and patriotism. Are these, indeed, drives in a psychological sense, drives that have been learned and are thus secondary rather than primary? It is relatively easy to show that these supposed motivations are indeed learned; it is more difficult to prove that they are drives.

Fear is demonstrably a primary drive—unlearned—but it may also be learned or conditioned. There is research evidence (17) that dogs conditioned to jump over a barrier to avoid shock are being reinforced by escape from the conditioned stimulus (darkness) preceding the shock. In view of the study by Miller, this conditioned stimulus may be called a *fear-inducing stimulus.* An *avoidance response,* then, is reinforced by removal of the fear-inducing stimulus and correspondingly of fear itself. What controls the amount of fear induced by such a stimulus?

An experiment by Kalish (68) showed that hurdle jumping by rats to avoid a conditioned stimulus was better learned if preceded by several fear acquisition trials rather than by a few. It appears that fear drive increases with the number of pairings of a conditioned stimulus and a painful stimulus, such as the electric shock used in fear acquisition trials in this experiment.

Conditioned fear is also increased by the increased intensity or duration of the painful stimulus during the fear-conditioning period. Overmier (101) found that dogs jumped over a hurdle faster to the sound of a tone that had previously been the conditioned stimulus (CS) in classical conditioning using a 50-second shock as the unconditioned stimulus (UCS). Slower jumps were made to a tone which had been a CS paired with a shock lasting only ½ second as the UCS.

Is the Fear Drive Irreversible? Many examples of fear as a secondary drive explore that question—one in a study in which the response of jumping over a barrier to avoid shock failed to extinguish or extinguished only after unusual measures were taken (113). The darkness which signals the beginning of a new avoidance trial has been paired with shock and therefore arouses fear (now we would say conditioned fear) which is removed by jumping. The jumping is reinforced (rewarded) by the removal of the darkness and the associated conditioned fear.

This use of fear drive theory almost explains the phenomenon in question, but not quite. Figure 11-14 presents a theoretical curve showing that the emotional response (fear) to a conditioned stimulus declines with the number of trials since the last shock. It further shows that in consequence the strength of the instrumental response (running) should increase for a while (due to further practice) and then decline due to the decline in fear drive. Why does the jumping response continue to become stronger in traumatic avoidance experiments, rather than decline as Fig. 11-14 predicts? Solomon and Wynne (114) propose a principle of partial irreversibility: ". . . a 'traumatic' or very intense 'pain–fear' reaction taking place in the presence of some conditioned stimulus pattern will result in a *permanent* increase in the probability of occurrence of an anxiety reaction in the presence of that conditioned stimulus pattern (whenever it reoccurs)." (Note the use of "anxiety reaction" rather than conditioned fear. In the discussion here, Solomon and Wynne's distinction between the two terms is not being followed.)

Solomon and Wynne ably defend the notion of partial irreversibility, but would not go so far as to explain a failure of extinction by saying

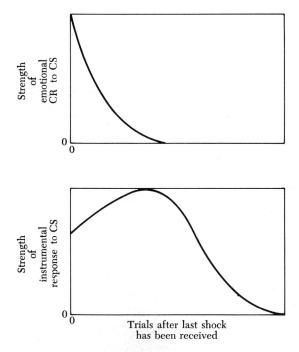

Fig. 11-14. Theoretical relationships between strength of emotional CR to CS and trials since last shock (upper graph) and strength of instrumental response to CS and trials after last shock (lower graph). [Figure 3 from Solomon and Wynne (114). Copyright 1954 by American Psychological Association, and reproduced by permission.]

extinction is impossible in certain situations. A cognitive theory like that of Tolman (127) might handle the problem by explaining that the dogs had learned that a jumping response in a short time interval led to no shock, and a response in a long time interval, or none at all, led to shock. Far from contradicting this *cognition*, the extinction procedure confirmed it because responses became faster and faster and could not provide the information that shock would be omitted even if the response were late. Only if a dog responded late could the original learning begin to break down, and this rarely occurs in the traumatic avoidance situation.

One of the complications in this problem is that extinction of conditioned fear responses does sometimes occur. Therefore, both in real life and in the laboratory a fear conditioning situation is considered traumatic if later extinction is difficult, thus making an exception to traditional learning laws in that case or invoking the cognitive principle just mentioned. However, in the nontraumatic situation (presumably associated with less painful stimuli) standard principles do apply. For example, Wagner, Siegel, and Fein (128) found greater extinction of a classically conditioned suppression of bar pressing if partial reinforcement with shock as the UCS had been used originally than if continuous reinforcement had been employed in the fear conditioning.

Summation of Fear and Other Drives. A student may be working on an assignment in order to reduce his fear of punishment and yet be motivated by other factors. A teacher could conceivably be offering positive rewards such as approval at the same time he was threatening punishment for not completing an assignment. In such cases the total motivation is increased, as predicted by Hull (64). While we might not approve of the use of fear in many classroom situations, the fact is that fear is often an effective element in preparing for examinations and in motivating working on assignments.

A laboratory demonstration of the additive properties of two kinds of motivation comes from Ley (78), who showed that animals which had to jump over a hurdle to avoid shock did so more quickly if they were also hungry and thirsty than if they were not.

The Concepts of Threat and Stress

Fear may be conditioned so that a single stimulus evokes it, but with humans, the fear stimulus may not be effective unless combined with other appropriate stimuli nor unless the person's knowledge and expectations are appropriate to the arousal of fear. Lazarus (77) tells of his family's nightly fear (while living in a Japanese city) that a nearby siren meant a house fire had broken out and would soon sweep through their block. Only when they learned that the siren belonged to an ambulance going to a nearby hospital did their fear subside. The siren could be called a *threat stimulus,* much like a conditioned stimulus for fear, except that few people have actually seen a fire in their own block just after hearing a siren. Lazarus emphasizes that people must appraise threat stimuli in the light of their own knowledge before they can respond with fear or some lesser emotion. Thus the physiological response to threat stimuli, such as seeing a movie of a sawmill accident, can be greatly reduced if the viewer is told that the accident shown is not real.

Psychological stress is a much broader term than threat, and refers to a range of stimuli, physiological reactions, and internal experiences associated with situations like crucial school examinations, physical danger as in military battles, and heated arguments between people. Lazarus (77) has summarized research evidence on a variety of methods used to cope with stressful situations. One response to stress is to become anxious.

Anxiety

Anxiety, to the clinical psychologist, is a state of uneasiness, apprehension, and/or fear sometimes experienced by psychologically disturbed persons. Its manifestations may be sweating palms, restless movements, failure to look directly at one's conversational partner, or expressed fear of certain situations or persons. Anxiety may be evoked by a situation such as standing near the edge of a cliff, in which case it is called *acute anxiety* or *temporary anxiety*. Or it may be a constant feature of one's personality, in which case it is called *chronic anxiety*. No doubt certain arousals of acute anxiety are greatest in persons having high chronic anxiety.

Several tests have been developed to measure chronic anxiety. The best known, perhaps, is Taylor's Manifest Anxiety Scale (122) consisting of 50 questions, each rated by at least four out of five clinical psychologists to have an answer indicative of manifest anxiety. The scale also contains some so-called buffer items which do not indicate presence or absence of anxiety but are included to prevent test-takers from recognizing the special purpose of the scale.

In another chapter, the fact that a sample of psychiatric patients showed higher anxiety scores than a sample of normal persons (121) would be of special importance. However, our interest now is in motivation, and about the relationship of the Manifest Anxiety Scale (MAS) to drive theory. Taylor developed the MAS to provide a new test for a proposition of Hull's theory (64), that *drive* (D) is multiplied by *habit strength* (H) (i.e., *learning*) to give *total response strength* (E). This proposition may be written as an equation: $D \times H = E$. As Spence (116) has stated, it would seem logical to think of anxiety as analogous to the emotional response aroused by electric shock in avoidance or escape conditioning situations. That emotional response is reasonably called a "drive," and so anxiety may also be considered a drive.

Several studies have compared persons with very high anxiety scores to persons with very low anxiety scores to see which group learns the faster. On simple learning tasks, such as classical conditioning, the highly anxious subjects learn more quickly, on the average, than do the less anxious subjects (117, 118). This confirms Hull's theory, for increased drive should have increased the response strength, and increased response strength should lead to an increased probability of a conditioned response.

Taylor and Spence (124) and Taylor (123) also predict that highly anxious subjects will learn complex tasks, such as a maze, more slowly than will less anxious subjects. This prediction, too, was generated by Hull's theory (64) or Spence's modification of that theory (115), but is the subject of some controversy (26, 60). One of Taylor's ways of predicting slow learning of complex tasks in highly anxious subjects seems invalid, but another appears logically acceptable, though it has empirical difficulties.

In comparing only two drive levels ($D = 1$ and $D = 2$) it can be assumed that the complex task involves two responses, one of which is correct and has a habit strength equal to H_c, the other being incorrect with a habit strength equal to H_I. Then if $D = 1$, the equation above for response strength, E, implies that $E_c = H_c$ for the correct response and $E_I = H_I$ for the incorrect response. But if $D = 2$, these equations become $E_c = 2H_c$ for the correct response and $E_I = 2H_I$ for the incorrect response.

Now, the response made depends primarily upon the difference between E_c and E_I. If $D = 1$, $E_c - E_I = H_c - H_I$. If $D = 2$, $E_c - E_I = 2H_c - 2H_I = 2(H_c - H_I)$. Late in training, the correct response is made and rewarded more often than the incorrect response. Therefore, H_c is greater than H_I, $E_c - E_I$ is positive, making a correct response highly probable, and $E_c - E_I$ is greater for $D = 2$ than for $D = 1$. This means that high drive facilitates the later stages of learning.

But what if H_c is less than H_I early in learning? Then $E_c - E_I$ is negative, making an incorrect response highly probable. If $D = 2$, $E_c - E_I$ is more negative than if $D = 1$ and an incorrect response is even more probable. Therefore, a high drive early in learning retards learning, provided the incorrect response originally had the higher H value. Learning will nonetheless occur eventually in most such situations because the incorrect response is never reinforced and the correct response is always reinforced, thus increasing H_c.

Based on these assumptions, if the early stage of learning predominates, high drive will have an overall effect of retarding learning. Otherwise it will facilitate learning, as a whole.

The Taylor–Spence predictions of inferior overall learning of complex tasks under high drive are usually confirmed. However, Hill (60) has pointed out that there is little evidence that a certain incorrect response is stronger than the correct response at the beginning of these studies. He also indicates that the predicted superiority of highly anxious persons late in training does not occur. Evidently, the theory of complex learning needs clarification to explain these data.

The question remains whether a difference between individuals on an anxiety scale or similar instrument should be considered a difference in motivation. There are problems of research design which make it difficult to be positive on this point: The highly anxious and less anxious persons may not be equivalent on all other characteristics which might have affected the learning being studied.

The most extensive test of this equivalence (88) shows no substantial correlation between anxiety and intelligence. However, because other studies present somewhat contradictory evidence, it is premature to attribute learning differences to anxiety differences rather than to differences in basic aptitudes or some other variable that also controls learning rate.

This objection applies to all differences between people alleged to measure motivation. It can be partially allayed by statistical analyses. The so-called *partial correlation* between anxiety and learning scores could be computed. Since it shows the relation between those two variables when others are held constant, a relatively large partial correlation would suggest that anxiety may, indeed, directly affect learning. There are so many pitfalls in this statistical interpretation, however, that complete confidence in any research conclusion would be unjustified.

An alternate method is to attempt to induce high or low anxiety, respectively, in two random groups of subjects and to study their subsequent learning. Experiments somewhat like this (82, 110, 111, 125) generally show no effect of induced anxiety upon learning or else show different effects for people who were already highly anxious before the experiment and for those who were already less anxious. There is also some question as to whether the anxiety-inducing instructions had the intended effect: If the MAS were given before and after those instructions, would a change in score actually have occurred? Knowing few answers, and just the facts reported, it seems best to consider anxiety a characteristic that differs from one person to the next, but which has not yet been proved subject to experimental modification in the same way that the hunger drive or other drives have.

Chapter 12 discusses the way in which classroom achievement depends upon the amount of anxiety a student possesses. We anticipate that material by discussing two such studies now.

McKeachie, Pollie, and Speisman (93) first reported, and Calvin, McGuigan, and Sullivan (21) confirmed, that students who took an objective examination and were allowed to write additional comments about any or all questions on the test had higher scores on the second half of the test than did students who were not given this opportunity. McKeachie *et al.* thought that this was because the tension that was building during the test was reduced by making comments. Calvin *et al.* give some scanty evidence that the tension or anxiety did not dissipate as McKeachie had anticipated, if measured by amount of perspiration. However, Calvin *et al.* also found that the more anxious students, as defined by scores on the Taylor MAS, improved more on the second half of examinations if they were allowed to make comments than did the less anxious students. These two studies suggest that allowing students to make comments during objective tests would be a very good idea, especially for the more anxious ones.

Conditioned Appetitive Drives

Can a primary drive such as hunger be induced by the introduction of stimuli which have accompanied hunger in the past? For example, do you genuinely become more hungry because you are standing in your dormitory's cafeteria line? And, do secondary reinforcements or other stimuli become so valued that people seem permanently motivated for them?

Wright (131) gives an affirmative answer to the first question, at least insofar as it applies to rats. For 18 days, his animals spent an hour in a distinctively colored box while under 22 hours of food deprivation. For another 18 days interspersed with the ones just mentioned, the rats spent an hour in a different-colored box while deprived of food for only one hour before being placed in the box. Then test trials were given to see in which box the animals would eat more. During the tests, the animals which had been in a black box when deprived for 22 hours and in a white box when deprived for 1 hour ate substantially more in the black boxes than in the white boxes. It cannot be explained by assuming that black simply makes animals hungrier, for if the training box colors were reversed, the animals ate more in white boxes. It appears that stimuli that have been present during strong hunger can produce a greater drive to eat than would otherwise be present.

The second question, relating to the motivational properties of secondary reinforcers, is hard to answer. It is clear that when under primary motivation, animals can learn new responses rewarded only by secondary reinforcements such as the color of a goal box (108). The secondary reinforcement in this and most other secondary reinforcement situations can be considered a determinant of the *incentive motivation* construct first discussed in Chapter 3. But as such, it is only the handmaiden of drive, increasing the expectation of reward rather than being the object sought for itself. If Saltzman's animals had been under zero motivation when tested for secondary reinforcement effects, he might have demonstrated that animals develop an acquired drive for stimuli which have been used as secondary reinforcers (108).

Something like this has occurred in a study with the apparatus illustrated in Fig. 11-15. Earl (37) trained mice to dig away 9 pounds of sand to obtain food. But when food was no longer there and the mice were not deprived of food, they nonetheless continued to dig. Apparently, a relatively permanent "digging drive" had been developed in which

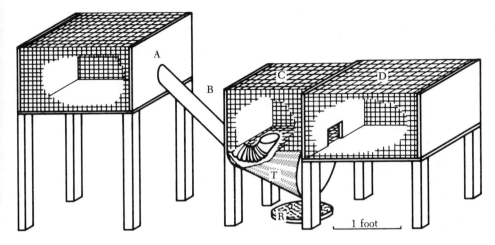

Fig. 11-15. A sand-digging apparatus. The mouse or rat must dig away all the sand coming into cage C through pipe B before going into cage A for reward. Cage D is optional equipment in case a living cage near the apparatus is desired. Figure 1 from Stone (120). The study by Earl (37) used a modified version of this apparatus.

secondary reinforcements associated with digging are now sufficient to maintain the response.

There have been objections to this interpretation. Perhaps some other primary drive was being satisfied; it is almost impossible to satiate all drives at once. One such objection is that an activity drive may be reduced by digging. But note that the activity drive was not enough to evoke digging until it was originally rewarded by food presentation. J. A. King and Weisman (69) have reported that several species of deer mouse will dig without other reinforcement. Therefore, Earl's experiment may have produced a secondary drive which was latent in his animals.

A further suggestion that a secondary drive can be developed for a secondary reinforcement comes from an ingenious experiment by Jensen (66). He found that rats trained to press a bar (lever) in a Skinner box to obtain food reward later preferred to press the lever for food even when food was also available on the floor of the box and could be obtained without further effort. Figure 11-16 shows that the degree of this preference increased with the amount of previous lever pressing experience. This figure could loosely be said to show that an acquired drive to work increases with the amount of previous rewarded work.

Since acquired appetitive drives do exist, despite the shortage of positive evidence and the objections to that evidence, what is their significance? The simple answer: It is enormous. Perhaps the major control of human behavior in civilized lands comes from acquired drives

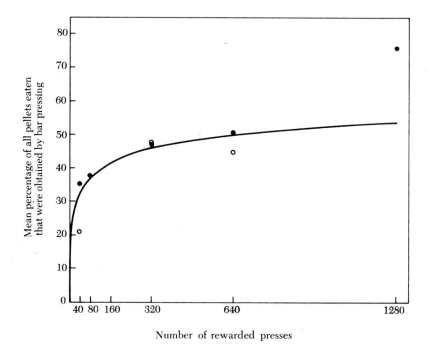

Fig. 11-16. Increased preference for "earning" pellets by bar pressing as a function of increased numbers of previously rewarded presses. [Based on Fig. 1 from Jensen (66). Copyright 1963 by American Psychological Association, and reproduced by permission.]

rather than from primary drives. People are motivated to earn money, to read, to play the piano, to be with relatives, and so on. To the extent that these motivations arose from secondary reinforcements, certain things should be true about them:

1. Deprivation of them should increase their motivational effects.

2. Their effects should be demonstrable in otherwise satiated persons.

3. They may persist somewhat beyond the time when lack of primary reinforcement might be expected to bring extinction effects.

Point 1, demonstrating the effects of deprivation upon motivation for reading, say, should easily be verified, but seems not to have been studied yet. It would be a natural follow-up to Jensen's study of "free-loading" to deprive well-trained rats of bar pressing, and to see if this further increases their preference for bar pressing over "free-loading." Only if deprivation does increase the effect, should we accept the Jensen phenomenon as one of secondary drive.

We have seen some laboratory evidence for points 2 and 3. Let us give further attention to 3. Allport (4) has asserted that this unusual resistance to extinction is a commonplace consequence of training. You learn to drive a car because it will lead to the primary reinforcements coming from getting to work on time; you continue because of an acquired drive to drive; stimuli associated with driving become secondary reinforcements and resistant to extinction.

Allport's theory, called the theory of *functional autonomy of drives,* sounds plausible and conforms to many historical events as well as to our personal experiences. It may account for at least some of the religious motivation of Saint Paul, the scientific motivation of Steinmetz, and the physical vigor of Theodore Roosevelt. However, very few experimental studies have attempted to test the theory—the sand digging study is one of the few such tests. It is reasonably easy to explain that study's findings on the basis of variables other than a relatively permanent acquired drive (functional autonomy), but it is easier still to find other explanations of historical instances of supposed autonomy. For example, Roosevelt's enthusiastic law enforcement as District Attorney of New York or his leading of the Rough Riders into battle during the Spanish–American War is understandable on the basis of reinforcement coming from newspaper publicity, attention from politicians, and winning elections.

To go even farther: In laboratory situations, the power of secondary reinforcements is very temporary. Until more studies demonstrating acquired drive, with some degree of functional autonomy accompanying it, are performed, it should be supposed that most alleged cases of acquired drive are contaminated by other reinforcements, notably the satisfaction of drives such as visual exploration and activity. Perhaps Brown (15) and Denny and Behan (36) are correct in saying that most "acquired drives" are habits of responding, not states of motivation.

Abundancy Motivation

Krech and Crutchfield (74) distinguish between *deficiency motivation,* resulting from shortages of food or other needed substances, and *abundancy motivation,* "desires to experience enjoyments, to get gratifications, to understand and discover, to seek novelty, to strive to achieve and create." While believing that the abundancy motives are not essentially different from deficiency motives in their effects, we welcome this emphasis upon the motives present in the well-fed person. Since we live in an affluent society (43) we must expect to behave more and more in response to these abundancy motives. Harlow (54) would say that except in famine, we have seldom been substantially controlled by deficiency motives. Some of the abundancy motives are surely primary; some may be acquired drives, some may be habits and not drives. But all are extraordinarily important in everyday life.

This is not to say that abundancy motives are intellectual, whereas deficiency motivations are physiological. It is simply to say that in the past individuals may often have had a strong drive for food of any kind, whereas, in the present the majority of Americans are deprived only of novelties or constant luxury. In fact, beggars today have been known to refuse a handout at a restaurant which can't provide pancakes.

While research evidence on the point is limited, many people believe that becoming accustomed to a state of affairs produces motivation for that state of affairs. Lockard (79) has shown that animals will select illumination levels in their cages similar to those in which they were raised. In a much different situation, John H. Patterson, founder of the National Cash Register Company, tried to increase motivation in his salesmen by giving them and their families free vacations in Chicago, New York, or Paris, to get the wives, particularly, accustomed to expensive living as well as acquainted with the company's policies. This, in turn, apparently spurred the husbands to greater sales (104). This may illustrate how abundancy motives may be learned.

Achievement Motivation

McClelland (89) and his co-workers (91) have conducted and inspired a large number of studies to test their conviction that a high need to achieve, as measured by achievement fantasies in response to the Thematic Apperception Test or similar pictures (see Chapter 13) or some comparable measure, can be induced experimentally. They further predict that the high need to achieve produces superior achievement of various kinds.

How do these authors measure the need to achieve (n Achievement)? The procedure is approximately that given below.

A picture of a man standing at an open doorway looking away from the viewer at the landscape is shown to a group of persons for 20 seconds. Then each person is given four minutes to write a story about the picture, answering the questions on the left below. On the right are two persons' answers to the four sets of questions after seeing the same picture (7).

A quick look at the stories of Person A and Person B is enough to show which person talked most about achievement. McClelland, Atkinson, Clark, and Lowell (91), have provided a scoring manual, however, for the achievement motive, so that standardized methods of assigning a numerical score to such stories will be used. Each person tested writes at least four stories to prevent inaccurately high or low scores which might be made on the basis of only one story.

Stories with frequent reference to achievement ("success in competi-

Question set	Person A	Person B
1. What is happening? Who is (are) the person(s)?	Son about to step out into the world of reality. He is thinking of the prospects of success ahead of him and the events he will have to face.	A young man is lingering hazily in a doorway in a daydreaming type of pose.
2. What has led up to this situation? That is, what has happened in the past?	He has graduated from college or high school and is about to start on his own. He wants to be away from the support of his parents and be self-supporting, successful, etc.	He evidently is free from care and responsibility. Somewhat the feeling you have on a vacation when you have nothing to do but relax.
3. What is being thought? What is wanted? By whom?	What will be ahead of him in the way of opportunities. Will he be able to capitalize on the breaks he receives.	Thoughts might be drifting toward his friends at home, the job he is away from, and his own sense of complete relaxation.
4. What will happen? What will be done?	He will go out into the real world, get settled and married and then spend the rest of his life in the Army.	Soon he will find an activity to engage in. Swimming, fishing, or possibly reading.

tion with some standard of excellence," as the scoring manual calls it), are assumed to indicate high motivation for achievement by the story writer. If this assumption is true, other consequences should follow:

1. It should be possible to produce high n Achievement scores by using instructions and experimenter variables which emphasize that a testing situation will indicate the subjects' capabilities for high level work. McClelland, Clark, Roby, and Atkinson (92) verified this prediction in a study in which paper and pencil tests were presented as measures of aptitude for high administrative posts (with falsely high or low performance reported at various times to the subjects) in two highly motivated conditions, whereas *relaxed* and *neutral* conditions de-emphasized their importance. Following the pencil and paper tests, each person wrote stories about four pictures. Achievement motivation scores were significantly higher with *success–failure* and *failure* the motivated conditions, presumably because of those conditions.

2. Parents of children with high n Achievement will show greater

encouragement for their children to succeed in experimental tasks than will parents of children with low n Achievement. Rosen and D'Andrade (106) took experimental materials into the homes of selected high n Achievement and low n Achievement boys, from 9 to 11 years of age, asking each boy, as well as his mother and father, to be present. As the boy was tested on such a task as blindfolded stacking of irregularly shaped blocks, the parents' reactions were also recorded. Mothers of high n Achievement boys gave more warm, approving responses to their boys during the task than did those of low n Achievement. A similar, non-significant trend was found with fathers. In addition, the average prediction of how well their son would do was significantly superior for parents of high n Achievement boys on one task.

3. Actual achievement will be greater, in some situations at least, for persons with high n Achievement than for those with low n Achievement. Lowell (81) found that male college students with high n Achievement learned to unscramble words such as WTSE (west) faster than did those with low n Achievement. The former group also was superior in performance of simple arithmetic addition problems.

In addition, Rosen and D'Andrade's study showed that for all tasks studied for high n Achievement boys the tendency was to do superior work.

However, Boverman, Jordan, and Phillips (14) found no greater indication of superior vocational achievement for persons with high n Achievement than for those with low n Achievement. In fact, the persons striving hardest for vocational advancement had the lowest mean n Achievement scores.

Results similar to those of Lowell and of Rosen and D'Andrade have been obtained by Gough (47, 48). His California Psychological Inventory was constructed to measure two kinds of achievement motivation, among other factors. Instead of telling a story about a picture, the person taking the test says "True" or "False" to a number of statements. Certain patterns of response give him a high or low score on what is called *achievement through conformance* (Ac); other patterns give him a high or low score on *achievement through independence* (Ai). Ac is high for persons who say they are self-disciplined, accept rules, and can perform narrowly defined intellectual tasks. (The last-named skill is called *convergent thinking* or *convergent production* and is discussed more fully in Chapter 14.) Ai is high for persons who say they are independent, like to create methods to use rather than follow other people's methods, and like to work on intellectual problems whose answers are unknown and may neither be unique nor even existent (*divergent thinking* or *divergent production*, as discussed in Chapter 14). Both in the United States (47) and in Italy (48) Ac and Ai have been successfully used to predict high school grades, with individuals having high Ac or high Ai scores also having high grades, on the average.

4. Goals set for themselves by high n Achievement subjects in experimental tasks should be different from those set by low n Achievement subjects. Atkinson, Bastian, Earl, and Litwin (9) confirmed this prediction, finding that high n Achievement male subjects tended to set goals in a shuffleboard game which were of intermediate difficulty, whereas low n Achievement male students tended either to set very difficult or very easy goals for themselves. The high n Achievement group members also preferred to make bets on their performance in which the subjective probability or expectancy (P_s) of success was intermediate ($P_s = 4/6$, $3/6$, or $2/6$) rather than extreme ($P_s = 5/6$ or $1/6$).

Atkinson and Feather (10) have developed a substantial theory concerning this phenomenon and present the results of many experiments related to that theory. This theory states that people find goals more attractive the harder they are to attain. This attractiveness is called incentive (I_s) and is defined by the equation: $I_s = 1 - P_s$. Despite the attractiveness of difficult goals, most people are pulled toward attainable goals as represented by the value of P_s. Consequently, when we further assume that the magnitude of one's n Achievement score (M_s) is a third factor in controlling choice behavior and that these three factors multiply to yield a total tendency to achieve success ($T_s = M_s \times P_s \times I_s$), it can be shown (10, pp. 328–330) that T_s is highest for intermediate probabilities of success (P_s) and lowest for extreme values of P_s. You can check this result of multiplying the three factors by assuming that $M_s = 1$ and solving for I_s and T_s with different values of P_s. Thus, if $P_s = 0.1$, $I_s = 1 - P_s = 0.9$, and $T_s = M_s \times P_s \times I_s = 1 \times 0.1 \times 0.9 = 0.09$. However, if $P_s = 0.5$, $I_s = 0.5$, and $T_s = 1 \times 0.5 \times 0.5 = 0.25$, which is larger than the T_s for $P_s = 0.1$ as expected. Figure 11-17 presents a graph relating T_s to M_s, P_s, and I_s. This graph confirms what has just been said: The tendency to achieve success (T_s) is higher for large values of the achievement motive (M_s or n Achievement) than for low values. Also, T_s is largest for intermediate values of subjective probability of success (P_s) and incentive (I_s). This figure and the theory on which it is based imply that students will tend to select tasks of intermediate difficulty. This is what Atkinson *et al.* (9) found for high achievement motivated students working on a nonacademic task; we will see supporting evidence from academic tasks in Chapter 12.

The theory just stated is an oversimplification because it ignores the possibility that some people may be motivated by a desire to avoid failure (M_{AF}) rather than by a need for achievement. Atkinson and

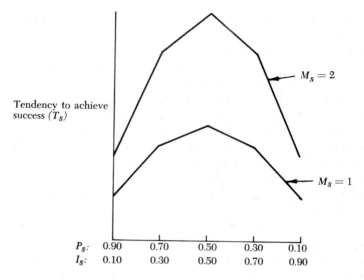

Fig. 11-17. Relation between tendency to achieve success (T_s), n Achievement (M_s), subjective probability of success (P_s), and incentive (I_s). Figure 2 from Atkinson (8).

Feather assume that persons with low n Achievement scores have high M_{AF} values. The total tendency to avoid failure (T_{AF}) for these persons is assumed equal to $M_{AF} \times P_f \times I_f = M_{AF} \times P_f \times (-P_s)$ where P_f and I_f are the subjective probability of failure and the incentive for failure, and this incentive is assumed equal to minus the probability of success because failure seems worse if the probability of success was large. The probability of failure P_f is obviously equal to $1 - P_s$ (one minus the probability of success).

Figure 11-17 shows what would occur if a person had achievement motivation (M_s) but no motive to avoid failure (M_{AF}). The above paragraph on T_{AF} implies that if the T_s axis in Fig. 11-17 were relabeled T_{AF} and its numbers made negative, then that figure would represent a pure case in which a person had a motive to avoid failure but no achievement motivation.

Most people are not pure cases; rather they have some achievement motivation and some motivation to avoid failure. Figure 11-18 shows how these two tendencies interact when the latter is stronger. Note that the difference between tendency to achieve success (T_s) and tendency to avoid failure (T_{AF}) is always negative in this case and is most negative for intermediate values of P_s, the subjective probability of success. Therefore, it is predicted that persons with higher M_{AF} values than M_s values will avoid tasks of intermediate difficulty, preferring either very easy or very difficult activities. If we use the Test Anxiety Scale (largely reflecting anxiety about taking examinations) of Mandler and Sarason (82) as a measure of motive to avoid failure, we can accept evidence from Atkinson and Litwin (11) as confirming this prediction: They found that only 31% of college students who had high test anxiety (M_{AF}) and low n Achievement (M_s) preferred goals of intermediate difficulty, whereas 77% of those with low M_{AF} and high M_s did so.

Atkinson is theorizing that test anxiety (or motive to avoid failure) operates to make people avoid situations, whereas Taylor assumes that anxiety is a drive which increases reaction potential even though it may retard the learning of complex skills. This may not be as contradictory as it seems. Atkinson's experimental subjects are usually given a choice of tasks and thus can let their anxiety control which task they do. However, if Atkinson requires his subjects to perform certain tasks, then anxiety may be expected to affect their performance in the manner Taylor predicts. This is a reasonably accurate statement of the present state of affairs; however, we know of no thorough attempt to combine the two theories in the way just outlined. Also, note the problem of comparing two theories about anxiety based on two different measurements of anxiety.

What can be concluded from consideration of the four points with

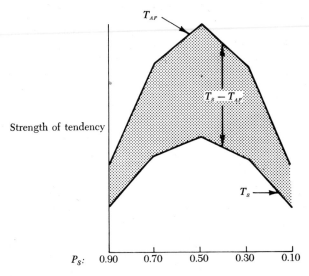

Fig. 11-18. The difference between tendency to achieve success (T_s) and tendency to avoid failure (T_{AF}) in a case where motivation to avoid failure (M_{AF}) is dominant. Figure 5 from Atkinson (8). Cross-hatching means that the difference is negative.

which this discussion of achievement motivation began? Despite many contradictory findings, it seems reasonable to say that n Achievement has exhibited many of the properties of a motive. Farber (40), however, while accepting the evidence cited here, might say that persons with high n Achievement simply have stronger habits of striving for achievement. The fact that parents of children with high n Achievement do set high goals for them and even exert pressure on them to excel in experimental situations (106) gives indirect support to the proposition that n Achievement is acquired by training. However, it is possible that parents could treat children differently because of their own inborn achievement motives and that the children's achievement motives would be again inborn.

A more telling indication that achievement motives are learned comes from McClelland's (90) book, *The Achieving Society,* which gives several examples of apparent changes in the strength of the motive during the history of a given country. McClelland [(90) based in part on Glotz (46a)] argues that the average strength of the motive in a country, from year to year, is controlled by social and family variables, while the achievement motive in turn controls economic growth:

> The simplest way to state the case is that some conditions arise in society, often based on an ideological movement . . . , which lead parents to give their children early achievement training of a certain special type. This, in turn, produces more boys with high n Achievement who, given at least some favorable conditions, are apt to become successful business entrepreneurs. . . . It is tempting to speculate that one reason why practically all great civilizations of the past have declined after a few generations of "climax" is because families have nearly always used their increased prosperity to turn over the rearing of their children to slaves or other dependents who "spoil" the children or keep them dependent too long. For a time, a civilization may draw its leaders with high n Achievement from the periphery, from portions of the society which have not as yet become wealthy enough to support slaves, but if prosperity becomes too general, the effect may be to diminish the number of children with high n Achievement below some critical point needed to maintain the civilization.*

As evidence for this view, McClelland cites de Charms and Moeller's finding (34) that n Achievement for popular fourth grade children's readers (as they rated it) in the United States rose and fell in the period 1800 to 1950 in phase but was a little ahead of the rate of patent issues per million population. This relationship, plotted in Fig. 11-19, suggests that American economic growth was spurred by factors which produced

---

* From *The Achieving Society* by David C. McClelland. Copyright © 1961 by Litton Educational Publishing, Inc., by permission of Van Nostrand Reinhold Company.

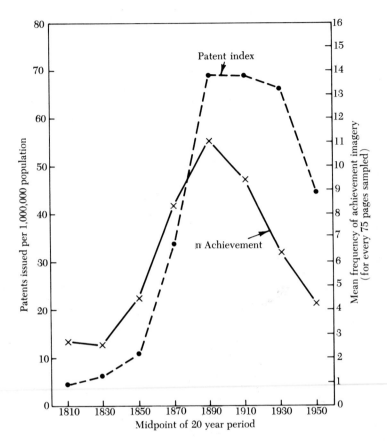

Fig. 11-19. Achievement imagery in children's readers and the patent index in the United States, 1800–1950. [Figure 4.4 from de Charms and Moeller (34). Copyright 1962 by American Psychological Association, and reproduced by permission.]

high n Achievement and has been declining as n Achievement declined. (An interesting sidelight of this article was the appearance of a consistent decline in the frequency of moral teaching in these readers, throughout the period graphed.)

Thus, there is a sense in which Farber and McClelland are in agreement that achievement motivation is learned, though they would part company on the question of its importance. McClelland calls it motivational, nonetheless; Farber apparently would not.

There are other considerations which cause us to be more conservative than McClelland and his associates about the usefulness of achievement motivation measures.

1. Different administrations of the n Achievement test to the same

people sometimes show consistent results (92), but sometimes do not (13).

2. The traditional measure of n Achievement has a very low relation with another measure accepted as appropriate (7). Other attempts to measure achievement motivation also show little or no relation with n Achievement (61, 83) even though they sometimes have interesting characteristics of their own.

3. Though achievement motive is typically higher in American college women than in American college men, it is not increased for women by achievement oriented instructions. It is, however, increased by instructions suggesting high or low social acceptability (91).

4. There is a tendency in experimental work to measure the effects of high n Achievement by academic tasks or laboratory tests of learning, whereas the conception of achievement motivation as striving to succeed with respect to some standard of excellence suggests that measures of athletic, artistic, and political achievement should receive equal attention, with economic achievement receiving even greater experimental attention in view of its theoretical importance to McClelland.

Despite some objections to this technique, we agree with the analysts (27) who said, "Of all the projective techniques with which we are familiar, more careful and experimentally oriented work has been conducted by McClelland, his co-workers, and others who have been intrigued with the technique for measuring n Ach than any other."

To conclude this section, we point out that the developers of the n Achievement measure have also produced measures of an "affiliation motive" and "power motive," among others. These contributions are perhaps not measures of motives in Farber's strict sense, but may be considered promising measures of motivated behavior. It should be noted that achievement, affiliation, and power motives had been discussed in Murray's (100) personality theory long before methods for measuring them were developed.

A Hierarchy of Human Needs

Maslow (85, 86) has hypothesized that people instinctively possess a set of needs arranged like a tower, with physiological needs at the base and needs to know and understand at the top. Figure 11-20 is an artistic rendering of Maslow's hierarchy of needs. The basic idea which determines the order in which the different needs are arranged in the tower is Maslow's conviction that if one need, such as a need for food, is more powerful than another, such as need for esteem, the former is more basic and must be located nearer the bottom of the tower.

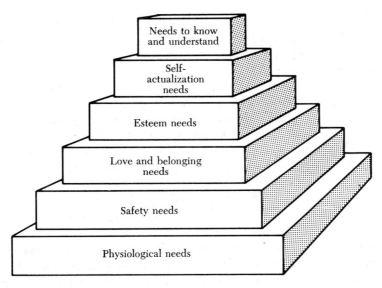

Fig. 11-20. A representation of Maslow's hierarchy of needs, with basic needs toward the bottom of the picture. Figure 12.1 from Klausmeier and Goodwin (73).

According to Maslow's theory, a person will not seek to satisfy a higher need so long as a lower need is strong. Since physiological needs such as hunger and thirst are at the bottom of the hierarchy, they must be well satisfied before the individual seeks to satisfy the next level of needs, the safety needs. Safety needs include the desire for health, for physical safety, and (in children) for a somewhat orderly routine and protection by parents.

If physiological and safety needs are both met, Maslow predicts that then people will seek to satisfy their needs to belong and their needs to love and be loved. The presence of friends, a sweetheart or a spouse, and of one's children will be particularly desired; a person lacking this experience of belonging and of mutual love will make great efforts to attain it. The next step up the hierarchy is to search for self-esteem and the esteem of others. This level of needs is closely related to the need for achievement.

Maslow assumes that if all the needs beneath it in the tower are satisfied, a person will direct his efforts toward self-actualization. This word means making of a person what he is most naturally fitted for. Thus, a person like Albert Schweitzer could and did have lower needs satisfied (such as the need for the esteem of others) but felt incomplete because he thought he was born to be a missionary, not an organist. Maslow (86, Ch. 12) has studied 45 contemporary or historical personages whom he considers to be in greater or lesser degree self-actualized. He reports that several characteristics are typical of these people, such as a capacity for efficiently perceiving reality and accepting it; an acceptance of one's self, of others, and of nature; and spontaneity.

Finally, at the top of the tower, as we show it, are the desires to know and understand. Maslow is convinced that all people, not just well-educated people, have these needs. However, if the more basic needs are not satisfied first, the intellectual needs will not be evident. A close relative of these highest needs is the need to experience and appreciate beauty. One can either think of it as one of the needs to know and understand, or one can add still another level to the tower.

It is difficult to evaluate Maslow's theory because so little empirical research has been done on it. On the one hand, much that it says is plausible—there is reason to suppose that one cannot focus on one's need for love when one is starving. On the other hand, our own experience suggests that some people have their needs arranged in a different order than Maslow supposes. Surely, many ambitious people are striving for esteem from others before they have satisfied their needs for love and belonging in more than a superficial way. Cofer and Appley (30) feel that the evidence for a hierarchy of needs is reasonably strong if one considers only the bottom two levels of the tower. They argue, however, that the theory as a whole must employ less vague concepts, and be based on more solid research evidence than now exists if that theory is to be considered scientifically established.

Summary

1. High food or water deprivation makes an organism work harder to obtain food or water, and makes it eat or drink more than if the amount of deprivation were lower.

2. The weak theory of drive reduction states that if a response is made in a certain situation and is followed by a reduction in drive level, the tendency for that response to be made in the same situation in the future is increased. This increase is called learning.

3. Increased drive level during training does not directly improve learning. However, teachers should note that a large difference between the rewards for the correct and incorrect choices in a task does facilitate learning.

4. Sexual activity is influenced by several factors, including hormonal activity, parental treatment, previous sexual experience, and marital status.

5. The curiosity drive is illustrated by the fact that a rhesus monkey will learn and repeatedly execute a response rewarded by the opportunity to look outside of his cage for a few seconds. Furthermore, this tendency is greater if the monkey has been deprived of such an opportunity for a long period of time, as compared to deprivation for a short period.

6. To frustrate is to do something to an organism to prevent certain customary responses. Frustration of a final act in a sequence will weaken (extinguish) previous acts in the sequence. Furthermore, if an animal is frustrated at a certain time, he will develop a frustration drive which will make the responses immediately after that time more vigorous.

7. Primary drives, such as hunger, thirst, and sexual motivation, have substantial unlearned components. A secondary drive, however, is developed through pairing of previously neutral stimuli with a primary drive state. The conditioned fear drive is an example of a secondary drive: A black wall may be present in a cage whenever an animal is shocked, and not present when the animal is not shocked. Fear responses originally made to the shock then become conditioned to the presence of the black wall and may be demonstrated by increased rapidity of escape or avoidance responses when the black wall is present, but the shock is not presented. An intensely painful stimulus may lead to what is called partial irreversibility in which a weakening of response during extinction is very difficult or impossible to produce.

8. Anxiety is a state of uneasiness, apprehension, or fear experienced in various degrees by different persons. Tests have been constructed to measure the amount of anxiety a person exhibits in everyday life. This anxiety has some properties of other drives: Persons with high anxiety develop conditioned responses more quickly than do persons with low anxiety. However, members of the former group generally learn complex responses more slowly than do members of the latter group.

9. A conditioned food drive can be induced by pairing previously neutral stimuli with high food drive. In later tests, when the organism has not been food deprived, presentation of those stimuli will cause an increase in eating. Possibly other drives, such as a drive to give speeches in public, are also conditioned—and so thoroughly conditioned that they do not extinguish even when the original drive and reinforcement are omitted. If this possibility is true, functional autonomy of the drive has been attained.

10. Achievement motivation is measured by evoking responses indicating an interest in such accomplishments as success in an occupation or gaining recognition for athletic or musical attainments. Some evidence exists that persons with high achievement motivation actually accom-

plish more in their work and/or studies than do persons with low achievement motivation. Not all psychologists would agree that achievement motivation is truly motivational, however. Some would prefer to call it a habit.

11. Maslow has hypothesized that human needs are arranged hierarchically, with physiological needs being basic, and safety needs, needs to belong and to love, needs for self-esteem and the esteem of others, a need for self-actualization (self-fulfillment), and needs to know and understand being higher needs, in the order given. By assumption, a person will not attempt to satisfy a higher need until all lower needs are reasonably well satisfied. This theory has not been thoroughly investigated and must, therefore, be considered possibly true, but unproved.

SUGGESTED READINGS

Berkowitz, L. Impulse, aggression, and the gun. *Psychology Today*, 1968(September), **2**, No. 4, 18–73.

The presence of guns in a room is shown to reduce inhibitions against violence when people are angry. In order to reduce violence, society should prevent frustration if possible, leave inhibitions intact, and remove stimuli which can trigger aggressive acts.

Cotton, J. W. Planaria; Lane, H. L. Empty planaria do not make the most noise; Royce, J. R. Noise from a non-Skinnerian non-planarian; Lane, H. L. On looking into Royce's taxonomy. *Worm Runner's Digest*, 1962, **14**, No. 1, 22–24.

A series of poems about the relevance of Hull's theory, Skinner's research, and evolutionary concepts to the conditioning of Planaria (flatworms). Planaria are alleged to be able to maintain conditioned responses even after they have been bisected and grown new tails. More amazingly, it is claimed that Planaria which eat "educated" Planaria then exhibit the conditioned behavior of the animals they have eaten. [See McConnell, J. V. *A manual of psychological experimentation on Planarians.* (2nd ed.) Ann Arbor, Mich.: Journal of Biological Psychology, 1967. Also Pronko, N. H. *Panorama of psychology.* Belmont, Calif.: Brooks, Cole, 1969. Pp. 32–44.]

Janis, I. When fear is healthy. *Psychology Today*, 1968(April), **1**, No. 11, 46–49, 60–61.

Dr. Janis tells how persons with moderate fear before undergoing surgery showed less anger and fewer complaints after the operation. Telling the patients what discomfort to expect also reduced anger and increased confidence in the surgeon.

REFERENCES

1. Acker, M., & McReynolds, P. The "need for novelty": A comparison of six instruments. *Psychological Record,* 1967, **17,** 177–182.
2. Adelman, H. M., & Maatsch, J. L. Learning and extinction based upon frustration, food reward, and exploratory tendencies. *Journal of Experimental Psychology,* 1956, **52,** 311–315.
3. Adolph, E. F. The internal environment and behavior. III. Water content. *American Journal of Psychiatry,* 1941, **97,** 1365–1373.
4. Allport, G. W. *Pattern and growth in personality.* New York: Holt, Rinehart & Winston, 1965. Pp. 244–246.
5. Amsel, A. The role of frustrative nonreward in noncontinuous reward situations. *Psychological Bulletin,* 1958, **55,** 102–119.
6. Amsel, A. Frustrative nonreward in partial reinforcement and discrimination learning: Some recent history and a theoretical extension. *Psychological Review,* 1962, **69,** 306–328.
7. Atkinson, J. W. (Ed.). *Motive in fantasy, action, and society.* Princeton, N. J.: Van Nostrand, 1958. Pp. 178, 248, 686–746.
8. Atkinson, J. W. The mainsprings of achievement-oriented activity. In J. D. Krumboltz (Ed.), *Learning and the educational process.* Chicago: Rand McNally, 1965. Pp. 25–66.
9. Atkinson, J. W., Bastian, J. R., Earl, R. W., & Litwin, G. H. The achievement motive, goal setting, and probability preferences. *Journal of Abnormal and Social Psychology,* 1960, **60,** 27–36.
10. Atkinson, J. W., & Feather, N. T. (Eds.). *A theory of achievement motivation.* New York: Wiley, 1966.
11. Atkinson, J. W., & Litwin, G. H. Achievement motive and test anxiety conceived as motive to approach success and motive to avoid failure. *Journal of Abnormal and Social Psychology,* 1960, **60,** 52–63.
12. Berkun, M. M., Kessen, M. L., & Miller, N. E. Hunger reducing effects of food by stomach fistula versus food by mouth measured by a consummatory response. *Journal of Comparative and Physiological Psychology,* 1952, **45,** 550–554.
13. Birney, R. C. The reliability of the achievement motive. *Journal of Abnormal and Social Psychology,* 1959, **58,** 266–267.
14. Boverman, D. M., Jordan, E. J., Jr., & Phillips, L. Achievement motivation in fantasy and behavior. *Journal of Abnormal and Social Psychology,* 1960, **60,** 374–378.
15. Brown, J. S. Problems presented by the concept of acquired drives. In J. S. Brown, H. F. Harlow, L. J. Postman, V. Nowlis, T. M. Newcomb, & O. H. Mowrer, *Current theory and research in motivation: A symposium.* Lincoln: University of Nebraska Press, 1953. Pp. 1–19.
16. Brown, J. S. *The motivation of behavior.* New York: McGraw-Hill, 1961. Pp. 89, 132.
17. Brush, F. R. The effects of shock intensity on the acquisition and extinction of an avoidance response in dogs. *Journal of Comparative and Physiological Psychology,* 1957, **50,** 547–552.
18. Butler, R. A. Discrimination learning by rhesus monkeys to visual-exploration motivation. *Journal of Comparative and Physiological Psychology,* 1953, **46,** 95–98.

19. Butler, R. A. The effect of deprivation of visual incentives in visual exploration motivation in monkeys. *Journal of Comparative and Physiological Psychology,* 1957, **50,** 177–179.

20. Butler, R. A., & Harlow, H. F. Persistence of visual exploration in monkeys. *Journal of Comparative and Physiological Psychology,* 1954, **47,** 258–263.

21. Calvin, A. D., McGuigan, F. J., & Sullivan, M. W. A further investigation of the relationship between anxiety and classroom examination performance. *Journal of Educational Psychology,* 1957, **48,** 240–244.

22. Campbell, B. A., & Kraeling, D. Response strength as a function of drive level and amount of drive reduction. *Journal of Experimental Psychology,* 1953, **45,** 97–101.

23. Cannon, W. B. *Bodily changes in pain, hunger, fear, and rage.* (2nd ed.) New York: Appleton, 1929.

24. Cannon, W. B., & Washburn, A. L. An explanation of hunger. *American Journal of Physiology,* 1912, **29,** 441–454.

25. Champion, R. A. Effect of competing responses as a function of deprivation time. *Journal of Experimental Psychology,* 1967, **73,** 503–508.

26. Child, I. L. Personality. *Annual Review of Psychology,* 1954, **5,** 149–170.

27. Christie, R., & Lindauer, F. Personality structure. *Annual Review of Psychology,* 1963, **14,** 201–230.

28. Cicala, G. A. Running speed in rats as a function of drive level and presence or absence of competing response trials. *Journal of Experimental Psychology,* 1961, **62,** 329–334.

29. Clayton, K. N. т-maze choice learning as a joint function of the reward magnitudes for the alternatives. *Journal of Comparative and Physiological Psychology,* 1964, **58,** 333–338.

30. Cofer, C. N., & Appley, M. H. *Motivation: Theory and research.* New York: Wiley, 1964. Pp. 681–692.

31. Cotton, J. W. Running time as a function of amount of food deprivation. *Journal of Experimental Psychology,* 1953, **46,** 188–198.

32. Davis, R. C., Garafolo, L., & Kveim, K. Conditions associated with gastro-intestinal activity. *Journal of Comparative and Physiological Psychology,* 1959, **52,** 466–475.

33. Davis, R. H. The effect of drive reversal on latency, amplitude, and activity level. *Journal of Experimental Psychology,* 1957, **53,** 310–315.

34. de Charms, R., & Moeller, G. H. Values expressed in American children's readers: 1800–1950. *Journal of Abnormal and Social Psychology,* 1962, **64,** 136–142.

35. Dember, W. N., & Fowler, H. Spontaneous alternation behavior. *Psychological Bulletin,* 1958, **55,** 412–428.

36. Denny, M. R., & Behan, R. A. Conditioned hunger drive or conditioned approach? *Psychological Reports,* 1956, **2,** 192–193.

37. Earl, R. W. Motivation, performance, and extinction. *Journal of Comparative and Physiological Psychology,* 1957, **50,** 248–251.

38. Ehrmann, W. Marital and nonmarital sexual behavior. In H. T. Christiansen (Ed.), *Handbook of marriage and the family.* Chicago: Rand McNally, 1964. Pp. 585–622.

39. Estes, W. K. Stimulus-response theory of drive. In R. Jones (Ed.), *Nebraska symposium on motivation.* Lincoln: University of Nebraska Press, 1958. Pp. 35–69.

40. Farber, I. E. The role of motivation in verbal learning and performance. *Psychological Bulletin*, 1955, **52**, 311–327.

41. Ford, C. S., & Beach, F. A. *Patterns of sexual behavior.* New York: Harper, 1951.

42. *Funk and Wagnalls standard dictionary of the English language, international edition.* Vol. I. New York: Funk and Wagnalls, 1961.

43. Galbraith, J. K. *The affluent society.* Boston: Houghton Mifflin, 1958.

44. Gewirtz, J. L., & Baer, D. M. The effect of brief social deprivation on behaviors for a social reinforcer. *Journal of Abnormal and Social Psychology*, 1958, **56**, 49–56.

45. Glanzer, M. The role of stimulus satiation in spontaneous alternation. *Journal of Experimental Psychology*, 1953, **45**, 387–393.

46. Glanzer, M. Curiosity, exploratory drive, and stimulus satiation. *Psychological Bulletin*, 1958, **55**, 302–315.

46a. Glotz, G. *Histoire Grecque.* Vol. 2. Paris: Les Presses Universitaires de France, 1925.

47. Gough, H. G. Academic achievement in high school as predicted from the California Psychological Inventory. *Journal of Educational Psychology*, 1964, **55**, 174–180.

48. Gough, H. G. A cross-cultural study of achievement motivation. *Journal of Applied Psychology*, 1964, **48**, 191–196.

49. Grossman, M. I. Integration of current views on the regulation of hunger and appetite. In R. W. Miner (Ed.), *The regulation of hunger and appetite. Annals of the New York Academy of Science*, 1955, **63**, 76–79.

50. Group for the Advancement of Psychiatry. *Sex and the college student.* New York: Atheneum, 1966.

51. Hall, J. F. *Psychology of motivation.* Chicago: Lippincott, 1961. Pp. 145–154.

52. Haner, C. F., & Brown, P. A. Clarification of the instigation to action concept in the frustration-aggression hypothesis. *Journal of Abnormal and Social Psychology*, 1955, **51**, 204–206.

53. Harlow, H. F. Studying animal behavior. In T. G. Andrews (Ed.), *Methods of psychology.* New York: Wiley, 1948. Pp. 319–347.

54. Harlow, H. F. Mice, monkeys, men, and motives. *Psychological Review*, 1953, **60**, 23–32.

55. Harlow, H. F. The heterosexual affectional system in monkeys. *American Psychologist*, 1962, **17**, 1–9.

56. Hess, E. H. Attitude and pupil size. *Scientific American*, 1965, **212**, 46–54.

57. Hess, E. H., & Polt, J. M. Pupil size as related to interest value of visual stimuli. *Science*, 1960, **132**, 349–350.

58. Hetherington, A. W., & Ronson, S. W. The spontaneous activity and food intake of rats with hypothalamic lesions. *American Journal of Physiology*, 1942, **136**, 609–617.

59. Hill, W. F. Activity as an autonomous drive. *Journal of Comparative and Physiological Psychology*, 1956, **49**, 15–19.

60. Hill, W. F. Comments on Taylor's "Drive theory and manifest anxiety." *Psychological Bulletin*, 1957, **54**, 490–493.

61. Himelstein, P., Eschenbach, A. E., & Carp, A. Interrelationships among three measures of need achievement. *Journal of Consulting Psychology*, 1958, **22**, 451–452.

62. Holder, W. B., Marx, M. H., Holder, E. E., & Collier, G. Response strength

as a function of delay of reward in a runway. *Journal of Experimental Psychology,* 1957, **53**, 316–323.

63. Horenstein, B. J. Performance of conditioned responses as a function of strength of hunger drive. *Journal of Comparative and Physiological Psychology,* 1951, **44**, 210–224.

64. Hull, C. L. *Principles of behavior.* New York: Appleton-Century-Crofts, 1943.

65. Hull, C. L., Livingston, J. R., Rouse, R. O., & Barker, A. N. True, sham, and esophogeal feeding as reinforcements. *Journal of Comparative and Physiological Psychology,* 1951, **44**, 236–245.

66. Jensen, G. D. Preference for bar pressing over "freeloading" as a function of number of rewarded presses. *Journal of Experimental Psychology,* 1963, **65**, 451–455.

67. Kagan, J., & Berkun, M. The reward value of running activity. *Journal of Comparative and Physiological Psychology,* 1954, **47**, 108.

68. Kalish, II. I. Strength of fear as a function of the number of acquisition and extinction trials. *Journal of Experimental Psychology,* 1954, **47**, 1–9.

69. King, J. A., & Weisman, R. G. Sand digging contingent upon bar pressing in deer mice (Peromyscus). *Animal Behaviour,* 1964, **12**, 446–450.

70. King, R. A. The effects of training and motivation on the components of a learned instrumental response. Unpublished doctoral dissertation, Duke University, 1959.

71. Kinsey, A. C., Pomeroy, W. B., & Martin, C. E. *Sexual behavior in the human male.* Philadelphia: Saunders, 1948.

72. Kinsey, A. C., Pomeroy, W. B., Martin, C. E., & Gebhard, P. H. *Sexual behavior in the human female.* Philadelphia: Saunders, 1953. Pp. 556, 685–687.

73. Klausmeier, H. J., & Goodwin, W. *Learning and human abilities. Educational psychology.* (2nd ed.) New York: Harper & Row, 1966.

74. Krech, D., & Crutchfield, R. S. *Elements of psychology.* New York: Knopf, 1958. P. 288.

75. Lambert, W. W., & Solomon, R. L. Extinction of a running response as a function of distance of block point from the goal. *Journal of Comparative and Physiological Psychology,* 1952, **45**, 269–279.

76. Larsson, K. Experience and maturation in the development of sexual behavior in the male puberty rat. *Behaviour,* 1959, **14**, 101–107.

77. Lazarus, R. S. *Psychological stress and the coping process.* New York: McGraw-Hill, 1966. Pp. 43–44.

78. Ley, R. Effects of food and water deprivation on the performance of a response motivated by fear. *Journal of Experimental Psychology,* 1965, **69**, 583–589.

79. Lockard, R. B. Self-regulated exposure to light by light- or dark-treated rats. *Science,* 1962, **135**, 377–378.

80. Logan, F. A., & Wagner, A. R. *Reward and punishment.* Boston: Allyn & Bacon, 1965. Pp. 46–50.

81. Lowell, E. L. The effect of need for achievement on learning and speed of performance. *Journal of Psychology,* 1952, **33**, 31–40.

82. Mandler, G., & Sarason, S. B. A study of anxiety and learning. *Journal of Abnormal and Social Psychology,* 1952, **47**, 166–173.

83. Marlowe, D. Relationships among direct and indirect measures of the achievement motive and overt behavior. *Journal of Consulting Psychology,* 1959, **23**, 329–332.

84. Marzocco, F. N. Frustration effect as a function of drive level, habit strength,

and distribution of trials during extinction. Unpublished doctoral dissertation, State University of Iowa, 1951.

85. Maslow, A. H. A theory of human motivation. *Psychological Review,* 1943, **50,** 370–396.

86. Maslow, A. H. *Motivation and personality.* New York: Harper, 1954.

87. Masters, W. H., & Johnson, V. E. *Human sexual response.* Boston: Little, Brown, 1966.

88. Mayzner, M. S., Sersen, E., & Tresselt, M. E. The Taylor Manifest Anxiety Scale and intelligence. *Journal of Consulting Psychology,* 1955, **19,** 401–403.

89. McClelland, D. C. (Ed.). *Studies in motivation.* New York: Appleton-Century-Crofts, 1955.

90. McClelland, D. C. *The achieving society.* Princeton, N. J.: Van Nostrand, 1961. Pp. 127–128.

91. McClelland, D. C., Atkinson, J. W., Clark, R., & Lowell, E. *The achievement motive.* New York: Appleton-Century-Crofts, 1955. Pp. 177–181.

92. McClelland, D. C., Clark, R. A., Roby, T. B., & Atkinson, J. W. The projective expression of needs. IV. The effect of the need for achievement on thematic apperception. *Journal of Experimental Psychology,* 1949, **39,** 242–255.

93. McKeachie, W. J., Pollie, D., & Speisman, J. Relieving anxiety in classroom examinations. *Journal of Abnormal and Social Psychology,* 1955, **50,** 93–98.

94. Melzack, R. The perception of pain. *Scientific American,* 1961, **204,** 41–49.

95. Michael, R. P. Estrogen-sensitive neurons and sexual behavior in female cats. *Science,* 1962, **136,** 322–323.

96. Miller, N. E. Studies of fear as an acquirable drive: I. Fear as motivation and fear-reduction as reinforcement in the learning of new responses. *Journal of Experimental Psychology,* 1948, **38,** 89–101.

97. Miller, N. E., Bailey, C. J., & Stevenson, J. A. F. Decreased "hunger" but increased food intake resulting from hypothalamic lesions. *Science,* 1950, **112,** 256–259.

98. Montgomery, K. C. The role of the exploratory drive in learning. *Journal of Comparative and Physiological Psychology,* 1954, **47,** 60–64.

99. Morgan, C. T., & King, R. A. *Introduction to psychology.* (3rd ed.) New York: McGraw-Hill, 1966. Pp. 215–224.

100. Murray, H. A. *Explorations in personality.* New York: Oxford University Press, 1938.

101. Overmier, J. B. Instrumental and cardiac indices of Pavlovian fear conditioning as a function of US duration. *Journal of Comparative and Physiological Psychology,* 1966, **62,** 15–20.

102. Peckham, R. H., & Amsel, A. Within-subject demonstration of a relationship between frustration and magnitude of reward in a differential magnitude of reward discrimination. *Journal of Experimental Psychology,* 1967, **73,** 187–195.

103. Rabedeau, R. G., & Whalen, R. E. Effects of copulatory experience on mating behavior in the male rat. *Journal of Comparative and Physiological Psychology,* 1959, **52,** 482–484.

104. Ratcliff, J. D. He rang the bell heard round the world. *Readers Digest,* 1956, **68**(March), 163–166.

105. Reiss, I. L. *Premarital sexual standards in America.* Glencoe, Ill.: Free Press, 1960. Pp. 227–239.

106. Rosen, B. C., & D'Andrade, R. The psychosocial origins of achievement motivation. *Sociometry,* 1959, **22,** 185–219.

107. Roth, L. M., & Willis, E. R. A study of cockroach behavior. *American Midland Naturalist*, 1952, **47**, 66–129.
108. Saltzman, I. J. Maze learning in the absence of primary reinforcement: a study of secondary reinforcement. *Journal of Comparative and Physiological Psychology*, 1949, **42**, 161–173.
109. Santa Barbara News Press, June 1, 1961.
110. Sarason, S. B., & Mandler, G. Some correlates of test anxiety. *Journal of Abnormal and Social Psychology*, 1952, **47**, 810–817.
111. Sarason, S. B., Mandler, G., & Craighill, P. G. The effect of differential instructions on anxiety and learning. *Journal of Abnormal and Social Psychology*, 1952, **47**, 561–565.
112. Schwarz, M. Instrumental and consummatory measures of sexual capacity in the male rat. *Journal of Comparative and Physiological Psychology*, 1956, **49**, 328–333.
113. Solomon, R. L., Kamin, L. J., & Wynne, L. C. Traumatic avoidance learning: the outcome of several extinction procedures with dogs. *Journal of Abnormal and Social Psychology*, 1953, **48**, 291–302.
114. Solomon, R. L., & Wynne, L. C. Traumatic avoidance learning: the principles of anxiety conservation and partial irreversibility. *Psychological Review*, 1954, **61**, 353–385.
115. Spence, K. W. *Behavior theory and conditioning*. New Haven, Conn.: Yale University Press, 1956.
116. Spence, K. W. A theory of emotionally aroused drive (D) and its relation to performance in single learning situations. *American Psychologist*, 1958, **13**, 131–141.
117. Spence, K. W. Anxiety (drive) level and performance in eyelid conditioning. *Psychological Bulletin*, 1964, **61**, 129–139.
118. Spence, K. W., & Spence, J. T. Sex and anxiety differences in eyelid conditioning. *Psychological Bulletin*, 1966, **65**, 137–142.
119. Stellar, E., & Hill, J. H. The rat's rate of drinking as a function of water deprivation. *Journal of Comparative and Physiological Psychology*, 1952, **45**, 96–102.
120. Stone, C. P. A sand-tube obstruction apparatus. *Journal of Genetic Psychology*, 1937, **50**, 203–206.
121. Taylor, J. A. The relationship of anxiety to the conditioned eyelid response. *Journal of Experimental Psychology*, 1951, **41**, 81–92.
122. Taylor, J. A. A personality scale of manifest anxiety. *Journal of Abnormal and Social Psychology*, 1953, **48**, 285–290.
123. Taylor, J. A. Drive theory and manifest anxiety. *Psychological Bulletin*, 1956, **53**, 303–320.
124. Taylor, J. A., & Spence, K. W. The relationship of anxiety level to performance in serial learning. *Journal of Experimental Psychology*, 1952, **44**, 61–64.
125. Taylor, J. A., & Spence, K. W. Conditioning level in the behavior disorders. *Journal of Abnormal and Social Psychology*, 1954, **49**, 497–502.
126. Teel, K. S. Habit strength as a function of motivation during learning. *Journal of Comparative and Physiological Psychology*, 1952, **45**, 188–191.
127. Tolman, E. C. Principles of purposive behavior. In S. Koch (Ed.), *Psychology: A study of a science*. Vol. 2. New York: McGraw-Hill, 1959. Pp. 92–157.
128. Wagner, A. R., Siegel, L. S., & Fein, G. G. Extinction of conditioned fear as a function of percentage of reinforcement. *Journal of Comparative and Physiological Psychology*, 1967, **63**, 160–164.

129. Welker, W. I. Some determinants of play and exploration in chimpanzees. *Journal of Comparative and Physiological Psychology,* 1956, **49,** 84–89.

130. Wharton, D. R. A., Black, E. D., Merritt, C., Jr., Wharton, L., Bazinet, M., & Walsh, J. T. Isolation of the sex attractant of the American cockroach. *Science,* 1962, **137,** 1062–1063.

131. Wright, J. H. Test for a learned drive based on the hunger drive. *Journal of Experimental Psychology,* 1965, **70,** 580–584.

132. Young, P. T. Reversal of food preferences of the white rat through controlled pre-feeding. *Journal of General Psychology,* 1940, **22,** 33–66.

133. Young, W. C., Dempsey, E. M., & Myers, H. I. Cyclic reproductive behavior in the female guinea pig. *Journal of Comparative and Physiological Psychology,* 1935, **19,** 313–335.

134. Zaretsky, H. H. Learning and performance in the runway as a function of the shift in drive and incentive. *Journal of Comparative and Physiological Psychology,* 1966, **62,** 218–221.

135. Zeaman, D., & House, B. J. The growth and decay of reactive inhibition as measured by alternation behavior. *Journal of Experimental Psychology,* 1951, **41,** 177–186.

12
MOTIVATION AND SCHOOLING

Chapter 11 focused upon motivation from a biological and general psychological viewpoint. We now turn to motivational processes as they affect students in our schools. The rewards used in animal learning experiments (food, water, etc.) become less important because most children have their biological needs satisfied routinely. But what of the 10-year-old boy who would rather play football than read, unless he has a very exciting space adventure story? Does the school satisfy his needs best by putting him on an intellectual treadmill in which five pages of reading in social science lead to a reward of five minutes of football? Should we expect obedient, compliant children in school, who study without external reward because that is what they are required to do? Or should we follow the example of A. S. Neill, founder of a well-known English boarding school, Summerhill:

> We set out to make a school in which we should allow children freedom to be themselves. In order to do this we had to renounce all discipline, all suggestion, all moral training, all religious instruction. All it required was what we had—a complete belief in the child as a good, not an evil being. For almost forty years, this belief in the goodness of the child has never wavered; it rather has become a fixed faith (60).

The Summerhill student is never required to attend class, to do assignments, or to take examinations. Our 10-year-old boy could play outdoors all day for years if he chose. A few Summerhill children have. But most of them go to class or study on their own, either because they really are interested in the material or because they have decided to try to pass college entrance tests.

A few modern American schools show the effects of viewpoints like Neill's, but other schools reflect the disciplinarian view of earlier generations of school teachers. Teachers often feel they know better than their pupils do what it is the students need to learn. Anxious lest they fall behind in occupational or social success as adults, teachers push their students to learn as much as possible each year and to learn enough in every subject matter field to be well-rounded, even though they have no interest in many fields they study.

Teachers are also tempted to say that children need to be controlled so that their behavior imitates adult activity as quickly as possible. Sometimes the feeling seems to be that childrens' behavior is naturally bad if they are free to make their own choices. Strict supervision becomes the aim, lest unrestricted children grow into unruly adults.

It makes a difference whether we believe that children's characteristics would continue in adulthood unless special training were given. In Chapter 9 it was pointed out that children both sleep and cry more as infants than they do as older children. But parents do not attempt to teach children to sleep less as they become older; they let "natural development" control changes in sleep habits. Although parents may try to reduce crying a bit by injunctions to be brave or to be a big boy, etc., basically they seem to accept children's tendencies to be more overtly emotional when young.

Until this century it was thought desirable to teach children to sit perfectly still in school because adults are relatively immobile in many places of business and work. It should be evident that sitting quietly in certain situations, such as during church services, requires the children to learn the proprieties of adult conduct, although in their most normal state children are active beings. It is not necessary to teach them now to be sedate when older; sedateness will come with age. Therefore, the schools may properly spend their efforts on tasks other than teaching quietness. This is recognized by most teachers today. Difficulties arise only when unwilling students or emotionally upset youngsters are more boisterous in class than the rest of the group find acceptable while they are carrying on their own activities.

In succeeding sections of this chapter the authors assume that academic achievement, in the subjects of a given school's curriculum, is a major goal of the teacher even though he personally may feel that Summerhill's de-emphasis of academic activity is desirable. We would urge upon even the most academically minded teachers the policy, however, that, where equal learning is produced by two methods, the more pleasurable one for the pupil be used as an act of simple kindness. In any case it seems wise to remember that we are first of all educators, not efficiency experts. McDonald (56) has emphasized this point, indicating that in some cases in which educational psychology has focused upon scientific research directed toward maximizing the amount of learning by school children, it has also shown a lack of concern for the individual child and in particular a lack of concern for the economically or culturally disadvantaged child. The authors hope that present-day research is more effectively combining scientific and humanitarian approaches to educational psychology.

One other prefatory remark: Hilgard (38) noted that motivation specialists working from physiological and learning theory bases and those working from what might be called a personality and social psychology orientation speak different languages and tend not to cite research performed in traditions other than their own. Chapter 11 reflected the former two positions; the present chapter takes the personality—social point of view and focuses as well on school problems. Rather than continually ask if a topic is really motivational, we now ignore such problems. Much of this chapter treats topics that would be considered learned behavior or problems of individual differences by learning theorists in the behavioristic tradition. These topics are clearly motivational, however, from the personality-social point of view. They are also motivational when viewed by the classroom teacher.

_____ **Relation between Affiliation Need
and Academic Achievement**

Affiliation need, to use Murray's (59) definition, is the need "To form friendships and associations. To greet, join, and live with others. To cooperate and converse socially with others. To love. To join groups." In research such a definition is too vague, and so investigators must use specific tests or questionnaires to measure the existence or amount of this need in a person.

If all of a child's needs worked together, a wise teacher could make use of them to produce appropriate learning. Perhaps when the personality development as well as the intellectual development of the child is considered, this is reasonably well done. However, other interests—play interests, for example—can interfere with purely academic achievement. This conclusion is supported by research on affiliation motivation and its relation to academic achievement: Ringness (66) and McGuire,

Hindsman, King, and Jennings (57) have reported that students whose academic achievement is high compared with their I.Q.'s are less motivated for companionship than students whose achievement is low, relative to their I.Q.'s. Similarly, Grinder (35) has found that high school students show less interest in dating and less need to assert independence if they are high academic achievers.

It would seem, then, that intellectual activity is not a social attribute. Certainly reading is usually done alone; perhaps most studying is. But classroom activity can be made more social through friendly, noncompetitive discussion and group projects, satisfying the affiliation needs of the present low achievers in an intellectual way and possibly awakening affiliative interests in the high achievers. However, E. G. French (29) has found that the adult with high achievement motivation but low affiliation motivation becomes bored or irritated when complimented for "praising each other for making good suggestions, giving everyone a chance to contribute, not becoming impatient with poor suggestions, failing to argue or keeping arguments friendly, etc." This kind of person also performs poorly on a group task following the feeling-oriented approval just mentioned. He will perform better if achievement-oriented approval is given in which the group is praised for working efficiently, reading off all stimuli immediately, trying to organize the task, etc. The opposite result holds for persons with high affiliation motivation but low achievement motivation. These results were secured with Air Force men, but they may be true for children as well. Teachers may wish to produce a better balance of affiliation and achievement needs in their pupils, but it is also important that they accept existing differences in the personality and aptitude of children. This study would suggest, then, that to improve the academic performance of high achievement—low affiliation oriented students may require a different approach from that required for high affiliation—low achievement oriented students.

The teacher must also expect to find some conflict within himself about whether to establish achievement goals or affiliation goals for his students. Ackerman (1) has cited evidence that the teachers whose pupils show the greatest progress in achievement test performance or in increased interest in the subject being taught are also the least considerate, friendly, or congenial. A teacher whose strong academic interest and need to communicate that interest to his pupils may be a good teacher in that he effects an improvement in their academic performance. He may do this, however, at the expense of his reputation as a likable person. But many teachers feel that their purpose is to teach pupils how to get along together, to accept their own feelings and those of their associates, and to be good citizens—and not necessarily to be outstanding in their academic attainments. The teacher who is heavily committed to achievement may lean in the direction represented by the Council for Basic Education (18); the affiliation oriented teacher may lean toward the Summerhill philosophy.

Use of Prestige as a Motive for Study

Coleman (17) advocates using prestige as a motive for study because he believes that the most intellectually talented students will not try to excel intellectually unless they gain recognition thereby. He argues by analogy: If football is the most popular sport in a school, all athletically inclined boys will attempt to excel in football. They will not try out for soccer unless they cannot make the football team. Thus the less talented athletes will engage in the less popular sports. Similarly, insofar

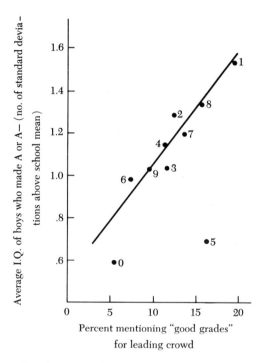

Fig. 12-1. Increased relative intellectual ability of A and A— students with increased percentages of boys mentioning "good grades" as a basis for entering the leading crowd at school. Average I.Q. values are number of standard deviations above school mean. [Figure 3 from Coleman, J. S. "The adolescent subculture and academic achievement," *American Journal of Sociology*, 1960, **65**. Copyright © 1960 by the University of Chicago Press.]

as a motive for recognition, prestige, or perhaps simple affiliation is dominant in a school child, he will pursue the school activities which are the most highly rewarded, shifting to less popular endeavors only if he must in order to gain prestige. This implies that if intellectual activity is not highly rewarded in a school the less intellectually talented youngsters will engage in it. Figure 12-1, taken from Coleman's article, supports this prediction by showing that the intellectual ability (relative to the other students in their school) of A and A— students is greater for schools with a higher frequency of students considering academic brilliance a social asset. Coleman believes that athletic competition serves to displace students' normal interests in classroom learning and advocates interschool competition in academic activities. According to him, if prestige could be gained by learning English literature, the most capable scholars would become the best achievers. As evidence for this belief he points out that two schools not represented in Fig. 12-1 showed a different trend, presumably because they were coeducational private schools in which athletics was de-emphasized. However, some educators would question the use of a competitive urge as a wise motivational device to improve educational achievement.

<hr>

Intrinsic versus Extrinsic Motivation

Should teachers employ extrinsic rewards and motivations for school-work, i.e., rewards not inherently part of the task at hand? Some educators would say, "No, the teaching process should rest on its own merits, with children participating only if they find the curriculum interesting to them, i.e., intrinsically motivating." The proposal for interschool academic competition would then be rejected as based on extrinsic motivation.

The teacher who is concerned with having pupils behave in a certain way right now is likely to find that intrinsic motivation leads the child into patterns of behavior other than what the teacher envisions. Horseplay by boys and primping by girls may be more popular than reading about the Civil War. Faced with disinterest, the history teacher tries to show his pupils that the Civil War is indeed interesting—he may show relics of a battlefield or tell about battles in Vietnam which are similar to those of the Civil War. The purpose of this technique is to help students realize the relations between their own interests in life and the school subjects they are studying. It may help them discover that they do have intrinsic motivations that are intellectual.

It would be folly to suppose, however, that teachers can keep students continually interested in conventional subject matter such as the history of the Civil War. The teacher must therefore do at least one of three things:

1. Introduce extrinsic motivations, either positive or negative, to keep the class working toward the academic goals originally established.

2. Maintain the original learning goals but recognize that children need guidance as a means of changing their motivational patterns to the point where they want to learn the material prescribed.

3. Sacrifice cognitive goals and let the class pursue only the content it currently finds of interest.

The first solution is very widely used. It is almost as widely criticized, even by teachers who employ it. Yet it seems effective—in the short run, at least. Teachers give assignments backed by the implicit promise of reward (good grades, praise, or honor roll listings) or punishment (poor grades, disapproval, or even suspension from school). As a result, pupils study more than they would have without such goals. Rewards and punishments are not always so obvious as this; sometimes teachers appeal more indirectly to extrinsic motives.

The second solution has the virtue of focusing on the end product, and thus tolerates temporary failures yet meets intermediate goals. Education becomes primarily the development of the person, not the implanting of knowledge per se. This view does not de-emphasize the cognitive side of education. The teacher using this technique has a very strong desire to impart an interest in learning; if the choice is between encouraging present acquisition of knowledge and discouraging future inquiry versus encouraging the development of an interest in learning at the expense of present acquisition of knowledge, he may often choose the latter. Later in the chapter is an example of this principle in action, based on research showing that science students develop an interest in previously unpopular topics, not by experience with the unpopular topics but rather by engaging in the activities they originally favor.

The difference between positions 2 and 3 above is largely one of the teacher's intention, expressed in action consistent with that intention. Position 3 implies that the teacher does not really care if pupils do not develop a motivation to learn the facts and skills presently characteristic of well-educated people. The teacher who feels this way may build a curriculum or a classroom schedule around the expressed needs of the children without making any effort to broaden their interests. Although this may be good for their emotional development, it may leave them unprepared to learn vocational skills and unappreciative of many aspects of intellectual life to which they have not been exposed.

The present authors advocate the use of intrinsic motivation when possible, with position 2 seeming most appropriate when intrinsic motivation flags. Position 3 is, on the whole, unsatisfactory even though A. S. Neill makes an interesting, nonempirical, case for it. We further feel that position 1, the use of extrinsic motivation, is often desirable even though potentially dangerous because it may teach children to value recognition rather than accomplishment. Extrinsic motivation seems to have been abundantly present in the highly publicized and apparently quite successful attempt by Samuel Shepard to upgrade school perform-ance in the 23 elementary schools of the Banneker area in St. Louis (7, 77). Thus the Banneker project conformed to the spirit of Coleman's suggestions by including academic contests, pep talks to students about studying, field trips, posters emphasizing the importance of learning, and very blunt talks to parents about why their children should learn more.

_____   **Effectance—The Drive for Competence**

White (85) has spoken of the need for intellectual achievement as one aspect of a general drive for competence. As the word implies, the drive for competence is a motive of desiring to do things well. This drive is called *effectance,* a coined word to insure a distinction between the act of desiring (effectance) and the thing desired (competence). One of the most striking things about White's concept is his emphasis on the im-portance of doing something competently rather than on the completion of the task. The satisfaction associated with this motive comes from the process itself—of reading, doing arithmetic, building a house—and not simply from the attainment of the final goal.

Effectance is central to human activity, particularly if physiological needs are satisfied reasonably well. Effectance is partially composed of the activity and curiosity drives discussed in the previous chapter; how-ever, one tends to speak of curiosity drive as a general, not a specific, drive. That is, a curiosity drive is not associated with seventeenth-century French history, whereas a drive for competence in seventeenth-century French history would be a natural concept for White to discuss.

White also believes that the exercise of competence is often playful, its underlying drive being a need for pleasant sensory stimulation. When competence gives such stimulation, the drive for competence is strength-ened. Teachers should seek ways in which academic accomplishment can yield the pleasant experiences of play.

The implication here is that the drive for competence is at least in part an acquired drive. Two kinds of reinforcements follow competent behavior: social recognition and satisfaction of manipulatory or curi-osity drives. The manipulatory and curiosity drives are *general,* nonphysiological *drives* in the terminology of Chapter 11. Thus much of the reinforcement is primary and may be a satisfaction of a broad general drive for pleasant stimulation, as noted above. However, the social recognition given for competence may in substantial part be a secondary reinforcement based on satisfaction of physiological needs.

After the pairing of social recognition and competent behavior, the person thus reinforced may want to do things well, and will continue his competent behavior—at least temporarily—in the absence of social reinforcement. When this occurs, there is an acquired drive for competence. This drive can be differentiated from a primary drive, such as manipulation, only insofar as some manipulations are competent and others are not. For example, a good tennis player is doing more than manipulating his racquet—he is manipulating it effectively. Therefore, he reflects a drive for competence as well as manipulation.

Achievement Motivation in the Classroom

One may properly ask what is the relation between the drive for competence and the need for achievement (discussed in the previous chapter). More experimental evidence exists about n Achievement, but it would seem that McClelland means much the same by achievement motivation as White means by a drive for competence. Both evidently focus on man's felt needs for accomplishment. Let us consider, however, some shades of meaning on which the two concepts may possibly differ.

McClelland (55) pointed out quite explicitly a connection between achievement motivation, occupational ambition, and industrial growth. In his view the person with high need achievement also shares the Protestant work-ethic which Max Weber (83) considered central to the development of a modern industrial society. This work-ethic is both a belief and a practice of the belief that work is morally good, to be valued for its own sake and as an expression of one's love for God. Not only is it good to work, but God may be expected to bless those who work hard. Thus, according to Weber, a religious basis for ambition was laid in the Protestant Reformation. Middle-class strivings for success—and for its manifestations—have their basis in such a belief.

Achievement motivation seems to include some of the duty-oriented striving Weber discussed. There is not so much emphasis on activity for the sake of the pleasure of the activity itself, the emphasis of White. Motivation for competence may be more concerned with present pleasures; the concerns of achievement motivation are with future accomplishment, future success, or with meeting one's current responsibilities to authority figures such as parents, teachers, employers, or even God.

Both achievement motivation and motivation for competence are useful; but because effort is essential to accomplishment, learning probably comes faster for persons with high achievement motivation than it does for those with low achievement motivation. It seems more likely that effort is expended if a need to achieve exists. A classroom verification comes from an experiment by Kight and Sassenrath (46), who taught high and low achievement motivation college students the principles of classroom achievement tests. After training with a programmed instruction technique like that discussed in Chapter 4, the high achievement motivation group was distinctly superior to the low achievement motivation group on a post-test to measure the amount learned.

Providing there is no job discrimination, motivation for educational achievement is particularly needed in working-class and minority-group children to qualify them for better jobs than their parents held. This poses a problem for the teacher who realizes that many Negroes hold distinctly poorer jobs than their education qualifies them for (81). Such a teacher must nonetheless help his pupils develop achievement motivation, and at the same time try to impart hope that recent legislation and future developments will create better opportunities than pertained in the past.

There is a feeling, among teachers and nonteachers, that certain racial groups have stronger motivations for accomplishment than do others. Although this may appear true, the reasons are not basically racial. Nonetheless, several minority groups still occupy the bottom of the economic ladder in the United States. If a person is poor, and particularly if his recent ancestors have also been poor, he can be expected to lack hope for the future or the motivation to work hard to escape what seems inevitable poverty. From this, it would seem that poor people, regardless of ethnic background, should have low achievement motivation and that middle-class or upper-class people of every ethnic origin should have high achievement motivation. This is very nearly what is found by empirical research on the relation between social class, race, and achievement motivation. For example, Rosen (67) compared American boys of French-Canadian, Italian, Greek, Jewish, Negro, and white Protestant origin from four social classes on achievement motivation scores obtained by the basic McClelland techniques. His principal finding is that boys from higher social classes have generally higher achievement motivation. There is no statistically significant difference among ethnic groups when social class is held constant.

Very possibly it is low achievement motivation with its concomitant reduced intellectual effort that leads to low intelligence scores. A piece of information consistent with this supposition (though not adequate to prove it) is Barberio's finding (6) that among eighth-grade Mexican–American and Anglo–American students matched for intelligence scores, the usual difference in average achievement motivation disappears. Thus either a control for socioeconomic level, as in Rosen's investigation, or a control for intelligence, as in Barberio's study, is sufficient to eliminate average achievement motivation differences between ethnic groups.

In view of these results, teachers often hope to increase their pupils' drive for intellectual and occupational accomplishment. They should be forewarned, however, that the values of the home and community are more influential than those of the school. Thus Kahl (43) reports from a study of minor white collar, skilled, and semiskilled occupational groups:

> There were no cases in which the boy found in schoolwork sufficient intellectual satisfactions to supply its own motivation. And there were no cases where a sympathetic and encouraging teacher had successfully stimulated a boy to high aspirations.

Kahl's results also include Table 12-1, which shows that few sons aspire to college without parental pressure toward college, and fewer plan not to attend college when parental pressure is toward college. The number of boys studied is small and the significance of Kahl's conclusion is limited, but his findings do confirm that teachers have less influence on academic interests and goals than do parents. Therefore, teachers may often feel that they can best influence children by helping parents understand their children's capabilities and the benefits to be gained by continued education.

There is evidence, too, that it is not always so difficult to help students become ambitious. During a summer session Kolb (47) tried to increase n Achievement in a group of high school boys who were of high intel-

TABLE 12-1

Relation between Parental Pressure and Son's Aspiration, 24 Boys[a]

	Parental pressure toward college	
Son's aspiration	No	Yes
College	4	8
No college	11	1

[a] From Kahl, J. A., "Educational and occupational aspirations of 'common man' boys," *Harvard Educational Review*, 1953, **23**, 186–203. Copyright © 1953 by President and Fellows of Harvard College.

ligence but had been doing poor schoolwork. These boys were told the characteristics of persons with high achievement motivation, they played a race car game which gave them an opportunity to see how risk-taking related to n Achievement, and they discussed the nature of their responses in that game. They also learned to score their own n Achievement stories, discussed the conflict between affiliation need and achievement need, underwent counseling about life goals, and played a business game which allowed them to exhibit their achievement motivation in something like real life. The boys trained in this manner showed a substantial increase in n Achievement over the summer, whereas comparable boys attending the same summer session but not trained in achievement motivation failed to show any increase. Much of this improvement was maintained for the following eight months. Among boys of a high social class, but not among boys of a low social class, there was also a greater improvement in course grades over the next semester and over the next year and a half for the trainees in achievement motivation than there was for the other boys, even though the summer session was intended to be remedial for both groups.

Similarly, Gray and Klaus (31) attempted to improve academic aptitude and achievement motivation for very young disadvantaged children, starting two or three summers before their entrance to first grade and measuring their performance in the first grade. Data on resulting achievement motivation changes have not yet been published; however, Gray, Klaus, Miller, and Forrester (32) have given a lengthy description of the philosophy and methods used to develop greater achievement motivation. They believe that achievement motivation includes two basic components: ability to continue effort toward a goal over a long period of time (persistence) and ability to postpone or accept postponement of gratification in order to achieve long-term goals.

Gray *et al.* gave training in persistence by such methods as requiring a child to throw a ball at a wastebasket from a position just beyond the greatest distance from which he could frequently land it in the basket. Adults then encouraged him every time he tried to throw the ball in the basket. Delay of gratification was taught by giving each child frequent opportunities to choose between immediate and delayed reward, with clear indications that the delayed reward would be greater. A 1-hour delay might be the maximum early in the study; later 2- or 3-day delays became possible.

In Chapter 11 we saw a mathematical prediction that students with high achievement motivation would prefer tasks of intermediate difficulty. On the other hand students with low achievement motivation or high test anxiety were predicted to prefer tasks of either very low or very high difficulty. Isaacson (41) checked this prediction, and found that men with high achievement motivation do indeed tend to select college "majors" of medium difficulty, defined by the ratio of average grades to average brightness of the students in the field. However, men with low achievement motivation or high test anxiety did not exhibit the predicted relationship, nor did either group of women except in minor data analyses. Thus the theory of achievement motivation received only partial confirmation in this study.

Level of Aspiration

Level of aspiration is the degree of performance a person expects of himself in a specific situation. It may be realistic, as when a high school student plans to finish a theme in an evening, or unrealistic, as when another student expects to study for an exam in half an hour. As children grow older, their levels of aspiration tend to be compatible with their abilities and past performance. Figure 12-2 summarizes the results of a college classroom demonstration (50) of such compatibility. In this demonstration the experimenter gave 21 trials on a letter substitution task, having each of 45 students count the number of substitutions made on each trial and predict the number to be made on the next trial. Each student was instructed to work as fast as he could. What the students

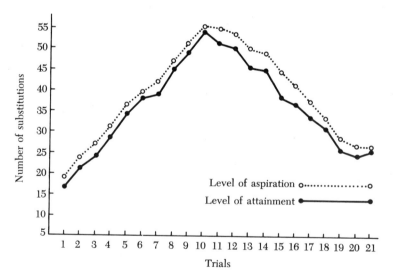

Fig. 12-2. Parallel increases and decreases in performance (attainment) and anticipated performance (aspiration) as trial length on a letter substitution task increases and then decreases. Figure 1 from Lachman (50).

did not know was that the first trial was 30 seconds long, the second was 35 seconds long, and so on with 5-second increases up to the tenth trial of 75 seconds, after which successive trials were 5 seconds shorter than their immediate predecessors. This procedure ensured that, on the average, the number of substitutions increased from trial to trial up to trial 10 and then declined on succeeding trials. Figure 12-2 shows such a performance curve, labeled *level of attainment*. Just above the attainment curve is the level of aspiration curve, which has a very similar shape. This figure shows that level of aspiration increases as performance increases, and decreases as performance decreases. Furthermore, the fact that the level of aspiration curve is above the level of attainment curve shows that the students continually thought they could do a little better the next time than they had just done. Figure 12-2 indicates that, on the whole, students are indeed realistic in their level of aspiration for a task they do repeatedly and receive information about. However, if teachers do not tell students what they accomplish, the students' levels of aspiration may become unrealistic.

A major difference between level of aspiration and achievement motivation is that the former is a specific expectation associated with a certain task, not a general motivational tendency applying to a broad class of achievement-oriented activities. As Fig. 12-2 shows, it is easy to shift the level of aspiration substantially by changing the amount accomplished. Corresponding changes in achievement motivation are more difficult.

Not only can level of aspiration be affected by controlling performance; one can also increase performance by suggesting what level a person should aspire to: Bryan and Locke (12) showed that students performing an arithmetic task could be trained to perform as well as an originally superior group if each subject were told how many addition problems to aim to complete on each trial. This motivational training also increased the trained group's judgment of effort expended per trial, compared with that of the untrained group.

Level of aspiration for an entire school course can also be measured. Rosenfeld and Zander (68) tried to predict the behavior of mathematics students from the behavior of teachers, as perceived by their students. They found that students desired to earn about the same grade they felt capable of earning. This congruence of desire and capability was greatest if students perceived their math teacher to be fair in grading and to approve of them relative to other members of the class. In general, students wanted to conform to their teacher's demands if they liked him, if he was fair, if he apparently approved of them, and if he gave approval when they had done something well. Unearned approval, and earned or unearned coercion, did not lead to a desire to conform. In summary, this study indicates that students work up to capacity or want to conform to school demands if they approve of their teacher because of his approval of them or if they appreciate his general likability or fairness.

Heretofore, level of aspiration was discussed as averaged across a group of people who were treated alike. However, there are wide differences in level of aspiration among the members of such groups. Sears (73) showed that different patterns of level of aspiration were associated with persons of different personality characteristics. Children whose levels of aspiration for school tasks were slightly above their attainments tended to be self-confident in their attitudes toward school, realistic, and extroverted. Children whose level of aspiration greatly exceeded their attainments had low self-confidence, were tense and sensitive, and were poorly adjusted socially. A group whose attainments exceeded their aspirations seemed self-conscious, defensive, and yet eager to impress others. Thus, several desirable personal qualities are found most frequently in persons whose levels of aspiration are realistic and least frequently in persons whose aspirations are unrealistic.

Motivational Aspects of Knowledge of Results (Informative Feedback)

The goal setting procedure used by Bryan and Locke (12) to improve arithmetic performance was a motivational device that required comparing one's goal with actual accomplishment on each trial. Occasionally such a device will stimulate students, but teachers hesitate to use it continually lest it become irksome or boring. A related procedure is routine in classrooms, however, and should be encouraged whenever possible: Students should learn whether their answers are correct and be told the correct answer again.

Learning whether an answer is correct is potentially a reward, just as food is a reward in an animal learning experiment. In order to be an effective reward, it must be desired by the student, probably either for its social value—approval from the teacher, parent, or classmate—or to satisfy the primary drive aspects of the drive for competence. Where approval is the motive, it would seem that warm and personal recognition would be most effective. For this reason teachers often write special approving notes on examination papers or homework papers.

Page (62) has demonstrated that such notes are indeed useful. He had 74 teachers divide their classes into three groups (No Comment, Free Comment, and Specific Comment). On one objective examination the No Comment group received normal scoring of their papers but no

additional comments. On the same examination the teacher put whatever special comment she thought appropriate on each paper in the
Free Comment group, and the following comments on the papers of
the Specific Comment group, depending on the grades obtained:

A   "Excellent! Keep it up."
B   "Good work. Keep at it."
C   "Perhaps try to do still better?"
D   "Let's bring this up."
F   "Let's raise this grade."

On the next objective examination it was found that the Free Comment group did best, the Specific Comment group next best, and the
No Comment group worst. The two comment groups were distinctly
better than the other group but did not differ appreciably from each
other. Interestingly, it was the F students who improved most after
receiving comments on their exam papers.

Another aspect of knowledge of results is that being told the correct
answer after a response is something in addition to a reward per se. It
facilitates learning over and above the effect of telling a person he was
correct or incorrect (52). This is because learning requires repeated
informational stimulus presentation as well as reward. Strictly speaking,
the presentation of information is not motivational; it is discussed here
because reward and knowledge of correct response are so often combined in teaching.

There is a difference between the value of knowledge of results (informative feedback) in the laboratory and in the classroom. A research
laboratory can isolate separate variables and determine their individual
effects; in the classroom several variables may act in combination. There
is little doubt that paired associates learning as described in Chapter 3
requires informative feedback, in that case, presentation of the stimulus
and response terms following the subject's guessing of a response to the
stimulus. But in many classroom situations there is so much information
provided by class discussion, teachers' lectures, and reading that failure
to provide specific knowledge of results on an examination may not
appreciably retard learning.

This seems to have happened in an experiment by Ross (69), in which
there was also informative feedback in that test questions missed by a
large number of students were discussed after the test. Four groups of
students all had that kind of knowledge of results but differed in the
degree to which they knew their own individual test scores or were
allowed to look at their individual test papers. Ross found no differences
in group performance and noted that most students who were not told
their test scores were able to estimate them fairly accurately nonetheless.

Brown (11) conducted a pair of experiments showing that having

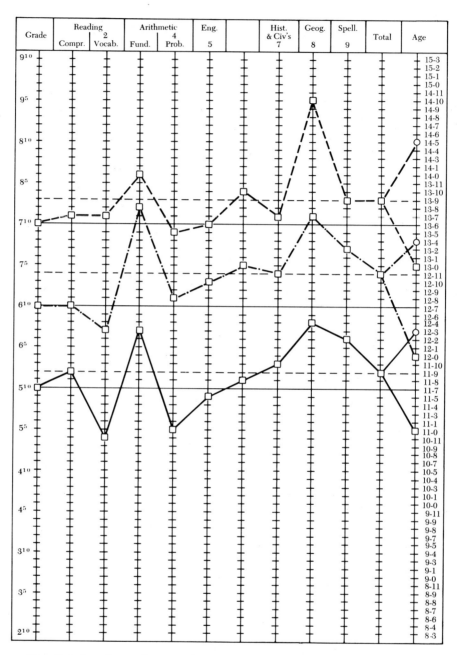

Fig. 12-3. Sample graphic record of pupil progress for the Metropolitan Achievement Tests. (The circles on the farthest entries to the right represent mental ages; the boxes on the far right represent chronological ages.) This figure is Fig. 16 from Greene, Jorgensen, and Gerberich (33) and was originally published in Allen *et al.* (2).

fifth- or seventh-grade children graph the number of correct arithmetic problems following each 10-minute drill period in a 10- or 20-day series led to superior performance compared with conditions in which the children could not check on their accomplishments.

Possibly students would benefit from more information even about their long-term progress. They typically receive feedback about performance on individual assignments, and they receive grades in most schools. However, there is relatively little review from year to year of information previously learned and there is little setting of long-term goals for children other than the mechanical ones of high school or college graduation. Perhaps encouraging children to keep year by year graphs of their performance on standardized achievement tests would be a helpful way of showing pupils how they are progressing from, say, the average performance of a fourth-grader one year to the average performance of a sixth-grader in the next if that is a year of rapid improvement.

Figure 12-3 shows a 3-year record of achievement in nine fields (2). It shows general improvement in all subjects tested from the fifth to the sixth and on to the seventh grades, with particular strengths appearing in arithmetic fundamentals and geography each year. Figure 12-4 shows the same data replotted in ten separate small graphs. This replotting would be particularly useful in a so-called *cumulative record blank* because several years' data could easily be plotted in each small graph to show the trend of progress in each subject year by year. Cumulative record blanks, either in graph or tabular form, are often used by school systems to record the physical, emotional, and intellectual growth of each pupil. It is our belief that they would also be useful motivational tools to show children and parents. [See Bauernfeind (9) for a discussion of "goal cards" which are used in a similar manner.] However, it seems important that when these tools are used, the emphasis should not be upon standings of children compared with others in their class. Rather, as in the present graph, the teacher should convey to the parent or child if the child is developing more quickly or more slowly than he did in former years and whether his performance is above or below the national average for that grade level. Some educators would hesitate to present the latter information lest children become discouraged at poor performance or elated by strong achievement. Neither reaction is necessary, however. Precise information on attainments, together with intelligent and sympathetic counseling of children, should help them to be realistic about their progress without feeling pride or shame for anything other than the degree to which they are fulfilling their capabilities.

One long-term effect of knowledge of performance is the effect of college grades upon occupational choice. Davis (22) found that men

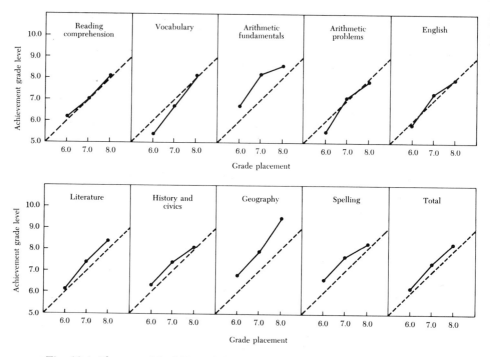

Fig. 12-4. The material of Fig. 12-3, except mental age and chronological age are replotted in separate growth curves for each subject and for total achievement. (Grade levels are expressed in decimal form rather than year and month, with 6.0 here corresponding to 5–10 in the previous figure, for example. Dotted lines show the trend to be expected if a student were at the national average every year.)

are more likely to enter the physical sciences, biological sciences, social sciences, humanities and fine arts, law, and medicine at professional levels if they have high college grade point averages. What makes Davis' finding surprising is that it is true regardless of the quality of the students in the college studied. Thus men who reached at least the semi-final stages of the National Merit Scholarship tests in high school are more likely to have good college grades and enter the fields mentioned above if they attend a college where the average scholastic aptitude of students is low than if their college has a higher quality of student. Since these semifinalists are all in the top 3% of American high school talent, they all have the intellectual ability to warrant entry into highly intellectual fields. However, rather than judge their talents by absolute standards, they apparently compare themselves with the people immediately around them and let grades based on that comparison affect their career choice. If a high school teacher wants to ensure that a student goes on to graduate school, it appears that she should encourage him to attend a college whose average student is less talented than he.

_____ **Praise, Reproof, and Discipline**

As a general rule schoolchildren perform better if they are praised for their work than if they are blamed or told it is of poor quality (45). This effect is somewhat independent of the knowledge of results effect just discussed. Knowledge of results confirms a correct response or corrects an incorrect one, and thus affects the response the next time the same problem appears. Any praise or reproof also affects the pupil's motivation to make responses of any kind related to the school situation. A child who is highly praised for making an effort in sports, drawing, arithmetic, or some other activity may be expected to put forth greater effort the next time.

Because these two effects function independently, it is possible to tell students their work is good or poor in order to motivate them without really giving accurate information about their performance. There is an ethical question as to the appropriateness of such action, which you must judge for yourself on the basis of its effects, the teacher's intentions, and whether the pupil eventually is told the truth. Thus in one experiment, Thompson and Hunnicutt (79) compared groups of fifth-grade students in a situation where certain children were to be told they did poorly on each trial of a clerical task and others were to be told they did well on each trial, regardless of their actual performance. Do you see the arguments for and against using such a procedure?

Teachers usually do well to praise all work that merits it, but the results summarized by Kennedy and Willcutt (45) suggest it is wise to consider special goading for underachievers (students who accomplish less than their aptitude allows) and for very bright adolescents. Teachers should adapt their practices to the individual, doing what seems most successful with each person. Reproof, when administered, should be gentle and should set standards for future performance, rather than simply judge the past.

What about punishment for misbehavior as contrasted with reproof for poor work or little effort? Should children have as little restriction on their behavior as is consistent with their health and safety, so long as they do not infringe on the rights of their associates? This policy is a desirable goal but it may have to be modified in highly structured school systems because some regimentation will become necessary if the structure is to survive. Thus rules about loitering in the corridors may become necessary to prevent pedestrian traffic jams even though the rights of other students are only indirectly infringed upon by the loiterers.

Many teachers believe in a more stringent policy than that advocated here. Our purpose is not to urge them to change but merely to examine the effects of various disciplinary procedures that are employed once a policy has been developed regarding limitations to be set upon student behavior. One line of research (48, 49) emphasized the nature of the disciplinary act: If a teacher is specific and clear in telling a kindergarten child what to do ("Johnny, stop shoving Billy!"), a child watching the disciplinary act is also more likely to follow that instruction. However, if a teacher is rough, shouts instructions, appears angry, or grabs an offender sharply, a child watching the act is likely to continue misbehaving himself or display signs of agitation. When pupils of punitive and nonpunitive first-grade teachers are compared, it is found that the former mention physically aggressive activities as serious school violations more often than do the latter, who point to breaches of school rules such as prohibitions against chewing gum or talking. The investigators also found evidence that pupils of punitive teachers emphasized lack of ability to control physical aggression, as if the disciplinary pressure of their teachers evoked aggressive responses against the will of the children.

The effect of physical punishment as a controller of behavior in animals was discussed in Chapter 11. Even if its effects were more permanent, physical punishment does not seem justifiable in the school system. In some instances (extinction of avoidance responses), a response continued after it became unnecessary as a means of preventing punishment. Such evidence and other information about children who continue acts which are punished (86) should make it apparent that in addition to the emotional effects just noted, punishment may sometimes have just the opposite effects of those implied by the proverb "Spare the rod and spoil the child."

Many aggressive, destructive children have received a fully adequate degree of punishment and may even have come to desire punishment as a means of recognition. Teachers concerned with disciplinary problems should become acquainted with the modes of treatment used by psychiatrists and psychiatrically oriented teachers in residential care of extremely aggressive children. Redl and Wineman* (65) say, for example,

> We, too, started out with the assumption that a child-acceptant and affectionate atmosphere is one of the most important primary conditions in a treatment home. We soon had to learn, however, that children, over and above wanting love, affection, and friendliness, demand an additional role from the adults who have charge of their lives. This role is that of the adult as a "protector."

* F. Redl and D. Wineman, *The aggressive child.* © 1957, Free Press, Glencoe, Illinois.

These authors go on to say that the children they were treating needed protection from the other children's temper tantrums and extremely destructive behavior. In addition to defining limits on the aggressive behavior of other children, adults in the home could help a particular child by protecting him from his own impulses and unintentional losses of emotional control. Furthermore, the children needed to be protected from moblike events in which the whole group became committed to an emotional outburst. Chamberlain (14) similarly emphasized the role of the group, rather than the individual, in producing a disciplinary problem in the classroom.

Although numerous other suggestions could be added, most teachers will find that maintaining discipline in the school depends upon developing a wise balance of the affectionate and the protective functions which Redl and Wineman discuss. The limits drawn for a classroom will be somewhat stricter than those in a home for delinquent children, of course. At the same time, the school schedule should include times (noons and recesses, for example) when very little restriction upon the children's activity is imposed. It is important, too, not to overemphasize the relationship between children's behavior and reward and punishment. Otherwise a child comes to feel that he is only liked if he is good. To some extent every child must experience rejection when he misbehaves; but in the extreme he loses a sense of self-worth because he is not permitted to be satisfied with himself as he is but must continually meet new demands of his teachers and parents in order to keep their favor. Similarly, it is easy to use punishment in such a way that school work seems degrading. If the penalty for misbehavior is an additional study assignment, the lesson to the pupil is obvious: Studying is unpleasant and to be avoided as much as is possible by being good. Fantini (26) is one of several educators who have discovered that it is possible to reverse this lesson by forbidding students to study or to do work projects in class if they are misbehaving. Such a policy helps to make school work a privilege rather than a duty.

_____ **Contingent Reinforcement versus Teacher Warmth:**
Contradictory Principles?

Some psychologists who are committed to the use of reinforcement principles in child rearing and education will take exception to the above discussion, particularly to its injunction not to overemphasize the relationship between children's behavior and reward and punishment. Here the possible conflict is between principles developed in the psychology of learning and those stemming largely from clinical experience. Gray *et al.* (32) have explicitly recognized that a problem of this kind existed in their project in which they attempted to develop greater achievement motivation and intellectual activity in preschool children from culturally deprived homes. On the one hand, the children seemed starved for affection; the experimenters wanted to satisfy that need without making the children so attached to them they would be unable to accept the end of the association between children and experimenters. On the other hand, the experimenters wished to use attention and encouragement as reinforcers of desirable behavior; therefore they did not wish to give it indiscriminately.

It should be clear that making reinforcement contingent upon desirable behavior can lead to effective teaching so long as the teacher keeps checking to be certain that the reinforcer is indeed reinforcing for each child receiving it. Harris, Johnston, Kelley, and Wolf (36) have shown, for example, that giving attention to a 3-year-old girl whenever she stood on her feet strengthened her tendency to stand on her feet whereas a later reversed procedure of reinforcing time spent off her feet strengthened the opposite tendency. Now why did this girl originally fail to stand up in the nursery school where she was observed? Apparently crawling or sitting on the floor was an infantile response which she made only in the presence of strangers. Harris *et al.* showed that standing could be either increased or decreased by appropriate reinforcement; they eventually instituted consistent reinforcement of standing. It is claimed that 5 weeks of about 12.5 hours of such training led to a degree of progress normal for at least 5 or 6 months under other methods of treatment. This claim requires documentation and may be overoptimistic in view of Seeman, Barry, and Ellinwood's (75) results in a different kind of situation. They found a significant improvement in an aggressive group of second- and third-grade children given play therapy for 37 once-a-week sessions of unstated duration, compared with no change among untreated aggressive children. If the play therapy sessions were 1½ hours or less in length, that method may have been more efficient than the reinforcement method just discussed. The important point here is that methods other than formal application of reinforcement are also effective with children. There is much to be said for play therapy, a treatment in which children are allowed to make responses in play which would be punished or at least nonreinforced in other settings. Very possibly some differential reinforcement of acceptable and unacceptable behaviors takes place in such therapy; the point is simply that the *procedures* of the play therapist and the "reinforcement therapist" do differ and may both be effective.

Sears and Hilgard (74) have called attention to warmth (also called *nurturance*) as a variable which facilitates school learning. One could call this warmth *noncontingent reinforcement,* i.e., reinforcement of everything a child does. If this is an accurate analysis, warmth would encourage children to follow their natural tendencies, which we would hope would be good ones. In actuality the warm teacher presumably more often rewards approaches to her than avoidance of her, thus increasing social behavior and possibly also increasing dependence on other people. In any case, Cogan (15) has found that teachers who are rated high (by eighth-grade pupils) on integrative, affiliative, and nurturant tendencies are also rated as teachers for whom these pupils do a great deal of both required and voluntary schoolwork. This result contradicts one by Ackerman (1) cited earlier in the chapter, however, and leaves the question of teacher warmth unresolved. A better established fact is that warmth provided by a woman in an experimental situation can lead a child to make that woman a model and to imitate her behavior in detail—even imitating her aggressive behavior (4a, 4b).

The authors believe that warmth expressed by an adult, independent of a child's behavior, will increase the child's liking for the adult and lead him to imitate the adult's behavior, and possibly to better learning, depending upon other aspects of the situation, such as pressures used by other teachers. Such warmth need not be a completely noncontingent reinforcement pattern but may represent reinforcement of a broader class of behaviors than some learning theorists would advocate. It may also involve reinforcing more behaviors selected by the child and fewer selected by the teacher than some psychologists would recommend.

<hr>

School Marks as Motivating Stimuli

Though the effect of school marks (grades) upon college admission or entry into certain professions is well known, much too little factual information (as opposed to opinion) exists about the motivational effects of those marks or of specific marking systems. One pair of empirical studies (3, 4) compared the eighth- and ninth-grade performance of pupils graded on a 1, 2, 3, 4, or F basis with the performance of pupils in the same school a year earlier who had been graded in the eighth grade on the basis of how well they were living up to their own capabilities and in the ninth grade on the 1, 2, 3, 4, F basis. These investigations, which were an attempt to evaluate the effects of an administrative change in policy on grading, showed no indication that the grading procedure affected the amount learned either in the eighth grade while the groups were being graded differently or in the ninth grade when delayed effects of differential grading might have appeared. This was true both for academic subjects and for course grades in a ninth-grade group guidance course in which the authors anticipated that mental health benefits attributable to being graded in accordance with a pupil's own potential might have appeared. One possible reason for the failure to find group effects in the ninth grade is that teachers may have adapted their old grading curves to a new group of students, giving about the same number of 1's, 2's, etc., as before, regardless of a change in performance. However, because the eighth-grade study measured achievement with standardized tests, it is probable that there was no learning difference in either grade.

An obvious effect of grading students' work is that it provides a means for teachers to exert pressure upon students. Wittrock (88) has shown how such pressure by a university professor upon student teachers can lead them to get their pupils to learn more than pupils of student teachers without such pressure. Fourteen student teachers in junior and senior high school classes were told that their educational psychology and student teaching grades would depend on the amount of gain their pupils showed in standardized achievement test performance, compared with the gains showed by pupils of 14 other student teachers who were not graded on this basis. The former group (experimental group) of student teachers did somehow induce their pupils to learn more on the average in their own social studies and English classes and perhaps also in their government and history classes. Since these student teachers did not know what achievement tests were being used, these learning differences are not to be explained by direct teaching of the test questions.

While this experiment shows that academic performance can be improved if a teacher is motivated to produce more learning by his pupils, it also shows that some undesirable consequences of this motivation may occur. Student teachers who had English classes (but not social studies or government and history classes) received substantially lower ratings from pupils in the course than did student teachers for the control group. This may reflect either resistance to the demands of the experimental teachers or a chance difference in the interest generated by the three experimental teachers of English compared with the three control teachers of English.

Another way grades may be used as a means of control is to require a good deal of written work in a course. Sometimes this is an absolute requirement; in other cases more is required for a high grade than for a low one. A variation of these procedures has been proposed as a way of maximizing the work done by the student and minimizing the grading done by the teacher. Lindsley (51) suggests that since learning will be improved by increased assignments, teachers can produce greater learning without burdening themselves if they will assign a weekly report but advise their students that a weekly drawing will be held in class to determine whose papers will be graded. The proportion of papers graded is set low enough to make the grading task feasible for the teacher but high enough to keep the students motivated. This is an application of the partial reinforcement principle described in Chapter 3. The weekly drawing in class is intended to show the students that the selection of papers to be graded is random and to increase their interest in the classroom activities.

Teachers should be aware that grades also may affect students' attitudes on controversial social issues. If, for example, students who disapproved of socialized medicine were assigned to write essays in favor of it, there would probably be a substantial change in their attitude toward the matter. This change would be large in any case but would be larger if an "A" grade were given than if a "D" grade were given. In the study being discussed (10), the grades were assigned randomly rather than on the basis of merit. However, one would expect the same phenomenon to occur if merit were the basis for grading. Note that the effect of the grade per se is smaller than the effect of writing contrary to one's previous view.

Grades also motivate students who have done well to continue to do well. Fay (27) found that students receiving an "A" on their first of four semester examinations in psychology maintained the same level of performance for the later exams and the final examination if they were told their grade for each examination. If they were not told how well they did, the students who received "A's" on the first examination wrote consistently poorer papers on later tests. Though this effect was minimal or nonexistent for students receiving other grades, its existence is one more reason to tell students about their progress in school.

_____ **An Alternative to School Marks: Token Reinforcers**

Teachers often doubt the advisability of assigning letter grades, particularly in elementary school, because some children derive so little encouragement or reinforcement from these grades. To the extent that pupils differ in their ability to do well in a course, grades seem to reward not only the people who work hard but also the people who find the work easy. For this reason many schools have abandoned letter grades for young children. Nonetheless, teachers need techniques of rewarding good academic performance in order to foster it.

One such reward method is token reinforcement. Pupils are told what is required of them to receive certain tokens such as blue, yellow, or pink stamps. They are also told the exchange value of the tokens, several yellow pages of stamps being worth a secondhand bicycle and a page of blue stamps being worth a trip to a movie, for example.

The use of these tokens has some resemblance to grading but differs in at least three respects: (a) Different standards can be set for each child if desired, in order to eliminate unequal competition due to different levels of ability. (b) The rewards offered are larger and more concrete than grades even though children do recognize the long-term importance of grades. (c) Rewards can be offered for increased quantities of work or for improved conduct, whereas grades usually emphasize quality of work.

Wolf, Giles, and Hall (89) compared 15 sixth-grade, poor reading students given token reinforcement of the kind described above (and other remedial techniques involving reinforcement procedures) with a control group of 15 sixth graders of equal reading ability who did not receive remedial treatment. In a year's remedial program the specially treated group gained 1.5 years in overall academic achievement, compared with a 0.8 year gain for the typical member of the control group. The remedial group also showed superior improvement in report card grades assigned in regular classes by teachers other than those giving remedial training (this training was given after school, on weekends, and on holidays).

The effectiveness of the token reinforcement program seems clear; however, its cost averaged $250.00 per student in the school year. This cost included $225.00 for redeeming stamps and $25.00 for parties given for improvement on a report card at the end of each 6-week period. There was additional cost for a teacher, two teaching assistants, and two Neighborhood Youth Corps employees. Since remedial sessions were conducted for 2½ hours on each weekday and 3 hours on Saturday mornings, the cost of the program was substantial.

In evaluating the practicality of a token reinforcement remedial program there is another factor to consider in addition to cost and achievement: The token reinforcement group learned more than the control group, but its members also spent about 15½ more hours per week in an educational program. Would a very different remedial program requiring the same additional time commitment be equally effective? It is probable that the degree of cooperation by the children involved would be greater with a token reinforcement method than with some other methods. However, there is no direct evidence that the overall effect of the token reinforcement method would be superior. Nor, despite the arguments in favor of token reinforcement in preference to class marks, is it certain that a token reinforcement program within regular class hours would be superior to a traditional classroom method. However, a minimum expectation is that the children would increase the frequency of specific responses rewarded by tokens. Wolf *et al.* found this to be true in their study, and O'Leary and Becker (61) found a substantial decline in disruptive behavior (such as pushing, chewing gum, and name calling) among emotionally disturbed schoolchildren following the institution of a token reinforcement system in which the tokens were ratings of good behavior and could be exchanged for candy, pennants, etc. Kolb's (47) use of remedial summer instruction, mentioned earlier in this chapter, seems to have been less successful than the token reinforcement method now under consideration.

—————————— **Fruitful Uses and Limitations of Competition**

To what extent should the schools foster competitive activity of any kind, be it athletic, academic, musical, or social? The popularity of athletic contests and the activities of advertisers and merchants make it clear that competition is popular and ever-present, at least in capitalistic societies. Even the laboratory rat will run faster in a two-rat race if the winner is consistently rewarded than if one or the other of the rats is rewarded on each trial but not on the basis of performance (44).

One problem with competitive rewards, whether with animals or people, is that they naturally provide more encouragement to winners than to losers. The study just mentioned had to be stopped prematurely because one animal in each competitive pair began to be the consistent winner; it may be inferred that once this occurred the inferior one would have extinguished his running response just as described in an earlier chapter for animals run individually. This suggests that classroom competition should be so arranged that children do not compete "out of their league" but rather are striving to excel with children so close to their own level that each will have a share of the recognition offered to the winners. This principle is followed in scheduling athletic contests between schools but is sometimes neglected in dealing with children who would like to develop certain skills but do not expect to be superior in them.

A great deal of expert opinion asserts that even the restrained competition favored above is excessive. One psychiatrist (21) makes the point that education for a vocation must teach that most occupations involve heavy competitive pressure, but that education for life in general should minimize competitive activity. He emphasizes that it is unnecessary to be competitive in going to the movies, in social contacts, in reading, hiking, or in making love. Therefore, it is urged that the schools teach youngsters to view each other as friends, not rivals, and to spend some of their leisure relaxing rather than transforming even the most intimate relationships into competitive ones.

One problem with expert opinion is that it is sometimes presented without evidence, so that one accepts it because of the eminence of the expert or rejects it because it does not ring true. Davidson (21) supports his argument by pointing to bad effects of extreme competition. He asserts that in competitive situations we often develop hostility toward rivals and anxiety over our own failure but cannot express them because of social demands that we be polite and restrained in the expression of emotion. This assertion is not documented by experimental material, but it is supported by the clinical experience of many psychiatrists and clinical psychologists.

Fortunately, there is also experimental evidence on the effects of competition. Hurlock (40) found that groups of elementary school children urged to outdo other groups on a test of arithmetic speed and accuracy did in fact excel children who were not instructed to compete. This shows that groups working together in competition will do better than groups working without instructions to compete. We may call the former groups *internally cooperative, externally competitive* groups, or *internally cooperative* groups, for a brief identification.

A related study by Deutsch (23) compared groups in which the members competed with each other for grades (internally competitive groups) with groups in which competition was between other groups (internally cooperative groups). The tasks were to find group solutions to puzzles and to problems in getting along with people. The reward was that the one individual in an internally competitive group judged to have made the most significant contribution to the group solutions over a period of several weeks would be excused from writing an assigned paper and be given a top grade. For internally cooperative groups, each member of the group received that reward if his group was judged best.

Deutsch found that the internally cooperative groups performed fully as well (if anything, slightly better) as the internally competitive groups. In addition to working effectively, they were more harmonious: They made more friendly remarks to each other during discussion and fewer aggressive remarks. When asked to rate their co-workers' performance, the internally cooperative group members replied more favorably than did the internally competitive group members. Furthermore, the internally cooperative group members were more practical in that they divided the job of writing solutions to problems; the internally competitive group members tended to let one person write the whole report without much help once the discussion of the problem was finished.

This study suggests that life may be more harmonious if one is allowed to compete by cooperating, i.e., to be motivated for higher accomplishment because of competition with outsiders but to be working with, rather than against, one's closest associates. Even here anxieties and hostilities may arise, but they are probably easier to express to one's co-workers with whom there is no competition. However, even intergroup competition of the kind involved in Deutsch's internally cooperative groups may have harmful effects. Presumably the psychiatrist's warnings against continual competition would apply even here.

We have seen earlier in this chapter that Coleman advocated interschool competition in intellectual achievement. Another of Coleman's papers (16) uses the Deutsch experiment just cited as support for this interschool rivalry. It is believed that those who live or work in institutions such as jails, factories, or even schools develop ways of opposing the people in charge. Workers learn how to keep from working too hard, and students learn to keep the grade curve low enough that A's can be earned without undue effort. Coleman suggests, however, that the efficiency of performance in Deutsch's internally cooperative group indicates that students can learn to do better work, or at least equally good work with less emotional stress, if interschool competition in scholarship is encouraged.

An experiment by Maller (53) appears to contradict Deutsch and therefore to raise questions about Coleman's proposals. Maller had over 800 children alternate between internally cooperative group instructions and internally competitive group instructions while doing simple addition problems. In six pairs of 2-minute sessions there were consistent differences in amount of work done, favoring the internally competitive condition, or "motive of self," as Maller calls it. The interpretation of this study is not clear because it is not known if knowledge of group performance was given after each 2-minute session. In view of this and other limitations of this very old experiment, it seems reasonable to accept Deutsch's conclusions rather than Maller's.

―――――――――――――――――   **Benefits of Having Students Work Together**

This section treats cooperation in learning, in contrast to the preceding section on competition. Some material here could be covered in a chapter on social psychology; however, we place it here as a means of emphasizing its motivational aspects.

A schoolchild may often profit more if he can do some of his studies in class, or even at home, with at least one other child. To some extent the advantage of working together is social: Because the affiliation motive is very high in human beings, people prefer to do things together than alone. However, there are also some nonmotivational variables operating in group situations. For example, working in large groups can be a disadvantage in that active participation is limited since not every one can talk at the same time. The following ten points are some of the factors to be considered in deciding whether to use individualized instruction or to have pupils work in teams. Note that teams may have different functions—some may do drill work as a unit, others may prepare reports together or hold discussions or construct apparatus in a laboratory. Some of the points listed below apply more to one type of team than to another.

1. Teachers tend to talk much more than students in a "discussion group" and to give a high proportion of pontifical statements.

2. The percentage of time a person talks in a discussion group decreases as the size of the group increases.

3. The percentage of time anyone says something to a specific person in a discussion group decreases as the size of the group increases.

4. The amount of information presented in a group tends to be constant regardless of the size of the group.

5. Individuals studying alone may get less feedback (knowledge of correctness or incorrectness) than when they work in groups.

6. Students often but not always do better work in groups than when studying alone or listening to lectures.

7. Working in an all-student team will focus the instructional task at the students' level rather than the teacher's perception of the students' level or the teacher's goal for the students' level.

8. Compatible student teams may be more effective than incompatible ones.

9. Nonparticipators may be helped by judicious grouping of team members.

10. Setting of educational goals by a group of students may lead to greater commitment to the task than if the goals are set by the teacher.

Learning Factors in Group Situations

Now let us consider these ten points more fully. Stephan and Mishler (78) studied 81 different 50-minute discussion class meetings at Princeton University to find out how much the most talkative person in each meeting talked, how much the second-most talkative person talked, etc. Figure 12-5 shows that they found the instructor or leader (L) the most talkative, supporting point 1 above. They did not investigate the degree to which the instructor was pontifical or directive in what he said; however, Flanders (28) has commented on this point. Figure 12-5 also shows that there is an uneven distribution of conversation by the members of the class, with the preponderance of discussion coming from the leader and a very few other class members.

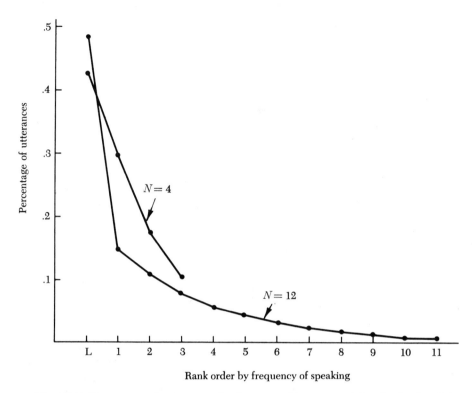

Rank order by frequency of speaking

Fig. 12-5. Percentage of utterances (uninterrupted statements) by the leader (L) and other discussion group members ranked by frequency of speaking. A comparison of trends for groups of different sizes ($N = 4$ and $N = 12$). Based on theoretical values from Table 2 of Stephan and Mishler (78).

Note, too, that Fig. 12-5 provides data for two class sizes—4 and 12. The leader does not decrease the amount of time he talks in the larger class (in fact he increases his amount slightly) but the most frequently participating students do decrease theirs, otherwise there would be no time for the least talkative members of a fairly large class. Data for group sizes between 5 and 12 were also obtained by Stephan and Mishler; they would lie between the two curves of Fig. 12-5 if plotted on the same graph. Thus point 2 above is also supported.

Stephan and Mishler also present data showing that the leader is spoken to about as often as he speaks. However, fewer remarks are specifically directed to other members of the group. In other respects the trend of these data are much like that shown in Fig. 12-5, combining points 2 and 3. The more frequent speakers also are more frequently spoken to. Assuming that point 4 is true, the amount of information presented in a group is approximately constant regardless of group size. In addition, a sizable proportion of comments are directed toward the group as a whole.

These four points have substantial implications for teaching practice because they relate to certain principles of learning. Learning depends to a considerable extent on the amount of information presented to the sense organs of the learner. If this were the only important factor in learning, teaching in very large classes or by educational television would be most desirable. The stimulus input should then be as fast as possible with the teacher doing the talking if he knows more about the topic at hand than his students do. (Possibly a book would do even better than the teacher because it can be read so quickly.) The only crucial educational question once the curriculum was prepared would be how to ensure that the students are exposed to the televised material and not turning off the TV set, playing cards in the back of the lecture hall, or if a book is being read, turning pages without reading.

A second learning principle discussed earlier is that making a response is important to learning it. Here the large group is at a disadvantage, for the student is less likely to ask questions in order to clarify matters which confuse him, less likely to repeat important statements aloud and thus strengthen his memory of them, and less likely to develop discussion and speaking skills. He may do some of these things subvocally, for pupils do think about material as they listen. However, he will usually need to make responses other than thinking in order to have mastered the material for any purpose other than passing examinations.

A third principle states that knowledge of results is crucial for learning. As class size increases the individual obtains less such knowledge or "feedback" because he speaks and is spoken to less frequently. Some knowledge of the correctness of his own ideas is obtained in the general discussion, but the procedure is inefficient because as class size increases the discussion focuses less and less upon his special points of interest or difficulty.

This third principle probably is one of the best arguments in favor of studying in pairs or small groups. An individual can take in information as quickly by himself as with others, and he can make as many responses. However, by himself, his feedback is poor. (This is point 5 above.) Even with a teaching machine or programmed textbook, with feedback built into the learning task, what an individual needs to know sometimes comes through most clearly from another person.

A major problem for the teacher, then, is to understand the relative importance of stimulus input, active responding, and knowledge of results for effective teaching. One point should be emphasized: Recent educational and psychological theory, while recognizing the great importance of stimulus input, suggests that it has been overemphasized by teachers. There should be no doubt that it is better for the student to make a response in class than for the teacher to make the same response. Teachers need not be passive, but the data in Fig. 12-5 suggest that there is no danger of this.

Is there any real benefit from choosing one kind of teaching over another? This question pertains to point 6: Students often, but not always, do better working together than studying alone or listening to lectures. Durell (25) found that fourth-, fifth-, and sixth-grade pupils working in very small groups or teams in spelling, arithmetic, reading, social studies, and language arts showed generally increased learning compared with their previous year of instruction without team assignments. Average achievements for sixth graders were 6 months better than previously; average achievements for fifth graders were 4 months greater. However, fourth-graders were not superior except in spelling. One-third of the pupils completed 2 years' work in arithmetic during the year.

McKeachie (58) summarizes unpublished work by Carpenter and Davage on teaching psychology at the college level. These investigators instituted a pyramid plan in which discussion groups consisted of six freshmen, six sophomores, two juniors as assistant leaders, and a senior as group leader. These pyramid groups met weekly for 2 hours to discuss personal and professional goals, requirements to enter their chosen professions, their college curriculum, and central concepts of psychology, and other pertinent topics. The discussion leaders were trained in the principles of working with small groups, and the effects of these discussions were spectacular: Compared with control groups that had no such discussion, the pyramid group students developed substantially more favorable attitudes toward psychology, more knowledge of the field, more scientific approaches to psychological questions.

A similar advantage appeared in a study on teaching tenth-grade English grammar to a group. Crispin (20) showed superior learning resulting from having one low aptitude student per team meet with one high aptitude student and three average students to study during the class period. The control or comparison group consisted of low aptitude students meeting all together with a single trained teacher. The lack of other control groups makes it impossible to infer which of several factors is responsible for the faster learning shown by low aptitude students trained in teams. Was the small size of the study team crucial, or was the important factor the instruction by someone the same age with the same viewpoint as the learner? Or was the segregation of low ability youngsters in a single class in the control group an inhibiting factor for learning? Further experimentation with this team teaching technique is clearly needed, but it nonetheless seems clear from the two studies just cited that point 7 is a relevant one: Students working together almost by definition share more common viewpoints than do teachers and students, which makes the students potentially better communicators of information—even though teachers may have more information to communicate.

Our eighth point, that compatible student teams may be more effective than incompatible ones, is a reminder that some students have strong preferences for working with particular persons. Westmeyer (84) has shown that among chemistry students the persons preferred for laboratory partners are superior in previous course grades and in their present laboratory proficiencies. General likability is presumably also a factor in students' selection of co-workers, as are personal friendships or animosities.

In reference to point 9, Witter (87) suggested that teachers develop complementary pairings so that a shy person is paired with a bold one; for example, in singing class, the shy child can become more expressive through imitation of, and motivation by, the bold one. Though this suggestion was made for grade school teachers, the problem of participation continues through the college level; and college instructors may sometimes wish to form groups that will increase participation by the quieter students. Thoresen (80) found that college students who do not participate in class discussion tend to show questionnaire responses characteristic of submissiveness, anxiety, meekness, and timidity. These students also study less and discuss material less outside of class. Thoresen cites evidence that operant conditioning procedures can increase the amount of participation in class discussion. Thus students may listen to audio tape playbacks of discussions and make comments when the playback stimulates them to do so. The experimenter reinforces such comments by approving verbally; this makes further comments in a discussion more likely to occur in the future.

Point 10 states that educational goals set by a group of students may lead to greater commitment to the task than if the goals were set by the teacher. Bany and Johnson (5) give an example of a low ability fourth-grade group which spontaneously established the norm that its members did not miss words on spelling tests. It is hard to imagine such norms being effectively imposed by the teacher. However, it should be realized that groups may also impose goals which limit the level of intellectual attainment. McKeachie (58) suggests that the greatest possible drawback of discussion methods or group-controlled classes may be a tendency for the class to have the power to implement a wish to accomplish less cognitive growth than the teacher might challenge them to do in a teacher-centered class. McKeachie reports that usually there is no difference in intellectual achievement between the two kinds of groups, however. It appears that if group leadership by class members involves setting lower academic goals than the teacher would set, other factors such as examination pressures compensate for that effect.

_____ **Test Anxiety and Defensiveness**

Anxiety as it relates to general theories of drive and motivation was discussed in Chapter 11. Every teacher is aware that some pupils become anxious whenever they take a test. Sarason and his co-workers (71) devised a way of measuring a child's anxiety about tests or schoolwork. This test, called the Test Anxiety Scale for Children (TASC), has 30 questions such as, "When you are in bed at night, do you sometimes worry about how you are going to do in class the next day?" A positive answer to this question would indicate anxiety, of course. It is interesting that elementary school girls have consistently higher average scores on the TASC than do elementary school boys. Table 12-2 shows this result as well as a trend for anxiety scores to increase from year to year as children are retested.

An interpretation of Table 12-2 suggests that the school situation breeds test anxiety, as might be supposed from the nature of the questions on which TASC is based. The longer a child attends school and faces the necessity of proving himself by taking tests and having homework graded the higher his test anxiety scores become. But why should these scores be lower for boys than for girls? Girls usually outperform boys in the early grades, particularly in reading. Why then should they be more anxious? Sarason's answer to this question is that boys are taught all their lives not to show fear or lack of self-confidence, on pain of being considered weak or a "sissy." Moreover, if a boy is not affected

TABLE 12-2
Longitudinal Average Test Anxiety Scores[a, b]

Grade	Boys ($N = 157$)	Girls ($N = 166$)
1	7.52	7.72
3	8.71	10.57
5	9.44	12.71

[a] Based on Table 21 from Hill and Sarason (39). Copyright 1966 by the Society for Research in Child Development, Inc., and reproduced by permission.

[b] The same children were tested repeatedly throughout the study.

by school demands, he will not have test anxiety, anyway. He can be a Huck Finn and ignore the requests of his teachers. Otherwise he must respond and because he must not show his anxiety, the emotions producing anxiety are rechanneled into a denial of a problem or defensiveness. Ruebush (70) has developed a way to measure this defensiveness, the Defensiveness Scale for Children (DSC).

The defensiveness scale not only indicates denial of anxiety (which, after all, could also have been measured by "No" answers on TASC) but also records denial of inadequacy or hostility. Defensiveness scores are expected to be high when test anxiety scores are low, and vice versa. The children whose scores are shown in Table 12-2 showed decreasing defensiveness scores from grade to grade as their anxiety scores increased.

Hill and Sarason (39) report that the 25% of children with the highest test anxiety scores in the fifth grade obtained significantly lower fifth-grade reading scores and fifth-grade arithmetic scores than did the children in the lowest 25% group on test anxiety. Such performance decrements among highly anxious subjects have frequently been reported, raising the question as to whether a major deterrent to learning may not be the presence of personality problems.

However, perhaps test anxiety arises primarily because a person has low intellectual ability. Then the personality problem is a consequence of being placed in a situation where one is bound to fail, rather than its being a cause of failure, as Hill and Sarason suppose. Either explanation is consistent with the fact that children with high test anxiety scores are, on the average, lower in I.Q. than those with low test anxiety scores (71), (39, Tables 5 and 8), (72). But, there is still a difference in achievement in favor of less anxious children if a comparison is made of less anxious and more anxious children with the same I.Q.'s (39), strengthening Hill and Sarason's supposition.

The teacher must expect some children of high intellectual ability to have poorer grades or poorer achievement test scores than they should have, simply because they are afraid of testing situations in which rapid and accurate work is demanded. The origin of this fear is unknown, but the personality theory advocated by Sarason asserts that the anxious child's parents have evaluated his performance when he was very young, perhaps expecting too early walking, talking, or toilet training, thereby arousing the child's hostility because he cannot meet his parents' demands. The hostility leads the parents to reprove the child, guilt feelings are bred within him, and the child begins to have self-doubts and to be dependent on his parents or other adults for approval. The child's strong dependency makes the testing situation stressful because it is so important that he not lose the approval of the teacher. In contrast, the child with low test anxiety has greater self-esteem and consequently will not press so hard for examination success since he does not need to prove himself to the adult world.

What can teachers do about the presence of high test anxiety in their pupils? It is of course important to learn which children have such anxieties; without a specific attempt to find this out, many teachers will not realize the feelings of inadequacy held by bright, highly motivated children who are obviously doing satisfactory work (39). Research by Grimes and Allinsmith (34) indicates (though does not definitively prove) that the more anxious children should have relatively structured teaching whereas the less anxious children should have unstructured teaching. In this work, structured schooling consisted of emphasizing phonics in reading instruction; unstructured schooling consisted of emphasizing word recognition before teaching analysis of words into separate sounds. Grimes and Allinsmith's findings must be viewed as preliminary because the two teaching methods were not controlled experimentally and the authors had more faith in the small effect of anxiety just noted than in a more substantial effect favoring phonics instruction for all students. An alternate approach to highly anxious children may simply be to talk with them reassuringly or to try in other ways to reduce their anxieties.

It will help the anxious children, too, if the teacher should realize that high test anxiety is not constant in the typical child. Over a period of 4 years there is usually a great shift within a class; some highly anxious children become less anxious and some less anxious children become more anxious. The teacher should watch for signs that anxiety is being replaced by defensiveness, leaving the child still unhappy but perhaps not as handicapped in the testing situation.

The teacher should be ready to adapt the teaching situation to the needs of individual pupils, placing less stress on highly anxious children than on others. This may mean using fewer examinations than usual or developing an evaluation procedure in which each child is assured approval for sincere effort commensurate with his abilities. Sarason and his associates realize that such recommendations may not increase strictly academic achievement, but they believe they might aid the healthy personality development of the child. Sarason *et al.* suggest that teachers would benefit from a clinical training procedure somewhat similar to that of psychiatrists, social workers, and psychologists (71). They also recommend longer periods of practice teaching than are now being given.

────────── **Intellectual Interests and Their Relation to School Activity**

Most of the material presented in this section is based on careful research, but a comment on intuition and expert opinion seems appropriate. In discussing intellectual interests, we are considering intrinsic motivation in its purest form. Almost every teacher hopes to develop strong intellectual interests in his pupils, or he at least hopes that such intellectual activity as the child does exhibit stems in some measure from internal rather than external motivation. As teachers, the authors have often proceeded from hunches and experts' advice to find ways to motivate students. No doubt teachers will always do so. Some evaluation of the success of these techniques can be made informally, based on student comments or performance in class. More satisfactory evaluation results from planning the innovation as part of an experiment so that performance under the new technique can be compared with performance under an older method.

In many cases, too little evaluating is done to provide a scientific basis for judgment as to an appropriate teaching method. For example, we have enormous respect for the work of A. S. Neill in Summerhill School, and feel that many of his recommendations make sense and either have been or will be adopted in many American schools. But our admiration for the techniques described in Neill's writings does not blind us to the fact that almost nothing except anecdotal evidence is provided to indicate the effectiveness of those techniques. The best support for them comes from psychiatric and clinical psychological theory, based largely on observation and interview data. For concreteness, many personality theorists have wished for more controlled data-gathering procedures, such as those used by Sarason in the test anxiety studies just discussed. Perhaps the best available evaluation of Summerhill is Bernstein's (9a) report of his followup interviews with 50 adults who had attended Summerhill. Five positive effects were most frequently reported by these adults: (a) a healthy attitude toward sex, (b) confidence with authority figures, (c) natural development in line with personal interests and abilities, (d) help in overcoming a need to play continuously, and (e) help in understanding their own children better. The one major complaint was the lack of academic opportunity and inspiration, coupled with a dearth of inspired teachers.

Our point is that the teacher needs to know when a new procedure is backed by intuition or expert opinion, when by clinical theory and clinical data, and when by careful experimentation or precise statistical information. Teachers should not hesitate to make innovations of their own or to follow innovations suggested by others. But they should recognize that there is a strong element of faddishness in many fields, including education. This faddishness may lead to heralding each new innovator who comes forth with a new technique or a new "experiment" which, when more closely examined, would not qualify as an experiment in the scientific sense.

With the above as a warning, let us examine some studies which do satisfy reasonable standards of research. First, note that rational analysis would suggest at least two reasons for wanting students to have intellectual interests: (a) There are very great practical rewards for knowledge and skills in a technological society. It is possible that intellectual interests will increase the likelihood of learning. (b) Whether or not there are other basic reasons for knowing something, so long as children are going to be forced to attend school, it would be desirable for them to enjoy what they do there. Point (b) is merely an expression of goodwill toward children, but point (a) leads us to seek data on the relation between interests and amount learned. The bulk of the evidence leads to the conclusion that amount learned is predictable in part from the degree of interest in a particular subject before a course in that subject is taken (8, 42). One can also predict the difference in achievement in two courses, such as English and geography, from interest in a school subject or interest in a certain occupation (30). This predictability is large enough to be real rather than accidental, but it is not as large as the predictability from intelligence tests to course grades. Therefore, one should realize that interest is not sufficient in itself to assure success in a subject.

Prospective elementary teachers interested in knowing exactly what topics interest children most may wish to begin by looking at one article showing that 1860 first-graders, in show-and-tell type sharing sessions in 34 different communities, shared the following items (13). Arranged in order from most frequent to least frequent, they are:

1. Science and nature
2. Possessions
3. Personal experiences
4. Family and home activities
5. Outdoor recreation
6. Books
7. Clothing
8. Events concerning friends and community
9. Moving pictures and television
10. Music and recordings

Prospective secondary teachers may wish to examine Shores' article showing that among 6614 high school students studied, 57% of those asked to name one topic they would like to receive a book about, said literature (49% preferring fiction), 14% said social science, 13% science, and 6% recreation and hobbies (76). (A particular reason for reading this article is Shores' report that junior and senior high school teachers are distinctly less aware of their students' reading interests and other intellectual interests than are elementary school teachers. Prospective teachers may find other references on this and related topics in the *Educational Index,* a journal published ten times a year in New York by the H. W. Wilson Company and available in many college and university libraries.)

Students often do less reading and perform less intellectual activity than teachers might wish. Thus the pyramid plan study of Carpenter and Davage cited earlier (58) had to give up using number of psychology books checked out as a measure of motivation because the number was so nearly zero for every student. Similarly, Hawk and De Ridder (37) found that, if anxiety about grades was reduced by assigning course grades at the beginning of the semester on the basis of grades in previous courses, students markedly reduced the level of their performance. Only one of the 62 students studied earned a higher grade than the one he had been assigned; most students earned lower grades than they obtained. It would seem that students taught in an environment where assignments and grade pressure are routine may not do very much reading or studying if it is not required. In another cultural situation such as at St. Johns College where grades are not emphasized or at Oxford University where the only important examinations occur at the end of four years of study, very different results might appear in experiments like the two just mentioned.

Another kind of environmental influence on intellectual behavior is revealed in a survey of library circulation statistics: A considerable part of the difference in per capita book circulation among 1350 communities studied could be predicted from per capita buying income, median* educational level of female adults, the community's population, and size of the average family (64). As income or female education increases, book circulation for the community increases. But as community size or family size increases, book circulation decreases. It is not clear whether these effects are true environmental effects in the sense that increasing the size of a city necessarily decreases average library circulation.

* Median is a statistical term for the middle value in some group. With reference to this particular study, if only five women lived in a particular community and they had completed 10, 10, 11, 12, and 13 years of school, respectively, the median years of school completed would be 11.

Alternative explanations would either be invidious ones, typing people or places, or indirect arguments speculating on other factors.

Probably the best explanations of effects like those just noted are indeed indirect ones. One such influence is suggested by a study showing that participants in one noncredit university evening class series were much more active in community organizations than were a representative sample of persons in the same area who did not sign up for the series (24). The participants in evening classes frequently told other people about the classes, making it appear that intellectual activity may spread through a community to persons who are active in similar groups. If physical crowding or other reasons cause urban dwellers to reduce their group participation (as seems to be true), one means of communication about adult education or about books is also reduced.

On the individual level, it has been shown that children who are rated by teachers as having more than average curiosity show better performance on reading comprehension than do children rated as having less than average curiosity (54). We do not know whether it would be possible to increase the other children's general curiosity or whether such an increase would lead to improved reading comprehension. However, there is evidence that the presentation of pictures of strange-looking or unfamiliar animals such as an elephant shrew will lead to better learning of written material that describes such an animal than if the same written material were presented with a picture of a familiar animal, with instructions in both cases being to learn the material describing each picture (63). This effect seems to result from heightened curiosity due to the unusual pictures presented. There is a related experiment reported in the same article showing that the college students used as subjects spent more time looking at the unusual animals than at the common ones. Taken as a whole, this study suggests that teachers can improve learning by arousing interest with novel stimuli. This study is an example of the close relationship between experimental psychology and educational psychology, for the earliest research hint of this principle for teachers came from verbal learning experiments as long ago as 1894, exhibiting the so-called *Von Restorff effect* that a vivid stimulus such as a red-colored nonsense syllable in the middle of a list of black-colored syllables will be learned fastest, with corresponding advantages in recall and relearning (82).

A final suggestion to teachers for increasing students' motivation for intellectual activity: One may ask pupils to attempt new tasks that are generally unpopular, on the ground that added experience will prove their value, whereupon the students will enjoy them. By and large this method will be less successful than its opposite. So long as students are receiving some minimal contact with all the experiences they really need (what is really needed being decided by curriculum specialists or general education theorists), a teacher is wise to leave time in his students' programs to engage in the preferred activities in the course being taught. One might suppose that this would leave the science student who liked to observe butterflies and disliked writing reports about his observations even happier about observing and less happy about writing reports. However, Craig and Holsbach (19) found the opposite to be true. In experiments with three eighth-grade general science classes, course material was subdivided into five sections: living things, the human body, the earth, the universe, and matter–energy. Each pupil filled out an interest questionnaire to indicate which of 18 aspects of each of the five sections he would enjoy working on. Under matter–energy he could, for example, indicate an interest in using a saw which would cut rocks in half or in using different chemicals on plants to see what would happen to the plants. When each section was taught, the supplementary activities of each person were based on whether he had many or few interests in that area. For one class the students with a low number of interests in the section were given a choice among the activities they liked; the other students were given a choice among the activities they disliked. In the second class both subgroups were allowed to choose supplementary activities they liked. In the third class there were no supplementary activities. Usually the students with few likes in an area increased the number of their likes by engaging in the activities they did like. The group with high numbers of likes occasionally showed an increase due to added experience with liked or unliked activities, but this was rare. There was very little change in interest in the class without special supplementary activities. This study seems worthy of application by many science teachers, and further research might show how related techniques could be used to produce interest in topics other than science.

Summary

1. There is some conflict between motives for affiliation (friendship) and academic achievement; since both are important, teachers should foster both but expect to be unsure at times just which must be temporarily sacrificed for the overall good of the child.

2. Extrinsic motivation based on grades, rewards from parents, and future occupational success for good classroom work can be at least temporarily effective. In some situations they seem essential. However, when used, they should be employed as tools to lead to intrinsic motiva-

tion so that learning is desired for the pleasures inherent in it. This can best be done if teachers encourage pupils to participate in the school activities they most enjoy, and not try to "broaden" their interests by assigning nonpreferred activities. This does not mean that a child who does not enjoy English will do no English, but that whenever possible, his work in English will be slanted toward his own individual preferences. Teachers should not hesitate to provide lists of possible activities for pupils who may not know what they would really like to do.

3. The motivation for competence is the desire to do things well. It has an aspect of fun to it; the satisfaction assumed in the theory is that it comes from the pleasure of actively doing something, not from the pleasure of having it accomplished.

4. High motivation for achievement (accomplishment) generally leads to higher achievement than does low motivation. Parents with high socio-economic status seem to instill high achievement motivation in their children.

5. Students generally expect to accomplish what they really can, or perhaps a little more than they can. This expectation (also called level of aspiration) can be modified by making a task more difficult or by setting slightly higher goals.

6. Being told how he performed on a test or an assignment (preferably as soon as possible) can improve a student's performance. Showing the student a cumulative record of his growth in knowledge of arithmetic, say, month by month and year by year, might also help to motivate him. Such a record should not emphasize comparisons with other children but how much more he knows this year than he did a year ago. Graphs of the age level at which he is performing may be useful. Students should be aware, however, of competitive factors: If a student attends a school or college with very capable students, more capable than he, he is more likely to obtain relatively poor grades and to enter a less intellectually demanding profession than he otherwise might.

7. Generally speaking, praise seems more desirable than reproof, and positive reinforcement of desirable behavior more appropriate than negative reinforcement of undesirable behavior. Some form of correction or even punishment may become necessary when children's behavior disrupts the class. Teachers should make clear what it is that should be stopped, and they should not frighten children by emotional displays of their own. Punishing a child by giving additional schoolwork is undesirable because it teaches children to think of schoolwork as unpleasant.

8. Groups that are rewarded as a whole (cooperative groups) are more friendly to group members than are the groups in which reward is based

on individual performance (competitive groups). Cooperative groups may learn as much or more than competitive groups.

9. Student leadership of classroom groups is desirable because it produces active responses by the students themselves, leading to more learning of certain things, such as thinking for one's self. Also, students are less likely to talk over other students' heads than are teachers.

10. Anxiety about tests or schoolwork increases each year in elementary school and is substantially less in boys than in girls. This may be because boys learn to deny anxiety and be defensive, in the image of the male stereotype in Western culture. Teachers should try to reduce the stress of the school experience, particularly in dealing with children who are highly anxious. It should be noted that the child who is highly anxious one year may be much less anxious the next.

11. High interest in a subject can lead to greater learning of that subject. Therefore, it seems desirable to use techniques—such as showing novel stimuli—to stimulate interest in a topic being covered.

SUGGESTED READINGS

Amidon, E., & Hunter, E. *Improving teaching; the analysis of classroom verbal interaction.* New York: Holt, Rinehart & Winston, 1966.

A book for teachers, designed to show how to assess the appropriateness of teachers' remarks to pupils.

Friedenburg, E. Z. *The vanishing adolescent.* Boston: Beacon Press, 1959.

This book asserts that adult society is hostile to adolescents and that schools would do better to foster feelings of competence and worth in adolescents.

Holt, J. C. *How children fail.* New York: Pitman, 1964.

An argument that schools teach children to act stupidly by frightening them, confusing them, and failing to challenge their intelligence.

Kuder, G. F., & Paulson, B. B. *Exploring children's interests.* Chicago: Science Research Associates, 1954.

A little booklet (complete with cartoons) designed to show adults how to understand children's interests.

REFERENCES

1. Ackerman, W. I. Teacher competence and pupil change. *Harvard Educational Review*, 1954, **24**, 273–289.
2. Allen, R. D., *et al*. *Supervisors' manual: Metropolitan Achievement Tests*. Yonkers, N. Y.: World Book, 1932. P. 32.
3. Baker, R. L., & Doyle, R. Change in marking procedure and scholastic achievement. *Educational Administration and Supervision*, 1957, **43**, 223–232.
4. Baker, R. L., & Doyle, R. Elementary school marking practices and subsequent high school achievement. *Educational Administration and Supervision*, 1958, **44**, 158–166.
4a. Bandura, A. *Principles of behavior modification*. New York: Holt, Rinehart, & Winston, 1969. Pp. 130–131.
4b. Bandura, A., & Huston, A. C. Identification as a process of incidental learning. *Journal of Abnormal and Social Psychology*, 1961, **63**, 311–318.
5. Bany, M. A., & Johnson, L. V. *Classroom group behavior: Group dynamics in action*. New York: Macmillan, 1964.
6. Barberio, R. The relationship between achievement motivation and ethnicity in Anglo-Americans and Mexican-American junior high school students. *Psychological Record*, 1967, **17**, 263–266.
7. Baron, H. Samuel Shepard and the Banneker project. In M. Weinberg (Ed.), *Learning together. A book on integrated education*. Chicago: Integrated Education Associates, 1964. Pp. 45–48.
8. Barrileaux, L. E. High school science achievement as related to interest and I.Q. *Educational and Psychological Measurement*, 1961, **21**, 929–936.
9. Bauernfeind, R. H. "Goal cards" and future developments in achievement testing. *Proceedings of the 1965 Invitational Conference on Testing Problems*, 1966, 73–84.
9a. Bernstein, E. What does a Summerhill Old School Tie look like? *Psychology Today*, 1968 (October), **2**, No. 5, 38–41, 70.
10. Bostrum, R. N., Vlandis, J., & Rosenbaum, M. Grades and reinforcing contingencies and attitude change. *Journal of Educational Psychology*, 1961, **52**, 112–115.
11. Brown, F. J. Knowledge of results as an incentive in schoolroom practice. *Journal of Educational Psychology*, 1932, **23**, 532–552.
12. Bryan, J. F., & Locke, E. A. Goal setting as a means of increasing motivation. *Journal of Applied Psychology*, 1967, **51**, 274–277.
13. Byers, L. Pupils' interests and the content of primary reading lists. *Reading Teacher*, 1964, **17**, 227–233.
14. Chamberlain, L. J. Group behavior and discipline. *Clearing House*, 1966, **41**, 92–95.
15. Cogan, M. L. The behavior of teachers and the productive behavior of their pupils: I. "Perception" analysis. *Journal of Experimental Education*, 1958, **27**, 89–105.
16. Coleman, J. S. Academic achievement and the structure of competition. *Harvard Educational Review*, 1959, **29**, 330–351.
17. Coleman, J. S. The adolescent subculture and academic achievement. *American Journal of Sociology*, 1960, **65**, 337–347.
18. Council for Basic Education. Some comments on mathematics achievement in

American schools. *Council for Basic Education Bulletin,* 1967(May), **11**, No. 9, 1–12.

19. Craig, R. C., & Holsbach, M. C. Utilizing existing interests to develop others in general science classes. An experimental study of the relationship between learning experience and science interests. *School Science and Mathematics,* 1964, **64**, 120–128.

20. Crispin, D. B. Learning under two different conditions. *Teachers College Journal,* 1966, **38**, 95–97.

21. Davidson, H. A. Should Johnny compete? Psychiatrist's view. *National Education Journal,* 1960(October), **49**, 30–31.

22. Davis, J. A. The campus as a frog pond: An application of the theory of relative deprivation to career choices of college men. *American Journal of Sociology,* 1966, **72**, 17–31.

23. Deutsch, M. The effects of competition and cooperation upon group processes. *Human Relations,* 1949, **2**, 199–231.

24. Dick, R. N. Gregariousness as a factor in adult participation in university non-credit evening classes. *Adult Leadership,* 1964, **12**, 271–272.

25. Durell, D. B. Implementing and evaluating pupil-team learning plans. *Journal of Educational Sociology,* 1961, **34**, 360–365.

26. Fantini, M. D. Reward and punishment. *Clearing House,* 1966, **41**, 252–254.

27. Fay, P. J. The effect of the knowledge of marks on the subsequent achievement of college students. *Journal of Educational Psychology,* 1937, **28**, 548–554.

28. Flanders, N. A. Using interaction analysis in the inservice training of teachers. *Journal of Experimental Education,* 1962, **30**, 313–316.

29. French, E. G. Effects of the interaction of motivation and feedback on task performance. In J. W. Atkinson (Ed.), *Motives in fantasy, action, and society.* Princeton, N. J.: Van Nostrand, 1958. Pp. 400–408.

30. French, J. W. Comparative prediction of college major-field grades by pure-factor aptitude, interest, and personality measures. *Educational and Psychological Measurement,* 1963, **23**, 767–774.

31. Gray, S. W., & Klaus, R. A. An experimental preschool program for culturally deprived children. *Child Development,* 1965, **36**, 887–898.

32. Gray, S. W., Klaus, R. A., Miller, J. O., & Forrester, B. J. *Before first grade.* New York: Teachers College, Columbia University, Bureau of Publications, 1966.

33. Greene, H. A., Jorgensen, A. N., & Gerberich, J. R. *Measurement and evaluation in the secondary school.* New York: Longmans, Green, 1954.

34. Grimes, J. W., & Allinsmith, W. Compulsivity, anxiety, and school achievement. *Merrill-Palmer Quarterly,* 1961, **7**, 247–271.

35. Grinder, R. E. Relations of social dating attractions to academic orientations and peer relations. *Journal of Educational Psychology,* 1966, **57**, 27–34.

36. Harris, F. R., Johnston, M. K., Kelley, C. S., & Wolf, M. M. Effects of positive social reinforcement on regressed crawling of a nursery school child. *Journal of Educational Psychology,* 1964, **55**, 35–41.

37. Hawk, T. L., & De Ridder, L. M. A comparison of the performance of pre-graded students with grade-motivated students. *Journal of Educational Research,* 1963, **56**, 548–550.

38. Hilgard, E. R. The motivational relevance of hypnosis. In D. Levine (Ed.), *Nebraska symposium on motivation.* Lincoln, Neb.: University of Nebraska Press, 1964. Pp. 1–46.

39. Hill, K. T., and Sarason, S. B. The relation of test anxiety and defensiveness to

test and school performance over the elementary-school years. A further longitudinal study. *Monographs of the Society for Research in Child Development,* 1966, **31**(2, Whole No. 104), 46–51, 265–268.

40. Hurlock, E. B. The use of group rivalry as an incentive. *Journal of Abnormal and Social Psychology,* 1927, **22,** 278–290.

41. Isaacson, R. L. Relation between n Achievement, test anxiety, and curricular choices. *Journal of Abnormal and Social Psychology,* 1964, **68,** 447–452.

42. Johnston, R. W. Are SVIB interests correlated with differential academic achievement? *Journal of Applied Psychology,* 1965, **49,** 302–309.

43. Kahl, J. A. Educational and occupational aspirations of "common man" boys. *Harvard Educational Review,* 1953, **23,** 186–203.

44. Kanak, M. J., & Davenport, D. G. Between subject competition: A rat race. *Psychonomic Science,* 1967, **7,** 87–88.

45. Kennedy, W. A., & Willcutt, H. C. Praise and blame as incentives. *Psychological Bulletin,* 1964, **62,** 323–332.

46. Kight, H. R., & Sassenrath, J. M. Relation of achievement motivation and test anxiety to performance in programmed instruction. *Journal of Educational Psychology,* 1966, **57,** 14–17.

47. Kolb, D. A. Achievement motivation training for under-achieving high school boys. *Journal of Personality and Social Psychology,* 1965, **2,** 783–792.

48. Kounin, J. S., & Gump, P. V. The ripple effect in discipline. *Elementary School Journal,* 1958, **59,** 158–162.

49. Kounin, J. S., & Gump, P. V. The comparative influence of punitive and non-punitive teachers upon children's concepts of school misconduct. *Journal of Educational Psychology,* 1961, **52,** 44–49.

50. Lachman, S. J. Level of aspiration: A classroom demonstration of phenomena and principles. *Journal of General Psychology,* 1961, **65,** 357–363.

51. Lindsley, O. R. Intermittent grading. *Clearing House,* 1958, **32,** 451–454. (Reprinted: *Clearing House,* 1966, **41,** 195–198.)

52. Lumsdaine, A. A. Instrumentation and media of instruction. In N. L. Gage (Ed.), *Handbook of research on teaching.* Chicago: Rand McNally, 1963. Pp. 583–682.

53. Maller, J. B. Cooperation and competition. *Teachers College Contributions to Education,* 1929, No. 384.

54. Maw, W. H., & Maw, E. W. Children's curiosity as an aspect of reading comprehension. *Reading Teacher,* 1962, **15,** 236–240.

55. McClelland, D. C. *The achieving society.* Princeton, N. J.: Van Nostrand, 1961.

56. McDonald, F. J. The influence of learning theories on education (1900–1950). In E. R. Hilgard (Ed.), *Theories of learning and instruction. Sixty-third yearbook of the National Society for the Study of Education.* Part I. Chicago: University of Chicago Press, 1964. Pp. 1–26.

57. McGuire, C., Hindsman, E., King, F. J., & Jennings, E. Dimensions of talented behavior. *Educational and Psychological Measurement,* 1961, **21,** 3–38.

58. McKeachie, W. J. Research on teaching at the college and university level. In N. L. Gage (Ed.), *Handbook of research on teaching.* Chicago: Rand McNally, 1963. Pp. 1118–1172.

59. Murray, H. A. *Explorations in personality.* New York: Oxford University Press, 1938. P. 83.

60. Neill, A. S. *Summerhill: A radical approach to child rearing.* New York: Hart, 1960. P. 4.

61. O'Leary, K. D., & Becker, W. Behavior modification of an adjustment class: A token reinforcement program. *Exceptional Children,* 1967, 33, 637–642.
62. Page, E. B. Teacher comment and student performance: A seventy-four classroom experiment in school motivation. *Journal of Educational Psychology,* 1958, **49,** 173–181.
63. Paradowski, W. Effect of curiosity on incidental learning. *Journal of Educational Psychology,* 1967, **58,** 50–55.
64. Parker, E. B., & Paisley, W. J. Predicting library circulation from community characteristics. *Public Opinion Quarterly,* 1965, **29,** 39–53.
65. Redl, F., & Wineman, D. *The aggressive child.* Glencoe, Ill.: Free Press, 1957.
66. Ringness, T. A. Identification patterns, motivation, and school achievement of bright junior high school boys. *Journal of Educational Psychology,* 1967, **58,** 93–102.
67. Rosen, B. C. Race, ethnicity, and the achievement syndrome. *American Sociological Review,* 1959, **24,** 47–60.
68. Rosenfeld, H., & Zander, A. The influence of teachers on aspirations of students. *Journal of Educational Psychology,* 1961, **52,** 1–11.
69. Ross, C. C. The influence upon achievement of a knowledge of progress. *Journal of Educational Psychology,* 1933, **24,** 609–619.
70. Ruebush, B. K. Children's behavior as a function of anxiety and defensiveness. Unpublished doctoral dissertation, Yale University, 1960.
71. Sarason, S. B., Davidson, K. S., Lighthall, F. F., Waite, R. R., & Ruebush, B. K. *Anxiety in elementary school children.* New York: Wiley, 1960. Pp. 147–151, 276.
72. Sarason, S. B., Hill, K. T., & Zimbardo, P. G. A longitudinal study of the relation of test anxiety to performance on intelligence and achievement tests. *Monographs of the Society for Research in Child Development,* 1964, **29**(7, Whole No. 98).
73. Sears, P. S. Level of aspiration in relation to some variables of personality: Clinical studies. *Journal of Social Psychology,* 1941, **14,** 311–336.
74. Sears, P. S., & Hilgard, E. R. The teacher's role in the motivation of the learner. In E. R. Hilgard (Ed.), *Theories of learning and instruction. Sixty-third yearbook of the National Society for the Study of Education.* Part I. Chicago: University of Chicago Press, 1964. Pp. 182–209.
75. Seeman, J., Barry, E., & Ellinwood, C. Interpersonal assessment of play therapy outcome. *Psychotherapy: Theory, Research and Practice,* 1964, **1,** 64–66.
76. Shores, J. H. Reading interests and information needs of high school students. *Reading Teacher,* 1964, **17,** 536–544.
77. Silberman, C. E. The city and the Negro. *Fortune,* 1962(March), **65,** 89–91, 139–154.
78. Stephan, F. F., & Mishler, E. G. The distribution of participation in small groups: An exponential approximation. *American Sociological Review,* 1952, **17,** 598–608.
79. Thompson, G. G., & Hunnicutt, C. W. The effect of praise or blame on the work achievement of "introverts" and "extroverts." *Journal of Educational Psychology,* 1944, **35,** 257–266.
80. Thoresen, C. E. Oral non-participation in college students: A study of characteristics. *American Educational Research Journal,* 1966, 3, 198–210.
81. United States Department of Labor. *The Negroes in the United States—Their economic and social situation.* Bulletin No. 1511. Washington, D. C.: United States Department of Labor, Bureau of Labor Statistics, 1966. Pp. 22–25.

82. Wallace, W. P. Review of the historical, empirical, and theoretical status of the Von Restorff phenomenon. *Psychological Bulletin,* 1965, **63,** 410–424.
83. Weber, M. *The Protestant ethic and the spirit of capitalism.* (Translated by T. Parsons.) London: Allen & Unwin, 1930.
84. Westmeyer, P. Some bases used by students in choosing partners in the chemistry laboratory. *Journal of Educational Research,* 1965, **58,** 355–357.
85. White, R. W. Motivation reconsidered: The concept of competence. *Psychological Review,* 1959, **66,** 297–333.
86. Whiteis, U. E. Punishment's influence on fear and avoidance. *Harvard Educational Review,* 1956, **26,** 360–373.
87. Witter, E. Pair the bold with the shy and get results! *Grade Teacher,* 1967 (September), **85,** 180–181.
88. Wittrock, M. C. Set applied to student teaching. In J. P. DeCecco (Ed.), *Human learning in the school.* New York: Holt, Rinehart & Winston, 1963. Pp. 107–117.
89. Wolf, M. M., Giles, D. K., & Hall, R. V. Experiments with token reinforcement in a remedial classroom. *Behaviour Research and Therapy,* 1968, **6,** 51–64.

13

PERSONALITY

Personality is many things to many people: It is the traits and the characteristics, the moods and the manners, and all the other qualities that make one person different from another. The sum of these differences—and similarities, too—is what some people call "personality" and others call "character"; either one describes what it is, aside from appearance, that makes it so easy to tell people apart, even after a brief acquaintance. That is, personality is a reflection of the consistency or "style" in an individual's behavior. This does not imply, however, that the field of personality is oriented solely, or even largely, to the uniquenesses of human beings.

It is often said that no two people are exactly alike (obviously an inductive proposition); and generally speaking, this is true. However, there is a difference between accepting that simple statement and accepting the idea that only individual differences among people are important. Certainly if no two people are exactly alike, no two people are different, either. The study of personality does not, then, concern itself only with the ways in which people are different from each other but also with the ways in which they are alike. There is a long-standing controversy in psychology about whether the differences or the similarities among people are more important. The choice, it would seem, depends on one's purposes. Most psychologists are interested in propositions that are true of groups or populations of individuals, for a science of the individual would be difficult to develop, requiring a new science for each individual.

The psychologist Gordon Allport has probably been the most consistent and influential proponent of the view that psychologists have neglected the individual in their search for broad generalizations they call *laws*. Allport (1) maintains that the behavior of any given individual may be quite predictable, that is to say, lawful, independent of the behavior of any other individual. Moreover, individuals may be "put together" in such different ways that their total personality is not comprehensible simply as the sum of all their separate traits. The same two traits, e.g., intelligence and friendliness, that produce one behavior in one person, may produce a very different behavior in someone else. It is the organization and interaction of the traits that is important. As Allport pointed out, there is, then, some conflict between the aim of the scientist to establish principles as broadly applicable as possible, and the aim of the student of the individual person, who may not care if the ideas he develops have any generality.

Certainly there is no need or desire to depreciate the importance of the individual; and in many situations, e.g., specific medical and educational settings, the individual is of paramount importance. It serves neither the patient nor the student if general principles do not work in his case. Nonetheless, for psychology *as a science,* it would seem necessary to strive for ideas that are general in the sense that they apply to a population of individuals. Consumers of psychological science should not presume that any psychological principles, no matter how well developed, can always be applied. They will only apply more often than other alternative principles. Limited application is not a weakness unique to psychology. Applications of principles from any scientific discipline must be limited by the recognition that they were derived under special circumstances and hold only on the average.

Just how different *are* individuals? Are the differences more marked than the similarities? Consider, for example, two situations, one in which a voice over a loudspeaker announces that a lion has escaped from a circus and is thought to be in the neighborhood, and the other in which a voice over a loudspeaker announces that free samples of cereal are being given away outside. Then consider all the people who live in a typical neighborhood and their reactions. Which would be more important, the differences among individuals in their tendencies toward anxiety or the differences between the situations in their tendency to provoke anxiety? In some data bearing on this point, Endler, Hunt, and Rosenstein (17) found that responses on an anxiety questionnaire were predominantly determined by the stimuli which might produce anxiety, i.e., by the situation, rather than by differences among subjects. Differences among individuals are likely to become an important source of variance in response only when the stimulus is relatively constant. Otherwise situational (stimulus) factors will probably contribute by far the greatest variance in response measures (69).

It is often somewhat difficult to discuss personality and personality research without borrowing some common everyday terms that have no special relevance to psychology. Yet these terms have no precise meaning and cannot be substituted finally for more rigorous, if more difficult, ways of thought. Such terms are used to describe inner or "experiential" states to which the psychologist has no access. For example, the statement "He believed that he was going to be shocked," describes a hypothetical inner state of the individual and is objectionable on various grounds. Note, however, that the statement "He said that he believed he was going to be shocked," would meet with no objections because the referent is very clear; it is the statement of the individual, what he said. Nonetheless, such commonsense terms as "believe" and "aware," will occasionally be used—in part, to avoid more cumbersome phraseology but also because these terms probably convey something more than is conveyed by strictly behavior-oriented statements.

_____   **Dimensions and Structure of Personality**

For many centuries, attempts have been made to describe personalities. The earlier attempts were probably various typologies consisting of a limited number of mutually exclusive categories, each based on a group of presumably interrelated characteristics. Thus, for example, Galen, elaborating on the doctrine of Hippocrates, thought it possible to classify people into four temperament types, temperament being determined by the dominance of one of the four body "humors" (35). If yellow bile was dominant, then the individual would be of a *choleric* temperament, i.e., disposed to anger. If black bile was in excess, then the individual would be given to *melancholy*. Phlegm produced a *phlegmatic* disposition, and blood produced *sanguinity* (optimism). There have been many other typologies, from Lombroso's "criminal" type, to Jung's extravert–introvert typology, to Sheldon's current system of three temperament types related to body build.

Although typologies have been a popular way of thinking about personality, they are fundamentally weak and unsatisfactory for the scientist. For one thing, it is implicit in a typology that most people or objects fall rather clearly into one or another of the various categories, the middle positions being unlabeled and vacant. Actually, however, characteristics are so distributed that considerably more people fit into the intermediate positions than at both extremes combined. Thus, an extrovert–introvert typology has to begin with the fact that most people seem to be neither. Forcing people into one category or another distorts nature so seriously that scientific integrity is imperiled.

A second weakness of typology is its use of mutually exclusive categories—its mutuality being more in theory than in fact. In employing typologies there is an inclination to allow classificatory decisions to be dependent, i.e., if an individual is a member of one class, he is automatically excluded from membership in all other classes. In fact, it seems the better course to make all decisions, classifications, and measurements independently. For example, there is the rather surprising finding that "good leader types" and "good follower types" turn out to be the same persons (see p. 685). Or, to take another example, it might be supposed that there are two types of children in a classroom, the "good" children who are usually praised by the teacher and the "bad" children who receive a disproportionate share of censure. However, praise and reproof administered to a given child tend to be positively correlated. Apparently the more active, alert, curious children are likely to be alternately the delight and the despair of their teachers. If both traits are independently assessed it is possible to find that some people are high in both introversion and extraversion.

A typology is based on the assumption of a fairly sizable number of characteristics that are highly associated with each other, i.e., that ought to occur together. However, such clustering of characteristics is not especially common, and the associations are disappointingly low from the standpoint of a type theorist. When methodologically independent measures of different attributes are obtained, the correlations are likely to be much closer to 0.00 than to 1.00. Of course, it is possible to form "types" from conjunctions (see p. 207) of any two or more traits, even if the traits are unrelated to each other, e.g., "the short, fat type." But it is absolutely necessary that the type so formed be shown to have a relationship to behaviors not involved in its definition. Thus, for example, it is probably possible to define a "criminal" type of physiognomy (or any other type for that matter) by specifying the characteristics which are sufficient for classification into the type(s).

One need merely specify a number of supposedly "criminal" features such as drooping eyelids, weak chin, and sloping forehead. Then to the extent that any individual has those features he will fit the "criminal type." However, unless it can be shown that a "criminal" physiognomy is in fact associated with criminal behavior, the typing seems pointless. And that, of course, is what has caused the difficulty in attempts to develop typologies. Moreover, it should be clear that the substantial variability and complexity of human behavior could not be accounted for in terms of such a simple system as is involved in typologies to date.

It appears that at present the most common use of the term type, e.g., "anxious type," "leader type," simply refers to individuals who are extreme in some dimension or other.

Traits

Another way of conceiving of personality is in terms of *traits*. A trait is quite similar to an *attitude* in that it refers to a disposition to respond in a certain way. That is, a trait name is an attempt to account for some more or less general response tendency, ordinarily not of an intellective or motor nature. However, unlike attitudes, which may be transient, traits are usually thought of as being more enduring. We speak of people "having" traits. Thus, it is possible for an individual to be anxious without "having" the trait "anxiety." The former suggests a temporary state while the latter suggests a consistent tendency to be anxious.

Even though it is usually said that someone is characterized by such traits as anxiety, shyness, or resourcefulness, traits are usually conceived of as dimensions, i.e., it is possible for a person to be high or low in some trait or to have the trait at some intermediate value. There is not, however, especially good agreement about what it means to be high or low in a trait. For example, if we consider anxiety as a trait, is the "high anxiety" individual someone who shows anxiety at a high level of intensity? With great frequency? With short latency? Or is it with a slow return to normal? (This is the same problem that is involved in evaluating the strength of any response.) At present, psychology is not in a position to resolve the issues involved here; and trait measures incorporate various conceptions of the specific kind of tendency which is involved in the trait.

If a trait is simply a term for a given response disposition, there must be about as many possible traits as there are responses. Unfortunately, that may be true. Allport and Odbert (2) once collected all the terms they could find that suggested some personality trait, and they came up with almost 18,000 terms. By eliminating obvious synonyms, rare terms, and the like, and by complex statistical procedures, Cattell (13) was able to reduce the list drastically, but he still had about 35 terms which seemed unique. In further analyses, Cattell was able to show that the 35 basic terms fell into 12 clusters when they were measured in individuals. His findings illustrate the point that traits can occur at quite different levels of generality. For example, it might be perfectly reasonable to suppose that there are a number of elemental traits such as passivity, optimism, and sociability, and at the same time secondary or subsidiary traits such as talkativeness, frankness, and gullibility. Although the number of possible personality traits seems large, there is an advantage in that, since all the uniqueness of personalities could be provided for quite easily. For example, even if the 35 traits were all represented by only two values, high and low, there would be 2^{35} unique patterns of personality, i.e., almost 40 billion different patterns.

An issue causing considerable controversy in psychology is whether a trait has the same meaning or function for all persons. For example, is dependency as a trait the same wherever it appears, or does its nature and meaning depend on the total context of traits in which it occurs? Is dependency really the same trait when it occurs in an anxious person as when it occurs in a calm person? Allport is probably the foremost exponent of the position that traits are only to be understood as they function *in a particular individual.* However, most psychologists today lean toward the view that personality traits can be safely viewed as having some common meaning and function across populations of individuals. Thus, when subjects are selected for participation in an experiment on the basis of their scores on some personality measure, there is an implicit assumption of identity of meaning of the measured variable across all the subjects studied.

The Structure of Personality

Is the individual's personality adequately described by an account of his standing on all the traits we wish to name? Certainly it doesn't seem that we, as individuals, can be adequately understood as a conglomeration of traits, no matter how precisely these traits are measured. To most of us it probably seems that we have a "style" or an overall theme to our lives that transcends any of our particular traits. Just as a building seems considerably more than a pile of bricks, some bags of cement, window frames, and the like, so it seems that personality has form, that there are special relationships among its parts. Expressed in another way we might say that personality is organized or that it has structure. Most unfortunately, however, very little is know about the structure of personality as a systematic, scientific construct in psychology. It is manifestly more difficult to study the organization of elements than the elements themselves.

As an example of an organizational variable in personality, consider the concept of *subsidiation* as proposed by Henry Murray (64). Murray tended to view personality in terms of *needs* toward whose satisfaction the individual is striving and *presses* or forces operating in the environment to push the individual in one direction or another. Murray says that some of the needs in a person's life seem to be more central than others, or more central than the same needs would be in another person's life. And some needs seemed to have the principal function of contributing toward the gratification of some other need. Thus, the structure in personality consists in part of the relationships among needs. For example, in one individual the need for power may be a central motive around which his many other motives are organized, and such needs as those for achievement, affiliation, and dominance may be important insofar as their gratification contributes to the attainment of power. But for someone else affiliation might actually be the more central need, and power might be important because it increases opportunity for affiliative responses. Although the preceding discussion is couched in terms of needs, it applies equally well to traits, e.g., scrupulosity may be a way of keeping guilt and anxiety at a minimal level.

Structure, then, in part means the relationships among various aspects of any person's personality. Structure implies that any changes which occur in one area of personality or in a trait will most likely have implications for various other areas or traits. If personality lacked structure, changes which occurred in one trait would not affect others. For example, a very dominant person might for some reason become markedly less dominant. The question then is whether he seems to have a generally different personality or whether he is the same person but simply less dominant.

Allport (1) has been one of the most eloquent spokesmen for the position that personality is more than the sum of its parts. He asserted quite vigorously that no individual personality can be understood simply as a set of scores on separate traits. The relationship among traits, the ways they modify each other, must be taken into account. Few persons would quarrel seriously with such a position, but psychologists differ in their opinions about the best place to begin studying personality, e.g., with the elements or the overall structure, and about whether the approaches to the study of structure which have been developed thus far have any scientific value.

Assessment of Personality

Obviously if any systematic use is to be made of personality variables, they must be in some way measurable. To say that personality variables must be measurable does not imply any particular method or any special level of precision. But at least we must be able to say with some consistency and with some fidelity that a certain person is high or low on some dimension. That is the basic measurement operation, and everything beyond that is a refinement. Moreover, the basic quantitative statement can come from casual observations of a bystander or from a very sophisticated, technically advanced scientific instrument. Ordinarily in psychology casual observations of bystanders are not relied on because they prove to be inconsistent and to lack fidelity. But it should not be supposed that there are any intrinsically unacceptable ways of assessing personality, nor any intrinsically desirable ways. Just as distance can be measured by visual inspection, pacing, tape measures, sound delays, triangulation methods, and the like, so personality can be assessed in a myriad of ways, all perhaps useful in particular situations and for particular purposes.

The same point about measurement of personality must be made at the outset as will be made later about measurement of attitudes. The only way to know about personality is from the way it manifests itself in behavior. To the extent that our personality variables go beyond mere description of some behavior, they are based on inferences. There are no ways of tapping directly into "the personality." This point must be clear. For example, suppose a group of young people is standing about with one fellow standing on the fringe of that group. When he is encouraged to move closer into the group, he seems flustered and refuses. It is obvious that he does not have much to say and that he does not look his conversational partner in the eye, but tends instead to glance downward. We, the observers, might say that the young man is shy. We have inferred from his behavior that at least at that time the trait of shyness is operating. But we could be wrong, for any number of reasons; e.g., he may be angry at someone in the group. Or suppose that someone replies "Yes" to the question "Do you ever cross the street to avoid meeting people?" His response is a bit of verbal behavior from which (given enough similar responses) shyness might be inferred. And, finally, suppose that a young man is shown inkblot and is asked to tell what it looks like. This time, too, there is a bit of behavior, predominantly a verbal response, from which some trait such as shyness could be inferred. In no instance can it be assumed that the behavior is directly revealing of personality.

One distinction that can be made among different ways of gaining knowledge about personality is in terms of the awareness* of the subject of what it is that is being measured. Obviously the more aware a person is of what a personality "test" is measuring, the greater the possibility

---

* Here is an example of a word referring to a private experience of the individual. We could substitute the phrase "ability of the subject to say what it is that is being measured" as one approximation to what is meant by awareness.

that the person's responses will reflect not so much what he is as the way he wants others to think of him. When an individual is asked whether he would cross the street to avoid meeting someone, it is likely that he has a pretty good idea of just what the question is supposed to reveal about himself. But it is probably more difficult to decide just what is specifically at issue when one is asked to indicate what an inkblot might be. Nonetheless, even for "camouflaged" measures such as the Rorschach Inkblot Test, it is likely that most subjects have an idea about what are probably "bad" responses and hence they are capable of some degree of "censoring" of their responses. Thus, Tutko (90) found that psychiatric patients who differed in their tendency to give unwarrantedly favorable descriptions of themselves on a set of objective questions also differed in their responses to various other measures including the Rorschach. Patients who gave unrealistically favorable pictures of themselves on objective questions, as indicated by marking numerous favorable items that are unlikely to be true of many people, produced shorter and more defensive responses on other tests. Personality tests of whatever variety cannot invariably lay bare the personality if the subject does not wish to be exposed.

Of course, many of the problems in assessing personality stem from the fact that many cues in the situation suggest that it involves assessment and hence the subject is motivated to produce responses which may not be characteristic. If it were possible to obtain measurements in ways which did not produce a reaction to the measurement operation itself, responses of a more "natural" or characteristic sort might be obtained. There are some ways psychologists have devised to obtain measurements that do not require the subject's cooperation and which do not affect his responses to any marked degree.

What are possible ways of assessing personality? If our interest is in measuring the more or less enduring dispositions of the individual, then the problem is the same as diagnosing any other response dispositions, although we are particularly fortunate with human subjects in that they can make verbal responses. Actually, there are many ways in which personality might conceivably be "diagnosed"—more than can be considered here. However, some of the most important approaches are described below.

Self-Report on Personality

First, and probably most evident, the subject is asked to report on his dispositions, i.e., his personality. This can be done by asking for reports on separate items which can be cumulated to arrive at a final score. For example, the California Personality Inventory (28) consists of many items such as "I often think about how I look and what impression I am making on others" and, "I often start things I never finish" to which the subject is to respond either "True" or "False." For a given trait such as "Dominance" the subject's score is the number of relevant items to which he makes an appropriate response. However, the subject may simply be asked to rate himself directly on the trait the examiner has in mind, e.g., "Rate yourself on the trait *dependability* using a seven-point scale on which 7 means "very high," 4 means "about average" and 1 means "very low." Although self-ratings are often scorned because of their obviousness, research evidence clearly indicates that for most people most of the time, self-ratings are the most valid predictors of behavior. It is probable that most people are not especially defensive, have little to hide, and can report pretty faithfully on their own personalities, at least insofar as their personalities are reflected in some kind of overt behavior. There is usually a good bit of asymmetry in the assessments people make of themselves. That is, if a group of adolescents is asked, "Do you hate your father?" a "Yes" answer has a high probability of being true, but a "No" would be given by a group lacking in hostility toward their fathers and also by a group of respondents who said "No" but should, to be truthful, have said "Yes."

Report on Stimuli

In addition to being asked to report on their own responses, respondents are also asked to report on their views of their environments (stimuli). Thus, for example, instead of asking "How do you respond to your father?" the question asked is "What kind of a person is your father?" Although descriptions of the stimuli one must face is not often explicitly recognized as a technique, it is an important one and is incorporated into many personality measurement devices. For example, the Minnesota Multiphasic Personality Inventory (32) asks for a true or false answer to the statement, "Most people are honest chiefly through fear of being caught" as a way of getting at a general tendency toward suspiciousness and distrust.

Report by Observer

Still another way of assessing a response disposition is to ask for a report from an observer. One form which the report may take is the rating of an individual by his peers. In a variety of situations, peer ratings have been found especially good predictors of behavior. For example, Williams and Leavitt (92) found that in a group of officer candidates, peer ratings on "leadership ability" were the best predictor of later success as an officer. Ratings can only be as good as the raters, but peer ratings have several strong points contributing to their probable validity even for fairly subtle personality factors. Observers, particularly peers, have had an opportunity to see the subject responding to a wide variety of stimuli over a long period of time. A one-half hour "test" consisting of a few responses to a limited number of stimuli would seem inherently limited in validity. It may be argued that peers are not objective or that their own problems will get in the way of the ratings they are asked to make. However, by employing a number of different raters it may be possible to cancel out biases introduced by individual raters. Moreover, it must not be assumed that raters, even unsophisticated ones, are insensitive to the nuances of personality. Certainly in their everyday speech and other behavior, people make distinctions on the basis of such personality traits as "sincerity" which imply an awareness of different levels of behavior and of subtleties of interpersonal responses. By employing peer ratings, Sechrest and Jackson (78) were able to achieve what appeared to be a distinction between "social intelligence" and "book learning intelligence," something which has been particularly difficult by other techniques. In most investigations of "social" intelligence, it has turned out that the measure used was nothing more than a test of general or verbal intelligence. Sechrest and Jackson, however, found that students can make a distinction with considerable apparent validity.

Symbolic Stimuli

As suggested earlier, information about personality may be obtained by asking the subject to report on his own response dispositions or to describe his stimulus situation. One might ask then, why not simply observe the individual making the response in question, obviously a much to be preferred way of finding out about responses. Psychologists have made some attempts at measurement by "real life" observations, but it is often difficult or inconvenient to make the kinds of observations which are necessary; for that reason psychologists have often employed symbolic stimuli which theoretically ought to elicit responses similar to those which would be elicited by the "real" stimuli in which they are interested. For example, if one wished to know how an individual might respond to "authority figures," one could look for stimuli which would symbolize authority and ask the individual to respond to them. Many interpretations of the Rorschach test, for example, are based on the assumption that the blots symbolically represent some common stimulus or other, e.g., many users of the Rorschach talk about certain cards as "Mother" or "Father" cards. The usefulness of symbolic stimulus tests is open to serious question although there is no dearth of advocates for them. There have been few really convincing demonstrations that they are better than, if as good as, self-reports and ratings by others (77).

Behavioral Observation

At the outset it must be admitted that the use of direct behavioral observations is often likely to be impractical in what are called "clinical" situations, but such observations are becoming considerably more frequent in research settings. Here is an example of a nonreactive behavioral observation, i.e., one which does not alter the individual's responses in any way, in a "real life" setting. Some time ago, Sommer (82) established the fact that there are systematic differences in the spatial distance which people like to have between themselves and other persons. Some like things close and cozy while others prefer a bit more space around them. It is not a far step from spatial distance to what we might call "social distance."

Leipold (49) suggested, then, that interpersonal factors which contribute to social distance should also contribute to spatial distance. Moreover, he supposed, with justification, that those persons high in "introversion" should prefer larger spatial distances than those high in "extroversion." So measures of introversion and extroversion were obtained from a large psychology class. Leipold reasoned that any condition which produced a threatening interpersonal situation should increase social distance. Therefore, after a midterm examination all the students who received a grade of "C" on the exam were randomly divided into three groups. One group received postcards stating that they had done poorly on the exam and asking them to report to Mr. Leipold, the teaching assistant, for a conference about their work. A second group received cards stating that they had done well on the exam and similarly asked them to report for a conference. The third group received cards which simply asked them to come in for a "course evaluation" conference.

When the students arrived for their "conference," they entered an anteroom where a secretary told them that Mr. Leipold was out but that they should go on into his offce and have a seat. When they entered the inner office they found a desk and three chairs arranged in such a way that they appeared naturally placed but at three distances from the desk. One chair was beside the desk, one was part way across the room, and one was just inside the door. The dependent measure was simply the chair chosen by the subject. As predicted, introverts tended to choose the more distant positions and extroverts the nearer ones. And the condition of interpersonal threat, i.e., which postcard message the subject received, also produced the expected difference. The "threatened" subjects stayed farther from the desk. Here, then, was an experiment in which an important trait was measured without the subject being the wiser. Moreover, the measurement operation probably left him essentially unchanged so that the measurement could be repeated at any time with consistent findings.

Although direct behavioral observations are still uncommon, the following have been employed with some degree of success: analysis of speech in spoken, recorded communications to assess tension or anxiety by way of the discomfort–relief quotient (16); eye-blink rate to measure tension or anxiety during interviews (44); choice between an immediate small reward and a promise of a larger one later to measure ability to delay gratification (62); cheating on a self-scored examination (29); and mailing of a "lost" envelope apparently containing money (61) to measure honesty.

It has already been suggested that one of the differences among personality measures is the degree to which it is apparent just what it is that is being measured. On some measures the subject may be quite aware of just what it is that is presumably being measured, and on other measures the subject may be considerably mystified. What is the relationship between comparable scores obtained from the two kinds of measures? Davids (14) tested two groups of subjects with both "direct" and "indirect" measures. One group was tested under conditions designed to engender the belief that the tests might be used in selecting them for a job. The other group was told simply that they were fulfilling a duty to science. It was found that the relationships among the measures were higher for the latter group and that the former group produced significantly "better" scores for the more direct measures. Other experiments (15, 25) produced evidence to suggest that better adjusted subjects perform more consistently on direct and indirect measures. More poorly adjusted subjects tend to show a discrepancy in performance on the two kinds of measures. For that reason it seems wise, as Allport (1) suggests, to include both direct and indirect measures in every personality assessment program.

Some Common Personality Tests and Devices

A. Tests with a marked limitation on the form of response:

California Personality Inventory (*CPI*) (28). Consists of 480 declarative statements to be answered "True" or "False." Sample items are:

I looked up to my father as an ideal man.
I think I would enjoy having authority over other people.
People today have forgotten how to feel properly ashamed of themselves.
My parents have often disapproved of my friends.

The CPI is scored simply by counting the number of items answered in the manner appropriate to each of the scales. It purports to measure 18 traits such as sociability, tolerance, intellectual efficiency, and femininity falling into four classes: I. Measures of poise, ascendancy, and self-assurance. II. Measures of socialization, maturity, and responsibility. III. Measures of achievement potential and intellectual efficiency. IV. Measures of intellectual and interest modes.

Minnesota Multiphasic Personality Inventory (MMPI) (32). Consists of 566 statements to be answered "True" or "False." The statements are very similar to those on the CPI, the CPI being a direct descendant of the MMPI. However, the MMPI was devised for use in psychiatric settings, and the scales on which the items are scored reflect its origins. The original scales were: hypochondriasis, depression, hysteria, psychopathic deviate, masculinity–femininity, paranoia, psychasthenia, schizophrenia, and hypomania. There have since been numerous additional scales developed for such traits as social introversion, ego strength, and social responsibility. Current interest in the MMPI is centered on ways to make automatic the personality interpretations which come from it.

B. Tests with a minimal limitation on the form of the response:

Thematic Apperception Test (63). Consists of 20 pictures, most containing human figures, suggestive of a wide variety of situations. The subject is requested to "make up a story" about each picture, telling what the people are doing, feeling, and saying. The stories can be scored by counting themes of a particular type, but it is common practice for the clinical psychologist to do only informal analyses. The interpretations are based predominantly on the assumption that the motives, actions, feelings and the like which characterize the central figure in the story are also characteristic of the subject whether he is aware of them or not.

Rorschach Inkblot Test (66). Consists of 10 inkblots made by dropping ink on paper and then folding it over to produce blots symmetrical around a midline (see Fig. 13-2). Some of the blots were made with black ink only, but they have rather marked gradations in shading. Others were made with ink of various colors. The subject is asked to look at each blot and to tell "What it looks like, what it might be." On the basis of both the content of the response, e.g., human vs. animal, and the characteristics of the blot which gave rise to the response, e.g., the shape of the blot, its shading, its color, the skilled clinician should be able to arrive at an insight into aspects of the personality not easily seen otherwise.

Figure Drawing Tests. The subject is usually presented with a blank piece of paper and asked to draw a figure. There are several versions of this task. In one common version called Draw-A-Person (55), the subject is asked to draw a person and then to draw someone of the opposite sex. Some clinical psychologists like to have the subject draw a family instead of one person, and another drawing test requires the subject to draw a house, a tree, and a person (10). The drawings may be "scored" for a variety of characteristics, but the interpretation of the drawings is still pretty much a function of whatever intuition the clinician has. Most of the principles of interpretation (e.g., 10, 55) are based on the assumption that the drawing in some way represents the subject himself, and specific interpretive suggestions make considerable use of both concrete translations of drawing features into personality traits (e.g., emphasis on the ear is a sign of suspiciousness) and symbolic translations.

Personality measurement, and for that matter, measurement in most other areas, has generally been accorded a good deal of importance in psychology, but the place of measurement should not be accepted uncritically. Measurement operations must serve some purpose, and that they actually serve a purpose—the purpose intended—is not always certain. When one wishes to evaluate some program, e.g., a remedial course, obviously it is necessary to make some measurements at some point following the enaction of the program, and when measurement operations are so used, there can be little objection although it may be possible to object strenuously to the particular measures used. However, another and very common measurement situation occurs when it appears desirable to minimize some errors by attempting to predict in advance how an individual or a group is going to perform. There are important considerations which limit the utility of any measurement for predictive purposes.

Specifically, if we engage in measurement for predictive purposes, we are assuming that employing such measures will enable us to avoid certain errors, to increase the efficiency of our efforts. For measures to have utility, several conditions must obtain. First, it must be shown that the probability of making an error actually decreases. That is the problem of test validity; although it might seem a simple matter, it is not always possible to be confident that errors are decreased, even with a valid measure. For one thing, no matter how valid a measure may be, it will be useless if no one pays any attention to the results obtained. Testing can be useful only if it leads to action. Moreover, it must be ascertained that the action implied is possible. Testing children to determine which ones are likely to become delinquent is of no value unless there is a program to deal with delinquent children. In fact, such testing may actually be harmful, for it may produce prejudice without producing amelioration. Informing a teacher that a child has a low I.Q. or that he has delinquent propensities may be harmful if it disposes the teacher to treat him as a stupid or evil child. R. Rosenthal (68) has shown that under some conditions, teachers' beliefs about the "growth potential" of children in their classrooms have a very great effect on the growth which actually occurs.

Second, for a measure to have utility, it must be shown that not only does the probability of making a mistake decrease, but that the overall cost of errors is reduced. An expensive testing program to reduce unimportant errors is no bargain. For example, a testing program to produce information for a teacher which she is very likely to gain for herself in a few days of contact with her class is of little value unless some very important decisions have to be made in those first few days. Moreover, we must assure ourselves that in reducing errors of one kind, we are not producing errors of another. If the measures used produce many errors of the kind that lead to labeling a child as "dumb" or "predelinquent," their value in correctly identifying other children as dumb or predelinquent will be vitiated.

This does not imply that measurement, and personality measurement, even for predictive purposes, has no place in psychology and in education. It merely suggests that it is unwise to suppose that because "good" measures are available, they are good under all circumstances. Testing should be done with a purpose in mind, and there should be some assurance that the purpose is worthy of the effort.

Genetics and Personality

Probably no idea about the basis for personality is more widespread than the notion that it is "inherited." Even among people who know nothing of a specific genetic mechanism it is often sufficient to account for someone's behavior by saying that his father was the same way. In view of the obvious physical similarities between parents and their children it is not remarkable that the idea of behavioral similarities should occur. However, it is not at all satisfactory to attribute behavioral similarity between parent and child to heredity in a genetic sense unless there is positive evidence of genetic transmission of the traits involved. Evidence for genetic transmission of personality characteristics is extremely difficult to produce, but it would consist of such findings as: (a) greater similarity between identical twins than among fraternal twins and siblings; (b) greater similarity between identical twins than among siblings even when the twins have been reared in separate and different environments; (c) greater similarity between adopted children and their real parents than between the children and their foster parents; and, perhaps, (d) evidence in controlled breeding studies for the genetic transmission of "personality" characteristics in animals. In the absence of knowledge about specific genetic mechanisms the interpretations of results obtained in studies of human personality should not violate current conceptions of genetic transmission. For example, a finding of greater similarity of a first-born child to parents than of later-born children to parents would not make sense genetically.

Before further discussion of the genetic basis for personality, it seems necessary to interject a comment about two mutually incompatible but frequently encountered positions. One is that personality is inherited; the other is that personality is learned. The implicit assumption of each position is that personality is *all* inherited or *all* learned. Neither position is tenable. However, there is no reason for anyone to have to take either position. It would be better to ask, "How much of the variance in some personality characteristic is accounted for by hereditary factors and how much by experience or learning?" Thus, in the discussion which follows, no inference should be drawn that heredity or learning is all there is to personality.

What are the possible ways in which personality might be related to genes? First of all, it is possible that a given personality trait might be directly transmitted, e.g., there *might* be a gene for a trait such as dependency. However, the probability of such direct transmission would be greater the more general and pervasive a trait is and lesser the more specific it is. It is easier to imagine that "aggressiveness" might be genetically transmitted than that "desire for status" might be. In fact, it seems very clear that something more than learning is involved in the differential aggressiveness of lions and lambs. Nonetheless, with fairly specific personality traits, it becomes doubtful whether there is a direct genetic basis for them.

However, it is entirely possible that more general traits or other kinds of dispositions are genetically transmitted and that those dispositions increase the probability of parent–child similarity in more specific traits. Take, for example, "activity level" as a characteristic which might be genetically transmitted. First it should be noted that it is easier to consider genetic transmission when there is a structural or somatic basis for a trait. Thus, it is not difficult to specify possible differences in the physiology of people who are quite active as compared with those who are inactive. And it is correspondingly easy to imagine the genetic basis for such a difference. In fact, good evidence of a genetic basis for activity level among animals already exists (23). It should be noted, too, that even very young infants are strikingly different in level of activity and that the differences are fairly persistent (18, 19, 22). If given equivalent environments, would a very active child, or a less active one, be more likely to develop dependent tendencies? Probably the less active child. There might be significant evidence for genetic transmission of a trait, e.g., from twin studies, without it being necessarily so that that trait is genetically determined, for what is transmitted is only a physiological disposition that either facilitates or impedes the development of the specific trait. To draw an analogy, no sophisticated person would say that tuberculosis is inherited, but certainly the kind of body structure that renders the person susceptible to tuberculosis might be. One example of the possibility of an inherited physiological reaction is afforded by the finding of Jost and Sontag (39) that a complex measure of autonomic nervous system "balance" (somewhat akin to reactivity) yielded correlations of around 0.46 for identical twins, about 0.32 for siblings, and 0.09 for unrelated pairs of children. (A common methodological problem with studies of identical twins, compared with studies of siblings, is that, in addition to being identical in heredity, twins are also identical in age, external environment, and other irrelevant factors at the time they are measured. Had Jost and Sontag included fraternal twins, the investigation might have produced correlations equal to those for identical twins, suggesting only that children are likely to be more similar if they are measured at the same age in life.)

There is another very subtle way in which an apparent genetic similarity may be produced in the absence of any specific genetic mechanism. Each individual may be said to produce, in part, his own environment. That is, a great deal of the environment in which we live, and especially our social environment, is a reaction to our own special characteristics. For example, few persons would doubt that a handsome child elicits different reactions from his environment than does a homely child. Those reactions then become a part of the handsome child's environment. Thus, a handsome child may, from the very early days of his life, live in a predominantly rewarding environment, one in which he tends to encounter positive reinforcements that may be irrelevant to the actual nature of his behavior. It does not seem remarkable that he should develop attitudes of confidence, dominance, and the like. On the other hand, the homely child may be evaluated more objectively by those around him, and he may grow up with less favorable attitudes toward himself. Therefore, for some variables there may be greater similarity in personality for identical twins than for siblings or for real parent and child than for foster parent and child even though no real genetic transmission of personality obtains. Obviously, caution is necessary in interpreting even what seems impeccable evidence for the inheritance of personality.

Having established these reservations, let us take a brief look at three kinds of investigations which have been used to support the hypothesis that some aspects of personality are inheritable. First, Tryon (summarized in 89) showed that rats could be bred to produce divergent strains of good and poor maze runners. However, subsequent tests of the animals suggested that instead of differing in maze running "intelligence," the rats may have differed in "emotionality," the better learners being less emotional (76). Then Thompson (88) was able to produce unequivocal evidence for inheritance of maze-running ability in rats. Shortly after Tryon's work, Hall (31) was successful in breeding a previously homogeneous strain of rats to produce divergent strains of "emotional" and "unemotional" rats. Since then there have been numerous successes in breeding strains of rats and mice differing in what might be called emotionality (53, 54). Although such investigations do not "prove" anything about human beings, they certainly do prove that a genetic mechanism exists by which the transmission of such a characteristic as emotionality could take place.

Other investigators whose work is reviewed by Fuller and Thompson (23) have shown that different breeds of dogs show marked differences in such traits as "timidity" even when reared under identical circumstances (74). Few persons would deny that such evidence favors a hereditary hypothesis for "personality" differences in dogs, but accepting the same hypothesis for humans is met with greater resistance. To be sure, no responsible scientist believes that results obtained from animal experimentation can be applied directly to human problems, but it is equally irresponsible to conclude that some results cannot be applied in some human cases.

A second type of evidence has been provided by Freedman and Keller (21), who examined a group of 20 sets of twins in their own homes on a monthly basis for a year. All sets of twins were of the same sex, but not until the completion of the study was zygosity, i.e., identity or fraternity, established by determination of blood group. Thus, the investigators did not know if the twins they were studying were identical or fraternal, and their observations should not have been biased. Of more than incidental interest is the fact that neither parents nor obstetricians were at all accurate in saying whether or not the twins were identical. The investigators point out that their observations occurred before the children could have had the opportunity for mutual imitation, and they are at some pains to establish that the reactions of the parents did not create differences where none were natural. The results of the study indicate that not only were the fraternal twins consistently more different within pairs on motor tasks, but they were just as different on measures of infant personality, even when personality was judged from movies rather than in person by the investigators themselves. The investigators made no attempt to estimate the relative importance of heredity in personality, but their prudent conclusion was that heredity does seem to play some role in the development of personality. That is a judgment with which few psychologists would disagree, but the task remains of establishing the exact role which heredity plays.

Finally, Kallman (41, 43) made an extensive series of investigations into the heredity of certain forms of mental disorder, investigations obviously relevant to some aspects of the genetics of personality. Kallman's analyses place considerable emphasis both on the study of identical twins and on the rate of "concordance" in mental condition between pairs of them. (Pairs are concordant if both are schizophrenic or if neither is; otherwise they are discordant.) He also emphasized complicated statistical analyses of the rates of mental disorder among persons related in varying degrees to a particular mental patient. An example of findings from identical twin studies is presented in Table 13-1 for the diagnosis of schizophrenia. It is evident that if one of a pair of identical twins is diagnosed schizophrenic, the expectancy is very high that the

TABLE 13-1

Expectancy of Schizophrenia for Persons Related in Various Ways to Known Schizophrenics[a]

Relationship	Expectancy[b] (%)
Unrelated person	0.85
Sibling	14.3
Fraternal twin	14.7
Fraternal twin: opposite sex	11.5
Fraternal twin: same sex	17.7
Identical twin	85.8
Children	
One schizophrenic parent	16.4
Two schizophrenic parents	68.1

[a] From Kallman (42).

[b] By expectancy is meant the probability that if one person is diagnosed schizophrenic that another person in the specified relationship will be similarly diagnosed. However, these expectancies have been "corrected" in certain ways and do not necessarily correspond to the actual percentages observed.

other twin will be similarly diagnosed. It is clear, too, that the expectancy for identical twins is much higher than for other groups of siblings. Note, too, the very great difference in expectancies for persons with two as opposed to only one schizophrenic parent. It seems that the closer the genetic relationship to a schizophrenic, the greater the probability of the same disturbance appearing in a given individual.

At face value, Kallman's data appear to justify the conclusion that certain kinds of serious mental disorder are genetically transmitted. Yet not all psychiatrists and psychologists are willing to accept Kallman's conclusions without serious reservations. For one thing, not all investigations have obtained results so favorable to the genetic hypothesis as Kallman's has. It is certainly instructive to examine the more general methodological and interpretive problems that arise in considering genetic hypotheses—but there is not the space here for a complete consideration of the issues, many of which are technically intricate. [For a more sophisticated but very readable treatment of this problem, see Jackson (36).]

Speaking broadly, then, about methodology and interpretative problems: First, for data on incidence of mental disorder in twins, etc., to be meaningful, it is necessary to assure ourselves of independent observations. Many persons in the field of psychopathology fear that judgments are far from independent; it is altogether too possible that when one of a pair of identical twins is adjudged insane, there will be a bias in judging the mental status of the other twin. Similar biases might well exist for persons closely related in other ways. Second, the genetic interpretation of findings about identical twins is premised on the supposition that they grow up in dissimilar environments, often "ensured" by their separation at an early point in their lives. However, there are very few cases on record of identical twins separated in their formative years, both of whom grow up to be insane. Jackson (36) claims there are only two such cases. In fact, most twin cases studied by Kallman were separated at a much later point in their lives, and then only for a mean of about five years (36). Moreover, since the social environment is reactive, it would be expected that the environment of identical twins would be considerably more similar than that of even fraternal twins, e.g., the very similar appearance of identical twins would tend to elicit the same kinds of reactions from other persons. And, to take one final issue, it appears that Kallman's interpretation of his data is at variance with current conceptions of genetic transmission. Although Kallman first suggested that a simple recessive genetic mechanism is responsible for the occurrence of scizophrenia, it can scarcely be as simple as that. For example, concordance is higher among related female pairs than among related male pairs, and higher among same-sex than opposite-sex pairs (67). Kallman's later elaborations strengthen his theory, but it would still seem to meet with serious problems in explaining data now available (23, 36).

It should be made clear that Kallman is not necessarily wrong in his belief that some genetic process is involved in the occurrence of mental disorder. However, the case has not been proved yet, and some of the available data are open to serious question. But for the reader who wishes to pursue some of the issues further, there is an account (67) of a set of identical quadruplets, all four of whom were diagnosed as schizophrenic, three of them requiring long-term hospitalization.

Physiological Bases for Personality

It is possible to go a step up the conceptual ladder from genetics and consider the somewhat broader possibility that personality might, in some degree, reflect the individual's basic physiological processes. This is not a question of the source of physiological differences—they may be genetic or they may arise in some other manner. One possibility, for example, is that physiological differences might stem from such factors as level of maternal nutrition during pregnancy or from the adequacy of the physical environment of the neonate.

Once more, some of the problems and issues are tricky, and it is easy to be misled about the findings of an investigation after it is complete. As one very interesting instance, consider the findings reported by Sontag (83). He and his associates developed measures of fetal activity, including the measurement of the fetal heart rate. Later they obtained behavioral ratings during nursery school on children whose fetal activity had been assessed. Sontag reports that there were significant positive correlations between activity during the last two months of fetal life and social apprehension, i.e., anxiety and timidity, at the age of 2½ years. There was a negative relationship between fetal activity and peer aggression at 2½ years, i.e., the very active fetuses tended to avoid conflict, which is consistent with their high social apprehensiveness. It is interesting that results in another sample showed that social apprehension at 2½ years was directly related to social apprehension at ages 22–25 years.

If asked to interpret the above findings, and one were not careful, it would be easy to conclude that some very fundamental constitutional differences detectable even before birth are related to later personality differences in children. However, such an interpretation assumes that the two groups of children have a comparable environment at the time of both observations, or that environmental characteristics at the two times, i.e., the last two months of fetal life and at 2½ years, are uncorrelated. But, as Sontag notes, there is certainly the possibility that both the observations of fetal activity and of later social apprehension are attributable to characteristics of the mothers. Perhaps a tense, anxious mother provides an intrauterine environment that is conducive to an increased heart rate, and the same kind of mother might well produce a later environment that is likely to result in her child's social anxieties. This explanation is not neccesarily true, but it is plausible. A variety of research findings have shown that fetal heart rate is affected by the behavior of the mother, e.g., by cigarette smoking, by the mother's emotional state (84, 85). Thus, we must be very cautious in interpreting research findings such as those above as evidence for a constitutional theory of personality.

Constitution and Personality

A very prominent theory of personality that has survived several centuries of "evidence" is based on the notion that personality is inextricably related to an individual's "constitution" or physical "type." At present, the foremost exponent of that theory is William Sheldon (80), who developed the idea that there are three basic body types (roughly approximated by the terms "thin," "muscular," and "fat") that are associated with three basic personality dispositions (approximated by the terms "withdrawn," "outgoing–aggressive," and "outgoing–dependent"). Sheldon has reported evidence in favor of his theory, but it has been criticized rather severely for nonindependence of observations, i.e., Sheldon decided both what the body type and the personality type of his subjects was. Moreover, even if a relationship between body build and personality should exist, there might be plausible alternative interpretations. For example, a weak, thin child is likely to meet repeated negative reinforcements when he attempts to interact with more capable and aggressive companions, and it would not be remarkable if a withdrawal reaction were the result. But we would be hesitant to assume the existence of an inescapable causal relationship between body type and personality.

However, some investigations into the relationship between physiology and personality are more convincing from a methodological standpoint. This is not to suggest that physiology "causes" personality. In fact, there are probably equally good reasons for supposing that differences in personality might be responsible for differences in physiological functioning. For example, many psychologists and psychiatrists are convinced that psychological conflicts and problems can give rise to physical symptoms, and a field of medicine called *psychosomatic medicine* is testimony to their belief—such symptoms as ulcers, asthma, headaches, and the like being typical examples. No opinion is being interjected here, only the wish to point to a possible relationship between the two systems. Present knowledge about possible bases in physiology for many aspects of personality, e.g., different traits, is limited, but an understanding of what we call "emotion" is increasing rapidly.

Physiology and Emotion

Both physiologists and psychologists—and those hardy, nonsterile hybrids, the psychophysiologists—have long been interested in the relationship between physiological states and those psychological states ordinarily called "emotion." Is it possible that fear and anger, so very obviously different at a psychological level, are accompanied by different physiological reactions? This would seem quite likely, yet it has taken years of effort to establish that they are, and the precise differentiation is still not certain. Funkenstein (24) has suggested that a hormone, epinephrine, which, when introduced into the bloodstream, produces an increased heart rate, elevated blood pressure, an increase in blood sugar, and other physiological changes, is associated with fear, while a closely related hormone, norepinephrine, which, when introduced in the bloodstream, produces effects similar to those of epinephrine but with higher blood pressure and lower blood sugar, is associated with anger. Funkenstein refers, for example, to work by others, indicating that "aggressive" animals which preserve themselves by fighting, e.g., lions, have a preponderance of norepinephrine while more passive and social animals which preserve themselves by flight or by "freezing," e.g., rabbits, have a preponderance of epinephrine. Funkenstein was able to make distinctions which were consistent with his hypothesis in the behavior of mental patients who were injected with the two different hormones.

Ax (3) made simultaneous recordings of several different physiological measures in a laboratory situation in which his subjects were "victims" of experimental conditions calculated to arouse fear or anger. For the fear situation, they were told excitedly that owing to an equipment failure they were in serious danger of a severe electric shock. Considering that the subjects were elaborately "wired" for the recording of various responses, fear was a very likely response. The anger situation was similarly perturbing, involving as it did a surly and "rough" assistant. The physiological reactions to the two situations were clearly different, suggesting the differentiation of fear and anger at the physiological level. Moreover, the overall patterns were somewhat similar to those produced by epinephrine and norepinephrine injections, thus supporting the ideas of Funkenstein. On the other hand, the correlations between reactions to the fear and anger situations were not so much negative as zero, i.e., it cannot be concluded that fear and anger are "opposite" reactions, rather the reactions which occur are peculiar to individuals. Some individuals respond one way and some another. The correlations among variables were higher for anger than for fear, supporting the notion that anger is a more unified state than fear.

Some very interesting evidence relating epinephrine and norepinephrine to behavior comes from studies by Hoagland (34) of hormones in urinary secretions of athletes and of psychiatric patients. Professional hockey players—and hockey is a game noted for its high level of aggressiveness—proved to have a very large increase in norepinephrine secretion from a pre- to a postgame sample. However, injured players, the goalie, and the coach showed relatively more epinephrine but a more variable pattern. Amateur boxers showed high levels of epinephrine in the period prior to a bout, although boxers who shadowboxed vigorously had high levels of norepinephrine. Finally, psychiatric patients, characterized by highly aggressive behavior, also had high levels of norepinephrine in their urine.

Lacey and his associates have proposed an important principle of physiological reaction which can be termed "autonomic response stereotypy" (47). What they have proposed and found is that individuals differ in their physiological responses to stressful situations. Everyone shows an extensive physiological response to stress, but each person is characterized by the predominant response of one or more of his various physiological responders. Thus, for example, when left for a period of time with his foot in a bucket of icy water, one person will show especially high blood pressure while another will show a relatively great increase in heart rate, and still another will show a marked increase in galvanic skin response (GSR). The autonomic nervous system will usually show a general state of arousal, but each person will have his own characteristic "peak" response. Such findings are important for a number of reasons; they also point to potential explanations of the formation of different medical symptoms among persons under stress. Perhaps the reason that some persons develop ulcers, some become hypertensive, and still others are stricken with "nervous" dermatitis is that they have differential somatic sensitivity to stressful situations, a possibility supported by the work of Malmo and his associates (56–58, 79).

It appears certain that people vary in their degree of sensitivity to stress as well as in their manifestation of it. Even casual observations reveal that some persons are calm in situations in which others may be very jittery or upset. Just what causes such sensitivity is not known for certain, although many hypotheses have been advanced. Some findings concerning hereditary and constitutional bases for personality have already been mentioned. Their relevance to sensitivity to stress is apparent, but the total amount of evidence is still scant. However, there are other lines of evidence. A number of investigations have shown that animals which have been exposed to "handling" or "gentling" experiences in the first few weeks of their lives are more resistant than unhandled animals to a variety of later stresses. For example, Wieninger (91) found that the rats he gentled by handling and stroking grew larger and had a lower mortality rate than rats not gentled. Moreover, they showed less evidence of physical damage, e.g., ulcers, following stress than the non-gentled animals did. Levine (50–52) confirmed these earlier findings and made the very important discovery that gentle handling was not the critical variable, for he found that rats exposed in infancy to electric shocks were also "superior" adult rats. Such a finding indicated that it was something about the handling and not the gentling that was important. Still other investigators (86, 87) have found that even moving the infant rats about without touching them can produce "better" adult rats. By just what means the handling of infant rats may affect their later responses to stress is not known, but an intriguing hypothesis suggested by Schaefer, Weingarten, and Towne (73) is that the forms of handling which have been employed result in a temporary lowering of body temperatures in the rat pups, and that the repeated lowering of body temperature might increase resistance to stress by altering physiological responses. These experimenters actually refrigerated infant rats for brief periods of time without handling them in order to substantiate their hypothesis. Their results were consistent with the hypothesis.

It should not be concluded that emotional states are the direct and inevitable products of particular patterns of physiological response. Although the previously cited work of Ax (3) suggests that fear and anger *can* be differentiated at the physiological level, differentiation at the level of feeling, i.e., at the level at which the subject is aware, need not necessarily occur. The fact that there are such extensive differences between individuals in the reactions they show to stressful situations, as shown by Lacey, indicates that each individual must, to at least some degree, learn to discriminate and label his own emotional states. An interesting question arises: How do you know you are angry? Could one be angry without being in a physiological state of arousal? Could the same physiological state be associated with different emotional states or feelings depending on the situation? Such questions cannot be given unequivocal answers just yet, but interesting experiments in recent years have cast light on them.

Epinephrine may be injected into the bloodstream, and when it is, it produces a state of physiological arousal. The heart beats faster, blood pressure increases, skin temperature drops, and the subject is likely to report feeling tense, alert and restless. Chlorpromazine has the opposite effect, producing a state of calmness and quiescence. What happens to people who are injected with such substances and are then exposed to an arousing stimulus? Schachter and Wheeler (72) gave subjects either epinephrine or chlorpromazine injections and then showed them a slapstick episode from a movie. An additional group of subjects had received a placebo injection that consisted of nothing more than saline solution. (A *placebo* is a chemically inert substance administered under conditions designed to suggest that it has specific properties.) The epinephrine-injected subjects rated the film funnier than either of the other groups, and they laughed louder during the film. The chlorpromazine-injected subjects were not amused. Thus, emotion (amusement) was correlated with physiological arousal. In a second experiment, Schachter and Singer (71) injected subjects with either epinephrine or a placebo, but the epinephrine subjects were variously informed about the effects they might expect. Some were correctly informed about the anticipated physiological effects, e.g., pounding heart; a second group was misinformed by being told to expect an itching sensation, that in fact would not occur; and a third group was not informed at all about what they might expect. Then the subjects were exposed to another subject (actually a confederate of the experimenter) who began to behave in either a "euphoric" or a "hostile" manner. In the euphoric condition the confederate made paper airplanes, played basketball with wadded-up paper, and twirled a hula-hoop. In the hostile condition (only for the informed, the uninformed, and placebo groups) the confederate expressed anger at the experimenters, tore up a questionnaire he was supposed to be working on, and finally stomped out of the room.

The results of the experiment were consistent with Schachter's (70) hypothesis that cognitive factors are major determinants of emotional states. The groups that were misinformed or uninformed about the effects of epinephrine tended to report more feelings of euphoria or anger, as appropriate to the confederate's behavior, and they tended to engage in more acts indicative of the appropriate state. Rather curiously the groups injected with the placebo solution, i.e., with salt water, also showed emotional arousal appropriate to the condition to which they were exposed. The explanation apparently lies in the fact that the injection the placebo subjects received led them to expect that something unusual might happen to them. They were uninformed about placebo effects. When they later became somewhat aroused as a result of the objectively exciting conditions of the experiment, their arousal apparently was augmented by the expectations they had from the injection. The epinephrine-injected subjects who were fully informed about the effects they might expect did not need an explanation for their state of arousal; they already had one.

To summarize the state of our knowledge about the physiological bases for personality, we would note several points. First, the biochemistry of the body is related to the kind of reaction an individual displays to stress. Substances with physiological effects, such as epinephrine, are also found in mammals lower than man, and their action in such mammals may be quite consistent with their actions in man. Second, emotion is quite complex at the physiological level. There are not highly uniform and predictable physiological reactions associated with each emotional state. There are patterns of response which are idiosyncratic to each individual, but such patterns may be fairly consistent. The basis for the development of individual patterns is unknown, but some investigators believe that early experiences are critical. Finally, the emotional experience that an individual will have is not the exclusive product of his physiology. Rather it is jointly produced by his physiological reactions and his cognition of what is happening to him. The same pattern of arousal can seemingly be interpreted as very different emotional reactions depending upon circumstances.

Development of Personality

To many persons, one of the most interesting and critical areas of inquiry in personality is the development of personality. How does personality begin in the infant? Can one plot the course of development of personality, i.e., do most children go through some common "stages" or "phases?" Are there critical points in the development of personality, points at which very important or even irreversible changes may take place? These and many other questions are necessarily of interest to those who have continuing contact with growing, changing, developing children.

To begin at the beginning. We have just discussed some of the work bearing on the issue of the importance of early experience in the development of the individual. The research cited was accomplished with animals, and with good reason, for one cannot intentionally treat human infants in a way that might permanently harm them. However, there have been human babies who have been treated in unusual ways, apparently out of ignorance of or indifference to the possible effects on them. The condition which has been studied most extensively is maternal deprivation, i.e., conditions in which, for whatever reason, the infant is deprived of the care of his mother or a mother substitute over an important period of time. The reasons for deprivation are diverse but they include death, desertion, abandonment, hospitalization of the child, and necessary separation from the mother as in wartime evacuation. Bowlby (8) has reviewed a large number of studies of maternal deprivation, all of which consistently led to a number of depressing conclusions. If the infant is deprived of close contact with a "mothering" person, especially during the second 6 months of his life, he is far more likely than other children are to grow up grossly lacking the capacity for affection toward others, to show many behavior problems such as stealing and lying, to do poorly in school, to show evidence of emotional apathy, and in general to show signs of personality disturbance. Thus, as an initial generalization we would say that important aspects of the personality develop out of the earliest experiences of the infant, particularly those involving his relationship with the person who mothers him. The evidence cited earlier on effects of early handling in animals corroborates such a conclusion.

A second aspect of Bowlby's findings is that the experiences during the second 6 months are of critical importance. There is, then, evidence for a critical period in personality development during which certain kinds of experiences must occur if the individual is to develop normally. Again, the results from studies of animals is corroboratory, for various investigators, including Levine (52) and Scott (75) working with rats and dogs, respectively, found that there are critical periods in the development of animals. Levine found that handling after the 20th day or so, i.e., after weaning, made little difference in the later development of the rat. Similarly, Scott found that there was a period in the development of puppies during which contact with humans was essential if they were to develop the usual friendliness of dogs for humans. Thus, for normal development of personality certain early experiences seem essential, and they may need to occur within a particular period of time to be effective.

There is a third conclusion drawn by Bowlby from his review of his own work and that of others. The effects of early maternal deprivation may be permanent and irreversible; at the very least they are difficult to reverse. If a child is deprived of maternal care for a period during infancy, and if compensatory care is not begun very soon afterward, i.e., before the age of 30 months or so, the child is likely to be permanently impaired. And, once more, data from studies of animals confirm other findings, for the animals deprived of handling or human contact during their infancy cannot be "cured" by compensatory handling or contact at a later date.

Considerations of the importance of early experience, critical periods, and irreversible learning lead naturally to the question of "stages" in personality development. It has often been suggested or implied that both intellectual and personality development proceeds by stages, but persuasive evidence is absent. If development does involve stages, a number of things should follow. First, there is the implication that changes should be discrete rather than gradual, and there should be periods of relative stability between changes. Second, the stages should be more or less uniform from one individual to another, i.e., the number and sequences of stages should be the same. If individuals go through different courses of development, if some pass through sequences that others do not, the validity of the assumption of stages becomes questionable. Thus far, there is very little evidence compatible with the idea that there are stages in personality development.

A number of personality theorists have made use of the idea of stages. Freud, the most prominent of these theorists, described a sequence of stages of personality development that was supposed to be universal. According to Freud, the course of development, i.e., the sequence of stages, is associated with shifting zones of erotic sensitivity. Thus, the first zone is the mouth, and the initial stage of development is "oral." Although it was assumed that each physically and intellectually normal individual would go through all the stages in the same order and, within limits, at approximately the same ages, experiences within stages were thought to be crucial. It was believed that during each stage the proper amount of erotic gratification had to occur in order for normal progression to the next stage to take place. If the individual did not receive sufficient gratification in a given stage, or if gratification during that stage was excessive, then "fixation" at that level occurred. Although fixation did not mean that the individual did not develop any further, it did mean that a pattern was formed so that for the remainder of his life he was likely to show distinct traces of his early development. Moreover, it was further supposed by Freud and his followers that if the fixated individual met excessive stress at some later point in his life, he was likely to revert ("regress") to the point of his earlier fixation. For example, an "orally fixated" person would show an exceptional interest in oral gratifications such as eating, smoking, and even talking, and when encountering severe stress would tend to respond to it by increased oral activity such as over-eating, excessive smoking, or verbal aggression. In Freudian theory fixations are irreversible except for such changes as might be brought about through psychoanalytic inquiry into the experiences associated with the acquisition of the fixation. Freud's speculations about early development have been provocative and fascinating to many people, but they have not proved susceptible to empirical confirmation. Many of his observations are easily explained by other theories, and some of his assumptions, e.g., of universal, sequential erogenous zones, are almost certainly untenable.

Although different theorists would place different emphasis on natural sequences or stages in development and on environmental experience, all would agree that the experiences of a child are of great importance in later personality development. However, it turns out to be very difficult to specify the relationship between the particular experiences of a child and his later personality. Take, for example, the much discussed issue of breast vs bottle feeding of infants. Theorists of a Freudian bent, and probably a good many others, say that breast feeding is superior, inherently so, to bottle feeding. On the other hand, because many other theorists are skeptical of the claim of superiority, the number of women in our culture who are breast feeding their babies is declining (11). There are several problems (11) which make it difficult to resolve the issue; moreover, analogous problems plague investigations into almost all other aspects of childhood experience.

1. We must assure ourselves that breast and bottle feeding do not differ nutritionally and hygenically, for otherwise the superiority of one practice or the other might be spurious. Recent developments in infant formula and simplification of sterilization make it possible for bottle feeding to be as nutritious and safe as breast feeding.

2. We must assure ourselves that breast and bottle feeding are carried out with the same warmth, attention, and interest. If breast-fed babies are held more closely, if they receive more attention, if their mothers are more relaxed, it may be very difficult to interpret differences between breast and bottle feeding. We would point out here that attitudes of mothers toward both practices are also of very evident importance.

3. The mechanics of breast and bottle feeding should not be artificially and unnecessarily dissimilar. Thus, the amount of sucking required for the infant to satisfy his nutritional needs does not have to differ and should not. The position in which the infant is held is not a necessary difference and should not be a determining factor.

These are only a few of the possible problems which arise. If the prescriptions implied in these issues were carried far enough could there possibly be any difference between breast and bottle feeding? But one of our principal and most powerful research strategies is to begin with things as nearly equivalent as possible and to try by introducing discrete changes to discover just what it is that makes a difference.

After sifting a great deal of evidence professing that infants are better fed from breast—or from bottle—Caldwell (11) concludes that there is no convincing evidence in favor of breast feeding, and there is no evidence at all in favor of bottle feeding. That does not mean that the choice is immaterial, for the mother's attitude is of very great importance. In short, what appears to matter is not the specific practice, but the attitude of the mother who is carrying it out.

In fact, the same conclusion can probably be drawn for most specific child-rearing practices. It is, of course, true that use of specific techniques in child rearing are usually confounded with attitudes of the mother (or father), e.g., mothers who use physical punishment frequently probably differ in many of their attitudes from mothers who use physical punishment rarely. But it appears quite likely that the overall attitudes of parents and the atmosphere in which they rear their children are of much greater significance than the specific techniques they employ.

Some generalizations relating personality development to parental attitudes and behaviors can be and have been made, particularly in the area of disciplinary efforts by parents. Becker (6) concludes that disciplinary practices can be understood only in the context of "the warmth of the parent–child relation, the prior history of disciplinary practices and emotional relations, the role–structure of the family, and the social and economic conditions under which a particular family unit is living." Much of what we know is probably fairly specific to the groups studied, which means working- and middle-class families. Even though warmth and permissiveness have consistently been found desirable for development of sociability and independence, while hostility seems quite undesirable, the extent of our knowledge is still limited. As Becker points out, what we know about is primarily the extreme forms of parental hostility. There is some evidence, however, to suggest that at milder levels, hostile interactions between parent and child may serve the valuable purpose of providing the child with opportunities to develop ways of coping with the world outside his home. We need more knowledge about the specific consequences of parental behaviors in these areas.

There is probably no better illustration of the development of personality than the evolution of sex-role identity in the childhood–adolescent years. Although the human infant may not be totally pliable, there is no question that the infant has the capacity to develop a wide variety of behavior patterns which may or may not be appropriate to his sex. Nor is there any denying that the variability in behavior within either male or female groups is very great; but the overall differences between males and females in almost every sort of behavior range from substantial to enormous. How, then, is the only marginally differentiated, asexual infant population transformed into two groups so different that they may seem two different species? That is a problem in personality development.

Kagan (40) has presented in considerable detail the research bearing on the acquisition of a sex-role identification. Probably the fundamental process involved is *identification* with a parental figure. Not all theorists agree completely on what identification is supposed to be but Kagan's definition is probably acceptable in general: "a belief that some of the attributes of a model . . . belongs to the self. . . . Moreover, if a child is identified with a model, he will behave, to some extent, as if events that occur to the model are occurring to him." Apparently identification is based largely on the child's desire to have the same power the model has to control reinforcements administered to others. Another widely held view has been that children identify with certain models because they wish to possess the reinforcements received by the model, but in a direct test of the two theories, Bandura, Ross, and Ross (5) found that when children had the opportunity to form a differential identification either with the dispenser or the recipient of desirable reinforcements, they showed a strong tendency to identify with the powerful model. Presumably, as the child identifies with the model, he will attempt to emulate the behavior and characteristics of the model. During the first few childhood years, it appears that both boys and girls very often identify with their mothers, who dispense the reinforcements most apparent to child. However, at a little later age, the father becomes more important as a dispenser of reinforcements, and identification with him increases. Presumably, children then also take on the masculine characteristics of the father.

Direct and differential reinforcement for identification becomes more important. If a little girl persists too long in displaying behaviors appropriate to the masculine sex role, she is likely to be actively discouraged by a wide variety of persons. Boys, of course, will be encouraged in such behavior. Each child will be encouraged to make an appropriate identification with the parent of the same sex. To the extent that the child has a parent whose behavior is appropriate to the culturally defined sex role, the child will, if he identifies with that parent, behave in an appropriate manner. If identification is weak, e.g., because the parent is absent from the home or is rejecting, or if the behavior of the same sex parent is inappropriate, the child may very well grow into adolescence with an impaired capacity to behave in a manner appropriate to his sex and age. What constitutes appropriate sex behavior is defined exclusively by cultural standards, so that what is considered "normal" male or female behavior in one culture might be totally inappropriate or "abnormal" in another. For example, in many places it is common for the women to go off to work in the fields while the men stay at home to care for the children and their homes.

A general principle might be that personality development proceeds in accord with approximately the same principles that determine sex-role identification and in accord with other principles of response acquisition. That is, behaviors will be acquired if they are followed by positive reinforcement or if they are perceived as potentially leading to positive reinforcement. If there are uniformities in personality development, or if it seems that development proceeds in the same way for sizable groups of persons, it is because there are uniformities in environments, mostly social and cultural, which make available a uniform schedule of reinforcements for a narrow range of behaviors.

The degree to which a personality can be altered once its development is well under way is an issue of obvious importance. If personality were completely pliable, there would be no concept of it, per se; but certainly, at any very early age, no personality is so fixed that it cannot be altered at all. There are many reasons for supposing that personality must become more and more stable with age, but whether it ever becomes immutable is questionable. Probably the answer depends on definitions, for personality could be so defined as to be quite fixed by early adulthood, but it could also be defined in such a way as to seem ever changeable.

The degree of alterability one sees in personality is probably related to one's views of the basis for personality. Certainly anyone who views personality as determined largely by genetics or constitutional makeup will be skeptical of the possibilities of producing any fundamental changes in personality. On the other hand, the view that personality develops from social learning is probably more consistent with the idea of personality changes. A physiological theorist might or might not accept the proposition that personality can be altered by experience.

Just what influence school experience does or can have on a child's personality is open to question. Probably the personalities of most children are little affected by school experience, in part because that experience is planned in such a way that it is relatively neutral in its impact on most children. Or, to say it another way, the nature of the school experience is controlled so that while learning is facilitated, neither the teacher nor the classroom has a strong emotional impact, positive or negative, on the child. The surroundings are pleasant, the teacher is usually pleasant but impartial, and even when she departs from a rather benign impartiality, the teacher is unlikely to engage—except momentarily—in highly charged interactions with the children. Moreover, the variety of reinforcements available in school, both positive and negative, is quite limited compared with a home situation, and the variety of behaviors which are likely to be reinforced one way or the other is also limited.

However, that is not to say that the school and the teacher cannot and do not have important effects on individual children. Children may find satisfactions in school not available to them outside, and they may find a teacher who fills an important gap in their interpersonal relations. Other children may meet with failure and rejection in school, and still others may meet with additional problems with which they are ill-prepared to cope, e.g., dealing with a playground bully. Thus, it is important that the school system and the individual teacher be alert for effects which may occur in relation to the personalities of children, and be prepared to make the most of the positive effects by contributing to the child's development of personal and interpersonal competence. Most children will be relatively unaffected, but those who are should be affected positively.

Adjustment and Failures of Adjustment

In one guise or another "personal adjustment" is one of the most widely used concepts in psychology. Various words may be used to express the ideas involved, and the negation of adjustment, i.e., maladjustment, is probably more widely employed than the affirmation of the idea. These terms are so commonly used that most laymen would not admit any particular confusion in their understanding and use of the idea of adjustment. It is evident, though, that from person to person and from occasion to occasion very different things are meant by "adjustment." Indeed, psychologists are in deep disagreement about the use of the term and sometimes seem to think that it would be better to abandon the term and the concept of adjustment altogether. What are the major difficulties inherent in the term, and what remains after the problems are resolved?

Adjustment, by itself, is predominantly neutral in its connotations, and as an evaluation is nearly always modified by some judgmental adjective, e.g., "good adjustment," "poor adjustment," or "maladjustment." It may not even be valid to ask whether someone is "making an adjustment" to his problem, for unless he is unconscious, he is responding in some manner—and that is exactly what is meant by adjustment. It is the adequacy of his response that we are concerned with—not merely the fact that he is responding. Another important point is that adjusting is a continuous process. It is not some final goal or ultimate state of nirvana toward which one strives.

It should be evident that adjustment means something other than statistical normality. Patterns of behavior are not good adjustments because they are common, nor are they poor adjustments because they are uncommon. In fact, it is obvious that some very superior and desirable forms of behavior are quite uncommon, and some inferior forms of response are, unfortunately, all too common. Nonetheless, thinking about adjustment often seems to be based on statistical notions. Many parents, for example, worry because their children are not "like other kids." A little probing of their feelings may often reveal other, perhaps more justified, concerns, but it also happens that the mere occurrence of a difference is sufficient to cause parents to worry about their child's adjustment. Neither differences nor similarities are cause for worry or elation in their own right.

Of course, a very important aspect of adjustment is the individual's relation to his fellows and to society at large. Adjustment is often thought of in terms of the adequacy with which a person manages his interpersonal relations and of his conformity to society's expectations. It follows, then, that the person who gets along well with others, who makes a decent living for himself and his family, who obeys the law, and who discharges his overall responsibilities to his family and his community is making a satisfactory, or even a good, adjustment. Conversely, argumentative people, lawbreakers, hippies, philanderers, and the like are considered "poorly adjusted." There may be some justice in each idea, but there is also a very important bias being introduced. It should be clear to just what kind of a society and to what aspects of society it is that an individual is being required to adjust. It has often been persuasively argued that in some societies, e.g., Nazi Germany, it is the dissident nonconformist who would be considered by outsiders to be making an excellent adjustment. Moreover, some people have argued that all innovation, all progress, stems from those who are discontent with their society and are largely outside it (30). Finally, we must remember that every individual is a member of many different societies and subsocieties, not all of which have congruent, compatible aims. When, in our own society, we find people who seem unaffected by the main currents and issues of our large, middle-class society, it is worse than gratuitous to evaluate their adjustment in reference to that society. Similarly, to make a social evaluation of the adjustment of the hippie, it is first necessary to be quite aware of the fact that the hippie may be a member of a subsociety in which he is getting along exceptionally well.

A second very important aspect of adjustment is the individual's own feeling about himself and his lot in life. The concept of adjustment is often invoked in relation to persons who, no matter how reasonable their social and other behavior, are evidently dissatisfied, tense, and unhappy. Of course, conformity to social expectations should not be at the cost of all personal satisfaction and happiness; it is expected that the person who is making a good adjustment will find personal satisfactions in his life and that he will often be very happy. It should be obvious that the well-adjusted person will not always be happy, for living inevitably involves disappointments and even tragedy. Happiness or personal comfort is not the sum total of adjustment. There are certain people in our society, many of them called *psychopaths*, who might be very happy if they were simply allowed to go about exploiting others to gratify whatever momentary urges they experience. And someone in a concentration camp might be persistently tense and distraught. It would be foolhardy to call psychopaths well adjusted and the prisoner maladjusted.

Although it is very difficult to arrive at a completely satisfactory concept of adjustment, a good definition of maladjustment was proposed by Cameron and Magaret (12). To paraphrase them, maladjustments are those behaviors which result in the person's being persistently tense, dissatisfied, incompetent, or ineffectual. Note that momentary or transient increases in tension, etc., are not particularly at issue, but the long-term, overall trends in an individual's behavior that are important. A more positive view is taken by Heyns (33), who states that responses represent good adjustments if they reduce tension (a) without unduly interfering with the satisfaction of the other motives of the individual, and (b) without interfering materially with the adjustment of other people. The first point is important because it acknowledges that there should be some balance in every person's life, and that the achievement of satisfaction in one area probably should not be at the cost of dissatisfaction in some other area of his life. The second point recognizes that a person who behaves in a way that brings distress to others in the fulfillment of his own needs is not adequately adjusted.

Many persons working in the field of adjustment are dissatisfied with what they consider minimal definitions of adjustment, e.g., "not maladjusted," and several have suggested that there is a need for a concept of positive mental health, i.e., something more than being not maladjusted. It is interesting that we do not even have a good word for what we want to talk about. Various criteria have been established for positive mental health (37), including positive and correct views of the self, an undistorted view of reality, and mastery over the environment. One idea that has received particular attention is self-actualization. Maslow (59) is currently the theorist most closely associated with that concept. Self-actualization means the fulfillment of the individual's unique capacities for development. Unfortunately it is very difficult to specify what each person's unique capacities are, and there are strong and obvious biases in Maslow's and others' nominations for self-actualized status (7). Eleanor Roosevelt and Albert Einstein were remarkable persons whose positions are unassailable. But why not list Ringo Starr, Natalie Wood, and Mickey Mantle? Who is to say that they have not fulfilled their special, unique capabilities for living? That we admire certain people more does not mean that others are not equally self-actualized. In practice, the specification of the qualities of the self-actualized person turns out to be little more than a list of qualities much admired by intellectual, politically liberal persons.

Although the possibility and usefulness of specifying the characteristics of self-actualized persons is doubtful, there is one aspect of self-actualization theory which seems important. It makes excellent sense to believe that there are many and diverse ways of adjusting to the stresses and strains of life and that the evaluation of adjustment must take into account the capabilities and circumstances of each unique individual. Two persons may be equally effective in life even though their "styles" are remarkably different. Wendell Johnson (38) describes an engineering concept of adjustment that is analogous to engineering standards applied to machines. An automotive engineer would not have much sympathy with complaints about the poor racing capability of the family auto. Johnson suggests that a similar view may be taken of human performance. Our expectations will be very different for a handcapped person or a culturally deprived person than for a person who has physical integrity and health, good education, and a stimulating environment. And expectations will differ for persons who are working under very good or very adverse circumstances. It is necessary to be cautious, then, in evaluating a person's level of adjustment on the basis of superficial observations.

Not all attempts at adjustment and at problem solving are successful, and when failures occur, the consequences may be of greatest importance. One important field of psychology, *psychopathology*, is wholly concerned with the problem of failures of adjustment. It should be made clear that failures of adjustment are common; no one is 100% effective in coping with his personal problems and dilemmas. For example, in one intensive investigation of a large urban community it was concluded that over 80% of the sample studied had psychological problems causing at least mild symptoms, and almost 25% would be described as "impaired" by their disturbance (48).

But psychopathology is something else; failures of adjustment are both extreme and persistent. A child's single, brief manifestation of "temper" is not of great concern, but if the manifestations of temper are extreme, prolonged, and repeated, they are "temper tantrums"—behavior distinctly undesirable and indicative of poor adjustment. This principle holds for most other behaviors. They are regarded as pathological or "abnormal" only if they are relatively extreme and persistent.

Failures of adjustment may seem like a euphemism for mental illness.

It is true that many of the same phenomena of adjustment failures are often called mental illnesses; but that term, because of its many unfortunate implications, is not being used in this text. The term "illness" seems to imply that there are separate and distinct entities, i.e., disease, which exist apart from any of their manifestations. That there is a disease of schizophrenia in the sense that there is a disease of tuberculosis is questionable. Moreover, the term "mental" implies that there is a separate but analogous system or structure called the "mind" that corresponds to the body—and that, like the body, can be "sick." That, too, is questionable. Finally, but without exhausting the undesirable implications of the term mental illness, there is a strong objection to the implication that what is called mental illness is clearly and properly a medical problem and only a medical problem.

Current thinking about adjustment failures has been heavily influenced by the fact that so very much of the early thinking occurred in the general context afforded by medical practice. An important consequence has been the development of a system of classifying mental disorders that is based on the "disease model." Thus, there are such terms as schizophrenia, manic–depressive psychosis, obsessive–compulsive neurosis and so on, all of which imply a homogeneous group of patients. Actually, patients with the same diagnosis are not especially homogeneous in any respect, and psychiatric diagnosis is notably unreliable. Moreover, it has been necessary to create many new categories which clearly do not fit the general notions of disease. For example, some patients are said to have character disorders, and some are described simply as having behavior disorders.

Many theorists in the field of psychopathology find it useful and consistent to think about failures of adjustment in terms of the ways people attempt to cope with stressful circumstances, including their own conflicts and anxieties. Failures of adjustment constitute patterns of reaction, and the fact that there are groups of people whose symptoms are similar may be accounted for by the limited number of human reactions. There is no clear indication that the reactions involved in failures of adjustment differ in kind from those considered more normal. Cameron and Magaret (12) suggest that all the symptoms and behaviors seen among psychiatric patients are seen among normal persons and are only distortions and exaggerations of ordinary behaviors. Failure of adjustment occurs when inadequate, inappropriate responses are prolonged.

A theoretically and practically important question is whether adequate adjustment can be measured on a continuous scale ranging from very good to very poor or whether there are breaks or discontinuities in the scale. For example, does behavior shade from normal to mildly inadequate, to very inadequate? Or are there places on the scale where the changes are abrupt? The application of medical thinking is seen in the development of such ideas as "neurosis" and "psychosis," which imply some discontinuities. It is a common supposition that the transition from normal to psychotic is very abrupt and drastic, with no gradations between. Moreover, it is also commonly supposed that people either are neurotic or are not neurotic. However, what is closer to the truth is that every degree of neurotic behavior may be found, i.e., gradual shadings of behavior from normal to what is called neurotic. There is even reason to suppose that more serious reactions ordinarily called psychotic may occur in every degree from normal to very extreme. The distinction between neurotic and psychotic is popularly made on the basis of the supposed seriousness of the case, and probably that is somewhat justified. Nonetheless, there are clearly many cases termed neurotic that are more difficult to treat than many cases called psychosis, and other distinctions such as "loss of contact with reality" are similarly imprecise.

There is not space enough to detail all of the varieties of reactions which constitute failures of adjustment, but it may be instructive to examine a few of the possibilities. For example, physical illness offers many opportunities for adjustment in our culture. Because we place such emphasis on being physically healthy, when a person becomes physically ill it is a source of some concern. But illness is also likely to provoke concern in others and to initiate sequences of dependent–nurturent interactions. Should an individual suffer from mild headaches when he is under stress, it would not be regarded as remarkable. But if his headaches came to preoccupy him and interfere with his ability to cope otherwise with the stress, and if he began to be chronically ill and dependent, the situation could be regarded as serious and in need of amelioration. There are some people who seem to retreat into invalidism as a way of avoiding the normal stresses and strains of life.

Withdrawal is another frequent reaction to difficult situations, often accompanied by wishful fantasies. Nearly everyone occasionally retreats from difficult situations and then daydreams about various, often highly gratifying, solutions to them. Again, within fairly wide limits, such withdrawal reactions are tolerable. However, as the withdrawal becomes more extreme and more persistent, it is likely to interfere with other attempts at problem solving, and it may even involve the individual in additional difficulties. And if the person who is withdrawing increasingly responds to his fantasies as if they were real, his adjustment is in serious doubt. Not all fantasies are necessarily pleasant, for one of the apparently strong motivations most persons have for fantacizing is to explain or rationalize their own situation and their behavior in relation to it. Para-

doxical as it may seem, most people would often rather have an unpleasant or threatening explanation for what is happening than to have
no explanation at all.

Often people seem to be caught in something of a maelstrom of events
for which they have no explanation, and if they hit upon a possible
explanation, even if it is an unpleasant one, they seize upon it. For
example, an adolescent boy had never developed sustaining confidence
in himself or a concept of himself as a worthwhile person. Consequently,
his interpersonal relationships were always strained and anxiety producing, and with some justification, he began to develop the belief that his
classmates did not like him, that they considered him odd, and that they
avoided him. He was rather agitated until he hit upon the notion,
apparently engendered by advertising, that he had an unpleasant body
odor. He then became notably less anxious although it should be said
that his relationships did not improve. For a while he was reassured that
there was a logical explanation for the reaction he sensed in others. If
unjustified beliefs about experience or interpretations of experience
become sufficiently extreme, they are called *delusions* and are regarded
as evidence of severe personality disturbance. Sometimes a person begins
to experience his own fantasies and thoughts as if real, and if they
involve distinct perceptual phenomena, he may hear voices or see visions
when there is no apparent justification; such reactions are *hallucinations*.

Finally, under many conditions of stress, some people respond with
attitudes of self-blame and self-derogation, often accompanied by
anxiety. If the reaction is sufficiently strong, that person is said to be
depressed. The depressed person is, of course, characterized by his
obvious unhappiness; he may weep and in other ways make his sad mood
manifest. Very often depressed persons become inactive and preoccupied
in much the way that a normal but sad person is likely to become quiet
and thoughtful. Given the self-blame and sense of worthlessness of
depressed persons, it is understandable that they might seek punishment
or attempt to do harm to themselves. In many ways the depressed person
has given up attempting to cope with his problems and is simply over-
whelmed by them.

There are, of course, many other ways people may adjust to stress, and
probably most of the ways eventuate in tension-producing, undesirable
patterns of response if they are inappropriate, distorted, or chronic. It
should be emphasized that to the outside observer, only a pattern of
behavior is evident. Whatever his inferences about "what really is wrong"
or about underlying states, they are based on something about the
individual which he can see and, at some crude level, measure. Thus, a
depressed person is someone who behaves "in a depressed manner." The

first stage in understanding or dealing with any adjustment problem is a careful detailing of the response patterns involved.

_____ The Modification of Inadequate Patterns of Adjustment

If a characteristic pattern of responses has been identified as inadequate, it then follows that we would want to change it, whether it is our own pattern or that of someone else. Since our concern is with responses, i.e., behavior, it is evident that the principles that apply to maladjustment are the same as those that apply to any other behaviors. Behavior patterns are altered by changing the stimuli or cues associated with the onset of the behavior and by changing the pattern of reinforcements contingent on the behavior. Once it is decided exactly what change in behavior is to be effected, it is necessary to determine what stimuli seem to elicit the behavior. Often behavior patterns can be changed by changing stimuli. For example, a group of dormitory counselors once complained that students were persistently dropping fire extinguishers down the stairwells. When asked where their fire extinguishers were kept, they replied that they were kept on walls adjacent to the stairwells. When the fire extinguishers were moved to the other end of the corridor, stairwell "bombing" declined greatly. Alternatively, stimulus patterns associated with highly desired behaviors can be strengthened. Probably many student complaints about problems of concentrating while studying could be reduced if not eliminated by making the stimuli more powerfully evocative of studious behavior, e.g., a special place for studying, removal of distracting stimuli.

The first requisite for altering reinforcement contingencies is to discover just what reinforcements are contingent on the response to begin with. Sometimes responses can be fairly quickly eliminated by removing a potent reinforcer. Temper tantrums are a good case in point. Nearly all authorities on child rearing are now agreed that tantrums are maintained because they are so effective in getting the child what he wants. When tantrums are ignored and are allowed to run their course, they quickly cease to occur. It is not always easy to discover just what the reinforcements for a particular response are, and it may not always be easy to change the reinforcement contingencies. The writers know several children whose rather serious behavior problems in the classroom seemed to be strongly reinforced by the attention they received from their teacher and classmates. How one gets a whole classroom of children to ignore a misbehaving child is a problem of considerable dimensions.

One very common hypothesis concerning children whose behavior is reinforced by attention from others is that they have a "need" for attention, and, hence, if they could get attention in other ways, they would not misbehave to get it. Perhaps a strategy based on that idea might sometimes work. One teacher decided that a still better idea might be to reduce the value of attention-getting as a reinforcement for a troublesome fourth-grade child whom we shall call Harry. The class was being disrupted several times each day by the clowning and obstreperousness of Harry, and the usual result of his behavior was that the whole class focused their attention on him. The teacher developed the idea of calling specific attention to Harry so that whenever he misbehaved, she would say, "Well, now. Let's all stop and look at Harry." The first day of her experiment he disrupted the class eleven times, but during the third week of the experiment he disrupted the class a total of only four times, and the experiment was discontinued. The teacher reported that Harry was a much improved if not a perfect pupil by the end of the term. Attention so freely gained may not be much of a reinforcement.

It is undoubtedly easier to see how the relatively simple behaviors such as classroom misbehavior can be manipulated than to see how one might produce changes in behavior of persons with serious personality problems. However, a number of investigators have been able to show critically important changes in behavior stemming from manipulation of reinforcements. Bachrach, Erwin, and Mohr (4) encountered a hospital patient who had suffered for many years from a severe loss of appetite without any medical explanation (*anorexia nervosa*), and who weighed only 47 pounds. The research team discovered that she was receiving a great deal of attention from her family and friends and that she was very sociable. Despite the protests of nursing personnel they put her in an impoverished environment without television, social contact, etc. Then they made such amenities contingent upon eating, and later upon weight gain, i.e., she could have visitors, watch television, or listen to music only after eating. The patient made considerable progress and on last report was out of the hospital and holding a job. Her weight had increased by about 40 pounds.

In a second case, Brady and Lind (9) dealt with a patient suffering from blindness without medical explanation (hysterical blindness). As is common in such cases the patient was not much worried about his condition, and got around very well despite his "blindness." Nonetheless, there was no doubt that his vision was actually impaired, i.e., he was not simply malingering. The experimenters put him in a problem-solving situation in which good performance was dependent upon vision and in which he was rewarded by attention and approval for good performance. Over a period of time the patient regained his vision and was able to leave the hospital in which he was receiving training for the blind. It should be noted that in neither of the above cases did the treatment depend on an analysis of the cause of the behavior or the nature of the underlying disorder.

The last example of behavior modification with very difficult problems comes from an experiment by King, Armitage, and Tilton (45), who worked with schizophrenic mental patients who had been hospitalized for a long period of time and were characterized by extreme withdrawal, including refusal to talk. The researchers began with a simple kind of conditioning problem in which the patients could get cigarettes and candy by pressing a bar, and progressed from these to more complicated problems requiring patients to cooperate and work in groups in order to solve the problems. Their procedures resulted in a considerable improvement in the behavior of the patients, such aspects as amount of speech, amount of activity, and cooperativeness being especially affected. Thus, even serious behavior problems are amenable to change by way of manipulation of reinforcement contingencies. Moreover, no cases have been reported of patients being made worse by such manipulations.

There are other methods for dealing with adjustment problems, and psychotherapy is often regarded the treatment of choice, i.e., the very best of the methods available. Except with children, psychotherapy almost always requires the patient to talk about himself and his problems while the therapist listens and occasionally offers comments meant to assist the patient in his attempts at self-understanding. Some psychotherapists place great emphasis on the understanding, called insight, which the patient gains, while other therapists emphasize the permissiveness and acceptance in the relationship which permits the patient to express himself freely and to grow as a person. Some theorists have suggested that psychotherapy may provide many opportunities for the patient to have his anxiety-producing responses extinguished since he emits them in the presence of an accepting, nonpunitive therapist (81). Other theorists have pointed out the many ways in which therapists may directly reinforce desirable responses (46). For example, the therapist may express verbal approval, he may smile or nod, or he may merely look more interested. Therapists may also offer communications which represent attempts at direct influence on the patient, and to the extent that they are credible and powerful as sources of communication, they may influence the patient (27).

Of course, psychotherapy is also a social situation, involving as it does at least two people, and there are very good reasons for considering the situation in terms of reciprocal relationships and influence. Thus, the patient emits some response to which the therapist replies, "Hmm. Good."

Presumably the patient is susceptible to the influence of the therapist and is more likely to emit the same or a very similar response on subsequent occasions. But presumably the therapist is also influenced in some degree by his patient. Therefore, the therapist's behavior may be shaped by the behavior of the patient. The therapist is likely to repeat those behaviors, e.g., saying "Good," that are reinforced by changes in the patient's behavior. And, in addition to the other things he is presumably learning, the patient is learning in at least some small degree to control the behavior of the therapist as well as to be controlled by him.

Unfortunately, the evidence for the effectiveness of psychotherapy is quite limited, and many psychologists doubt that it has any specific efficacy at all. One psychiatrist (20) has indicated his belief that any effects of psychotherapy are the result of the prestige of the psychotherapist and the suggestibility of the patient. Goldstein (26) has shown that whether patients do well in psychotherapy is very strongly related to their own and their therapists' expectancies that they will make good progress. That psychotherapy should have a considerable component stemming from suggestion should not be especially surprising, for in physical medicine the power of placebos has long been known. Evidently, in a good many areas of behavior the most powerful stimulant to change is the expectation that change will occur.

We would not want to suggest that all problems in adjustment boil down to simple but bad habits, nor would we want to suggest that attempts to modify behavior should consist of simple attempts to modify those bad habits. In many instances there is probably much to be gained from examining the pattern or structure implicit in an individual's behavior and also from discovering what the behavior seems designed to achieve. Producing even relatively limited changes in responses may ramify in such a way as to produce widespread changes in patterns of behavior is that limited changes in the environment may disrupt plans or intentions. Just as a plan for a 100-mile trip may be changed completely by the collapse of a 100-foot bridge, so may elaborate patterns of behavior be disrupted by indications of the failure of one part of the pattern. When the hysteric blind patient finds his blindness being alleviated, many other changes in his behavior may also have to occur to maintain the integrity of his behavior. Although it may often be expedient to deal with fragments of behavior, with isolated responses, it may also be expedient in other instances to think of behavior in terms of a structure or plan which may underlie it and to try to change that structure. Thus far our knowledge of the ways of changing broader aspects of behavior is slight, but it is often more to that question that the efforts of psychotherapists are directed. In their view, changing the individual's view of himself, which is often called the self-concept, and by which they mean more than simply what he says about himself, may have widespread effects on behavior.

One final word about behavior modification. We assume that when behavior is modified in some limited or controlled situation it will transfer to other situations and be positively reinforced in them. Neither assumption necessarily obtains. In all attempts at changing an entire pattern of behavior, special effort must be made to ensure the transfer of the behavior in question (27). For example, in the case reported by Bachrach, Erwin and Mohr, there was a distinct possibility that the woman might eat more in the hospital but that her eating would not carry over into her extra-hospital life. Therefore, the experimenters took special precautions to have eating outside the hospital brought under appropriate stimulus control and to have it reinforced, e.g., by social contact and approval. But no matter what our efforts to modify behavior, we may be frustrated if the behavior we want to change is reinforced differently under situations outside our control. It will be very difficult to make great progress in decreasing aggression in children who find it persistently rewarding in their natural habitat. A better understanding of patterns of reinforcement prevailing in situations in which responses are to be performed may aid us immeasurably in modifying behavior or in comprehending our failures.

Personality and Psychology

There is not a distinction to be made between the variables of personality and the variables of the rest of psychology although there is often an inclination to act as if there were. The same factors that account for other aspects of behavior can account satisfactorily for the data of personality. Some behavior is reflexive, and some may in a general sense be constitutional, but the bulk of the behavior in which personality psychologists are interested in is unquestionably learned. It is, as there is reason to believe, learned in the same way as other behaviors.

There is, of course, always some degree of organization to behavior, and various responses are likely to affect each other. So it is with personality. We do not find it surprising that variables thought of as reflecting personality should affect other responses such as learning, retention, and perception. Indeed, we would be surprised if it were not so. We should be very careful to be sure that we know in just what manner variables do influence each other, and we might often be surprised at the truth if it were known. For example, a number of years ago there was considerable excitement in psychology because it appeared that a fundamental perceptual phenomenon, the absolute recognition threshold, was greatly influenced by personality. Specifically, it was shown that when taboo and neutral words were tachistoscopically presented at very fast speeds, subjects reported seeing the neutral words before the taboo words (60). However, later results have shown that recognition of words is delayed about in proportion to their infrequency in the language, and many of the taboo words are considerably less frequent in occurrence than the neutral words that were originally used as controls. Moreover, it very quickly became apparent that a distinction had to be made between "seeing" and "saying" a word, and subjects were more reluctant to say taboo words even if they did see them (65). Thus, the initially exciting findings concerning the relationship between personality (defensiveness against threatening material) and perception were largely dissipated in the light of general psychology.

That is not to imply that personality variables and other psychological variables would have no direct, first-order relationship. Certainly it seems reasonable that anxiety should be related to the manner and speed with which people learn. That people might find material closely related to their personal problems either more or less difficult to learn than material without personal relevance would not be surprising. We do not yet know many of the details of the relationship between personality and other psychological processes, but we know enough to conclude that personality is comprehensible in the same terms as the rest of the field of psychology.

Summary

1. Personality is a difficult term to define. Although psychologists have studied many variables associated with personality, there is less than unanimous agreement as to what personality is or what the term means. The authors of this book have chosen to view personality as those characteristics of people which make it easy to tell them apart. Personality from this point of view is a reflection of the consistency of "style" in the behavior of any individual.

2. An examination of the scientific literature on personality reveals many different ways of approaching the study of personality. Two of these approaches are through the use of typologies and traits. A typology represents a limited number of mutually exclusive categories, or types, into which individuals may be placed. Typologies have two fundamental weaknesses. Forcing people into a category tends to do violence to the

fact that many people do not fit neatly into an "either–or" categorization. For example, some people may be neither introverted or extraverted. Secondly, the mutually exclusive nature of typology systems excludes persons from membership in all other classes if he is a member of one class.

3. Trait systems of classification for personality types represent another way of dealing with the problem of the structure of personality. A trait is usually thought of as a more or less enduring behavioral disposition. A trait name is a way of accounting for a general tendency to respond in a particular way. One of the major problems with traits is whether a trait, such as dependency, has the same meaning for one person as it has for another.

4. Although the systems that are used to investigate the structure of personality all have some problems associated with them, most psychologists agree that personality does have a structure which is represented by the organization and interrelationship of the elements of personality. Unfortunately, very little is known about this structure as a scientific, systematic construct.

5. One way the psychologist can study personality is through some technique of assessment. There are no ways of studying the personality directly. We can only know about personality from the way it manifests itself in behavior. One technique of assessment is the personality test. A problem with tests of personality is that the more a person is aware of what a test of personality is measuring, the more the person's responses will tend to reflect the way he wants others to think of him. Personality can be assessed through self-reports in which the person tested responds to questions about his own behavior or items from which his behavior can be inferred, through the reports of observers of the individual's behavior, through direct behavioral observations, as well as through individual responses to stimuli which permit the person to "project" a behavior. Some of the more formal tests of personality which require the individual to give a specific response to a statement or a question are the *California Personality Inventory* and the *Minnesota Multiphasic Personality Inventory*. Some tests such as the *Thematic Apperception Test* and the *Rorschach Inkblot Test* place very little demand on the structure of the response of the individual.

6. Many people believe that personality is inherited. The observation that a child may have some behavioral similarities to one or the other of his parents does not mean that these similarities were genetically transmitted. Some evidence does exist to suggest that some behavioral characteristics may have a hereditary basis, but no conclusive proof is presently available to support the assumption of inheritance for personality struc-

ture or for any part of that structure. While the evidence for a hereditary basis for personality is sketchy, at best, the evidence to support a relationship between personality and an individual's basic physiological processes is stronger. One should not conclude, however, that physiological processes cause behavior simply because a relationship has been demonstrated.

7. Several points can be noted from studies of the physiological bases for personality. Some biochemical substances, and processes, in the body are related to the kinds of reactions an individual might display in stress. Second, emotional behavior has associated with it some highly uniform and predictable physiological reactions. Third, an emotional experience is not the exclusive product of physiological change but is rather the result of a complex interaction between physical and psychological factors.

8. Many studies support the conclusion that many important aspects of the personality develop from the earliest experiences of infancy. The role of the mother during infancy is most important. The experiences of childhood are important in establishing basic aspects of the personality. One of the most basic influences parents have is on the development of a sex-role identification in the child. It appears that personality can be altered during early adulthood, if one assumes that personality is not genetically determined, but the influence of school experiences on the development of personality is not known.

9. The relationship between personality and adjustment is a topic of some concern to most people. The degree to which adjustment means meeting the demands of society at large as opposed to considering one's own feelings as more important represents a dilemma which most people face at some time during their lives. The meaning of adjustment has been debated extensively by psychologists and others who are concerned with the problem of mental health. Much of this debate centers around a definition of what is normal and what is abnormal in behavior. One of the more frequent concerns of the behavioral scientist during the past decade has been the development of techniques of behavioral modification, usually involving some form of reinforcement, to change behavior which interferes with the adjustment of the individual. While techniques of behavioral modification seem promising, more research is needed before these techniques can be used in education.

SUGGESTED READINGS

Allport, G. W. *Becoming: Basic considerations for a psychology of personality.* New Haven, Conn.: Yale University Press, 1955.

In this slim volume the late Gordon Allport presented his views of personality as an entity that is constantly in the process of attaining a structure, or of becoming. This point of view is in opposition to those of the theorists who tend to speak as if personality is a structure that is unchanging after the initial stages of its development.

Sechrest, L., & Wallace, J. *Psychology and human problems*. Columbus, Ohio: Merrill, 1967.

The authors have assembled in this text a wide variety of research in psychology dealing with the general area of human problems. Much of the book concerns the topic of adjustment and its relationship to learning, cognitive, and environmental factors.

Ullmann, L. P., & Krasner, L. (Eds.). *Case studies in behavioral modification*. New York: Holt, Rinehart & Winston, 1965.

The articles collected here all report on some aspect of the modification of behavior in humans. The introduction by the editors presents a clear and concise explanation of behavioral modification and its development in the field of psychology.

REFERENCES

1. Allport, G. W. *Pattern and growth in personality*. New York: Holt, Rinehart, & Winston, 1961.
2. Allport, G. W., & Odbert, H. S. Trait names: a psycho-lexical study. *Psychological Monographs*, 1936, **47**(Whole No. 211).
3. Ax, A. F. The physiological differentiation between fear and anger in humans. *Psychosomatic Medicine*, 1953, **15**, 433–442.
4. Bachrach, A. J., Erwin, W. J., & Mohr, J. P. The control of eating behavior in an anorexic by operant conditioning techniques. In L. P. Ullman & L. Krasner (Eds.), *Case studies in behavior modification*. New York: Holt, Rinehart, & Winston, 1965.
5. Bandura, A., Ross, D., & Ross, S. A. A comparative test of the status envy, social power and secondary reinforcement theories of identificatory learning. *Journal of Abnormal and Social Psychology*, 1963, **67**, 527–534.
6. Becker, W. C. Consequences of different kinds of parental discipline. In M. L. Hoffman & L. W. Hoffman (Eds.), *Review of child development research*. New York: Russell Sage Foundation, 1964. Pp. 169–208.
7. Bonner, H. *Psychology of personality*. New York: Ronald Press, 1961.
8. Bowlby, J. M. Maternal care and mental health. *World Health Organization Monograph Series*, 1951, No. 2.
9. Brady, J. P., & Lind, D. L. Experimental analysis of hysterical blindness: operant conditioning techniques. *Archives of General Psychiatry*, 1961, **4**, 331–339.
10. Buck, J. N. The U.T.P. technique. *Journal of Clinical Psychology, Monograph*, 1948, No. 5.
11. Caldwell, B. M. The effects of infant care. In M. L. Hoffman & L. W. Hoffman (Eds.), *Review of child development research*. New York: Russell Sage Foundation, 1964. Pp. 9–37.
12. Cameron, N., & Magaret, A. *Behavior pathology*. Boston: Houghton Mifflin, 1951.

13. Cattell, R. B. *Description and measurement of personality*. Yonkers, N. Y. World Book, 1946.
14. Davids, A. Comparison of three methods of personality assessment: direct, indirect and projective. *Journal of Personality*, 1955, **23**, 423–440.
15. Davids, A., & Pildner, H., Jr. Comparison of direct and projective methods of personality assessment under different conditions of motivation. *Psychological Monographs*, 1958. **72**(11, Whole No. 464).
16. Dollard, J., & Mowrer, O. H. A method of measuring tension in written documents. *Journal of Abnormal and Social Psychology*, 1947, **42**, 3–32.
17. Endler, N. S., Hunt, J. McV., & Rosenstein, A. J. An S-R inventory of anxiousness. *Psychological Monographs*, 1962, **76**(17, Whole No. 536).
18. Escalona, S. K. The use of infant tests for predictive purposes. *Menninger Clinic, Bulletin*, 1950, **14**, 117–128.
19. Escalona, S. K., & Heider, G. M. *Prediction and outcome: A study in child development*. New York: Basic Books, 1959.
20. Frank, J. D. *Persuasion and healing*. Baltimore: Johns Hopkins Press, 1961.
21. Freedman, D. G., & Keller, B. Inheritance of behavior in infants. *Science*, 1963, **140**, 196–198.
22. Fries, M. E. Psychosomatic relationships between mother and infant. *Psychosomatic Medicine*, 1944, **6**, 159–162.
23. Fuller, J. L., & Thompson, W. R. *Behavior genetics*. New York: Wiley, 1960.
24. Funkenstein, D. H. The physiology of fear and anger. *Scientific American*, 1955, **192**(5), 74–80.
25. Getzels, J. W., & Walsh, J. J. The method of paired direct and projective questionnaires in the study of attitude structure and socialization. *Psychological Monographs*, 1958, **72** (1, Whole No. 454).
26. Goldstein, A. P. *Therapist–patient expectancies in psychotherapy*. New York: Macmillan (Pergamon), 1962.
27. Goldstein, A. P., Heller, K., & Sechrest, L. *Behavior change and psychological research*. New York: Wiley, 1966.
28. Gough, H. G. *California psychological inventory*. Palo Alto, Calif.: Consulting Psychologists Press, 1957.
29. Gross, Sister M. M. The effect of certain types of motivation on the "honesty" of children. *Journal of Educational Psychology*, 1946, **40**, 133–140.
30. Hagen, E. E. *On the theory of social change*. Homewood, Ill.: Dorsey Press, 1962.
31. Hall, C. S. The inheritance of emotionality. *Sigma Xi Quarterly*, 1938, **26**, 17–27.
32. Hathaway, S. R., & McKinley, J. C. *Manual and booklet for the MMPI*. New York: Psychological Corporation, 1943.
33. Heyns, R. W. *The psychology of personal adjustment*. New York: Dryden, 1958.
34. Hoagland, H. Some endocrine stress responses in man. In J. M. Tanner (Ed.), *Stress and psychiatric disorder*. Oxford: Blackwell, 1960. Pp. 76–93.
35. Irwin, J. R. Galen on the temperaments. *Journal of General Psychology*, 1947, **36**, 45–64.
36. Jackson, D. D. *The etiology of schizophrenia*. New York: Basic Books, 1960.
37. Jahoda, M. *Current concepts of positive mental health*. New York: Basic Books, 1958.
38. Johnson, W. *People in quandaries*. New York: Harper, 1946.
39. Jost, H., & Sontag, L. W. The genetic factor in autonomic nervous system function. *Psychosomatic Medicine*, 1944, **6**, 308–310.
40. Kagan, J. Acquisition and significance of sex typing and sex role identity. In

M. L. Hoffman and L. W. Hoffman (Eds.), *Review of child development research.* New York: Russell Sage Foundation, 1964. Pp. 137–168.

41. Kallman, F. J. *The genetics of schizophrenia.* New York: Augustin, 1938.
42. Kallman, F. J. The genetic theory of schizophrenia: an analysis of 691 twin index families. *American Journal of Psychiatry,* 1946, **103,** 309–322.
43. Kallman, F. J. *Heredity in health and mental disorder.* New York: Norton, 1953.
44. Kanfer, F. H. Verbal rate, eyeblink and content in structured psychiatric interviews. *Journal of Abnormal and Social Psychology,* 1960, **61,** 341–347.
45. King, G. F., Armitage, S. G., & Tilton, J. R. A therapeutic approach to schizophrenics of extreme pathology: an operant-interpersonal method. *Journal of Abnormal and Social Psychology,* 1960, **61,** 276–286.
46. Krasner, L. The therapist as a social reinforcement machine. In H. H. Strupp & L. Luborsky (Eds.), *Research in psychotherapy.* Washington, D. C.: American Psychological Association, 1962. Pp. 61–94.
47. Lacey, J. I., & Lacey, B. C. Verification and extension of the principle of autonomic response stereotypy. *American Journal of Psychology,* 1958, **71,** 50–73.
48. Langner, T. S., & Michael, S. T. *Life stress and mental health.* London, Ont.: Free Press of Glencoe, 1963.
49. Leipold, W. D. Psychological distance in a dyadic interview as a function of introversion-extraversion, anxiety, social desirability and stress. Unpublished doctoral dissertation, University of North Dakota, 1963.
50. Levine, S. Infantile experience and resistance to physiological stress. *Science,* 1957, **126,** 405.
51. Levine, S. Infantile experience and consummatory behavior in adulthood. *Journal of Comparative and Physiological Psychology,* 1957, **50,** 609–612.
52. Levine, S., & Otis, L. The effects of handling before and after weaning on the resistance of albino rats to later deprivation. *Canadian Journal of Psychology,* 1958, **12,** 103–108.
53. Lindzey, G. Emotionality and audiogenic seizure susceptibility in five inbred strains of mice. *Journal of Comparative and Physiological Psychology,* 1951, **44,** 389–393.
54. Lindzey, G., Lykken, D. T., & Winston, H. D. Infantile trauma, genetic factors and adult temperament. *Journal of Abnormal and Social Psychology,* 1960, **61,** 7–14.
55. Machover, K. *Personality projection in the drawing of the human figure.* Springfield, Ill.: Thomas, 1948.
56. Malmo, R. B., & Shagass, C. Physiologic studies of symptom mechanisms in psychiatric patients under stress. *Psychosomatic Medicine,* 1949, **11,** 25–29.
57. Malmo, R. B., Shagass, C., & Davis, F. H. Specificity of bodily reactions under stress. A physiological study of somatic mechanisms in psychiatric patients. *Research Publications, Association for Research in Nervous and Mental Disease,* 1950, **29,** 231–261.
58. Malmo, R. B., Shagass, C., & Davis, F. H. Symptom specificity and bodily reactions during psychiatric interview. *Psychosomatic Medicine,* 1950, **12,** 362–376.
59. Maslow, A. H. *Motivation and personality.* New York: Harper, 1954.
60. McGinnies, E. Emotionality and perceptual defense. *Psychological Review,* 1949, **56,** 244–251.
61. Merritt, C. B., & Fowler, R. G. The pecuniary honesty of the public at large. *Journal of Abnormal and Social Psychology,* 1948, **43,** 90–93.

62. Mischel, W. Father-absence and delay of gratification: cross-cultural comparisons. *Journal of Abnormal and Social Psychology,* 1961, **63,** 116–124.
63. Morgan, C. D., & Murray, H. A. A method for investigating fantasies: the Thematic Apperception Test. *Archives of Neurology and Psychiatry,* 1935, **34,** 289–306.
64. Murray, H. A. *Explorations in personality.* New York: Oxford University Press, 1938.
65. Postman, L. The experimental analyses of motivational factors in perception. In M. R. Jones (Ed.), *Nebraska symposium on motivation.* Lincoln, Neb.: University of Nebraska Press, 1953.
66. Rorschach, H. *Psychodiagnostics.* Bern: Huber, 1921.
67. Rosenthal, D. Familial concordance by sex with respect to schizophrenia. *Psychological Bulletin,* 1962, **59,** 401–421.
68. Rosenthal, R. *Experimental effects in psychological research.* New York: Appleton-Century-Crofts, 1967.
69. Rotter, J. B. The role of the psychological situation in determining the direction of human behavior. In M. R. Jones (Ed.), *Nebraska symposium on motivation.* Lincoln, Neb.: University of Nebraska Press, 1955.
70. Schachter, S. *The psychology of affiliation.* Stanford, Calif.: Stanford University Press, 1959.
71. Schachter, S., & Singer, J. E. Cognitive, social and physiological determinants of emotional state. *Psychological Review,* 1962, **69,** 379–399.
72. Schachter, S., & Wheeler, L. Epinephrine, chlorpromazine and amusement. *Journal of Abnormal and Social Psychology,* 1962, **65,** 121–128.
73. Schaefer, T., Jr., Weingarten, F. S., & Towne, J. C. Temperature change: the basic variable in the early handling phenomenon. *Science,* 1962, **135,** 41–42.
74. Scott, J. P. Critical periods in the development of social behavior in puppies. *Psychosomatic Medicine,* 1958, **20,** 42–54.
75. Scott, J. P. *Animal behavior.* Chicago: University of Chicago Press, 1958.
76. Searle, L. V. The organization of hereditary maze-brightness and maze-dullness. *Genetic Psychology Monographs,* 1949, **39,** 279–325.
77. Sechrest, L. Testing, measuring and assessing people. In E. Borgatta & W. Lambert (Eds.), *Handbook of personality research.* Chicago: Rand-McNally, 1968.
78. Sechrest, L., & Jackson, D. N. Social intelligence and accuracy of interpersonal predictions. *Journal of Personality,* 1961, **29,** 167–182.
79. Shagass, C., & Malmo, R. B. Psychodynamic themes and localized muscular tension during psychotherapy. *Psychosomatic Medicine,* 1954, **16,** 295–314.
80. Sheldon, W. H., & Stevens, S. S. *The varieties of temperament.* New York: Harper, 1942.
81. Shoben, E. J. Some observations on psychotherapy and the learning process. In O. H. Mowrer (Ed.), *Psychotherapy, theory and research.* New York: Ronald Press, 1953. Pp. 120–139.
82. Sommer, R. Studies in personal space. *Sociometry,* 1959, **22,** 247–260.
83. Sontag, L. W. Somatopsychics of personality and bodily function. *Vita Humana,* 1963, **6,** 1–10.
84. Sontag, L. W., & Wallace, R. F. The effect of cigaret smoking during pregnancy upon the fetal heart rate. *American Journal of Obstetrics and Gynecology,* 1935, **29,** 77–82.

85. Sontag, L. W., & Wallace, R. F. The movement response of the human fetus to sound stimuli. *Child Development,* 1935, **6,** 253–258.
86. Spence, J. T., & Maher, B. A. Handling and noxious stimulation of the albino rat: I. Effects on subsequent emotionality. *Journal of Comparative and Physiological Psychology,* 1962, **55,** 247–251.
87. Spence, J. T. & Maher, B. A. Handling and noxious stimulation of the albino rat: II. Effects on subsequent performance in a learning situation. *Journal of Comparative and Physiological Psychology,* 1962, **55,** 252–255.
88. Thompson, W. R. The inheritance and development of intelligence. *Research Publications, Association for Research in Nervous and Mental Disease,* 1954, 33, 209–231.
89. Tryon, R. C. Genetic differences in maze-learning ability in rats. *39th yearbook of the National Society for the Study of Education.* Bloomington, Ill.: Public School Publishing Co., 1940. Pp. 111–119.
90. Tutko, T. A. Need for social approval and its effect on responses to projective tests. Unpublished doctoral dissertation, Northwestern University, 1962.
91. Wieninger, O. Physiological damage under emotional stress as a function of early experience. *Science,* 1954, **119,** 285.
92. Williams, S. R., & Leavitt, H. J. Group opinion as a predictor of military leadership. *Journal of Consulting Psychology,* 1947, **11,** 283–291.

14

INTELLIGENCE MEASUREMENTS
AND THEIR USES

Scope of Intelligence Testing

Since teachers use intelligence scores as one indication of the academic progress their pupils are capable of making, the present chapter is intended to survey what is known about intelligence, thereby providing background for the wise use of intelligence scores. In addition to considering the definition of intelligence and means of measuring it, we will discuss multiple-factor approaches to intelligence; creativity; genetic factors in intelligence; depression of intelligence by poor environments; changes in intelligence during the lifespan; intelligence scores in different ethnic, national, and socioeconomic groups; and practical uses of intelligence testing, among other topics.

Perhaps the most important single product of psychological research in education is the intelligence test. It takes many forms, serves many purposes, and has many interpretations; nonetheless, it seems to have satisfied its users reasonably well. The magnitude of the effort expended on intelligence testing is illustrated by the facts that 131 different intelligence tests (plus several other tests which could also have been so classified) were listed as of current interest in *Sixth Mental Measurements Yearbook* (24) and that approximately 35,000 copies of *SRA Tests of Educational Ability* (137) were printed in 1967 despite there being other tests even more widely used in the United States.

Types of Intelligence Tests

By and large test makers agree as to what are intelligent answers to most questions, but they often disagree on the questions to be asked. Accordingly, though most intelligence tests give very similar results, there is reason to admit that there is no single official definition or test of intelligence. Alfred Binet and Thomas Simon, who devised the first standardized intelligence test in 1908, conceived of intelligence as a capacity to make rational judgments in situations requiring a minimum of formal schooling (18). The Stanford–Binet Scales (130, 131, 132), American descendants of the Binet–Simon tests, preserve this emphasis in questions like this verbal absurdity item: "Some bowlers feel that they knock down more pins with the second ball they roll than with the first one. So they have decided to skip the first ball and roll the second one first. What is foolish about that?"

Similarly, Wechsler (145) believes, "Intelligence . . . is the aggregate or global capacity of the individual to act purposefully, to think rationally and to deal effectively with his environment." This led him to use supplementary questions of a more verbal nature, with such items as the assembly of simple objects or animals that have been cut into several pieces, similar to a jigsaw puzzle.

Tests of intelligence which emphasize verbal tasks are called, quite naturally, *verbal tests*. Intelligence tests which use nonverbal items are called *nonverbal tests* or *performance tests*.

Some psychologists think that intelligence is a single general ability or factor, and the Cattells (27) emphasize that their most recent intelligence test measures that general ability. Others produce statistical evidence that several factors are involved, and so the Thurstones (138) developed the SRA Primary Ability Tests to measure verbal, perceptual, quantitative, motor, spatial, reasoning, and word fluency factors.

Just as test makers differ in their conception of the meaning of intelligence and its amenability to measurement by a single test or several tests by response to verbal or relatively nonverbal inquiry, so they differ on methods of test administration and scoring procedures. Tests like the Otis Quick-Scoring Mental Ability Tests (111) are designed to be administered to a group which records its answers in test booklets. But only one person at a time can be examined with the Revised Stanford–Binet Test because the person being tested has to respond orally or by some sort of demonstration to most items. In addition, responses to several items have time limits; and the order of presentation of items and even the number presented depends on how the individual responded to earlier items. The Otis is a *group test* and the Stanford–Binet is an *individual test.* If many people are to be tested, group tests are clearly faster to administer, and often they may be scored electrically. Individual tests are generally considered better measures of intelligence and are often given in cases where the result of a group test is questioned. One reason for this preference is that the examiner in a group situation cannot make allowances for handicaps such as visual impairment, hearing loss, or inability to read, whereas there are individual tests which do. Also, some children who respond poorly on a paper-and-pencil test do better in a face-to-face situation. And the enormous effort devoted to the standardization of the Stanford–Binet Test in particular has made it the reference by which all others are judged. Finally, there is some evidence that the long-term predictive value of at least the first Stanford–Binet has been greater than that of other tests (54).

The Intelligence Quotient (I.Q.)

Scores are generally recorded either as intelligence quotients or as point scores. Since the I.Q. is the more common, we consider it first. I.Q. was originally a quotient in the mathematical sense: 100 times the ratio or quotient of the mental age (M.A.) and the chronological age (C.A.), where each is expressed to the nearest month. An M.A. score is simply a statement of the age level at which the person tested functions. Intelligence tests are standardized to yield average mental ages equal to the chronological age for members of each age bracket. Children who are 10 years and 2 months old have an average mental age of 10 years, 2 months, and this average M.A. is expressed as an I.Q. of 100:

$$\text{I.Q.} = 100 \times \frac{\text{M.A.}}{\text{C.A.}}$$

$$= 100 \times \frac{10 \text{ years, } 2 \text{ months}}{10 \text{ years, } 2 \text{ months}}$$

$$= 100 \times \frac{122 \text{ months}}{122 \text{ months}}$$

$$= 100$$

At any age level, the child of average intelligence has an I.Q. of 100. A child whose mental age is lower than his chronological age has an I.Q. of less than 100; a child whose mental age is greater than his chronological age has an I.Q. of more than 100.

Variability of I.Q. Scores

While it is easy to recognize whether an I.Q. score is above or below average, it is harder to know how important a given deviation from average may be. An I.Q. of 130 sounds impressively high, and an I.Q. of 70 sounds depressingly low. Yet, the importance of these deviations depends upon the standardization procedure used. If an intelligence test is constructed so that most people's I.Q.'s range from 80 to 120, scores of 70 and 130 are surely extreme cases. If, however, the I.Q.'s of most people taking a particular test range from 20 to 180, I.Q.'s of 70 and 130 would not be out of the ordinary. The amount of variability in most intelligence tests is much nearer the former example than the latter: Generally an I.Q. of 70 is very low and may even indicate mental deficiency while an I.Q. of 130 is very high. However, there is as yet no standard variability for all intelligence tests. One index of variability, the *standard deviation** has values that range from 9.7 to 24.4 for different tests; most tests now used have standard deviations of 15, as in the Wechsler Preschool and Primary Scale of Intelligence (146), or 16, as in the Stanford–Binet Form L–M deviation I.Q. (115, 132). The interpretation of an I.Q. value thus depends upon the test used, both because content varies and standard deviations differ.

Correlation—A Statistical Measure Essential to the Study of Intelligence

In psychological research, correlation—the measure of relatedness of two quantities—is an important parameter. When one quantity, such as intelligence, is high, is a second quantity such as school grades also high? One measure of the relation between such quantities is the *product–moment correlation coefficient* (33, 125).

To understand this term think first of a group of identical twins (twins of the same sex, developed from a single fertilized ovum). Everyday experience makes us expect them to look alike and act alike. Great similarities can be seen in identical twins raised together in a single home; but some of these similarities disappear if the twins are separated. We see less similarity in fraternal twins (twins not developed from a single ovum, though possibly of the same sex). Consider the similarity in Stanford–Binet I.Q.'s of 19 pairs of identical twins whom Newman,

---

* A formula defining the standard deviation is given in almost all statistics books [e.g., (33, 125)] but will not be presented here because the necessary exposition of such a formula would be out of place in this book. Suffice it to say that the standard deviation measures how much the scores of a set spread around their average. In many circumstances 34% of the cases studied will lie between the average value and a value 1 standard deviation above the average. Another 34% will lie between the average value and a value 1 standard deviation below the average. With an average I.Q. of 100 and a standard deviation of 15, then, 34% of the cases would lie between 85 and 100 and another 34% would lie between 100 and 115.

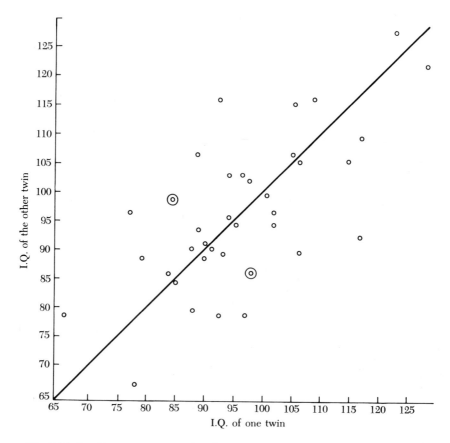

Fig. 14-1. Intelligence quotients (I.Q.'s) for 19 pairs of separated identical twins in Table 87 of the Newman *et al.* study (108).* Copyright © 1937 by the University of Chicago Press.

Freeman, and Holzinger tested in adulthood after they had been separated from each other very early in life. (Twelve pairs were separated before age 1, all 19 pairs by age 7.) Figure 14-1 shows I.Q. scores for each pair. The circled points show that one member of one pair had an I.Q. of 85 while the other had an I.Q. of 97. Notice that data points do not occur

---

* A careful reader may note that there are 38 rather than 19 data points in Fig. 14-1. Each pair of scores for a set of twins is plotted twice in opposite orders. For example, the circled point with 87 for one twin's score and 97 for the other twin's score is matched by another point with 97 and 87, respectively, because no convenient and important reason existed for saying which twin in the pair should be called "one" and which "the other." The *r* was calculated using all 38 data points and is called an *intraclass correlation coefficient* because of the double plotting even though in all other respects it was obtained like any product–moment correlation coefficient.

in the upper left- and lower right-hand segments of the graph: Seldom does a person with a relatively low I.Q. have a twin with a relatively high I.Q., or vice versa. We say there is a *positive correlation* (similarity) between twins' I.Q.'s because identical twins tend to have similar scores. If high I.Q.'s were almost always paired with high I.Q.'s and low I.Q.'s with low I.Q.'s, we could say that there is high positive correlation (or high predictability), and if all data points were on a straight line from the lower left- to the upper right-hand corner of the graph, there would be *perfect positive correlation* (perfect predictability) between the I.Q.'s of the twin pairs. However, if the study results had shown that twins tend to have disparate I.Q.'s, there would have been a *negative correlation* between twins. If all data points fell exactly on a straight line from the upper left- to the lower right-hand corner of the graph, there would have been a *perfect negative correlation* between I.Q.'s of the twin pairs. Finally, there would have been *zero correlation* (no relation) between these I.Q.'s if twin pairs had shown as many disparate I.Q.'s as identical I.Q.'s.

From a graph like that of Fig. 14-1, general statements about correlation or similarity can be made. More precision is obtained by using formulas which give a numerical value for the *product-moment correlation coefficient* of the data in question. This value may be anywhere from -1 (perfect negative correlation) through 0 (zero correlation) to $+1$ (perfect positive correlation). By comparing these values the degree of correlation between pairs of psychological variables can be obtained. It is significant that the product-moment correlation coefficient (often called r) for Fig. 14-1 has a value of $+0.67$, indicating a relatively high positive correlation between the I.Q.'s of identical twins who were separated early in life. A comparison of this value with correlations between identical twins raised together and between other pairs of family members, can be used to infer the effects of heredity and environment upon I.Q.

Scoring Problems with Adolescents and Adults

The second type of scoring, using a point scale rather than an I.Q. system, arose because cross-sectional studies of various age groups indicated that mental age stopped increasing sometime after the chronological age of 16 years. As a result I.Q. calculation could work well for children but would yield an I.Q. of only 50 for an average man of 32 years if his M.A. were only 16. Three ways were available to handle this problem: (a) to seek out new items of a clearly intellectual sort that would be increasingly mastered throughout youth and adulthood; (b) to stop increasing C.A. in computing I.Q. after a certain age; (c) to give up the fiction that a ratio of M.A. to C.A. is meaningful beyond childhood and score intelligence tests like other tests, assigning the number of points attained by the person tested rather than assigning him a mental age as the basis for an I.Q. calculation.

Option (a) has not received a full consideration though there have been recent longitudinal studies suggesting that it might be feasible, at least for people of superior intelligence; these studies will be discussed in a later section of this chapter. Option (b) has been used with the Stanford–Binet test in all its recent forms. Thus Pinneau (115) gives corrected C.A. values in the range from actual ages of 13 to 18 years, corrected C.A. growing more slowly than the actual C.A. so that a person of 18 years or older has a corrected C.A. of 15 years. Option (c) has been widely used in intelligence tests such as the Wechsler Adult Intelligence Scale (144) which were developed almost exclusively for use with adults. However, Wechsler provides a conversion table for shifting a point score into a pseudo-I.Q. score or "deviation" I.Q. score, so named because the deviation of the point score from the mean is used to produce a corresponding deviation of the I.Q. score from 100. This deviation I.Q. score is not a ratio at all; it is simply a score devised to have an average of 100 and variability similar to ratios used in I.Q. determination.

The newest version of the Stanford–Binet test (132) also uses a deviation I.Q., a change from previous forms. This new test which is called the Stanford–Binet Form L–M allows one either to compute an I.Q. in the conventional way and then convert it to a deviation I.Q. or to determine the M.A. first and use a table to find the deviation I.Q. Because of the great influence of the Wechsler and Stanford–Binet scales, it would not be surprising to see the I.Q. as a ratio of M.A. to C.A. abandoned in a few years, replaced in most major intelligence tests by the deviation I.Q.

Criteria of a Good Intelligence Test

Direct Measurement, Correctness of Answer Key, and Objectivity of Scoring

Intelligence seems to depend for its definition on common usage. Those responses which laymen think of as expressions of opinion rather than memory, fact, or logic are excluded from direct measures of intelligence. Note that, from a standpoint of prediction alone, this exclusion may not be necessary. There is some evidence that attitudes may be very effective in predicting success or failure in college, for example (76). Accordingly, it would be possible to give a very controversial set of questions, scoring each on a practical basis—do successful students say "yes" more often than unsuccessful students?—and use the resulting "intelligence" test quite successfully to predict next year's good and bad students. This would be a good, though indirect, measure of intelligence; and, in fact, Gough (61) constructed a test composed of 52 personality items which can be used quite successfully to estimate intelligence.

We can say, then, that in an indirect measure of intelligence the answers themselves are neither intelligent nor unintelligent even though the test may be valid in the sense that it works. In a direct measure of intelligence the answer itself is classified as intelligent or unintelligent, however, with the classification being in part a logical one. Thus, it is wrong to say 1, 2, 3, 4, 5 when instructed to repeat 1, 7, 4, 1, 9; or it is wrong to cut out a square when instructed to cut out a diamond.

This is not to say that the scoring of an answer can always be automatic. When answers appear neither wholly correct nor wholly incorrect, the scorer uses standard procedures given by the test manual to decide whether zero, partial, or full credit is allowed. For example, a partly accurate drawing might receive half credit as a reproduction of the standard drawing in a 9-year-old task of the Stanford–Binet test (132).

Intelligence tests must fulfill two initial criteria. There must be a logically or factually correct answer or set of answers to each item, and the scoring procedure must be so explicit that everyone scoring the response to an item can reasonably be expected to assign the same amount of credit for that response. The first criterion rules out items whose answers are not yet completely verified; the second rules out items for which scoring procedures are ambiguous. Tests which fulfill the second criterion only are sometimes called *objective* tests; however, both criteria seem essential to true objectivity. The first criterion is not, however, intended to rule out the kind of divergent thinking responses discussed later in this chapter under the topic of creativity. Some original or creative responses to intelligence test items may not be logically or factually correct, but neither will some quite traditional answers; thus no inherent penalty is intended for either type of response.

Relative Independence of Special Experience

Because an intelligence test is designed for wide usage, throughout an entire country in most cases or even throughout the entire world, it should not focus on some form of knowledge or skill attainable only in certain localities, social classes, or occupations. One way to meet this requirement is to use items which are subject to very little improvement with practice. A second way to avoid geographical, social, or occupational bias is to test infants before they have learned language skills. This method has been unsuccessful because it does not lead to efficient prediction of school performance or I.Q. at a later age (4). A third procedure, and the one most widely used until recently, has been to seek materials so widely circulated as to be within the experience of almost everyone tested. Thus, Binet and Simon (18) retained only questions which were not closely tied to special training by teachers or parents. Under Binet's procedure, or similar procedures, specialized questions are excluded, leaving only very broad academic questions common to the overall school system or questions of everyday experience.

A fourth method of eliminating bias attributable to previous experience is to introduce almost completely novel tasks but ones whose answers nonetheless meet the criteria of intellectual objectivity in scoring. Such tasks often are stated in pantomime or with very few words, making them particularly useful with deaf children and persons with other handicaps. Thus in the Grace Arthur Performance Scale (6) a child is asked to fit a stencil set together to match a pattern shown by the examiner. This is an example of a task rarely performed in ordinary life which nonetheless seems reasonable in a test of intelligence.

Reasoning Rather Than Knowledge or Memory

Many of the criteria for intelligence tests just given could also be demanded of many other tests. However, the prime requisite of an intelligence test is that it measure what was earlier defined as intelligence. This means that reasoning rather than knowledge, memory, or other attainments is the principal object of study. Our emphasis on reasoning is akin to Binet and Simon's[*] emphasis on judgment:

> But here we come to an understanding of what meaning to give to that word so vague and so comprehensive, "the intelligence." Nearly all the phenomena with which psychology concerns itself are phenomena of intelligence; sensation, perception, and intellectual manifestations as much as reasoning. Should we therefore bring into our examination the measure of sensation after the manner of the psycho-physicists? Should we put to the test all of his psychological processes? A slight reflection has shown us that this would indeed be wasted time.
>
> It seems to us that in intelligence there is a fundamental faculty, the alteration or the lack of which, is of the utmost importance for practical

[*] A. Binet & T. Simon, *The development of intelligence in children.* © 1916, The Williams & Wilkins Co., Baltimore, Maryland.

life. The faculty is judgment otherwise called good sense, practical sense, initiative, the faculty of adapting one's self to circumstances. To judge well, to comprehend well, to reason well, these are the essential activities of intelligence.

We would prefer not to go as far as Binet and Simon in accepting initiative or the faculty of adapting one's self to circumstances as an index of intelligence. Those capacities are obviously useful ones; yet they seem to have strong emotional or motivational as well as intellectual aspects.

Examination of existing intelligence tests certainly shows a large number of items that require reasoning for solution. Consider, for example, the names of the items included in the 11-year-old level of Form L of the Revised Stanford–Binet Scale (131).

1. Memory for designs
2. Verbal absurdities III
3. Abstract words I
4. Memory for sentences IV
5. Problem situation
6. Similarities: three things

Except for number 3, these six kinds of items bear very little similarity to the questions on an achievement test, for they are unlikely to have been specifically covered in the school curriculum and they do not depend heavily upon a foundation of knowledge. Two of these test short-term memory; and it is an ability rather than a content that is desired. In the other four cases there must be a logical argument if an answer is to be correct. The items do not reveal that argument but only whether the conclusion reached is logical. This process of reaching logical conclusions may be called reasoning; the purpose of an intelligence test is to measure it when stripped of as many extraneous factors as possible. Since technical jargon may obscure this issue, or emotionally tinged subject matter may divert people from correct responses, or the general tone of statements made may produce a mental set toward agreement or disagreement (151), the test maker tries to structure the framework of a question as innocuously as possible. It makes no difference whether we ask, "What do you think will come next in this list? Brown, white, brown, white . . . ," or ask, "What do you think will come next in this list? Red, yellow, red, yellow. . . ." The logic of the question is identical, and the terms in each are equally well known. We would not consider the item "What do you think will come in the blank? 'Coco___'" equivalent to the items above because a new sort of answer is possible, completing the word "Cocoa" rather than saying "c" to carry on the alternation as before. Nor would we ask, "There were five major battles in the Civil War. The first four were won as follows, by the South, the North, the South, the North. Who won the fifth one?"

Intelligence, Not Achievement Tests

Any useful intelligence test employs items which require the use of a language which had to be learned or of skills taught in school or acquired at home. In fact J. S. Coleman *et al.* (31), in their extensive study of the effects of integrated and segregated education, took intelligence scores to be the best measure of the effectiveness of previous instruction. Why, then, are intelligence tests not achievement tests? First, they do not attempt to measure one's knowledge in a specific subject, such as English, geography, biology, or arithmetic as a battery of achievement tests might. Second, makers of intelligence tests try to include test items on topics which everyone probably has had an equal opportunity to learn. Third, these tests emphasize skills, not specific knowledge.

However, in Chapter 15 we shall see that new achievement tests are increasingly de-emphasizing knowledge in favor of measuring skills such as problem solving. Does this mean that the difference between achievement tests and intelligence tests is disappearing? To some degree, the answer is "Yes," and yet the rate of this disappearance is very slow. To a still very large extent achievement tests present problems that are specific to practical situations. For example, the Iowa Every-Pupil Tests of Basic Skills (126) has a section on use of references which begins as follows:

> Directions: After each question there are listed four things that might be used in answering the question. Only one of these things might be used in answering the question. Only one of these things is correct or better than any of the others. Place an X in the box in front of the one that you think is best.

A typical item is

> 16. What would you use to answer the question: When it is midnight here, in what countries would it be midday?
> ☐ An encyclopedia
> ☐ A globe
> ☐ A world almanac
> ☐ A map of the United States

Clearly the focus of this question is on getting the specific task done. An appropriate answer depends not only on general reasoning ability such as might be measured by an intelligence test but also on specific training in geography.

A Measure of Mental Products, Not Processes

Our emphasis above on reasoning has the trappings of 19th century psychology texts in which authors like Williams James (77) listed such abilities as attention, instinct, and will among their chapter headings. This was the era of "faculty psychology," which emphasized differentiation of mental abilities or skills, an approach much scorned by psychologists and educators recently for different reasons. Psychologists have seen in it the mentalism or emphasis on mental processes rejected by Watson, and educators have seen it as the basis for defending outmoded educational systems. However, even though one cannot go back to the time before either intelligence testing or motivation received widespread attention from psychology, by now it is apparent there is much to be gained in studying reasoning, if not entirely as faculty or mental process, certainly as an end product of behavior. The philosopher Spinoza's emphasis on reasoning as the very heart of the human enterprise may or may not be extreme. But surely reasoning *is* at the heart of scholarship and scientific inquiry. Without logical organization, theory becomes a shambles and experimentation a cluttered attic. No wonder, then, that our society prizes reasoning, or that intelligence tests are designed to show the degree to which a person's responses to standardized instructions are reasonable. There is nothing unscientific in this; we do not try to "weigh" a ghostly mind but only to compare intellectual behaviors of different people under testing conditions which are constant enough to make the differences due to the persons themselves.

And yet the emphasis upon products rather than processes may have diminished in recent years. Hunt (73) suggests that intelligence testing has been too concerned with measuring people's intellectual status, a static property, and too little concerned with the way that status was acquired, a dynamic property of intelligence. We see this same concern in Piaget's work on the development of cognitive skills, discussed in Chapter 10. Where conventional intelligence tests have used items that do not closely relate in intellectual content, psychologists, following Piaget's work, have been constructing sets of items that have more unity because of their relation to Piagetian stages of development. Tuddenham (142) has modified 25 of Piaget's experiments to form intelligence test items for research purposes only, not for identification of children with high or low I.Q.'s. These items were passed more frequently by older children than by younger ones, a desirable characteristic of an intelligence test. Furthermore, several items on conservation (of volume, mass, length, etc.) are highly correlated, requiring a unity of behavior corresponding to the unity of logical content built into them. For items of different kinds (conservation versus ordering, say), intercorrelations are less than is the case with the Stanford–Binet test. This latter fact indicates that the Piaget items as a whole do not have more psychological unity than the items of traditional I.Q. tests.

Tuddenham is not the only person working with Piagetian tests of intelligence. Kohlberg (87) refers to his own and his associates' work at the University of Chicago, showing correlations of about 0.70 between total scores on Piagetian tasks and on Binet tests, a further indication that this new type of test may be a useful one.

Limitations of Intelligence Tests

The question arises, "Does an I.Q. test measure what the real person is like or only what he can do with a standardized test?" It can only be answered that an intelligence test permits a person to show what he can do at a certain time with a certain carefully selected, but small, set taken from all the possible items which test intelligence. No one should suppose that this small set can tell as much about him as if 100 times as many items were available. Nonetheless, it tells a great deal, and inordinate increases in length of tests suffer the usual consequences of the law of diminishing returns (66, Fig. 1, p. 91). Similarly, we know that one person may be more fatigued than another when he takes the test, possibly reducing his score. Yet we also know that the effect of this fatigue is on the whole very small (75).

What we are saying is that these tests are as fair assessments of a person's present status as anyone knows how to make them. They tell what a person can do right now, handicapped or favored as he may be by his inherited characteristics, his home and school background, and his sensory, motor, or general bodily state. They do not tell how well he would have done with better inheritance, better home or school background, or better sensory, motor, or bodily states. They do not tell how he would have done if tested ten years ago or if tested ten years hence, with or without ideal conditions during those ten years. Consequently, it is always possible to second-guess such a test and conclude that it doesn't tell what we really want to know. But no test can.

The foregoing remarks should not be taken to mean that inaccurate I.Q. scores never are obtained. Jensen (78) reports he has often had cause to believe that the first intelligence test given to certain children underestimates their I.Q.'s. After 2 to 4½ days of getting acquainted with such children, Jensen typically found that a retest on a different form of the same test yielded an I.Q. of 8 to 10 points higher. Kagan (81) has mentioned similar unpublished findings by Palmer. These reports confirm what common sense should tell us. Children may be so frightened in a testing situation with a tester they do not know and when confronted with tasks that are completely novel that they do not exhibit nearly the intellectual capacity one would expect from other evidence about them. Particularly with young children, it may be important to spend much more time building rapport for testing than the few minutes that are sometimes employed before formal testing begins.

_____   **Factor Structure and Special Abilities**

General Intelligence versus Many Abilities

Now let us consider a controversial point: Is it more defensible intellectually and more useful practically to treat intelligence as an entity to be measured with a single score (the I.Q., M.A., or a point score) than to treat it as a congeries of perhaps 15 separate abilities or factors such as verbal reasoning, numerical ability, abstract reasoning, spatial reasoning, etc.? The makers of the SRA Primary Abilities Tests (138), among others, hold the latter view. The present section presents a defense of the former followed by a critical but, nonetheless, sympathetic look at investigation by factor analytic methods.

It is important to know what is meant by saying that a test measures only one factor (e.g., general intelligence or *g*, for short) or several factors (e.g., verbal reasoning, numerical ability, and abstract reasoning). Precise mathematical definitions have been given, but an intuitive description may be more meaningful.

A single-factored test measures only one thing (except what is called an *error factor* resulting from the imperfection of every measuring instrument). If one test or measuring instrument were a yardstick and another were a meterstick, each would be measuring the same factor, length, because yards and meters are proportional to each other by definition. Now suppose we have five or six such equivalent measures of length, but that a good deal of error is associated with each, due to poor construction of the measuring sticks. Then the correlations between the different tests (measuring sticks), as applied to the measurement of various objects, would not be unity and might even vary from one pair of measuring sticks to another because of different amounts of error in each test. However, certain patterns would show up in the set of correlations and would prove that only one factor was involved.

Now consider a different measuring device which yields the sum of length in inches plus weight in ounces—a measure the Post Office Department might use to determine if a package were too large to be shipped conveniently. Two factors, length and weight, by definition, are involved. However, most tests are devised empirically, and the factors which determine the measurements are not known, only the scores that were obtained with each test on each object measured. *Factor analysis,* a form of statistical analysis of correlation coefficients, can be used to determine how many factors such as length, width, height, and weight are involved in each test and to what degree. Thurstone (136) has, in fact, presented such an analysis for certain properties of a set of boxes. But most factor analyses concern psychological factors; physical measurements can usually be more simply understood.

What happens when the factor structure of an I.Q. scale is investigated? One procedure is to correlate scores from different subtests of a test such as the Wechsler Adult Intelligence Scale (144) and examine the correlations for evidence of single- or multi-factoredness. Unfortunately, though most test specialists would agree on the principles involved here, they would disagree on what method should be used to analyze a set of correlations. Probably no one claims that the typical intelligence test measures only one factor and nothing else. But some theorists (48, 99) argue that a single factor is the major contributor to the correlations between pairs of subtests while others (63, 137) hold that the use of suitable factor analysis techniques reveals several factors as substantially involved.

McNemar (99) has pointed out that English factor analysts, who are predisposed in favor of a single factor theory of intelligence, tend to find a single factor most important but minor factors also present. The methods favored by some American factor analysts yield several factors of nearly equal strength but apparently not completely uncorrelated. While no absolute standard exists to say that one factor analytic method is superior to the other, we prefer the single-factor approach because it does not require the further awkward assumption that factors are correlated and does not require movement away from a first result which typically shows a very substantial first factor.

Are Single-Factor Subtests Desirable? A secondary disagreement is whether it is desirable to try to construct an intelligence test consisting of several subtests so developed that each measures only one discrete factor.

Guilford (63, 64) answers the second question by indicating that logical and psychological analysis of psychological activity shows that many abilities are present and deserve measurement. His structure-of-intellect theory says that there are three basic variables to be studied.

1. Operations, including cognition, memory, divergent production, convergent production, and evaluation
2. Products, including units, classes, relations, systems, transformations, and implications
3. Contents, including figural, symbolic, semantic, and behavioral contents

Most of Guilford's terms are either known to the layman or defined in standard dictionaries. However, two should be defined here. *Convergent production* is activity that produces a response or responses such as a correct choice between a singular noun and a plural noun to complete a sentence. These responses are intended to converge upon a basic, already known answer to the problem. *Divergent production* is activity that produces a response or responses in situations where a large group of responses may be almost equally acceptable and a "correct" answer may not yet be known by anyone, not even the person asking the question. Many inventions, such as the very simple snaptop shoe polish can and twist-off beverage can tops, stem from divergent production.

Since any one of the five operations can be paired with any one of the six products and with any one of the four contents, there are $6 \times 5 \times 4 = 120$ possible factors, of which Guilford has found evidence for 80.

The ultimate hope of multiple factor theorists is that not only will many factors be identified but also that prediction of school performance or specific job effectiveness will be improved by using tests of certain factors rather than general ability tests. We agree that some special tasks, such as identification of musical tones or running the 100-yard dash, require such different abilities from those of ordinary classroom work as to warrant special tests. However, there seems to be no reason to believe that separate measurement of intellectual factors is desirable. McNemar (99), discussing the Differential Aptitude Test (DAT) in some detail, has shown that ordinary performance on a particular job like clerical work is predicted as well by the verbal comprehension section of the DAT or by the total DAT score as by the spelling section or any other section thought logically to be most closely related to clerical work. Milholland and Fricke (106) also assert that special aptitude tests rarely predict much better for their intended purpose than for other purposes. Thus, a linguistic test may be only slightly better for predicting foreign language learning than for predicting science and mathematics learning. This makes it seem that special abilities tests, or separate parts of intelligence tests, are less useful than intelligence tests as a whole.

One exception to this statement should be noted: If instead of defining a factor logically or constructing a single-factored test, one simply uses item selection procedures (2) which maximize the correlation between the resulting test and performance on a criterion, the resulting correlation will usually be at least slightly higher than if an intelligence test were used. Thus, Milholland and Fricke mentioned one study showing that the best predictor of shop grades in school is a set of personality traits not appreciably correlated with I.Q.

Creativity—One Example of a Special Ability?

Recently there has been much interest in creativity, which may be thought of as an example of an ability that is evidenced by important vocational contributions, that is predictable by tests which are only moderately correlated with intelligence, and that is, perhaps, improvable with special training or experience. This section supplements the discussion of creativity in Chapter 6.

Definition of Creativity

Common usage says the creative person has the capacity to do work which is superior in quality, originality, or importance—not simply in quantity, general dependability, or accuracy. We will distinguish between *creative performance,* which we shall call the criterion, and tested creativity or simply *creativity,* which we shall call the predictor or the intermediate criterion. This corresponds to the practice of letting intellectual performance (for example, grade point average) be the criterion and I.Q. be its predictor. If this distinction is used, there are several measures of creativity (e.g., 10, 62, 102) just as there are several measures of intelligence.

The Guilford tests of divergent thinking (62) measure unusual or clever responses to questions such as one in which a story is told of a wife who is unable to speak until after an operation. Then her husband finds her too talkative and asks a surgeon to eliminate his hearing, thus restoring peace in the family. Titles for this story are requested, and responses such as, "Operation—Peace of Mind," and "Yack, Yack, Hack," receive high scores for originality. The Barron–Welsh Art Scales (10) measure preference for simplicity versus complexity in pictures [and preference for symmetry versus asymmetry (107)], and the Remote Associates Test (102) measures unusual responses in a testing situation where a person is asked, for example, to mention all the words which come to mind when he is told a word such as "bicycle."

Thorndike (133) has pointed out that different creativity tests are generally less highly correlated than are different intelligence tests. Also different subtests within a creativity test (even one which is not intended to be multi-factored) are less highly correlated with each other than are different subtests within an intelligence test. This means that creativity as presently defined seems more multi-factored and has a more equivocal definition than I.Q. (Possibly this appears to be the case because creativity tests are now in their infancy, so there is less agreement about their ideal content and there has been less work on their statistical refinement.)

Defining Creative Performance

Creative performance is typically measured by ratings of experts. MacKinnon (92) asked five professors of architecture to nominate the 40 most creative architects in the country. M. T. Mednick (101) asked faculty advisors to judge whether certain psychology graduate students were high or low in research creativity. McDermid (95) had co-workers and supervisors of engineers and technical workers in an organ company evaluate the creative work of those persons.

Use of ratings to identify creative persons in a field is rather indirect; it would also seem desirable to point to the work a person has done and assess its creative qualities directly. People might then be termed highly creative if the average task they accomplished was rated highly creative or perhaps if the highest rating they received on any task was "highly creative." McPherson (100) has advocated such a direct rating of specific work products and illustrated its relation to the patent law's standards for "inventivlevel," i.e., an adequate level of novelty to make a new process or mechanism patentable.

Predictive Power of Creativity Tests

M. T. Mednick (101) has shown a correlation of 0.55 between rated research creative performance of psychology graduate students and performance on the Remote Associates Test. Personality and creativity test items were generally poor predictors of rated creative performance of engineers and technical personnel in McDermid's (95) study, but the creativity rating of the Biographical Information for Research and Scientific Talent (BIRST) form correlated 0.43 with the criterion.

Relation of Creativity Tests to Creative Performance

These two correlations are the highest we have seen between creativity and creative performance; in general, prediction of creative performance is less successful than this and definitely less successful than the prediction of school grades from I.Q. scores. It appears, however, that some creativity test may predict creative performance as well as, or better than, an intelligence test would. Thus in the McDermid study the BIRST creativity score was apparently a better predictor than the Concept Mastery Test (an intelligence test), but the Concept Mastery Test was a better predictor than the Welsh Art Scale, another creativity test. Much more work on creativity tests is needed to test their validity; very possibly different creativity tests will be needed to predict different kinds of creative performance.

Relation of Creativity to I.Q.

Getzels and Jackson (55) have indicated their belief that high creativity is a better predictor of good high-school academic achievement than is I.Q. McNemar (99) has reinterpreted their data, indicating that the creativity measure used in that study was at most about equal to I.Q. in predictive power.

One reason that some creativity tests can predict school achievement or creative performance is that these tests are correlated with I.Q., which is also correlated with school achievement and creative performance. Ohnmacht (110) found that two of Getzels and Jackson's creativity tests were highly related to verbal and nonverbal intelligence tests. Guilford and Hoepfner (65) have shown the correlation of 45 creativity tests with I.Q. ranges from -0.07 to 0.70 with a mean (corrected statistically) of 0.42. On the other hand, McNemar (99) cites a correlation of 0.80 (corrected statistically) based on a very large study $(N = 7648)$ (119). When low correlations between creativity and I.Q. are obtained, it may be because only highly intelligent persons were studied, producing the so-called *restriction of range effect* in which a correlation is lower than if all levels of ability were studied or because the creativity test has low reliability. To the extent that creativity tests measure something different from I.Q. and make useful predictions, they are a promising addition to the educator's test battery. For further information on creativity the references cited at the end of this chapter should be consulted.

Evidence for a Relationship between I.Q. and Learning Ability

Intelligence tests have been very successful in predicting success of students in academic courses. By this we do not mean that perfect prediction is possible. However, as will be shown later, the use of an I.Q. test affords a more accurate prediction than is possible without a test. In view of this effectiveness in predicting course grades, it is paradoxical to note that rate of learning laboratory tasks such as memorizing paired-associates lists is not always higher for persons with high I.Q.'s than for persons with lower I.Q.'s. When one thinks about this problem, one decides that memory questions on an I.Q. test should help predict purely rote learning and reasoning questions should help predict problem-solving ability. However, school grades may be more easily predicted than learning rates on laboratory problems because laboratory experiments may take only an hour rather than a semester or a year, thus not giving a student enough time to display his overall intelligence when performing a laboratory learning task. Furthermore, school grades are typically based on what a person knows at the end of a course (even though he may have known most of it before the course began) rather than how much he actually learned. Since very few I.Q. tests measure learning rate directly, it is not too surprising that a relationship between I.Q. and learning ability in laboratory tasks has not always been found.

Duncanson (44) reviewed some of the evidence, both positive and negative, on this point. In addition, he performed an experiment in which three kinds of concept formation, three kinds of rote memory, and three kinds of paired-associates learning tasks were performed; and several kinds of intelligence and achievement tests were administered. His findings give somewhat more evidence for a relationship between learning rate and intelligence than most of the studies he cites. Scores on the six paired-associates or rote memory tasks are fairly closely related to the intelligence tests used. However, concept formation performance seemed quite unrelated to intelligence. This latter result does not seem logical in view of the need for conceptualizing in intellectual work. But it may only reflect the unusual difficulty of the particular concept formation tasks employed by Duncanson, or it may merely be a further example of the difficulty of finding a consistent relationship between learning rate and intelligence.

——————— **Determiners of Intelligence: Heredity and Environment**

Heredity: Its Genetic Basis

It is known that I.Q. scores are more closely correlated in identical twins than in like-sexed fraternal twins. Genetics, the science of heredity, which deals with the mechanisms for the transmittal of characteristics from parent to child, suggests there are ways intelligence may be transmitted from one generation to another.

Microscopic examination of human body tissue shows that the nucleus of each cell, except the sperm and the ovum, contains 23 pairs of microscopic entities called *chromosomes* (139, 140). Figure 14-2 shows these pairs for one normal human male. When originally viewed under a microscope, the pairs are randomly arranged except when they are dividing. This figure pictures a standardized arrangement geneticists employ to permit comparison from one cell to another (49). Chromo-

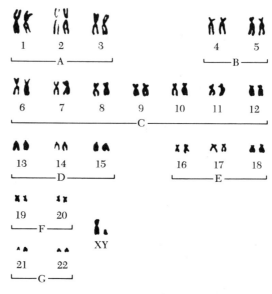

Fig. 14-2. Photomicrograph of the 23 pairs of chromosomes of a normal human male. The pairs have been rearranged in a standard order for further scientific analysis. Figure VI-3B from A. Falek and R. Schmidt (49), Human cytogenetics. In H. J. Van Peenen (Ed.), *Biochemical Genetics*, 1966. Courtesy of Charles C Thomas, Publisher, Springfield, Illinois.

somes in different cells of the same individual have the same basic structure.

Chromosomes are the carriers of all hereditary characteristics from parent to child. In the case of spermatogenesis (sperm production) or oogenesis (ovum production), one member of each chromosome pair goes into the nucleus of the newly formed germ cell. At conception, when sperm and egg unite, the fertilized cell has 23 pairs of chromosomes once more. One particular pair of chromosomes is of special interest to us: note the X and Y pair at the lower right of Fig. 14-2. The corresponding pair of the human female is two X chromosomes. The ovum will therefore always contain an X chromosome. Approximately one-half the sperm produced will contain an X chromosome; the remainder will contain a Y. Consequently, about one-half of the fertilized ova will contain X,X pairs, and females will result; the remainder will contain X,Y pairs, and males will result.

By various techniques, such as electron microscopy and ultraviolet photography, it is possible to examine chromosomes of various species to see what geneticists knew long before they could observe it directly: chromosomes contain smaller units called *genes* which are the basic determiners of specific traits. (This is somewhat of an oversimplification but is approximately correct.) A brief description of the revolutionary findings of biochemical genetics in the past 20 years or so will help to explain the operation of the genes. The genes contain molecules of a biochemical substance known as DNA (deoxyribonucleic acid). This substance can produce more of itself through a series of complex biochemical reactions. Each DNA molecule consists of alternating biochemical units called nucleotides. These, in turn, are made up of a 5-carbon sugar, a phosphate group, and any one of four basic-reacting, nitrogen-containing compounds [adenine (A), guanine (G), thymine (T), and cytosine (C)]. The basic DNA structure was elucidated by Watson and Crick (14) as a double helix (Fig. 14-3).

Because an almost infinite variety of arrangements of nucleotides can occur, and because one gene can influence the action of another gene in a variety of ways, all the genetic information required to produce a unique individual is contained in the genes on the 23 chromosomes of the sperm and the 23 chromosomes of the ovum. The complexity of genetic coding can be seen in Asimov's recent book on the subject (7). It is also of interest to note that a common bacterium discussed by Engel has only one chromosome but contains 4000 genes (47).

For many years it has been known that a specific characteristic can be transmitted from one generation to another by means of one or more genes. The best-known process of this kind employs only one gene pair for this transmission. An example from Mendel (103), the founder of genetic theory, explains the effects of mating pure strains of yellow garden peas with pure strains of green garden peas: In modern language we say that there is a gene pair for color, and that pure strains of peas will either have two genes for yellow (*YY*) or two genes for green (*gg*). The abbreviations used here are obvious; the capitalization of the *Y*'s indicates that yellow is *dominant,* and the lower-case form of the *g*'s indicates that green is *recessive.* When these pure strains are mated, one

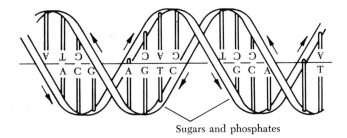

Sugars and phosphates

Fig. 14-3. A representation of the Watson–Crick double helix model for DNA. Figure 92 from *The language of life* by George W. Beadle and Muriel Beadle. Copyright © 1966 by George W. Beadle and Muriel Beadle. Reprinted by permission of Doubleday & Co., Inc.

gene from the YY pair is joined to one gene from the gg pair to form a Yg pair. All such matings yield yellow peas. Thus yellow is dominant, and green is recessive—since, when two different kinds of genes are paired, the resulting characteristic is always like the characteristic of the dominant gene and never like the characteristic of the recessive one in this example.

The second generation of Mendel's hybrid peas is particularly interesting. We can form a grid to show all the possible results of pairing genes from a sperm cell having Yg and an ovum having Yg for their respective gene structures.

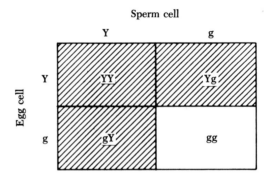

There are four possible results of this union, as indicated in the grid, and each has a probability of 0.25 since a sex cell is as likely to have a Y as a g. Since Y is still dominant, the only green peas in the second (hybrid) generation are represented in the gg square of the grid. One-quarter of the pea plants will be green, then. Based on the shaded parts of the grid, it can be said that three-quarters of the pea plants will be yellow even though they are not all the same in their genetic structure. It will be useful sometimes to distinguish between the *phenotype* or observable characteristic of an organism and its *genotype* or genetic characteristics. Thus YY and Yg have the same phenotype but different genotypes. Yg and gY have the same phenotype; they also have the same genotype since it is irrelevant in a body cell whether a gene came from the male or the female once one knows what characteristic is determined by that gene.

Not all genes are dominant or recessive. Stern (128) tells us that skin color in humans depends upon two gene pairs, and that there is no completely dominant alternative in either case. A person with four genes for black skin will be black; a person with four genes for white skin will be white; a person with some genes for black and some for white will be intermediate in skin color. Thus, interracial marriages in humans produce a blending of skin color, rather than the classic Mendelian result.

Genetic Influence in Intelligence

Eminence as a Family Trait

The genetic principles just discussed may be applied, with reservations, to human intelligence, though no genes for intelligence or eminence have been discovered. The fact that intellectual ability and social contribution may be high in one family and low in another, for virtually all its members, is obvious to any layman and well documented in the history of psychology. Galton (52) showed that eminent men are often grouped together in a single family. He also showed that eminent men more often have close relatives who are eminent. Galton made or obtained lists of eminent judges, statesmen, military commanders, literary men, scientists, poets, musicians, painters, and clergymen, totaling 966 persons living over the space of many centuries and in many countries. Of these persons 397, or 41%, had at least one eminent relative. On tracing the genealogies of these 397 persons from 300 different families, Galton found a total of 977 people who could be classed as eminent in some field

TABLE 14-1

Number of Eminent Relatives of Each Degree of Relationship in Galton's 300 Distinguished Families[a, b]

Relationship	Number of eminent relatives per family	Estimated number of relatives of any degree expected per person	Proportion of relatives who are eminent
Father	.31	1.0	.310
Brother	.41	1.0	.410
Son	.48	1.0	.360
Grandfather	.17	2.0	.085
Uncle	.18	2.0	.090
Nephew	.22	3.0	.073
Grandson	.14	4.5	.031
Great-grandfather	.03	4.0	.008
Great-uncle	.05	4.0	.012
First cousin (male)	.13	6.0	.022
Great-nephew	.10	9.0	.011
Great-grandson	.03	13.5	.002
All more remote	.31	?	?

[a] From Sir F. Galton, *Heredity genius: An inquiry into its laws and consequences.* New York: Horizon, 1952. (Reprinting of 2nd ed. of 1892.)

[b] This table corresponds to columns B, C, and D at the far right of the table on p. 308 of Galton (52). However, column C is here corrected under the assumption that a constant number of children per family (two) reach maturity of whom half are males. Since column D is the ratio of corresponding entries from B and C, it too is different from that appearing in Galton's book.

or another. Table 14-1 shows how eminence followed blood lines within those 300 families.

As Table 14-1 indicates, the absolute and proportionate numbers of eminent relatives decrease as the degree of relationship declines, i.e., as a shift is made from one group of relatives to another separated by an empty line in the table. This decrease is not always great: An eminent man is almost as likely to have an eminent male first cousin as an eminent grandson. Note that there were not enough eminent female relatives to justify including them in the table. Because this study was completed in 1892, sociological factors may have influenced this parameter. Nor did Galton find a high proportion of occasions where the eminent relative of his reference person was from the maternal side of the family. Under the influence of Galton, Charles Darwin, Julian Huxley, and others, many scholars have advocated careful planning of human marriages and childbearing to improve the human race. The study of the principles of such planning (selective mating) has been called eugenics.

This study overlooks the possibility that a highly able father may have more opportunity because of his own vocational achievements to aid the career of his son than would a mother with equal ability but lesser professional status. Also, we will see much evidence that I.Q. scores (though not necessarily eminence) can be raised or lowered by appropriate training or experience. However, it is quite possible that several gene pairs contribute to intelligence (51) just as two gene pairs are thought to control skin pigmentation in man. Such a multi-gene theory of intelligence could be used to predict Galton's findings; and, of course, it is also appropriate to include environmental factors in any serious theory of intelligence.

Mental Deficiency as a Family Trait

Just as high ability runs in families, so does gene-linked mental deficiency, as compared with that caused by infection, injury, or malnutrition. Goddard (59) has traced six generations of the descendants of Martin Kallikak (a pseudonym), a Revolutionary War soldier, and a feebleminded girl who bore him a son. Goddard also traced six generations of Kallikak's descendants from a legitimate union to a woman of normal intelligence. Of the former union there were at least 143 feebleminded descendants out of 480. There were also 24 alcoholics and a wide variety of persons with other deficiencies. Of the latter union, there were no mentally retarded persons among 496, only two alcoholics, and hardly any others with behavioral deficiencies of any kind. While the "bad" wing of the Kallikak family was afflicted by an inferior environment and by many other marriages or clandestine unions with feebleminded persons outside the Kallikak strain, it is nonetheless striking to consider how strongly Martin Kallikak affected the lives of his offspring when he selected his two mates.

Selective Mating and Its Effects

The differences in the two wings of the Kallikak family show the effects of selective mating, or assortative mating, as Jensen (78) calls it. Once the two wings were established, they continued because persons tend to marry similar persons. Highly intelligent people are likely to attend college where they meet prospective mates like themselves. Members of high-income groups tend to have high intelligence and to live in the same neighborhoods and to mix socially. Highly intelligent people often prefer the companionship of people of similar abilities. For these and other reasons, the correlation between the I.Q.'s of husbands and wives averages about +0.60 (78). Theoretical calculations of the effects of this selective mating, together with empirical evidence, indicate that it tends to increase the average intelligence of our citizenry. There are about 20 times as many persons with an I.Q. above 160 as would be seen if there were no assortative mating; in general, the number of persons of high I.Q. of any level is increasing. Since assortative mating tends to increase the standard deviation of I.Q.'s, we might also expect that there would be more persons with very low I.Q.'s than if there were no assortative mating. However, persons with I.Q.'s below 75 have difficulty finding marriage partners and therefore produce fewer children than other adults (78).

Similarity of Intelligence of Twins

From our conviction that much of a person's intelligence derives from inherited characteristics, we would expect closely related persons to be more similar in intelligence scores than distantly related persons. This expectation was indirectly confirmed by Galton's study cited above. A more direct test of this hypothesis is to compare the similarity of the test scores themselves among brothers and sisters, fathers and sons, grandfathers and grandsons, etc.

In our illustration of the meaning of the product–moment correlation coefficient, we stated that the data of Fig. 14-1 showed a correlation of +0.67 between the I.Q.'s of identical twins who had been separated early in life. This correlation is slightly larger than the 0.64 value obtained by Newman, Freeman, and Holzinger (108) for like-sexed fraternal twins who were reared together, but who, since they did not come from the same ovum, did not have identical genes. A much higher r, 0.91, was obtained by Newman, Freeman, and Holzinger for 50 identical twin pairs who grew up together. Evidently the correlation between I.Q.'s of pairs of family members is increased both by increasing the genetic similarity between them and by having them grow up together rather than apart.

Similarity of intelligence scores in other siblings. If the above is correct, pairs of siblings other than twins, triplets, etc., should show positive but lower correlations of I.Q. scores than should twins. McNemar (98) reports that 384 pairs of ordinary siblings have an *r* of 0.53. This is as expected except that it is lower than that for fraternal twins of like sex whom we saw earlier to have an *r* of 0.64 when their I.Q. scores were considered. Two possible reasons for this are (a) that the difference between the 0.53 and 0.64 obtained for ordinary sibs and for fraternal twins is an accident due to the particular samples of persons studied and that no difference would appear if all such pairs could be studied and (b) that fraternal twins though no more alike genetically than ordinary sibs are treated as if they were alike by their parents because they are passing through the same developmental stages at the same, or nearly the same time. Possibility (b) is more widely accepted though (a) cannot be wholly excluded.

Now if (b) is true, similarity of rearing also explains at least some of the similarities in intelligence of identical twins. They are surely treated as similarly by parents and others as are fraternal twins. Those who minimize the effects of heredity on intelligence argue that all the increase in similarity of intelligence scores of identical twins over fraternal twins is due to this similarity of treatment. There is evidence to refute this: Newman, Holzinger and Freeman's 19 pairs of identical twins who had been reared apart through most of their early life had a correlation of intelligence scores of 0.67, which is substantially the same as the 0.64 for fraternal twins, whereas a complete environmentalist would contend that with widely different environments the identical twin pairs should have been less similar in I.Q. than the fraternal twin pairs.

Family Resemblances in Intelligence

The same emphasis on similarity of treatment or of environment as a controller of similarity of intelligence leads to the expectation that foster children should become like their foster parents and foster siblings. When we look for evidence of this in adoptive parents and their children, we are disappointed. Leahy (89) found that the average Otis intelligence score of the two foster parents and the Stanford–Binet I.Q. of the foster child correlated only 0.18 whereas the corresponding correlation for parents and their own children was 0.60. It seems that much of the similarity of parent and child depends on hereditary factors rather than on the home environment.

Leahy's study does not imply, however, that level of performance on I.Q. tests is unrelated to that of the foster parents. Work by Skodak and Skeels (122) showed that 100 illegitimate children adopted before six months of age had mean I.Q.'s (at an average age of 13½ years) of 106. This is quite high considering that the mean I.Q. for those of their real mothers who were tested (63 of them) was only 85.7; those fathers on whom data were available were disproportionately concentrated in the lower occupational classifications. These children's I.Q.'s showed an *r* of 0.44 with their 63 true mothers' I.Q.'s but no correlation with their foster parents' educational levels. It seems that foster parents (whose background was superior to everything known about the true parents' background) contributed to a general raising of these children's I.Q.'s. However, the children's *relative* standings were apparently controlled by the intelligence of their true parents, not their foster parents. [But see McNemar (97) for an argument that the true parents of the adopted children were more intelligent than Skodak and Skeels believed.] In view of evidence suggesting that the level of intelligence in each generation may be rising, it is possible that these foster children would have shown about the same I.Q.'s if raised by their true parents. Note, however, that Skeels (121) has shown that retarded orphans who were given special attention in infancy were better adjusted and had a higher adult intelligence than a comparable control group left in a standard orphanage situation.

An Estimate of How Much Heredity Controls I.Q.

Theoretical genetics provides formulas for assessing the relative contribution of heredity to variation in observed characteristics (phenotypes). Jensen (78) reports that one such measure, called *heritability*, yields a value of 0.77 for I.Q.'s in a large group of persons of varying relationships. This means that about 77% of the variance (*variance* being technically defined as the standard deviation squared) in these I.Q. scores could be predicted from a knowledge of family relationships. Such facts as the positive correlation of the I.Q.'s of unrelated foster parents and their foster children could not be predicted from genetic theories, however, except by assuming that the assignment of foster children took into account the genetic background of those children and of their prospective foster parents.

Kagan (81), Hunt (74), and Cronbach (34) have called attention to the fact that heritability may be high without implying that differences between racial or socioeconomic groups are inherited. Height, for example, is definitely inherited; but its average in certain countries may shift markedly with such changes in environment as improved nutrition. Jensen (78a) cites evidence for a 2½ to 3½ inch average mature height increase in European countries since 1870. Jensen (78) recognizes that severe malnutrition can reduce I.Q. by as much as 20 points, a reduction which can be compensated for by nutritional improvement if provided by the age of 2 years. He appears, however, to think that such severe malnutrition is much less common in the United States than Cronbach (34) and Brazziel (23) suppose.

Environmentally Produced Shifts in Intelligence Scores

Depression of Intelligence Scores by Poor Environments

It is a pity that this chapter must be written so soon after intelligence testing was begun or that intelligence testing should have begun so late, for many hints about intelligence need a generation more of research before they can be understood. One such hint is the manner and degree to which poor surroundings can depress intelligence scores. Had these tests been available 100 years ago, before women had generally begun to receive the same education as men, we have no doubt that women would have scored much lower, leading to the conclusion that they were an inferior sex (82). Further, we should expect that with added educational opportunities for people in isolated communities and for underprivileged races, those people's scores should increase markedly.

From what is known already, however, it is clear that something is happening to children in impoverished environments. Hirsch (69) long ago found that a group of mountain children in geographical and cultural isolation were noticeably lower in intelligence than those in urban areas and that older children were lower in intelligence than younger ones. Presuming that no older children left the mountains, this would be strong evidence for a reduction in intelligence with time in a poor environment. Since that presumption is not wholly correct, migration of persons with above-average intelligence may account for part of the inferiority of the mountain group as a whole and of the older group in particular. Wheeler (148) has presented similar data showing a decline in mean I.Q. with age, as represented in Table 14-2. Chapanis and Williams (29) found a similar decline more recently.

These studies, though they suggest certain trends, suffer from the handicaps underlying cross-sectional analyses. We cannot expect mountain children to show progressive declines in intelligence with age on the basis of this study. We do not know what their I.Q. changes would have been had these children lived elsewhere or had they been tested longitudinally. Such studies need to be supplemented either with long-term studies of the same persons or by comparisons of older and younger

TABLE 14-2

Decline in Average I.Q. Score (Dearborn Intelligence Test) as a Function of Age of 557 Children in East Tennessee Mountains[a]

Chronological age	Median I.Q.	Number of cases
9	95.3	27
10	89.7	63
11	87.2	81
12	81.8	98
13	79.4	102
14	75.7	122
15	72.5	64

[a] From Wheeler (148).

children of the same family to show what happens in people with more similar genetic backgrounds.

Effects of Nursery School Training

Direct or indirect practice upon intelligence tests, affecting I.Q. values, are accepted by one and all as the natural consequence of formal instruction. If, however, the instruction is less formal, as in nursery schools, what a research worker finds and what a reviewer concludes seems to depend more on his personal biases than on the nature of the population studied.

What would a psychologist expect if he had never studied the effects of nursery schools and had no preconceived notions about the susceptibility of intelligence scores to external influence? Surely, if he knew something about the problem of transfer of training, he would expect improvement to be greatest if the nursery school activities were very similar to intelligence test problem solving and least if the nursery school activities were very unlike such problem solving. This influence is verified by the data once the literature on this topic is searched carefully and questions of research design are put in their proper place. Unfortunately, some studies (19, 127, 147) purporting to show increases in I.Q. following nursery school instruction merely compare such I.Q.'s for children in nursery school at the beginning of a year and at the end of the year for one or two years without comparison to groups of children not in school. Accordingly, the gains observed may be no more than would be observed if the children were not in nursery school. It is also possible that they result from changes in the standard deviation of the I.Q. from one age to the next, so that an I.Q. of 110 at one age might correspond to an I.Q. of 113, say, at another age. However, it does seem that I.Q.'s for the nursery school children were truly increasing, regardless of the reason for the increase.

Two studies in which comparison groups (or control groups) were employed are those of Goodenough and Maurer and of Messenger (60, 105). In each study approximately as many children not in nursery school as those in nursery school were tested at 1-, 2-, and (in the Goodenough and Maurer study only) 3-year intervals. Some attempt was made to ensure equal ability of nursery and non-nursery school children at the beginning of each study. However, this matching procedure was not ideal because the experimenters did not use a random process to decide which child would be in the nursery school and which would not. Rather, the decision depended on which parents asked that their children be admitted to nursery school and whether there were vacancies in the school for them.

Goodenough and Maurer found no evidence that nursery school attendance in Minneapolis improves intelligence more than would non-attendance, whether for 1, 2, or 3 years. However, in the first year of her study Messenger found a 10 point average increase in I.Q. for Iowa City nursery school attendants and a 7 point increase for Stillwater, Oklahoma, nursery school children compared with a 1 point decline for nonattending children. The same four groups, using children remaining in the study for the second year showed average losses of 1 or 2 points or no change from the scores for the first year. Thus, some advantage accrued to the nursery school groups over the 2 years but not a large one. The decline during the second year is a phenomenon frequently observed in these studies and suggests that nursery school benefits come from nonspecific training which is concluded very quickly. Presumably part of the first year gain and part of the second year loss is attributable to chance. Some instances of gains may also result from unequal standard deviations of the I.Q. from one age to the next.

Dawe (40) has done one of the finest experiments in this field. She gave an average of 50 hours of training with words, books, pictures, and excursions to 11 preschool or kindergarten children while giving no special training to 11 children matched with them for age, mental ability, and other factors. The specially treated group gained an average of 14 I.Q. points while the untreated group lost an average of 2 points. This confirms our expectation that experience with material fairly similar to the tasks of intelligence items should appreciably facilitate gains in I.Q. scores.

After a lapse of about 25 years, investigations of the possibility of increasing I.Q. scores by appropriate preschool experiences have again become popular, with special emphasis being given to work with so-called "disadvantaged children," a designation that is often though not always a euphemism for ethnic minority children. Chapters 9 and 10 discussed some such studies without indicating the magnitude of I.Q.

changes which had been reported. Before reviewing those studies and related experiments further, we must mention that two problems apparent in the 1930's and 1940's are still present; too few investigations include a true control group, and I.Q. increases often disappear after the training program ends. For example, Hodges and Spicker (70) report that the Perry Preschool Project showed a mean advantage in I.Q. of 8.9 points over a control group after a year of preschool, with the advantage over a control group dropping to 1.6 points by the end of the second grade. Bereiter and Engelmann's highly academic preschool environment (17) led to gains of about 7 points in Stanford–Binet I.Q. over an 18-month period. This average I.Q. improvement was retained for the subsequent 11 months, at least.

The size of these gains due to special training is comparable to that obtained with direct coaching and practice on intelligence tests. Only if such gains are maintained on later tests with new items can we feel sure that they represent real changes in I.Q. In addition to possibly being the consequence of practice on similar items or to being the result of improved rapport on later tests (which should also be true for a control group if it exists), changes in I.Q. following training may be due to a change in attention to class material or test material. Kohlberg (87) mentions one of his own research efforts in which an average Stanford–Binet I.Q. increase of 14 points occurred in the first 6 months of a program for Headstart children of ages 3 and 4. Because Piagetian tests did not exhibit a comparable improvement, Kohlberg believes this I.Q. change not to be an improvement in cognitive development. He provides evidence instead which indicates that individuals who improved in degree of attention paid in class also improved in I.Q. scores.

Deloria (40a) reports that the successor of the Perry Preschool Project, the Curriculum Demonstration Project, yielded average Stanford–Binet gains of 27.5, 28.0, and 30.2 points for 3-year-old children given traditional, Piagetian, and Bereiter–Engelmann preschool instruction in 1967–1968. A 1968–1969 replication yielded similar but slightly lower gains.

Obviously an I.Q. change in the course of preschool training may or may not indicate future high performance on I.Q. tests. From a practical standpoint, there is promise in Bereiter and Engelmann's (17) finding that greater gains can be made in psycholinguistic abilities, reading, and arithmetic, than in I.Q. per se.

Effects of College Training

If nursery school makes some difference in intelligence, possibly later periods of education should do so as well. To find out if this is true, Lorge (91) tracked down 131 persons for whom he had intelligence records from 20 years before and gave them a new test. When he compared the scores of the people who had gone on to obtain 15 to 17 years of school and of those who had obtained only 8 to 10 years of school, he found that the former, though equal 20 years ago to the latter in I.Q., had since gained an average of 2 more years of mental age than the latter. Smarter people go to college; and going to college makes people smarter. Both conclusions appear plausible, but the latter assumes that college itself, rather than motivational or other differences, is the crucial factor. This assumption has not been verified.

Now, whether or not increased intelligence scores obtained under favorable circumstances other than direct practice of test items or very similar items do occur often enough to be significant, dramatic changes cannot be expected. An increase in I.Q. score following special instruction or a change in environment may or may not be permanent, and it may or may not be reflected in other aspects of life such as school performance or occupational success. Furthermore, to offer hope for dramatic improvement in intellectual performance to anyone, be he mentally retarded, dull normal, normal, or quite superior, is overoptimistic.

Effects of Practice on Intelligence Tests

Psyche Cattell's study (25), to be discussed shortly, shows a zero change in I.Q. from one testing to another to be most frequent. However, there are other data where the whole trend is toward improvement. Consider the most trivial possible situation. If persons were repeatedly reinforced with knowledge of results on the exact items to be used in later tests, they would surely improve very greatly, on the average, in test scores. After such training, the test is obviously not very useful in predicting academic performance and is no longer a valid measurement. But what if the test is simply given two or more times, with no intervening practice? Here, too, some improvement in average score may be expected, as much as 10 I.Q. points in one study (96). As mentioned above, different forms of tests were introduced to minimize this unintentional direct improvement (or transfer, see Chapter 3) from the first testing to the second testing. However, some transfer will nonetheless occur from one form to another of almost any test (41, 114, 149).

Effects of Practice with Related Materials

Nor is this the end of the effects of practice. Sometimes material other than intelligence test items themselves is used for extended practice, as in the study presented in a thesis by Sarason. He gave 6 hours' training over a period of 6 weeks, either in verbal knowledge and skill, geometrical problems in pictorial form, form boards and other performance tasks, or arithmetic and algebraic problems, to each of 4 groups. Improvement on the retest was marked with almost any test employed, even those intended to be insensitive to experience and, therefore, termed culture-free (28). Hunt (73) has reviewed much of this research, mentioning methodological arguments as well as factual evidence on the questions of the effects of practice and improvability of I.Q. scores.

Possible I.Q. Increase Resulting from Teachers' Expectations

Rosenthal and Jacobson (116, 117) have reported the results of telling elementary school teachers that certain children—selected quite randomly by the investigators—were expected to show substantial intellectual growth during the year. There was in fact a net gain of 3.8 I.Q. points in 8 months over the performance of comparable children from whom their teachers were not told to expect such growth. This is a startling finding and potentially an important one in that it indicates that teachers who believe in their students' potential for improvement can bring it about. However, this report has been criticized, largely on the grounds of improper use of statistics (34, 78, 135). Note, too, that an attempt to duplicate this finding with another group of children was unsuccessful (29a). Therefore, teachers should treat all normal children as having the potential for substantial intellectual growth even though it remains to be proved whether this will improve their I.Q. scores.

Intelligence as Related to Experience and Maturation

It would seem apparent that everything a person receives credit for on an intelligence test is something he could not do at birth. In one sense, then, intelligence is the sum total of acquired skills in intellectual tasks. Certainly children and adults learn many things which, directly or indirectly, relate to the content of intelligence tests. Even if the test maker tries to present completely novel items, he must fail; something similar has appeared before, making the solution a little easier. It would be wrong to suggest, though, that intelligence is limited only by opportunities for learning and not by genetic or physiological factors. For example, we saw indications in Chapter 9 that children raised in isolation show very little measurable intelligence. This deficiency need not entirely be attributed to lack of cultural experience. Some such children apparently lacked normal neurological apparatus as well, a second reason for their limited intelligence.

Growth in Childhood

Thus both maturation of inherited characteristics and acquired learning are required for intelligent behavior to show itself. Some of the evidence for each process is presented here. From a cross-sectional analysis (98), it can be shown that ease in answering test items increases with age. Longitudinal data also reveal this improvement. Because intelligence is increasingly used to mean I.Q. or *relative intelligence,* considering C.A., and because I.Q. does not systematically increase with age, we choose to use a separate term, *intellectual power,* to denote the quantity which is growing. Often M.A. scores will be available as measures of intellectual power; in other cases point scores will be used.

Baldwin and Stecher (9) found regular increases in intellectual power with increased age, as did Bayley (11, 12), Bradway and Thompson (21), Honzik (71), and Honzik, MacFarlane, and Allen (72), among others. Figure 14-4 presents growth curves for five individual boys in a study by Bayley (11). Since any single intelligence test is appropriate only to a limited age range, several different tests were employed. By analysis of results from the different tests, Bayley constructed what might be called a "universal unit" or measure of intellectual power, the 16D unit, to compensate for the fact that mental age or point score units on the different tests were not originally equivalent.

The five individual curves show sizable differences in final level of performance. Within each curve some irregularities occur, due partly to shifts in the content of the tests given and partly to irregularities in development of these individuals. Such irregularities are to be expected in most persons, and certain means of tallying them may magnify their apparent importance unduly. For example, Fig. 14-5 shows the results of converting the intellectual power measure for Case 5M of Fig. 14-4 to an I.Q. or *relative intelligence* measure. Figure 14-5 might cause a parent or teacher to think of Case 5M as highly inconsistent in intellectual growth while Fig. 14-4 makes clear that the general trend is upward and the net result above average. Thorndike (134) has also shown evidence for inconsistency in intellectual growth; he finds only a slight relationship between intellectual power shown on one testing and the gain displayed in a few years.

When we emphasize intellectual power or M.A., we are calling attention to the fact that intelligence increases even when the I.Q. remains relatively constant. Bloom (20) has particularly emphasized that intellectual growth is cumulative, with the skills developed one year being added to those available in the previous year just as height increases by

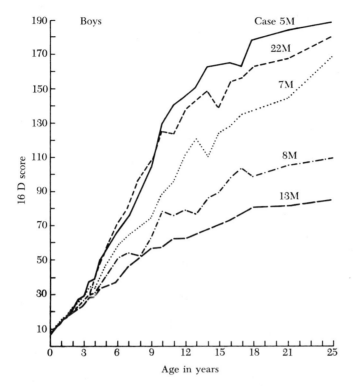

Individual curves of 16 D scores (intelligence)

Fig. 14-4. Growth of intellectual power for five individuals. Based on Figure 13 of Bayley (11). Copyright 1955 by American Psychological Association, and reproduced by permission.

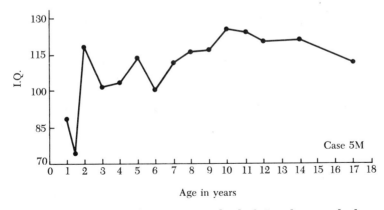

Fig. 14-5. Change in I.Q. with age in one individual. Based on standard scores for Case 5M of Figure 7 of Bayley (11). Copyright 1955 by American Psychological Association, and reproduced by permission.

additions to previous height. Partly because of this cumulative process, the correlation between I.Q.'s at different ages increases with age up to about 8 years, after which I.Q.'s for any 2 years will yield correlations above 0.90. Even by the age of 4 or 5, I.Q. correlates about 0.70 with I.Q.'s at age 17 (78). Information of this kind has led Bloom and others to conclude that, if I.Q.'s are to be increased or reduced by environmental processes, those processes must take effect in the first few years of life. This argument has been widely used to support Headstart programs and other preschool programs for economically disadvantaged children. However, there is evidence that I.Q. also increases in adulthood under some circumstances. This is one reason why we recommend that attempts to improve the educational attainments of persons in economically disadvantaged groups (or ethnic groups who have suffered from discrimination) involve extra opportunities at every age level. A second reason is that the rate of learning in a mature person may be expected to be greater than in a child even though their I.Q.'s are identical. A third reason to be offered is that education of older persons may be seen by them to have immediate occupational advantages, thus increasing the incentive to learn, while a young disadvantaged child may not be certain that any degree of learning can bring him greater financial security than his parents possess.

Changes in Adults

From studies of the growth of intelligence in children and adolescents it is natural to move toward the question of further growth, stability, or decline in adult intelligence. Figure 14-4 showed increases in intellectual power up to age 25 for the five individual cases; Bayley found such increases for 14 of 15 persons tested. However, cross-sectional data have long suggested that this growth must stop in adolescence or early adulthood and, like physical stature and vigor, begin a decline. Thus, Jones and Conrad (80) administered the Army Alpha examination to 1911 representative inhabitants of 19 New England villages. When persons of various ages were compared, the graph in Fig. 14-6 was obtained. The peak ability is shown by 18-year-olds, followed by a decline from ages 18 to 60, with 60-year-olds performing at the level of 14-year-olds. Assuming that their demonstration of homogeneity of the different age groups with respect to occupation and social level implied homogeneity of intelligence for all groups except for the effects of aging and minor random fluctuations, Jones and Conrad inferred that individuals studied longitudinally would exhibit similar declines in intelligence from ages 18 to 60. However, recently obtained longitudinal evidence as well as more indirect evidence indicates that other factors than age are at least

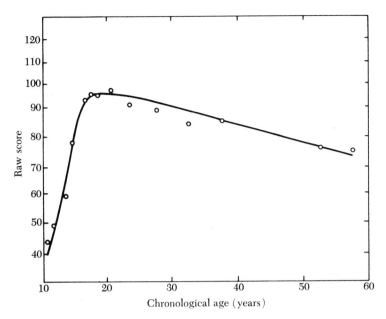

Fig. 14-6. Growth and decline of Army Alpha scores from 10 to 60 years as suggested by Jones and Conrad's (80) cross-sectional study.

partially responsible for the decline in intelligence found by Jones and Conrad and other investigators.

First of all, each generation in this country receives a more lengthy education than its predecessor. This alone might cause the new generation to score higher than the older one. This presumption is strengthened by Tuddenham's research on World War II soldiers using the Army Alpha test, a World War I instrument, in which he found substantially higher average scores than those for World War I (141). Tuddenham's data are by no means intended to make a complete case for intelligence increase with a new generation, either because of improved education or for genetic or physiological reasons. However, they do indicate that serious attempts to demonstrate whether this increase occurs should be made. Kuhlen (88) has emphasized the possible effect on I.Q. of changes in intellectual activity as well as education from generation to generation. He also points to other factors, such as the effects of practice, which increase intelligence scores with age, indicating that errors in longitudinal data should counteract those of cross-cultural data.

A second major reason for skepticism about I.Q. decline with age is the smaller declines exhibited in cross-sectional analyses of college educated people. Gurvitz (67) found less decline of I.Q. with age among college educated persons than others. Ghiselli (57) has reported no decline in intelligence with age in a cross-sectional study of persons with at least one year of college training.

A third reason for expecting a different result once longitudinal data are obtained is that such data are becoming increasingly available and do show less decline or even an increase in intelligence with years. In 1949 and 1950 Owens (112) tried to find and retest persons given the Army Alpha test as a scholastic aptitude test at entrance to Iowa State College in 1919. With a 65% survival of his subjects, both literally and figuratively (though he studied only 127 of the 1000 originally tested), he concluded, "There was a significant increase in the total Alpha score which was of the order of magnitude of one-half of a sigma" (i.e., a standard deviation).

Owens (113) went on to retest 96 persons who had been retested in 1949–1950. This third testing, performed in 1961 when the persons retested had an average age of 61, showed no further increase in intelligence. In fact there was a very slight, though statistically insignificant, decline in the average total Alpha score compared to 1949–1950. Owens also presented some evidence in this latest study that the net gain from 1919 to 1961 could be attributed to increased sophistication in taking tests and general cultural growth in that period. Male freshmen at Iowa State University in 1961 had almost as high total Alpha scores as the 61-year-old group.

Manifestly, longitudinal data may be misleading in some respects. Perhaps Owens' subjects remembered some test items over the years. Some may have shown effects of practice because they looked up answers to questions following the first or second examinations. Perhaps those who died or disappeared before the two retests were those who would have shown the greatest decline had they been available for retesting. Nonetheless, Owens' data are as definitive as anything we have. His results are reasonably consistent with most longitudinal studies (13, 15, 94, 109).

Since most longitudinal studies have been performed on persons of college caliber and with few retests, it is premature to conclude that intelligence increases or decreases during maturity for persons who did not attend college or to conclude that Owens' findings imply that a maximum is reached between ages 50 and 60.

Variability of I.Q.'s from Test to Retest

Given the sort of items which appear in tests of intelligence or scholastic aptitude and given that answers to them can be learned just as if they were school assignments, it is not surprising to see some

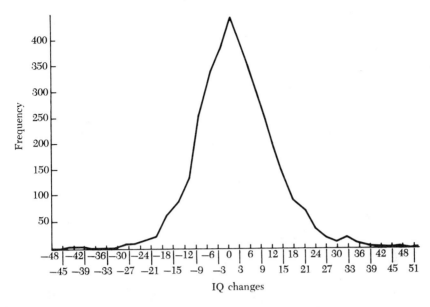

Fig. 14-7. Test–retest changes in Stanford–Binet I.Q. based on 3331 comparisons. Figure 2 from P. Cattell (25).

people's scores change from one testing to another. Figure 14-7 shows a typical finding (25) on the degree of change from one testing to the next. Note that the most frequent result is that of no change but that many shifts of great magnitude occurred. Some variations could be explained as happenstance fluctuations in the person or the testing situation from one time to the next. Earlier in this chapter the standard deviation was defined as a measure of variation among a group of persons. The standard deviation can also be measured among several scores for the same person; this indicates the amount of "happenstance fluctuation" just mentioned. However, statistical theory implies that bright pupils should appear duller on retest and dull pupils brighter, whereas the reverse occurred in Cattell's study. Apparently some of the change in I.Q. scores results from a change in the person tested, either in his biological rate of development or his intellectual experience.

_____ **Intelligence Scores in Ethnic and National Groups**

Some Facts about Ethnic Group Differences

Just as family resemblances appear in intelligence scores or in attainments partially reflecting those scores, so may intellectual similarities appear in the inhabitants of different nations or in members of ethnic groups. First, let it be said that the homogeneity of intelligence in national or ethnic groups is very small. Whereas no member of the Kallikak family rose to the level of the average of the eminent men of Galton's study, every national or ethnic group has a noticable percentage of its members above the average I.Q. of each other such group. This percentage is technically known as the *overlap.* Thus we would expect 50% of Chinese–Americans to be above the average for Americans of Caucasian origin if these two ethnic groups were of equal average intelligence. The use of the term overlap is regrettable because its meaning to the layman is not the same as to the specialist. As used here, 100% overlap means that the overlapping group is distinctly more intelligent, on the average. To the layman, 100% overlap would imply equality, and 50% overlap (approximate equality) would imply a great difference between groups.

Because the question of differences between different ethnic groups is the subject of much controversy, let us examine the data. Take for granted that differences in educational and vocational opportunity, as well as possible differences in interest patterns and motivations, in Indian–American, Mexican–American, Oriental–American, and Anglo–American subcultures (among others) do not permit assessment of the relative intellectual potential of different racial groups by comparing their intelligence test scores. But assume also that these scores permit prediction of relative performance in school for a few years after they are given. Then it becomes important to know the amount of overlap in I.Q. test scores of blacks and whites, for example, as a means of characterizing their present capacities. Further evidence will suggest how differences (if any) between these groups arise and what the prospects are for their disappearance.

Data from the nationwide study entitled *Equality of Educational Opportunity* (31) indicate that children in most of the minority groups of the United States have median intelligence test scores (i.e., scores for the middle person in the group when persons are arranged according to their scores) which are lower than scores for children of the majority group—the Anglo–Americans or so-called whites. Table 14-3 shows Coleman's results for first and twelfth graders and for verbal and non-verbal tests. (Further consideration of these data is presented in Chapter 17.) Though it is not surprising in view of the fact that intelligence tests have been constructed by whites for use in a white-dominated society, it is noteworthy that no median scores for any minority group exceeds the corresponding median for the majority group, except in the case of the nonverbal test scores for first-grade Oriental–Americans. There is also

TABLE 14-3

Nationwide Median Test Scores for First- and Twelfth-Grade Pupils, Fall 1965[a]

Grade	Racial or ethnic group					
	Puerto Ricans	Indian– American	Mexican– American	Oriental– American	Negro	Majority
1st						
Nonverbal	45.8	53.0	50.1	56.6	43.4	54.1
Verbal	44.9	47.8	46.5	51.6	45.4	53.2
12th						
Nonverbal	43.3	47.1	45.0	51.6	40.9	52.0
Verbal	43.1	43.7	43.8	49.6	40.9	52.1

[a] Abridged from Coleman *et al.*, Table 9 (31).

some evidence within the Coleman Report, as it is often called, for a decline in minority group test scores from the first to the twelfth grade, an indication that the school system may not be serving minority groups as well as it serves the majority.

Shuey (120) examined 194 studies of intelligence test scores of black elementary school children, 55 studies of intelligence test scores of black high-school children, and studies of intelligence scores of 24,640 black college students. Among children from ages 2 to 6 she reports an average I.Q. of 94.0 for 1541 blacks and an average I.Q. of 105.6 for 13,816 whites. For both groups these means are higher than among older children. Also the mean difference between racial groups is smaller for younger children. Shuey further reports that the mean I.Q. difference between racial groups is reduced when the children compared live in the same neighborhood, attend the same school, and have fathers in the same occupational group.

Shuey reports that, among 23 studies using individual intelligence tests for white and black school children, only two showed mean I.Q.'s as high for the black as for the white children. An additional 20 investigations of black school children alone showed 17 averages below the national norms for whites. Similar results were reported by Shuey for high-school and college students. Black high-school students showed a mean I.Q. of 84.1 and whites showed a mean of approximately 100 (97 in studies prior to 1945; 102 in studies from 1945 to 1965). Black college students had an average score (on the American Council Psychological Examination for College Freshmen) which fell at a point where only 12% of the overall population was lower. Shuey has computed the mean overlap between black I.Q. scores and white median I.Q.'s to be 11%, based on 71 studies.

Are Mean I.Q. Differences among
Different Ethnic Groups Eradicable?

Shuey and other students of blacks' intelligence find the data above most convincing evidence that a natural inferiority in intelligence is characteristic, on the average, of the black. It is surely convincing evidence that black performance on intelligence tests averages below that of whites. Nonetheless, most psychologists hold that natural differences between these or other racial groups could only be concluded as an established fact after testing a very large sample from a population in which discrimination and prejudice had been absent for so long that genuine equality of opportunity held for all members of each group.

What data point to environmental depression of black intelligence scores? Because blacks are found disproportionately often to hold menial jobs and live in blighted areas, the data cited earlier about decline of intelligence as a function of malnutrition or intellectually impoverished environments are surely applicable to many blacks. This may be a factor in any town or community or city; it is also a factor from state to state and from region to region. Bagley (8) and others have emphasized that Army Alpha scores from World War I, though showing inferior scores of blacks, on the average, also showed that certain Northern states had black soldier populations with higher median Alpha scores than the white soldier populations from several Southern states. Thus Klineberg (84) reported that blacks from the four Northern states where they scored highest (Pennsylvania, New York, Illinois, and Ohio) had medians which were all above or almost all above the medians of whites from the four Southern states (Mississippi, Kentucky, Arkansas, and Georgia) which scored the lowest (Georgia whites were slightly above Pennsylvania blacks). This suggests that the advantages of a Northern environment somewhat compensate for the intellectual disadvantages of being black. It should be noted, however, that this comparison of Alpha scores is a comparison only for literate blacks and whites. Table 14-4 shows the results when scores for all soldiers tested, either with the Alpha or the Beta (for use with illiterates) examinations, are examined in these eight states selected as the most superior in the North or most inferior in the South. Table 14-4 shows that, for the soldiers studied (at least 3900 in each of the four categories), average scores were higher for these Northerners than these Southerners, higher for whites than blacks, and slightly higher for Southern whites than Northern blacks. The fact that the difference between Northern whites and Northern blacks is less, on the average, than that for

TABLE 14-4

Mean Intelligence Test Scores (Either Alpha or Beta) from the Four Highest Scoring Northern and the Four Lowest Scoring Southern States[a]

Race	States	
	Northern	Southern
Black	12.0	9.8
White	14.1	12.7

[a] Based on Alper and Boring (1). Copyright 1944 by American Psychological Association, and reproduced by permission.

Southern whites and Southern blacks could be because of a more nearly equal education of blacks and whites in the North. This would suggest that differences between whites and blacks will indeed disappear as segregation decreases. Indications from World War II data (36) are that the years between wars did not reduce the difference. However, this was a period without major changes in segregation patterns in either North or South, and one would expect that a reduction in the black–white differential in intelligence would only occur in a period like the present one, with its strong emphasis on integration in the armed forces, schools, and places of employment. Until such a reduction is demonstrated, it is always possible to suppose that superior educational advantages, such as those in the four Northern states under consideration, will simply raise the intelligence of whites and blacks alike but not bring their scores nearer equality.

A further possible explanation for the discrepancy between mean intelligence scores in the North and in the South would be that selective migration, i.e., northward movement of the abler persons, is taking place. This seems unlikely for blacks, at least, since Klineberg (83) has shown no consistent difference of average grades for black migrants from Birmingham, Alabama; Nashville, Tennessee; and Charleston, South Carolina, to Northern cities, compared with average grades of the entire black school population in those three cities. Klineberg (84) has shown further that, on the average, blacks who have been in the North for some years have higher intelligence test scores than those who have migrated more recently. Figure 14-8 illustrates this trend from part of his studies. This, too, suggests that the Northern environment may be favorable for intellectual development; we believe it is beneficial for whites as well as blacks, partly since Northern schools are usually characterized by longer school years and higher per capita school expenditures than Southern schools.

Because Klineberg's comparison was a cross-sectional one, it may be

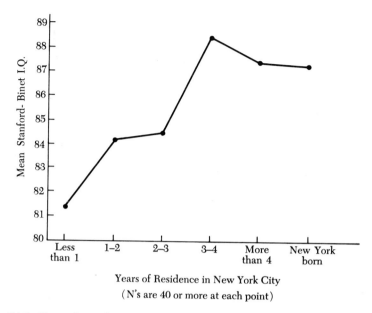

Years of Residence in New York City
(N's are 40 or more at each point)

Fig. 14-8. Upward trend in intelligence scores as a function of number of years since leaving the South. Based on Table 24 of Klineberg (84).

that his results are due to original differences between the groups tested. Therefore, longitudinal data on this question also seem desirable. Research by Clark (30) found little, if any indication that retests of Southern-born black children in Cleveland or Detroit schools showed improvement in I.Q. over original tests in those schools, with the time between the two tests variable from person to person and experiment to experiment, but with averages on the order of 2 years. However, Lee (90) found the records of 424 black children who had been born in Philadelphia, had not attended kindergarten, and had received the I.Q. testings regularly given in grades 1A, 2B, 4B, 6B and 9A. He compared results for these children with those of migrants from the South (also blacks) who had not attended kindergarten and had received all regular testings following their arrival in Philadelphia. There were five such groups: those who had first been tested in grade 1A and always thereafter, those who had first been tested in grade 2B and always thereafter, and so on. These groups all were 109 or more in size. Though the Philadelphia-born group showed an average gain of only 1.6 points from grade 1A to grade 9A, the migrant group which had reached Philadelphia in time for the grade 1A testing showed an average gain of 6.3 points in the same period. Later-arriving groups showed lower gains, with a consistent trend indicating the longer the time spent in Philadelphia the greater the gain. Since the migrant groups were all below the Philadelphia-born students, on the average, even at the end of the study, it seems that earlier depressions in intelligence scores were not completely eradicated by experience in Philadelphia schools and neighborhoods. There is no reason to think that the 1.6 point average increase of the Philadelphia-born group represents anything other than the effects of practice or random fluctuation in I.Q. scores. Note, too, that there is conflicting evidence in at least one study (118) which shows a decline over a period of years in mean I.Q. of black school children in some segregated schools in the North. Klineberg (85) has pointed out that overlap statistics and mean differences can be misleading because they lead one to forget such facts as the following. An overlap of 30% of blacks compared to whites means that approximately 99% of blacks will reach or exceed the lowest score of whites. Also, two groups may show mean differences despite the fact that the low scores of the two groups are essentially identical and the high scores of the two groups are essentially identical. (Shuey objects to Klineberg's statement because of its presumption of a 30% overlap rather than the 11% mentioned earlier in this chapter. This weakens Klineberg's argument but does not destroy it. Even with 11% overlap, most blacks would have higher I.Q. scores than the lowest member of the white group.)

The Coleman Report (31) presents an interesting position on this question of the eradicability of ethnic differences in intelligence. Coleman *et al.* in that report call the verbal and nonverbal test scores shown in Table 14-3 achievement scores and attempt to determine what school characteristics lead to the highest achievement by minority and majority group members. The authors of that report show by statistical means that when socioeconomic level is held constant the achievement of white students is less affected by the school's facilities, curricula, and teachers than is the achievement of minority group members. The existence of science laboratories seems to favor the development of high test scores, but this variable is minor compared to the amount of education and verbal ability of the teacher. Both the latter measures of the quality of teachers affect the achievement of students, and, particularly, of minority group students, with the effect being in the expected direction; more intelligent and better educated teachers produce brighter students. Furthermore, a minority group child is more likely to show high achievement if he attends a school in which most of the students have a high motivation for attending college.

Jensen (78), in what is proving to be a very controversial paper, has stated his opinion that the mass of evidence indicate a genetic contribution to the average difference between white and black persons' I.Q.'s. Several rebuttals to this article have been published; we mentioned some of them in our discussion of heritability earlier in this chapter. It should be noted that Jensen does not assert that his hypothesis has been proved, but only that his position is stronger currently than one which clearly assigns group differences to environmental causes. We believe his evaluation to have greatly underestimated the difficulties of finding comparable environments for whites and blacks in which meaningful genetic comparisons can be made.

The interested reader is encouraged to examine Jensen's article, the early commentaries on it (16, 23, 34, 35, 46, 74, 81), and Jensen's reply (78a).

An even more recent article by Light and Smith (90a) questions Jensen's conclusions on two grounds: (a) It is possible to predict the mean intelligence differences between racial groups on the basis of genetic variation within races and existing environmental differences between races, plus a small interaction effect between heredity and environment, without assuming any racial effect upon the genetic contribution to intelligence. (b) The original data on which estimates of heritability are based are inconsistent, incomplete because of the absence of data on black twins, and subject to large variability, preventing precise determination of genetic differences in intelligence between races.

Dreger and Miller (43) have written a sequel to an earlier summary of black–white comparisons which is extremely thorough and has the further advantage of referring to a variety of data other than intelligence test scores. One of their important contributions is showing the difficulty of drawing genetic inferences about racial differences in average intelligence in the absence of careful procedures for identifying members of different ethnic groups. They also stress the need for research on the effects of using only white examiners to test both white and black children instead of having some testers from each ethnic background examine children in each group.

This section can be closed, as it was begun, by stating that a comparison of intellectual potential of different ethnic or national groups is still impossible. To use the words of Dreger and Miller (42), "We are not satisfied that either those who . . . believe that genetic differences in psychological functions or those who maintain that no such differences can be found have succeeded in establishing their position."

Dreger and Miller's position is consistent with that of the famous geneticists, G. and M. Beadle (14): "As of now there is no compelling evidence that any race is genetically superior to any other race—in health, in behavior, or in ability to acquire a specific cultural pattern.

And, on the domestic scene, there is considerable evidence that the alleged cultural inferiority of Negroes is the result of less favorable opportunity, on the average, for education and employment, and their being raised in poorer social and economic environments than whites. One way to settle the question is to equalize Negro and white opportunity and environment—and then compare intelligence and achievement."

One final source of differences between national and ethnic groups must be the cultural background of the test constructor. He is usually a psychologist, a Caucasian, an urbanite, and a member of the middle class. Even though he does not intentionally build tests to favor people like himself, it is little wonder to find that psychologists, Caucasians, city-dwellers, and middle-class citizens generally show superior scores on his tests.

From a humanitarian point of view we feel compelled to add that the important question is not whether a person or a group of persons has high intelligence, but rather whether such persons have the opportunity to use their abilities effectively. Ginzberg (58) points out that one out of every four white soldiers in the top two mental groups during World War II became an officer; only one out of every ten blacks in those groups did so. Several comparable statistics also provided by Ginzberg make it apparent that, on the average, highly talented blacks are not reaching the same levels of education and professional status they would were they equally able Caucasians.

_____   **Are Intelligence Tests Socially Biased?**

Three Explanations for Social-Class Differences in Intelligence Scores

This brings us, quite naturally, to the question of whether intelligence tests give higher scores to members of one social class than to another because of bias in the items rather than because of differences in the original or attained ability of those group members. From the time of Binet and Simon (18) on, superior mean intelligence test scores have been found for members of higher social classes. As Hess (68) and others have indicated, there are at least three possible explanations for this well-established superiority: "(a) the superior test performance of high socioeconomic groups represents a genetic superiority in intelligence; (b) the superior performance of the high-status samples indicates a true difference in intelligence—a difference which results from environmental rather than genetic factors, and (c) the differential performance of high- and low-status levels arises from cultural factors within the testing instruments and testing situations themselves and does not necessarily reflect either genetic or environmental differences in intelligence between groups." Explanations (a) and (b) are surely plausible when one reflects on the material presented earlier in this chapter. How defensible explanation (c) may be remains to be seen.

First of all, is explanation (c) different from explanation (b)? If the present content of an intelligence test is central to the concept of intelligence, then one cannot have high intelligence without mastering culturally defined skills such as a middle-class vocabulary. Then (c) is unnecessary and can be forgotten. However, there seems to be no reason why intelligence test items could not be given the same logical structure as before but, nonetheless, be couched in a vocabulary and problem setting more typical of lower-class and nonbookish environments than presently. Possibly the altered intelligence test would then either show superiority for the lower-status children or equality with other groups. We would, in fact, consider it crucial that lower-status children would show superiority on some clearly intellectual task required by such a test. Explanation (c) implies that these children are developing different skills, not fewer skills, than other children. If we give an English language test to a French child, the child's score will be depressed but no more depressed than an English child's score on a test presented in French. It seems perfectly reasonable, then, to suppose that if intellectual development has been equal but different in different socioeconomic groups, intelligence tests for lower-class children could be so devised as to make their scores average above those of other groups. There is a hint in one study (5) that the Davis–Eells test, intended to be "fair" to members of all socioeconomic levels and thus to be expected under explanation (c) to give equal averages to each, may actually lead to this superiority of lower-class children at the first-grade level.

Possible Cultural Bias

Granted that explanation (c) is conceivable, just as are (a) and (b), what support can be found for it? Some authors have strongly emphasized the fact that most of the items on the tests, as well as intelligence tests as a whole, are generally easier, for children from higher socioeconomic levels. For example, Davis (37) reported that the percentage of items significantly easier for high-status children at the 9- and 10-year-old level ranged from 46 for the Otis Alpha nonverbal test to 93 for the Henmon–Nelson test, with even greater percentages occuring at the 13- and 14-year-old level. But this finding does not itself cast doubt upon the argument that genetic or environmental differences in the status groups have produced superior mean intelligence in the higher-status groups. Because of the similarity of content and purpose of intelligence test items, it is reasonable to expect most items to be easier for any group or person who will score above some other group or person on the entire test.

A second and more convincing argument for explanation (c), the implication of cultural bias in intelligence tests, is Eells' finding (45) that the items which were clearly easier for high-status children usually were vocabulary items or other verbal items demanding a fairly extensive vocabulary, often academic in nature. Correspondingly, items on which high- and low-status children performed equally usually were "performance" tasks, such as interpreting geometrical relations, or they were verbal tasks with minimal vocabulary requirements. This finding is not entirely compatible with a genetic interpretation of class differences, though it can be reconciled with it if one is really committed to that interpretation.

Producing Culturally Fair Tests

The person who suspects the presence of strong cultural bias in tests is left, then, with no data consistent with that hypothesis alone. His strategy must be to make a culturally fair test and demonstrate its superiority over other tests in a few situations at least. Davis and Hess (39) have presented an example of an item which is easier for high-status children than for low because of difficult vocabulary: "A symphony is to a composer as a book is to what?

☐ paper; ☐ sculptor; ☐ author; ☐ musician; ☐ man."

and an item which has equal difficulty for high- and low-status children because of easy vocabulary even though the item itself is difficult: "A baker goes with bread the same way a carpenter goes with what?

☐ a saw; ☐ a house; ☐ a spoon; ☐ a nail; ☐ a man."

Note that, except for a reversal in the order of mentioning the person and his creation, both items have similar logical structure: each is asking the child to pair a worker and what he produces. The context of the second question is more clearly within the experience of lower-status children, however.

Hess (68) has gone to some pains to produce a 16-item intelligence test whose items not only appear to refer to situations common to the experience of all social classes, and which use everyday vocabulary, but for which evidence could be adduced that they do actually meet these requirements. On his test, 188 high-status whites from 6½ to 9½ years of age showed no superiority over 178 low-status whites in the same age range even though appreciable differences in mean M.A. existed between the groups according to school records. Differences between high-status whites and a low-status black sample also appeared reduced by the Hess test, although they did not disappear. Since the Hess test seemed as successful for predicting reading achievement as the standard tests, except with blacks, it apparently achieved a reduction of class differences in intelligence scores without substantial impairment of its predictive function and, thus, of its practical adequacy as an intelligence test. Presumably lengthening of the test and very careful refinement of the sort employed for the Stanford–Binet could make it serve all conventional purposes and still remain a culturally fair test.

Whereas the Hess test was produced for research purposes only and has not been commercially distributed, two other tests intended to be culturally fair have been circulated more widely. They are the Davis–Eells Test of General Intelligence or Problem Solving Ability (38) (also known as the Davis–Eells Games) and the IPAT Culture Free Test (26). The Davis–Eells test, however, has not yet proved successful in eliminating or consistently reducing discrepancy in mean scores of high- and low-status children. Angelino and Shedd (5), Coleman and Ward (32), Knief and Stroud (86), and T. W. Smith (124) all found appreciable increases in the Davis–Eells Index of Problem Solving Ability (IPSA, the Davis–Eells counterpart of the intelligence quotient) with increases in socioeconomic status, except in the one part of the Angelino and Shedd study previously noted which yielded higher mean scores for lower-class 6-year-olds. This failure to reduce social status group differences may either be taken as a demonstration that the Davis–Eells test is not culturally fair or that "true" intelligence differences exist due to genetic and/or environmental factors. Although Hess's own test did suggest that some reduction of class differences was possible and Scale 2 of the IPAT Culture Free Test has been shown (93) only mildly sensitive to social class, we believe it unreasonable to call the Davis–Eells test culturally unfair solely on the grounds that differences remain despite an attempt to select items common to the experience of all children. Presumably, most of the mean difference is attributable to genetic or environmental background, not to characteristics of the test.

Whereas the Davis–Eells test focused on elimination of social class differences, the IPAT Culture Free Test and related editions such as the Culture Fair Test (27), have attempted to minimize nationality biases by omitting all language content except as required in general instructions given orally at the beginning of the test. That this has been successful is indicated by the fact that Puerto Rican children living in New York City and tested twice, once with English instruction and once with Spanish instruction, showed no effect in intelligence scores due to the language used (3). There is also some indication that, though not all national groups have the same mean I.Q. scores on the IPAT test, the means for American, Australian, British, and French populations may be equal (123).

Jensen (78) has reported that various measures of associative learning ability do not reveal mean differences between members of different socioeconomic groups. Such tasks as remembering digits orally presented, learning to associate pairs of pictures of familiar objects, and recalling names or objects which have been presented one to five times in random order can be as easily performed by children from low-income groups as from high-income groups. But Jensen does not think of these items as the basis for a culturally fair test. Rather he presumes they represent what factor analysis might reveal as a second factor in an intelligence test, a measure of associative learning in contrast to conceptual learning or abstract problem solving, which Jensen thinks of as general intelligence or g.

--------------------- **The Practical Value of Intelligence Testing**

Prediction of Academic Success

In the face of day-to-day problems of teaching, personnel selection, and counseling, an intelligence test is good or bad inasmuch as it succeeds or fails in assessing a person's likelihood of success or failure in a given task. The teacher wants to know if a pupil can keep up with work in the third grade; the personnel director wants to know if the applicant can work at the intellectual level required by the position applied for; and the high-school counselor wants to know if his student can be successful in study at a certain college.

Note that many questions of scientific importance are more or less irrelevant to the practical situation. If a mentally retarded child has an I.Q. so low that almost no child of that level ever completes third grade work successfully, the child will not be kept in a conventional third-grade class. In the face of evidence that success in that class is almost impossible, it becomes relatively useless to discuss whether the mental deficiency was inherited or developed by intellectually poor surroundings, whether the child is retarded on a general ability of intelligence, whether a multiple set of abilities constitutes the intelligence factor on which the child is retarded, or whether M.A. stops increasing after the age of 16. Except when understanding the nature of intelligence or the source of mental retardation can be shown to lead to means of increasing the likelihood of success in school, college, or vocation, the user of the intelligence test is forced to place most of his emphasis on the relations between the I.Q. and the measure of success.*

In a general way the identification of people of low, moderate, or high intelligence is self-validating; and little verification by future performance is needed. We know from Merrill's (104) work on the Stanford–

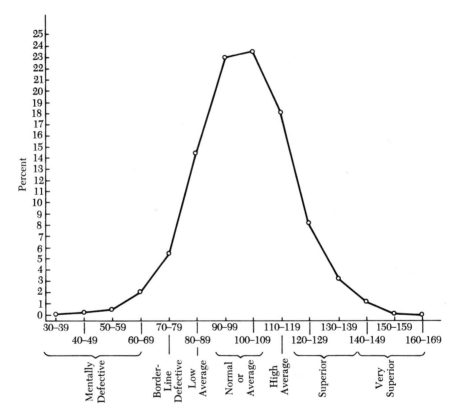

Fig. 14-9. Distribution of I.Q.'s in Revised Stanford–Binet Scales. Based on Table VII of Merrill (104).

* Inflexible or inconsiderate use of intelligence tests and similar devices can lead to predictive failures which are frightening in magnitude. One of the intellectual giants of this generation was once denied admission to a great university when a visual handicap depressed his test scores and the person in charge of selection overlooked other signs of extraordinarily high ability. Similar errors have no doubt occurred on other occasions.

Binet Revised Scale what proportion of people in the standardization group were of each level. Figure 14-9 shows these proportions, together with Merrill's labels for certain ranges of intelligence. These proportions should be taken as approximating rather than fully representing the characteristics of the nation as a whole. Recent evidence is that the general population is somewhat superior to the sample used.

Consider the group of people who are mentally defective, i.e., have I.Q.'s below 70. (This is an arbitrary classification, as Merrill took pains to emphasize. Legal declaration that a person is mentally defective would sometimes be based on a different dividing line and would consider other evidence in addition to I.Q.) It was to identify these people that intelligence tests were first made. In France by 1904 the problem of educating mentally handicapped children had become so acute that a commission which included Alfred Binet and Thomas Simon was formed to recommend solutions, partly by the measurement of relative abilities among handicapped children. Consider the following report* on one of their cases, Albert, with a M.A. of 7 and a C.A. of 26.

> . . . he is one of our most brilliant imbeciles. We have never found a more docile school boy nor one more submissive. Never a moment of impatience, an expression of weariness nor fatigue. Albert would be a model laboratory subject, such as foreign psychological laboratories made a specialty of some time ago. . . . The definitions of Albert belong to the same category; definitions by use, with a childish turn.

Q. What is a house?	A. A house . . . well . . . a house is to rent.
Q. A fork?	A. It is to eat with.
Q. A mamma?	A. She is to get ready things to eat.
Q. A table?	A. It is to eat on.
Q. A chair?	A. It is to sit on.
Q. A horse?	A. It is to work.
Q. A snail?	A. It is to eat.
Q. Charity?	A. It is those who do good in the world.
Q. Justice?	A. It is those who do evil.
Q. Goodness?	A. Ah, goodness, it is to get angry.
Q. Virtue?	A. (after thinking a long while) I don't know.
Q. How many fingers have you on the right hand?	A. Five.
Q. Altogether on the two hands?	A. Six.
Q. How many eyes have you?	A. Two.
Q. And how many ears?	A. Two.
Q. 2 eyes and 2 ears, how many ears does that make?	A. Three.

* A. Binet & T. Simon, *The development of intelligence in children.* © 1916, The Williams & Wilkins Co., Baltimore, Maryland.

Clearly, Albert and his fellow patients had substantial intellectual deficits which revealed themselves in the answers above as well as in inability to perform useful work or to attain an education. For Albert, the I.Q. test was able only to specify his limitations, not to help him surmount them except by keeping him from attempting the impossible.

Identifying persons with high intelligence is much more valuable because it provides information that certain people can profit immensely from academic experience. Brandwein (22) has shown how a science honors program can function on a volunteer basis, admitting all high-school students with a genuine vocational interest in scientific work whether or not their intelligence is high or their grade record good. Despite the presence of some students of decidedly mediocre ability, it is nonetheless true that 40% of the students in one of Brandwein's analyses had I.Q.'s of over 140. Furthermore, a group of 54 of them who entered graduate programs in science had I.Q.'s of 135 or above.

By and large, then, it seems that a high I.Q. is necessary for advanced study in science; institutions of higher learning are increasingly using intelligence tests or similar tests as one basis for selecting students. However, as Brandwein has emphasized, selection of students for scientific training will require demonstration of certain skills (such as mathematics) which would not be required of equally capable students in other fields. Brandwein also rated his students on the intensity of their motivation for scientific achievement, as evidenced largely by promptness of performance of assigned work and the amount of voluntary experimentation performed in clubs, contests, or hobby activities. When highly motivated students are compared with poorly motivated students of equal ability as shown on intelligence tests, the highly motivated students show a much greater frequency of successful entry into the scientific professions. The moral is evident; while intelligence and special vocational abilities are necessary to many types of work, they are not sufficient to make a person either happy or capable in those fields. Motivation, partly innate and partly created or at least aroused by the student's experience, is absolutely essential for high attainment in any field.

Turning from the consideration of persons of exceptionally high or low talent, we may ask how well I.Q. tests predict scholastic performance for the mass of students. The best data available are on predicting success in college: Garrett (53) has summarized 94 studies or substudies correlating the scores on intelligence tests with grade point averages for stated portions of the students' college careers. The median correlation found was 0.47, showing that intelligence is an excellent indicator of college success. Nonetheless, intelligence is not the best, nor perhaps even the second best, predictor of college grades; for 29 studies show a median correlation of 0.55 between student's rank in their high-school graduating class and their grades in college, while 24 studies show a median correlation of 0.49 between performance in general achievement tests and college grades.

Still the fact that school performance does so closely relate to intelligence encourages psychologists to use intelligence scores as bases for encouraging students to enter or not enter certain schools or fields of study. When academic performance is predicted to be low, admissions officers may reject applicants, particularly if other indications such as high-school rank and general achievement test scores support the implications of the intelligence score. While many persons might question the advisability of rejecting applicants who have some real chance of doing better in school than the tests indicate, we feel that none would deny that it is a disservice to encourage students to invest several years in training of a particular kind without realizing what his chances of success might be. This has been well known since the 1920's. Figure 14-10 shows the likelihood of students entering the Arts College of the University of Minnesota in 1923, 1924, or 1925 for graduating from that college if they had certain college aptitude ratings based on high-school

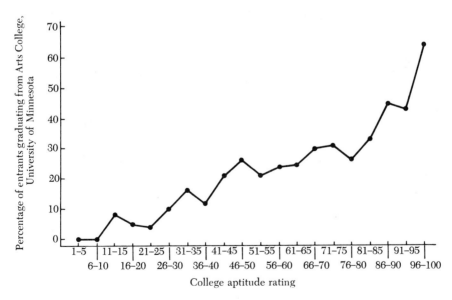

Fig. 14-10. Likelihood of graduation from the Arts College, University of Minnesota, as a function of college aptitude rating. Based on part of Table I of Johnston and Williamson (79).

rank and a psychological test (79). Clearly, a person with a rating of less than 26 should have thought long and hard about the future before entering that college in those years.

More recent data on this topic using intelligence alone as a predictor show similar results for both high-school and college performance (150). Note, from Fig. 14-11, that a person of any ability level has a much higher probability of entering high school than of entering college. These probabilities in turn are much higher than the probabilities of graduation—except for high intelligence, where pairs of curves join. These joinings mean that persons of sufficient ability are almost certain to graduate from high school or college provided they enter. (This fact seems to contradict the previous figure showing a maximum percentage of 63.9 graduating from a specific college. One reason for this discrepancy is that the current figure refers to graduation from any college, not necessarily the one first entered.)

Nothing above should suggest that intelligence tests alone or in combination with several other measurements lead to perfect or nearly perfect prediction of school performance. The correlations mentioned on pp. 586–587 (0.47, 0.55, and 0.49 for correlations between college grades and intelligence, high-school rank, and achievement test scores, respectively) are so far from perfect that a prediction for any one person may be greatly in error. Nonetheless, the correlations are high enough that the prediction for any one person will usually be less in error than if one

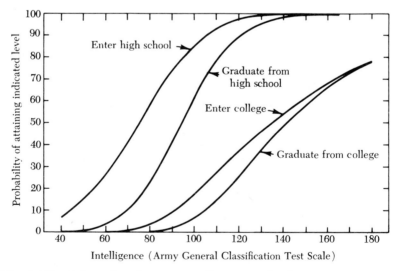

Fig. 14-11. Relationship between intelligence and educational level attained. Figure VI.4 from Wolfle (150).

threw away his predictor variables and just expected everyone to show average performance.

Intellectual Requirements of Different Occupations

If intelligence level so clearly affects success in school, it must also affect entry, at least, into different occupations. A person whose intelligence is high enough to permit college graduation is preferred or required in many occupations. Stewart (129), as well as others earlier, has verified this expectation. Among 83,618 white enlisted men studied in 1944 there were strong tendencies for persons from occupations with high requirements of academic training to show higher Army General Classification Scores than persons from occupations with lower requirements. Furthermore, persons from skilled trades showed higher scores, on the average, than persons from unskilled trades. As Fig. 14-12 illustrates, the average scores of soldiers from a general field sometimes depended greatly upon the specific category within that field. (The general fields mentioned are the usual ones, not Army classification systems.) Because the entire list of 179 occupations discussed by Stewart is too lengthy for reproduction, a limited number of them are presented in Fig. 14-12.

Stewart mentions that the occupations with higher median intelligence scores have relatively few members with low scores but that the converse

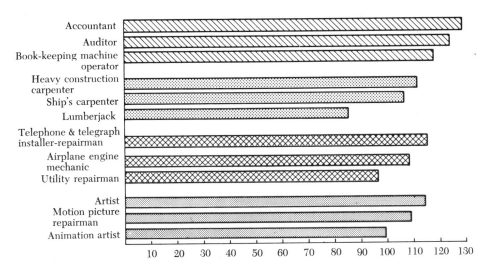

Fig. 14-12. Median Army General Classification Test scores for several occupations. Groups of three show variations within closely related occupations. Based on part of Table I of Stewart (129).

is not true. It is much less unusual to find highly intelligent people in unskilled work than relatively unintelligent people in high level jobs. Table 14-5 shows an example of this from a study of a Scottish photographic manufacturing company. As this table indicates, none of the persons in the directive and executive positions who were tested ranked in the lowest fourth (fourth quartile) of scores in the Progressive Matrices Test even though 12% of the unskilled workers ranked in the highest fourth (first quartile). Evidently a minimum level of ability is necessary to hold a high level position, but many persons of high ability will be found in relatively unskilled positions because of limited training, lack of motivation, lack of opportunity, or other reasons.

The presence of so many men of superior intelligence in unskilled work serves to emphasize the fact that intelligence alone is not sufficient to ensure occupational success. Note that since most occupations have their top positions filled with workers of high ability, the remaining persons of high intelligence are automatically relegated to lower level work. In other cases, as where minority group members are excluded regardless of ability, a person cannot attain the employment he merits; but it is also clear that other abilities such as affability or good work habits are essential in addition to a stated level of intelligence for success in many positions. An indicator of this fact is a survey by Ghiselli (56) which shows little, no, or even negative validity of intelligence tests in predicting success within certain occupations. Figure 14-13 shows the percentage of correlation coefficients of stated values between intelligence scores and proficiency measures in eight occupational areas. Note that wide ranges of values have been found for most areas, and that high intelligence seems to be of negative value for sales clerks though not for salesmen.

TABLE 14-5

Intelligence Categories of 920 Men of Differing Employment in a Scottish Photographic Manufacturing Concern[a]

	Quartile on Progressive Matrices Test				
Occupational level	1st	2nd	3rd	4th	Total
Directive and executive	79%	9%	12%	0%	100%
Highly skilled	48%	23%	19%	10%	100%
Skilled	29%	25%	27%	19%	100%
Qualified	18%	26%	28%	28%	100%
Unskilled	12%	15%	28%	45%	100%

[a] Based on Foulds and Raven (50).

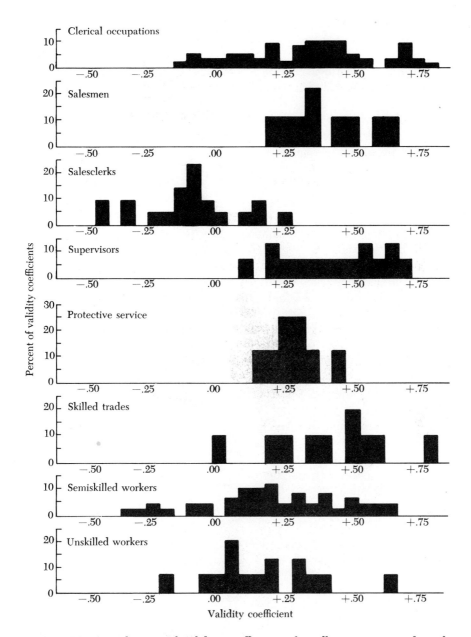

Fig. 14-13. Distributions of validity coefficients of intelligence tests used in the prediction of proficiency of workers in various occupational groups. Figure 1 from Ghiselli (56).

-- **Summary**

1. An intelligence test is intended to measure the overall contribution of a variety of special abilities, of which reasoning as generally defined is primary.

2. Intelligence tests are constructed to include as few items as possible with which persons tested will have had different amounts of practice.

3. The use of intelligence tests which have separate scores for each of several pure factor subtests does not appear to be generally as useful as the application of an overall intelligence test in predicting grade point average or even specific course grades. However, tests constructed by item analysis methods to have high predictive power for a single course or profession may be somewhat superior for that purpose to tests of general intelligence.

4. Different creativity tests show less consistent results to date than different intelligence tests. Creativity test scores appear to be moderately correlated with intelligence and, at best, to predict creative performance as well as, or perhaps slightly better than, intelligence scores. Among persons selected for high intelligence, creativity tests may allow additional discrimination. This is because those qualities measured by the creativity tests, such as certain personality traits, are not components of intelligence scores.

5. The intelligence scores of members of the same family are very similar, with greater similarities for more closely related members. This similarity is associated with similarities in both heredity and environment for the family members; since foster children (with different genetic backgrounds from their foster parents) show relatively little similarity to their foster parents in intelligence, it seems that genetic factors are of primary importance.

6. Relative intelligence (the I.Q.) declines with added years in an intellectually limited environment; the reverse effect in extremely favorable environments may occur but is probably smaller in magnitude.

7. Mental age increases throughout childhood, but cross-sectional research has indicated an intellectual decline beginning at about 18. This decline would be considered genuine if the comparison groups were of equal genetic origin and education. However, there are indications that the intelligence of this generation is higher than that of its predecessors. Also longitudinal studies show that persons of age 55 and older have superior scores to those they made on entrance to college. These two findings suggest that there is little or no decline in a person's intelligence prior to advanced old age.

8. At the present time representative samples of Americans from some national or ethnic groups may be expected to differ widely in average I.Q. scores from those of other groups; these differences will be mirrored by differences in average scholastic attainment.

9. Such facts as the absence of average differences between many national groups tested in their native lands, large geographical differences in average I.Q.'s of Americans, increases in black intelligence with added years in the North, and inferiority of girls' intelligence to boys' intelligence under conditions of unequal opportunity suggest that some, and perhaps all, of the difference in average performance between groups, is produced by the environment. Attempts to conclude that none of the difference is environmental or that all of it is environmental seem to flow more from theory or from philosophic conviction than from the data, which are still inconclusive. However, it is clear that all levels of intelligence are so well represented in every group that ability must always be judged directly rather than inferred from stereotypes about race or national origin.

10. Large differences in average I.Q. exist between members of different socioeconomic classes. While these may result in part from selection of employees of one status level from candidates of a corresponding level, it also is a consequence of reduced intellectual opportunity for children in lower-class homes. The major attempts to produce a culturally fair test seem not to have reduced these social class differences in I.Q., indicating that the differences are not simply attributable to asking questions inappropriate to the experience of lower-class children.

11. Nationality fair tests seem to be feasible, giving equal average scores for samples from several different countries and making testing of bilingual children equally successful with either language.

12. School performance is positively related to intelligence scores.

13. Mean intelligence scores vary widely from occupation to occupation. Furthermore, certain occupations have almost no workers below certain levels. However, people of very high intelligence appear in every occupation. Intelligence and quality of work within an occupation are often, but not always, positively correlated.

SUGGESTED READINGS

Bitterman, M. E. The evolution of intelligence. *Scientific American*, 1965(January), 212, 92–100.

   A comparison of the intelligence of different animals, indicating that higher animals not only have more intelligence but also have a higher kind of intelligence.

Cattell, R. B. Are I.Q. tests intelligent? *Psychology Today,* 1968(March), **1,** No. 10, 56–62.

This article gives information about two kinds of intelligence. *Crystallized intelligence* depends upon previous learning and is measured by vocabulary, numerical skills, etc. *Fluid intelligence* is less culturally determined and may be evident in high degree among uneducated people. It is measured by tests of classifications, analogies, etc.

————————————————————————————————— **REFERENCES**

1. Alper, T. G., & Boring, E. G. Intelligence-test scores of northern and southern white and Negro recruits in 1918. *Journal of Abnormal and Social Psychology,* 1944, **39,** 471–474.
2. Anastasi, A. *Psychological testing.* (2nd ed.) New York: Macmillan, 1961. Pp. 168–172, 432–436.
3. Anastasi, A., & Cordova, F. A. Some effects of bilingualism upon the intelligence test performance of Puerto Rican children in New York City. *Journal of Educational Psychology,* 1953, **44,** 1–19.
4. Anderson, J. E. The limitations of infant and preschool tests in the measurement of intelligence. *Journal of Psychology,* 1939, **8,** 351–379.
5. Angelino, H., & Shedd, C. L. An initial report of a validation study of the Davis-Eells tests of general intelligence or problem-solving ability. *Journal of Psychology,* 1955, **40,** 35–38.
6. Arthur, G. A. *Point scale of performance tests, Revised Form II. Manual for administering and scoring the tests.* New York: Psychological Corporation, 1947.
7. Asimov, I. *The genetic code.* New York: Orion Press, 1962.
8. Bagley, W. C. The Army tests and the pro-Nordic propaganda. *Educational Review,* 1924, **67,** 179–187.
9. Baldwin, B. T., & Stecher, L. I. Mental growth curve of normal and superior children. *University of Iowa Studies,* 1922, **2,** No. 1.
10. Barron, F., & Welsh, G. S. Artistic perception as a possible factor in personality style: its measurement by a figure preference test. *Journal of Psychology,* 1952, **33,** 199–203.
11. Bayley, N. On the growth of intelligence. *American Psychologist,* 1955, **10,** 805–818.
12. Bayley, N. Data on the growth of intelligence between 16 and 21 years as measured by the Wechsler-Bellevue scale. *Journal of Genetic Psychology,* 1957, **90,** 3–15.
13. Bayley, N., & Oden, M. H. The maintenance of intellectual ability in gifted adults. *Journal of Gerontology,* 1955, **10,** 91–107.
14. Beadle, G., & Beadle, M. *The language of life. An introduction to the study of genetics.* New York: Doubleday, 1966. P. 236.
15. Bentz, V. J. A test-retest experiment on the relationship between age and mental ability. *American Psychologist,* 1953, **8,** 319–320. (Abstract)
16. Bereiter, C. The future of individual differences. *Harvard Educational Review,* 1969, **39,** 310–318.
17. Bereiter, C., & Engelmann, S. An academically oriented preschool for dis-

advantaged children: Results from the initial experimental group. In D. W. Brison & J. Hill (Eds.), *Psychology and early childhood education. Ontario Institute for Studies in Education,* 1968, No. 4, 17–36.

18. Binet, A., & Simon, T. *The development of intelligence in children.* (Translated by E. S. Kite.) Baltimore: Williams & Wilkins, 1916. Pp. 25, 42–43, 88, 100–101, 275, 316–329.
19. Black, I. S. The use of the Stanford-Binet (1937 revision) in a group of nursery school children. *Child Development,* 1939, **10,** 157–171.
20. Bloom, B. S. *Stability and change in human characteristics.* New York: Wiley, 1964.
21. Bradway, K. B., & Thompson, C. W. Intelligence at adulthood: A twenty-five year follow-up. *Journal of Educational Psychology,* 1962, **53,** 1–14.
22. Brandwein, P. F. *The gifted student as future scientist: The high school student and his commitment to science.* New York: Harcourt Brace, 1955.
23. Brazziel, W. F. A letter from the South. *Harvard Educational Review,* 1969, **39,** 338–347.
24. Buros, O. K. *The sixth mental measurements yearbook.* Highland Park, N. J.: Gryphon Press, 1965.
25. Cattell, P. Stanford-Binet I.Q. variations. *School and Society,* 1937, **45,** 615–618.
26. Cattell, R. B., & Cattell, A. K. S. *IPAT culture free intelligence test.* Urbana, Ill.: Institute for Personality and Ability Testing, 1951.
27. Cattell, R. B., & Cattell, A. K. S. *Culture fair intelligence test.* Urbana, Ill.: Institute for Personality and Ability Testing, 1963.
28. Cattell, R. B., Feingold, S. N., & Sarason, S. B. A culture-free intelligence test: II. Evaluation of cultural influence on test performance. *Journal of Educational Psychology,* 1941, **32,** 81–100.
29. Chapanis, A., & Williams, W. C. Results of a mental survey with the Kuhlman-Anderson intelligence tests in Williamson County, Tennessee. *Journal of Genetic Psychology,* 1946, **67,** 27–55.
29a. Claiborn, W. L. Expectancy effects in the classroom: A failure to replicate. *Journal of Educational Psychology,* 1969, **60,** 377–383.
30. Clark, R. M. The effect of schooling upon intelligence quotients of Negro children. Unpublished doctoral dissertation, Western Reserve University, 1933.
31. Coleman, J. S., Campbell, E. Q., Hobson, C. J., McPartland, J., Mood, A. M., Weinfeld, F. D., & York, R. L. *Equality of educational opportunity.* Washington, D. C.: U. S. Government Printing Office, 1966.
32. Coleman, W., & Ward, A. W. A comparison of Davis-Eells and Kuhlman-Finch scores of children from high and low socio-economic status. *Journal of Educational Psychology,* 1955, **46,** 418–422.
33. Cotton, J. W. *Elementary statistical theory for behavior scientists.* Reading, Mass.: Addison-Wesley, 1967.
34. Cronbach, L. J. Heredity, environment, and educational policy. *Harvard Educational Review,* 1969, **39,** 338–347.
35. Crow, J. F. Genetic theories and influences: comments on the value of diversity. *Harvard Educational Review,* 1969, **39,** 301–309.
36. Davenport, R. K. Implications of military selection and classification in relation to universal military training. *Journal of Negro Education,* 1946, **15,** 585–594.
37. Davis, A. *Social class influences upon learning.* Cambridge, Mass.: Harvard University Press, 1951.
38. Davis, A., & Eells, K. *Davis-Eells test of general intelligence or problem-solving ability.* Yonkers, N. Y.: World Book, 1953.

39. Davis, A., & Hess, R. How fair is the I.Q. test? *Science Digest,* 1951(May), 43–47.
40. Dawe, H. C. A study of the effect of an educational program upon language development and related mental functions in young children. Unpublished doctoral dissertation, University of Iowa, 1940.
40a. Deloria, D. J. Personal communication, March, 1970.
41. Dempster, J. J. B. Symposium on the effects of coaching and practice in intelligence tests. III. Southampton investigation and procedure. *British Journal of Educational Psychology,* 1954, **24,** 1–4.
42. Dreger, R. M., & Miller, K. S. Comparative psychological studies of Negroes and whites in the United States. *Psychological Bulletin,* 1960, **57,** 361–402.
43. Dreger, R. M., & Miller, K. S. Comparative psychological studies of Negroes and whites in the United States: 1959–1965. *Psychological Bulletin,* 1968, **70**(3, Part 2), 1–58.
44. Duncanson, J. P. Learning and measured abilities. *Journal of Educational Psychology,* 1966, **57,** 220–229.
45. Eells, K., Davis, A., Havighurst, R. J., Herrick, V. E., & Tyler, R. *Intelligence and cultural differences: A study of cultural learning and problem solving.* Chicago: University of Chicago Press, 1951.
46. Elkind, D. Piagetian and psychometric conceptions of intelligence. *Harvard Educational Review,* 1969, **39,** 319–337.
47. Engel, L. *The new genetics.* New York: Doubleday, 1967.
48. Eysenck, H. J. Intelligence assessment: A theoretical and experimental approach. *British Journal of Educational Psychology,* 1967, **37,** 81–98.
49. Falek, A., & Schmidt, R. Human cytogenetics. In H. J. Van Peenen (Ed.), *Biochemical genetics.* Springfield, Ill.: Thomas, 1966. Pp. 281–322.
50. Foulds, G. A., & Raven, J. C. Intellectual ability and occupational grade. *Occupational Psychology,* 1948, **22,** 197–203.
51. Fuller, J. L., & Thompson, W. R. *Behavioral genetics.* New York: Wiley, 1960. Pp. 222–226.
52. Galton, Sir F. *Hereditary genius: An inquiry into its laws and consequences.* New York: Horizon, 1952. (Reprinting of 2nd ed. of 1892).
53. Garrett, H. F. A review and integration of investigations of factors related to scholastic success in colleges of arts and sciences and teachers colleges. *Journal of Experimental Education,* 1949, **18,** 91–138.
54. Gates, A. I., & LaSalle, J. The relative predictive value of certain intelligence and educational tests together with a study of the effect of educational achievement upon intelligence test scores. *Journal of Educational Psychology,* 1923, **14,** 517–539.
55. Getzels, J. W., & Jackson, P. W. *Creativity and intelligence.* New York: Wiley, 1962.
56. Ghiselli, E. E. The validity of commonly employed occupational tests. *University of California Publications in Psychology,* 1949, **5,** 253–288.
57. Ghiselli, E. E. Relationship between intelligence and age among superior adults. *Journal of Genetic Psychology,* 1957, **90,** 131–142.
58. Ginzberg, E. *The development of human resources.* New York: McGraw-Hill, 1966.
59. Goddard, H. H. *The Kallikak family: A study in the heredity of feeblemindedness.* New York: Macmillan, 1921.
60. Goodenough, F. L., & Maurer, K. M. The mental development of nursery-school children compared with that of non-nursery school children. *Intelligence: Its*

nature and nurture. Yearbook of the National Society for the Study of Education, 1940, **39**, Part II, 161–178.

61. Gough, H. G. Nonintellectual intelligence test. *Journal of Consulting Psychology,* 1953, **17**, 242–246.
62. Guilford, J. P. Factors that aid and hinder creativity. *Teachers College Record,* 1962, **63**, 380–392.
63. Guilford, J. P. Intelligence: 1965 model. *American Psychologist,* 1966, **21**, 20–26.
64. Guilford, J. P. *The nature of human intelligence.* New York: McGraw-Hill, 1967.
65. Guilford, J. P., & Hoepfner, R. Creative potential as related to measures of I.Q. and verbal comprehension. *Indian Journal of Psychology,* 1966, **41**, 7–16.
66. Gulliksen, H. *Theory of mental tests.* New York: Wiley, 1950.
67. Gurvitz, M. S. Unpublished data. Cited by D. Wolfle, *America's resources of specialized talent.* New York: Harper, 1954. Pp. 223–224.
68. Hess, R. D. Controlling culture influence in mental testing: an experimental test. *Journal of Educational Research,* 1955, **49**, 53–58.
69. Hirsch, N. D. M. An experimental study of the East Kentucky mountaineers. *Genetic Psychology Monographs,* 1928, **3**, No. 3.
70. Hodges, W. L., & Spicker, H. H. The effects of preschool experiences on culturally deprived children. In W. W. Hartup & N. L. Smothergill (Eds.), *The young child: Reviews of research.* Washington, D. C.: National Association for the Education of Young Children, 1967. Pp. 262–289.
71. Honzik, M. P. The constancy of mental test performance during the preschool period. *Journal of Genetic Psychology,* 1938, **52**, 285–302.
72. Honzik, M. P., MacFarlane, J. W., & Allen, L. The stability of mental test performance between two and eighteen years. *Journal of Experimental Education,* 1948, **17**, 309–324.
73. Hunt, J. McV. *Intelligence and experience.* New York: Ronald Press, 1961.
74. Hunt, J. McV. Has compensatory education failed? Has it been attempted? *Harvard Educational Review,* 1969, **39**, 278–300.
75. Huxtable, Z. L., White, J. H., & McCartor, M. A. A re-performance and re-interpretation of the Arai experiment in mental fatigue with three subjects. *Psychological Monographs,* 1946, **59**, No. 5. P. 52.
76. Jacob, P. E. *Changing values in college: An exploratory study of the impact of college teaching.* New York: Harper, 1957.
77. James, W. *Psychology, briefer course.* New York: Holt, 1908.
78. Jensen, A. R. How much can we boost I.Q. and scholastic achievement? *Harvard Educational Review,* 1969, **39**, 1–123.
78a. Jensen, A. R. Reducing the heredity–environment uncertainty: A reply. *Harvard Educational Review,* 1969, **39**, 449–483.
79. Johnston, J. B., & Williamson, E. G. Follow-up study of early scholastic predictions in the University of Minnesota. *School and Society,* 1934, **40**, 730–738.
80. Jones, H. E., & Conrad, H. S. The growth and decline of intelligence: A study of a homogeneous group between the ages of ten and sixty. *Genetic Psychology Monographs,* 1933, **13**, No. 3, 223–298.
81. Kagan, J. S. Inadequate evidence and illogical conclusions. *Harvard Educational Review,* 1969, **39**, 274–277.
82. Kamat, V. V. Sex differences among Indian children in the Binet Simon tests. *British Journal of Educational Psychology,* 1939, **9**, 251–256.
83. Klineberg, O. *Negro intelligence and selective migration.* New York: Columbia University Press, 1935.

84. Klineberg, O. *Race differences.* New York: Harper, 1935. P. 182.
85. Klineberg, O. Negro-white differences in intelligence test performance: A new look at an old problem. *American Psychologist,* 1963, **18,** 198–203.
86. Knief, L. M., & Stroud, J. B. Intercorrelations among various intelligence, achievement, and social class scores. *Journal of Educational Psychology,* 1959, **50,** 117–120.
87. Kohlberg, L. Early education: a cognitive-developmental view. *Child Development,* 1968, **49,** 1013–1062.
88. Kuhlen, R. G. Age and intelligence: The significance of cultural change in longitudinal vs. cross-sectional findings. *Vita Humana,* 1963, **6,** 113–124.
89. Leahy, A. M. Nature-nurture and intelligence. *Genetic Psychology Monographs,* 1935, **17,** No. 4, 235–308.
90. Lee, E. S. Negro intelligence and selective migration: a Philadelphia test of the Klineberg hypothesis. *American Sociological Review,* 1951, **16,** 227–233.
90a. Light, R. J., & Smith, P. V. Social allocation models of intelligence: A methodological study. *Harvard Educational Review,* 1969, 39, 484–510.
91. Lorge, I. Schooling makes a difference. *Teachers College Record,* 1945, **46,** 483–493.
92. MacKinnon, D. W. Personality and the realization of creative potential. *American Psychologist,* 1965, **20,** 273–281.
93. Marquart, D. I., & Bailey, L. L. An evaluation of the Culture Free Test of Intelligence. *Journal of Genetic Psychology,* 1955, **86,** 353–358.
94. McCulloch, T. L. The retarded child grows up: psychological aspects of aging. *American Journal of Mental Deficiency,* 1957, **62,** 201–208.
95. McDermid, C. D. Some correlates of creativity in engineering personnel. *Journal of Applied Psychology,* 1965, **49,** 14–19.
96. McIntosh, D. M. The effect of practice in intelligence test results. *British Journal of Educational Psychology,* 1944, **14,** 44–45.
97. McNemar, Q. A critical examination of the University of Iowa studies of environmental influences upon the I.Q. *Psychological Bulletin,* 1940, **37,** 63–92.
98. McNemar, Q. *The revision of the Stanford-Binet Scale.* Boston: Houghton Mifflin, 1942. Pp. 40, 87–88.
99. McNemar, Q. Lost: our intelligence? Why? *American Psychologist,* 1964, **19,** 871–882.
100. McPherson, J. H. A proposal for establishing ultimate criteria for measuring creative output. In C. W. Taylor & F. Barron (Eds.), *Scientific creativity: Its recognition and development.* New York: Wiley, 1963. Pp. 24–29.
101. Mednick, M. T. Research creativity in psychology graduate students. *Journal of Consulting Psychology,* 1963, **27,** 265–266.
102. Mednick, S. A., & Mednick, M. T. A theory and test of creativity. In G. Nielsen (Ed.), *Proceedings of the 14th International Congress of Applied Psychology.* Vol. 5. *Industrial and business psychology.* Copenhagen: Munksgaard, 1962. Pp. 40–47.
103. Mendel, G. *Versuche über Pflanzenhybriden.* 1866. (Translation: *Experiments on plant hybridization.*) Cambridge, Mass.: Harvard University Press, 1948.
104. Merrill, M. A. The significance of I.Q.'s on the revised Stanford-Binet Scales. *Journal of Educational Psychology,* 1938, **29,** 641–651.
105. Messenger, V. M. A longitudinal study of nursery school and non-nursery school children. Unpublished doctoral dissertation, University of Iowa, 1940.
106. Milholland, J. E., & Fricke, B. G. Development and application of tests of special aptitudes. *Review of Educational Research,* 1962, **32,** 25–62.

107. Moyles, E. W., Tuddenham, R. D., & Block, J. Simplicity/complexity or symmetry/asymmetry? A reanalysis of the Barron Art Scales. *Perceptual and Motor Skills*, 1965, **20**, 685–690.
108. Newman, H. H., Freeman, F. N., & Holzinger, K. J. *Twins: A study of heredity and environment.* Chicago: University of Chicago Press, 1937.
109. Nisbet, J. D. Intelligence and age: retesting with twenty-four years' interval. *British Journal of Educational Psychology*, 1957, **27**, 190–198.
110. Ohnmacht, F. W. Achievement, anxiety, and creative thinking. *American Educational Research Journal*, 1966, **3**, 131–138.
111. Otis, A. S. *Otis quick-scoring mental ability tests.* Yonkers, N. Y.: World Book, 1962.
112. Owens, W. A. Age and mental abilities: A longitudinal study. *Genetic Psychology Monographs*, 1953, **48**, 3–54.
113. Owens, W. A. Age and mental abilities: a second adult follow-up. *Journal of Educational Psychology*, 1966, **57**, 311–325.
114. Peel, E. A. A note on the practice effects in intelligence tests. *British Journal of Educational Psychology*, 1951, **21**, 122–125.
115. Pinneau, S. R. *Changes in intelligence quotient, infancy to maturity.* Boston: Houghton Mifflin, 1961. P. 205.
116. Rosenthal, R., & Jacobson, L. Teacher's expectancies: determinants of pupils' I.Q. gains. *Psychological Reports*, 1966, **19**, 115–118.
117. Rosenthal, R., & Jacobson, L. *Pygmalion in the classroom.* New York: Holt, Rinehart & Winston, 1968.
118. Scott, R. First to ninth grade I.Q. changes of Northern Negro students. *Psychology in the Schools*, 1966, **3**, 159–160.
119. Shaycoft, M. F., Dailey, J. T., Orr, D. B., Neyman, C. A., Jr., & Sherman, S. E. *Project Talent: Studies of a complete age group—age 15.* Pittsburgh: University of Pittsburgh, 1963.
120. Shuey, A. M. *The testing of Negro intelligence.* (2nd ed.) New York: Social Science Press, 1966.
121. Skeels, H. M. Adult status of children with contrasting early experience. *Monographs of the Society for Research in Child Development*, 1966, **31**(3, Whole No. 105).
122. Skodak, M., & Skeels, H. M. A final follow up study of one hundred adopted children. *Journal of Genetic Psychology*, 1949, **75**, 85–125.
123. Smith, I. M. Review of the IPAT Culture Free Intelligence Test. In O. K. Buros (Ed.), *Fifth mental measurements yearbook.* Highland Park, N. J.: Gryphon Press, 1959. Pp. 473–474.
124. Smith, T. W. Comparison of test bias in the Davis-Eells Games and the CTMM. *California Journal of Educational Research*, 1956, **7**, 159–163.
125. Spence, J. T., Underwood, B. J., Duncan, C. P., & Cotton, J. W. *Elementary statistics.* (2nd ed.) New York: Appleton-Century-Crofts, 1968.
126. Spitzer, H. F., in collaboration with E. Horn, M. McBroom, H. A. Greene, & E. F. Lindquist. *Iowa Every-Pupil Tests of Basic Skills, new edition. Test B: Work-study skills—form L. Elementary battery—grades 3–4–5.* Boston: Houghton Mifflin, 1940. Pp. 3–4.
127. Starkweather, E. K., & Roberts, K. E. I.Q. changes occurring during nursery-school attendance at the Merrill-Palmer school. *Intelligence: Its nature and nurture. Original studies and experiments. Yearbook of the National Society for the Study of Education*, 1940, **39**, Part 2, 315–335.

128. Stern, C. *Principles of human genetics.* (2nd ed.) San Francisco: Freeman, 1960.
129. Stewart, N. AGCT scores of Army personnel grouped by occupation. *Occupations,* 1947, **26,** 1–37.
130. Terman, L. M., & Merrill, M. A. *Measuring intelligence.* Boston: Houghton Mifflin, 1937.
131. Terman, L. M., & Merrill, M. A. *Revised Stanford-Binet Scales.* Boston: Houghton Mifflin, 1937. (Forms L and M.) Pp. 108–110.
132. Terman, L. M., & Merrill, M. A. *Stanford-Binet Scale.* Boston: Houghton Mifflin, 1960. (Form L-M.) Pp. 104, 251.
133. Thorndike, R. L. The measurement of creativity. *Teachers College Record,* 1963, **64,** 422–424.
134. Thorndike, R. L. Intellectual status and intellectual growth. *Journal of Educational Psychology,* 1966, **57,** 121–127.
135. Thorndike, R. L. Review of R. Rosenthal and L. Jacobson, *Pygmalion in the classroom. American Educational Research Journal,* 1968, **5,** 709–711.
136. Thurstone, L. L. *Multiple-factor analysis.* Chicago: University of Chicago Press, 1947. Pp. 139–146.
137. Thurstone, L. L., & Thurstone, T. G. *SRA tests of educational ability.* Chicago: Science Research Associates, 1962.
138. Thurstone, L. L., & Thurstone, T. G. *SRA primary abilities.* Chicago: Science Research Associates, 1963.
139. Tjio, J. H., & Levan, A. The chromosome number of man. *Hereditas,* 1956, **42,** 1–6.
140. Tjio, J. H., & Puck, T. T. Genetics of somatic mammalian cells. II. Chromosomal constitution of cells in tissue culture. *Journal of Experimental Medicine,* 1958, **108,** 259–268.
141. Tuddenham, R. D. Soldier intelligence in World Wars I and II. *American Psychologist,* 1948, 3, 54–56.
142. Tuddenham, R. D. A "Piagetian" test of cognitive development. Paper presented at the Symposium on Intelligence, sponsored by the Ontario Institute for Studies in Education, Toronto, May 1969.
143. Wechsler, D. *Wechsler Intelligence Scale for Children Manual.* New York: Psychological Corporation, 1949.
144. Wechsler, D. *Wechsler Adult Intelligence Scale.* New York: Psychological Corporation, 1955.
145. Wechsler, D. *The measurement and appraisal of adult intelligence.* (4th ed.) Baltimore: Williams & Wilkins, 1958. P. 7.
146. Wechsler, D. *Manual for the Wechsler Preschool and Primary Scale of Intelligence.* New York: Psychological Corporation, 1967.
147. Wellman, B. L. Iowa studies on the effects of schooling. *Intelligence: Its nature and nurture. Original studies and experiments. Yearbook of the National Society for the Study of Education,* 1940, **39,** Part II, 377–399.
148. Wheeler, L. R. The intelligence of East Tennessee mountain children. *Journal of Educational Psychology,* 1932, **23,** 351–370.
149. Wiseman, S. Symposium on the effects of coaching and practice in intelligence tests. IV. The Manchester experiment. *British Journal of Educational Psychology,* 1954, **24,** 5–8.
150. Wolfle, D. *America's resources of specialized talent.* New York: Harper, 1954.
151. Woodworth, R. S., & Sells, S. B. An atmosphere effect in formal syllogistic reasoning. *Journal of Experimental Psychology,* 1935, **18,** 451–460.

15

THE ASSESSMENT
OF EDUCATIONAL ACHIEVEMENT

Educational assessment has a long history. Oral examinations began in 1219 at the University of Bologna. In the United States classroom tests became prevalent under the influence of Horace Mann in the middle of the nineteenth century. Written classroom examinations probably began in Cambridge, England (41) in 1702, though written examinations of a very rigorous sort were used in China by 29 B.C. to select government officials (15). But not until the end of the nineteenth century did psychologists begin to focus upon methods of test construction and development. Ebbinghaus [see Watson (91)] invented the completion question in 1897, and J. M. Rice popularized objective questions in the United States in the 1890's and early 1900's (68).

There are many uses for educational assessment: determining whether one topic has been well enough covered that another may be begun; helping decide about promotion or graduation; providing a basis for or against admission to college or professional school. In its most extraordinary and surely least formalized application, it led Dr. Isaac Barrow to conclude that his student, Isaac Newton, deserved the Lucasian Professorship of Mathematics held by Barrow himself. Thereupon, Barrow resigned on condition that Newton be named his successor (71).

One of the major contributions of psychologists to testing or other methods of assessment is theoretical, stemming from mathematical work by Spearman (73) on the properties of tests. The present chapter will review relevant theory and factual knowledge about the use of assessment devices in educational settings.

_____ **Some Terms Distinguished**

Evaluation and Measurement

This entire chapter is concerned with the purposes as well as the techniques of educational assessment. Before introducing the theoretical material necessary to discuss this topic in detail, we should indicate something of the scope of the area of evaluation and measurement. Educators speak of *evaluation* as the overall process of assessing pupils' development. Evaluation may be either quantitative or qualitative. Most classroom tests and nationally distributed achievement tests are quantitative because they lead to numerical scores or letter grades which imply levels of performance. For obvious reasons quantitative evaluation is usually known as *measurement.*

Qualitative evaluation is exemplified by a teacher's day-to-day notes: "Jane cried when Bill made fun of her drawing. Alice seemed poised as she introduced the fourth-grade number at assembly," etc. Many report cards and cumulative record folders kept by the school to summarize a child's progress and school experience include a good deal of qualitative information. Particularly in the lower grades, a report card may consist primarily of the teacher's written sentences describing the academic and social development of the child.

Quantitative measurement usually focuses upon learning something such as the plot of *Hamlet* whereas qualitative evaluation often deals with affective processes such as awareness of other people's feelings. Despite the usefulness of qualitative evaluation, it is difficult to do research on means of improving it; therefore, teachers may feel that it is too vaguely defined to be approached effectively. Still it is important; a good deal of a teacher's career is properly devoted to it and it must be done conscientiously. The Krathwohl, Bloom, and Masia handbook (52) on educational goals in the affective domain can be of real help in clarifying one's own teaching goals and in suggesting means of evaluation and measurement.

Discrimination and Mastery

The theory of educational testing has largely centered on the problem of discriminating between the best, next best, . . ., next to the worst, and worst performances on a given test. Such testing for discrimination is important if one must pick the most talented applicants for a job or for admission to college. It is also necessary if one is assigning letter grades and wishes to be fair, not giving one person an "A" and another person of greater achievement a "B."

A second purpose of educational testing is to determine if students have mastered a lesson or set of lessons. In a physical education class the teacher may want to be certain that every student can swim 50 yards or more. One could find this out by testing for discrimination, letting each person swim as far as he can, and also checking to be sure if anyone stopped before 50 yards. In that case, testing for mastery and testing for discrimination would be performed at the same time. However, if one is testing for mastery it is much more efficient to have each student try to swim exactly 50 yards and stop.

The classroom teacher must decide which skills or information should be mastered; a test for mastery should be given on that material. In many cases it will be useful to test on other material as well so that one can tell how far some students have exceeded the minimum progress expected on the unit being tested. By telling each student what he has accomplished beyond that minimum, the teacher can keep students from being complacent about less than their best possible achievement.

Tests of Educational Achievement

Achievement tests are usually classified on the basis of who constructed them, whether they are standardized, and whether subjective judgment is required to score them. A teacher-made test is often used only once, but some teachers save their tests and use them again, or at least use some questions or items from a test two or more times. Tests constructed by the staff of professional firms such as the Educational Testing Service or the Psychological Corporation are intended to be used in many schools and for several years. Copies of such tests must therefore not be made available to persons who might show them to students preparing to take them. Even the teacher may not administer certain tests because it is considered so important to keep their contents confidential.

A commercially produced test is usually *standardized.* By this we mean that it has been administered to a large enough group of students so that certain crucial statistical facts about the test can be determined, and that this determination has been made. The principal facts needed are the value of the mean (i.e., the average), the standard deviation, and the reliability and validity coefficients. (The first two concepts have been treated earlier in this book; reliability and validity will be discussed later in this chapter.) Standardization is important because it permits comparison between students in one class and a much larger group. Thus, a teacher may learn that a boy who is doing average work in his fifth-grade class is above average for all fifth-grade boys in his state or in the country. Standardization also helps ensure that a test yields consistent results and measures what it is intended to measure. A teacher who wishes to do so can partially standardize the tests he constructs if he is able to administer the test to several hundred students and then do some statistical calculations with the resulting data. An advantage of this procedure is that the teacher can then develop what are called *local norms,* standards appropriate to his own school. Such norms can be used, for example, to help determine the likelihood of a high-school senior being admitted to the nearest university.

Subjectively scored tests include essays of some length, short essays written in response to specific questions, and very short answers to questions. We will see in this chapter that long essays are the hardest to grade fairly. Very short answers are almost as easy to grade as objective tests, which can be scored by machine once it has been decided what answers the machine should accept. True–false items, matching questions, and multiple-choice items are all used in objective tests.

Since to give a correct answer on a paper-and-pencil test is not nearly as important as performing a complex task, teachers often give performance tests. To take a simple example, a driving instructor is better advised to measure actual driving performance than abstract knowledge of how to drive. In some cases his measurement of performance will be subjective, as when he sits beside a student driver on an hour's ride and then says, "I think you did quite well today." However, simulators used for teaching driving sometimes are equipped to score errors automatically so the testing is objective. The instructor can also increase the objectivity of his grading by developing a way of counting errors and correct responses as they occur.

Theory of Testing: True Scores and Error Scores

The first presumption of test theory is that a test score is the sum of a true score and an error score on the characteristic being measured. The true score cannot be measured directly, nor can the error score. Yet performance on educational tests (and most other tests) is dependent on error or chance factors as well as on actual achievement. Students sometimes complain that their teachers seem to have assigned test grades by drawing them at random from a hatful of numbers or tossing the test papers downstairs and giving an "A" to the one which fell the farthest.

What they are saying is that they think the whole set of test grades consists of error scores and none at all of true scores. A very bad test or a badly graded test could have that property, but usually a sizable part of the test score does depend upon a true score. The better the test is, the more consistent (*reliable*) its scores will be on two testings of the same people. The contribution of true scores to total scores should then be higher. Teachers can minimize error by increasing the reliability coefficients (to be discussed later in this chapter) of the test. One particular word of advice should be given here; if misunderstanding the instructions can decrease a test score greatly, then it is vital to make sure the instructions are grasped before the test is begun. Otherwise, a large part of each test score can represent error scores.

The Information Provided by Test Scores

The second presumption of test theory is that assessment is relatively uninformative if a measurement device gives the same score to everyone. Figure 15-1 shows the *amount of information,* in a technical sense (70), provided about individuals. This amount depends on the proportion of

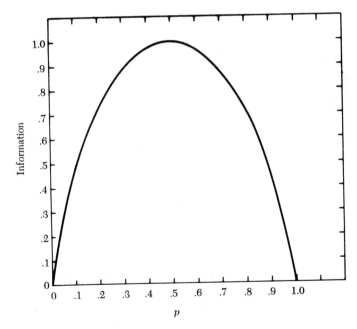

Fig. 15-1. Amount of information provided as a function of proportion (p) of persons passing a test item. Figure 7, with modified legends, from Shannon (70).

them passing a test item. The figure may seem nonsensical: it says that no information is provided if all persons fail a test item, or if all persons pass a test item. Obviously, though, we have learned something—that all persons failed or passed. The figure actually shows how much additional information may be gained by looking at individual scores once we know how many passed. Nothing remains to be learned from them if everyone passed the item. Very little added information is to be gained if 99% of pupils passed the item; more is to be gained if 50% of pupils passed it.

The implications to classroom situations are fairly obvious. A first-grade teacher in Pendleton, Oregon, need not begin the school year by testing her pupils to see how many can speak English. She estimates subjectively that 100% or very nearly 100% can do so. [See Savage (67), for a discussion of subjective estimates like this one.] Consequently, little information on this point will be provided by testing. However, a first-grade teacher in a Miami, Florida, school with many Cuban refugees may subjectively estimate that only one-half her pupils speak English. Therefore a large amount of useful information about her pupils may be obtained by asking each if he speaks English. The moral, an obvious one, is that people need not be tested if it is known that almost all of them will pass the test or almost all will fail. However, sometimes a teacher may want to be sure that a group's members have all mastered a multiplication table or other learning task before beginning the next stage of instruction. In that case it is hoped that everyone will pass the test, and it is appropriate to give it in order to find out.

A further consequence of the information presented in Fig. 15-1 is that an item, to give maximal information, should be made so difficult that one-half the test takers miss it. This requirement appears to conflict with old-fashioned rules of thumb in grading, of which one example is given:

$$A = 94\text{--}100\% \text{ correct}$$
$$B = 88\text{--}93\% \text{ correct}$$
$$C = 80\text{--}87\% \text{ correct}$$
$$D = 70\text{--}79\% \text{ correct}$$
$$F = \text{less than } 70\% \text{ correct}$$

With an *absolute standard* such as this one, an item missed by one-half the pupils would be considered too difficult to include. The question arises: Which procedure is to be considered correct?

Test theory does not automatically require rejection of the assignment of grades on the basis of these absolute standards. It emphasizes two facts, however: A teacher can adjust the difficulty of test items so as to control roughly how many students have a given percentage score. Therefore, the so-called absolute standard for grading is not an absolute one in fact. Second, since a major purpose of assessment is to gain information about students, one should use methods which maximize that information, if possible. A good teacher may often use items which will be missed by one-half her students, but she will also help them to understand that perfect performance on tests made up of such items is not to be expected, even by very good students. This may seem a lowering of standards to some people. However, it should be viewed as a reminder that there is no neat package of exactly 1000 things to be learned in a grade or a course. Rather what can be learned is large, perhaps infinite. Perfect mastery is not within human power.

The Reliability of Test Scores

Definition of Reliability

A third consideration of test theory is the search for reliable measures. *Reliability* means consistency of results and is commonly measured by the *correlation coefficient* (r) mentioned in Chapter 14. When a test is standardized, i.e., evaluated to show how well it works and whether it is well enough constructed to be widely used, its reliability is measured.

As Cronbach (17) points out, a measure of reliability is the extent to which true scores rather than error scores contribute to a test. There are, however, several ways of measuring reliability, which are not equivalent either in the numerical values they yield or in their definitions of what true scores are. But these methods do closely relate theoretically.

Cronbach (17) has distinguished between *lasting general, temporary general, lasting specific,* and *temporary specific* components of tests. These four categories are *factors,* as defined by the factor analysis methods mentioned in Chapter 14. We can clarify their psychological meaning by considering fifth-grade arithmetic achievement tests as an example. (a) The lasting general factor would be the arithmetic ability reflected by answers to one set of arithmetic questions and answers to the same set of questions presented a second time or to a different set of very similar questions. (b) The temporary general factor would be shown by answers to similar questions given at the same time; it would not be reflected by results from two tests administered with a time interval between them, regardless of whether the same questions were asked both times. (c) The lasting specific factor is relatively permanent. It is shown by scores from two administrations of the same test, regardless of whether a time interval elapsed between them, but not by scores from two different tests. (d) The temporary specific factor fluctuates in scores from

TABLE 15-1

Influences on Assignment of Factors to True or Error Scores

Type of factor	Contributes to true scores?	Contributes to error scores?
Lasting general	Always	Never
Temporary general	In other measures	In delayed test–retest measures either of the same or related items
Lasting specific	In test–retest measures of the same test	In other measures
Temporary specific	Never	Always

item to item and from administration to administration. It is the one factor which produces error scores by every kind of reliability measuring procedure.

Although we will talk about a variety of reliability measures, these four factors will always be relevant. Table 15-1 shows the conditions under which each factor contributes to true scores or to error scores. Note that there are two basic considerations in specifying those conditions: whether two testings are performed with a delay between them (test–retest procedure) and whether performance on similar items or identical items is compared. Reliability measures based on a test–retest procedure with the same items are called *coefficients of stability;* their values will depend upon how long the interval between test and retest is, with long intervals leading to smaller coefficients than short intervals. Correlations based on comparison of scores from similar items are called *coefficients of equivalence.*

Coefficients of Stability—Test–Retest Correlations

From Table 15-1 we can infer that a test followed by an immediate retest using the same items will yield a reliability coefficient whose only source of error scores is temporary specific factors. Such a procedure has the advantage of requiring construction of only one set of items; it has the disadvantage of requiring that the test be administered twice. For some purposes a teacher may feel that a test followed by an immediate retest gives too high an estimate of reliability because of its inclusion of temporary general factors such as memory of items and answers from one test to another.

The use of a delayed test–retest procedure will reduce or eliminate the contribution of these temporary general factors to the coefficient of stability, depending upon how long the delay is. Note that a long delay may result in changes in the characteristics of persons being tested, as occurs when an intelligence test is administered twice at an interval of a year or more and will result in a lowering of the coefficient of stability. This does not mean that the test is poor, but rather that the people tested have changed.

Coefficients of Equivalence

Parallel Forms Reliability

Any test, such as a measure of knowledge of art history, may be constructed to have two forms which are intended to give equivalent scores, often by having similar pairs of items assigned in parallel, one to each form. A teacher administering an important examination may distribute the two forms so that students in adjacent seats have different forms. Or a teacher may wish to give one form at the beginning of a course and the other at the end in order to measure reliability without including in the estimate of true score contribution any temporary general factors such as memory of the first test. We can see from Table 15-1 that this delayed retesting with parallel forms yields a low reliability or coefficient of equivalence value, with only lasting general factors contributing to true scores.

We illustrate the use of parallel forms with the following hypothetical scores.

Person tested	Form A score	Form B score
A.K.	119	114
E.J.	108	121
C.P.	100	109
L.R.	99	94
H.M.	94	92

As can be seen, persons high on form A are usually high on form B.

Because of this tendency the parallel forms reliability will be high, 0.76 in this case. High reliability between parallel forms is desirable because it implies that the two forms are, indeed, approximately equivalent and may be used interchangeably just as two yardsticks are interchangeable.

Split-Half Reliability

Because of difficulties with reliability estimates by the parallel forms and test–retest methods, a third method has gained favor. This is the *split-half* reliability measure. In this method students' scores on one-half the items are correlated with their scores on the remaining items. For example, a student might have received 42 points on the odd-numbered items and 46 points on the even-numbered items. Once pairs of scores for the other persons in the group are known, the whole series of pairs can be correlated. A high correlation between the scores on odd-numbered items and even-numbered indicates high reliability for the test as a whole.

Why was a comparison of odd-numbered versus even-numbered items used instead of some other comparison? This procedure arose because such comparisons as the first half versus the second half were unsatisfactory. Typically, some of the second half items are not attempted by the test taker unless the time allowed is quite long. Also, the items in the second half of the test are frequently more difficult than those in the first half, making comparison difficult. But the odd–even comparison is not ideal, however.

From Table 15-1, it can be seen that split-half measures of reliability will have lasting general and temporary general factors contributing to true scores. Such reliability measures should be smaller than coefficients mentioned earlier as based on similar items but also including lasting specific factors in the true scores. A further problem with any split-half reliability is that it is reduced in value because it is based on a test only half as long as the original test. Consequently, a correction is made to indicate the reliability which should have been found with a full-length test. Readers interested in more sophisticated measures are referred to Kuder and Richardson (53) and Cronbach (16).

Effect of Length of Test on Reliability

This leads to the question of the specific effects of length of tests on reliability. Spearman (72) and Brown (6) independently and simultaneously reported finding an equation to express how this reliability increased with an increase by twofold, threefold, or more in the length of the test. The length increase may be called, in general, K-fold. Figure 15-2 summarizes the Spearman–Brown findings for several original correlation values (r) and K-values.

The bottom curve of Fig. 15-2 shows that $r = 0.2$ for $K = 1$ (original test length) leads to R (augmented reliability) $= 0.33$ for $K = 2$ and $R \cong 0.72$ for $K = 10$. In theory, lengthening a test enough times would make even this test (of originally low reliability) yield a reliability as nearly perfect ($r = 1$) as desired. If the lower curve of Fig. 15-2 is extended, it reaches an R of 0.99 when K is 400.5. Though it can only attain unity if the test is infinitely long, an R of 0.99 certainly is not far from perfection.

Figure 15-2 represents a theoretical situation. In many real life cases

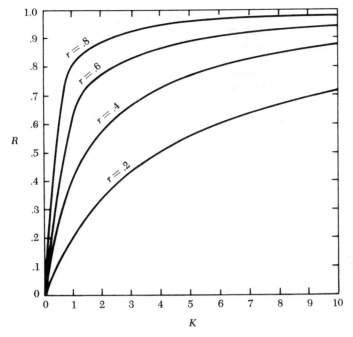

Fig. 15-2. Augmented reliability (R) resulting from a K-fold increase in test length for different initial reliabilities (r). Figure 2 from Gulliksen (43).

the assumptions made by Spearman and Brown seem untrue, and Fig. 15-2 must be corrected to account for the discrepancy between real life and theory.

However, a practical procedure is to consider that Fig. 15-2 indicates approximately what the new reliability of a test will be if it is increased K-fold under nearly ideal conditions.

_____ **The Validity of Test Scores**

Content Validity

The fourth and final important consideration in test theory is that a test should make possible certain measurement goals in addition to being reliable. To take an extreme example, a highly reliable test purporting to measure intelligence would be quite unsatisfactory if it measured musical aptitude instead. In general, we say that a test which measures what it is intended to measure has high *validity*. As is seen from the *Standards for Educational and Psychological Tests and Manuals* (51), a test is not simply valid or invalid. It may be valid for pupils but not for adults. It may also have one kind of validity and not another. To make this latter point clear three different kinds of validity emphasized in the report just cited are discussed.

Content validity is the property a test possesses if its items are representative of all possible items relevant to the subject of the test. If one is testing knowledge of fourth-grade geography, then there might be 1000 questions the students could be asked. Assume the test actually constructed contains 50 of these. For such a test to have high content validity, all 50 must come from the 1000, and they must not unduly emphasize certain topics. If all 50 questions concerned rivers and none concerned mountains, cities, countries, oceans, or lakes, the test would not have high content validity. One may check the content validity of a test by deciding what kinds of knowledge or skills are to be developed in a certain course and the proportionate emphasis to be given to each topic. Then one checks the test to see that approximately the same proportions of items are devoted to each topic and that the right kinds of questions are asked. Thus, if one desires to develop skill in interpreting graphs, one does not test for this by measuring how much algebra is known. Rather, one presents certain graphs and asks each pupil to draw conclusions from them.

Criterion-Related Validity

Another purpose of a test is to make possible an accurate prediction of success in college, athletic accomplishment, or some other event before it happens. This is called *criterion-related validity* because validity is judged by the correlation (or simply the relation) between the test and some criterion. Sometimes one can tell fairly well if a test and a criterion are highly related just by looking at the test. One looks at a test of arithmetic achievement, decides it looks like a good test, and assumes that it will predict performance in ninth-grade algebra because arithmetic and algebra seem closely related logically. Making a judgment of this kind is saying that a test has high *face validity*—it looks right. One should always check face validity; however, one cannot be certain criterion-related validity exists until one computes the correlation coefficient between the test and the criterion.

Construct Validity

Construct validity is validity indicated by a test's having properties which are explainable by some psychological construct (or concept) which cannot be observed directly but rather must be inferred from a combination of theory and data. For example, Taylor's Manifest Anxiety Scale, discussed in Chapter 11, gains its validity this way. Hypotheses were formulated as to how highly anxious and less anxious people should perform on different kinds of learning tasks and then those hypotheses were tested experimentally. General confirmation of the hypotheses led to the conclusion that the test was valid. Thus, the Taylor scale has construct validity.

Relation between Reliability and Validity

A highly reliable test which measures the wrong thing is clearly an invalid test. Test theory tells us that the reverse is not possible: there are no highly valid tests which are unreliable. The reason for this is that inconsistency of measurement (*unreliability*) prevents achieving the purposes of the test.

Essay Testing

The Distinction between Essay Tests and Objective Tests

Stalnaker (77) defines an essay question as "a test item which requires a response composed by the examinee, usually in the form of one or more sentences, of a nature that no single response or pattern of responses can be listed as correct, and the accuracy and quality of which can be judged subjectively only by one skilled or informed in the subject." The prototype of an essay question comes from English courses: "Write a 300-word composition entitled, 'How I feel about modern art.'" In such an essay, correctness or incorrectness is largely impossible to assess (except for the mechanics of grammar, spelling, etc.), and the grader ultimately makes a subjective judgment of quality.

Essay questions in other subject matter fields typically lead to less subjectivity of grading but yet satisfy Stalnaker's definition. Thus, a history professor may ask, "What were the principal factors leading to the Declaration of Independence of 1776?" No single pattern of responses will be correct but many of the possible answers will be clearly correct or clearly incorrect.

Certain examination questions only satisfy that part of Stalnaker's definition which refers to the composition of a response by the examinee. Thus, "Tell how to multiply 320 by 34," is a question for which a limited number of correct answers can be stated. While it may not be quite objective enough to be scored by a machine, answers to the question should not prove very controversial; most persons grading the answer would agree as to its correctness or incorrectness.

Within-Reader Reliability

When an objective test is graded twice by the same *grader* (also called *reader* or *marker*), exactly the same score is obtained both times, barring clerical errors or changes in the answer key. Essay tests do not have this degree of consistency. Knowing whose essay paper one is grading may cause a "halo" effect, the marker grading, in effect, the person not the paper. To be fair, a teacher should probably hide the names of the students while grading their papers.

Great inconsistency in grading may be expected in many cases where grading is done. One highly experienced grader, Diederich (21), reports that, in the case of an examination question he thought to be particularly good, he regraded all the essays six months later and found a correlation coefficient (r) of only 0.54. Other scholars report somewhat larger correlations. Finlayson (29) compared two gradings of the same papers with a 6-month period between gradings. Six different graders were studied. On the average, the correlation between the two gradings was 0.81. In a similar study Wiseman (92) found eight such correlations over a 3-month period between gradings. Only one was below 0.70, and two were 0.85 or over. Though Finlayson's and Wiseman's correlations are higher than Diederich's, all three investigations indicate that within-reader reliability for essay tests is lower than the value expected with objective tests.

Inter-Reader Reliability

If a reader cannot agree with himself, it is doubtful that he can agree with anyone else. At their worst, graders of essay examinations are notorious in their disagreement (93):

> One of the five or six expert readers (college professors of history) assigned to a certain group of history papers, after scoring a few, wrote out for his own convenience what he considered a model paper for the given set of ten questions. By some mischance the model fell into the hands of another reader who graded it in perfectly bona fide fashion. The mark he assigned to it was below passing, and in accordance with the custom, this model was rated by a number of other expert readers in order to insure that it was properly marked. The marks assigned to it by these readers varied from 40 to 90.

We need not be convinced by a single anecdote like the one above.

Many careful investigations of inter-reader reliability have been made. A few decades ago the English composition of 350 words used by the College Entrance Examination Board (CEEB) yielded an inter-reader reliability of only 0.55, even though the graders were excellent teachers using very careful methods (76). More recent studies (79) of the CEEB General Composition Test (an essay test) yielded inter-reader reliabilities of about 0.70. Compared with inter-reader reliabilities of near unity for objectively scored tests, these values for essay test results seem very low.

All essay tests are not so difficult to grade reliably. In 1937, most CEEB essay examinations (75, 76) yielded inter-reader reliabilities over 0.90. In 1956 the same value was obtained (81). The reason for the high reliabilities with these tests is that they were designed to measure factual knowledge, as in a physics test, or vocabulary, as in a French test. Questions requiring relatively short answers, where expert opinion is pretty well agreed on the correct answers, may be expected to yield high within-reader and between-reader reliability.

Many of these essay tests with high reliability may not be essay tests at all by Stalnaker's definition given above. It is the existence of well-defined correct answers which makes them easy to grade reliably, but such answers do not exist for Stalnaker's category of essay questions. This is an important point because some people seem to feel short-answer questions cannot be graded reliably. Because they know that English compositions have low reader reliability, some teachers never use an open-ended test item such as, "What was the Kellogg-Briand Pact?" This is regrettable because persons who can recall facts of this kind may not be the same ones who are good in recognizing such facts in multiple-choice questions.

Tests designed solely to measure writing skill are the ones most likely to be scored inconsistently. However, Traxler and Anderson (88), as well as others since their time, have found ways to make even tests of writing skill so highly structured or well-graded that the within-reader or between-reader reliabilities become acceptable.

Increasing Reliability by Adding Readers

Because many teachers and educational administrators wish to continue giving essay examinations, even in English composition where interreader agreement is so low, methods for increasing reliability are desirable. The most common one is to average the grades assigned independently by several different readers for each paper. The theoretical work of Kuder and Richardson (53), previously cited, implies that this averaging process would increase reliability. Empirical studies verify it: Finlayson (29) and Wiseman (92) both report that the average of four grades from separate graders correlates over 0.90 with the same average when papers are regraded by the four graders. This might be called an increase in "intra-reader team reliability," as the team size increased from one to four. Wiseman further reports that the inter-correlation between average grades based on the work of four graders and four other graders is 0.92. This might be called "*inter*-reader team reliability."

In many situations the use of reader teams may be desirable even though it obviously increases the work involved in grading papers. They are used in England for the grading of English essay papers which decide in part which 11-year-old students enter the Grammar School system, the academically oriented secondary school system of the country. Unjust decisions would be much more likely if only a single reader graded each paper.

American schoolteachers often feel that objective tests should be employed rather than the school system having to involve itself with the complications and financial costs of the use of reader teams. As far as educational testing or evaluation is concerned, they may very well be right. However, there are situations in which objective measurement is even more difficult and in which teams of raters or readers are desirable. The unreliability of boxing judges and flower show judges is well known. Yet combining the judgments of several persons gives more satisfactory results than would otherwise occur. It should also be noted that increasing the number of essay questions can increase reliability.

Despite the American predilection to avoid the time-consuming grading of each examination by several readers, a modified English system has recently been used here. In typical American fashion, Godshalk, Swineford, and Coffman (see 34, 38a, 60) have found that five readers can appraise a 20-minute essay in one and one-half minutes each, assigning grades of "superior," "average," or "inferior" to every essay. When the five readers' grades for five different essays by the same person are added to form a single essay score, an intra-reader team reliability of 0.92 results. This grading method, then, gives approximately the stability of the British method with the speed desired by American readers.

Still another attempt to secure good reliability on essay tests has been the interlinear measure used by the College Entrance Examination Board (80). It provides a sample of a poorly done essay with room between each pair of printed lines for corrections by the test taker. If the person taking the test finds and properly corrects most of the specific errors in the original essay, he earns a high score. He is warned in advance not to add ideas of his own. Inter-reader reliability of the interlinear test is about 0.95.

An example of an interlinear test taken from Findley (27) is presented below:

Specimen of the New CEEB Experimental "Interlinear"
Exercise
PART III
(Suggested time—30 minutes)

Directions: This part consists of a poorly written passage which you are to improve. Wide spaces have been left between the lines so that you can write the necessary improvements. Do not omit any ideas and do not add any ideas of your own. You may, however, change any word which you think is express- ing an idea inexactly; and you may omit words, phrases, or sentences that are unnecessary.

If you wish to change a word or a phrase, blacken it out with heavy lines and write your own version above it. If you wish to change the position of words, either draw a circle around them with an arrow pointing to the new position or, if it is more convenient, cross them out where they stand and write them in wherever they should go, indicating their position by means of a caret ($\wedge$).

If you wish to omit a mark of punctuation, draw a circle around it. If you wish to change it, draw a circle around it and write the new mark above it.

If you have time, you should check your work to make sure that you have indicated your changes clearly.

The Spanish Armada really was not a navy but a transport fleet. The Spaniards had the idea in their heads to capture the English vessels. After that, they were going to land and give battle on shore. But they didn't know anything about English ships, or the strategy that the English were accustomed to use, and the English people were unfamiliar to them. It is possible that the British admirals Drake and Hawkins were foggy about their own strategy beforehand, but they also knew a good opportunity when they saw it. Their ships were half as small or less than the great Spanish galleons, and they could sail twice as fast, and four shots could be fired by their guns to the Spaniards one shot. Therefore the British admirals decided that the English vessels were to move in behind the Spanish transports, and taking advantage of the winds and currents, the Spanish ships would soon be overtaken, which is the well known tactics of pirates.

The English strategy was successful. On account of the Spanish guns were so high, the English vessels could sail beneath their shots and get plenty close. Pursuing the Spaniards up the Channel and by shooting through the towering hulks, many of the enemy's ships were put out of action. Every once and awhile a Spanish ship sunk. They let it as they sailed on. Completely demoralized, one thought was in the mind of the Spaniards only. To get away from these fiend pursuers. If a storm had not sprang up, it might have been done. But a great storm had arose and the south wind had become a tearing racing hurricane. Whose dread anger far outran the wrath of the Englishmen. The Spaniards were always superstitious and they ceased to struggle and fight back at the fate which was their destiny. Indeed before they perished by shipwreck both on the shores of Scotland and Ireland, they were most dead in spirit. No more than hardly a third of the vessels and half of the men was ever to get back to Spain. The flower of Spanish chivalry had perished never to rise again, which was a fatal blow to the Spanish domination of Europe.

End of English Composition Test

Increasing Reliability by Having a Computer Score Essays

Garber (37) has developed a method by which student essays are first transformed, errors and all, into holes on IBM cards, whereupon they are fed into an electronic computer which measures 31 different characteristics of the essays. These characteristics include such things as whether the essay has a title, the average sentence length, the number of commas, and the variability in word length in the essay. Garber used advanced statistical methods to derive an equation to predict the average grade which four English teachers would assign to each essay. This predictive equation proved quite successful: The correlation between the grades assigned by the computer and the average grades assigned by the teachers was 0.71. Though computer scoring of essays is not yet widely in use, it seems to be a promising technique. However, a high score might be assigned by the computer to an essay which is not logical or otherwise fails to make sense to a human reader. One ought to be able to construct such an essay intentionally.

If an essay is written and graded for the purpose of helping a teacher help a pupil, at least two other objections to computer grading must be considered. First, a computer can give feedback to the author in the form of a total score and in terms of scores on each of the characteristics being scored, but it cannot yet give a personalized assessment of how interesting or how well organized the essay is. Some improvement may be expected as computers come to print out messages such as, "Your topic sentence in paragraph 2 is fascinating; keep up the good work." But development of objective criteria for such judgments by the computer will be difficult and will also have to face the difficulty of giving students the impression that interest is a fixed property which does not differ from reader to reader. The second and more basic objection is that a teacher who does not read his students' papers will know less about them, making it more difficult for him to develop a personal relationship with each one. It may be argued that the efficiency of formal instruction will not be impaired thereby. However, we believe that student morale will suffer greatly, which is undesirable even if instructional efficiency remains high.

Validity of Essay Tests as Compared with Objective Tests

Theoretically, the validity of essay tests should be small because of their unreliability and because so few different items can be included in any one test. The objective test includes more items because less time is required for each one. Therefore, a more representative sample is taken from the total set of possible items on a topic. Proponents of essay tests reply that objective tests do measure things but the wrong things in many cases. The objective test, it is alleged, does not require creative activity. It may test for recognition of facts, for recognition of correct versus incorrect spelling or punctuation, for selection of correct versus incorrect solutions to logical or semi-logical problems. But, they say, the objective test (at least in its multiple-choice form) does not require the student to recall and write down facts, to spell or punctuate properly in his own writing, to write down his own solutions to problems, or to write essays which attain a measure of literary excellence.

In defense of the objective test, let it be said that it is often possible to assess ability or achievement without measuring it directly; therefore, a test with high criterion-related validity rather than high content validity is employed. For example, selection tests for salesmen work very well even though they do not require the prospective salesman to demonstrate his sales technique in a real life situation (54). Indirect measurement also is successful in assessing writing skills. Diederich (21) reports that an intelligence test predicts writing skill better than an English composition test. He was describing research by Olsen (63), using as criteria teacher ratings of students in five categories: mechanics, style, organization, reasoning, and content. Since each student had been taught for at least one year by the teacher rating him, these ratings were a plausible criterion measure of writing ability. Yet scores on the five categories never correlated higher than 0.43 with corresponding category scores from the General Composition Test, a test that has been carefully constructed to measure writing skill directly. But for every category an intelligence test score (the Scholastic Aptitude Test Verbal Score) correlated higher than 0.43, going as high as 0.60.

Not only were the ratings in the five categories poorly predicted by the essay test, but so were the total ratings obtained by adding the five category ratings together. For juniors in high school the essay grades correlated 0.52 with total rating whereas the verbal intelligence score correlated 0.70. Interestingly, an objective English test showed a correlation of 0.65 with total rating, almost but not quite as high.

Even though there are many other indications of lower validity with essay tests (14); the argument that the wrong thing is measured in objective tests still has some merit. The classroom teacher would be silly to administer an intelligence test five times during a semester to measure progress in writing skill. It might be better to administer an objective English test five times, but once at the beginning and once at the end of the semester would be adequate for measuring progress. Though giving an essay assignment or test five times may be less valid for refined measurement, it does provide practice in an important task. If essay papers are graded carefully, with adequate comments to the student, the amount of improvement in quality of writing should be greater than with any other method.

In this connection, Diederich (20) has demonstrated that improvement in English composition can be shown over a period of a semester or a year's instruction in English as follows. Have students write two essays on the same subject, one at the beginning and one at the end of the course, giving no hint as to the time of writing. Have all names removed from the papers to prevent a bias in grading. Have someone other than the teacher grade both sets of essays at the same time, with the essays picked at random so that it is impossible to tell which were written earlier. Diederich found in one class that only 14% of the first papers received any grade higher than a D, whereas 70% of the second papers did.

There is also evidence that essay tests do measure something in addition to what is obtained from objective tests. Diederich (21) reported that the prediction of rated writing ability was slightly improved by using the General Composition Test in addition to the Scholastic Aptitude Test Verbal Score. Similarly, in an early summary, Noyes (60) reported that the total score on four essays was better predicted from objective English test items plus an essay score than from a test battery of equal length having all objective items or all essay material. Godshalk, Swineford, and Coffman (38a, Table 12) also found that the total score on four essays was better predicted from two objective English tests, a verbal aptitude test, and an essay than from the same battery of tests with an interlinear test replacing the essay. (An interlinear test was generally superior, however, to most of the objective English tests studied.) The slight degree of improvement attributable to the essay means, however, that an essay test *measures* little that is not available from objective test items.

Relation of Factor Analysis to Validity Studies

French (34) has given a further answer to the question of the unique contribution of essay tests. To appreciate his findings, it is necessary to consider the technique of factor analysis which was discussed in Chapter 14.

The theory of factor analysis states that several tests may be measuring the same property or factor. For situations that are not quite that simple, the theory states that the several tests measure more than one factor. Tests 1 and 2, for example, might both measure a factor of verbal comprehension (85). Test 3 might measure a factor of memory, and test 2 might also depend on memory in addition to its previous measurement of verbal comprehension. In such a situation the theory predicts (under special assumptions not discussed here) that the correlation coefficient between tests 1 and 3 should be zero because they measure different things. However, there would be a positive correlation coefficient between tests 1 and 2 because both measure verbal comprehension, at least in part. Similarly, there would be a positive correlation between tests 2 and 3 because both measure memory, at least in part. Table 15-2 illustrates these relations between the three tests and gives hypothetical values for the correlation coefficients.

Unfortunately, it is usually not known what factors a test measures. Instead of predicting the correlations between tests from a knowledge of the amount of each factor represented on each test, the reverse is true: starting with known values of r such as those given in Table 15-2, an inference is made of how many factors were being measured and in what degree. Techniques for doing this have been thoroughly developed and are described by French (34) and others.

Once the inference is made that certain tests measure certain factors, factor analysis can become quite useful. The example of Table 15-2 suggests that one of the three tests may be unnecessary because only two factors are being measured. Very possibly, test 2 should be discarded, with the other tests being kept because they are *pure-factor* tests, i.e., they measure only one factor at a time.

In other cases, factor analysis may lead to other decisions. If, for example, two tests both measure the same factor and no other, one test can be discarded. This suggests a new way to evaluate essay tests. A factor analysis of essay test scores and objective test scores can be performed. If the essay tests do not measure factors different from those measured by the corresponding objective tests, then one type of test is superfluous. French (34) performed such a factor analysis of grades on essays (tests of writing skill) marked by different graders, together with

TABLE 15-2

Hypothetical Example of Three Tests Which Measure Two Factors

Test number	Factors measured	Hypothetical correlation coefficient
1	Verbal comprehension	$r = 0.54$ between test 1 and test 2
2	Verbal comprehension and memory	$r = 0.43$ between test 2 and test 3
3	Memory	$r = 0$ between test 1 and test 3

grades on the Scholastic Aptitude Test (Verbal and Mathematical scores reported as separate values) and the English Composition Test. He found that the Scholastic Aptitude Test sections and the English Composition Test, all of which are objective tests, measured the same factor. None of the different graders measured that factor. Rather, they seemed to measure (a) relevance and number of ideas, (b) spelling and clarity of expression, (c) quality of ideas and style, (d) punctuation and grammar, and (e) general wording and word choices. The graders, however, were inconsistent with each other in that they emphasized different factors; but all were measuring qualities not assessed by the objective tests. Someone should improve either essay or objective testing procedures so that some, at least, of these five factors can be measured separately and reliably.

There is further indication that different types of tests give non-equivalent results. Hurlburt (47) found that the ability to recognize and associate the meanings of words was only moderately correlated (r about 0.61) with the ability to recall and use the same words. Recognition tests are common forms of objective examinations. Hurlburt's results suggest, however, that a teacher really wishing to help students recall and use words should assess their achievement by measuring it directly. An objective recall test will have good reliability and may be more to the point than the more common recognition test. Presumably a factor analysis would show that different factors are involved in these two kinds of tests.

Suggestions to Teachers Who Use Essay Tests

D. A. Wood (94) has provided a set of rules for developing essay test questions and for scoring essay tests. Those rules are quoted below, almost without elaboration. Interested readers may wish to examine the original statement by Wood to learn her reasoning about these rules.

Rules for Developing Essay Test Questions

1. The teacher must plan to devote sufficient time to constructing the questions.
2. The questions should precisely define the direction and scope of the answers desired.
3. A large number of questions each of which demands a short answer is often preferable to a small number of questions calling for long answers.
4. The time available for responding to the question should be carefully considered in relation to the amount of writing required for adequate responses.
5. The same examination should be administered to all the students whose relative degrees of achievement in a particular area are to be compared.

One comment about rule 5 seems appropriate here. This rule forbids the use of optional questions except in unusual circumstances. The reason for the rule is that it is difficult to be fair in grading two persons who responded to different questions. Optional questions are usually used to be sure that a student need not respond to a question about which he knows very little because of an unlucky sampling of essay questions. This will occur sometimes unless rule 3 is followed. Rule 3 is important because content validity is hard to obtain in an essay test with a very few items.

Rules for Evaluating Essay Test Papers

1. Preferably at the time the test is constructed, the teacher should prepare a tentative scoring key.
2. The tentative key should be applied to an assortment of answers as a preliminary check on its adequacy.
3. In order to reduce "halo effect," one question should be graded [for every student and then the next question graded for every student, etc., rather than all questions for one student, then all questions for the next student, etc.] [The bracketed material above uses slightly different words from Wood's terminology but preserves the original meaning.]
4. If a large number of papers must be graded, the teacher should periodically recheck papers graded earlier to ensure that standards have not shifted appreciably.
5. When resources permit and an essay test has unusually important consequences, the pooled ratings of equally competent judges should be obtained because they are more reliable than the ratings of a single judge.

Time Limits and Test Performance

Students typically prefer tests with almost unlimited time to complete the answers rather than tests that are impossible to finish. However, the time spent in testing will be very great if students are given no limit whatever. One student may complete an examination in 15 minutes, whereas another might take 3 hours. For this reason Nunnally (61) recommends that time limits be set with the goal of leaving 90% of students feeling that they had enough time and only 10% feeling rushed.

The foregoing advice applies to teacher-made tests. However, in standardized tests a time limit has been set by the test constructor; the teacher should not deviate from the instructions given in the manual provided for administrators of the test. The reason it is important to follow instructions completely is that no comparison between students in a given class and in the original standardization group can be made if the class is allowed less or more time than the persons originally taking the test, or given some other different treatment which might reasonably be expected to change the scores.

Test specialists also emphasize that the abilities required for doing fast work are somewhat different than the abilities required for doing accurate work. Drastically reducing the time allowed for taking a test, therefore, has the result not only of reducing the number of correct answers for most people, but also of changing the rank order so that persons with good scores on a test with almost unlimited time do less well on the short test than some persons with poor scores on the test with almost unlimited time. Now the question of validity arises: Which test gives the proper indication of performance? Obviously, the answer depends upon the purpose of the test. However, if we are talking about criterion-related validity, with high-school or college grade point averages as the criterion, it is well known that aptitude tests with almost unlimited time (sometimes called *power tests*) are more valid than aptitude tests with a short time for completion (sometimes called *speeded tests*) (2, 17). The use of a speeded test can affect the reliability values obtained with it. Ordinarily, the parallel forms reliability and test–retest reliability coefficients are the most satisfactory measurements for speeded tests, whereas any of the reliability coefficients may be appropriate for power tests (22, 94).

_____ **Item Analysis, Selection, and Revision**

If a test with many items in it is to be useful and more useful than a test with only one item, a paradoxical balance must be maintained between two conflicting principles: (a) the questions must all measure approximately the same thing, or factor and (b) the questions must not all give exactly the same result. Principle (a) implies a correlation between scores for the different items. Principle (b) implies that the correlation should not be perfect because then all items but one would be unnecessary. Test constructors have many ways of checking whether these principles apply. The simplest is to check each item in the test to see whether persons who have a high score on the total test are more likely to pass the item than persons with a low score. For example, Lange, Lehmann, and Mehrens (55) give an example of a psychology test item which was passed by 63% of the better students taking the test, and 52% of the poorer students. The difference in these percentages, 11%, is a measure of the discrimination of the item and is called D. To interpret a D value of 11, Fig. 15-3 shows the relationship between D and the Kuder–Richardson reliability coefficient for a 100-item test composed of items which all have the same difficulty. It can be seen from Fig. 15-3 that this D value would yield a reliability of approximately zero if it were

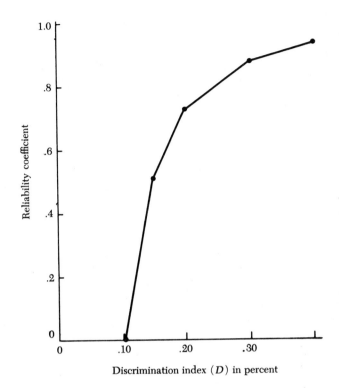

Fig. 15-3. Predicted relationship between average discrimination index (D) and Kuder–Richardson reliability coefficient (r) when 100 items of equal difficulty are used. Enlarged points are taken from Table 4 of Ebel (23). Straight lines connect the points, for simplicity, but the theoretical relationship is a curved one.

the average D for all items. This means that the item was a poor item and should not be used in future tests.

Item selection consists largely in finding a D value for each item of a test and dropping the poor items in order to make the test better the next time it is used. Lange, Lehmann, and Mehrens have shown that it is also possible to rewrite poor questions so that the difference between the proportions of good and poor students passing the item is increased. The psychology question previously mentioned as having a D value of 11% was modified to yield a D of 21%. Modified questions can be prepared in about one-fifth as much time as new questions; they are also more likely to discriminate well than new items.

One gap in the discussion above was the definition of the quality of the students. The better group of students is the 27% who received the highest score on the total test; the poorer group is the 27% who received the lowest scores on the total test. The number 27 has been selected because statistical theory shows that it is most efficient. However, other percentages such as the highest and lowest 33% or the upper and lower halves also work quite well and can be more convenient (25).

--------------------------------- **The Use of Test and Evaluation Procedures**

Evaluation of an Individual Pupil

All the theory and research on testing described above acquires social importance as tests are developed and used in school situations. As suggested at the beginning of this chapter, tests help indicate which children require extraordinary attention, typically either because they are ahead of or behind their peers in some area. Some children will enter classes for the gifted, others will "skip a grade" (acceleration), others will receive special instruction in art, others will enter technical high schools, and so on.

On solely scientific grounds it might seem most reasonable to make these decisions automatically after collecting all examination material, whether objective or essay, and statistically predicting the success of each student in each possible environment. In fact, studies by Meehl (58) and by Cronbach and Gleser (18) give us good reason to think that prediction is best when performed statistically. Yet, assignment of students to special programs usually involves a more subjective element. Parents are consulted to see if they believe the proposed special instruction is as good for the child's emotional and social development as it is for his intellectual development. Where the parents and teacher usually agree on these points, the inquiry becomes simply an act of courtesy and information. If they disagree, it may, nonetheless, be true that "scientific" judgment now or 100 years from now could give a better answer than the parent. Members of a democratic country will hope, nonetheless, that parents and children keep their freedom to make apparently wrong decisions, unless they are of major significance. In matters of life and death, like vaccinations against smallpox, the schools have insisted that parents conform to their recommendations. But teachers can use only their powers of persuasion in attempting to convince parents that a talented youth should go on to college.

Not only does educational guidance assume communication and freedom of choice, it also uses nonacademic and almost intuitive information. Qualitative evaluation may be most useful in assessing personal qualities such as citizenship, sociability, and the practice of the fine arts. Since these qualities are desirable and since the schools have responsibility for the children during a large proportion of their waking hours, these qualities may be weakened by schools which ignore them. Evaluation, therefore, becomes a means of judging nonacademic development and helps suggest means of fostering it.

Other Evaluations

The foregoing paragraphs refer to the evaluation of academic and nonacademic behavior of the individual pupil. We must also consider the evaluation of a curriculum section, of the teacher, or of a whole class or school.

The same test used to determine individual pupils' progress may serve these added purposes as well. If the testing program was planned carefully enough to have scientific meaning, it may show that the high-school physics curriculum material concerning electricity was less well learned than that concerning mechanics. This may lead to a revision of the teaching plan for the electricity section. Similarly, controlled studies may show situations wherein one teacher is more effective than another. Later in the chapter comparisons between different schools will be considered.

Evaluation goes on in many cases, however, where the scientist would hesitate to pass judgment. The teacher notices that his pupils seem less interested in electricity than mechanics, and he asks himself why. Or from time to time he conducts a review session of a class which also serves for evaluation: He discovers that he has said things which were misunderstood, so he repairs the damage and plans to present the material differently next year. Or he may simply ask the pupils what material was most boring and could have been covered very quickly because it was known already, or what material was too difficult and required more time for learning. Not everything the teacher concludes from these evaluation procedures could be proved true if scientifically tested. However, probably enough of it is true to make the attempt worthwhile.

Achievement tests are also widely used as means of assessing the effectiveness of different methods of instruction or of different teachers. We illustrate this practice by referring to a book by Goldberg, Passow, and Justman (40) which was primarily concerned with the effects of so-called "ability grouping." This is the device of making school classes more homogeneous in scholastic aptitude than would be true if random assignments were employed to divide a large group into several classes. Ability grouping is often employed in the upper elementary grades and above. Usually it provides that persons with a high, medium, or low I.Q.

or other aptitude test scores are placed with similarly rated students in all or most of their classes.

An immense amount of research has been performed on the effects of such grouping, most of which is alluded to in Goldberg *et al.* However, we will discuss only the particular experiment performed by Goldberg and her co-workers while cautioning the reader to remember that this is only an illustrative discussion, not a definitive pronouncement on the effects of ability grouping.

The experiment involved 2219 fifth-grade children in New York City and compared 15 different patterns of class assignments ranging from a class consisting only of students with I.Q.'s of 130 and above, through a class with pupils whose I.Q.'s covered the entire available range, to a class all of whose pupils had I.Q.'s of 99 or below. Membership in these classes was assigned according to an experimental design rather than the principals' or teachers' preferences. Students attended their regular schools; they were not transferred to other schools nor were class sizes adjusted. All students involved were tested at the beginning of the fifth grade and again at the end of the sixth grade; the 2219 children reported on all stayed in the same school for two years and were assigned to the same groupings but not necessarily to the same teachers for both years. Teachers were instructed not to use special methods as a function of the presence or absence of ability grouping in their classes.

The study showed the effects of grouping upon learning to be minimal. However, the grouping pattern with the greatest ability spread did give some evidence of producing the largest academic gains for all pupils. Members of certain classrooms learned more of one subject than another, apparently because of the interests and knowledge of the different teachers. It appears that assigning teachers to subjects which they prefer may have more effect upon learning than modifying the range of ability among students in each classroom. If ability grouping is to be used, it may be best to do it only by individual courses. In that case a person might be placed in a high ability English course and a low ability science course, for example, with assignment based on previous performance in these fields.

_____ **Misuse of Achievement Tests**

Aptitude and achievement tests have both been strongly criticized in recent years, primarily by nonpsychologists. Teachers tend to feel that such tests are impersonal and that their usefulness is mitigated by the special circumstances of many children being tested. Humanists and other scholars outside the field of psychology often object to the use of objective questions and in particular to the specific answers which are scored correct. In many cases they feel that a strong case can be made that some other available answer is equally good.

We have discussed the former objection briefly in the chapter on intelligence measurement; the same considerations apply with achievement tests: relatively good prediction can be made from an achievement test score to later test scores in the same field even when different children have had different opportunities to learn. There is some evidence, however, of greater achievement by southern black students when brought to integrated northern colleges than would have been expected from their high-school aptitude scores (12). This does suggest that prediction sometimes breaks down because of special factors not considered in test construction. In addition, it no doubt is true that achievement tests are sometimes administered under very adverse conditions in which many students' scores are lower than they should be.

An excellent presentation of the one correct answer feature of many tests is made by Hoffmann (45). He gives examples of some objective examination questions in commercially produced tests which have clearly incorrect answers in their scoring keys. Hoffman also provides several examples of items where the allegedly correct answer is subject to considerable discussion. Hoffman is well aware of the arguments which are given to justify ambiguous questions; he is also aware of the difficulties involved in using essay questions. It is the writer's personal belief that achievement test constructors in the future must pay much more attention to the correctness of their item answers than they have in the past.

Standardized Tests of Achievement

Though any classroom test of achievement could be standardized sufficiently for its reliability and validity to be approximately known, most standardized tests are used by many classes in many different schools. By 1954 achievement testing had become so common that 26 states offered statewide testing programs (87). New York had such a program in 1865, long before objective tests were available. All other states introduced their programs in the present century.

Statewide testing is most common for twelfth-grade students, being used as a basis for college entrance and specialization counseling. However, in eight states it occurs in grade four or lower. Testing in the lower grades may often attract special attention to pupils with unusual talent. It is also true that achievement testing is being done at more and more advanced levels. Because graduate schools need some basis for selecting their students, the Graduate Record Examination has been developed.

No estimate of the total number of achievement tests given in a year can be quite complete. We get an idea of the size of the enterprise because some years ago 16 of the states made estimates of their own programs' sizes and the total came to 4,455,000 tests per year. This is only the beginning. Thirty-eight of the forty largest school systems in the United States were using system-wide testing programs at the same time, often in addition to the statewide programs (86).

The principal standardized achievement tests of the United States include, among others, the California Achievement Test (grades 1–14), College Entrance Examination Board Achievement Tests (candidates for college entrance), Cooperative General Achievement Tests (grades 9–12 and college entrants), Iowa Tests of Basic Skills (grades 3–9), Graduate Record Examination: Area Tests and Advanced Tests (grades 14–17), Iowa Tests of Educational Development (grades 9–12), Sequential Tests of Educational Progress (grades 4–14), SRA Achievement Series (grades 1–9), and the Stanford Achievement Test (grades 1.5–9). In addition, the National Merit Scholarship Qualifying Test is administered to second-semester juniors and first-semester seniors in high school as a basis for selecting National Merit Scholars (35). Project Talent, a long-term study of 440,000 representative high-school students, 5% of the students in grades 9 through 12 in the United States in 1960, has used tests of its own construction, including several types of information tests and several tests of language skill (32).

Several of the above tests have been standardized nationally. This means that they were administered in enough states and in enough schools to permit calculation of nationwide norms showing the estimated scores on each test for each age level for the lowest 1%, 2%—and on up to 100% of the students. These scores are called the *percentiles* of the test at each age level. We refer to *estimated scores* or *estimated percentiles* because the exact percentiles could be known only by testing all school children of a given age.

Not all the tests have nationwide standardization, however. Certain tests were originally developed primarily for certain states or regions, and their original standardization groups were primarily from the localities of origin. However, because of the tests' wide acceptance elsewhere, national norms have often been added.

What are the reasons for using one achievement test rather than some other at a particular school and grade level? First, of course, the test must have a form appropriate to that level. Thus, the Stanford Achievement Test breaks its range down into five grade levels (1.5–2.5, 2.5–3.9,

4–5.5, 5.5–6.9, and 7–9), to provide appropriate tests at each grade in the spectrum intended for coverage. Second, the test standardization must give evidence of accuracy.

If a research report states that one test yields mean achievement scores almost one-half grade higher than any one of four other tests given to children of similar average intelligence (74, 82), the school superintendent or director of testing seeks evidence to verify or refute that information. He may decide that the test in question is less satisfactory than others available and use another. Or he may decide that the evidence just mentioned is either erroneous or not significant for the test because correction can be made for the systematic overestimation reported. Similarly, if an article reports that two supposedly equivalent forms of a test give substantially different average scores (46), he tries to determine if the article is correct. He also decides to what extent that information, if true, militates against the use of the test, or (more likely) requires a particular sort of interpretation of testing results.

The requirement of content validity has already been noted; in addition to appropriate age level and accuracy of normative material, an achievement test must sample from an appropriate set of possible items. One school system will have a heavily fact-oriented curriculum and may, therefore, choose one particular test battery. Another may have a curriculum emphasizing creativity or problem solving and, therefore, choose some other test battery.

This is only the beginning of the analysis of coverage, however. One administrator may not only wish to emphasize educational skills but also to emphasize precisely those indicated by Bloom (4) for the cognitive domain. This may lead him to use the Graduate Record Examination Area tests, if he is testing at the college or graduate level (5). Someone else may want assurance that the items of the test refer to material from commonly used textbooks and school courses of study across the nation. This may impel him to consider the Stanford Achievement Test, for one (36).

Many other considerations arise in selection of an achievement test, including some very practical ones such as price and legibility. A standard source of information about these tests, as well as many other kinds of tests is the *Mental Measurements Yearbook* edited by O. K. Buros (8), and revised every few years. It prints at least one review of each major test and lists or provides other information about most research studies concerning each test.

One consideration related to the matter of content validity is overlap with aptitude tests. If an achievement test has the same items as an aptitude test, its content validity is low because items highly dependent on specific instruction are lacking. This can often be established by looking at specific items of a test. In other cases statistical arguments have been presented for the proposition that a given achievement test measures nearly the same thing as an aptitude test (49).

In the former case the content validity is low as measured directly. In the latter case the content validity could still be high because the text-books and other materials used as a source of items contain much material that would be known by a bright pupil without special instruction. Presumably, such a test would lack criterion-related validity in either case.

——— **Implications of Achievement Tests for Psychology in General**

Growth Curves of Achievement

Data from achievement tests tell us a great deal about normal intel-lectual development. Just as height or weight can be plotted year by year for an individual child, so a child's achievement scores can be graphed as a function of grade level. Given a home and school environ-

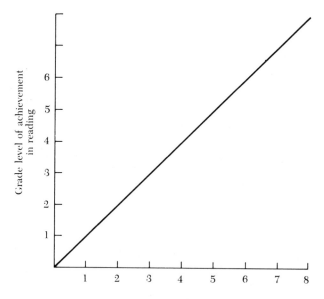

Fig. 15-4. Straight-line function relating idealized achievement in reading to actual grade in school.

ment conducive to normal learning, an average child should show a growth in reading ability displayed in Fig. 15-4. Figure 15-4 shows that achievement level always equals grade level in this idealized case.

The trend shown in Fig. 15-4 is a straight line rather than a curve such as those for height and weight growth. Because there are few "natural" units, such as inches or pounds, for achievement, the units for grade school level tests have usually been average attainment for each grade, forcing the straight line shape as seen in the figure, except for chance fluctuations above or below the norm of a grade of achievement growth for every actual grade change. At higher levels, the unit of achievement may be points on a scale with a mean of approximately 500 and a standard deviation of approximately 100 (as in the Graduate Record Examination). Unfortunately, very few attempts to record year-by-year achieve-

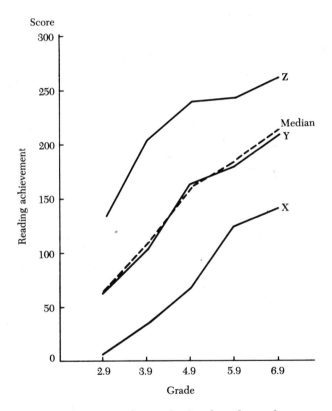

Fig. 15-5. Relation between grade in school and reading achievement (based on the Stanford Achievement Test) for three children of varied intelligence and for the median of 42 students in a class. Child Z had an I.Q. of 150, child Y an I.Q. of 118, and child X an I.Q. of 97. Figure 8 from Hildreth (44).

ment growth of individuals have been made. Where comparisons as a function of age have been made, they have often been cross-sectional.

Figure 15-5 presents growth curves in reading achievement from a study by Hildreth (44). Though these data were first reported many years ago, they are still correct in showing that achievement is typically greatest for children of high intelligence and that it increases consistently with grade in school. This figure may be compared with Fig. 15-4 for the idealized average child, someone whose I.Q. is a little higher than the I.Q. of child X. (Also see the achievement growth curves in Fig. 12-4.)

Osborne and Sanders (64, 65) found that the relatively younger graduate students entering the University of Georgia had higher achievement scores on the Graduate Record Examination at entrance. These investigators took this to indicate that there is a substantial loss of information with age for adults. However, it is probable that some of this decline is due to different ability levels, with the older students having lower intelligence originally or knowing less originally.

Need for Bench Marks in Achievement Testing

Increasing numbers of research workers have tried to obtain achievement scores with units of absolute meaning rather than meaning relative only to representatives of a given age or grade level. Findley (28) has commented favorably upon a method of scaling vocabulary growth by statistical means. Flanagan (30, 31) has also argued for the use of absolute units so that *bench marks* as he calls them may be established to show how well students performed in one year, permitting comparison with students of the same age in later years. Though this could be done with relative scores also, if standards of scoring were held constant, Flanagan feels that a unit such as the percentage of words correctly spelled out of 5000 test words would be a more meaningful unit for comparison from year to year. The Project Talent tests mentioned earlier in this chapter reflect Flanagan's interests. On the basis of those tests, we know, for example, that the average ninth grader can do about 3.95 simple arithmetic problems per minute. By comparison, the average twelfth grader can do about 4.6 such problems per minute (31).

The final version of the Project Talent test battery gives primary emphasis to an achievement type test without absolute standards of measurement but includes absolute measurements (also called *domain tests*) of vocabulary, spelling, and reading comprehension (32). Figure 15-6 shows the resulting proportions of the most commonly used 5000 English words which can be properly spelled by boys and girls in grades 9 through 12. These percentages are quite high, ranging from 77.2% for ninth-grade boys to 95.2% for twelfth-grade girls, with a consistent

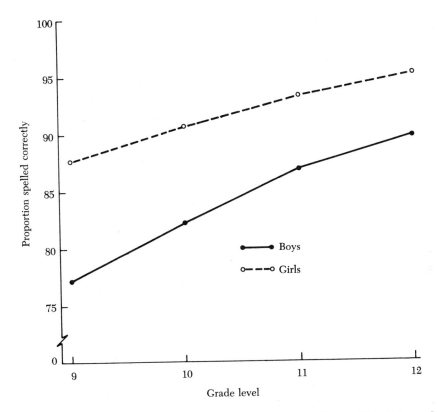

Fig. 15-6. Estimated proportions of the 5000 most commonly used English words which can be spelled correctly by high-school boys and girls at each grade level. Based on Table 3-13 of Flanagan *et al.* (32), with the 5000 words taken from E. L. Thorndike and Lorge (83).

superiority for girls and improvement with every increase in grade level. An indication of the level of difficulty of words in the most frequent 5000 is that the Preamble to the Constitution of the United States contains only three words ("ordain," "posterity," and "tranquility") which are not in that group; all three are in the second 5000 most commonly used words.

A Nationwide Assessment Program

In 1964 planning was begun for a so-called national assessment much like Project Talent. Under the leadership of the Committee on Assessing the Progress of Education (with subsequent direction by the Education Commission of the States), specific objectives in 10 areas were developed and corresponding tests constructed. Beginning in March, 1969, 32,000 persons in each of three age groups (9, 13, and 17) and 20,000 young adults were to be tested. Three of the designated areas were to be tested in 1969, three more in 1970, and the remaining four in 1971. Further testings with other children in the three age groups are planned for later years in order to show whether improved teaching occurs in later years. The first results from this study will be reported in the fall and winter of 1970–1971 (58a).

Achievement Growth as a Function of Subject Matter

Achievement test scores may generally be expected to increase age by age regardless of subject matter, assuming the subject matter is in the formal curriculum or is informally presented to the child in some other way. Conceivably, an American child might improve his annual achievement test scores on American history without even studying it in school; he would be much less likely to do so for Australian history because it is so rarely mentioned in the American child's culture.

Restricting ourselves to subjects which are commonly taught formally or informally to American children, we find that almost all children show some annual growth in the traditional school areas. However, growth may be so slow in young childhood as to make it impractical to introduce instruction until later, as indicated in the discussion of readiness to learn in Chapter 9.

In order to have an increase in achievement test scores with age continued education is required, whether it be from newspapers or in school or through some other medium. One indication of this fact is that physical science achievement does not grow significantly among social science and humanities majors from the second to the fourth year of college (56). These students take little or no physical science in college after their sophomore year and they use it, read about it, or talk about it so little in daily life that they simply do not exhibit improvement in it thereafter. In contrast, in the study just cited natural science majors showed substantial gains in social science achievement in their last two years of college.

Obviously, much that is learned is forgotten. Chapter 5 reported that the loss may be as much as 100%, with most of it occurring within a day after learning. Consequently, many specific test items passed by a fourth grader may have been long forgotten by an eighth grader. The latter, though, may have learned much more in four years than would appear from the growth curve for his achievement scores. He probably also learned enough to make up for forgetting of fourth-grade material and to allow some forgetting of more recent material as well. If all the material once forgotten were lost forever, our educational system would seem grievously inefficient. However, Chapter 5 showed that relearning after forgetting is faster than original learning. Therefore, though a student may feel certain subject matter is lost to him forever, some saving will occur if he ever needs to relearn it.

Despite the fact that apparently forgotten material may be relearned quickly, it does seem inefficient for so much material to be learned and then forgotten. Could not fewer topics be treated, and they more thoroughly so that most of what is learned is retained permanently? Probably our schools will increasingly follow this proposal, which is a partial return to the emphasis upon drill and overlearning in eighteenth- and nineteenth-century schools. While an argument could be presented for partial adoption of such a proposal, another argument can be presented in favor of the diffuse instruction now offered.

Every 15 years the amount of information about physical science doubles (50). Much of the increase deserves no place in our public schools, but neither did much of the information available 100 years ago. However, there is much more worthwhile information of all kinds, empirical, theoretical, artistic, etc., available now for learning by students. Since no comparable increase in learning ability has occurred, either different people must know different things or everyone must learn how to find and use information which it is not practical to learn. The former solution, specialized instruction, is increasing, particularly at the college and professional school levels. But side by side with this, if specialists are to be able to work or even get along with each other, they must employ the second solution of learning how to find and use information. Consequently, achievement tests place an increasingly high premium upon knowledge of the use of maps, dictionaries, encyclopedias, reference books, and the like. However, in earlier parts of this book we discussed "learning-how-to-learn." It may be that the greatest achievement of any student is this learning how to learn something. The college-trained student, then, may have only a limited advantage over others in actual skills or remembered information but an enormous advantage in ability to acquire the information necessary for a task and integrate it with what he already knows.

—————————————————— **Prediction of Achievement Scores**

Predicting from Aptitude Scores

Achievement test scores may be expected to have relatively high correlations with aptitude test scores, and this expectation is repeatedly confirmed. Only one illustrative study need be mentioned. Stroud, Blommers, and Lauber (78) found a correlation of about +0.66 between I.Q.'s from the Wechsler Intelligence Scale for Children (WISC) and scores on the reading comprehension, arithmetic, and spelling tests of the Iowa Tests of Basic Skills for 775 children in grades 3 through 6.

Sometimes it is difficult to infer from a correlation coefficient just how successful individual predictions will be. For that reason *expectancy tables* have been developed to tell the probability of certain outcomes as a function of test scores. (This topic was also mentioned in the preceding chapter.) In a survey of such expectancy tables Schrader (69) has presented some information which will help to interpret the 0.66 correlation just reported. From Schrader's Table 2 it can be seen that—given certain assumptions it is not necessary to state here—a correlation of 0.6 implies that persons in the top fifth of the WISC score group would have a 2% chance of being in the bottom fifth on achievement scores, a 48% chance of being in the middle three-fifths, and a 50% chance of being in the top fifth on achievement. Persons in the middle three-fifths on the WISC would have a 16% chance of being in the bottom fifth on achievement, a 68% chance of being in the middle three-fifths on achievement, and a 15% chance of being in the highest fifth on achievement. Persons in the bottom fifth on the WISC would have corresponding percentages of 50, 48, and 2. Slightly better prediction would be possible with an *r* of 0.66; in any case a WISC score in the top fifth or bottom fifth tells a good deal about a person's probable achievement.

Predicting from Other Achievement Scores

Even better predictions of achievement can result if the predictor variable used is earlier achievement scores. Gates and LaSalle (38), testing 75 pupils every 4 months for 2 years, found the correlations between scores on the first administration of a spelling achievement test and on each later administration to be no lower than 0.87. These correlations were noticeably higher than those between the Stanford–Binet intelligence test or the National Intelligence Test and subsequent spelling lists. They were also distinctly higher than the correlations between a composite of all achievement tests and subsequent spelling achievement tests. Similar findings were obtained when scores on reading comprehension, reading rate, and arithmetic tests, respectively, were used as the variables to be predicted over the 20-month period. It would seem that prediction is generally most successful when exactly the same variable is used in the predictor test as in later measures of the criterion.

                              Variations of Achievement Test Scores
                                        in Different School Systems

Rural versus Urban Schools

Studies of Tennessee grade-school children (13) and of University of Georgia freshmen (66) show that achievement test scores, on the average, are worse for students from rural environments than from urban backgrounds. This was not true, however, for every possible grade or subtest studied.

Because of its careful nationwide sampling of 5% of American high schools, the Project Talent survey previously discussed (32) may be taken as definitive on this topic, at least for high schools. That investigation also found a sizable superiority in achievement by urban students, if attention were limited to mathematics, science, and foreign language. Quite possibly this superiority resulted from the fact that many rural high schools have very few courses in those subjects. For other subjects, Project Talent showed negligible achievement differences between the students of urban and rural high schools.

Socioeconomic Factors

Project Talent also reported that nearly all sections of the United States contained high schools with students of high average achievement and others with students of low average achievement. A principal predictor of high average achievement in a school was a high teacher salary scale. While the salary scale did not directly cause high achievement, it probably attracted more talented teachers, thus leading to better student achievement. It may also have resulted from the high-school district having parents of greater intellectual capacity and (correlated with it) greater financial resources, thus making it feasible to provide higher salaries.

A related study of R. L. Thorndike (84) shows that communities with students having high average scores on the Metropolitan Achievement Test battery differed sociologically from those whose students had low average scores. The most substantial effect found was a 0.26 correlation between average achievement score and the number of professional workers per 11,000 population.

The inference is obvious that communities with large numbers of professional workers also have large numbers of academically talented students who therefore perform well on achievement tests. Parental pressure may also ensure greater effort by these children than by talented children in other groups.

Differences between Student Achievement in the United States and Great Britain

Many claims have recently been made that educational achievement is poorer in the United States than in other countries. Evidence in favor of this proposition is often tenuous, being contaminated by noncomparable tests or student groups in the two countries being studied. One of the best of these reports, however, provided convincing evidence in 1958 that Central Californian schools were not keeping up with English schools in teaching arithmetic at the 11-year-old level. Buswell (9) compared 3191 children from a random sample of 91 English schools and 3179 children from 70 schools in Central California, on 70 arithmetic items appropriate to both localities, with the following results:

	Central California	England
Average number correct	12.1	29.1
Standard deviation	6.8	18.7

The difference in average number correct may properly be called enormous, and the difference in standard deviations is even more striking. Finally very high scores were much more frequently obtained in England than in central California.

Note that no Central Californian student had 70 correct or even as many as 54, whereas seven English students had 70 correct and 428 English students had 54 or more correct. It would seem that instruction in the California schools studied had served to make all students similar in performance and to eliminate extremely high performance. (This study cannot be taken to indicate superior performance by English children in any area other than the one just discussed. It may or may not be true that other subjects or other tests in arithmetic would show similar results.)

A Twelve-Nation Comparison of Mathematical Achievement

A more comprehensive international study, a 5-year evaluation of mathematics teaching, was performed by Husen (48) with the assistance of specialists in 12 different countries. That study indicates that typical American school children learn less mathematics than children in most other countries do. At the age of 13 the average score for the United

States was 16.2, for England 19.3, and for Japan 31.2. Since all countries studied required all 13-year-olds to attend school, the inferiority of the American students, who ranked tenth out of 12 countries, seems a genuine one. Possibly this is attributable in part to the fact that U. S. teachers ranked seventh out of 8 countries from which reports were made on whether the topics tested had been taught to the students (48).

The United States also ranked low (twelfth) in mathematics achievement of students in their final year before university entrance (48). However, Carnett (11) pointed out that 70% of U. S. children of their age group are in school during their last preuniversity year, compared with 57% in Japan, 12% in England, and 8% in The Netherlands. Carnett would apparently agree with Husen's (48) conclusion that the low average performance of mathematics majors in the United States in their last preuniversity year is predictable solely from overall international scores plus the large proportion of American students still in school who are specializing in mathematics. A further indication that by some criteria the United States is doing a good job of mathematics instruction is Foshay's (33) interpretation of this study, showing that 65 American students per 10,000 at the age of the last preuniversity year have achievement scores high enough to lead them into graduate work in mathematics or closely allied fields. In this respect the large number of American students in school compensates for low average scores, allowing the United States to rank third among the 12 countries studied.

Possible Changes in School Achievement in Succeeding Generations

In addition to the charge that school achievement is poorer in the United States, there is the further claim that American school children are learning less than they did in former years. On the one hand, such a claim must be qualified by reminding ourselves that much greater proportions of American children are now attending school. We know that only 7% of persons of high-school age were attending high school in 1890. On the other hand, for those who were in school some generations ago, it may be that academic achievement was greater.

Comparisons between school achievement of different generations of school children have been relatively common in the United States. Consider the first large-scale written examinations in the country. In 1845, the annual examining committees of the Boston grammar and writing schools prepared examinations in history, arithmetic, geography, definitions, grammar, natural philosophy, and astronomy. From 10 to 31 questions were used for each subject. In addition, handwriting samples were collected and graded. A representative question from each test is given in Table 15-3 below.

It should be noted that these examinations were given only to students in the "first classes" of each school, that is, those students about to graduate. Their average age was about 14 years, 2 months. In the 1845 examinations only the superior students—less than half—within the first classes were tested. Even so, the examining committee was shocked by the poor performance of the students tested. Recent complaints about the effectiveness of our schools are nothing new, then.

The book *Then and Now in Education* (10) reports a comparison between the approximately 500 Boston students tested in 1845 and about 12,000 children of the same age tested in 1919. In some ways it is most regrettable that exactly the same tests were not given each year. However, the authors of the book reduced the test to five questions on each of six subjects, excluding astronomy completely because it was no longer taught in the schools, and many questions were excluded as being no longer important to a well-educated person. (The sample question for history given in Table 15-3 deserved exclusion on that basis.) Some were excluded because almost no one passed them in the original testing. Some, particularly in arithmetic, were excluded as not relevant to practical

TABLE 15-3

Questions Asked in 1845 Examinations[a, b]

Subject	Question (or word to be defined)
History	What are the eras the most used in Chronology?
Arithmetic	The City of Boston has 120,000 inhabitants, half males, and its property liable to taxation is one hundred millions. It levies a poll tax of $\frac{2}{3}$ of a dollar each on one half of its male population. It taxes income to the amount of $50,000, and its whole tax is $770,000. What should a man pay whose taxable property amounts to $190,000?
Geography	Draw an outline map of Italy.
Words to be defined	Hades
Grammar	Punctuate the following sentences; correct all the errors you may find in them; and write them out grammatically if you think them to be ungrammatical: . . . "The property of such rules are doubtful."
Natural philosophy	Which occupies the most space, a pound of water when liquid, or when in the state of ice?
Astronomy	What do you understand by the transit of planet?

[a] From Caldwell and Courtis (10).

[b] Examples of questions asked by the Annual Examining Committees of the Boston Grammar and Writing Schools.

situations. With this much excluding, bias in favor of the 1919 children becomes a possibility, but one that we cannot really evaluate. Recognizing though the very real problem as to what was worth testing, we turn to the results of the 1919 survey. Though the median score was 45.5% for the 30 questions in 1919, compared with 37.5% in 1845, the most striking result is that very few items received similar scores in the two years. On half of them the students did better in 1919, but on half they did poorer. On a punctuation question the change was upward from 32 to 80% correct. On an arithmetic question the change was downward from 92 to 16%.

A fair summary of the changes from 1845 to 1919 was that the later tests showed lower scores on pure memory and arithmetic computations but higher scores on thought and reasoning questions. Spelling, punctuation, and parsing also were superior in 1919.

The difference in educational emphasis and achievement is well illustrated by the following quotation (10). "In 1845, 35 per cent of the children knew the year when the embargo was laid by President Jefferson, but only 28 per cent knew what an embargo was. In 1919, only 23 per cent knew the year, but 34 per cent knew the meaning."

Cubberley (19) summarizes a similar study by Riley, who reused written examinations first given in Springfield, Massachusetts, schools in 1846. Riley had these examinations in spelling, arithmetic, geography, and penmanship given again in 1906 to Springfield students of the same level (ninth grade). The pupils in 1906 were superior in each field, particularly so in arithmetic.

Important comparisons of achievement over about a generation span have been made with standardized tests comparing data from the 1930's and later. Burke and Anderson (7) compared 162 Kansas pupils in grades 1 to 6, tested in 1939, to 216 in those grades and from the same school, tested in 1950. The same tests, Metropolitan Achievement Tests, were used in both cases though new forms of the tests had to be administered in 1950 and conversions made to provide scores comparable to those for the earlier forms. Of 27 comparisons made, 11 showed statistically significant superiority for the 1939 group and 3 for the 1950 group. The remaining 13 showed smaller differences which can be presumed to result from chance. This investigation may be taken as indicating some inferiority in achievement in 1950, particularly for arithmetic.

Lanton (57) and Miller (59) made similar comparisons of 886 third-, fourth-, fifth-, and eighth-grade children from schools in Evanston, Illinois, tested in 1932–1934 and 1049 children from the same grades and geographical areas tested in 1952–1954. Exactly the same achievement tests were administered in both years under the supervision of the same research director. The pupils tested in 1952–1954 showed generally superior performance on achievement tests as compared with the pupils tested earlier. Consistently superior reading was found for recent students. However, a few comparisons in arithmetic favored the earlier group.

At the high-school level there is some indication of improved achievement recently (3). A normative study of five General Educational Development tests (English grammar, social studies, natural sciences, literary materials, and mathematics) testing 38,773 seniors from a well-constructed sample of 1506 American senior high schools showed that the median score on each test improved over a comparable sample taken in 1943. Despite this improvement in performance of the typical student, there is an indication that the superior students were not better in 1955 than in 1943. Particularly in mathematics it was apparent that the standard deviation was reduced in 1955, making students at the higher percentiles have lower scores than before. This reduction in variability reminds us of the article by Buswell showing smaller variability among Central Californian students than among English students. It should be a source of concern to all educators. We conclude, then, that no consistent evidence has been produced of a change in amount learned from one generation to the next, but that possible trends toward imposing uniform mediocrity deserve further study.

_____ Relation of Testing and Evaluation Methods to Teaching

Three Points of View: Conventional Subject Matter, Test Theory, and Behavioral Objectives Approaches

Among other possibilities, teachers can approach the evaluation of student progress with a conventional subject matter emphasis, a test theory emphasis, or a behavioral objectives emphasis. The *conventional subject matter emphasis* is what one experiences as a student in most college classes; the *test theory emphasis* is reflected by most of the research reported in the present chapter. A new approach, the *behavioral objectives position*, emphasizes the setting of definite goals for a course, so that a teacher can observe the behavior of the students in the course and tell whether or not those goals have been reached. A discussion of these three positions follows in order that the reader may learn some of the strengths and weaknesses of each. Each position will be compared in its approach to a variety of educational issues. There is no intention to distort any of the three positions, but each is oversimplified as presented here.

Methods of Course Content Selection

The conventional subject matter approach is for the teacher or curriculum developer to select a series of topics to be covered within the course in question. This selection may be done alone, with the advice of a number of specialists in the field or specialists in teaching methods, or with students. At the same time the teacher is selecting these topics he may be selecting a textbook or curriculum package which will cover those topics. The reverse may also be true; the teacher may select the textbook he likes and use the topics selected by the author.

The test theory approach may not even be involved at the time of course content selection. If the teacher knows something about test theory, however, he may ask himself, "How do I know that the students don't know this material before they take the course?" or "How can I be sure the course will be pitched at a level of difficulty the students will find challenging but not too difficult?" Such a teacher will check his students' backgrounds to determine if they have studied similar material previously; he will give a pretest to see how much class members know at the beginning of the course; and he will give a carefully constructed final test to determine if students learned as much as he hoped of them.

A teacher pursuing behavioral objectives will first decide exactly what it is that he wants the students to accomplish and then will build the course in such a way that it seems reasonable to expect his goals to be met and that he can tell if they are. This method is more specific about goals than either the conventional subject matter approach or the test theory approach. It is more specific about measuring techniques than the conventional subject matter approach but not more than the test theory approach. Thus the following goal from Walbesser (89) would be appropriate under either the test theory or behavioral objectives approach. "The child can demonstrate whether or not a figure is symmetrical by pointing out its matching (or non-matching) parts."

Advocates of the behavioral objectives approach do not always agree with each other as to what a behavioral objective is. Probably they agree that at least the following is required: We should be able to state what a student has to do if we are to accept it as "evidence that we have achieved, or had a reasonable hope of achieving over time, the objectives toward which curricular or extracurricular experiences were aimed" (39). If this is all that is meant, then any good paper-and-pencil test item may be considered a measure of whether a certain behavioral objective has been met. Either learning the contents of a chapter or learning skills such as the operation of a Bunsen burner could be defined in such a way that we could tell whether a person has accomplished it, whereupon it would be a behavioral objective which one could introduce into a course. Walbesser (89) seems to accept this usage when he says, "Whether this accomplishment is content assimilation or performance is of no real consequence." The behavioral objectives approach emphasized in this paragraph may be termed the *unrestricted behavioral objectives position*.

One possible reason for restricting the behavioral objectives approach is that many educators feel that paper-and-pencil tests measure mere transmission of book knowledge when more important objectives could be established. These educators tend to desire testing procedures which will show improvement in laboratory skills rather than recall of facts or procedures and that will show changes in the ways children behave outside the classroom. Ojemann (62) notes that a pupil may be able to pass a written test on nutrition but might not select a nutritious lunch in the cafeteria except under duress. Therefore, Ojemann urges that special attention be given to behavioral objectives concerning activities pursued when students are not directly under school or parental discipline.

Because of the objections to overemphasis of bookish instruction, Walbesser and Carter (90) reject recall of previously acquired classroom skills as evidence of the meeting of behavioral objectives. They seem to be further troubled by a belief that a behavior was not really acquired if taught directly. This does not appear logical. Regardless of whether a skill was taught directly or transferred from some other learning, it is available for further use. Walbesser and Carter naturally want to teach material which will have transfer value, but it seems unnecessary to require that all tests measure transferred learning. Walbesser and Carter's view is that the unrestricted behavioral objectives position is too broad. It is not sufficient that a behavioral objective be one that can be scientifically tested as met or not met; only certain objectives requiring somewhat more action and more evidence of transfer from the teaching situation than conventional tasks are acceptable. This position is called the *specialized behavioral objectives position* or the *active behavioral objectives position*.

Regardless of how behavioral objectives are defined, courses having this emphasis should be built around the objectives the teacher or course planner selects. This means that the philosophies of teaching and testing become heavily intertwined because almost nothing is presented in class except for the purpose of meeting some behavioral objective for which a test has been devised in the course of specifying the objective.

Standards for Adequacy of Course Planning and Presentation

A conventional subject matter specialist defines the adequacy of his course in relatively subjective terms, considering whether other qualified instructors in the same course would approve of his selection of topics, his analysis of these topics, and his selection of books and other teaching materials. The conventional subject matter specialist also wants to know if his students wrote good term papers and examinations and whether they thought the course was worthwhile. If the specialist is evaluating more than one class, perhaps the teaching of social studies in California, he may seek information and advice from a wide variety of people thereby becoming less subjective in identifying his goals. However, he will still focus upon appropriate content and tend to de-emphasize test theory and behavioral objectives, without necessarily completely overlooking them any more than test theorists or behavioral objectivists will overlook traditional content considerations.

The test theorist looks at the quality of a course from the standpoint of one who knows little about how the teaching was done but knows what at least some of the students should have been learning. Perhaps a test on American History has been developed by a national testing service, and the teacher feels that the test covers the material he wishes his students to have learned. This test may or may not have been selected when the course was planned at a particular school, but now it is administered to a class completing the history course. If the students taking the test score higher, on the average, than the national average score on that test, the course is considered to be more successful than the average course in the nation. (We already know that this may be because the students in this school are more intelligent than the national average; therefore, if possible, this class should be compared to a national average for persons of the same intelligence level as in the class.) The test theorist may also ask if some absolute standard of knowledge, such as that of Flanagan (discussed earlier in this chapter), was achieved, in which case he has moved toward the behavioral objectives position.

The user of behavioral objectives evaluates the effectiveness of a course by asking if his objectives were attained. Usually, though not necessarily, he is concerned with minimal objectives which every student or almost every student should reach. For example, in an extremely important paper Walbesser and Carter (90) have set the following criterion for the course series *Science—A Process Approach* developed under the leadership of Robert Gagné and Henry Walbesser and under the sponsorship of the American Association for the Advancement of Science.

At each grade level from kindergarten through grade 6 about 26 exercises have been prepared which define what every student should be able to do at the end of that grade. Because children do differ in ability, in previous knowledge, and in whether they have taken part in this science series in previous years, Walbesser and Carter established the goal that 90% of the children at each grade level should each pass 90% of the exercises at that grade level by the time they finish that grade.

Walbesser and Carter studied only kindergarteners through third graders. The instructional materials for these children had been developed and revised one summer and tried out for 3 years in the schools, with revision each summer. The tests were given in the third year of use with each set of materials. At least 48 students were tested in each grade. Now how well did the curriculum work? Figure 15-7 graphs the percentage of students meeting the 90% success criterion at each grade level. Note that in no grade were 90% of the students performing at the

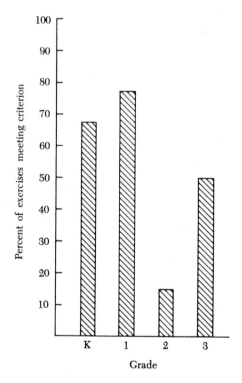

Fig. 15-7. Percentage of students passing 90% of exercises in the *Science—A Process Approach* curriculum at each of four grade levels. Data from Walbesser and Carter (90).

90% level as required. Walbesser and Carter discuss the possibility that further revision of the science teaching materials may permit meeting those goals. However, it seems likely that some of the behavioral objectives for the course series may have to be dropped or deferred to a later year. In part this problem arises because students in the first grade and above who did not receive *Science—A Process Approach* instruction in earlier years do more poorly currently than those who have been in the program continuously since kindergarten. However, the 90–90 criterion was not met even with the latter group, a further indication of difficulty with these materials. Very possibly these behavioral objectives are just too high to be reached by the students for whom they were established.

Okey (62a) points out that averaging data points within each of the first four graphs of Walbesser and Carter yields the following average percentages of persons passing any one of the approximately 26 exercises at each level: K—89.7, 1—90.0, 2—83.2, and 3—84.4. These results seem more favorable than those of Fig. 15-7. However, because students are not perfectly consistent in choosing which exercises they find easiest, these new data *do not* imply that the average kindergarten student passes 89.7% of the items, for example.

In a sense, the Walbesser and Carter study shows that the science curriculum investigated has been a great failure. Yet the strength of the behavioral objectives approach lies right here, in the possibility of showing that a course or curriculum has failed. By comparison, it is somewhat difficult to decide whether the Physical Science Study Committee high-school physics course was or was not successful, even after reading a report of an evaluation conducted in the test theory tradition (26). About the most meaningful indication of the degree of success of the Physical Science Study Committee course is the assertion that the validating tests were designed to be so hard that getting half the questions right would be a creditable performance and that the students did achieve this average level.

With the Walbesser and Carter approach it is possible to establish behavioral objectives for a course, test to see if they are met, and revise instructional procedures until the objectives are met or until it becomes evident that the objectives cannot be attained within the course time available, in which case some new objectives may be developed and some old ones dropped. This method is no magic solution for educational problems; it may often be expected to fail the way it did for Walbesser and Carter. But even then, teachers will know exactly what has been achieved; this is a very real advantage. This method will take a good deal of time to use effectively. In some cases teachers will be best advised to wait for organizations such as the American Association for the Advancement of Science to establish committees to develop and test new curricula. However, there will be other courses or parts of courses for which individual teachers will wish to establish their own behavioral objectives and test for accomplishment of those objectives.

Standards for Adequacy of Student Performance

Conventional subject matter specialists tend to judge the quality of student work in a course by comparing each student's written (and perhaps oral) contributions to the class with other students' contributions and some "absolute standard" the teacher has developed, which may be completely subjective or may be as specific as the numerical standards for letter grades mentioned at the beginning of this chapter.

Test theory specialists may do a similar evaluation procedure but will emphasize the need to establish reliable and valid measures of performance in a course. Grades will be assigned either on the basis of how high a student ranks compared to other past or present students of the course or on the basis of meeting certain absolute standards, i.e., specific score values.

The advocate of behavioral objectives wants all students to meet certain minimal standards. Walbesser and Carter (90) felt it impractical to require 100% of students to meet a criterion of correct on 90% of the test exercises, but it appears that they would have desired 100% to do so. In a highly developed instructional system using the behavioral sciences approach, we would expect that 100% of students would be required to meet a certain minimal criterion. Students who did not do so after the system had been sufficiently revised to seem practical would be given remedial training before being advanced to the next stage.

We believe that it is also necessary to establish behavioral objectives of greater than minimal level, expecting that whereas 100% of students might be expected to pass level 1, and 70% might be expected to pass level 2, only 40% might be expected to pass level 3, and so on. This procedure would take into account that students differ in the amounts they can learn and that classroom material differs in whether it is universally useful or important only for certain persons to learn. We also believe that the standards should be flexible enough to allow all students to learn some materials which are most interesting to them personally.

Summary

1. Evaluation is the overall process of assessing pupils' development in school. Evaluation may be either quantitative or qualitative. The

former is called measurement and receives primary attention in this chapter.

2. The reason for standardizing a test is to learn such properties as the mean score, standard deviation, value of a reliability coefficient, and value of a validity coefficient of the test.

3. Reliability means consistency of results. It is typically expressed as a correlation coefficient. Three ways in which reliability may be measured are (a) by correlating scores obtained on successive administrations of the same test, (b) by correlating scores obtained on equivalent or parallel forms of the same test, and (c) by correlating the scores obtained on half the items of the test with the scores obtained on the other half.

4. Validity is the measurement of the degree to which a test meets the goals for which it was constructed. Three types of validity are (a) content validity (the degree to which the questions asked are representative of the entire body of material to be taught), (b) criterion-related validity (the degree to which test scores correlate with a criterion such as college grades or success in an occupation), and (c) construct validity (the degree to which all theory and knowledge about the construct being measured seems consistent with the measurement procedure actually used).

5. A major problem with essay tests is that within-reader reliability (consistency of one reader in grading the same papers twice) and inter-reader reliability (consistency of two or more readers in grading the same papers once each) are low. This problem is greatest for the sort of essays employed as assignments in English composition classes. Within-reader or inter-reader reliability may be quite satisfactory in certain kinds of short answer tests, however.

6. Reliability of essay grading can be increased by having several persons grade each paper and using the average grade for each paper as the officially recorded grade. Computer scoring of essays is also being used experimentally as a means of improving reliability of essay grading.

7. Despite the difficulty of grading English composition papers reliably, scoring can be made unbiased enough to demonstrate a definite improvement in students' essays over a semester or two.

8. A basic procedure used in deciding which test items to keep after an objective test is tried out is as follows. Discover which persons had the highest total test scores and which had the lowest. (Various proportions of such persons are acceptable, but there is some reason to use 27% in each group.) Then determine the proportion of persons in the high group who pass each item and the proportion in the low group who pass each item. If the difference between these two proportions for any item is high, that item is discriminating between the two groups of people. Keep such items and discard or revise all others.

9. A major recent study of ability grouping indicates that, by itself, the practice of dividing a group of students in one grade into different classroom units with each unit having students of a homogeneous and different intelligence level has very little effect, if any, upon course achievement.

10. Project Talent, a nationwide survey of high-school students, has developed some achievement tests which tell how much a student knows in absolute terms rather than merely in test scores whose meaning must be derived from a comparison with other persons' scores. Project Talent found, for example, that, on the average, twelfth-grade girls can spell 95% of the 5000 most commonly used English words.

11. A correlation of 0.60 between academic aptitude and achievement test scores will not permit precise prediction of individual achievement scores. However, there is only a 2% probability that a person in the highest fifth of the aptitude score distribution will score in the lowest fifth on achievement or that a person in the lowest fifth on aptitude will score in the highest fifth on achievement. Better predictions than this occur with higher correlations; poorer with lower correlations.

12. Mathematics achievement in schools in the United States is lower for 13-year-olds than in several other highly developed countries. However, when the fact of universal education in the United States is taken into account, the further inferiority of American high-school seniors in mathematics disappears or nearly disappears. Furthermore, the United States ranks high in its development of persons with potential for graduate study in mathematics or allied fields.

13. Comparisons of academic achievement of American school children over periods of 11 or more years give inconsistent results: In some cases performance by the newer generation is superior; in others it is inferior. If one takes as the most important data the final level of achievement for most students, one should emphasize that there is some indication of recent improvement in achievement at the high-school level.

14. Teachers and other educational planners have formerly taken a conventional subject matter approach or a test theory approach to the evaluation of curricula and of student progress. Test theory has largely provided concepts such as reliability and validity for subject matter specialists to consider in making or selecting measuring devices for their courses. Recently a third approach, that of establishing behavioral objectives, teaching in such a way as to achieve them, and checking to see if they are achieved, has been advocated. A behavioral objective is a goal which is so specifically stated that a procedure can be devised to see whether a student has reached that goal. (Some educators prefer that such goals represent changes in everyday behavior rather than

ability to pass conventional classroom tests.) The behavioral objectives approach has the advantage that, when fully practiced, it includes a testing stage which definitely tells whether or not the behavioral objectives of a class have been satisfied. Further use of the method is required before we can tell whether it actually produces better teaching and evaluation than older techniques requiring the same amount of planning and effort.

SUGGESTED READINGS

Maynard, F. B., & Mainwaring, M. The cat who went to college. In R. A. Baker (Ed.), *Psychology in the wry*. Princeton, N. J.: Van Nostrand, 1963. Pp. 82–90.

This is a poem ridiculing the excessive use of test scores as bases for counseling students about which courses to take.

Ricks, J. H., Jr. On telling parents about test results. In W. H. McGinitie & S. Ball (Eds.), *Readings in psychological foundations of education*. New York: McGraw-Hill, 1968. Pp. 175–180.

Some advice to teachers and counselors about whether or how to tell parents their children's standardized test results. This article emphasizes the importance of conveying the real information from a test, not simply a test score or even a percentile ranking.

REFERENCES

1. Basumallik, T. Reliability of essay-type examinations: a review of studies. *Journal of Educational Psychology, Baroda*, 1959, **17**, 127–156.
2. Bauernfeind, R. H. *Building a school testing program*. Boston: Houghton Mifflin, 1963. P. 87.
3. Bloom, B. S. 1955 normative study of the tests of G.E.D. *School Review*, 1956, **64**, 110–124.
4. Bloom, B. S. (Ed.) *Taxonomy of educational objectives*. Handbook I. *Cognitive domain*. New York: Longmans, Green, 1956.
5. Bloom, B. S. Cooperative General Culture Test, college, 1930–1956. In O. K. Buros (Ed.), *Fifth mental measurements yearbook*. Highland Park, N. J.: Gryphon Press, 1959. Pp. 15–17.
6. Brown, W. Some experimental results in the correlation of mental abilities. *British Journal of Psychology*, 1910, **3**, 296–332.
7. Burke, N. F., & Anderson, K. E. Comparative study of 1939 and 1950 achievement test results in the Hawthorne Elementary School in Ottawa, Kansas. *Journal of Educational Research*, 1953, **47**, 19–33.
8. Buros, O. K. (Ed.) *The sixth mental measurements yearbook*. Highland Park, N. J.: Gryphon Press, 1965.
9. Buswell, G. T. Comparison of achievement in England and central California. *Arithmetic Teacher*, 1958, **5**, 1–9.

10. Caldwell, O. W., & Courtis, S. A. *Then and now in education.* Yonkers, N. Y.: World Book, 1925. Pp. 87, 275–281.

11. Carnett, G. S. Is our mathematics inferior? *Mathematics Teacher,* 1967, **60**, 582–587.

12. Clark, K. B., & Plotkin, L. *The Negro student at integrated colleges.* New York: National Scholarship Service and Fund for Negro Students, 1963.

13. Coleman, W., Fish, L. E., & Ward, A. W. Community size and educational outcome. *High School Journal,* 1955, **38**, 138–141.

14. Cowles, J. T., & Hubber, J. P. A comparative study of essay and objective examinations for medical studies. *Journal of Medical Education,* 1952, **23**, 14–17.

15. Cressey, P. F. The influence of the literary examination system on the development of Chinese civilization. *American Journal of Sociology,* 1929, **35**, 250–252.

16. Cronbach, L. J. Coefficient Alpha and the internal structure of tests. *Psychometrika,* 1951, **16**, 297–309.

17. Cronbach, L. J. *Essentials of psychological testing.* (2nd ed.) New York: Harper, 1960. Pp. 129, 133, 221–223.

18. Cronbach, L. J., & Gleser, G. G. *Psychological tests and personnel decisions.* Urbana, Ill.: University of Illinois Press, 1965.

19. Cubberley, E. P. *Public education in the United States.* (Rev. ed.) Boston: Houghton Mifflin, 1934. Pp. 332–333.

20. Diederich, P. B. Making and using tests. *English Journal,* 1955, **44**, 135–140, 151.

21. Diederich, P. B. The problem of grading essays. Paper presented at the College Testing Conference, Mount Union College, Alliance, Ohio, February, 1957.

22. Durost, W. N., & Prescott, G. A. *Essentials of measurement for teachers.* New York: Harcourt, Brace & World, 1962. P. 17.

23. Ebel, R. L. The relation of item discrimination to test reliability. *Journal of Educational Measurement,* 1967, **4**, 125–128.

24. Engelhart, M. D. Examinations. In W. S. Monroe (Ed.), *Encyclopedia of educational research.* New York: Macmillan, 1950. Pp. 407–414.

25. Engelhart, M. D. A comparison of several item discrimination indices. *Journal of Educational Measurement,* 1965, **2**, 69–76.

26. Ferris, F. L., Jr. An achievement test report. *Science Teacher,* 1959, **26**, 576–579.

27. Findley, W. G. How objective can free-style measures of writing ability be? *English Record,* 1953, **4**, 19–25.

28. Findley, W. G. Progress in the measurement of achievement. *Educational and Psychological Measurement,* 1954, **14**, 255–260.

29. Finlayson, D. S. The reliability of marking essays. *British Journal of Educational Psychology,* 1951, **21**, 126–134.

30. Flanagan, J. C. Units, scores, and norms. In E. F. Lindquist (Ed.), *Educational measurement.* Washington, D. C.: American Council on Education, 1951. Pp. 695–763.

31. Flanagan, J. C. Maximizing human talents. *Journal of Teacher Education,* 1962, **13**, 209–215.

32. Flanagan, J. C., Davis, F. B., Dailey, J. T., Shaycoft, M. F., Orr, D. B., Goldberg, I., & Neyman, C. A., Jr. *Project Talent. The identification, development, and utilization of human talents. The American high school student.* Pittsburgh: University of Pittsburgh, 1964. Pp. 1/4, 3/96–3/113.

33. Foshay, A. W. International study of mathematics achievement. *Education Digest,* 1967(November), **33**, 40–42.

34. French, J. W. The creativity dimension in student writing. In M. H. Elliott

(Chmn.), *11th annual western regional conference on testing problems. Creativity: Its assessment and measurement.* Los Angeles: Educational Testing Service, 1962. Pp. 45–59.

35. Fricke, B. G. National Merit Scholarship Qualifying Test. In O. K. Buros (Ed.), *Fifth mental measurements yearbook.* Highland Park, N. J.: Gryphon Press, 1959. Pp. 42–46.

36. Gage, N. L. Stanford Achievement Test (1953 revision). In O. K. Buros (Ed.), *Fifth mental measurements yearbook.* Highland Park, N. J.: Gryphon Press, 1959. Pp. 75–80.

37. Garber, H. The digital computer simulates human rating behavior. In J. T. Flynn & H. Garber (Eds.), *Assessing behavior: Readings in educational and psychological measurement.* Reading, Mass.: Addison-Wesley, 1967. Pp. 367–373.

38. Gates, A. I., & LaSalle, J. The relative predictive value of certain intelligence and educational tests together with a study of the effect of educational achievement upon intelligence test scores. *Journal of Educational Psychology,* 1923, **14**, 517–539.

38a. Godshalk, F. I., Swineford, F., & Coffman, W. E. *The measurement of writing ability.* New York: College Entrance Examination Board, 1966.

39. Gideonse, H. D. Behavioral objectives: continuing the dialogue. *Science Teacher,* 1969, **36**, No. 1, 51–54.

40. Goldberg, M. L., Passow, A. H., & Justman, J. *The effects of ability grouping.* New York: Teachers College, Columbia University, Bureau of Publications, 1966.

41. Greene, H. A., Jorgensen, A. N., & Gerberich, J. R. *Measurement and evaluation in the secondary school.* New York: Longmans, Green, 1953. P. 22.

42. Gulliksen, H. The content reliability of a test. *Psychometrika,* 1936, **1**, 189–194.

43. Gulliksen, H. *Theory of mental tests.* New York: Wiley, 1950.

44. Hildreth, G. H. Results of repeated measurement of pupil achievement. *Journal of Educational Psychology,* 1930, **21**, 286–296.

45. Hoffmann, B. *The tyranny of testing.* New York: Crowell-Collier, 1962.

46. Howell, J. J., & Weiner, M. Note on the equivalence of alternate forms of an achievement test. *Educational and Psychological Measurement,* 1961, **21**, 309–313.

47. Hurlburt, D. The relative values of recall and recognition techniques for measuring precise knowledge of word meaning—nouns, verbs, adjectives. *Journal of Educational Research,* 1954, **47**, 561–576.

48. Husen, T. *International studies of achievement in mathematics. A comparison of twelve countries.* Stockholm: Almqvist & Wiksell, New York: Wiley, 1967. 2 vols. Vol. II, pp. 135–138, 170–174.

49. Jackson, R. W. B. Sequential tests of educational progress. In O. K. Buros (Ed.), *Fifth mental measurements yearbook.* Highland Park, N. J.: Gryphon Press, 1959. Pp. 62–67.

50. Johnson, E. A. The crisis in science and technology and its effect on military development. *Operations Research,* 1958, **6**, 11–34.

51. Joint committee of the American Psychological Association, American Educational Research Association, and National Council on Measurement in Education. *Standards for educational and psychological tests and manuals.* Washington, D. C.: American Psychological Association, 1966.

52. Krathwohl, D. R., Bloom, B. S., & Masia, B. B. *Taxonomy of educational objectives. The classification of educational goals.* Handbook II. *Affective domain.* New York: McKay, 1964.

53. Kuder, G. F., & Richardson, M. W. The theory of the estimation of test reliability. *Psychometrika*, 1937, **2**, 151–166.

54. Kurtz, A. K. Research in the selection of life insurance salesmen. *Journal of Applied Psychology*, 1941, **25**, 11–17.

55. Lange, A., Lehmann, I. J., & Mehrens, W. A. Using item analysis to improve tests. *Journal of Educational Measurement*, 1967, **4**, 65–68.

56. Lannholm, G. V. Educational growth during the last two years of college. *Educational and Psychological Measurement*, 1952, **12**, 645–653.

57. Lanton, W. Proof of the pudding. *Phi Delta Kappan*, 1954, **36**, 136.

58. Meehl, P. E. *Clinical versus actuarial prediction.* Minneapolis: University of Minnesota Press, 1954.

58a. Mehrens, W. A. National assessment through September, 1969. *Phi Delta Kappan*, 1969, **51**, 215–217.

59. Miller, V. V. Reading achievement of school children, then and now. *Elementary English*, 1956, 33, 91–97.

60. Noyes, E. S. Essay and objective tests in English. *College Board Review*, 1963, **49**, 7–10.

61. Nunnally, J. C. *Educational measurement and evaluation.* New York: McGraw-Hill, 1964. Pp. 103–104.

62. Ojemann, R. H. Should educational objectives be stated in behavioral terms? *Elementary School Journal*, 1968, **68**, 223–231.

62a. Okey, J. Personal communication, November, 1969.

63. Olsen, M. *The validity of the College Board General Composition Test.* Statistical Report No. 55–4. Princeton, N. J.: Educational Testing Service, 1955.

64. Osborne, R. T., & Sanders, W. B. Comparative decline of Graduate Record Examination scores and intelligence with age. *Journal of Educational Psychology*, 1954, **45**, 353–358.

65. Osborne, R. T., & Sanders, W. B. Recency and type of undergraduate training and decline of G.R.E. performance with age. *Journal of Educational Psychology*, 1956, **47**, 276–284.

66. Sanders, W. B., Osborne, R. T., & Greene, J. E. Intelligence and academic performance of college students of urban, rural, and mixed background. *Journal of Educational Research*, 1955, **49**, 185–193.

67. Savage, L. J. *Foundations of statistics.* New York: Wiley, 1954.

68. Scates, D. E. Fifty years of objective measurement and research in education. *Journal of Educational Research*, 1947, **41**, 241–264.

69. Schrader, W. B. A taxonomy of expectancy values. *Journal of Educational Measurement*, 1965, **2**, 29–35.

70. Shannon, C. E. *The mathematical theory of communication.* Urbana, Ill.: University of Illinois Press, 1949.

71. Snow, C. P. On magnanimity. *Harpers*, 1962(July), **225**, 37–41.

72. Spearman, C. Correlation calculated with faulty data. *British Journal of Psychology*, 1910, 3, 271–295.

73. Spearman, C. The proof and measurement of association between two things. *American Journal of Psychology*, 1940, **15**, 72–101.

74. Stake, R. E. Overestimation of achievement with the California Achievement Test. *Educational and Psychological Measurement*, 1961, **21**, 59–62.

75. Stalnaker, J. M. Essay examinations reliably read. *School and Society*, 1937, **46**, 671–672.

76. Stalnaker, J. M. Question VI, the essay. *English Journal (College Edition)*, 1937, **26**, 133–140.

77. Stalnaker, J. M. The essay type of examination. In E. F. Lindquist (Ed.), *Educational measurement*. Washington, D. C.: American Council on Education, 1951. Pp. 495–530.

78. Stroud, J. B., Blommers, P., & Lauber, M. Correlation analysis of WISC and achievement tests. *Journal of Educational Psychology*, 1957, **48**, 18–26.

79. Swineford, F. Reader reliability of the General Composition Test, Form H. In-house publication of the Educational Testing Service, Princeton, N. J., 1954.

80. Swineford, F. Reliability of an inter linear test of writing ability. *School and Society*, 1955, **81**, 25–27.

81. Swineford, F. Test analysis of the CEEB Advance Placement Tests, Form EBP. In-house publication of the Educational Testing Service, Princeton, N. J., 1956.

82. Taylor, E. A., & Crandall, J. H. Study of the non-equivalence of certain tests approved for the California state testing program. *California Journal of Educational Research*, 1962, **13**, 186–192.

83. Thorndike, E. L., & Lorge, I. *The teacher's word book of 30,000 words*. New York: Teachers College, Columbia University, Bureau of Publications, 1944.

84. Thorndike, R. L. *Community factors related to intelligence and achievement of school children*. 1949 Official Report. Washington, D. C.: American Educational Research Association, 1949. Pp. 265–271.

85. Thurstone, L. L., & Thurstone, T. G. Factorial studies of intelligence. *Psychometric Monographs*, 1941, No. 2.

86. Traxler, A. E. The status of measurement and appraisal programs of large city school systems. *Educational Records Bulletin*, 1953, No. 61, 75–86.

87. Traxler, A. E. The status of statewide testing programs. *Educational Records Bulletin*, 1954, No. 63, 86–92.

88. Traxler, A. E., & Anderson, H. A. Reliability of an essay examination in English. *School Review*, 1935, **43**, 534–539.

89. Walbesser, H. H. Science curriculum evaluation: observations on a position. *Science Teacher*, 1966, **33**, 34–39.

90. Walbesser, H. H., & Carter, H. Some methodological considerations of curriculum evaluation research. *Educational Leadership*, 1968, **26**, No. 1, 53–64.

91. Watson, R. I. *The great psychologists from Aristotle to Freud*. Philadelphia: Lippincott, 1963. P. 267.

92. Wiseman, S. The marking of English composition in grammar school selection. *British Journal of Educational Psychology*, 1949, **19**, 200–209.

93. Wood, B. D. Measurement in higher education. Yonkers, N. Y.: World Book, 1923. P. 193.

94. Wood, D. A. *Test construction. Development and interpretation of achievement tests*. Columbus, Ohio: Merrill, 1960. Pp. 14–16, 102–107.

16

THE SOCIAL PSYCHOLOGY
OF THE CLASSROOM

Man's tendencies toward social behavior are so strong and so uniform that they are sometimes said to be instinctual. Although social behavior cannot qualify as instinctual, it is evident that man is especially characterized by his social heritage and social environment. Even the human infant, who depends on his adult caretaker for the gratification of physical demands for food and relief from pain, is at the same time being indoctrinated in normal patterns of social interaction that will characterize him the remainder of his life. Indeed, some investigators (see Chapter 13) believe that if at a certain critical period in the infant's life he does not receive the care and loving attention of a human "mother," he will be permanently impaired in his capacity for establishing social relationships (17, 32, 33, 81). The likelihood of anyone's choosing to live like a hermit is so remote that the benefits of early socialization are most important. Thus, even though man is not instinctively sociable, the nature of his experience and the pressures of his social environment make him inescapably so.

Although the basic principles of learning, the nature of intelligence, and psychophysiology may all be examined without reference to man's social environment and social behavior, it is not possible that man's social behavior can be adequately considered independently. Ultimately, psychology must put man in his social context, and it is the purpose of this chapter to consider some of the implications for behavior of man's social heritage and environment.

Each child begins life in a social environment and is susceptible to a wide variety of influences that will mold him and substantially influence his view of the world and his responses to it. Although infants may go through a period critical to their social development, the major research that can serve as a basis for our discussion has been done with children of school age.

The Classroom as a Social Situation

Of course, the school classroom is itself a society, the creator of its own social situation. This obvious fact is often overlooked, so that discussions of teaching and learning usually describe the typical classroom as if it had one teacher and one pupil. Discussions of disciplinary measures often seem to be based on the assumption that a teacher may do as she pleases with a given pupil, as if their interaction could be carried on in perfect privacy instead of before a classroom of 29 other pupils. Except for some consideration of the effects of competition on performance and, perhaps, of popularity, the relationships among pupils are largely ignored. But a classroom is, among other things, a laboratory in social behavior. Everything that takes place within the classroom makes its impact on the social situation that is inherent there.

Of the many aspects of the classroom the few listed here particularly define the social forces that are operative.

First, although the classroom is a social situation involving a sizable number of persons who find themselves interacting quite regularly, there is a final and inescapable emphasis on the individual outcomes of the educational experience. At the end of the term it is the individual, not the group, who will be judged. Thus, the classroom differs from situations in which the performance of the individual is of less, even of little, importance in comparison to the performance of the group. In a baseball game it makes little difference if a batter strikes out but his team wins the game. But it makes a good deal of difference if one child fails to learn but the rest of the class does well. One consequence of the emphasis on individual merit is that a class may often be engaged in parallel but not cooperative activity. In fact, cooperation may be actively discouraged although it is considered quite desirable in most other social activities.

A second distinguishing aspect of the classroom situation is the emphasis on accomplishment. Some social psychologists have made a distinction between *task orientation* and *group maintenance orientation* (e.g., 84). The former refers to an intent to accomplish some task of extrinsic value, something "worthwhile." Group maintenance orientation is simply a primary interest in seeing to it that the group survives, ordinarily in good harmony, whether it accomplishes anything or not. Indeed, some groups, e.g., social fraternities, have as their avowed purpose maintenance goals, i.e., harmonious social relations, fellowship. In the classroom maintenance activities are usually considered secondary to the accomplishment of the primary task of instruction.

Task orientation in the educational situation can be seen in two different ways, depending upon whether it is from the viewpoint of the teacher or of the pupil. However, their joint task is, in part, to develop particular attitudes in the pupils. It may be said that it is not the task of the school to influence attitudes, yet the school most certainly is influential with respect to science, democracy, books, personal hygiene, and a host of other things.

If the teacher is fortunate, attitudes need to be developed from scratch, i.e., no prior disposition exists in those areas or the attitudes merely need to be strengthened. Most students begin school with no particular attitude toward science, and it is partly the school's task to develop one. In other instances, however, attitudes may need to be developed that counter existing attitudes or are being fostered in the larger community of which the child is a part. It might seem simple to foster favorable attitudes toward science, but there are other beliefs with which such attitudes conflict, e.g., superstitions. In either case the school and the teacher are inevitably involved in the complex tasks of communication and persuasion. The conditions under which effective communication occurs and which are conducive to attitude changes are discussed later in the chapter.

One of the important factors bearing on communication within a group is the intragroup structure or organization, for the organization will determine the channels of communication, the importance of various messages, and even their content. The group structure of the classroom is relatively uniform, which distinguishes it from many other, but certainly not all, groups. For example, there are gross age and status differences between the teacher and the pupils; the teacher is appointed to the pupils and cannot be removed by them; the goals of the teacher are often at considerable variance with the goals of the pupils; all the members of the group save the teacher are presumably equal in status and function within the group.

Finally, the classroom group is different in size from other groups, different in the inherent patterns of participation by group members, and different in the patterns of leadership which are likely to emerge. It is apparent that size has a lot to do with the kinds of interactions one group member has with other members of the same group—a fact often ignored in discussions of classroom activities. Moreover, it is fundamental to our educational philosophy that learning proceeds best when it is planned and guided, hence the continual discussions about curriculum planning. Therefore, there are limitations on the leader–follower patterns which can possibly be worked out in the classroom. Considerations such as these will lead to a discussion of the kinds of factors conducive both to individual and group problem solving and to the maintenance of those conditions in the educational situation.

Reinforcement and Learning in the Social Situation

Suppose a small boy, Johnny, saw his friend Billy approach a box on the playground, put his hand in, and come away with a fine lollipop. Wouldn't Johnny's tendency be to approach the box and put his hand in? Just such experiments have been done (67), and children do in fact learn very quickly to copy the behavior of a child who has been successful in, say, getting candy out of a box. Suppose, though, that Johnny saw Billy put his hand in and then pull it out quickly and shake it as if it had been hurt. What would happen to Johnny's box-approaching disposition then? Nothing has really happened to Johnny. Yet his behavior will probably change just as if he, himself, had performed Billy's acts and received the consequences. Somehow, Johnny has acquired a habit by observation. This interesting phenomenon turns out to have many facets and many ramifications for learning and behavior in social situations.

First, what are the ways in which one person might acquire the capacity to model his behavior after that of another person? Probably the first answer to that would be "imitation." But that is not much of an answer until we are able to specify why imitation occurs and the conditions under which it will occur. It was toward that end that some early experiments by Miller and Dollard (67) were directed. They were reinforcement learning theorists, and they did not see why it should be necessary to suppose the existence of any special characteristics in order to account for imitative behavior. They suggested that it is possible for the behavior of one organism to become a discriminative stimulus for the behavior of another organism, and that, depending upon the pattern of reinforcements associated with either imitating or not imitating another organism, imitative or nonimitative behaviors will be established. So they designed some experiments in which a rat ran down a short runway while being observed by a second rat. At the end of the runway the first rat went either right or left, and the second rat was then allowed to follow or not. When the second rat got to the choosing point, he could either go the same way as the first rat (imitate) or go the other way (nonimitate). It was found that the behavior of the second rat was a function of the reinforcements administered. If he was reinforced for imitating, he would imitate. If he was reinforced for nonimitation, he would not imitate. The behavior of the second rat became dependent upon the behavior of the first rat, and Miller and Dollard used the term *matched-dependent* behavior in lieu of the less precise term imitation. Other experiments were done to show that matched-dependent behavior was generalizable, i.e., that once it was established as a pattern for one situation or one response, it would carry over to other situations and other responses and also to other leaders. Thus Miller and Dollard showed that for rats (and, in other experiments, for children) the behavior of imitating others can be acquired in the same way as other habits, i.e., by repeated elicitation and reinforcement.

Probably every child has a history of many reinforcements for doing as others do, particularly when it looks as if the consequences for other persons have been favorable. And when it appears that the consequences of a behavior for another person have been unfavorable, children have had many opportunities to learn by negative reinforcement not to engage in that behavior. What Billy is spanked for, Johnny is likely to be spanked for. The capacity to learn from the experiences of others is immensely important in maximizing the economy of learning, for it means that many people should be able to learn from the experiences of only one person. It is probably especially valuable for behaviors with dangerous or otherwise undesirable consequences which we would not like everyone to experience. In fact, an important theory about the control of criminal behavior suggests that criminals will learn to be better citizens by seeing (or reading about) their fellow criminals punished for their crimes.

Actually the situation is considerably more complicated than indicated thus far, for a number of different things can be learned from observing the behavior of another person and its consequences (20). Obviously one may learn a specific response and its consequences from seeing it performed and observing the outcome. However, one may also learn a specific response without observing any particular consequence. A child may learn to walk like his father even though he has never seen his father reinforced for walking the way he does, nor is the child ever obviously reinforced for that behavior. If the father is generally successful in the eyes of the child, i.e., is admired, his behaviors may be acquired even though they are largely or completely irrelevant to the father's actual success in society. It is also clear that totally irrelevant responses may be acquired by observation just as they may be acquired directly. The observer may also learn in a general way the responses appropriate to a particular situation even though he has never seen anyone actually reinforced for those responses.

If it can be assumed that the net reinforcement experiences of people are positive (otherwise behavior would be extinguished), then it can also be assumed that where there is uniformity in behavior, that behavior is positively reinforced. Finally, through observation a person may learn about the kinds of reinforcements which are likely in a given situation even though he does not learn the specific ways of gaining those reinforcements. This kind of learning has been the source of some persistent misunderstandings. A child may easily learn that the attention of the teacher is valued, but he may not learn how to get that attention. Similarly, visitors to the United States from many economically less fortunate countries can more easily discern the rewards for desirable behavior—e.g., fine houses, automobiles—than they can discern the behavior by which those rewards are obtained.

In their review of research on observational learning Bandura and Walters (6) point to three possible bases for behavioral change as a function of observing the behavior of a model. First, a model may display behaviors which are novel to the observer (modeling), and the observer may then try them himself, especially if the consequences are positive. Bandura, Ross, and Ross (5), for example, had children watch models behaving aggressively in a playroom, and they found that the observing children later went through very similar patterns of behavior in the same situation, patterns which they had almost certainly never before displayed.

A second effect of observing may be to change the level of inhibition with respect to a particular response. For example, in our society it is typical that children are punished for aggressive responses, and they learn to inhibit many forms of aggression. However, an aggressive model who goes unpunished may serve as a cue to the observer that aggression is "safe" in that particular situation, and the level of inhibition may be decreased. On the other hand, observing a passive, compliant model in a situation which would seem likely to produce frustration might serve as a cue to the inappropriateness of aggression, and in the same situation an observer might have an increased level of inhibition with respect to aggressive responses.

And third, Bandura and Walters suggest that the responses of a model may simply serve as a "releaser" for similar responses by the observer, an effect which they refer to as *eliciting*. Presumably there might be responses which do not occur at a particular time because the observer just has not thought of them but which are not being inhibited in any way. The responses of a model might serve as cues for the appropriateness of the given response. For example, an adolescent boy might see a friend on his way to the hangout wearing a particular kind of jacket and think to himself, "Say, I think I'll wear my new jacket tonight." That no cognitive elements are necessary in the eliciting process is indicated by the example of Bandura and Walters of the way in which people returning to their home communities revert to accents and speech patterns which they would ordinarily no longer display.

Obviously, not all "models" are equally likely to be emulated. Some persons are imitated, some are not. If one had to make a blind bet at a race track and could follow either a prosperous looking gentleman or a seedy looking bum to the $5 window, the choice would be obvious. And in experimental situations it is easily established that successful, consistently rewarded models are likely to be imitated by those who have an opportunity to observe them (67, 74). In a typical classroom situation a popular, successful child is more likely to be imitated by other pupils than a student who is notably unsuccessful.

Two varieties of success are relevant to deciding whether or not an individual is likely to be emulated. First, a potential model may be generally successful and may inspire imitation even though he has never been observed in the specific situation in question. The prosperous gentleman at the racetrack would be an example of the generally successful person who inspires confidence. However, there may also be specific competencies that will override considerations of overall success. The batting stance of a champion slugger will be imitated by small boys whether the champion is successful or not in other ventures, e.g., intellectual pursuits. Some people may be imitated simply because they look as if they *could* be successful in a given field—whether they have actually been observed or not. The studious *looking* boy may be imitated in the classroom on the first day of school even though no one really knows him, and the athletic *looking* boy may be imitated on the playground even though his athletic competence has never been demonstrated. Finally, those people who are likely to be imitated look as if they are well endowed with the kind of reinforcement valued by the observer, e.g., the studious boy will be imitated chiefly by those students who value the reinforcements which come from studious behavior. One possible factor in nonimitation which remains to be investigated experimentally is that a model may be too successful, i.e., he may be so perfect that he is not regarded by possible imitators as an appropriate model for them because they do not conceive of the possibility of matching his performance. The brightest child in a schoolroom will not necessarily be most often imitated. Other children may think of him as so bright, so perfect, so different from themselves that he is nonimitatible.

Their model may well be a student who sets a more reasonable standard of performance.

There are some kinds of responding based upon observational learning that seem not to involve imitation. Some other process is involved. For example, suppose one person witnesses another person being hurt. Even though there is no special relationship between the two persons, the observer may experience an emotional arousal much as if he himself were being hurt. The observer's experience is "vicarious." Berger (10) has shown that it is possible to condition an observer's galvanic skin response (GSR) to electric shocks being administered to someone else. The capacity for that kind of vicarious experience probably has its genesis in a complex series of early happenings by which the child learns that his welfare and fate are inextricably tied up with the welfare and fate of other persons. Part of this process is *identification,* a state that can be defined in terms of *the tendency to respond to reinforcements administered to another person as if they had been administered to oneself.** The individual who has learned to identify with others quickly and easily can suffer or bask in reflected glory depending upon the fortunes of his momentary "identity." In fact, if someone's vicarious experience is strong enough, he may even be relieved of some of the necessity for personal action. This may be regarded as a danger for the boy who is so gratified at the exploits of a hero that he does nothing himself, but there are also circumstances when being relieved of pressure of the need for personal action could be desirable. A good example is provided by the research of Rosenbaum and deCharms (73) who put Ss in an experimental situation in which they thought they were being very much insulted by another experimental S, and in which, it might be assumed, they had rather strong dispositions to some sort of counteraggression. However, the aggressive tendencies were reduced by vicarious aggressions carried on by a third, nonparticipating person. Thus, pressures for personal action of an aggressive nature were reduced without any overt action.

Vicarious gratification of desires is possible to all of us in some degree, but the critical test for gratification of a desire is whether on some subsequent occasion the strength of that desire has been decreased. For example, is it likely that watching another person eat a good meal would decrease one's own hunger?

On the other hand, books and plays and conversations are full of accounts of parents who have supposedly gratified some of their own desires through the activities of their children, wives who have ex-

---

* This definition differs slightly from the one by Kagan (47) which is quoted in Chapter 12, but we believe that the two definitions are substantially equivalent.

perienced gratification of their own wishes for power through their husband's actions, and the like. However, it would be difficult to demonstrate that the motives involved actually decreased in strength. Indeed, in some of the accounts there is little evidence of diminution in the strength of the motivation. Moreover, it is necessary to distinguish the true vicarious effect from the direct reinforcement that might accrue as the result of the actions of another person. For example, a woman whose husband gains greater power is herself likely to be rewarded directly with material incentives. It might be asked then whether it is the power of her husband she appreciates or the power she exercises through her husband. There is nothing vicarious in the gratifications one could get through the actions of a robot under one's own control.

Effects like those discussed may operate in the classroom, as proved by a variety of investigations. Barnwell and Sechrest (7) found that first-grade children are likely to choose to work on a task for which one of their classmates has been rewarded and to avoid the task if a classmate has been reproved for his performance on it.

Kounin and Gump (52) have described the "ripple effect" in classroom discipline which is the spreading of the impact of the teacher's disciplinary efforts from their direct object to the remainder of the class. Additionally, it has been shown that when a class sees a disciplined student submit to a teacher's control techniques, the teacher is perceived to be more expert and powerful, and the control technique is judged to be fairer than if the student is successfully defiant (31).

An amusing example of spreading the effect of a disciplinary effort and proof that the effect has long been recognized at the practical level is provided by Fielding in his novel *Tom Jones*. In the scene in question, Black George, the untrustworthy gamekeeper, has become angry, and he has just taken a switch to his wife and beaten her. "The whole family were soon reduced to a state of perfect quiet; for the virtue of this medicine, like that of electricity, is often communicated through one person to many others who are not touched by the instrument" (27).

Competition for Reinforcement

The matched-dependent and imitative situations already discussed are characterized by the implicit understanding that the supply of reinforcements is not limited in any way. Or, for imitation to make sense, the occurrence of a reinforcement for a given person should not *decrease* the probability of similar reinforcements for observers. However, there are many situations in which individuals may see themselves in competition for an exhaustible supply of reinforcements. A good example is the dispensing of school grades and honors on the basis of a percentage system. If one child is known to have received an "A," that results in a decrease in every other child's chances. In fact, it is likely that even if a strict percentage system, i.e., a "curve," is not followed, in the eyes of the students the supply of "A" grades is not as large as the number in the class, and competition still results.

It does not really matter whether the supply of a given kind of reinforcement is unlimited or limited. What is important is what people believe to be true, the hypothesis to which they cling. We have labeled the two somewhat opposite hypotheses about the world, or parts of it, the "infinite pool of reinforcements" hypothesis, and the "finite pool of reinforcements" hypothesis. In order to make the implications of the two hypotheses clear and to dispel any notions that people do not really have such beliefs, let us consider two very different but important examples.

Sigmund Freud was rather cynical about many ethicomoral abjurations to "love thy neighbor" and "love thine enemies." The reason is that Freud believed that love exists in every individual as a definite quantity (based on his conception of psychic energy which he called *libido*). Now if each of us has only a limited amount of love to bestow, then the more widely we bestow it, the less of it there will be for any one person. Freud felt that we dilute our love for those close to us by investing it in strangers, (see 29). Consider the reaction of a girl whose boyfriend seriously attempted to expound an "infinite pool" hypothesis about love!

A somewhat bizarre (to us) example of a "finite pool" theory is related by the late Ruth Benedict (9) in her description of the Dobu culture on some small islands near New Guinea. The Dobu are a very suspicious and fear-ridden people who believe strongly in various forms of magic. One of their most important food crops is yams, which they plant in plots near their houses. They believe that the total supply of yams is limited and that every night the yams detach themselves from their vines and migrate underground to new vines. The fear of every gardener is that he will come out on the short end of the migration, and an important part of his magical skills consists in getting his own yams to stay put while attracting as many as possible from the gardens of his neighbors. The Dobu do not recognize differences in agricultural skill and the "fact" that any one gardener's crop is being drawn from a theoretically infinite pool. They believe that if a gardener has a better crop than his neighbors, it can only have occurred at the expense of his neighbors. Among the Dobu such beliefs lead to intense competition associated with suspiciousness and hostility.

In situations in which a person is led to believe that the action of another person has depleted in some measure the pool of reinforcements available, imitation would not always be expected to occur. If a child who is watching another child remove candy from a box suspects that it might have been the last piece, he may try what looks to him like an untapped supply. In fact, Miller and Dollard (67) found just such behavior among children. Most children had to be *taught* to imitate in their situation. Or, if a child believes that a teacher's affections are limited and that they are already invested in several favored children, he may seek attention and affection elsewhere.

Implicit Reinforcement of Responses

There is another social situation in which reinforcements given may not lead to imitation. Consider a situation in which two children are working simultaneously on individual but similar tasks, when an adult appears, looks at their work, and then says "Max, that is very good work." What would Sam's reaction be? It is easy to believe that his subsequent performance might be affected. Such a circumstance is known as *implicit reinforcement,* i.e., it is a circumstance which permits one individual to infer a reinforcement to himself by noting the reinforcement to another person. Note that implicit reinforcement need not be negative. Had the adult's comment been "Max, that work is terrible!" Sam might have taken the adult's silence about his own work as an implicit commendation. Situations involving implicit reinforcement are common. What is their outcome likely to be? Sechrest (76) studied implicit reinforcement in a setting in which children were working on simple puzzles in which speed of solution was the criterion measure. In that experiment the implicitly reinforced children behaved as if they had received a reinforcement opposite to the one received by the directly reinforced child. When the directly reinforced child was commended, he worked faster on the second puzzle, but the implicitly reinforced child worked more slowly. When the directly reinforced child was told that his performance was not so good, his subsequent performance was poorer and his partner's was better. These results suggest that caution must be exercised in such public commendation of children as is involved in "setting an example," for those children whose performance has been inspected but ignored may well believe that they have been by comparison reproved. Similar mechanisms may operate for adults.

We have discussed only a few of the many ways in which an individual's behavior may be affected by his observations of the experiences of other persons or of their actions. Undoubtedly the reader will be able to discern for himself many of the additional complexities of social learning. We would, however, affirm that all of the general principles discussed above are subject to the moderating or even radical influence of individual experience. Thus, even though it is reasonable to expect that an individual will imitate a successful person, if his imitative efforts are negatively reinforced, e.g., if he is a poor imitator, then his final behavior cannot be expected to resemble the behavior of the initially imitated person. And certainly not every individual will be susceptible to implicit reinforcement. An individual's unique history of reinforcements may have made him relatively impervious to implicit comparisons, e.g., either by engendering a firm confidence or a firm insecurity about his own efforts. Nonetheless, these principles are generally valid and useful for the understanding of behavior.

Attitudes

At this point it is desirable to introduce in a more formal way the discussion of attitudes, a topic of long-standing interest to social psychologists. It is our general inclination to eschew rigorous and formal definitions of terms, particularly terms which are in common usage and which have a consensual if imprecise meaning. Therefore, we will not insist on a special definition of the term attitude but will only indicate that the term is used generally to denote a prior disposition to make some response, usually of a judgmental or evaluative nature, to a stimulus. Similarly, we will speak of likes, dislikes, etc., since they have a common-sense meaning even though a rigorous definition of them may be difficult. Thus, when someone is asked what his attitude toward socialized medicine is, we have in mind his general disposition toward the topic, before any new information or problems are introduced. It is worth noting that "attitude" refers to a *general* disposition, or tendency, to respond, and perfect consistency of performance is not implied (20). Thus someone may have an unfavorable attitude toward members of a minority group without necessarily having an unfavorable attitude toward every individual member of that minority group. Before becoming acquainted with a particular person, one's inclination may be unfavorable, but subject to modification.

Campbell (20) made an exceptionally helpful analysis of the concept of attitude in psychology, and among his contributions is a revision of views concerning the consistency between attitudes and behavior. A problem that has long plagued social psychologists is the fact that a person may express an attitude which would seem to imply a particular form of behavior and yet act in quite a different manner. One experiment which seemed confusing to social psychologists was by LaPiere (54), who made an extensive trip with a young Chinese couple and took advantage of the opportunity to do a valuable bit of research. He noted the hotels and restaurants along the way where he and his Chinese friends asked for, and in nearly every case, received service. Very often it was the Chinese male who entered first and requested the service. Later LaPiere wrote to the establishments in question and asked whether they would be willing to serve Orientals. Somewhat to the dismay of attitude theorists and probably contrary to what most persons would have expected, a great many of the replys expressed an intent to refuse service to Orientals. From this and similar experiments many social psychologists were led to question the relationship between "mere attitudes" and "real behavior."

If an attitude is a general behavioral disposition, how do we know what someone's attitude is? Attitudes cannot be seen nor palpated. An attitude can only be determined or more properly, inferred, *from the behavior that an individual displays.* How, then, could an attitude be inconsistent with behavior if it is inferred from behavior? It can not. Only the inference can be wrong. Obviously the attitude of the businessmen contacted by LaPiere was *not* what was inferred from their responses to the questionnaire. Actually the problem of diagnosing attitudes is a difficult one. There are many possible indicators of an attitude, ranging from responses the person is not even aware of, through verbal statements, to gross motor behaviors such as moving closer to a favored stimulus or hitting an unfavored one.

Campbell suggests that we can order various indicators of an attitude, i.e., behaviors, in terms of the probable strength of the underlying attitude that would be necessary to ensure their occurrence. What then appears to be an inconsistent attitude is simply an attitude of intermediate strength, i.e., strong enough to support some of the weaker attitude indicators but not all of the stronger ones. For example, several behaviors which might have occurred in the experiment devised by LaPiere: (1) replying to the questionnaire with an offer of a firm welcome to Chinese; (2) replying to the questionnaire indicating a reluctant acceptance of Chinese patrons; (3) replying to the questionnaire indicating an intent to refuse service to Chinese patrons; (4) turning away a lone Chinese who appears at the business establishment; (5) turning away a well-dressed Chinese couple accompanied by a similarly well-dressed westerner; (6) summarily ordering the Chinese couple and the westerner out of the establishment. Certainly it must be easier to say on a questionnaire that one does not wish to serve a Chinese than to actually turn away a cultured Chinese couple who appear in the company of a western customer. Therefore, what appears to be inconsistency of attitude is really only an attitude of moderate strength.

Presumably attitudes can differ from each other along a number of dimensions, but the evaluative dimension, i.e., favorable–unfavorable, certainly predominates. An extensive series of investigations by Osgood and his associates (69) into the structure of attitudes has consistently shown the importance of the evaluative factor in attitudes toward almost everything. However, attitudes may also differ in strength, ranging from very strong attitudes to very weak ones. And obviously associated with strength of attitudes is their resistance to change. Some attitudes are seemingly easy to alter while others seem very nearly unassailable, resisting the strongest efforts to change them. Finally, attitudes differ in their centrality or importance to the individual. Some attitudes seem peripheral, of little significance, while others are important to an individual's very sense of self-identity. Some attitudes are so important to the person that he might imagine that he would not be himself without it. Obviously the centrality of attitudes is related to their resistance to change. Other things being equal, a very important, central attitude will probably be more resistant to change, for by being central it is involved with more of the person's other attitudes, including his all-important self-attitudes. Probably most central attitudes are relatively strong or "polarized," but they need not be.

Development of Attitudes

The way in which attitudes develop is in no way remarkable. Attitudes, like dispositions, develop out of a person's experiences. When a person has negatively reinforcing experiences with some complex stimulus pattern, it may be expected that avoidance of hostile tendencies will become attached to certain aspects of the stimulus pattern. Just which aspects are affected will depend on a variety of circumstances. Elements that are constant in a changing stimulus pattern will ultimately develop the strongest propensity to elicit the "negative" response tendencies. For example, if a small child has several frightening experiences with different animals, all of which are striped, then the child may come to have a "prejudice" against striped animals. However, some aspects of a stimulus pattern may be far more salient than others, and the response tendency may not be equally likely to become attached even to the constant elements in a stimulus pattern. The "stripedness" of animals may be more salient than, let us say, whether they have hoof or paw-like feet. Attitudes become attached to salient characteristics of a stimulus, and disassociated with characteristics that are difficult to observe. An attitude depending on very subtle distinctions is difficult to develop—and to maintain. Some characteristics of a stimulus pattern may be made more forceful. For example, when it became apparent in Nazi Germany that the physical characteristics of Jews did not really serve as a cue for anti-Semitism, the Jews were forced to wear distinguishing armbands.

It is quite evident that many attitudes in no way develop out of an individual's direct, firsthand experience with the object of the attitude. But they can be developed by "direct tuition" (19) of the attitude. That is, the attitude, like other behaviors, can be taught. Children can be taught that members of certain minority groups are repugnant or dangerous, and the children can then be reinforced for their speed, accuracy, and intensity of acceptance of the adult (or peer) "knowledge." Many such attitudes are well established before the child can possibly have had direct experience of the kind necessary to develop the attitude independently. Moreover, to use one of Cameron and Magaret's terms describing social acquisition of responses, attitudes can be acquired by "adoption of the prevailing pattern." It is likely that even without any special instruction a child will be strongly inculcated with the attitudes that are prevalent in his environment. By observation and imitative learning a child will probably acquire attitudes much like those of his parents and, a bit later, his peers.

Once developed, attitudes may or may not change. Change may occur by the same methods that are involved in the initial development of the attitude; i.e., direct experience, direct tuition, and adoption of the prevailing pattern. However, Campbell (20) points out that there is a very interesting and important difference between favorable and unfavorable attitudes that are erroneous, i.e., attitudes that are not justified by the facts. A favorable attitude is ordinarily indicated by an approach tendency toward the object(s) of the attitude, and an unfavorable attitude is indicated by an avoidance tendency. As an example, suppose that a young man who has never tasted Greek food but has heard about the use of grape leaves and the like, simply believes that he would not like Greek food. However, let us suppose that *if* he tried it, he would, in fact, like it very much. Let us further suppose that this same young man has read about the interesting customs of Mexico and has decided that he would like Mexican food. And, suppose that, in fact, the young man would not like Mexican food because he does not like "hot" foods. Which attitude could be corrected more easily? Obviously, the unwarranted favorable attitude, because that very attitude would lead to trying Mexican food. However, the unfavorable attitude toward Greek food would lead to his avoiding Greek food, so he may never have the opportunity to "unlearn" his error about it. Whenever attitudes lead to avoidance responses, they become less susceptible to change, particularly if they are in error.

An interesting and illustrative investigation into interpersonal relations was carried out by Priest and Sawyer (71), who studied the development of interpersonal attractions in a new college dormitory for male students. They found that sheer proximity, i.e., location of rooms and belonging to the same college class, was a strong determinant of attraction. For those students who initially thought they would like each other and who were living in close proximity there was little change in attraction, i.e., it remained high. And there was correspondingly little change when the initial attraction was low and when the two persons lived far apart. Dislike could be better modified when proximity provided opportunities for unlearning the initial attitude.

Prejudice

An attitude of great interest to lay persons as well as to social scientists is "prejudice." Actually, the term could be applied to any attitude, for the word simply means "pre-judge"—and that is very much what an attitude is, a prejudgment. However, prejudice usually refers specifically to unfavorable dispositions toward racial, religious, or national minority groups. An associated term, nearly complementary in meaning, is *ethnocentric*, an unwarranted regard for members of one's own group with the associated expectation of hostility toward members of other groups. A person described as "prejudiced" is inclined to judge certain other persons unfavorably even without personal experience with them. Prejudice consists of assumptions about individual members of a group on the basis of beliefs or knowledge about the characteristics of the group as a whole. Prejudice is not necessarily negative, but it usually is.

Professor Donald T. Campbell (20a) has been engaged in studies of prejudice and has found that prejudice consists not so much in erroneous observations of behavior but in the interpretations of the observations. Thus, two groups with mutually negative attitudes toward each other are likely to agree in describing their own behavior and that of the other group, but their interpretations of the behaviors may be exactly opposed. Thus, Groups A and B may agree that people in Group A do not spend their money readily, but while Group B views Group A as "stingy," Group A views itself as "provident." Prejudice, then, also consists of tendencies toward unwarrantedly unfavorable interpretations of the behavior of other groups.

There is strong reason to believe that the roots of prejudice extend back to the early childhood environment. Triandis and Triandis (85), for example, in studying reports of home backgrounds of subjects both high and low in tendency to reject association with members of certain minority groups, found that the prejudiced subjects more often came from homes described as cold and rejecting, in which the father rather than the mother was the chief disciplinarian, and in which the children were inconsistently punished.

On the other hand, Pettigrew (70) has suggested that pressures toward conformity are perhaps the strongest single factor operating to maintain prejudice. Pettigrew believes that many people express prejudiced attitudes, both verbally and in other modes of behavior, because they fear being different from others. Such people would fear rejection if they took unpopular positions in the community. To the extent, then, that everyone believes that the prejudiced view is the current norm or correct view it will tend to persist. The study by Triandis and Triandis (85) suggests that the less critical and more conforming people are the prejudiced ones.

Different hypotheses about the sources of prejudice lead to different approaches in dealing with it as a problem. Obviously, if prejudice goes back to the earliest childhood years, the way to reduce it is to alter the way parents rear their children—a difficult task, to say the least. However, Pettigrew thinks that racial prejudice could be greatly reduced by directly attacking the belief—or misbelief, actually—that the prejudiced opinion is the norm in the community. If community leaders could be persuaded to take a forthright position against racial prejudice, if newspapers would give greater publicity to the anti-prejudice position, then the ordinary citizen would not feel so strongly compelled to conform to no-longer-in-vogue prejudiced position.

However, racial or religious prejudices are rooted in diverse sources, particularly in a large community of individuals. Therefore, the approaches to the elimination of prejudice must be multidimensional, attacking at once the various sources of prejudice (51). For example, the changed image of a minority group, accomplished by a better educational level, would make it difficult to support other prejudicial attitudes about the group. A reduction of pressures to conform to a possibly spurious community "norm" would make possible a greater personal latitude, both in public expressions and in personal associations. And although dealing at the individual level with a broad social problem is highly inefficient and slow, some small impact on total amount of prejudice might be made by a therapy for the individual deficiencies that give rise to "prejudice proneness."

Altering negative attitudes is a difficult task. Negative attitudes, leading as they do to avoidance responses, are likely to go uncorrected if they are wrong because in that person's experience there is no basis for change. It is reasonable to think, then, that some changes in negative attitudes toward racial or religious groups might follow as a result of contact with those groups. The complaint of minority group leaders about the "image" of their group in all communications media is probably realistic in that members of minority groups are rarely shown in "normal" activities—shopping in a store, playing with their children—making it easy to maintain the belief that "they" are really not like "us."

There have been important investigations of attitude changes resulting from enforced contact of blacks and whites which show an overall change in the direction of a more favorable attitude toward blacks. In the United States Army it finally became the official policy to integrate blacks into the ranks of soldiers. However, the integration occurred in various ways and at a varying pace so that not all white men actually served with black soldiers. During the later stages of World War II some platoons of black infantrymen were found and placed in otherwise white companies. Stouffer *et al.* (82) took advantage of the opportunity to study the attitudes of white soldiers in reaction to the experience of serving in combat with black soldiers. Even though many of the whites studied were Southerners, and approximately two-thirds of them had initially been opposed to the idea of integration, nearly all the white soldiers reported having been favorably impressed with their black comrades. The investigators asked the following question: "Some Army divisions have companies which include Negro platoons and white platoons. How would you feel about it if your outfit was set up like that?" The marked difference in replies is shown in Fig. 16-1. Clearly, a favorable response to the suggestion of integrated fighting units was related to the degree of previous close contact with blacks in that situation.

A similar and possibly even more convincing result of enforced contact was discovered in a study of segregated and integrated housing projects by Deutsch and Collins (24). In the Army study just cited, it appeared that serving in combat with blacks is a rather special experience, and soldiers who were willing, even glad, to contemplate doing so were not necessarily willing to participate in social activities with blacks. However, living in close proximity to blacks is both a more complete and a more commonplace kind of experience. The results were also favorable. It was found that white women in integrated projects used such words as "dangerous" or "troublemakers" in describing blacks far less frequently than did women in segregated projects. (Note that the result is exactly what would be expected for an erroneous belief subjected to a test, enforced or not.) Moreover, white women in the integrated projects were *far* more likely to express a desire to be friendly with blacks than to avoid them than were women in the segregated projects. There were many other indicators of profoundly improved attitudes toward blacks

Question: Some army divisions have companies which include black
platoons and white platoons. How would you feel about it
if your outfit was set up something like that?

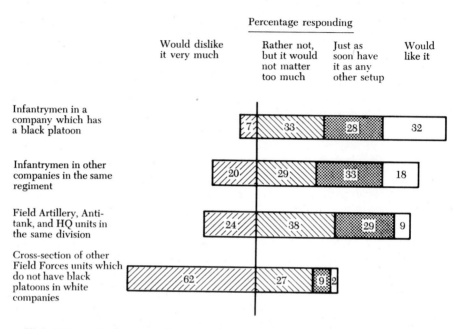

Fig. 16-1. Attitudes toward serving in a company containing black and white
platoons among men who have done so and men who have not (Europe, June, 1945).
From Stouffer *et al.* (82).

as a result of the experience of living with them. Apparently the dictum
"You cannot legislate beliefs!" is questionable if not completely incorrect.

―――――――――――――― **Social Influence on Behavior**

We are all susceptible to the influence of our social environment. However, in our culture we are inclined to place a rather high value on
independence and individual initiative, and we often decry attempts to
influence others as if by definition they are undesirable. Sociologist
David Riesman (72) coined the term "other-directed" to refer to people
who are especially sensitive to guidance and influence by others; and it
is very clear from Riesman's use of the term that it is a term of oppro-
brium. If other-directedness is undesirable, it is unfortunate that Riesman
finds it so widespread in our society.

However, instead of making any *a priori* judgments about the desirability of social influence, it would be better to examine the nature of
social influence and the conditions under which it occurs.

Conformity

Very often people talk about susceptibility to social influence as if it were a mindless conformity, an automatic response in obedience to the will of the group. An experiment which is often cited as an example of rather extreme conformity, and one which has been repeated numerous times, was done by Asch (3) to show the effects of judgment of group pressure. In his experiment, Asch required his Ss to match a line of a given length with one of three comparison lines. The task was done in groups of eight, but the Ss did not know that the first seven "subjects" were actually confederates of the experimenter. After several routine judgments the seven confederates suddenly gave a unanimous but erroneous judgment. The experimental data consisted of the number of times the real S would "conform" to group pressure rather than remain "independent" and give a judgment consistent with his own sense impressions. In one run of 50 Ss, 37 yielded to group opinion on one or more of 12 possible occasions, and the mean number of times yielded was 3.84.

Why would anyone give an erroneous judgment in such a situation? There is, of course, the possibility that the Ss actually "saw" the line as matching the erroneous comparison rather than the true comparison line. Interviews with Ss in such experiments have always shown, however, that there is little effect on perception. The yielding Ss usually recognize that the erroneous judgments are *apparently* in error. The yielding is more in the report than in the perception. The interviews also reveal that the yielding Ss arrive at a number of different hypotheses to justify their behavior. For example, they sometimes suppose that there is some sort of an illusion to which they are not susceptible. Or they decide that "obviously" the experiment involves some sort of trick or secret to which they are not a party. Thus, even though unanimously uncomfortable about it, some Ss do yield to the group opinion. Note, however, that about one-fourth of the Ss do not yield at all, and very few of the Ss yield more than a few of the total number of possible times. It was also found that when even one confederate of the experimenter was instructed to give a correct judgment, the frequency of yielding was drastically reduced. In other words, if the S had even one ally, reducing the majority from 7-1 to 6-2, then he was very much more independent. Moreover, yielding did not occur with any appreciable frequency until the majority became at least 3-1 against the S. Finally, the degree of yielding is a direct function of the ambiguity of the situation, i.e., when the errors of the majority are large, yielding is less. When the discrepancy from the true comparison is small, the yielding is greater. Is this really such mindless conformity?

The ideal of the sternly independent respondent who makes up his own mind is realistic only in situations in which he is truly as well informed as the others are and is equally good in evaluating information. Crutchfield (23) found that conformity was negatively related ($r = -.63$) to rated intelligence. We have all been in situations in which for one reason or another we were not especially well informed or were lacking certain skills necessary to make a judgment. What is the best course of action in such a situation? It would seem sensible to observe what others in that situation are doing—and to do the same. There is much to be said—in certain instances—for blind but sensible conformity. Similarly, if a student looking for a barber shop sees a busy one on one side of the street and an empty one on the other side, there is good rationale for his "conforming" and choosing the popular one.

There is more to learn from the Asch experiment. Most of us have had experiences in which we were not privy to a secret shared by a group and so came out looking somewhat ridiculous by behaving inappropriately. A student who enters a psychological experiment and finds himself faced by a majority of 7-0, even about a rather obvious matter, may be forgiven for supposing that "something is up" and going along with group opinion. Having had experiences in which our own judgment was wrong, and many experiences in which the judgment of others was correct, makes it easier to yield to group opinion. When faced with seven unanimous opinions on some matter that you, the subject, feel uncertain about, yielding to group opinion may be the more intelligent thing to do. Asch's experiment, as well as subsequent ones, indicates that yielding judgments are easy to produce only in situations with some degree of ambiguity about the correct response (21, 87).

On the other hand, some of the Ss in Asch's experiment did not yield, and that, too, may be explained by their previous experiences in related situations. For example, perhaps the nonyielders had often been reinforced for going against the judgments of other persons. Or perhaps they had learned that with some degree of frequency the "trick" is on the majority. In such a case it is sensible to remain independent. It has been found in a number of experiments that a prior experience of success on a task reduces later conformity in response to group pressure (12).

Other investigators have attempted to elicit conforming or obedient behavior of a more extreme sort, often with a success that has been surprising and perturbing to many people. Thus, Milgram (66) has conducted experiments in which Ss were led to believe that they were administering very dangerous levels of electric shock to another person, but at the insistence of the experimenter they continued to perform the frightful response. Milgram's research was upsetting to many people for a variety of reasons, but perhaps chief among them is the implication that many people are so blindly obedient to authority that they will do anything they are told, even in our democratic nation.

On the other hand, Orne (68) has suggested, and has described considerable research to prove his point, that people will behave in very unusual ways if they believe that they are in a scientific experiment, "doing something for science." Probably one important reason is that people have a trust of scientists, however naive, that makes them believe that everything will turn out all right. It could be argued that people should not trust scientists quite so implicitly; but there is some difference between reasonable faith based on proof and simple obedience to the commands of an authoritative person. Many of the issues are far from being resolved, and it would be incautious to conclude that most of our society has arrived at the point of stupid conformity and blind obedience.

This is not to say that the authors are in favor of unthinking conformity; but neither do we stand in favor of unthinking independence. Whether one should conform or remain independent in any situation depends on the nature of that situation. For example, in matters like using the "proper" fork or wearing the currently popular clothing, whether one conforms or not is not of great consequence. On the other hand, when a jury is debating the guilt or innocence of a defendent in a criminal case, a great deal is at stake. In such a situation one would want to be very careful *either* in yielding to group opinion or in remaining obdurately opposed to it.

Social Facilitation of Behavior

A number of years ago, Bayer (8) noted that hens given free access to food would, after a time, stop eating, apparently being satiated. However, if other hungry hens were introduced into the situation, the apparently satiated chickens would resume eating and eat considerable additional quantities of food. Other investigators have found the same results with rats (91). Such a phenomenon is probably not unlikely in humans. The changes in probability of behavior in group or social situations over what would be found in individual situations is known as social facilitation of behavior.

Examples of social facilitation of human behavior are not difficult to find. The behavior of people in mobs and crowds provides obvious examples. People will do things under the influence of a mob of people that they would certainly hesitate to do under other circumstances. Social facilitation may result in very undesirable behavior, e.g., lynch mobs [see Miller & Dollard (67), for a fascinating, if repelling, account];

boisterous behavior, e.g., during conventions; and very desirable behavior, e.g., during solemn occasions.

One special type of social facilitation is competition. It is widely believed that people will work a little harder, do a little more if they believe they are in competition with some other person(s). Yet, ours is a culture that is strangely ambivalent about competitive activity. Competition is idealized in our conception of the development of American business and industry; yet there are often overtones of concern that competition may lead to the trampling of the weak. The public school system simultaneously believes that the highest grades should go to the best competitors and yet is concerned that the students who are intellectually less capable may suffer psychological damage in their losing efforts. Even in some kinds of athletic competitions there are special arrangements to lessen the blows of losing, e.g., by granting handicaps, having separate teams for different sized competitors.

What is the effect of competition? First, there are certainly experimental results to show that among school children competitive conditions are likely to produce an improvement in level of performance. Leuba (55) gave fifth-grade children multiplication problems to work on, and found that competition was as effective as a candy reward in improving performance over a "practice" situation. Although Hurlock (43) found that inducing group competition improved performance, other investigators (61, 80) found that individual competition resulted in a better performance than group competition did. However, in the above experiments the competition was over a brief period of time. It is not possible to say what the effects of prolonged competition might be. There is reason to doubt that the kind of competition usually created in experiments would be likely to sustain a prolonged performance.

People may appreciate competition because they value the consequences of competitive activity, e.g., prizes and recognition. Even if the competitor loses, there may be considerable reinforcement of competitive activity, e.g., "You played a great game!" However, competition may come to be valued for its own sake. Competitive activity provides heightened stimulation and excitement that may result in a pleasurable level of "arousal" (11).

That competition can also facilitate behaviors other than increased excellence in performance is suggested by other experiments. Sherif and Sherif (79) found that intergroup competition produced a greater sense of cohesiveness and "belongingness" within the groups, a finding substantiated by others (12, 53). Meyers (65) reports a study of ROTC cadets organized into three-man rifle teams and firing either against each other or against an "objective standard." Competition apparently contributed to team adjustment and was reflected in their behaviors toward and liking for each other, even when the team was not notably successful in its task. Wilson and Miller (89) report a similar increase in mutual appreciation of team members under conditions of competition.

Cooperation is usually viewed as the opposite of competition, and it, too, involves some degree of social facilitation. However, the rewards consequent to cooperative behavior are probably much less clear than they are for competition. It may be inevitable, and this is a "finite pool" notion, that the narrowly distributed rewards for competitive activity seem larger than the more widely distributed rewards for cooperation. It seems clear, however, that if cooperation is valued for its own sake, as a "higher" form of human activity, it should be made comparably rewarding to competition.

Competition and cooperation are both responses and possible stimuli to other responses. Competition is likely to be heightened by a limitation on the potential supply of reinforcements. On the other hand, it is also true that cooperation can be produced when the cooperative response is reinforced. Oddly enough, one of the first demonstrations of the learning of a cooperative response was the production of cooperation between a cat and a rat by Tsai (86). Tsai was able to train a cat and a rat to work together in order to obtain access to food. Similarly cooperative responses have been developed in mental patients who would otherwise have no interaction (50). Wright (90) subjected pairs of children (ages 3 to 6) to frustration and found an increase in cooperative behavior and a decrease in conflict behavior. The effect was especially marked for children who were already good friends. It appears, then, that adverse circumstances, if shared, can produce a higher level of cooperation. Such a research finding is consistent with the common observation that groups of all kinds become more cohesive under stressful conditions. Thus, cooperation is likely to result from stress, especially if the basis for cooperation already exists. Azrin and Lindsley (4) have shown that children can be "taught" to cooperate in a game situation if they are reinforced for cooperative responses. Moreover, the cooperation is subject to extinction if reinforcement ceases.

Another area exemplifying social facilitation is in problem solving. Some years ago Shaw (78) compared individual problem solving with the performance of four-person groups and found a larger number of correct solutions in the group condition. Shaw believed that the superiority of the groups came from the greater probability of rejection of incorrect suggestions and from more checking of errors. Such findings as Shaw's led many people to suppose that group performances were in every way superior to individual performances and that for almost any problem the preferred method of solving it was to turn it over to a group. That, however, is not exactly true.

More recent experiments by Taylor and Faust (83) and Marquart (62) have shown that groups are superior to individuals only for certain kinds of problems and only in certain ways. It appears that when problems require a novel solution, something creative, or when they involve a special technical knowledge, the performance of groups is seldom likely to be better than the performance of the better individual problem solvers—and probably not as bad as the performance of the poorer ones. Groups probably minimize the really bad mistakes, but they probably also minimize the really good solutions. Obviously, however, this is valid only for certain kinds of problems. If the problems involve easy steps which can be accomplished simultaneously by various group members, then an individual could not be expected to do as well. Moreover, the relative effectiveness of group and individual problem solving often depends on the way the group works together. A group might be expected to improve considerably after a period of working together. It has often been said that the *Mona Lisa* could never have been painted by a committee; however, some remarkable woodblock prints were seen by one of the authors in a Japanese elementary school, where the work had been done by a group. The prints' design had been created by the group and the various sections had been produced by individual workers.

A somewhat different but related problem was investigated by Hudgins (42), who was interested to know whether experience in group problem solving might contribute to subsequent improvement in individual problem solving. Presumably by working in a group for a period of time an individual might have an opportunity to observe a wider variety of problem-solving attempts, some perhaps more effective than his own. Hudgins' Ss were fifth-grade students, and their task required the solution of arithmetic problems. Both the Ss working in groups and those working individually had problem-solving practice on three consecutive days before each was tested individually. Contrary to expectations, group experience did not facilitate, i.e., *transfer* to, individual problem solving. Apparently it is well to be cautious in assuming very much about the value of group experience in the problem-solving area.

The Nature of Group Membership

Everyone belongs to groups—many groups—with differing functions, characteristics, and demands. However, just what is meant by "membership" varies just as widely as the groups. One is a voluntary member in some groups, e.g., fraternal orders, religious organizations; an incidental member of some groups, e.g., teenagers, theater audiences; and an involuntary member of still other groups, e.g., juries, some military units. Obviously, membership in the different groups is accompanied by very different feelings: strong commitment, a sense of obligation, liking, disliking, and even negative or no feeling. Many factors determine whether one likes a group or feels committed to it: similarity to other persons in the group, agreement with group goals, restrictions on individual initiative.

One particular factor on which research has been done illustrates the current thinking of social psychologists about membership in groups. There are various ways in which one may enter a group. Some groups may be joined easily, merely by a display of interest. Other groups are difficult to join. Some groups even put prospective members through an initiation ceremony. Aronson and Mills (1) became interested in the initiation of members into a group as a determinant of subsequent attitudes toward a group. One might suppose that a severe initiation would dispose an individual toward an unfavorable impression, but their data argue otherwise. For example, did the hazing that routinely accompanied entry into college fraternities weaken the commitment of fraternity men toward their organization? Moreover, some rather clever theorizing by Festinger (25) which he presents as a "theory of cognitive dissonance" leads to the prediction that a severe initiation might actually produce a stronger commitment to a group. Put very simply, Festinger's theory states that when a discrepancy develops between two related beliefs or between a belief and an action, the discrepancy, or *dissonance* as he calls it, must be reduced in some manner. Suppose that someone has just permitted himself to be put through a severe initiation ceremony into a group which he believes to be of little worth. Festinger's theory states that the person will be uncomfortable until the discrepancy between the severity of the initiation and his conception of the worth of the group is reduced in some way. The discrepancy is most easily reduced by increasing one's regard for the group, convincing oneself that it is such a good group that membership in it is worth the initiation.

Aronson and Mills (1) did an experiment in which college women who volunteered to participate in discussion groups were randomly assigned to a severe, mild, or no initiation condition. In the severe condition the Ss were required to read some rather blatantly sexual material before joining the group, and in the mild condition the Ss read only some sex-related words. Through a series of subterfuges the Ss were led to believe that they were about to join a group discussing sex, and they listened to a very dull, banal recorded discussion by "their group." Later, when asked to rate the attractiveness of the group, the Ss in the severe condition rated both the discussion and the participants higher than Ss in the mild or control conditions rated them.

Among individuals who are members of a group there are almost certain to be differences both in attraction to the group and in acceptance by the group. When attraction to the group is low, individuals could be expected to be less susceptible to group pressures—and that has been verified experimentally (12). However, nonacceptance does not necessarily lead to less conformity if attraction to the group is high, perhaps because conformity is seen as one of the routes to acceptance (44).

Leadership

Although nearly everyone has a fairly definite idea of what is meant by leadership and of what a leader is, it is difficult to define leadership in a really satisfactory way. Status is often related to leadership, but there are many instances of high-ranking group members who do very little "leading." Moreover, leadership is a shifting role. The leader in one situation may not be the leader in another. Therefore, the conception of leadership advanced by Hemphill (36) is the one discussed here. After examining many instances of supposed leadership behavior and after observing many groups in operation, Hemphill concluded that it is better to talk about the *leadership act* than simply leadership. He further concluded that what characterizes leadership acts is that they *initiate structure* in the processes or activities of the groups. In other words, leadership acts reduce, or attempt to reduce, uncertainty about the ongoing behavior of the group. For example, when a group member makes a statement beginning, "Why don't we . . ." "Well, we could . . ." "How about . . ." he is attempting to initiate structure. From this viewpoint anyone in a group is a leader any time he initiates structure in the group's activities.

Note that the member was *attempting* to initiate structure, i.e., he was attempting a leadership role. However, people will differ in their ability to actually influence the group, and the same person may differ from time to time. Therefore Hemphill suggests that an important aspect of leadership is success in influencing the group, and he refers to the leadership act, which does influence the group, as a successful leadership act. A successful leader is someone who succeeds in getting his group to follow his suggestions. Every group has some goals, and some leadership acts may help the group progress toward its goals, and some may not. Some may even result in disaster for the group. Hemphill suggests that if a leadership act results in an acceptable amount of progress toward group goals, it is an effective act. If it does not, it is ineffective. An effective leader is one whose acts, when followed, result in progress toward group goals. Obviously a leader must be successful to be effective.

What determines whether a leader is successful or not? Some leaders have power over their groups so that their attempts to initiate structure must be followed, and in some instances the group is in no position to question the leader. A military commander, for example, must be obeyed. Many of the leadership acts of teachers are of the same kind. When a teacher says, "Now, take out your spelling books," that is a leadership act, and whether it is a good idea or not it is likely to be successful.

But for leaders without commanding status and in groups in which participation is voluntary the situation is probably different. In such circumstances a number of other factors come into play. First, of course, the group members may evaluate the leadership act themselves. If it appears to be similar to leadership acts which in the past have been proved ineffective, it may be ignored. Second, the person making the suggestion may be evaluated. If he is a new person, an unknown quantity in the group, the evaluation of him will be based on his similarity to other persons who have made such suggestions in the past. If he resembles people whose suggestions have been effective, his suggestions are likely to receive serious consideration. But if he resembles persons whose suggestions have proved bad, his suggestions may be ignored. But if the potential leader is a known member of the group, his success is likely to be a function of the effectiveness of his previous leadership attempts. In other words, when a group is reinforced for following suggestions from a particular source, suggestions from the same source are more likely to be followed on subsequent occasions.

An interesting question is whether there is such a thing as a "leader type." But if the foregoing question makes any sense, it does so only insofar as it is possible to distinguish a "good leader" from other good men. Thus, findings that good leaders are more intelligent, more popular (30), and the like only suggest that superior people make good leaders. There are few findings which suggest traits peculiar to leaders. In fact, in one investigation it was even found that the correlation between nominations for good leader and good follower was 0.92 (37).

Communication, Persuasion, and Attitude Change

A great many of the interactions among people involve attempts on the part of some to bring about changes in the beliefs and attitudes of others. A politician hopes to convince you that he can serve your interests better than his opponent can—or perhaps the cynical would say that he simply hopes to get you to vote for him for whatever reason. A soap manufacturer hopes to persuade you to switch to his brand. An instructor hopes to convince you that Keats is superior to Shelley. And your father hopes to persuade you to study more and play less. All of these persuasive attempts involve communications of some sort. Some of the attempts will succeed and others will fail.

Obviously, it is important whether a communication is accepted or not. For example, suppose a toothpaste manufacturer claims that his brand resulted in 65% fewer cavities than any other brand. That is an impressive claim, but will you believe him? If in your experience similar claims have been true, you may believe him. Have such claims by other manufacturers proved true? And you may believe this manufacturer if the claim is made through persons whose right to be believed has been established in other connections, e.g., you may be more credulous if the claim is "verified" by the seal of a national dental society. On the other hand, if the source of a communication is unacceptable, the communication may be distrusted, whatever its nature. A number of experimenters (38) have shown that identical communications were accepted or rejected depending upon whether the readers believed they came from either Thomas Jefferson or Lenin.

Some kinds of persuasive efforts are effective through negative approaches. For example, in advertising toothpaste one might either emphasize the dangers of not using the toothpaste, or one might emphasize the positive values to be obtained from its use. In one investigation of communications directed toward improved dental hygiene, fear-provoking communications were less effective than communications addressed to more positive goals (45). A similar investigation was done by Blomgren and Scheuneman (13) on attempts to persuade people to purchase seatbelts for their automobiles. One set of materials featured pictures of accidents in which it was claimed lives could have been saved by seatbelts. The other set of materials featured endorsements by racing car drivers with assertions that seatbelts contribute to good driving skills. The results clearly favored the latter approach. The nonresponsiveness of most smokers to propaganda about lung cancer is another case in point. The effect of fear-provoking propaganda may simply be that people "close their ears" to all communicative efforts. Fear-provoking propaganda may arouse such anxiety that it is preferable to ignore the whole issue. In another context, there are the attempts to motivate students by arousing fear of failure. Although it may be believed that inciting students to increase their effort by pointing out how possible it is that they may fail, the effect may be that they inhibit all responses— including thinking—connected with the work they are to do. However, the research on fear-arousing communications is not totally consistent, and some investigators have found fear communications to be effective, e.g., Leventhal and Singer (55a) in a study of communications about dental practices.

Another aspect of persuasive communication that must be considered is whether it is better to present people with only one side of an argument, i.e., the side favoring the attitude change one wishes to induce, or whether it is better to present both sides of an argument. An early investigation (39) on this point occurred during the late phases of World War II when it was thought that troops in the European command believed that the war was nearly over, and that Japan would succumb easily. In the higher echelons it was deemed desirable to counter such a belief, for some still foresaw a prolonged war in the Pacific. Therefore, systematic efforts were made to effect a change in belief in the direction of greater congruence with official beliefs. Accordingly, some of the troops received propaganda of a one-sided nature to produce a belief that the war in the Pacific would be difficult and prolonged. Other troops received the same argument but also were informed of the possible counterarguments, i.e., that the Japanese could not hold out long, based on such factors as Russia's active entry into the Pacific war.

The results are not surprising, but they are instructive. It was found that the effectiveness of the *pro/alone* versus the *pro/con* propaganda depended upon the educational level of the troops. At the lower educational levels the one-sided presentation was most effective. Probably the presentation of the opposite side was only confusing. However, at higher educational levels the two-sided presentation was more effective. What seemed to happen to better educated soldiers is that the presentation of a one-sided argument stimulated them to think of counterarguments, thus reducing the effectiveness of the presentation. However, when the source presented the opposing arguments the implicit assumption was that authoritative analysis arrived at the belief in a prolonged war *in spite of* possible arguments against it.

One must also consider what is likely to happen to the recipient of a communication who later is subjected to counterpropaganda. To revert to our previous example, what happens when a person who hears the claim that Brand X is 65% more effective later hears a similar claim from the makers of Brand Y? Fortunately, there are research results on this point, and they indicate rather clearly that initial exposure to both sides of an argument reduces susceptibility to later counterarguments (59). Somewhat the same mechanisms are probably involved as were described above. When the counterarguments come from the initial source, the buyer is likely to think that they have already been taken into account. But if he meets them for the first time on some later occasion, he may assume that they were not considered initially and that they merit additional thought.

An interesting question is, Does the effectiveness of communications depend on the order in which they are presented? If there is an audience to persuade, as in a debate, is it preferable to have the initial or the final position? Hovland and his associates (41) have made extensive studies of the effects of order of arguments; what follows summarizes some of their findings. First, regarding the order of presentation, it depends on what happens in the interval between the first and second arguments. If the listener is asked to take a public stand after the first argument, then certainly *primacy* of argument holds, i.e., the change following the second argument will be slight. Once having committed themselves publicly people are reluctant to reverse their stand. However, if no commitment by the listener is required, or if he is not required to take a public stand, then the primacy effect does not occur, and the first argument has no superiority over the second argument. Second, it depends on the source of the two arguments. If the source of both arguments is the same, then primacy is likely to operate. When one argument is made by a particular source, subsequent arguments are likely to be interpreted in terms of the initial argument, and so lose much of their impact. However, if the two arguments come from different sources, *recency* is probably the more powerful effect, and the second argument is likely to be more persuasive.

Very often in presenting arguments on any position it is possible to take a variety of positions differing in extremeness. Again reverting to the toothpaste example, an advertiser might say either:

1. This toothpaste shows some superiority to others in current use.
2. This toothpaste is markedly better than any other toothpaste.
3. This is clearly the finest toothpaste science can provide, and it is the only one an informed person could consider using.

This may not read like the ads you are familiar with; but it does illustrate a point, which is that arguments may differ in extremeness. If an individual's original position is measured on an attitude scale, the magnitude of the difference between his original position and the position taken in the argument can then be determined. What change can be expected? Apparently when other things are equal, the change induced by a communication is proportional to the magnitude of the change advocated (2, 18). What that means is that for individuals at a given point on an attitude scale advocating a big change is likely to produce a larger change than advocating a smaller change, even though the change achieved in either case is likely to be less than the minimum advocated.

It is as if persons listening to an argument had made a prior decision to meet the argument halfway. But these effects may be greatly attenuated or even reversed if the S is unwillingly exposed to opinions contrary to his own (18) or if the source of communication is not viewed as trustworthy (2).

Finally, it is necessary to discuss what has come to be known as the "sleeper effect" in persuasion and propaganda. Very often people are subjected to arguments from a discredited source, and such arguments are likely to be rejected. But is there any reason to suppose that there might be a delayed effect from hearing arguments, even though, at the time, they are rejected? Apparently so, for Hovland and Weiss (40) and Weiss (88) found that discredited arguments were rejected at the time of first hearing, but one month later there were measureable effects from such arguments. This is termed the "sleeper effect" in propaganda. It simply suggests that there are certain dangers in exposing people to arguments from untrustworthy sources. However, the results of experiments also suggest that the sleeper effect occurs only when subjects are not reminded of the source of the arguments.

Let us summarize very briefly a few of the points about persuasion. First, communications are more persuasive if they come from a trustworthy source and if they are similar to previous trustworthy communications. However, even if the communications come from an untrustworthy source, evidence suggests that they may have a delayed effect. Communications which arouse fear responses may be less effective than those which make a more positive appeal. At least for better educated Ss it is better to present both the arguments in favor of a position and the arguments against it; the latter are especially important in inducing resistance to later counterpropaganda. Primacy and recency are both possible effects in order of arguments, but neither is a consistent effect. Primacy is probably more powerful if both pro and con arguments come from the same source, and recency is more powerful if the arguments come from different sources. Finally the amount of attitude shift induced will be proportional to the discrepancy between the position held and the position advocated.

Improvisation and Attitude Change

There is evidence suggesting that when people are forced to take a public stand, to commit themselves, on some issue, their attitudes on that issue become relatively fixed. How would someone's attitudes be affected if he were persuaded to commit himself on some issue to a position that was discrepant with his own privately held opinion? Ordinary experience and folklore are replete with instances of people who have been changed during the course of "playing a role." There is also scientific evidence for such phenomena. In one of the early studies, Janis and King (46) had Ss give speeches on different topics, working from a prepared outline but encouraged to improvise. Other Ss followed the outline and listened to the speeches. Measures of attitudes on the topics had been obtained before the experimental situation and measurements were obtained subsequently. For two of the three topics the speechmakers (active participants) changed more in the direction of the view advocated in their speech than did those Ss who merely listened to the speech (passive controls), and on the third topic the active participants were more confident of their changed estimates than were the passive controls. Thus, it appears that merely requiring the Ss to play the role of advocates of a position resulted in a change in their own attitudes.

In the experiment of Janis and King the topics were rather trivial— e.g., how many years will it be until a cure is found for the common cold—and the induced attitude shifts were all in one direction, viz., toward a decrease in estimate. Moreover, the extent to which the speech-making part of the experiment was divorced from the measurement of attitudes is open to question. However, in a later experiment Salman (75) obtained similar results with a somewhat more important question, whether it is better to pry into the personal problems of others in order to be of help or whether they should be left to their own devices. Different Ss were required to improvise a speech in favor of one of the other positions so that attitude shifts occurred in both directions.

There are a number of reasons why improvisation of a speech on some issue might produce a change in attitude toward the issue, e.g., heightened but selective awareness of the arguments, but a number of observations point in an interesting direction. It has been found that amount of opinion change is correlated with the amount of improvisation and other indices of the energy or interest invested in the topic by the improvisers (22, 46, 49). It will be recalled that Festinger's *theory of cognitive dissonance* deals with the discomfort which is aroused in a S when two parts of his cognitive system are dissonant, i.e., in disagreement. Dissonance is aroused when Ss are led publicly to espouse a belief which they, themselves, do not hold. The dissonance can be reduced only by (a) changing the private attitude or (b) renouncing the publicly espoused position. In certain circumstances, at least, it appears that the former is easier and more likely.

Some readers may be reminded of the many essay contests in which children are enticed to participate and they may wonder whether writing the essays might not have a salutary (or other) effect on the children's attitudes since that situation so closely parallels the experiments described above. Unfortunately there is another aspect of Festinger's dissonance theory and of the empirical evidence that we must point to that would be less comforting. It seems that dissonance is aroused only when a person finds himself doing something contrary to his beliefs for no special reason. If an individual has a good reason for taking a public position on some issue, e.g., to win a prize, then dissonance is apparently not produced and there will be no necessity for a private attitude change. In one experiment, for example, Festinger and Carlsmith (26) offered one group of Ss one dollar to espouse a position at variance with their own, and a second group was offered twenty dollars for the same task.The latter group showed almost no effect from the public espousal. The former group, which presumably found it more difficult to rationalize their behavior, showed more change in the direction of their public statements. An example from everyday life; the people who write advertising copy are almost never persuaded by their own arguments, for which they are well paid. Essay writing contests are likely to have little impact on the writers' attitudes when handsome prizes are offered. If people can be persuaded to write essays without thinking of any reward, there may be some good results.

Group Atmosphere

Probably most groups, if not all, are characterized by an "atmosphere" or "climate" which distinguishes them from other groups. It is difficult to define "atmosphere" and to specify just what is meant by it, but what it does not mean is something ineffable and unmeasureable. What Hemphill (35) has called "hedonic tone," i.e., pleasantness, is a part of the atmosphere of a group, and such variables as "tension" and "restriction" would further define the overall atmosphere of a group.

The atmosphere characteristic of a group is probably a function of a number of variables. The type of leadership which a group has certainly has something to do with its atmosphere. A number of studies show that groups led in diverse ways differ on many variables (15, 16, 57, 58, 60). The types of leadership which have been studied fall pretty much on a single continuum ranging from democratic-permissive through laissez-faire to authoritarian-restrictive. Unfortunately, there have not been attempts to disentangle some important variables. For example, studies of "authoritarian" leadership have involved a cold, rejecting, aloof leadership, and a type of leadership which might be termed "benevolent" or "paternal" authoritarianism has not been sufficiently explored. [For a more complete discussion of this point, see Sechrest (77).]

A second variable related to group atmosphere is the kind of relationships characteristic among members of a group. The cohesiveness of a group, which is related to the attraction which the group has for its members, is related to forces producing conformity within the group. Moreover, some groups are characterized by pleasant relationships among their members; in fact, for a very good reason most groups have predominantly pleasant intragroup relations. However, some groups may have a good bit of unpleasantness and tensions among group members and still persist as groups if members share an imporant common goal. Some groups are *task-oriented* while others are *maintenance-oriented*.

Ordinarily such groups as infantry squads, program committees, and school faculties are task-oriented and can be expected to have a relatively work-minded approach to problems. Other groups, e.g., social fraternities, families, and bridge clubs, are more concerned with the maintenance of harmonious relations within the group, even at the expense of accomplishing any realistic goals. That is not to say that there will be great consistency for groups and agreement among group members. At times, groups which are ordinarily task-oriented may become preoccupied with harmony, and maintenance-oriented groups may at times sacrifice some degree of harmony in order to get on with a task. And within a group some members may be the stern taskmasters while others are the arbitrators and peacemakers. But the major orientation of a group at any one time will contribute to its overall atmosphere.

Finally, the relationships which a group has with other groups or other aspects of its environment will contribute something to the atmosphere that pervades it. A group under attack or threatened in some way will certainly have a different atmosphere from a group existing in safety. Threats to a group often produce a greater cohesiveness within the group, and threats also may crystallize the goals of a group at any particular time, whether they are task or maintenance goals.

Group-Centered Processes

One of the several ways in which a group might be guided is by itself, i.e., with a minimum of external intervention. Instead of imposing structure and leadership on a group, it might be allowed to develop its own processes and to guide itself. Groups which are permitted to develop with a relatively great amount of freedom are referred to as *group-centered*.

The genesis of much interest in group-centered processes was the early series of experiments by Lewin (56) on group discussion and group decision making. During World War II the continuing threat of serious meat shortages led to an attempt to persuade housewives to make greater use of so-called "variety meats." Lewin took advantage of an opportunity to do some experimentation and compared the effects of a 45-minute lecture on variety meats and ways of preparing them with group discussions by the housewives, themselves, of variety meats and their advantages. A follow-up showed that only 3% of the housewives in the lecture group served any of the meats after hearing the lecture, whereas, 32% of the women in the discussion group did do so. That experiment was repeated twice, once in an attempt to increase milk consumption and another time to instruct mothers on the desirability of feeding orange juice and codliver oil to their babies. In both additional experiments the results were the same. The group discussion method proved more effective than the lecture method in producing the desired change. Such findings led to many speculations concerning the reason for the effectiveness of group decision making, and the answer may still not be totally clear. However, it seems possible that several factors may be operating. Personal participation is, of course, elicited in group discussion to a greater degree than it is in lectures, and such participation may increase the sense of personal commitment. Moreover, personal participation may increase the sense of "belonging" and arouse feelings for conformity in what *appears to be* a group decision. (Note, however, that in a more realistic sense the "conformists" were the ones who did *not* try the new meat.) Also, the level of activity may have been higher in the discussion group, with the resulting higher level of attention. There is evidence to suggest that attention level remains higher for discussions than it does for lectures (14).

The results obtained by Lewin seem to have relevance to many other situations, notably instruction, and various efforts have been made to determine whether instruction is best carried out by traditional lecture or by group discussion methods. Pleasant though they are, group discussions rarely produce better performances than lectures do on examinations, particularly when the examinations depend upon the absorption of a great deal of information. Since group discussion is undoubtedly an inefficient way of transmitting information, it is remarkable that lectures are not consistently superior to group discussions. However, with other goals of education, e.g., continuing interest in a field, it appears that group discussion is likely to be the superior teaching method. Nonetheless, the differences within methods are still much larger than the differences between methods, and many other variables, such as the skill of an individual instructor in using a particular method, will have to be taken into account before a blanket recommendation of a particular teaching method can be made (63, 64).

Democratic-Authoritarian Leadership

Many writers have more or less equated "democratic" with "group-centered," and tend to view certain other forms of leadership as inherently authoritarian. Contrasting the lecture with "democratic" group discussion is an implicit condemnation of the lecture as authoritarian. But is it the form of instruction, i.e., the lecture, or the person conducting it that might be authoritarian? Thus, an authoritarian lecturer is one who places more restrictions on the freedom of his audience than are necessary in order for him to complete his lecture. And an authoritarian group discussion leader is one who places more restrictions on the group than are necessary in order to accomplish the goals of the discussion. Both can permit—or limit—the freedom inherent in these situations.

The most widely cited experiment on group leadership was one done by Lewin, Lippitt, and White (57, see also Lippitt & White, 58). In their experiment, clubs for 11-year-old boys were formed, and adult leaders assigned to the clubs were instructed to use a particular leadership technique. Three techniques were studied, and two of the clubs experienced all three types of leadership. The three types studied were aloof, arbitrary, authoritarian; warm, democratic; and passive, friendly laissez-faire (leave 'em alone). Clearly the boys preferred the democratic leader, although a few boys liked the authoritarian leader best. There were, in fact, two somewhat different reactions to the authoritarian leader, one being aggressive resistance, the other apathetic submission. In both types of authoritarian reaction the boys were more dependent upon the leader, although that was virtually insured by the nature of the authoritarian leader's role, and demands for the leader's attention were more frequent. Authoritarian leadership also seemed to induce a higher level of work activity when the leader was present. However, when the authoritarian leader left the room, the work activity dropped sharply. Although work activity was never quite so high for democratic and laissez-faire clubs, there was much less drop in activity when the leader was absent. In fact, level of work activity actually increased in the laissez-faire leader's absence. As might be expected from data on level of work activity, the clubs produced more (they worked on various projects) under the authoritarian leaders. Although the boys were not especially fond of either the club or its leader under the authoritarian condition, they were equally friendly to each other under all three conditions.

Another experiment on type of leadership was conducted by Flanders and Havumaki (28), and is of considerable interest. High school students were brought by bus to a laboratory, ostensibly to form a school team for a city-wide "Quiz Kid" type show. They participated in a discussion as to whether television or radio would be a better medium for the show. Each group had a teacher-leader, who opposed the students' preference; in all groups, the preference was for television. During the discussion each student had a lever which he could move in order to record his opinion in favor of either radio or television, and all the students could see a panel on which they had been led to believe their overall preferences were being registered continuously. However, the panel visible to the students was actually controlled by the experimenters. In some of the groups the students were led to believe that their group was gradually yielding to the dominative influence of the teacher, and in the other groups the students were led to believe that their group was resisting. During the discussion the leader directed his arguments to individual members in half of the groups, and in the other half he directed his arguments to the group as a whole.

The results of the experiment are not surprising; in fact, they confirm our expectations. Compliance increased when the students saw that others were yielding—it was contagious. And the individual approach of the leader produced more compliance than the group approach did. Perhaps the cohesiveness of a group is reduced when a leader singles out individual members for attention and pressure, thus leaving the group more open to influence. When the approach of the leader is to the group and when the members perceive that the group is in firm opposition, yielding is minimal, with only 15% changing their original preference for television. But when the arguments are directed to individuals and when members see that others are yielding, 58% changed their own preference. Very interesting, however, is the fact that the individual–compliant condition produced the greatest overt compliance, it also produced the greatest covert resistance as measured by actual recordings of the movements of the levers by which Ss thought their private opinions were being registered. Although they "voted" publicly for radio, the students "conned" into compliance still privately continued to register resistance.

The results of such studies as Lewin, Lippitt, and White's (57) and Flanders and Havumaki's (28) do not necessarily support an unqualified recommendation of any one variety of leadership. To a very great extent the best kind of leadership of a group depends on the goals that have been set for a group. For example, it seems clear that if for some reason a high level of productivity is necessary in a group, a relatively authoritarian leader is likely to be more successful. If, on the other hand, promoting a positive attitude toward a group is important, a democratic leader may be more successful—with most group members. Apropos here is Hemphill's (34) finding that the type of leadership preferred by a group is a function of the size of the group. Larger groups have a much greater tolerance for authoritarian leadership than small groups do. Larger groups appear almost of necessity to be less permissive. And the larger the group, the smaller the proportion of members who will participate actively (48). It would appear, then, that some degree of flexibility in leadership is eminently desirable. Whether any one leader is capable of the kind of flexibility that is required is an important question. Moreover, in an ongoing group it is questionable if a leader can really change his style with perfect freedom. It might also be mentioned here that some research has shown that the kind of leadership which occurs in a group is in part a function of the kinds of members who are in the group (30). To a certain extent the followers determine the behavior of the leader.

There is another issue which must be considered, however, especially in a complex society such as ours. What must always be considered is not only the immediate effect of any action or procedure but the long-range effects. Thus, a nondemocratic type of leadership may be acceptable or even desirable at a particular time and in a particular situation, but is it conducive to the development of desirable longer term habits? For example, there are certainly children who prefer an authoritarian leader, and they might even do better under the guidance of such a leader. But can such leadership prepare them to be the kind of responsible citizens needed in our democratic society? These questions deserve consideration. Valuable as research findings may be, a good bit of caution must be exercised in transposing research findings into situations that are so very different in so many ways.

Summary

Although most people think of the classroom as a place where students learn what is prescribed by the curriculum, the classroom is also a social situation in which students learn specific attitudes about themselves and about others. Children in the classroom are reinforced both positively and negatively in their social behavior. A child may change his behavior by modeling his behavior after another person, i.e., by imitation. Experiments have shown that the behavior of imitating others can be acquired in much the same way as other habits, that is, by repeatedly eliciting the imitating behavior accompanied by reinforcement.

Bandura and Walters (6) give three possible bases for behavioral changes which result from observing the behavior of a model. First, the observer may wish to imitate the model because the model's behavior represents something novel. Second, the effect of observing may produce a change in the level of inhibition associated with a particular response. Third, the responses of a model may serve to elicit the responses of the observer simply because they occur at a particular time when it is appropriate for the observer to imitate.

Not all observational learning is based on imitation. The process of identification which represents a tendency to respond to reinforcements administered to another person as if they had been administered to one-self is also a basis for behavioral change. Vicarious gratification of this kind can operate in a number of different situations. Vicarious reinforcement is an important mechanism for behavioral change in the classroom. Observing other children being rewarded for specific behaviors can increase the probability of that occurance in the behavior in the observer.

Implicit reinforcement is another use of reinforcement in producing behavioral change. Implicit reinforcement usually occurs in those situations which permit one individual to infer a reinforcement to himself by taking note of the reinforcement given to another person.

Attitudes represent behavioral predispositions which are important to the social psychologist. The term "attitude" is usually used to denote a prior disposition to make some response, usually of a judgmental or evaluative nature, to a stimulus. Attitudes cannot be seen; their existence is inferred from the behavior which an individual displays. Attitudes can differ from each other along a number of dimensions, but the dimension of evaluation, that is, favorable–unfavorable, appears to be predominant in comparison with other dimensions.

Attitudes may develop out of first-hand experience, or they may be the result of learning. Prejudice and ethnocentricism represent attitudes that have been studied extensively by social psychologists. The reasons for prejudice are obscure, but most research points to the origins of strong prejudical judgments in the childhood of the individual who displays prejudice. No one technique for eliminating prejudice seems to be more effective than others in all situations involving ethnocentric attitudes.

Susceptibility to social influence has been studied in psychology through experiments that attempt to control conformity behavior. Many people will conform to the judgmental will of others even though the data forming the basis for the judgment are false. The reasons for conformity are not known, however, it appears that conforming behavior is more prevalent in situations in which the evidence is ambigious.

Social facilitation of behavior, or the change in the probability of a particular behavior occuring in group situations over what would be found in individual situations, has been studied through experiments involving cooperation and competition. Competition over brief periods of time does produce a change in performance for the better. Cooperation, under certain conditions, is also a stimulus for the improvement of performance. Although many people think that group problem solving that requires cooperation produces better results, data exists which suggest just the opposite. The value of group experience in problem solving has not been demonstrated to the extent that group experience is advisable in all problem solving situations.

One of the aspects of social behavior which has been studied extensively by the social psychologist is that of persuasion and communication between individuals and groups. Communications have been found to be more persuasive if they come from a trustworthy source and if they are similar to previously trustworthy communications. Communications which arouse fear may be less effective than those which make a positive appeal.

Group "atmosphere" or "climate" represents one variable which distinguishes one group from another. Atmosphere within a group could result from the type of leadership, the relationships among group members, whether a group is task-oriented or maintenance-oriented, and the relationships a group has with other groups.

SUGGESTED READINGS

Bandura, A., & Walters, R. H. *Social learning and personality development.* New York: Holt, Rinehart & Winston, 1963.

The authors present an interesting and provocative account of the learning which is involved in the development of social responses. Their discussion of models for behavior and of imitation is of special interest.

Brown, R. *Social psychology.* New York: Free Press, 1965.

Prof. Brown's recent textbook in social psychology ranges over a wide selection of topics which are presented in an interesting and clear manner. The material covered is indicative of the wide range of interests represented by social psychology.

Festinger, L. *A theory of cognitive dissonance.* New York: Row, Peterson, 1957.

Cognitive dissonance represents a theoretical approach to behavior which helps to explain why we often are involved in both logical and seemingly illogical behavior. Prof. Festinger's theory has attracted much attention in the behavioral sciences and represents an inventive way of seeking explanations for behavior.

Webb, E. J., Campbell, D. P., Schwartz, R. D., & Sechrest, Lee. *Unobtrusive measures; nonreactive research in the social sciences.* Chicago: Rand McNally, 1966.

The authors discuss and present examples of research in the social sciences obtained from data in which the procedures of the experiment did not intrude into the behavior being studied. The beginning student gets a perceptive view of the inventiveness of some social science researchers from this book.

————————————————————————————————— REFERENCES

1. Aronson, E., & Mills, J. The effect of severity of initiation on liking for a group. *Journal of Abnormal and Social Psychology,* 1959, **59,** 177–181.
2. Aronson, E., Turner, J. A., & Carlsmith, J. M. Communicator credibility and communication discrepancy as determinants of opinion change. *Journal of Abnormal and Social Psychology,* 1963, **67,** 31–36.
3. Asch, S. E. *Social psychology.* New York: Prentice-Hall, 1952.
4. Azrin, N. H., & Lindsley, O. R. The reinforcement of cooperation between children. *Journal of Abnormal and Social Psychology,* 1956, **52,** 100–102.
5. Bandura, A., Ross, D., & Ross, S. A. A comparative test of the status envy, social power, and the secondary-reinforcement theories of identificatory learning. *Journal of Abnormal and Social Psychology,* 1963, **67,** 527–534.
6. Bandura, A., & Walters, R. H. *Social learning and personality development.* New York: Holt, Rinehart & Winston, 1963.
7. Barnwell, A., & Sechrest, L. Vicarious reinforcement in children at two age levels. *Journal of Educational Psychology,* 1965, **56,** 100–106.
8. Bayer, E. Beiträge zur zweikomponoten-theory des hungers. *Zeitschift für Psychologie,* 1929, **112,** 1–54.
9. Benedict, R. *Patterns of culture.* New York: Mentor Books, 1946.
10. Berger, S. M. Conditioning through vicarious instigation. *Psychological Review,* 1962, **69,** 450–466.
11. Berlyne, D. E. *Conflict, arousal and curiosity.* New York: McGraw-Hill, 1960.
12. Blake, R. R., & Mouton, J. S. Conformity, resistance and conversion. In I. A. Berg & B. M. Bass (Eds.), *Conformity and deviation.* New York: Harper, 1961. Pp. 1–37.
13. Blomgren, G. W., Jr., & Scheuneman, T. W. Psychological resistance to· seat belts. Research Project Report RR–115, The Traffic Institute, Northwestern University, 1961.
14. Bloom, B. S. Thought processes in lectures and discussions. *Journal of General Education,* 1953, **7,** 160–169.
15. Bovard, E. W., Jr. Experimental production of interpersonal affect. *Journal of Abnormal and Social Psychology,* 1951, **46,** 521–528.
16. Bovard, E. W., Jr. Clinical insight as a function of group process. *Journal of Abnormal and Social Psychology,* 1952, **47,** 534–539.
17. Bowlby, J. M. *Maternal care and mental health.* Monograph Series No. 2. Geneva: World Health Organization, 1951.
18. Brehm, J. W., & Cohen, A. R. *Explorations in cognitive dissonance.* New York: Wiley, 1962.
19. Cameron, N., & Magaret, A. *Behavior pathology.* Boston: Houghton Mifflin, 1951.
20. Campbell, D. T. Social attitudes and other acquired behavioral dispositions. In S. Koch (Ed.), *Psychology: A study of a science.* Vol. 6. New York: McGraw-Hill, 1963. Pp. 94–172.

20a. Campbell, D. T. Stereotypes and the perception of group differences. *American Psychologist,* 1967, **22,** 817–829.

21. Coleman, J. S., Blake, R. R., & Mouton, J. S. Task difficulty and conformity pressures. *Journal of Abnormal and Social Psychology,* 1958, **57,** 120–122.

22. Crowne, D. P., & Marlowe, D. *The approval motive.* New York: Wiley, 1964.

23. Crutchfield, R. S. Conformity and character. *American Psychologist,* 1955, **10,** 191–198.

24. Deutsch, M., & Collins, M. E. *Interracial housing: A psychological evaluation of a social experiment.* Minneapolis: University of Minnesota Press, 1951.

25. Festinger, L. *A theory of cognitive dissonance.* New York: Row, Peterson, 1957.

26. Festinger, L., & Carlsmith, J. M. Cognitive consequences of forced compliance. *Journal of Abnormal and Social Psychology,* 1959, 203–210.

27. Fielding, H. *Tom Jones.* London: Pan Books, 1963.

28. Flanders, N. A., & Havumaki, S. Group compliance to dominative teacher influence. *Human Relations,* 1960, **13,** 67–82.

29. Freud, S. *Civilization and its discontents.* London: Hogarth Press, 1930.

30. Gibb, C. A. Leadership. In G. Lindzey (Ed.), *Handbook of social psychology.* Vol. II. Reading, Mass.: Addison-Wesley, 1954. Pp. 877–920.

31. Gnagey, W. J. Effects on classmates of a deviant student's power and response to a teacher-exerted control technique. *Journal of Educational Psychology,* 1960, **51,** 1–8.

32. Goldfarb, W. Infant rearing and problem behavior. *American Journal of Orthopsychiatry,* 1943, **13,** 249–265.

33. Harlow, H. F., & Harlow, M. K. The effect of rearing conditions on behavior. In J. Money (Ed.), *Sex research: New developments.* New York: Holt, Rinehart & Winston, 1965. Pp. 161–175.

34. Hemphill, J. K. Relations between the size of the group and the behavior of "superior" leaders. *Journal of Social Psychology,* 1950, **32,** 11–22.

35. Hemphill, J. K. Group dimensions: A manual for their measurement. *Ohio State University Studies of Bureau of Business Research Monograph,* 1956, **87,** 66.

36. Hemphill, J. K. Administration as problem-solving. In A. W. Halpin (Ed.), *Administrative theory in education.* Chicago: Midwest Administration Center, University of Chicago, 1958. Pp. 89–118.

37. Hollander, E. P., & Webb, W. B. Leadership, followership and friendship: An analysis of peer nominations. *Journal of Abnormal and Social Psychology,* 1955, **50,** 163–167.

38. Hovland, C. I., Janis, I. L., & Kelley, H. H. *Communication and persuasion.* New Haven, Conn.: Yale University Press, 1953.

39. Hovland, C. I., Lumsdaine, A. A., & Sheffield, F. D. *Experiments on mass communication.* Princeton, N. J.: Princeton University Press, 1949.

40. Hovland, C. I., & Weiss, W. The influence of source credibility on communication effectiveness. *Public Opinion Quarterly,* 1951, **15,** 635–650.

41. Hovland, C. I., et al. *The order of presentation in persuasion.* New Haven, Conn.: Yale University Press, 1957.

42. Hudgins, B. B. Effects of group experience on individual problem solving. *Journal of Educational Psychology,* 1960, **51,** 37–42.

43. Hurlock, E. B. The use of group rivalry as an incentive. *Journal of Abnormal and Social Psychology,* 1927, **22,** 278–290.

44. Jackson, J. M., & Saltzstein, H. D. The effect of person–group relationships on

conformity processes. *Journal of Abnormal and Social Psychology*, 1958, **57**, 17–24.

45. Janis, I. L., & Feshbach, S. Effects of fear-arousing communications. *Journal of Abnormal and Social Psychology*, 1953, **48**, 78–92.
46. Janis, I. L., & King, B. T. The influence of role-playing on opinion-change. *Journal of Abnormal and Social Psychology*, 1954, **49**, 211–218.
47. Kagan, J. Acquisition and significance of sex typing and sex role identity. In M. L. Hoffman & L. W. Hoffman (Eds.), *Review of child development research.* New York: Russell Sage Foundation, 1964. Pp. 137–168.
48. Kelley, H. H., & Thibaut, J. W. Experimental studies of group problem solving and process. In G. Lindzey (Ed.), *Handbook of social psychology.* Vol. II. Reading, Mass.: Addison-Wesley, 1954. Pp. 735–785.
49. Kelman, H. C. Attitude change as a function of response restriction. *Human Relations*, 1953, **6**, 185–214.
50. King, G. F., Armitage, S. G., & Tilton, J. R. A therapeutic approach to schizophrenics of extreme pathology: An operant-interpersonal method. *Journal of Abnormal and Social Psychology*, 1960, **61**, 276–286.
51. Klineberg, O. *Social psychology.* New York: Henry Holt, 1954.
52. Kounin, J. S., & Gump, P. V. The ripple effect in discipline. *Elementary School Journal*, 1958, **59**, 158–162.
53. Lanzetta, J. T., Haefner, D., Langham, P., & Axelrod, H. Some effects of situational threat on group behavior. *Journal of Abnormal and Social Psychology*, 1954, **49**, 445–453.
54. LaPiere, R. Attitudes versus actions. *Social Forces*, 1934, **13**, 230–237.
55. Leuba, C. J. A preliminary experiment to quantify an incentive and its effects. *Journal of Abnormal and Social Psychology*, 1930, **25**, 275–283.
55a. Levanthal, H., & Singer, R. B. Affect arousal and positioning of recommendations in persuasive communications. *Journal of Personality and Social Psychology*, 1966, **4**, 137–146.
56. Lewin, K. Group decision and social change. In T. M. Newcomb & E. L. Hartley (Eds.), *Readings in social psychology.* New York: Henry Holt, 1947. Pp. 330–344.
57. Lewin, K., Lippitt, R., & White, R. K. Patterns of aggressive behavior in experimentally created social climates. *Journal of Social Psychology*, 1939, **10**, 271–299.
58. Lippitt, R., & White, R. K. An experimental study of leadership and group life. In G. E. Swanson, T. M. Newcomb, & E. L. Hartley (Eds.), *Readings in social psychology.* New York: Holt, 1952. Pp. 340–354.
59. Lumsdaine, A. A., & Janis, I. L. Resistance to "counterpropaganda" produced by a one-sided versus a two-sided "propaganda" presentation. *Public Opinion Quarterly*, 1953, **17**, 311–318.
60. Maier, N. R. F., & Solem, A. R. The contribution of a discussion leader to the quality of group thinking. *Human Relations*, 1952, **5**, 277–288.
61. Maller, J. B. Cooperation and competition. *Teachers College Contributions to Education*, 1929, No. 384, 176 pp.
62. Marquart, D. I. Group problem solving. *Journal of Social Psychology*, 1955, **41**, 103–113.
63. McKeachie, W. J. Anxiety in the college classroom. *Journal of Educational Research*, 1951, **45**, 153–160.
64. McKeachie, W. J. Research on teaching at the college and university level. In

N. L. Gage (Ed.), *Handbook of research on teaching*. Chicago: Rand McNally, 1963. Pp. 1118–1172.

65. Meyers, A. Team competition, success and the adjustment of group members. *Journal of Abnormal and Social Psychology*, 1962, **65**, 325–332.

66. Milgram, S. Some conditions of obedience and disobedience to authority. *Human Relations*, 1965, **18**, 57–75.

67. Miller, N. E., & Dollard, J. *Social leaning and imitation*. New Haven, Conn.: Yale University Press, 1941.

68. Orne, M. T. On the social psychology of the psychological experiment. *American Psychologist*, 1962, **17**, 776–783.

69. Osgood, C. E., Suci, G. J., & Tannenbaum, P. H. *The measurement of meaning*. Urbana, Ill.: University of Illinois Press, 1957.

70. Pettigrew, T. F. Social psychology and desegregation research. *American Psychologist*, 1961, **16**, 105–112.

71. Priest, R. F., & Sawyer, J. Proximity and peership: changing bases of interpersonal attraction. *American Psychologist*, 1965, **20**, 551. (Abstract)

72. Riesman, D., Denney, R., & Glazer, N. *The lonely crowd*. New Haven, Conn.: Yale University Press, 1950.

73. Rosenbaum, M. E., & deCharms, R. Direct and vicarious reduction of hostility. *Journal of Abnormal and Social Psychology*, 1960, **60**, 105–111.

74. Rosenbaum, M. E., & Tucker, I. F. The competence of the model and the learning of imitation and nonimitation. *Journal of Experimental Psychology*, 1962, **63**, 183–190.

75. Salman, A. R. The need for approval, improvisation and attitude change. Cited in Crowne & Marlowe, reference 22. Pp. 117–132.

76. Sechrest, L. Implicit reinforcement of responses. *Journal of Educational Psychology*, 1963, **54**, 197–201.

77. Sechrest, L. Studies of classroom atmosphere. *Psychology in the Schools*, 1964, **1**, 103–118.

78. Shaw, M. E. A comparison of individuals and small groups in the rational solution of complex problems. *American Journal of Psychology*, 1932, **44**, 491–504.

79. Sherif, M., & Sherif, C. W. *Groups in harmony and tension*. New York: Harper, 1953.

80. Sims, V. M. The relative influence of two types of motivation on improvement. *Journal of Educational Psychology*, 1928, **19**, 480–484.

81. Spitz, R. A. Hospitalism: an inquiry into the genesis of psychiatric conditions in early childhood. In A. Freud, E. Kris, & H. Hartmann (Eds.), *Psychoanalytic study of the child*. Vol. I. New York: International Universities Press, 1945. Pp. 53–74.

82. Stouffer, S. A., Suchman, E. A., Devinney, L. C., Star, S. A., & Williams, R. M. *The American soldier: Adjustment during Army life*. Vol. I. Princeton, N. J.: Princeton University Press, 1949. P. 594.

83. Taylor, D. W., & Faust, W. L. Twenty questions: efficiency in problem solving as a function of size of group. *Journal of Experimental Psychology*, 1952, **44**, 360–368.

84. Thibaut, J. W., & Kelley, H. H. *The social psychology of groups*. New York: Wiley, 1959.

85. Triandis, H. C., & Triandis, L. M. A cross-cultural study of social distance. *Psychological Monographs*, 1962, **76**, No. 21.

86. Tsai, L. S. Cats help rats. *Life*, 1951(March 12), **30**, No. 11, 111–112.

87. Walker, E. L., & Heyns, R. W. *An anatomy for conformity.* Englewood Cliffs, N. J.: Prentice-Hall, 1962.
88. Weiss, W. A. A "sleeper" effect in opinion change. *Journal of Abnormal and Social Psychology,* 1953, **48**, 173–180.
89. Wilson, W., & Miller, N. Shifts in evaluations of participants following intergroup competition. *Journal of Abnormal and Social Psychology,* 1961, **63**, 428–431.
90. Wright, M. E. The influence of frustration upon the social relations of young children. *Character and Personality,* 1944, **12**, 111–122.
91. Zajonc, R. B. Social facilitation. *Science,* 1965, **149**, 269–274.

17

URBAN SCHOOLS AND LEARNING

When the historians of the next century examine the crises in education occurring during the latter half of the twentieth century, the recurring theme will be the inability of our country's large metropolitan centers, or urban areas, to provide the kind of mass education we have come to expect by tradition as a heritage of all our citizens. The gradual discovery that the quality of educational accomplishment and the socioeconomic level of those being educated tend to go hand-in-hand has profoundly affected the conscience of an educational establishment which in the past has usually cast education in the mold of a middle-class model of motivation. That the difficulties of the urban school have been associated with racial minorities in our society is not irrelevant, since these minorities, particularly blacks, form a majority among those citizens whose income is classified as below median to substandard. Low income together with population density and substandard living conditions has created problems for the urban school system, and for society generally. The continual decline of the quality of urban education can be predicted unless positive steps are introduced to solve these problems. Many of the difficulties of the urban school are the result of factors over which the educational system has little direct control but which greatly influence the programs and policies of the metropolitan school system. The growth in population in our metropolitan centers has placed a severe strain upon the ability of our tradition-oriented educational institutions to absorb the impact. That this increase in population has usually been the result of minority groups, especially blacks, moving into our cities to seek better economic opportunities has added another dimension to the problem by bringing students into city schools who are not as ready to learn as the white middle-class child whose image has tended to dominate the educational establishment.

This chapter will attempt to illuminate some of the problems of the urban school system by presenting the results of a recent national survey which had much to say about educational opportunity in the United States. We will also discuss some attempted solutions to these problems, particularly Head Start. The reader should keep in mind, however, that urban education and its problems do not yet lend themselves to direct prescriptive solutions.

Equal Education—The Coleman Report

One provision of the Federal Civil Rights Act of 1964 required that the United States Office of Education, under the direction of the Commissioner of Education, undertake a survey to assess "the lack of availability of equal educational opportunities for individuals by reason of race, color, religion or national origin in public educational institutions" (8, p. iii). The resulting survey, called the Coleman Report from the name of its senior author, James S. Coleman, represents one of the most massive assessments of public education ever undertaken in this country. This national evaluation sought to determine the extent of ethnic and racial segregation in the public schools of all states, to estimate the degree of inequality among racial and ethnic groups in the educational resources available, to measure the levels of performance of students with differing backgrounds by means of achievement tests, and to relate achievement, type of student, and school background.

Such an imposing survey has not been without its critics. Factors such as the method of statistical analysis of data and the use of data to answer some of the questions asked of the survey have been criticized by some reviewers of the report (20, 22). The study has received wide acceptance, however, as the report to Congress which it was intended to be. The survey involved 4000 public schools in all fifty states plus the District of Columbia. All teachers, principals and district superintendents together with all pupils in grades 3, 6, 9, and 12 in these schools participated in the collection of data. More than 645,000 persons were involved in contributing data to the study. The survey obtained information for five minority groups (Puerto Ricans, Indian–Americans, Mexican–Americans, Oriental–Americans, and blacks) and one majority group (whites). Comparisons were made for the nation as a whole and for the nonmetropolitan north, west, south, and southwest together with the metropolitan north-east, midwest, south, southwest, and west. While comparisons involving all of these minority groups are presented in the report, black–white comparisons dominate the conclusions.

The following major findings were reported from an analysis of the data obtained:

1. For the nation as a whole, white children attended elementary schools with a smaller average class size (29) than did any of the minority groups (average class sizes ranged from 30 to 33). This national average can be deceiving, however, when class size is analyzed for white and nonwhites by region. In the nonmetropolitan north, west, and southwest, black pupils in the elementary grades attended schools with a smaller average number of pupils per room than whites.

2. In the secondary schools of the nation, the average classroom size for whites (31) was also smaller than for the minority groups (34), with the exception of Indian-Americans. Regional differences were apparent at the secondary level also; for example, the average classroom size for blacks in metropolitan midwest cities was 54 while for whites the average number of pupils per room was 33. In the metropolitan regions of the southwest; however, this trend was reversed with an average class size in secondary schools of 28 for blacks, compared with 42 for whites.

3. Minority groups tended to have less access to physical facilities for their educational experiences related to school achievement than did whites. Regional variations in facilities were apparent in the data; however, the overall trend in fewer and less varied facilities for minority groups was supported for all regions of the country. According to the Coleman Report (8, p. 12):

> Secondary school Negro students are less likely to attend schools that are regionally accredited; this is particularly pronounced in the South. Negro and Puerto Rican pupils have less access to college preparatory curriculums and to accelerated curriculums; Puerto Ricans have less access to vocational curriculums as well. Less intelligence testing is done in the schools attended by Negroes and Puerto Ricans. Finally, white students have more access to a more fully developed program of extracurricular activities, in particular those which might be related to academic matters.

4. The average black student attended a school where a large percentage of the teachers appeared to be less able than the teachers in the average white student's school. Teacher ability was measured by such factors as highest degree earned, the percent of teachers who attended colleges which white students attended, the percent of teachers majoring in academic subjects, salary, together with a measure of verbal ability.

5. The average black student attended a school with fewer classmates whose mothers were high school graduates, and the families of these classmates were larger than the families of the average white student. The average black student tended to be less often enrolled in a college preparatory curriculum and to have taken a smaller number of basic courses such as English, mathematics, foreign language, and science than the average white student. These differences tended to be greatest in the South.

6. Achievement tests administered to students in grades 1, 3, 6, 9, and 12 indicated that, with the exception of Oriental-Americans, the median scores for the

minority students were lower at every level when compared with median scores for white students. Table 17-1, taken from the survey report, summarizes these achievement test results for the first and twelfth grades. One should remember that the achievement tests which were used did not measure intelligence nor were they constructed to be "culture-free." In the words of the report, "what they measure are the skills which are among the most important in our society for getting a good job and moving up to a better one and for full participation in an increasingly technical world (8, p. 20)." An examination of Table 17-1 shows that the median scores for black and white students indicate a sizable difference at the first-grade level. This difference increases so that, at the twelfth-grade level each of the minority groups has a lower median score on verbal and nonverbal measures than the median scores for the first-grade pupils in the same minority group. Although the majority students have slightly lower median scores at the twelfth-grade level also, the difference between the first and twelfth-grade majority students is not as great as that same comparison for the minority students. The most startling difference, however, can be seen in the disparity between the median scores for the minority and majority students at the twelfth-grade level. In all instances, the median scores for the minority students are lower than the median scores for the white students. An indication of this difference and its progressive increase from one grade to the next can be seen in the example of Negroes in the metropolitan northeastern region of the United States. At grade 6 the difference represents a lag of only about 1.6 years. At grade 9 this increases to 2.4 years and at grade 12 the median achievement scores for blacks in this region represents a lag of about 3.3 years when compared with the median achievement scores of the white students in the same region. According to Coleman *et al.* (8, p. 21):

> For most minority groups, then, and most particularly the Negro, schools provide no opportunity at all for them to overcome this initial deficiency; in fact, they fall farther behind the white majority in the development of several skills which are critical to making a living and participating fully in modern

TABLE 17-1
Nationwide Median Test Scores for First- and Twelfth-Grade Pupils

	Racial or ethnic group					
Test	Puerto Ricans	Indian– Americans	Mexican– Americans	Oriental– Americans	Black	Majority
First grade:						
Nonverbal	45.8	53.0	50.1	56.6	43.4	54.1
Verbal	44.9	47.8	46.5	51.6	45.4	53.2
Twelfth grade:						
Nonverbal	43.3	47.1	45.0	51.6	40.9	52.0
Verbal	43.1	43.7	43.8	49.6	40.9	52.1
Reading	42.6	44.3	44.2	48.8	42.2	51.9
Mathematics	43.7	45.9	45.5	51.3	41.8	51.8
General information	41.7	44.7	43.3	49.0	40.6	52.2
Average of the 5 tests	43.1	45.1	44.4	50.1	41.1	52.0

society. Whatever may be the combination of nonschool factors—poverty, community attitudes, low educational level of parents—which put minority children at a disadvantage in verbal and nonverbal skills when they enter the first grade, the fact is that schools have not overcome it.

In considering the findings of this survey, especially those reported in Table 17-1, the use of a comparison which emphasizes average and median type indices should be kept in mind. Obviously, many *individual* minority pupils surpass *individual* majority students in achievement.

7. One surprising finding of the survey was the conclusion that the characteristics of a school (library facilities, science laboratories, teachers, etc.) had little effect on the achievement of both majority and minority pupils. When the socioeconomic background of students was taken into account, schools appeared to be remarkably similar in the effect they had on pupil achievement. When the socioeconomic factor was statistically controlled, differences between schools, in terms of strengths and weaknesses in facilities, curriculum, and teachers, accounted for only a small portion of the differences between pupils in achievement. Differences did exist in the degree of impact the school had when minority pupils were compared with majority pupils; however, this difference itself was small. For example, the statistical method used to compare schools with pupil achievement indicated that about 20% of the achievement of black students in the south was associated with the school they attended, while only 10% of the achievement of white students in the south was associated with the school they attended. Although the influence of the school itself seems to be minimal in influencing differences in achievement, one should remember that the data obtained for the Coleman Report represented primarily responses from standardized tests which did not measure many aspects of school influence. The following quotation from the report indicates the school factors which the authors feel contribute to the small amount of variations in achievement as a function of the school attended (8, p. 22):

> Among the facilities that show some relationship to achievement are several for which minority pupils' schools are less well equipped relative to whites.' For example, the existence of science laboratories showed a smaller but consistent relationship to achievement [with] minorities, especially Negroes, in schools with fewer of these laboratories. . . . The quality of teachers shows a strong relationship to pupil achievement. Furthermore it is progressively greater at higher grades, indicating a cumulative impact of the qualities of teachers in a school on the pupils' achievement. Again teacher quality is more important for minority pupil achievement than for that of the majority. . . . Finally, it appears that a pupil's achievement is strongly related to the educational backgrounds and aspirations of the other students in the school.

Criticism of the Coleman Report has centered upon this last conclusion emphasizing the relationship between school facilities and achievement. Levin (20) contends that the statistical technique used in the analysis of achievement differences, together with sample bias, tended to produce statistical results which were weighted in a direction which understated the importance of school resources in explaining variations in achievement. Nichols (22) takes the investigators to task for failing to control important sources of variation in their sample, particularly student dropout and migration. He feels that causal relationships have been suggested on the basis of nonexperimental correlational data which indicate only gross relationships and not causation.

Supporters of the report generally praise the results—not for their specificity—but rather for the broad conclusions which the study offers for the guidance of public policy relative to education. Jencks (16) praises the report for what it contributes to our understanding of how schools effect the individual learner. He offers as a hypothesis for the findings of the report the observation that:

> . . . all American children, regardless of race, know they will need verbal skills to get ahead, and acquire them if given half the chance. If they come from good homes they pick these skills up from their parents and neighboring children, and even a good school adds relatively little. If they come from poor homes, however, they cannot acquire verbal skills from their parents or on the streets. In that case school, and more specifically, schoolmates, are crucially important.

Figure 17-1 presents a comparison of the verbal achievement skills of blacks and whites by showing urban and rural differences in the

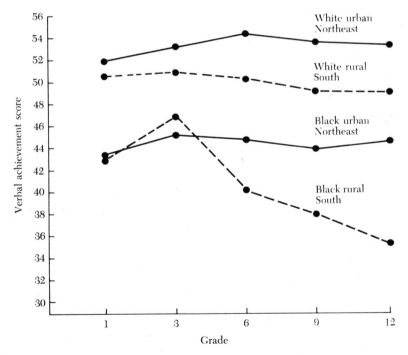

Fig. 17-1. Verbal achievement by grade level, race, and region. National mean score at each grade = 50 ± 10. Adaptation of figure in Coleman (7).

northeast and in the south. These data from Coleman (7) show only too well the cumulative deficits in verbal skills which tend to build up as the black student progresses through school. Jencks concludes that the evidence cited by the report suggests that the narrowing of the educational gap between blacks and whites is being facilitated to a greater degree by forces outside the school system than by schools themselves. An increased expenditure in black schools will not bridge this gap unless increased spending goes to those factors which most influence achievement in schools. Closing the educational gap between blacks and whites will require radical changes in the whole structure of society, and not just changes in schools themselves.

Bronfenbrenner (5) has reacted to the Coleman Report by commenting on two of the findings of the survey as being the most significant. One impressive, but expected, result was that the home background of the child was of critical importance in determining the extent of achievement in school. This was true for all pupils in the study except southern blacks, for whom the characteristics of the school seemed to be the more important. When the home provided the primary sustenance, its importance was dominant; when the school was the source of primary support for achievement, the school became the more important source of sustenance. A second impressive, but unexpected, finding was the basic importance of the characteristics of schoolmates in determining pupil achievement. A lower-class child with schoolmates from advantaged homes usually achieved better than the lower-class child who was with other lower-class children. Bronfenbrenner points out that the report supports the crucial importance of home background and age mate influences on achievement in today's classroom.

In a recent issue of the *Harvard Educational Review* devoted to an assessment of *Equality of Educational Opportunity*, Moynihan (21) summarizes the possible influences on black and white educational achievement from Coleman's data as follows:

    1. The influence of race (white medians were consistently above Negro medians).
    2. The influence of residence (urban pupils, with few exceptions, scored higher than rural groups of the same race and region).
    3. The influence of region (with few exceptions, northern groups scored above southern groups of similar race and region).
    4. The influence of a home with both parents present (almost all groups showed a tendency for achievement to decline in instances where the structural integrity of the home was missing through the absence of the father).

Moynihan feels that blacks in the south have largely been the victim of a caste system which has institutionalized few, if any, socially available educational opportunities. Changes in the institutions which perpetuate the caste should be the first step in correcting inequalities in education in the south. On the other hand, as blacks move farther away from caste conditions they come in contact with a wide variety of socially provided opportunities for education. These opportunities, however, provide circumstances in which the individual characteristics of the student and his peer group begin to control the incidence of success and failure. The lack of a structural integrity more frequently in the homes of black students than in the homes of white students suggests that many of the personal and individual characteristics which are important for success in school, and which are usually learned in a white society at home prior to school, are not generally available to the black child who has not had the socially provided opportunity of a stable home environment (21).

In a personal evaluation of the Coleman Report, Pettigrew (24) has this to say about the survey:

> Let it be clearly stated that Coleman and his associates achieved a landmark contribution in an amazingly short span of time. Though not without its problems of sampling, non-response, and analysis, this ambitious study should influence educational research and practice for years to come . . . the social implications for practical school policy are reasonably clear: equal educational opportunity for both Negro and white children requires socially and racially integrated, and not merely desegrated, schools.

Pettigrew (24) feels that one of the most significant consequences of the Coleman Report is the conclusion that desegregation is only a minimum and beginning condition for the provision of equal education opportunities for minority and white students. Desegregation involves only a prescription of the racial mix of a classroom. It indicates only the quantity involved and says nothing about the quality of the interracial contact between students in a classroom. Desegregation, in and of itself, does not produce "good schooling." Integration involves desegregation, but it goes beyond racial mixing to specify a climate of interracial acceptance.

Pettigrew (24) believes that "many of the consequences of interracial classrooms for both Negro and white children are a direct function of the opportunities such classrooms provide for cross-racial self-evaluation." To the degree that a classroom provides for positive cross-racial self-evaluation which leads to the development of patterns of internal self-control, which is necessary for success in an achievement-oriented society, effective integration has taken place for purposes of the educational task. Coleman *et al.* (8) speculated that every child faces a two-stage problem in developing those personal characteristics which lead to achievement. First, the child must learn that he can control and effectively manipulate his surroundings; and, second, that he can realistically evaluate his own relative capabilities for mastering the environment. Pettigrew indicates that the critical step for the white child is the second stage while the critical step for the black child is all too often the first stage, in which the black child is caught up in the critical activity of learning to manipulate an impersonal, harsh, and overpowering environment. Thus, the black child comes to the classroom with much less preparation for evaluating his own capabilities than the preparation he has had for doing battle with a hostile world. In a supportive integrated classroom setting the black child should have the opportunity to learn this process of self-evaluation from his classmates—provided many of them have this characteristic and provided his own prejudices do not prevent him from using classmates as models. Desegregation at the elementary school level is of special importance as a first step in the establishment of opportunities for cross-racial self-evaluation. The elementary school child has not developed a firm commitment to a uniracial peer structure and is able to identify across race to a much greater degree. According to Pettigrew (24):

> . . . integrated education in the early grades seems to have important benefits for both Negro and white children in terms of improved interracial attitudes and preferences. . . . And if social evaluation processes during interracial contact are as critical contributors to these benefits as they appear in these [Coleman's] data, even the most academically successful "compensatory program" in ghetto schools cannot rival genuine integration.

The Coleman Report provides no ready solutions to the inequalities in education which it documents. The authors present clear evidence of a segregated system of schools which, it is hoped, is becoming more de-segregated as this is being written. The conclusion suggesting that school facilities themselves have little influence on the achievement of the pupil represents a result which could lead to several interpretations. Taken at face value without an analysis of the variables involved in assessing facilities, and without an understanding of the statistical techniques used in analyzing these data, one could incorrectly conclude that schools can do very little to improve the achievement of their pupils. According to Dyer (10) ". . . possibly the major contribution [of the Coleman Report] is its massive challenge to the simplistic notion that counting educational dollars, or the things dollars buy, is a sufficient measure of the equality of educational opportunity."

The influence of home background and classmates on achievement points to the long known fact that early opportunities for learning socially acceptable verbal skills is related to later success in school. Unfortunately, children do not usually start their formal school experiences until they are about 6 years of age. Children whose backgrounds are not conducive to the development of school readiness therefore have an extensive period of time before entering school to learn behaviors and attitudes which are not helpful in learning to achieve in school. Preschool experiences have been advocated as one way to compensate for these deficiencies. One of these programs—Head Start—is supported by the Federal Government.

Head Start

One of the most outstanding involvements of the Federal Government in education has been through preschool programs such as Head Start which, in 1967, was providing learning and health care for some 3 million children. In a special message to Congress asking that Head Start be expanded to include the early grades, President Johnson (25) had this to say about the Head Start program:

> Head Start, a preschool program for poor children, has passed its first trials with flying colors.
> Through this program hope has entered the lives of hundreds of thousands of children and their parents. The child whose only horizons were the crowded rooms of a tenement discovered new worlds of curiosity, of companionship, of creative effort. Volunteer workers gave thousands of hours to help launch poor children on the path toward self-discovery, stimulating them to enjoy books for the first time, watching them sense the excitement of learning.

Head Start was conceived as a concentrated effort to prepare the disadvantaged child for the experiences of school. Its activities are centered in those areas where poverty is greatest. The influence of Head Start on urban education patterns, especially at the elementary level, should be great because of the incidence of economically disadvantaged families in large urban centers. In addition to educational goals, Head Start also provides needed health care for the children it serves, with such care based on the well-established observation that healthy children learn best.

The relationship between physical health and learning in the young child has been underscored in a recent summary of research on learning and infant malnutrition, reported by Scrimshaw (28). He points out that the correlation of physical size with conditions of poverty strongly suggests that nutritional and not genetic factors are the cause of the appearance of both factors together. During the 1920's, animal experiments produced data which suggest that these nutritional deficiencies not only depress physical size but affect the central nervous system, particularly the growth of the brain. Accumulative results from animal studies demonstrate that central nervous system damage is most pronounced when the animal's diet is deficient in protein, even though adequate calories may be present. Infant malnutrition in most sophisticated societies involves an absence of adequate protein after about the second or third year of development, when the child is weaned and put on a diet which may be adequate in calories but deficient in proteins. This type of malnutrition is called kwashiorkor. In experimental animals even when this protein deficiency is reversed they exhibit the results of central nervous system damage, which is irreversible. Studies of malnutrition in young children and in experimental animals lead to the conclusion that nutritional factors in the early years of life, especially during those years involving maximum brain growth, can contribute to mental retardation and mental "dullness" during the school years and in later adult life, especially if the nutritional deficit involves protein support. Scrimshaw concludes that malnutrition and early infection should be considered along with early cultural and sensory deprivation as important contributing factors to deficits in the ability to learn and adapt to one's environment. By the time a child of 6 is introduced to learning tasks in school his neurological capacity to respond to learning tasks and to perform at an expected level may be irreversably damaged by earlier patterns of nutrition involving protein deficits.

The need for a Head Start program in education has been stimulated by a number of factors, among them the changing pattern of child rearing in this country, which has shifted from a system in which the parent had the basic responsibility for the development of the child to a system in which the parent is only one of a number of agents and institutions which shape the child. The family is still recognized as the major setting for the child's development, but other sources, especially the child's age mates, increasingly influence the behavior of children and adolescents. In many instances this shift of responsibility to institutions outside the family has not been clearly accepted as a responsibility by these social settings. One factor alone—the decrease in the amount of time children spend with parents in situations involving training and development for socialization—is indicative of the shift in time commitments to other agents in society. Children are growing up in a different kind of environment from that which influenced their parents.

According to Bronfenbrenner (5) one significant change which has been brought about by this shift away from the family as the dominant influence in development has been the emergence of the influence of peers on early development. Children now spend much more time with other children in formal and informal relationships. Even when the child must stay home, his time is usually occupied with TV-watching and not in any kind of meaningful interaction with parents. Bronfenbrenner (5) states that ". . . whereas American children used to spend much of their time with parents and other grownups, more and more waking hours are now lived in the world of peers and of the television screen."

While the reality of these changes is apparent, the influence of the peer group and of TV on the development of children has not been studied sufficiently to be understood. Bronfenbrenner mentions the results of some studies which relate to these influences. He and his colleagues have found that children who indicated that their parents were away from home for long periods of time had significantly lower ratings on such factors as leadership and responsibility. The absence of the father seemed to have a greater influence than the absence of the mother, particularly with boys. Several studies have shown that in boys the absence of the father is associated with low achievement motivation, low self-esteem, the inability to delay immediate for later gratification, susceptibility to group influence, and juvenile delinquency.

In a 1959 study of Bowerman and Kinch, reported by Bronfenbrenner (5), a turning point at about the seventh grade away from parental influence and toward peer influence was identified. The children in the study reported that before that time they turned more often to their parents for advice, opinion, and company in various activities. Parents were perceived as models, companions, and guides to behavior. After that time, the influence of peers superceded that of parents. This trend in the dominance of influence has probably been accelerated during the ten-year time span since the study, so that peer influence may appear much earlier than the seventh grade today.

Bronfenbrenner feels that society needs to develop an opportunity structure for young children which will allow the many forces involved in the development of children, especially the family, the peer, and the whole community, to come together to focus the influence of these three forces on constructive learning and socialization. The beginnings of this type of opportunity structure clearly exist in Head Start programs, which attempt to involve parents, older children, and the whole community in care for the young.

Head Start programs are now established throughout the United States and, for the most part, have been met with enthusiasm from the parents of children involved. Many attempts to evaluate Head Start programs are under way. One such evaluation made during the beginning months of the program has been reported by Wolff and Stein (29). Their study compared children who had participated in Head Start with children who had not. The sample consisted of children who attended four kindergartens in public elementary schools in New York City. The Head

Start children in the study had attended three Head Start centers. One center was all-black, another was predominantly Puerto Rican, and the third was racially and ethnically mixed. According to Wolff and Stein (29):

> Four measures of social and educational "readiness" for first-grade work were selected for comparisons: the child's initial adjustment to classroom routines and the length of time it took him to become fully adjusted to school routines; his behavior towards his peers and towards the teacher; his speech, work habits, and listening habits, and his educational attainments.

In addition to data collected from Head Start and non-Head Start children, the parents of both groups were interviewed. The results indicated a support for the Head Start experience, especially for the black and Puerto Rican children. Specifically, the investigators found that:

> 1. Head Start children in the all-Negro school and the Puerto Rican school tended to be ranked higher in their kindergarten classes by the teacher in greater proportions than non-Head Start children. In the mixed kindergarten the opposite results were obtained, with non-Head Start children being ranked higher in greater proportions than Head Start children.
> 2. Parents were unanimous in their enthusiasm for the Head Start program in all the schools. Parents approved of the program mainly because they felt that their children were better prepared for kindergarten. The children who had the Head Start experience were favorable in their recall of the experiences.
> 3. Teachers were divided in their impressions of the effectiveness of the Head Start experience. Teachers with fewer than 25% of their kindergarten class consisting of Head Start children were less likely to feel that the experience made any difference than teachers who had 50% or more children in their class who had been through the Head Start program.
> 4. Head Start children as a group were judged by their teachers to have adjusted to the kindergarten experience better than non-Head Start children did.
> 5. Head Start children were not significantly different from non-Head Start children 6 to 8 months after the Head Start experience in their general readiness for kindergarten, as measured by a preschool inventory.

The report of Wolff and Stein (29) agrees with other observations concerning the enthusiasm of parents, particularly those whose children are generally judged "culturally deprived." In addition, the favorable response of teachers to children who have had the Head Start experience has been confirmed in other studies. The program has had its widest effect in poverty areas and so has become associated with other antipoverty programs even though economic need is not an absolute criterion for inclusion in Head Start programs.

During its second year of activity, Project Head Start enrolled approximately 1.3 million children in 2400 communities throughout the United States (4). It has been referred to as one of the largest mobilizations during peacetime of resources and efforts. Head Start is designed to be a short-term experience for children who have been socially, emotionally, and intellectually retarded by the experience of living in substandard surroundings. According to Brazziel (4) Project Head Start attempts to provide a program which emphasizes educational development, health services and nutritional support, social and psychological services, and parent participation. The educational program emphasizes the development of vocabulary and word fluency, learning to express oneself spontaneously, familiarization with the routine of school, getting to know teachers and learning to relate to them, developing an interest in books and reading, and developing a broader concept of the world. Classroom experiences are much like those in a nursery school or a kindergarten and the development of readiness for later school experiences is stressed.

Since the great majority of children participating in Head Start come from environments which are less than adequate in health care and eating habits, special attention is given to health problems and to nutritional deficits. Head Start emphasizes the fact that ill and/or hungry children are not able to learn. Midmorning snacks and lunches are provided in most programs and breakfast is usually made available to children who are not provided this meal at home. Most programs include comprehensive health examinations and provide required care through referrals to other agencies within the community.

In many programs psychological counseling is provided for the child and for parents when the need is present. Psychological evaluations of emotional and social factors in the life of the child, which keep him from learning adequately, are usually undertaken and referrals made to appropriate agencies as needed.

One of the unique aspects of Head Start is the involvement of the parents of Head Start children in the program. This involvement can take many forms such as direct participation as a teaching aide or meeting as a group to discuss the progress of the children. While the type of involvement is important, the act of involvement is itself felt to be the crucial factor since the family that helps plan activities for children is more likely to support that activity than the family that is given a plan which is developed apart from the parents. According to Brazziel (4):

> . . . both tangible and intangible gains are hoped for by Head Start planners. Readiness for formal schools is the prime wish; gains in achievement and achievement motivation are important corrollaries. It is also hoped that parents and other adults will know more and do more about preparing underprivileged children for school by providing the psychological, social, and physical support necessary for achievement motivation and success. Put differently, it is hoped that a change in community ethos will result. . . . A minimum academic gain from Head Start experiences is coming to be regarded as an increase of from 5 to 10 points in I.Q. and 20 to 25 points on school readiness tests.

While average gains in I.Q. scores and in scores on readiness tests have been observed as an apparent function of preschool programs such as Head Start, these gains have in many cases been transitory. Changes in rapport between the child and the psychologist on the first testing as compared with the second testing as well as problems of motivation with the child could account for a significant portion of these differences.

Many of the present positive feelings about Head Start which have been offered in support of this type of activity may, to some extent, be due to the enthusiasm engendered during its first few years of operation. As the results of more objective assessments become available, we will probably find that such programs are not the total answer to the problem of the child who is penalized by an environment which makes him begin the crucial activity of school at a pronounced disadvantage. Head Start, however, together with programs designed to erase the environmental disadvantage, should provide the factors which are needed to give all children a maximum opportunity to profit from school experiences.

One section of the Coleman Report deals with the effects of Project Head Start on black and white pupils who participated in this program during the summer of 1965. No firm conclusion concerning an evaluation of the program could be made, but one result did indicate that the program was reaching those pupils for whom it was intended. A black child from a metropolitan region had a probability of participating in this first summer Head Start program which was nearly seven times as great as that of a white child in the same region. In nonmetropolitan regions the probability of participation for the black child was nearly five times as great as that for the white child. Coleman *et al.* (8, p. 492) conclude "that the Head Start programs are being offered where background deficiencies are most prevalent and are being taken advantage of by those students most likely to have deficient backgrounds." Thus, Head Start programs in the summer of 1965 were generally attended by pupils who had the most to gain from this participation; i.e., students from lower socioeconomic backgrounds. These participants also appeared to have higher educational motivation than comparable nonparticipants, with the association between higher motivation and lower socioeconomic status being quite apparent for black children. The effects of participation, however, appeared to be less noticeable in test performance than in educational motivation. Such an observation is not surprising when one considers that these students were participants in the first summer experience of the program. Gains over average test performance would not be anticipated as an immediate result of the first few months of Head Start if the majority of pupils had entered the program with a deficiency in achievement. Reports of Head Start experiences during 1965, 1966, and 1967 have presented no indications that these first conclusions are basically incorrect.

Head Start will undoubtedly be regarded as one of the most innovative activities of the Federal Government in the field of education. Only the future will decide whether Head Start will receive the funding needed to allow it to reach all children who could profit from it. In addition to adequate funding, programs such as this will need to remain free from the politics of the cities where these efforts are more desperately needed. Since its beginning, Head Start has been a most attractive target for those forces within the Federal establishment that wish to see programs such as this funded through local governmental units. Depending on the integrity of the local unit, such a move could produce Head Start programs which would become nothing more than sources of patronage positions. Any program which brings together parents, children, and community resources in an attempt to prepare children for their first formal school experiences deserves the serious attention of all citizens. Head Start is by no means the total answer to the problems which cultural deprivation and poverty create for education; however, Head Start places the emphasis on intervention at a time in life when intervention can be most effective. Support for this conclusion comes from a recent study of Bloom (2) in which he discusses the problem of intervention in changing human characteristics. Let us consider his findings briefly, since they have implications for Head Start and for compensatory education programs generally.

Bloom (2) undertook an analysis of approximately 1000 longitudinal studies having as their major concern the development and shaping of human characteristics from infancy to adulthood. These studies dealt with such factors as physical characteristics, intelligence, achievement data, interests, attitudes, personality, and the general environment. One finding was that the correlations between the measurement of a specific characteristic at particular ages was quite similar from one study to another. This degree of similarity suggests that the data which Bloom analyzed produced measures which have some degree of stability associated with them and which support general conclusions about the characteristics measured. An analysis of growth curves from one study to another leads to the conclusion that growth and development are not in equal units per unit of time. In other words, for each characteristic studied, a period of rapid growth and a period of slow growth could be identified. With few exceptions, the period of most rapid growth corresponds to the first five years of life. For example, when development by ages 18 to 20 is taken as the maximum level of growth, one-half of this level for height is reached by age 2½; for general intelligence by age 4

(I.Q. at age 4 accounts for 50% of the variance in I.Q. at age 16); for aggressiveness in males by age 3; for dependence in females by age 4; and for intellectuality in males and females by age 4. Among these characteristics, general school achievement is the only exception with one-half of its level of growth being reached by grade three (2).

Bloom refers to these as stable characteristics as opposed to human characteristics which change very rapidly over shorter periods of time. These stable characteristics have in common the factor of being either irreversible or only partially reversible, and they appear to undergo very rapid growth and development during their early phases followed by less rapid change. Changes through time in a particular characteristic are basically dependent upon the environment as the agent influencing the extent and kind of change. With this observation in mind, Bloom (2) offers the hypothesis that "a characteristic can be more drastically affected by the environment in its most rapid period of growth than in its least rapid period of growth."

Bloom advances three reasons why early environment is important for growth and development. The first is based on the evidence of the rapid growth of basic characteristics during the early years. The importance of early environment is crucial in shaping stable characteristics during a time involving their most rapid periods of formation. Second, these characteristics interact so that each is built upon the base of the same characteristic at an earlier time or on the base of other characteristics at earlier stages of development. Theories of development based upon the concept of developmental stages emphasize the importance of initial development and interaction between characteristics on the later stages of development. A resolution of developmental problems at one stage has consequences for subsequent stages. Development which takes place during the early years is crucial in shaping the direction and consequences of later developmental stages. And, third, early learning, if correct to begin with, avoids the later problem of having to unlearn non-reinforcing patterns of behavior in order to learn behaviors which are rewarding. According to Bloom (2), "it is much easier to learn something new than it is to stamp out one set of learned behaviors and replace them by a new set."

These findings of Bloom point to the tremendous importance of the early years, particularly those before the start of formal schooling, in influencing development and growth that follows. The difficulty of changing many characteristics becomes more pronounced with advanced age. Massive environmental interventions are required to produce changes at later stages of life. The implications of these findings for education are, of course, obvious. If basic characteristics that are important for success in learning and achievement—and most of the characteristics studied by Bloom are—need to be changed, programs of intervention must be started early, before the child enters kindergarten. Intervention should involve all of those environmental forces which are important in stimulating the direction of development for these characteristics. Any compensatory program, for example, which attempts to increase the holding power of the school and decrease the number of dropouts must begin before the junior high or high school level. By that time the amount of intervention necessary to produce change is so great it may be prohibitive.

Higher Horizons—New York City

Head Start programs provide a type of intervention designed to produce changes in characteristics important for success in school. Let us examine one other program which received much attention when it was begun in New York City. This is the Higher Horizons Program for Underprivileged Children in the New York City School System (30). Higher Horizons was designed to bring quality education to the socially disadvantaged child in New York. The program is a compensatory one which attempts to overcome the influence of low income, frequent moving, poor housing, bad health conditions, broken or incomplete families, racial problems, and other social disadvantages. The Higher Horizons Program is based on the assumption that to improve the pupils' abilities to learn and achieve in school the environment must be controlled in a way that brings about a direct influence on the child, the teacher, and the parent (19). In order to raise his aspirations, the child must first be convinced that it is possible. Higher Horizons emphasizes enrichment and compensatory educational programs which give the disadvantaged child the close attention and frequent stimulation needed to succeed.

The goals of Higher Horizons are presented in Fig. 17-2. These goals do not differ significantly from those which should apply to all students. They do emphasize, however, the extent of the intervention necessary to bring about changes in the abilities, interests, and aspirations of children. The success of such a program depends upon the system's ability to provide additional personnel necessary to make the program function as planned. During the 1962-1963 school year Higher Horizons in New York City cost approximately $3,800,000. This money provided 290 program teachers and 157 guidance counselors plus books and supplies. The total additional cost of education for the Higher Horizon student during that school year produced an estimated total cost of over $200 per pupil (19). The increase in personnel needed for Higher Horizon schools can be

Guidance

1. To identify abilities, interests, and needs of children.
2. To raise levels of aspiration of children, and to stimulate them to attain levels commensurate with their ability.
3. To create for all children the aspiration to complete high school, and for those with appropriate ability, the aspiration to go on to higher education.
4. To carry on programs of intensive individual and group counseling which will:
   —assist each child in making and following appropriate educational and occupational plans.
   —provide for the early introduction of occupational information.
5. To carry on programs of education of parents in guidance objectives.
6. To assist with in-service training of teachers.
7. To develop new guidance tools, techniques, procedures, and materials to help realize these objectives.

Teacher Training

1. To train teachers in identification of ability, particularly academic ability.
2. To train teachers in methods of helping children to realize their potential, particularly in academic areas.
3. To help teachers to set goals for children which are realistic in terms of potential rather than in terms of past achievement.
4. To define the role of the classroom teacher in the total program to help the educationally disadvantaged.
5. To stimulate teacher participation in the total program.

Cultural Experiences

1. To raise children's cultural sights by giving them experiences not usually provided by the home or community.
2. To help children see themselves as part of the cultural mainstream of our country.
3. To supply educational, occupational, and cultural experiences which will raise the aspirations of the children while simultaneously improving their self-image.
4. To provide a firm basis for other educational experiences, particularly those of a verbal nature.

Curriculum Enrichment and Adaptation

1. To enrich the curriculum in academic and cultural areas in order to discover and develop pupil potential.
2. To make such curriculum adaptations as may be necessary to develop the academic potential of pupils.
3. To utilize existing school facilities, such as libraries, in reaching these goals.

Remedial Services

To supply remedial services for children with good academic potential, particularly in reading but also in other academic areas.

Parent and Community Education

1. To help parents understand the value of the school in terms of their hopes for their children.

Fig. 17-2. Goals of the Higher Horizons Program of New York City. Taken from Landers (19), pp. 11–12.

2. To give parents a better understanding of the community resources and educational opportunities available to them and to their children.
3. To encourage and assist parents in providing an atmosphere of encouragement and stimulation for their children.
4. To raise the levels of educational, vocational and cultural aspiration of parents for their children.
5. To enlist the assistance of community agencies in supplying necessary services, and to coordinate such services.
6. To develop new approaches which will encourage parents to cooperate with the school in raising the educational, vocational, and aspirational level of children.

Inspiration
1. To give to teachers and parents that faith in children, and children that faith in themselves, which alone makes progress possible.
2. To enable teachers, pupils, and parents to identify themselves with a successful enterprise of great importance.

Evaluation and Record-Keeping
1. To develop techniques for the identification and stimulation of the educationally disadvantaged.
2. To organize and maintain meaningful records.
3. To evaluate the success of the Higher Horizons program.

Fig. 17-2 (*Continued*).

seen in the comparison between a school in a middle-class residental area which was not part of the Higher Horizon effort with a school that was. The non-Higher Horizon school had 34 professional workers per thousand pupils while the Higher Horizon school had 61 professional workers per thousand. Both of these elementary schools had approximately 860 pupils in grades 1 through 6, but the Higher Horizon school had a total professional staff of 52 while the non-Higher Horizon school had a professional staff totaling 29. These comparisons are not presented to imply that increases in staff are the answer to remedial and compensatory needs, but rather to indicate the increases needed to accomplish the goals set for Higher Horizons. In addition to lower class size and increased opportunities for personal contact with teachers and professional workers, the students in the Higher Horizons Program were given large doses of cultural stimulation designed to acquaint them with aspects of the life of New York City which they might not know about or might not be willing to expose themselves to. Field trips and special projects, many involving parents, were planned as part of the formal educational activities of the students. During 1962-1963, the Higher Horizons Program reached 33,757 elementary pupils in grades 3, 4, 5, and 6 of 52 schools in New York City. During the same school year, 19,338 junior high school students were involved in grades 7, 8, and 9 of 13 schools (19).

Wrightstone (30) reported on an evaluation of Higher Horizons which was undertaken to assess professional and staff reaction, parental reaction, the personal and social development of pupils, and their scholastic aptitude and achievement. The major findings of this evaluation were:

1. Fewer disciplinary problems were found in the elementary schools among the fifth graders who were in Higher Horizon schools.
2. Pupils who were not in the Higher Horizons Program reported higher self-concepts but not higher ideal concepts than their counterparts in the program did.
3. Truancy was lower in Higher Horizon elementary schools than in non-Higher Horizon schools.
4. Attendance was better at Higher Horizon elementary schools.
5. No significant gains in I.Q. were reported in a comparison of Higher Horizon students with non-Higher Horizon students.
6. No significant differences in reading comprehension test scores were observed in comparing program and non-program students.
7. Junior High School students in Higher Horizons tended to be rated better behaved than the non-Higher Horizon student.
8. Attendance at Higher Horizon Junior High Schools was better than at non-program schools.
9. Parents indicated that the features of the program which they liked best were the trips of cultural interest, the increased student interest in school work, the improved school achievement, and the increased attention to the needs of the individual.

An examination of these evaluation results of the Higher Horizons Program in New York City suggests that Higher Horizon students emerge from the program with the same general level of achievement as those students who were in regular elementary and junior high schools. This in itself is an achievement when one considers the backgrounds of the Higher Horizon students and the characteristics which were brought to the program by them. The enthusiasm shown by the professional staff and by the parents indicates support for the efforts of the program and a degree of implicit motivation which is needed if the Program is to succeed. The Higher Horizons Program represented one of the most prominent examples of a compensatory educational program. The program is no longer operational.

Compensatory Education and Cultural Deprivation

During the summer of 1964, a conference sponsored by the United States Office of Education, was held at the University of Chicago to review the problems of education and cultural deprivation and to make recommendations about what could be done to solve some of these problems. Bloom, Davis, and Hess (3) have reported the results of these deliberations by some 31 specialists, research workers, and teachers.

Compensatory education addresses itself to those students who do not make normal progress in their school learning and achievement. These are the students whose home experiences are marginal, whose motivation is not supportive of constructive efforts in school, and whose goals for the future are a handicap to success in learning. For the most part these are the students who do not complete high school. Bloom, Davis, and Hess (3) refer to this group as "the culturally disadvantaged or culturally deprived because we believe the roots of their problem may in large part be traced to their experiences in homes which do not transmit the cultural patterns necessary for the types of learning characteristic of the schools and the larger society." Cultural deprivation should not be defined in terms of race or ethnic origin although one does find a high incidence of culturally disadvantaged in minority groups. Instead, the concept should be defined on the basis of individual characteristics and/or the characteristics of the environment. According to these authors (3):

> The task of changing the schools of the U. S. from a selective system which rewards and finally graduates only the more able students to one which develops each individual to his fullest capabilities is a difficult one. . . . What is now required [in education] is not equality of *access* to education. What is needed to solve our current as well as future crises in education is a system of compensatory education which can prevent or overcome earlier deficiencies in the development of each individual. Essentially, what this involves is the writing and filling of educational prescriptions for groups of children which will enable them to realize their fullest development. Compensatory education . . . is not the reduction of all education to a least common denominator. It is a type of education which should help socially disadvantaged students without reducing the quality of education for those who are progressing satisfactorily under existing educational conditions.

The conference stressed that the new demands being placed on education will likely involve goals which place increasing emphasis on higher mental processes and problem solving as opposed to the learning of discrete information. The new goals will emphasize the basic methods of inquiry in each field of study together with the ideas and structure of the discipline as opposed to the learning of minutiae about a field of study; will place stress on the process of learning or "learning how to learn" as opposed to stress on the product of learning; and will emphasize the development of interests, attitudes, and personality which will enhance the further growth and satisfaction of the individual as opposed to educational programs which submerge the individual through an emphasis on skill learning and retention of information.

The recommendations of the conference stress the factors which should be supplied through compensatory efforts. These are:

1. An attention to basic needs. Each child should be provided with an adequate breakfast if none is available at home. Each child should have competent and

frequent physical examinations provided by the school if not provided by the home. Each child should have adequate clothing for school attendance.

2. The early experiences provided by nursery school should give the culturally deprived child the conditions of stimulation which are available in favorable home environments. A national commission should be created to develop materials and curricula for this type of early school experience.

3. Special training should be provided for teachers in nursery schools for the culturally deprived so that they could be prepared to do for the child many of the things which parents do not do.

4. Parents should be involved in this type of nursery school experience so that they could be committed to its objectives.

5. Detailed data should be obtained on each child when he enters the first grade in order to diagnose the verbal and nonverbal problems the child might have as he progresses through learning activities.

6. Individual programs of learning should be available so that the approach most appropriate for each child could be provided.

7. The first three years of elementary school should emphasize the development of the child through continual success at small tasks. During these early years the child should not be failed or be expected to repeat a grade.

8. Teachers for the first three years should be carefully prepared to accomplish the tasks of helping children learn the basic verbal and arithmetic skills which are necessary for future progress. A national commission of teachers and specialists should be formed to guide the development of materials and curricula for the first three grades.

9. For children who have not had the advantages of a curriculum designed for the culturally deprived during the first three years of schooling, efforts should be directed toward language development, reading, and arithmetic with maximum priority being given to these skill areas. Every effort should be made to involve the parents of these children in the program of the school.

10. Integration in the schools can serve the purposes of a compensatory program when it allows children of different racial and ethnic backgrounds to engage in common activities on a one-to-one basis.

11. Major efforts should be made by the beginning of secondary school to identify those culturally deprived students who can successfully complete high school and begin college. These students should be given the attention necessary to prepare them for the college experience.

12. Culturally disadvantaged adolescents should have available to them work-study programs which allow them to learn and at the same time prepare for a contributing work role in society.

13. For all youth, peer societies should be organized by community agencies to provide opportunities for youth to engage in meaningful and positive social relations, to provide service to others, and to develop meaningful value patterns.

While these recommendations are phrased in the most general terms, they do represent an attitude about schooling for the socially disadvantaged which is shared by many more specialists in education than the 31 involved in the conference. Most of these attitudes about compensatory efforts can be summed up by pointing out that compensatory education demands a maximum assessment of the characteristics and abilities of the child, a maximum effort to create learning programs which are designed for the individual learner, and the provision of logistical support for these efforts which would maximize their effectiveness.

A recent review of compensatory education programs (13) is critical of those efforts now being undertaken in the United States because the authors feel that they are based primarily on sentiment and not on fact. Most of what is being done for the culturally disadvantaged in schools, according to these investigators, is based on unscientific innovation involving, for the most part, hit-and-miss shotgun-type programs, with little attempt being made to evaluate the efforts of the program. Most programs seem to be designed to make the child fit those educational methods which have traditionally been successful. Instead, attempts should be made to design and implement new methods based on the unique needs of the type of child being educated. Gordon and Wilkerson (13) feel that compensatory programs need to break the traditional molds of the educational establishment and experiment with methods, techniques, and designs which concentrate efforts on the individual child rather than dissipate efforts through nothing more than rearranging class schedules or lowering class size.

Many educators feel that for education in a free society to be maximally effective, intervention programs must begin long before the age of 4—the age now generally taken as a minimum age for entrance into compensatory programs. Edwards (11) believes that programs involving significant intervention before the age of 2 must be tried in order to learn how to help the disadvantaged child before he becomes a deprivation statistic. Some few programs are being tried which involve cognitive development—a dimension which has traditionally been missing from nursery school education. Edwards (11) reports on one such effort designed by Bereiter and Engelmann which is described as "perhaps at the moment the most controversial program in pre-school education." These two educators use what they call a "pressure-cooker approach" to cognitive development. Groups of 4- and 5-year-olds from lower-class homes are taught verbal and number patterns through a direct academic force-feeding technique. An example of the type of exercises used is as follows (11):

> This is a ball.
> This is a piece of clay.
> Is this a ball?
> Yes, this is a ball./No, this is not a ball.
> This is a what? This is a ball. . . .

This exercise has as its goal the development of the ability to label "ball" and "clay" and to know the use and significance of words such as "not" which are essential carriers of meaning. The exercises used by Bereiter and Engelmann involve verbal skills, reading, and numbers. Drill is the medium of instruction. The adult involved in the instruction pressures the child to learn through the use of praise, exhortation, and tangible rewards and punishments. Through an intense atmosphere which emphasizes giving the child those skills which will enable him to enter into a world created by an adult society, the child is encouraged to develop his own desire for competence. Programs such as this must be given an opportunity to be used and evaluated. Only through experimenting with different approaches to programs of education for the disadvantaged will we be able to organize our efforts in the most efficient manner possible. A continuation of the practice of merely rearranging the traditional ingredients of instruction to emphasize or de-emphasize selected factors leaves success to the chance combination of factors which might be effective in preparing children for adult roles. Some evaluation of Bereiter and Engelmann's results was given in earlier chapters.

Jensen (17), in a recent widely quoted article states that compensatory education programs have failed because they do not produce the anticipated lasting effects on I.Q. and achievement which are expected of these programs. He points out that one of the basic assumptions supporting compensatory programs is the belief that differences in I.Q. are almost entirely the result of the cultural bias of intelligence tests and environmental differences among individuals tested. We saw in Chapter 14 that Jensen presents arguments to support the thesis that I.Q. can be separated into genetic and environmental components. He feels that environmental influences on I.Q. are not nearly as important as genetic factors. Compensatory programs of enrichment may allow a child to achieve at a level which more realistically represents a genetic potential, but programs of enrichment cannot push a child past his hereditary endowments. He believes that educational efforts should be directed toward teaching specific skills represented by mental abilities which are much more responsive to educational programs than the general characteristic of I.Q. Jensen's criticism of compensatory programs will certainly not signal the demise of such efforts. Rather, a critical re-evaluation of the objectives of compensatory efforts should be stimulated by timely examinations such as the one offered by Jensen.

Much attention has recently been directed toward the black child and his interaction with an educational system which has been dominated by a white middle-class model of what it takes to be successful in school. The relationship between blacks and the disadvantaged is direct and immediate. Only in recent years could it be said that to be black in the United States was not to be disadvantaged. Even today, in spite of the great progress which has been made in erasing the stigma of racial differences in our society, to be black in some parts of the nation is to be culturally disadvantaged. Many teachers who emerge from teacher preparation programs which emphasize teaching in the systems of middle-class suburbia find themselves unable to relate to students in inner city schools where the rules of the game are completely different. More teachers are ambivalent about teaching in ghetto schools than they are about teaching in the suburbs. Havighurst (14), in his survey of the Chicago Public School System, reported a deep ambivalence in teachers about teaching in a school which is in a high transiency–low income area.

Ausubel and Ausubel (1), in a discussion of ego development among segregated black children, point out that the unstable family structure which is typical of the lower income black family creates conditions in the black child which lead to the development of unstable ego structures. They feel that the black child gradually learns the negative implications of his status which in turn leads to a resistence toward positive identifications with his own racial group. The unstructured family situation leads to a disproportionate dependence on the black peer group for many of the cues for socialization normally provided by the family. Clark (6) feels that by the time the black child starts school his major disadvantage is his feeling of low self-esteem and his anticipation of failure. Clark sees the fundamental task of the school, in stimulating academic achievement for the black child, as the provision of conditions which would allow the minority child to build a positive image of himself. Basic to this is an integrated school situation which provides opportunities to have successful experiences and meet challenges in an atmosphere which would support rewarding outcomes. According to Clark (6) "a child cannot be expected to respect himself if he perceives himself as rejected and set apart in a compound for those of inferior status or caste."

Rosenthal and Jacobson (26, 27) have helped to define the dimensions of the classroom which reinforces the poor performance of the lower-class child in an educational system with a middle-class orientation. Reasons usually given for this poor performance are directed toward the factors which have made the child disadvantaged and toward the child's characteristics which result from his background. Rosenthal and Jacobson conceptualized the problem by hypothesizing that the child from a deprived background might do poorly because of what is expected of him rather than because of his background. According to the investigators (26):

> We have explored the effect of teacher expectations with experiments in which teachers were led to believe at the beginning of a school year that certain of their pupils could be expected to show considerable academic improvement during the year. The teachers thought the predictions were

based on tests that had been administered to the student body toward the end
of the preceding school year. In actuality the children designated as potential
"spurters" had been chosen at random and not on the basis of testing. Nonetheless, intelligence tests given after the experiment had been in progress for
several months indicated that on the whole the randomly chosen children
had improved more than the rest.

The investigators clearly showed that children who were expected by
teachers to show greater gains in intelligence did show such gains. The
greatest gains were shown by children in the lower grades. The authors
feel that the explanation for this "self-fulfilling prophecy" is to be found in
the interaction between the teacher and the student in which the teacher's
facial expression, tone of voice, touch, and posture serve as subtle communicators of expectations. The communication of these implicit expectations may help the child change his conception of himself and his motivation for cognitive skills. These results very clearly suggest that many
disadvantaged children do not show gains in school, especially during
the early grades, because their teachers do not expect them to show gains.
Many teachers, in other words, expect the culturally disadvantaged child
to perform poorly because he is disadvantaged, consequently he does
perform poorly. This explanation is, of course, oversimplified in that it
concentrates on only one factor which influences performance among
culturally deprived children. Nevertheless, Rosenthal and Jacobson have
made a significant contribution by investigating their hypothesis and
producing data to support it. Their conclusion has many implications for
the preparation of teachers of the disadvantaged, but must be considered
tentative in view of the criticisms of the study noted in Chapter 14.

The Urban School—Some Observations

The urban community has become for many the battleground that will
determine the continuation or destruction of many of the traditional
institutions of our society. Public education is one of these institutions.
Unfortunately, knowledge about education has not kept pace with the
problems the schools are forced to solve. Schools are not able to stop their
activities while the educational researcher finds out the best way to teach
a black child or to stimulate the underachiever. The solutions to many
problems which confront the metropolitan schools are arrived at not by
the objective application of experimental data but by a process akin to
baking a cake by trial and error without a receipe. In the absence of
scientific data to support decision making, the power of opinion dominates
the scene. An examination of many of the programs of education which
have been started by big city schools in recent years leaves one with the

impression that the guiding rule is to try something, try anything, until you find a combination of factors which leads to some improvement over what you had to begin with—but, above all, try something. Only recently have educational researchers become interested in the inner city ghetto school. Federal funding for compensatory education programs has stimulated much of the interest. In one sense, research money goes where researchers want it to go, since much of the funding for research, at the Federal level at least, is based upon recommendations made by researchers themselves.

Many educators feel that the problems of big city school systems will not be solved until those who have the greatest benefits to gain from education become personally involved in the educational system itself. These, of course, are the minority groups of our cities. In many ways the problem of education in metropolitan areas becomes the problem of blacks and their relationship to the school, simply because blacks represent the largest minority group in the large cities of the United States (23). A recent assessment of population trends in thirteen cities revealed that the concentration of whites in the suburbs and blacks in the central cities is continuing (12). Population projections made through the year 2000 indicate that blacks will be in a majority in many of our large cities by the beginning of the twenty-first century (18). For example, these projections predict that the percentage of blacks in the population of these cities will be as follows in the year 2000: Washington, D. C., 75%; Cleveland, 67%; Newark, 63%; Baltimore, 56%; Chicago, 55%; New York City, 50%; Philadelphia, 50%; Detroit, 50%; St. Louis, 50%. During this time the black population will also increase in the suburbs, but this gain should leave blacks as less than one-fourth of the total suburban population. Were blacks to increase their economic base dramatically during the next ten years these statistics might show a greater increase in the suburbs and less of an increase in the city. Income, however, is tied closely to education. Generally, the more education one has, the higher his income is likely to be. Housing opportunities in the suburbs are more readily available to those who have the money to purchase a home, and housing is usually more expensive there than in the city. Even though recent evidence supports the conclusion that there is an increasing rise in support of integration in both the North and the South, integration depends upon much more than supportive attitudes (15).

The development of an effective power base within the black community which will compete with, and eventually amalgamate with, the power base of the white majority is only beginning to be assembled. Unlike the Irish or the Italian immigrant, blacks have not been able to evolve group power in the United States. Comer (9) believes that this is due to an unrecognized disunity among blacks which has remained since the first slave contingents were brought out of Africa. Many of the excessive manifestations of "black power" may represent temporary over-reaction to the discovery of a common identity, which should help to establish the unity necessary for the expression of a democratic power base through the ballot and through economic advancement.

Relevant education is crucial to the entrance of blacks into the main-stream of the American culture. In order for relevant education to be available to this minority, it must be present in the place where the Negro can get to it—in the large cities of the United States. The major changes and the most inventive innovations in educational practice must arise from the urban centers where the greatest need exists. In order to be relevant to the problems faced by minority groups in the United States, and especially relevant for blacks, we must develop within our educational institutions the kinds of educational programs which reach children early enough to prevent them from being burdened by the effects of cumulative deprivation; programs which have as a central concern the development of reinforcing attitudes about learning, and which make the process of achievement a factor of worth in the home and with the parents. The problem of relevant learning for the culturally deprived is not just a problem of classroom management. It involves the total social milieu which spawns deprivation. The schools of the inner city will need to become vitally involved in the home and in the community in a way which may be foreign to our traditional conceptualizations of public education. The battle lines for education in the decades ahead will be on the boundary between the central city and the suburb. The nurture and the support which the suburb offers to education must be directed toward the inner city where the critical problems remain unsolved. Leadership for relevant and constructive educational innovation must be available to the schools which serve minority groups. Unless education can successfully meet these challenges in the decades ahead the schools as we know them may take their place in museums as historical curiosities.

Summary

The quality of education in urban areas has emerged as the major educational problem of this decade. A close examination of this issue reveals that the educational efforts in major cities in this country are in difficulty largely because of the disparity between what the schools accomplish with the typical child, who is usually white and from a middle-class background, compared with what schools accomplish with children from minority backgrounds. The Coleman Report has indicated that the minority child does not do as well in school and usually emerges from public school experiences less well prepared than the child from a majority background. Another way of stating this observation is to say that schools do not provide programs which are as effective with the black pupil, or the Puerto Rican, the Indian–American, the Mexican–American, or the Oriental–American. These inequalities in educational opportunity for minority groups are most apparent in our large metropolitan areas.

Many attempts have been initiated to provide changes in our traditional concepts of education to help erase the achievement differences which exist between white and nonwhite children in our public schools. One such program is Head Start, which provides an early preschool experience for children from low-income families. Head Start is a Federal program supported by funds from the United States Office of Education. Its worth as a compensatory program to help raise the achievement level of children from minority backgrounds has yet to be finally decided. However, Head Start has won the support of many educators who see it less as a compensatory program than as an experience which helps the child get ready for the formal school experiences of the first grade. Other programs, such as the Higher Horizons efforts in New York City, attempt to provide a more meaningful approach to education for minority groups. One of the basic assumptions underlying the Head Start efforts is that changes in behavior are best attempted when children are young. To create positive attitudes about school and learning in children, the best time to do it is before the child has started school, thus preventing attitudes of negativism reinforced by unsuccessful school experiences.

Not all educators feel that compensatory programs are useful in helping to raise the achievement level of students. Jensen (17) suggests that compensatory programs will fail if they state their major objective to be increases in pupil I.Q. He argues that I.Q. is more of a genetic component than a factor which is influenced by the environment. While a compensatory program might help a child to work up to his genetic potential, it will not help him surpass that hereditary level.

Rosenthal and Jacobson (26) believe that children from minority backgrounds do not perform well in school largely because their teachers do not expect them to perform well. Their lack of achievement becomes a self-fulfilling prophesy. These authors have dramatically called attention to the role of the teacher and the teacher's perceptions in influencing pupil behavior by suggesting that students usually try to live up to, or live down to, the teacher's expectations.

Many educators feel that the problems of urban education will not be solved until direct efforts are made to involve minority groups in planning for their own education. Certainly a greater involvement of minorities in the educational enterprise should produce a greater commitment to the objectives which emerge from this process. However, until metropolitan school systems have access to the money needed, until these systems can recruit the teachers needed, and until they can effectively deliver teachers, money and educational planning involving those to be educated, we will continue to see in our large urban centers the effects of educational atrophy into the 1970's.

SUGGESTED READINGS

Goldstein, B. *Low income youth in urban areas.* New York: Holt, Rinehart & Winston, 1967.

Today's concerns in education have focused dramatically on the programs of education available in the inner city areas of our metropolitan regions. Poverty and the inner city go hand in hand, and this book is a critical review of the literature concerning the young who are from low-income backgrounds in urban areas. The author has reviewed and summarized many of the relevant studies which provide a background for our understanding of the interaction between poverty and education.

Jensen, A. R. How much can we boost I.Q. and scholastic achievement? *Harvard Educational Review,* 1969 **39**(1), 1–123.

Professor Jensen's article has been given much attention in the popular press because of his suggestion that social class and racial variations in I.Q. are due, in part, to genetic factors. The article is a well-reasoned assessment of possible reasons for the failure of compensatory educational programs such as Head Start to have the effect on I.Q. which supporters of these programs predicted. Anyone reading this reference should follow it with the following two issues of the *Harvard Educational Review* for discussions of the Jensen article by a group of educators and psychologists.

Rosenthal, R., & Jacobson, L. *Pygmalion in the classroom.* New York: Holt, Rinehart & Winston, 1968.

The authors of this volume advance the thesis that children from minority group backgrounds do not perform as well in school as children from nonminority backgrounds because their teachers do not expect them to perform as well; thus, they fulfill a prophesy made before they start to learn. Although the experimental data used to test this hypothesis have been criticized, the report has already become a minor classic because it calls attention to an alternate and equally plausible explanation for the poor performance of some minority group children. It could be said that the teacher expects that minority group children will not learn as well as other children and proceeds to treat minority group children in a way which rewards inferior performance.

Smith, L. M., & Geoffrey, W. *The complexities of an urban classroom.* New York: Holt, Rinehart & Winston, 1968.

This slim volume concisely presents many of the factors involved in the interaction of a middle-class teacher with a class of seventh-graders in a slum school. While the report goes beyond description to an analysis and interpretation which becomes at times complex, the student who wishes to learn about the unique features of the urban classroom will find much in this book to help him accomplish that objective.

REFERENCES

1. Ausubel, D. P., & Ausubel, P. Ego development among segregated negro children. In A. H. Passow (Ed.), *Education in depressed areas.* New York: Teachers College, Columbia University, Bureau of Publications, 1963. Pp. 109–141.
2. Bloom, B. *Stability and change in human characteristics.* New York: Wiley, 1964. Pp. 210, 215.
3. Bloom, B., Davis, A., & Hess, R. *Compensatory education for cultural deprivation.* New York: Holt, Rinehart & Winston, 1965. Pp. 4, 6.
4. Brazziel, W. F. Two years of head start. *Phi Delta Kappan,* 1967, **48**, 344–348.
5. Bronfenbrenner, U. The split-level american family. *Saturday Review,* 1967 (October 7), **50**(40), 60–66.
6. Clark, K. B. Educational stimulation of racially disadvantaged children. In A. H. Passow (Ed.), *Education in depressed areas.* New York: Teachers College, Columbia University, Bureau of Publications, 1963. Pp. 142–162.
7. Coleman, J. S. The concept of equal educational opportunity. *Harvard Educational Review,* 1968, **38**, 7–22.
8. Coleman, J. S., Campbell, E. Q., Hobson, C. J., McPartland, J., Mood, A. M., Weinfeld, F. D., & York, R. L. *Equality of educational opportunity.* OE 38001. Washington, D. C.: Office of Education, 1966.
9. Comer, J. P. The social power of the negro. *Scientific American,* 1967, **216**(4), 21–27.
10. Dyer, H. S. School factors and equal educational opportunity. *Harvard Educational Review,* 1968, **38**, 38–56.
11. Edwards, E. P. Kindergarten is too late. *Saturday Review,* 1968(June 15), **51**(24), 68–79.
12. Farley, R., & Taeuber, K. E. Population trends and residential segregation since 1960. *Science,* 1968, **159**, 953–956.
13. Gordon, E. W., & Wilkerson, D. A. *Compensatory education for the disadvantaged: Programs and practices, preschool through college.* New York: College Entrance Examination Board, 1966.
14. Havighurst, R. J. *The public schools of chicago.* Chicago: Board of Education, 1964.
15. Hyman, H. H., & Sheatsley, P. B. Attitudes toward desegregation. *Scientific American,* 1964, **211**(1), 2–7.

16. Jencks, C. Education, the racial gap. *New Republic,* 1966(October 1), **155,** 21–26.
17. Jensen, A. R. How much can we boost I.Q. and scholastic achievement? *Harvard Educational Review,* 1969, **39,** 1–123.
18. Kahn, H., & Wiener, A. J. *The year 2000.* New York: Macmillan, 1967.
19. Landers, J. *Higher Horizons progress report.* New York: Board of Education, 1963.
20. Levin, H. M. What difference do schools make? *Saturday Review,* 1968(January 20), **50**(3), 57–67.
21. Moynihan, D. P. Sources of resistance to the Coleman report. *Harvard Educational Review,* 1968, **38,** 23–36.
22. Nichols, R. C. Schools for the disadvantaged. *Science,* 1966, **154,** 1312–1314.
23. Pettigrew, T. F. *A profile of the negro american.* Princeton, N. J.: Van Nostrand, 1964.
24. Pettigrew, T. F. Race and equal educational opportunity. *Harvard Educational Review,* 1968, **38,** 66–77.
25. Johnson, L. B. President Johnson's special message to congress. *PTA Magazine,* 1967(March), **61,** 20–22.
26. Rosenthal, R., & Jacobson, L. F. Teacher expectations for the disadvantaged. *Scientific American,* 1968, **218**(4), 19–23.
27. Rosenthal, R., & Jacobson, L. F. *Pygmalion in the classroom.* New York: Holt, Rinehart & Winston, 1968.
28. Scrimshaw, N. S. Infant malnutrition and adult learning. *Saturday Review,* 1968(March 16), **51**(11), 64–66.
29. Wolff, M., & Stein, A. Head start six months later. *Phi Delta Kappan,* 1967, **48,** 349–350.
30. Wrightstone, J. W. *Higher Horizons Program for underprivileged children, a summary.* Cooperative Research Project No. 1124. Washington, D. C.: Office of Education, 1965.

AUTHOR INDEX

Numbers in parentheses are reference numbers and indicate that an author's work is referred to although his name is not cited in the text. Numbers in italics show the page on which the complete reference is listed.

A

Aarons, L., 309, *327*
Acker, M., 390, *421*
Ackerman, W. I., 431, 451, *473*
Adams, P. A., 94(70), *114*
Adelman, H. M., 396, *421*
Adolph, E. F., 377(3), *421*
Aiken, E. G., 80, *111*
Aldrich, C. A., 303(1), *325*
Allard, M., 77(18), *112*
Allen, L., 566, *597*
Allen, R. D., 444, 445, *473*
Allinsmith, W., 465, *474*
Allport, G. W., 406, *421*, 479, 482, 484, 490, *527*
Alper, T. G., 575, *594*
Altus, W. D., 311, *325*
Amatruda, C. S., 283(27), 284(27), *326*
Ames, L. B., 283(27, 29), 284(27), 290 (35, 36), 320, *326*
Ammons, C. H., 256, *276*
Amsel, A., 181, 182, *187*, *188*, 395(102), *421*, *425*
Anastasi, A., 547, 583(3), *594*
Anderson, A. R., 317, *327*
Anderson, H. A., 615, *657*
Anderson, J. E., 540(4), *594*
Anderson, K. E., 643, *653*
Angelino, H., 580(5), 582, *594*
Apell, R. J., 290(36), *326*

Appley, M. H., 418, *422*
Archer, E. J., 92(2), *111*, 208, 209, *215*
Arling, G. L., 354, *371*
Armitage, S. G., 521, *529*, 681(50), *701*
Arnold, C. R., 72(7), 73, *111*
Aronson, E., 683, 688(2), 689(2), *699*
Arthur, G. A., 540(6), *594*
Asch, S. E., 677, *699*
Asimov, I., 553(7), *594*
Atkinson, J. W., 408(7, 91), 409, 411, 412, 413, 416(7, 91, 92), *421*, *425*
Atkinson, R. C., 77(47), *113*, 133(1), 134, *146*, 173, *188*, *190*
Austin, G. A., 197(12), 207(12), *215*
Ausubel, D. P., 51(5), 85(3, 4), 86(4, 6), *111*, 161, 162, 169, *188*, 729, *735*
Ausubel, P., 729, *735*
Ax, A. F., 501, 503, *527*
Axelrod, H., 680(53), *701*
Azrin, N. H., 681, *699*

B

Bachrach, A, J., 520, *527*
Baer, D. M., 176(8), *188*, 390, *423*
Bagley, W. C., 574, *594*
Bahrick, B. O., 164, *188*
Bahrick, H. P., 164, *188*
Bailey, C. J., 391, 392(97), *425*
Bailey, L. L., 582(93), *598*

STATISTICAL INDEX

Many introductory psychology and educational psychology texts contain a chapter summarizing several statistical concepts with conceptual examples. The present textbook provides very brief mention of such concepts in several chapters, as needed for describing specific research studies. Computational examples are not provided, but may be found in standard statistical texts. The present statistical index has the advantage of telling the reader where all mention of statistical concepts may be found. Most terms in test theory, however, are listed in the subject index, not in the statistical index.

SUBJECT INDEX

A

Ability grouping, 627–628, 652

Absolute standards of measurement, 606, 634
  compared to domain tests, 634

Abstraction, development of, in normal growth, 338–339

Abundancy motivation, 407–408

Academic achievement
  academic and affiliation motivation, 430–432
  as determiner of level of aspiration, 440–441
  longitudinal records of, 444–445
  of minority groups, 706–708
  predictability from intellectual interest, 467
  prediction of
    by creativity tests, 550
    by intelligence tests, 583–589

Academic performance, improvement through teacher motivation, 452

Achievement
  academic, see Academic achievement
  change over time, 652

classroom, relationship to amount of anxiety, 403–404
  through conformance, 410
  educational, 601–657
  growth curves of, 632–634
  growth in
    amount of information and, 637
    as function of subject matter, 636–637
  through independence, 410
  tests of, 603–604

Achievement motivation, 408–416, 419–420, 436–440
  affiliation motivation and, 470
  in classroom, 436–440
  compared to competence motivation, 437
    to level of aspiration, 441
  duty and, 436–437
  ethnic groups and, 437–438
  as habit, 414, 420
  measures of, 415–416
  motivational training as determiner of, 438–439, 450
  persistence as component of, 439